Cambridge Yearbook of European Legal Studies

Vol 16, 2013–2014

The *Cambridge Yearbook of European Legal Studies* provides a forum for the scrutiny of significant issues in European Union Law, the Law of the Council of Europe, and Comparative Law with a 'European' dimension, and particularly those which have come to the fore during the year preceding publication. The contributions appearing in the collection are commissioned by the Centre for European Legal Studies (CELS), Cambridge, which is the research centre of Cambridge University Law Faculty specialising in European legal issues.

The papers presented are all at the cutting edge of the fields which they address, and reflect the views of recognised experts drawn from the University world, legal practice, and the civil services of both the EU and its Member States. Inclusion of the comparative dimension brings a fresh perspective to the study of European law, and highlights the effects of globalisation of the law more generally, and the resulting cross-fertilisation of norms and ideas that has occurred among previously sovereign and separate legal orders.

The *Cambridge Yearbook of European Legal Studies* is an invaluable resource for those wishing to keep pace with legal developments in the fast moving world of European integration.

This volume can be cited as (2013–2014) 16 *CYELS*.

The Cambridge Yearbook of European Legal Studies

VOLUME 16, 2013–2014

EDITED BY
Albertina Albors-Llorens
Kenneth A Armstrong
and
Markus W Gehring

·HART·
PUBLISHING
OXFORD AND PORTLAND, OREGON
2014

Published in the United Kingdom by Hart Publishing Ltd
16C Worcester Place, Oxford, OX1 2JW
Telephone: +44 (0)1865 517530
Fax: +44 (0)1865 510710
E-mail: mail@hartpub.co.uk
Website: http://www.hartpub.co.uk

Published in North America (US and Canada) by
Hart Publishing
c/o International Specialized Book Services
920 NE 58th Avenue, Suite 300
Portland, OR 97213-3786
USA
Tel: +1 503 287 3093 or toll-free: (1) 800 944 6190
Fax: +1 503 280 8832
E-mail: orders@isbs.com
Website: http://www.isbs.com

British Library Cataloguing in Publication Data
Data Available

ISBN: 978-1-84946-628-8

Typeset by Compuscript Ltd, Shannon
Printed and bound in Great Britain by
CPI Group (UK) Ltd, Croydon CR0 4YY

Editors' Preface

On behalf of the Centre for European Legal Studies (CELS), Faculty of Law, University of Cambridge, the editors are pleased to present the contributions to this year's *Yearbook*. As in previous years, many of the contributions were presented as papers in the CELS' lunchtime seminar series. We are also pleased to include the text of the 2014 Mackenzie-Stuart Lecture delivered by Viviane Reding. Annual lectures are often a way of giving a focus to a contemporary issue or to a particular theme. In the *Symposium* section of this year's *Yearbook* we include the texts of some of the recent Lasok Lectures delivered annually at the University of Exeter. These lectures—edited by Leone Niglia and supplemented by his own contribution—focus in different ways on issues of 'balancing' in adjudication.

We are grateful not only to the contributors but to all the reviewers who have helped in the editing process. As ever, we owe an enormous debt of gratitude to Felicity Eves-Rey for providing much needed administrative support and guidance.

As editors we have been fortunate enough to work with the fantastic team at Hart Publishing and we take this opportunity to thank them for their professionalism and dedication to the publication of the *Yearbook*. Indeed, it is appropriate for us, on behalf of all the past editors of the *Yearbook*, to record our sincere gratitude to Richard Hart, Mel Hamill and to Hart Publishing for its outstanding contribution to European law scholarship. In so many ways, Hart Publishing has helped define 'European law' as a distinctive field of legal scholarship within academic publishing in the English language. Its willingness to work with authors and institutions in collaboration and partnership has been valued by the entire European law community. Now forming part of Bloomsbury Publishing and with Sinead Moloney as its new General Manager and Publisher, Hart Publishing enters a new phase in its development. We wish all those involved continued success and express our gratitude for making the *Yearbook* possible.

Albertina Albors-Llorens
Kenneth A Armstrong
Markus Gehring
Cambridge, July 2014

Contents

List of Contributors

ANCA CHIRITA is Lecturer in Competition Law at Durham University.

SAMUEL DAHAN is a Référendaire at the Conseil d'Etat in France.

NIAMH DUNNE is a Lecturer in Law at King's College London.

MARK FLEAR is Lecturer in Law at Queen's University Belfast.

JULIAN GHOSH QC is a Barrister at Pump Court Tax Chambers, London, Visiting Fellow Clare Hall, Cambridge and Senior Fellow of the International Tax Centre, University of Leiden.

TATJANA JOSIPOVIĆ is Professor of Civil Law at the University of Zagreb.

NIALL LENIHAN is Assistant General Counsel and Senior Adviser in Legal Services at the European Central Bank. Solicitor of the Senior Courts in England and Wales (1999), Solicitor of the Courts in Ireland (2003), Attorney of the US District Court for the Southern District of New York (1994) and Attorney and Counsellor at Law of the Courts of New York State (1992).

AMY LUDLOW is Affiliated Lecturer at the Faculty of Law, University of Cambridge and Fellow of Gonville & Caius College.

VIRGINIA MANTOUVALOU is Reader in Human Rights and Labour Law and Co-Director of the Institute of Human Rights at University College London.

PAOLO MENGOZZI is Advocate General at the Court of Justice of the European Union.

ELISA MORGERA is Senior Lecturer in Global Environmental Law at the University of Edinburgh School of Law.

LEONE NIGLIA is Associate Professor in Law and Director of the Centre for European Legal Studies at the University of Exeter.

VIVIANE REDING was Vice-President of the European Commission. Member of the European Commission 2009–14. Elected to the European Parliament in 2014.

ALLAN ROSAS is Judge at the Court of Justice of the European Union.

TAKIS TRIDIMAS is Professor of European Law at King's College London.

Table of Cases

Court of Justice of the European Union

Alphabetical

Numerical

General Court

Alphabetical

Numerical

European Court of Human Rights

EFTA Court

International Court of Justice

World Trade Organisation

Commission Decision Cases

National competition authority's decision

National

Cyrpus

Germany

South Africa

United Kingdom

United States of America

Table of European Legislation

Treaties, Agreements, Charters and Conventions

Decisions

Directives

Regulations

Table of International Legislation

International Agreements, Charters and Conventions

NATIONAL LEGISLATION

Croatia

Cyprus

France

Germany

Greece

Hungary

Ireland

Latvia

Netherlands

Portugal

Romania

Spain

United Kingdom

United States of America

Statutory Instruments

The 2014 Mackenzie-Stuart Lecture

The Mackenzie-Stuart Lecture is an annual public lecture in honour of Lord Mackenzie-Stuart, the first British judge to be nominated to the European Court of Justice and, later, its President. The lecture is hosted at the University of Cambridge Faculty of Law by the Centre for European Legal Studies. The lecture is sponsored by the law firm Shearman and Sterling.

1

The United Kingdom and the European Union: Inevitably Drifting Apart?

VIVIANE REDING

I. INTRODUCTION: THE UK'S DEBATE ON MEMBERSHIP OF THE EU

I AM DELIGHTED and truly honoured to be able to speak to you tonight to deliver the 2014 Mackenzie-Stuart lecture. President Barroso was speaking in London last Friday where he said: 'The European Union would not have become what it is today if it weren't for British politicians and entrepreneurs, British thinkers and British ideas'. Scholars from this University and from its Centre for European Legal Studies have contributed enormously. Looking just to the Union's Courts, Judges Lord Mackenzie-Stuart, David Edward, Konrad Schiemann, Christopher Vajda and Nicholas Forewood, Advocates-General Francis Jacobs and Eleanor Sharpston are true architects of our Union.

It is tremendously inspiring to come to a university that has been inextricably linked to excellence and culture for centuries. A place that puts great value on acquiring and passing on knowledge, but also encourages people—especially young people—to question and to debate. In doing so, your university is nurturing that great British debating culture which pervades not only academia and politics, but the whole of British society. Because the people of this country love to scrutinise. To challenge the establishment and hold the powerful to account. For you it comes naturally not to accept, but to probe; not to shout, but to reason; not to walk away, but to engage. Independent-minded, yes, but usually settling for the rational, the pragmatic view. This is a great strength of this country, something to be proud of.

How astounding, then, that the most important questions we are faced with in Europe are debated so very differently in this country. As soon as the issue of the United Kingdom's relationship with the European Union is raised, a strange reflex seems to kick in, pushing the public debate away from the facts.

I believe, to make this clear from the start, that the United Kingdom should be a central part of the European Union. This country has so much to gain from being in our Union, and the EU benefits greatly from having the UK as a confident member. To my mind, all the arguments, the hard facts, indicate that it is in the UK's national interest to remain part of the EU. Yet, what we have been seeing over the last couple of years is a sense that the UK is gradually, inexorably drifting away. As other countries, in particular the members of the Eurozone, have integrated much more strongly, the UK has remained apart. And it is preparing to loosen its ties to the rest of Europe in a number of policy areas. Will it sever them in the coming years? I sincerely hope not. This can be avoided, though the politicians and the people of this country will have some crucial choices to make. Do you still want to be part of this Union? How closely do you want to work with the other Member States? How do you want to (re-)define your relationship with the rest of the EU? Of course we, Continental Europeans, also have to seek answers. Most importantly, we will all have to decide on a way of reconciling the closer integration of the Eurozone countries with the wish of others, like the UK, to stay away—at least for the time being—from the new architecture being set up.

II. THE HARD FACTS: IT IS IN THE UK'S NATIONAL INTEREST TO REMAIN PART OF THE EU

Let us now look at some of those hard facts. The UK benefits enormously from EU membership, both economically and politically. The Confederation of British Industry (CBI) estimates that four to five per cent of British Gross Domestic Product (GDP) can be attributed to the fact that it is a member of the European Union. And that each British household would be £3,000 worse off each year if the UK were outside the EU, for this simple reason: that the UK conducts half of its trade with the EU.

EU membership brings British companies the biggest prize: unfettered access to the Single Market of more than 500 million people. Around 3.5 million British jobs are linked to the single market. That is around one in every ten jobs in this country. The EU's clout allows it to negotiate valuable trade deals with other trading partners around the world—opening up a plethora of further markets for British businesses.

Only as a member of the EU can the UK safeguard these privileges. Because, as President Barroso also rightly said, 'size matters'. Leaving our powerful trading bloc would severely restrict British companies' access to this goldmine—and make the UK a much less attractive trading partner for third countries. The example of the financial services sector demonstrates this very clearly. This sector is vital for the British economy, employing more than one million people and providing over 10 per cent of the government's tax receipts. It is often pointed out—rightly so—that the City competes with financial centres outside the EU, like Hong Kong, Singapore and New York. In this context, the UK's EU membership matters enormously. The City would most definitely lose its unhindered access to the single market in the case of an exit. Because EU Member States would obviously have no interest in supporting what would then be an offshore financial centre competing with their own financial firms. And companies from third countries would find London a much less attractive location to do business, since it would no longer be a gateway to the EU's single market.

I can see why one of the leading NGOs for keeping Britain in the EU has given itself the name 'British Influence'. The truth is, outside the EU, the UK would lose influence. Every day, banks and other financial services firms in the City carry out a huge number of transactions with their counterparts in the rest of Europe. In 2012, the City's trade surplus with the EU was £16.6 billion—more than a third of the UK's total finance sector surplus. This trade in financial services is extremely valuable for the British economy. That is why it is in the UK's interest to have a say on the rules that govern these transactions. If the UK were to leave the EU, however, it would no longer be able to influence EU regulation. It would have to live with the rules decided on by the EU countries—and these countries, some of them with little or no financial services industry of their own, would have very little incentive to take the City's needs into account.

This is the hard truth. So why do some Euro-sceptics argue that the UK would be leaner and meaner on the outside, rid of all that alleged red tape imposed by the EU? After Britain's exit, they say, special access to the EU Single Market would be negotiated, this time at an advantage. They add that focus should shift to trade with other parts of the world. Maybe, also the Commonwealth could be revived.

So many ideas, so many lazy assumptions: 'fatally flawed', to use the words of the think tank, 'the Centre for European Reform'. First, to get access to the Single Market, you have to apply its rules. Just ask the Norwegians. It's difficult to see why the other Member States would grant the UK unfettered access to their markets without requiring it to apply the EU's rules. The equation would be simple—the more EU rules you apply, the more access to its market you will get. Secondly, the share of the UK's trade with the rest of the world is rising precisely *because* it is a member of the EU. It is testament to the effectiveness of the EU's trade policy in opening new markets for EU exports. The UK alone would not have the clout. And as for the Commonwealth, it represents only eight per cent of the UK's trade.

I would like to echo the words of Prime Minister Cameron, who very recently said the following with regards to the Scottish referendum on independence: 'The plain fact is we matter more in the world together'. Well, the same is true in the case of the EU.

III. DRIFTING APART: THE EUROZONE INTEGRATES AS THE UK SHUFFLES AWAY

In spite of the strong business case for UK membership of the EU, there is a clear sense, not just that the UK is semi-detached, but that it is drifting away. Dissatisfaction has moved well beyond the traditional bugbears like the Working Time Directive—whose impact on the private sector is limited, by the way, as even business representatives admit. Because British companies widely use an opt-out clause in the directive that allows individual employees to work more than the regulated 48 hours a week.

While we are used to people in this country fretting about issues like this one, their unease in other areas is more unexpected. Take the issue of free movement of EU citizens. You would think that a country as traditionally open to the world as the UK would embrace this fundamental freedom wholeheartedly. And for a long time it did. Let me give you a concrete example: Lord Mackenzie-Stuart was one of the judges sitting in the *Van Duyn* judgment of 1974.[1] In this case, it was a UK jurisdiction that asked the Court for the first time whether the provisions of the Treaty on free movement of workers were directly applicable. And the Court for the first time answered 'yes'. It held that workers in the Union can avail themselves directly of the freedom of movement without any discrimination on grounds of nationality.

Now something has changed. Openness is no longer seen as opportunity, but as a threat. Across political parties, there is talk of curbing immigration, of closing doors. Politicians have even abandoned their policy of pushing for ever more enlargement of the EU and are now taking a much more cautious stance. Whilst I welcome the fact that they finally agree with me on this topic, I still have to say this is a remarkable U-turn.

I have made my position clear: the four freedoms enshrined in the EU Treaties come as a package. You either enjoy all of them—or none. Those who benefit from the free flow of capital, goods and services must also accept that our citizens are free to move in the EU to travel, study and work. And the European rules allow Member States to fight abuse of this right.

I understand that in economically difficult times, people are worried about jobs, about opportunities for their children, about their ability to access public services. That is why all of us, but particularly politicians and businesspeople in this country need to reassure people. The people have a

[1] Case 41/74, *Van Duyn v Home Office* [1974] ECR 1337.

right to know the facts—for instance that 77 per cent of those EU citizens coming to the UK are in employment, a higher share than nationals, and a much higher share than third country migrants. They also deserve to hear that the UK hurts itself by making it more difficult for bright young people to come here to study and work, and by hampering the many employers who are looking to fill vacancies but cannot find suitable employees within the British workforce.

Politicians also need to work on the quality of education and welfare, so that people in this country can find employment and enjoy reasonable social standards. Simply trying to project all problems onto the supposed issue of too many foreigners moving into the country is certainly not the answer.

The discussion about EU policy in the area of police and judicial cooperation in criminal matters displays the same pattern. Of course, this is a challenging area in which the UK's common law tradition must interact with the civil law heritage of the majority of Member States. Yet all the elements that should ensure the UK's participation are in place. At present, the UK is only bound by instruments it has voluntarily opted into: all the measures were adopted under Protocols which give the UK broad opt-out rights. Most of these measures are not developments of the Schengen *acquis*, meaning that the UK can decide whether or not to participate on a case-by-case basis.

It is astounding to see the caution gripping the UK in this area. After all, the principle of mutual recognition, which underpins the European Arrest Warrant, was first advocated by the UK itself. Far from being an alien concept foisted on the UK by the EU, it is in fact a system which originated in this country and one which is still applied today between the different parts of the UK. Even more than this: the principle of mutual recognition was introduced for the first time into European law by the famous *Cassis de Dijon* judgment of 1979.[2] Lord Mackenzie-Stewart, to whom this lecture is dedicated, was again one of the sitting judges.

So why has the prospect of full judicial control by the Court of Justice shaken these foundations? The UK's Government has notified its intention to opt out of 135 measures in this area. This has raised considerable concern—voiced by practitioners, Police Chiefs and even a former Director of MI5. Cambridge's Centre for European Legal Studies has warned that the UK could become 'the Brazil of the EU' were it to opt out. Regardless of these warnings, the Government has pressed on. It has announced that it will request to opt back into certain measures. But this is an uncertain process in which decisions are taken by a qualified majority of the Member

[2] Case 120/78, *Rewe-Zentral AG v Bundesmonopolverwaltung für Branntwein* (*Cassis de Dijon*) [1979] ECR 42.

States, without the participation of the UK. It will lead to uncertainty in an area where clarity is needed to ensure our mutual security.

Just as the UK drifts away from the EU, there has been a strong push for integration in the Eurozone. This integration has been extraordinary. The economic crisis brutally exposed how incomplete and inadequate governance of the Eurozone was before the crisis. As a consequence, major reforms were undertaken. The economic and fiscal policy is much now more strongly coordinated and supervised at EU level. The aim is to spot difficulties early on and stop them spreading from one country to others. The European Commission is now even responsible for analysing the budgetary plans of euro area countries before national Parliaments have had their say—this development would have been unthinkable of a few years ago.

And stronger integration does not merely concern fiscal policy, it goes much further. A key plank is the European Semester, a yearly cycle of economic policy coordination. Member States draw up programmes for economic and structural reforms designed to improve competitiveness and drive economic growth and job creation. The Commission then analyses them and issues detailed recommendations for the next 12–18 months. The scope of these recommendations is broad—they cover issues such as taxation and pensions, public administration and the labour market. Suggested reforms include initiatives as diverse as improving companies' access to finance, promoting research, adapting wage-bargaining systems and making it easier to set up a business. Even though these are recommendations, the degree of coordination is remarkable.

Similarly huge leaps are being taken in the financial sector. To make our banks more stable and to ensure they fulfil their role of responsibly lending to businesses and consumers, we are building a Banking Union. We have already set up a central supervisor. This will soon be complemented by a common system for restructuring and resolving failing financial institutions that involves pooling money at EU level to be used in such cases. Again, a few years ago no one could have imagined Member States being prepared to cede sovereignty in such a sensitive area. But we learned the lessons of the crisis and created the necessary instruments to avoid problems in the future.

In order to strengthen the Single Currency, the Union had to address the causes of the crisis which lay in Member States' fiscal bases, their financial sectors and the potentially fatal link between the two.

All these reforms have serious implications for the EU's Single Market. Whereas in the past, the Single Market and the single currency developed side by side, the crisis made clear how interconnected the two are. For the Eurozone members, the ultimate goal is to ensure the stability of the euro. They view and approach the new rules and architecture first and foremost with this objective in their minds. While a stable currency union is obviously also essential for Member States outside the Eurozone, their main interest may lie elsewhere—for instance in preserving the Single Market for all 28 EU countries and their unimpeded access to it.

These different starting points create strong tensions. And these tensions are likely to grow as the process of stronger integration of the Eurozone advances further. We have made great strides, but more bold reforms will be needed. Of course the debate on the future of the EU is ongoing, but there is a strong case for a true fiscal and ultimately political union. In my personal view, the Eurozone should become a kind of 'United States of Europe'. Like Winston Churchill, I believe that the UK will not be part of this, but it should remain a close ally with the federated Eurozone, with which it would continue to share a common market, a common trade policy and hopefully a common security agenda.

How then do we ease the tension and reconcile the interests of Member States which share a currency with the interests of others? This is the crucial challenge we will have to master over the next 5 to 10 years. Given its dependence, for better or for worse, on its financial services sector, resolving this issue is the key to the UK's future in the European Union.

IV. A SEPARATION IS AVOIDABLE: FINDING THE RIGHT LINK BETWEEN THE SINGLE MARKET AND THE SINGLE CURRENCY

This will require two preconditions. First, the UK should accept that it is in its interest to allow the Eurozone members to do what it takes to strengthen the euro. This was not immediately clear to British politicians. The UK opposed the proposed Fiscal Compact, forcing the remaining Member States to proceed on an inter-governmental basis to save the single currency. Since then, the tone and the policies have changed. The Chancellor has said very clearly that a stable euro on the UK's doorstep is good for growth and jobs in the UK.

Secondly, the Eurozone members must acknowledge the need to find solutions where their interests are different from those of the Member States who do not share the single currency. Otherwise, they risk pushing the UK out of the EU before it decides of its own accord, as it might, to jump.

Striking this balance has so far not proven easy. That might explain why the views of the European Court of Justice are in high demand. Take the lawsuits against EU rules curbing bonuses and against plans by some Member States to introduce a financial transaction tax, or the latest one concerning 'short selling'. Obviously, it is neither in the UK's interest nor in that of the other Member States to negotiate their relationships through court cases. And there are signs that when the two sides are willing to find solutions, progress is possible.

In a positive tone, the area of banking regulation offers some interesting examples of how the other Member States and the Commission accommodated the UK's interests and concerns. Take the rules governing the European Banking Authority (EBA) in London. By developing the single rulebook for Europe's financial institutions and promoting consistency of supervision across all 28 EU Member States, the EBA has a crucial role in ensuring a level playing-field for European banks and preserving the Single Market in financial services. While the Eurozone countries were setting up the Single Supervisory Mechanism, the UK was worried that they would form a bloc to outvote it on the EBA's Board of Supervisors which is the main decision-making body of this institution and where each of the national supervisors is represented. This was resolved through the creation of a double majority voting system: now, when the EBA decides, for instance, on binding technical standards, a majority of both Eurozone and non-Eurozone countries need to agree for the standards to come into force. Another example: Eurozone countries agreed to insert a non-discrimination clause into the Regulation setting up the Single Supervisory Mechanism. It states that 'no action, proposal or policy of the ECB shall, directly or indirectly, discriminate against any Member State or group of Member States as a venue for the provision of banking or financial services in any currency'. This clause recognises that London's role as a leading financial centre is based in part on the euro-denominated banking services it provides. The purpose of the clause is to prevent any restriction of London's role as a financial centre in the Single Market through measures connected to the euro.

What's more, when drawing up its proposals for the structural reform of banks, the European Commission took the situation in the UK into account. One of the key elements of the draft regulation would give supervisors the power to require large banks to separate certain potentially risky trading activities from their deposit-taking business if the pursuit of such activities threatens financial stability. In the context of the Banking Union, the ECB would be the supervisor taking this decision for the countries taking part in it. Rather unusually, for a regulation grounded on a single market legal basis, it opens up ways for a Member State to apply its own rules on this particular point: a derogation may be granted to individual banks that are already subject to equivalent measures in another Member State. This means that banks in the UK, if already subject to British ring-fencing rules, would not necessarily have to apply a second set of EU rules.

Of course, this could still be changed during negotiations by the Member States and the European Parliament. But if the provision stays, the UK could use it, as it is already in the process of implementing its own rules designed to reach the same objective, but in a different way (by requiring banks to ring-fence the deposit-taking part of their business against difficulties arising from their riskier activities).

V. CONCLUSION: A DEBATE THAT LIVES UP TO BRITISH STANDARDS

This brings me back to what I said in the beginning. The debate in this country about the UK's place in the EU is distorted. All that talk about opt-outs, renegotiations and referenda distracts from the real issue. Finding more solutions like the ones I have described is what we should all be focusing our energy and creativity on.

Unfortunately, the debate is distracting from the real challenge in the relationship between the UK and the EU. And it is even inflicting wider damage by holding back our Union as a whole. We don't need this. What we need are great ideas and solid arguments about how we can strengthen the EU and make it more competitive on the world stage. What we need is to push for valuable policies: creating a real single market in services, strengthening small and medium-sized enterprises, boosting free trade with other parts of the world.

The UK could make a real difference here, and this is one of the reasons why I would argue that the EU is stronger with the UK in it. Indeed, it is one of the reasons why I want it to stay in—and why I also want to say to you: if this country decides one day to be part of a stronger integration, you know where to find us. The door is open, and there is a seat at the table for you.

Right now, however, we have a problem: the potentially constructive and forward-looking arguments are overshadowed by the negative debate on the relationship between the UK and the EU. The solution? It should be clear to everyone in this room; everyone in this country, in fact. Mark Carney, Governor of the Bank of England, made it very clear in a recent statement. We need to replace the current debate, which leads to uncertainty for business and holds off investment, with constructive proposals that bring about certainty, investment and progress. This would be beneficial for both the UK and the EU.

The British can still do what comes naturally to them and debate their way out of this. They have every right, and even a duty, to be critical, to scrutinise and to question. But whatever they do, I just hope they do it in true British style.

2

The Public Procurement Rules in Action: An Empirical Exploration of Social Impact and Ideology

AMY LUDLOW[1]

Abstract

Governments are increasingly turning to the market to provide public goods, works and (perhaps most controversially) services. Markets, and market values, have come to govern our lives as never before and the financial crisis appears to have done little to dampen governments' faiths in markets. The public procurement rules define some of the parameters within which governments must engage with the market but the ideology of these rules, particularly how much 'space' they afford Member States to pursue non-commercial policies in their procurement decision-making, is deeply contested. This chapter argues that there is a missing empirical dimension to these ideological discussions. It seeks to partially redress this by presenting findings from an ethnographic study of a competitive tendering exercise at a British prison, from which it is argued that a more complex ideological picture emerges than appears from doctrinal analyses of the rules.

I. INTRODUCTION

UNLIKE PRIVATE PARTIES, government bodies are not permitted to conclude contracts by whatever process they wish or, arguably, with whomever and on whatever terms they wish. Government bodies must instead comply with public procurement rules, which regulate how they are able to acquire goods, works and services from the market. Justifications for these additional restraints vary, and are contested, but

[1] I am grateful to the AHRC for funding the fieldwork upon which this chapter draws and to Catherine Barnard and Nicky Padfield for our many useful discussions that shaped my thoughts during fieldwork and beyond. Thanks also go to Niamh Dunne, Oke Odudu and Kenneth Armstrong for their helpful comments when an earlier draft of this work was presented at a CELS lunchtime seminar. All errors, of course, remain my own.

most commonly include concerns about corruption, cronyism and inefficiency in the spending of taxpayer money.[2]

In the EU, national public procurement rules have become increasingly coordinated by a series of EU public procurement directives. Though discriminatory public procurement practices have been prohibited since the EU's infancy through the free movement provisions in the Treaties, non-tariff barriers to trade (such as preferential procurement practices) were not at the top of the (then) EEC's original legislative agenda. As Trepte explains, this was because tariff barriers were more easily identifiable and remediable obstacles to trade than non-tariff impediments.[3]

However, as the Common Market matured, tariff barriers became less common and national preferential procurement practices crept up the legislative agenda. In 1961, the Council adopted two General Programmes that sought the abolition of national procurement rules and practices that placed limitations upon the participation of non-national companies in procurement processes for public works contracts.[4] These were implemented from 1964 onwards by a series of liberalisation directives. At first, the directives were confined to reiterating the principle of non-discrimination but they have since gone much further by imposing an ever-increasing degree of procedural coordination upon state procurement bodies. In February 2014, the EU Council adopted three new directives on public procurement: two amending previous directives (Directive 2014/24/EU replacing Directive 2004/18/EC on public works, supply and service contracts, and, Directive 2014/25/EU replacing Directive 2004/17/EC on procurement in the water, energy, transport and postal services sectors); and the third, a new directive (Directive 2014/23/EU) on concession contracts.[5]

During the last 30 years, the importance of these public procurement rules has increased. In 2008–09, the UK Government spent £220 billion on public procurement,[6] amounting to 19 per cent of the UK's GDP in 2008.[7] Although private finance has become more difficult since the financial crisis of 2007, there remains strong support for the procurement and privatisation of public services, not least among the Troika—the European Commission, the European Central Bank and the International Monetary Fund—as reflected in the conditions it has imposed upon Member States in

[2] O Dekel, 'The legal theory of competitive bidding for Government contracts' (2008) 37 *Public Contract Journal* 237–67.

[3] P Trepte, *Public Procurement in the EU: A Practitioner's Guide*, 2nd edn (Oxford, OUP, 2007) 5.

[4] General Programme for the abolition of restrictions on freedom to provide services (JO 2/32; English special edition, series II, vol IX, p 3) and General Programme for the abolition of restrictions on freedom of establishment (JO 2/36; English special edition, series II, vol IX, p 7).

[5] For all three directives, see [2014] OJ L94/1–374.

[6] HM Treasury, *Public Expenditure Statistical Analyses 2009* (April 2009).

[7] D Audet, 'Government procurement: a synthesis report' (2002) 2 *OECD Journal on Budgeting* 149–94.

receipt of 'bail-outs'[8] as a way for governments to deliver 'more for less'. Notwithstanding powerful critiques of austerity policies and neoliberal assumptions about markets and market actors,[9] the UK Government has made strong commitments to procure public services from deregulated markets. In its 2011 *Open Public Services* White Paper, the UK Government said: 'Apart from those public services where the Government has a special reason to operate a monopoly (eg the military) every public service should be open so that ... services can be delivered by a diverse range of providers'.[10] Regulation is seen as 'red tape' that needs to be cut as far as possible to create the conditions under which the market is said to work best.[11]

In this context of 'market triumphalism',[12] the public procurement rules have become a site of ideological conflict, crystallising and refracting deeper, related dissatisfactions about the future of the EU and the balance of power between the EU and the Member States,[13] particularly in areas where national social policy has been 'forced' to acquiesce to EU free movement rights (see especially the *Viking* and *Laval* cases and their progeny).[14] Some recent scholarship has contributed to these debates by exploring the scope and purposes of the public procurement rules with a view to shedding light on how much discretion is left, or ought to be left, to Member States

[8] See for example the privatisation of Thessaloniki Water and Sewage Company in Greece (www.popularresistance.org/troika-demands-privatization-of-greek-assets-workers-push-back/) and public utilities in Cyprus (www.euractiv.com/euro-finance/cyprus-parliament-rejects-troika-news-533830).

[9] See for example M Blyth, *Austerity: The History of a Dangerous Idea* (Oxford, OUP, 2013), S Deakin and F Wilkinson, 'Rights v. efficiency? The economic case for transnational labour standards' (1994) 23 *Industrial Law Journal* 289–310 and K Busch et al, *Austeritätspolitik und das Europäische Sozialmodell: Wie die Krisenpolitik in Südeuropa die soziale Dimension der EU bedroht* (Berlin, Friedrich Ebert Stiftung, 2012). See also the European Parliament's recent criticism of the Troika: www.europarl.europa.eu/news/en/news-room/content/20140307IPR38407/html/Troika-helped-to-avoid-the-worst-but-flawed-structure-harmed-recovery.

[10] www.cabinetoffice.gov.uk/sites/default/files/resources/open-public-services-white-paper.pdf.

[11] See especially the British Coalition Government's 'Red Tape Challenge': www.redtapechallenge.cabinetoffice.gov.uk/home/index/.

[12] M Sandel, *What Money Can't Buy: The Moral Limits of Markets* (London, Allen Lane, 2012).

[13] For recent academic reflections see A Giddens, *Turbulent and Mighty Continent: What Future for Europe?* (Cambridge, Polity Press, 2014).

[14] C-438/05 *International Transport Workers' Federation and Finnish Seamen's Union v Viking Line ABP and OÜ Viking Line Eesti* [2007] ECR I-10779; Case C-341/05 *Laval un Partneri Ltd v Svenska Byggnadsarbetareförbundet and Others* [2007] ECR I-11767; Case C-346/06 *Rüffert v Land Niedersachsen* [2008] ECR I-1989; and C-319/06 *Commission v Luxembourg* [2009] ECR I-4323. See related debates about the meaning of Services of General Interest. On their relationship with the public procurement rules see N Fiedziuk, 'Putting services of general economic interest up for tender: reflections on applicable EU rules' (2013) 50 *Common Market Law Review* 87–114. On their relationship with internal market law more broadly see M Cremona (ed), *Market Integration and Public Services in the European Union* (Oxford, OUP, 2011).

in their procurement decision-making. Such regulatory autonomy might be used by Member States to fulfil other national policy objectives (a power described by Kunzlik as 'dominium'[15]), which might include social or environmental protection (described by Arrowsmith as 'horizontal procurement policies'[16]).

In this chapter, I build upon a trio of recent and influential contributions to this field: Graells' 2011 monograph, *Public Procurement and the EU Competition Rules*,[17] Arrowsmith's response to Graells' monograph in the 2012 *Cambridge Yearbook of European Legal Studies*[18] and Kunzlik's reply and partial dissent from Arrowsmith's paper in the 2013 *Cambridge Yearbook of European Legal Studies*.[19] My arguments are three-fold. First, that although doctrinal and theoretical arguments are important, they ought to be viewed alongside, and enriched by, empirical research that explores the significance and operation of the law in practice. Notwithstanding important recent efforts to stimulate methodological debate,[20] there remains a dearth of empirical research in EU law fields that ought to be redressed.[21] Secondly, I argue on the basis of an ethnographic study of the operation of the public procurement rules that empirical data paints a more complex and less certain picture about the ideology of public procurement than a doctrinal analysis of the rules would suggest. Notwithstanding Kunzlik's persuasive doctrinal account of the procurement rules as 'broadly conform[ing] to the preferred neo-liberal model of international (or in this case supranational) regulation' and strong pressures particularly from the European Commission and Graells to deploy and interpret the rules in an increasingly neoliberal manner, empirical data suggests that public

[15] P Kunzlik, 'Neo-liberalism and the European public procurement regime' in C Barnard et al (eds), *Cambridge Yearbook of European Legal Studies 2012–2013* (Oxford, Hart Publishing, 2013) 283–356.

[16] S Arrowsmith, 'The purpose of the EU procurement directives: ends, means and the implications for national regulatory space for commercial and horizontal procurement policies' in C Barnard and M Gehring (eds), *Cambridge Yearbook of European Legal Studies 2011–2012* (Oxford, Hart Publishing, 2012) 1–47. See generally on horizontal procurement policies S Arrowsmith and P Kunzlik (eds), *Social and Environmental Policies in EC Procurement Law: New Directives and New Directions* (Cambridge, CUP, 2009) and C McCrudden, *Buying Social Justice: Equality, Government Procurement, and Legal Change* (Oxford, OUP, 2007).

[17] A Sánchez Graells, *Public Procurement and the EU Competition Rules* (Oxford, Hart Publishing, 2011).

[18] See n 16, above.

[19] See n 15, above.

[20] See particularly T Hervey, R Cryer, B Sokhi-Bulley and A Bohm, *Research Methodologies in EU and International Law* (Oxford, Hart Publishing, 2011).

[21] Though notable exceptions include S Bekker, *Flexicurity: The Emergence of a European Concept* (Cambridge, Intersentia, 2012), scholarship in the social cohesion field such as J Bachtler, C Mendez and F Wishlade, *EU Cohesion Policy and European Integration* (Farnham, Ashgate, 2013), and T Daintith, *Implementing EC Law in the United Kingdom* (Chichester, John Wiley & Sons, 1995).

procurement regulation is not necessarily mobilised as a neoliberal construct in practice. Neoliberalism may be simultaneously both an overstatement and an understatement of how these rules operate. Finally, I argue that these empirical findings might suggest that the efforts of those who seek to highlight or enlarge the scope for national autonomy within the public procurement framework might be better directed by engaging more directly with procurement practitioners and commissioners.

The remainder of this chapter is structured as follows. Section II provides a more detailed account of the features of the public procurement rules that are central to any assessment of their 'ideology' and, more particularly, the balance that is struck between market and non-market values. This section also outlines the key arguments posited by Graells, Arrowsmith and Kunzlik in their publications, arguing that all three contributions could be enriched by an empirical dimension. Section III introduces the empirical context and methods used to gather the data upon which the rest of the section draws, in order to probe the ideology of the public procurement rules. Sub-section A addresses procurement at national level (an 'overstatement') and B addresses procurement at local level (an 'understatement'). Section IV concludes and reflects upon the implications of the study's empirical findings for the direction of future public procurement reform, practice and research.

II. THE PUBLIC PROCUREMENT RULES AS A SITE OF IDEOLOGICAL AND SCHOLARLY CONFLICT

Society has an interest in obtaining public services at the best price and ensuring that the public procurement rules achieve optimum economic outcomes. However, society also has non-economic interests, such as employment rights or environmental protection, which go beyond finding the lowest price for its goods and services.[22] Particularly in times of financial crisis, there is strong pressure on national governments to use public money to support national industry. Where jobs are lost to non-national service providers, society has to bear the costs of rising social security payments. Consequently, procurement decisions that have these sorts of social consequence may not represent best value in its broader (national) societal sense. This is why procurement decisions can prompt such intense political debate and public reaction.

But this desire to further local non-economic (or even economic) interests comes into conflict with the EU's ethos of dismantling national trade barriers and cultivating efficiencies across the whole European market. From

[22] For discussion, see for example C McCrudden, *Buying Social Justice: Equality, Government Procurement and Legal Change* (Oxford, OUP, 2007).

a European perspective (and particularly from the European Commission's perspective), the pursuit of interests that do not have tangible and immediate economic benefits, suggests national protectionism and discrimination, the very antithesis of the European free market.[23] In designing the public procurement rules, European legislators must therefore strike a 'balance' between these competing interests or, perhaps more realistically, determine which set of interests (global or national) is to take precedence.[24]

As Kunzlik helpfully outlines in his *Yearbook* paper, the European Commission has long argued that there is little scope within the public procurement rules for contracting authorities to take non-economic interests into account in their procurement decisions. In the Commission's view, the public procurement rules seek to achieve best value for taxpayer money by creating the competitive and procedural conditions under which public procurement bodies behave so far as is possible like private sector, economically rational market actors. Consequently, the Commission has argued, for example, that technical specifications (the documents setting out what government bodies want to buy) must only include requirements affecting consumption characteristics and not the manner of production. Furthermore, the Commission has argued that contracting authorities must be able to demonstrate that a direct economic advantage flows from all contract award criteria, and that contracting authorities cannot demand compliance with contractual conditions that are unrelated to the functional needs of the subject-matter of the contract (narrowly construed). These interpretations of the public procurement rules preclude commissioners from using social or environmental award criteria, since they mostly do not affect the characteristics or performance of the product or service that is being purchased; they cannot be objectively assigned a direct economic value. Applying this reasoning, electricity that is produced from renewable energy works just as well from a functional perspective as electricity produced from coal-powered sources and so source should not form part of any technical specification. Equally, office furniture that is manufactured at factories that pay below the living wage (but above any statutory minimum wage) is just as serviceable as furniture produced by higher paid staff.

However, there is little textual evidence on the face of the public procurement rules to support the Commission's interpretation: the text is arguably ideologically inconclusive.[25] More significantly, the CJEU has, in

[23] Views reflected in, for example, the Commission's *Green Paper on the Modernisation of EU Public Procurement Policy: Towards a More Efficient European Procurement Market* COM(2011) 15/47.

[24] Catherine Barnard has recently coined 'glocalisation' as a term to describe this tension between globalisation and localism: www.youtube.com/watch?v=wMN6N8yWfbU.

[25] I acknowledge though that the procurement rules have an internal market legal basis and the Court has used this before as a means of prioritising internal market objectives over competing social objectives. See for example interpretation of the Posted Workers' Directive

some of its case law interpreting the procurement rules, cast doubt upon the Commission's views of what the rules entail. In *Concordia Bus*[26] for example, the CJEU rejected the Commission's argument that each contract award criterion must confer a direct economic advantage on the contracting authority, holding instead that indirect economic advantage is sufficient so long as the award criterion is 'linked to the subject matter of the contract'. The Court also rejected the Commission's argument that technical specifications may only impose requirements that affect consumption characteristics and not the manner of production, in *EVN*[27] (concerning renewable source electricity) and *Commission v Netherlands*[28] (concerning organic and fair trade coffee). In *Beentjes*[29] and *Nord-Pas-de-Calais*[30] the Court validated the inclusion of award criteria that go beyond the narrow functional needs of the contract by imposing, for example, a condition on contractors that they employ some of the long-term unemployed.

Yet, notwithstanding this case law, some of the CJEU's other decisions have served to reinforce the Commission's (neoliberal) stance. Perhaps most significant is the shift in the Court's free movement case law from the traditional discrimination model to market access.[31] Unlike the discrimination model, market access enables restrictions upon free movement to be challenged if they are likely to prohibit or impede access, even if the restrictions apply without distinction to both nationals and non-nationals and do not have a national protectionist purpose. This approach tends to have a deregulatory effect since both home and host state rules can be challenged and almost anything can constitute an impediment to free movement. As Snell has argued, 'When pressed, the notion of market access collapses into economic freedom or anti-protectionism, and obscures the need to choose between the competing paradigms of free movement law'.[32] Moreover, although restrictions may be justified by reference to an unlimited number of public interest motivations, which include the protection of social interests, the defendant (state) bears the burden of proving justification

(96/71/EC), which is based upon free movement of services. See further R Blanpain, *Freedom of Services in the European Union: Labour and Social Security Law* (The Hague, Kluwer Law International, 2006) 184–85 and T Novitz, 'UK Implementation of the Posting of Workers Directive 96/71/EC' in S Evju (ed), *Cross-Border Services, Posting of Workers, and Multilevel Governance* (Oslo, University of Oslo, 2013) 329–57.

[26] C-513/99 *Concordia Bus Finland* [2002] ECR I-7251.

[27] C-448/01 *EVN AG & Wienstrom GmbH v Austria* [2003] ECR I-14527.

[28] C-368/10 *Commission v Netherlands* [2012] ECR I-284.

[29] C-31/87 *Gebroeders Beentjes BV v Netherlands* [1988] ECR 4635.

[30] C-225/98 *Commission v France (Nord-Pas-de-Calais)* [2000] ECR I-7445.

[31] See, for example, C-76/90 *Säger v Dennemeyer & Co Ltd* [1991] ECR I-4221 and C-110/05 *Commission v Italy (trailers)* [2009] ECR I-519. For general analysis of this case law see C Barnard, *The Substantive Law of the EU: The Four Freedoms* (Oxford, OUP, 2013).

[32] J Snell, 'The notion of market access: a concept or slogan?' (2010) 47 *Common Market Law Review* 437–72.

and proportionality, and the Court has taken a narrow approach to social justification in its recent case law.[33] This is why Barnard has argued that the market access approach 'inevitably prioritises the economic right over the social interest'.[34]

The consequences of this case law for the public procurement field are that it becomes much less certain what sort of procedural or substantive requirements imposed as part of the procurement process will be considered prima facie discriminatory and harder to predict how the CJEU will approach potential justifications, especially in the field of social policy. All in all, this produces an uncertain and contested legal landscape as a potential consequence of which some European Member States appear to have been much less ambitious in their horizontal procurement policies and commissioning guidance than others. Scottish guidance, for example, is generally more ambitious than its Westminster counterpart. According to the Scottish Procurement Directorate's website, in March 2010 John Swinney, Cabinet Secretary for Finance and Sustainable Growth, said: 'The first question that we should ask when developing any contract specification should be: "Can we include a community benefit clause?"'.[35] The Directorate has produced extensive, positive guidance on corporate social responsibility (covering social, economic and environmental issues)[36] and community benefits in public procurement.[37] However, the paucity of empirical evidence in this field means that it is difficult to determine whether policy differences are merely rhetorical or whether they produce divergent procurement practices.

In this context of few textual indicators in the public procurement rules, some inconsistency and tensions in the CJEU's guidance on their interpretation, and divergence between the Member States in how the rules are understood, attention has shifted in recent scholarship to explore the purposes of the procurement rules, informed by the history of their development and their relationship with other aspects of internal market regulation. By identifying the purposes of the rules, scholars are able to posit how the rules ought to be interpreted and, more particularly, what balance should be struck between EU (the global) and Member State (the local) power. Graells and Arrowsmith present strongly divergent views in this respect, with Kunzlik's account sitting between the two, albeit closer to Arrowsmith than Graells.

Graells presents a 'manifesto' for the neoliberalisation of the public procurement rules. In Graells' view, public procurement is exclusively

[33] See n 13, above.

[34] C Barnard, 'Procurement law to enforce labour standards' in G Davidov and B Langille (eds), *The Idea of Labour Law* (Oxford, OUP, 2011) 256–72.

[35] www.scotland.gov.uk/Topics/Government/Procurement/policy/procurecombenefits.

[36] www.scotland.gov.uk/Topics/Government/Procurement/policy/corporate-responsibility.

[37] www.scotland.gov.uk/Topics/Government/Procurement/policy/procurecombenefits.

concerned with achieving economic goals. Consequently, he argues that their dominating norm should be competition to achieve efficiency. Graells argues that competition and public procurement law should be largely immune from other social policy objectives which, he suggests, are more appropriately pursued (if at all) through labour regulation and tax and social security law. By contrast, by tracing the history and legal bases of the procurement rules, Arrowsmith argues that the purpose of the rules is to promote the internal market *only* through the removal of access barriers and the imposition of non-discrimination and transparency obligations. In her view, the EU does not have the competence to mandate competition in its normative sense (a neoliberal definition of 'value for money') through its procurement rules as Graells suggests. Competition, in Arrowsmith's view, plays only an instrumental role in public procurement: it is a mechanism to remove discrimination and barriers to entry into markets and a means to ensure transparency. Thus, while increased competitiveness (and value for money) may be a by-product of the introduction of competitive procedures and a non-discrimination obligation, it is not a function of the rules. As she explained: 'This [Graells' thesis], however, puts the cart before the horse ... the purpose of competitive procedures is to secure transparency to prevent discrimination, rather than transparency being required to secure competition in general'.[38] Kunzlik adopts much of Arrowsmith's analysis but he departs from it by agreeing with Graells that competition is an aim of the public procurement rules. In contrast to Graells however, he defines competition much more narrowly as referring to the 'structure of competition', meaning that it is concerned to 'protect the structure of the market and equality of competitive opportunity' between traders. In his view, competition does not relate to the neoliberal efficiency concept that Graells suggests.

All three of these authors make important contributions to the field by offering different conceptions of what the procurement rules should achieve. I have found Arrowsmith's account particularly influential and helpful in some of my other work;[39] undoubtedly in part a reflection of my allied interests in research that explores the cultural and performance benefits of social protection, from which my view has developed that there ought to be space for national proactivity and diversity in social policy, particularly in the face of CJEU case law that arguably does not take social rights 'seriously'.[40] My task here though is not to explain why I might

[38] Arrowsmith, see n 16, above at 26.

[39] A Ludlow, *Privatising Public Prisons: Theory, Law and Practice* (Oxford, Hart Publishing, 2015, forthcoming).

[40] See for example the divergence between the CJEU and ECtHR's approaches to Art 11 ECHR described in A Ludlow, 'The right to strike: a jurisprudential gulf between the CJEU and ECtHR' in K Dzehtsiarou et al (eds), *Human Rights Law in Europe* (Abingdon, Routledge, 2014) 121–36.

prefer one author's view over another, but rather to highlight a dimension that is missing from all three accounts, namely the empirical experience of the public procurement rules and to suggest that all three accounts could be enriched by reference to empirical data. Empirical questions might include: how do procurement practitioners understand and operationalise the rules? Do they feel that their horizontal procurement policy discretion is constrained? What do they see as the purposes and ideology of the rules? The CJEU's understanding of the issues in public procurement practice is conditioned by the few cases that come before the Court each year. In practice, the vast majority of procurement activity happens without the Court or Commission ever hearing about it. How do things work in the vast majority of procurement exercises that 'fly under the radar' and what might we learn from that about the ideology of public procurement and how we might best shape it?

III. EMPIRICAL INSIGHTS

This section begins to address some of those questions by drawing upon an 11-month ethnographic study conducted between November 2010 and October 2011 of a competitive tendering exercise for the contract to manage HMP Birmingham, a local, mostly Victorian-built prison in the West Midlands of England, housing just short of 1500 men. The study proceeded from a broad interest in how social rights were safeguarded during a competitive process, with a particular focus upon the operation, effectiveness and interaction between of a set of employment law regulations (with EU origins), the Transfer of Undertakings (Protection of Employment) Regulations 2006 (more commonly referred to as 'TUPE'), and the public procurement rules. It is acknowledged that prison services formally fall within Annex IB of Directive 2004/18, with the consequence that the Birmingham competition was not in theory subject to the full rigours of the procurement rules. However, in practice since many of the constraints imposed by the procurement rules are replicated in the CJEU's case law which still applies to Annex IB services, it was thought likely that the Birmingham competition would shed useful light upon the operation of the procurement rules. As it transpired in fieldwork, the contracting authority (the National Offender Management Service (NOMS), an agency of the Ministry of Justice) was running the competition as if the procurement rules applied in full. There was limited understanding of the distinction drawn in the Directive between 'part A' and 'part B' services (see further below).

The primary mode of data collection was 11 months of participant observation which yielded extensive, often verbatim, fieldwork and interview notes, totalling over 1000 pages. 86 semi-structured interviews were conducted with Birmingham's staff and managers, trade union officials and staff running the competition or managing employment and industrial relations as NOMS employees. This was supplemented by focus groups with a total of 24 participants and documentary analysis of internal communications and records and contract and tendering papers. Fieldwork in Birmingham spanned publication of the contract notice in the Official Journal of the EU (OJEU) (November 2010) to one month after contractual vesting with the new selected provider, G4S (October 2011). I have since returned to Birmingham twice (in December 2011 and 2012) as part of a research group invited into the prison by its new Governor to provide his team with an indication of the prison's performance and direction of travel.[41]

What light does this data shed upon the ideology of public procurement? In short, the data paints a more complex and conditional ideological picture than the neoliberalism that emerges from a doctrinal analysis of the rules and their EU policy context. Evidence about the chaotic and costly nature of the procurement process and the inclusion of some social policy parameters within it suggests that neoliberalism may be an ideological 'overstatement' of procurement practice at a national level. However, neoliberal characterisations of public procurement seem simultaneously too 'thin' ('understatements') when account is taken of the local procurement picture. The following two sub-sections explore the data in respect of each of these dimensions in turn. Although I recognise that the definition of neoliberalism is itself contested, Kunzlik's definition is adopted, since my intention is to build upon his and other previous contributions and probe neoliberalism empirically more than conceptually. Our shared broad concern is about the balance between market and non-market values within the procurement framework.

A. An 'Overstatement' at National Level?

While Kunzlik acknowledges that public procurement is in some senses inherently challenging for neoliberals, because, for example, public purchasers are public bodies having public functions and they generally do not compete with each other, his overall argument is that the public procurement regime 'broadly conforms to the preferred neo-liberal model of international (or in this case supranational) regulation'. This argument seems (at least implicitly) accepted by many scholars active in the field of horizontal procurement policy: the starting point and challenge is how to 'overcome' the neoliberalism bequeathed as part of the

[41] See further on methods Ludlow, n 39, above.

procurement rules.[42] But data from the Birmingham competition suggests a less straightforward picture: while on their face the procurement rules may be neoliberal, they do not necessarily produce procurement processes and contracts that are neoliberal. Four key themes and issues can be drawn from the data in respect of the contracting authority's understanding and accommodation of the public procurement rules: (1) competition as an end in itself; (2) displacement of substance and social; (3) chaotic and costly process; (4) unrealised social boldness. The first two themes broadly support a neoliberal account of public procurement but the last two complicate the picture and provide a counter-narrative to neoliberalism.

In his notes on writing up qualitative research, Back encourages researchers to begin by thinking about the project's 'primal scene', the moment when they realised 'I am on to something'. The aim is to take the reader 'to the place where the social action is going on'.[43] There are two 'primal scenes' from the Birmingham data that encapsulate the first two themes of 'competition as an end in itself' and 'displacement of substance and social'. Both interactions took place in HMP Birmingham shortly after the decision to transfer management of the prison to G4S in April 2011, but the contrast between the perspectives of the two individuals could scarcely be starker:

> *Researcher:* Do you think this competition has been a success?
>
> *NOMS Senior Manager:* Yes it has. It's been a clean process. Obviously the bidders that didn't win weren't pleased but everyone agrees that it was a fair process. We managed to avoid any leaks. Nobody knew until the Minister stood up in the House of Commons. That was a big achievement. We've proved to the private sector that the prisons market is worth investing in.
>
> *Birmingham Senior Officer:* Success? I dunno what they were trying to achieve. Four staff were sent off duty during the last 10 days because they were crying and shaking uncontrollably. We sent another two off in the last week for alcohol related issues. You see everyone in the car park before work psyching themselves up, in tears, doing their best to come into work. If that's what they wanted then I guess they've got it, yeah. We're broken. I don't know anymore.

The divergence in these responses reflects the different perspectives from which each individual had participated in, and experienced, the competition. The officer had no knowledge of the manager's high-level decision-making and no understanding about the purpose and process of competition, or its next steps. This is reflected in the officer's choice of words, which express feelings of hopelessness and futility. By contrast, the manager's evaluation

[42] For a somewhat different view see D Damjanovic, 'The EU market rules as social market rules: why the EU can be a social market economy' (2013) 50 *Common Market Law Review* 1685–718.

[43] L Back, 'Take your reader there: some notes on writing qualitative research', Durham University Department of Anthropology, 'writing on writing' series ((last accessed 26 September 2014).

of success bore no trace of the competition's human impact, upon which the officer's response focused. While both individuals were intimately involved in the process of competition, their worlds had remained entirely separate: there was an almost total disconnection between the process of competition and the people whom it affected.

The substance of the manager's response is also an interesting reflection of NOMS' priorities. The manager's focus upon the integrity of the process ('clean', fair and no leaks), and the capacity of such a process to build a dynamic prison market, comes at the expense of any consideration about whether the competition has laid solid foundations for the prison's future improvement, despite this being a central outcome promised by the Government. It seems likely that this is partly a product of the 'high-stakes' political context in which Birmingham was competed. The Government had only tried to subject a 'traditional' local prison to competition once before (at HMP Brixton in 2001) and that process was abandoned, reportedly for want of bidders interested in running an old, costly prison with a poor industrial relations history. The Government could not (in reputation terms) afford another Brixton. It needed to take on the Prison Officers' Association (POA) and win; show its staff and private company bidders that it could be tough and commercially rigorous.

Rather than using competition, then, as a tool to achieve higher values, competition was seen by the contracting authority as an end in itself: jumping through 'the hoops' of the process of competition took precedence over outcomes. In such a context it was perhaps unsurprising to find that there was little explicit consideration of horizontal procurement policies. Despite problems with staff culture and practice being core to the prison's historically poor performance, the contracting authority had not developed a 'social vision' for the future of the prison or its staff beyond ensuring compliance in the final contract with fairly minimal statutory obligations. The process of competition alone was thought to provide the 'cure' for Birmingham's problems and there was little appetite for trying to shape how the new service provider would achieve change. There was little attempt to 'align values, institutions and markets'.[44] Decisions about the competition process, such as the decisions to use competitive dialogue (a process where bidders construct their bid incrementally in light of feedback they receive during a series of dialogue sessions with the contracting authority), to put out a call for tenders in respect of five prisons simultaneously, and to outsource *all* services at the prisons rather than just parts of what they provide, were taken without evidence of much thought being given to their impact on the ongoing performance of the prisons, their staff or their future

[44] T Brown, M Potoski and D van Slyke, 'Managing public service contracts: aligning values, institutions and markets' (2006) *Public Administration Review* 323–31.

improvement trajectories. In interview, procurement staff seemed mostly unaware of the distinction between 'part A' and 'part B' services or the potential in this instance (because prison ('part B') services were sought) to apply the public procurement rules in a more limited, 'relaxed' manner than if the services had fallen with part A. It might have been a deliberate policy choice to apply the public procurement rules in full, owing to concerns about the potential risk and cost of litigation brought by unsatisfied tenderers, but I did not find evidence of this.

As the competition progressed, the already limited appetite for 'pro-social' process shaping appeared to wane further. Alongside the OJEU contract notice, NOMS' procurement team produced a statement of the 'Principles of Competition'. This was provided to all bidders as part of the pre-qualification documentation in November 2009. A revised second version was published in August 2010. One of the most significant differences between the two versions of the Principles was decreased emphasis upon social protection. Most strikingly, the November version included an extract from the Cabinet Office Statement of Practice (COSOP) that read:

> The government is committed to ensuring that the public sector is a good employer and a model contractor and client. The people employed in the public sector, directly and indirectly are its biggest asset and critical in developing modern, high quality, efficient responsive, customer focused and environmentally friendly public services.

This was omitted from the later version of the Principles published in August.

These first two themes, 'competition as an end in itself' and 'displacement of substance and social' resonate strongly with a neoliberal procurement thesis. NOMS operationalised the procurement rules in a way that supported the belief that markets produce the 'best', most 'efficient' outcomes where they are as unencumbered by state interference as possible. However, this would tell only half of HMP Birmingham's 'story' at national level. First, notwithstanding the resonance between a neoliberal account of procurement and some of the data, procurement law or even procurement policy was not often 'present' in the field. Save references to the 'paralysing complexity' of the process that the procurement rules required them to follow, interviewees did not really engage with the public procurement rules; less still cite them as ideologically coercive. This begs the question whether it is really law that is driving a neoliberal ideology in procurement practice or whether the socio-political context in which procurement teams operate in fact exerts the more significant influence. Perhaps it is both law and context, because the procurement rules do not give contracting authorities any clear guidance on horizontal procurement policy. If context is shaping procurement ideology, then the impression of at least some British politicians that Britain takes the procurement rules more 'seriously' (perhaps 'neoliberally') than other EU Member States is significant and merits evaluation. The decision in June 2011, for example, to award a train-building contract (Thameslink) to (German) Siemens in preference to UK-based Bombardier, prompted the then Secretary of State for Transport, Philip Hammond, to comment before Parliament:

> I firmly believe that free trade and open markets are the best way for us to proceed, but I believe also in the concept of the level playing field, and there is a case for looking at the way in which some of our neighbours and competitors operate the EU procurement directive, because it seems quite astonishing that, complying with that directive as we do, they [France and Germany] have managed to achieve very high percentage penetrations of French-built trains on the French railway and of German-built trains on the German railway.[45]

A crude search of Tenders Direct's database (which publishes all OJEU tenders) for tenders between April 2013 and 2014, suggests that the UK has published more tenders in the OJEU during that period compared to other Member States: 53,276 records were retrieved for the UK compared to 423,999 for the rest of Europe excluding the UK and Ireland. If all Member States were publishing approximately the same number of calls for tender the UK would be expected to have published approximately 17,000 tenders in that period.[46] Such tentative insights underline the importance of collecting comparative empirical evidence about the operation of the public procurement rules in different socio-political environments.

The account given of Birmingham's 'story' so far is also partial in that it has given the impression of a 'lean, mean, neoliberal procurement machine'. In reality, two further themes emerged from the data at national level, namely 'chaotic and costly process' and 'unrealised social boldness', which produce a more complex and uncertain picture. Notwithstanding NOMS' concerns about process integrity and rigour, and how those factors might shape private sector bidders' perceptions about the value of investing in the prisons 'market', the course of the competitive process at Birmingham was far from smooth. There was little evidence that NOMS had fully understood or evaluated the demands and impacts of its procedural choices. The use of competitive dialogue in the Birmingham competition, for example, seemed objectively justifiable on the basis of the complexity of the services that were sought. However, competitive dialogue is more complex than its procedural alternatives. It almost inherently entails a more costly and lengthy process because bidders are required to develop their vision for the service incrementally in light of feedback they receive from the contracting authority during dialogue sessions. These process dynamics make it especially

[45] L Maer, 'Public Procurement' (2012) Economic Policy and Statistics Section, House of Commons Library Note SN/EP/6029, p 6.

[46] See www.tendersdirect.co.uk/Search/TenderSearch.aspx. Tenders Direct is licensed by the European Commission.

important for contracting authorities to be competent commissioners; but this was not, unfortunately, how the competition was experienced.

Deficiencies in preparation, particularly of documents that ought to have been reasonably foreseeable (such as a survey of the existing fabric of the prison and a compendium of staff terms and conditions of employment), caused multiple delays and work to be repeated. This increased costs for NOMS and bidders and prolonged the uncertainty and anxiety for Birmingham's staff. There was a pervasive lack of cultural reflection upon what this sort of procurement meant for NOMS as an organisation. There was no 'joined up' thinking. As a NOMS Senior Manager explained:

> What the [NOMS management] Board seemed not to realise is that the idea and reality of competition are actually very different. There was no consideration about the level of resource, or appropriate balancing of resource. We haven't thought about what competition means for us as an institution. There is lots of responsibility sitting with not many people who are not quite sure what competition means or how to deliver it. It is all a bit amateurish.

Despite the obvious human resources implications of the Birmingham competition, the exercise did not feature in NOMS' human resources business plan. Moreover, the 'ethical walls' erected between NOMS' staff who were involved in commissioning and those who were not did not work as intended in practice. Staff did not understand the purpose of the 'walls', and so struggled to identify with whom they could talk and about what. This was exacerbated by the lack of clear organisational structural delineation between commissioners and non-commissioners within NOMS. The HR Directorate of NOMS comprised commissioners, non-commissioners and, most controversially, the public sector bid team, who were putting together the in-house public sector bid for Birmingham.

Problems with NOMS' delivery of the competition process were compounded by the political context in which the exercise was being undertaken. During the course of the (almost two-year) competition, Government reformed, or attempted to reform, public sector pensions and a policy guaranteeing pension protection for public sector staff transferred to private sector employment (known as 'Fair Deal'). Both of these policies have major impacts on how bidders calculate their costs and therefore how they price their bids. Moreover, although HMP Birmingham was undoubtedly a poor performing prison there was evidence that the prison had not been selected for competitive tendering on the basis of its poor performance alone. The Birmingham branch of the Prison Officers' Association (POA) had been very vocal in its opposition to a package of reforms known as Workforce Modernisation. Competition was therefore seen by the prison's staff and sometimes acknowledged by Ministers as the 'price' Birmingham had to pay for not 'toeing the line' and an attempt by NOMS finally to 'break' the power of the POA. This caused many Birmingham staff to feel that the competition was a 'personal attack' on them and their prison, which further delegitimised the process in their eyes, prompting varying combinations of anger, disbelief and disengagement. It also complicated the message that the competition was intended to send: was competition a mechanism to improve service performance or a mechanism to realign industrial relations?

All in all, the competition at Birmingham took just short of two years to complete (against a Government target of 120 days for 'all but the most complex procurement processes'[47]) at a cost to the taxpayer of £5.84 million.[48] It produced a contract between the Government and G4S with a value of £316.5 million that is impenetrable to all but lawyers in its length and language. This casts public procurement processes and the ideology of the rules that (at least partly) produce those processes in a rather different light to neoliberal analyses. Far from offering cheap, straightforward and quick 'fixes', as we might expect if the procurement rules were truly neoliberal, the public procurement rules structured a process (in Birmingham at least) that was complex, costly, protracted, deeply political and 'messy': a long way from being a 'lean, mean, neoliberal procurement machine'.[49]

The picture of 'unbridled neoliberalism' is further complicated by the fourth theme to emerge from the data at national level, 'unrealised social boldness'. Although Birmingham's staff experienced their prison's selection for competition, the process and, by extension the system (and perhaps rules) that administered it, as deliberately complex, dysfunctional, uncaring and unfair (see sub-section B, below), the final contract between G4S and the Government contained a number of performance conditions on staff matters. Notwithstanding the absence of any articulated vision or ambition on NOMS' part for achieving social policy objectives through its procurement, parts of the final contract with G4S imposed social and employment obligations that went beyond securing compliance with minimum statutory employment standards. Part 8 of the contract, for example, covered apprenticeships, and obliged G4S to 'use reasonable endeavours to employ apprentices, and report to the Authority [NOMS] the numbers of apprentices employed and wider skills training provided, during the delivery of this Contract.' Most significantly, the contract obliged G4S to comply with 'Fair Deal' and provide its transferring public sector staff with broadly comparable pensions. This provides staff with significantly more protection than they could expect on

[47] The Government refers to this as 'lean sourcing': Government Procurement, 'Government Sourcing: A New Approach Using LEAN' (2012).

[48] Prison Reform Trust, 'Bromley Briefings Prison Factfile' (December 2011) 72.

[49] For some similar reflections see H Cox, 'Questions about the initiative of the European Commission concerning the awarding and compulsory competitive tendering of public service concessions' (2003) 74 *Annals of Public and Cooperative Economics* 7–31 and P Bajari, R McMillan and S Tadelis, 'Auctions versus negotiations in procurement: an empirical analysis' (2009) 25 *Journal of Law, Economics & Organization* 372–99.

the basis of the statutory framework alone and adds significant additional cost to bids and constraints upon successful bidders. This social 'boldness' might have been a product partly more of accident than design (there was evidence in the contract's drafting to suggest that NOMS had 'recycled' a previously concluded contract with another prison) but these are still not the sorts of constraints that one would expect contracting authorities to impose or bidders to accept if the procurement rules were truly neoliberal.

B. An 'Understatement' at Local Level?

In the foregoing sub-section I have argued that the empirical picture at national procurement level is not straightforwardly neoliberal. There is instead evidence from the Birmingham case study that public procurement processes are costly, burdensome, difficult, and suffused with some interests and concerns that are not confined to commercial efficiency or profit-making. Although it is difficult to disentangle the rules from their delivery, and cause from effect, the rules played a role in shaping this process, which makes it hard to sustain the argument that the public procurement rules are truly neoliberal.

By contrast, I argue in this sub-section that when the public procurement rules are analysed through a local lens, through the eyes of those working in organisations that are subject to competitive tendering exercises, neoliberalism is conceptually too 'thin', or an 'understatement', in that it fails to capture adequately the 'lived experience' and broader social impacts of competition. I suggest that it would be better to situate neoliberalism within the broader sociological picture to provide a more empirically grounded conceptual language with which to think about the ideology of public procurement.

The Senior Officer's statement, in the primal scenes that introduced the previous section, was undoubtedly shaped by anger at NOMS' ultimate decision to award the contract to G4S. The dominant view amongst Birmingham staff at all levels was that the procurement process had been a betrayal: 'I'm used to the Winson Green way of having a knife stuck in your back but now they're sticking it between your eyes'. (Birmingham Manager). However, the statement also reflected the experience of a two-year process that had been beset by uncertainty. NOMS' failure to prepare adequately for the Birmingham competition, as was described above, meant that staff did not understand the process, did not feel involved in it and had to endure that experience for twice as long as had been promised:

> There has been a total disconnect between the business process and the people. The Authority [NOMS] is running the competition with a business head on and hasn't put anything in place to help staff get to grips with it. Maybe it's not for the Authority to do. Maybe it should have been NOMS sorting it out. The point is that nobody has done it. (Birmingham Senior Officer).

Staff struggled to come to terms with the initial decision to subject Birmingham to competition. This makes it difficult to disentangle the parts of their relayed experiences and sentiments that related to the manner in which the procurement rules were operated from the parts that resulted from the mere fact that the prison had been put out to tender. Nevertheless, staff expressed sustained and significant frustrations about the commissioning process to such an extent that it seems fair to conclude from the data that this was *a* source, if not *the* source, of their negative experiences. Staff described a lack of information about, and involvement in, an unsustainably protracted process:

> All the managers and the bid team keep saying is trust us, we've got your best interests at heart. So we have to pretend that we are wholeheartedly behind the bid but we don't have a clue what it is we're behind! And we're supposed to trust them when this thing has been going on all this time and so badly organised. (Birmingham Prison Officer).

Given that competence is a key ingredient of legitimacy,[50] it is unsurprising that Birmingham's staff experienced the process of competition as illegitimate and its outcome has proved difficult for staff to accept.

The procurement process was emotionally and psychologically destabilising for staff. Staff described the process as a 'weight' or 'sword' above their heads. After the local bid development team (of which some of Birmingham's staff had been part) disbanded,[51] staff felt that they had no control or influence over the process. There was a significant information void. Information from NOMS was sporadic, and often delayed without explanation. Staff felt that there were few people speaking a language that they could understand: 'We get some information about the bid and stuff from the POA. But it's not in normal language, you can't really understand it. It's in union-speak'. (Birmingham Prison Officer). The POA was torn between a position of principled non-engagement with competition processes, because of their objection to the policy, and the realities of what their membership in Birmingham were experiencing. The result was that staff felt that there was no-one to 'speak up' for them locally or nationally. There were few managers who staff described as effective but those who were, were over-burdened and simultaneously worried about their own futures:

> It's very hard to soak up staff concerns. It affects you. I try to care, support, and give as much information as I can, make their working lives easier and try to

[50] A Bottoms and J Tankebe, 'Beyond Procedural Justice: A Dialogic Approach to Legitimacy in Criminology' (2012) 102 *Journal of Criminal Law & Criminology* 119–70.

[51] The team was disbanded because it was thought to be no longer necessary in light of NOMS' decision to run the competition using the competitive dialogue process. The local bid development team had expected the restricted procedure to be used as had been the case in previous competitions in the prison sector. Competitive dialogue was seen as a more complex process requiring high levels of ongoing national coordination, which displaced local participation.

> develop them for the future. It's what we're paid to do but it's hard. It's very hard to be a manager here now. (Birmingham Manager).

The competition process 'changed the tone of the prison' (Birmingham staff member). Staff reported that they had 'lost their corporate identity' and that 'money rather than people now ruled the roost' (Birmingham Prison Officer). One Birmingham prison officer described it as: 'Basically it's been a case of keep your mouth shut, do as you are told and a bit more, and you might just be lucky to have a job'. NOMS was seen as 'flogging willing horses' who were 'scared' to express themselves for fear of being 'blacklisted' as 'Mr Negative'. Staff felt 'out of control'. This manifested itself in low morale, decreasing trust between staff and apathy towards their work:

> There are three types of officer in this jail. Those who do, those who do a bit and those who don't. Because of this bid, those who do now just do a bit and those who just did a bit before do nothing now. (Birmingham Senior Officer).

Staff sickness levels escalated for a short period following some of the announcements of process delays or missed procurement deadlines, suggesting a close relationship between staff experiences and how the public procurement rules were operationalised: 'Just as you get closer to a resolution, they move the goalposts and staff morale takes another hit'. The prison's occupational health professional noted a 'big increase in occupational health issues since the bid', with 'many more staff just dropping by and asking for a quick five minutes'. Many staff described themselves as avoiding talking about the competition, or talking about it with colleagues only 'indirectly', masked by humour, for fear that 'if [they] sat down and thought about it cold and clinically, about the effect on [their] family, Pandora's Box would be opened and [they'd] be a mess'.

There was a feeling of hopelessness and deflation: 'There is no light at the end of the tunnel. We need a light at the end of the tunnel, no matter what colour it is'. (Birmingham Prison Officer). This was reflected even in the appearances and habits of some staff; effects that were exacerbated as the process protracted: 'I've actually lost weight, not that that's a bad thing necessarily but sometimes I come in here without shaving. I'd have never have done that before this bid. I wake up, feel sick and think why even bother shaving'. (Birmingham Senior Officer). Cooperation between staff, which had previously lubricated the cogs of the prison's machine, began to erode and was displaced by individual self-interest:

> I don't want to come into work anymore and when I'm here I don't want to do anything. If I do, I do it as slow as possible—it feels like a bit of payback for what they're putting me through. (Birmingham Prison Officer).

'Infighting' between groups of staff intensified as informal trust diminished. Staff perceived that it had become more difficult, even for well-liked junior managers, to get staff to extend their shifts to cover staffing shortfalls. The tone of the prison became 'flatter'; 'there [was] less banter, less give and take'.

Many staff felt that this was bound to have had a detrimental impact upon staff-prisoner relationships. Some partly attributed the high number of self-inflicted prisoner deaths during 2010 to the competition process.[52]

Declining morale and cooperation were symptoms of more fundamental damage to the prison's workforce. While some staff overly romanticised their past working lives in the Prison Service, there was a predominant consensus that the mere fact that the prison had been put out to tender marked a negative turning point in their careers and the Service. Many staff experienced the competition as de-professionalising. The process per se expressed a shift in their employer's values, which empowered a flexible, short-term private sector employment model and stigmatised their stability and longevity. Compounded for many by NOMS' inattention to staff information and consultation throughout the competition, the process appeared to staff to deny the importance and value of contextual knowledge and experience of prison work and prison life ('jail craft'). It suggested that 'anyone' could do their job and that they were readily replaceable, over-priced 'commodities': 'After, they told us someone put as his employment status on Facebook: "unemployable" and that said it all, it just broke my heart'. (Birmingham Prison Officer).

The competition forced a clear gap in staff minds between NOMS' new 'vision' of custodial work and prison officers' understandings of their work and value. Market language 'hollowed out' the service ethic of their work.[53] Staff felt that working for the Prison Service was now 'just a job' rather than a career and 'moral task'. Although some staff had the 'wrong' professional identity (they over-used their authority, for example), and all staff had a clear interest in protecting their own jobs, almost all staff felt that something valuable and worth protecting was being lost by the process of competition and privatisation. The prison's 'Investors in People' sign, which was displayed at the prison's gate, was described by staff as 'a joke'. One officer imagined that the future of the Service would 'look like Tesco, people will come and go'. Many talked about the return of the 'turn-key prison officer' or 'robots with keys', 'de-skilling the service to save money'.

IV. MAKING SENSE OF THE DATA: NEOLIBERALISM AND SOCIOLOGY

Neoliberalism does not capture these 'lived experiences' of competition. In general terms neoliberalism accounts only for (crudely put) 'pro free market' and 'non-interventionist' policy preferences: it does not concern itself

[52] There were six self-inflicted deaths in Birmingham in 2010, compared to none in 2009, two in 2008 and 2007 and one in 2005 and 2006: www.gov.uk/government/publications/safety-in-custody.

[53] A Patterson and P Pinch, 'Hollowing out the local state: compulsory competitive tendering and the restructuring of British public sector services' (1995) 27 *Environment and Planning* 1437–61.

with the broader social impacts of its policies (of which public procurement is part) that are reflected in the Birmingham data. This is because neoliberalism's central concern is with the market, not society, since it is the free 'efficient' market, unencumbered by non-economic interests and state interference that is said to be the best way to achieve global prosperity. The social impacts of a free market are therefore mostly unacknowledged 'necessary evils', to which the market will respond and provide a solution if it is efficient to do so. The experience of competition for Birmingham's staff, in terms of both the prison being put out to tender and the manner in which the process was run, was much 'deeper' and socially more fundamental and far reaching than most normative accounts of neoliberalism could accommodate.

It might be better then, to think about public procurement at a local level through Sennett's 'new capitalism' lens and Giddens' 'late modernity' lens. Giddens argues that we are living in an era ('late modernity') where tradition, localism and predictability have been replaced by doubt, globalism, the erosion of trust, unfettered marketisation and insecurity: the 'disembedding processes of modernity'. These processes have restructured and social relationships at both institutional and individual levels. Social institutions have become fragmented, globalised, marketised and increasingly technological. Social relations have become individualistic and individual identities are fragile.[54] As Liebling and Lacey have argued, the late modern 'psychological habitus' includes 'economic and ontological insecurity, resentment, powerlessness, anxiety and lack of trust'. 'For the excluded, there is humiliation and disrespect, along with a sense of alienation which comes with relative deprivation in a world which prizes material success and purports to offer equal opportunity'.[55]

Sennett has also sought to articulate the sociological nature of the current era and its cultural impacts. Unlike Giddens, Sennett has focused solely upon current experiences of capitalism as one of the institutions of late modernity.[56] He describes an impatient and short-term capitalism, 'the new capitalism', and the structural changes that have been involved in dismantling the 'iron cage of bureaucracy'. He argues that this dismantling process has produced three 'social deficits': low institutional loyalty, diminished informal trust among workers and weakened institutional knowledge. Taken together, these social deficits reduce 'social capital' and

[54] A Giddens, *The Consequences of Modernity* (Stanford CA, Stanford University Press, 1990) and *Modernity and Self-Identity: Self and Society in the Late Modern Age* (Cambridge and Oxford, Polity Press, 1991).

[55] A Liebling and N Lacey, *Submission to the British Academy project on Crime, Punishment and the Prison* (2014).

[56] R Sennett, *The Corrosion of Character* (New York, WM Norton & Co Ltd, 1998), *The Culture of the New Capitalism* (New Haven CT/London, Yale University Press, 2006) and *Together: The Rituals, Pleasures and Politics of Cooperation* (London, Penguin, 2012).

create 'the spectre of uselessness'. A new form of power has been situated simultaneously within the flexible organisation. Flexibility is demanded in terms of both employee number and function. This increases job insecurity and labour commodification. It decreases the role for collective institutions, most notably trade unions. Employment in both an individual and institutional sense has been transformed: 'In these ways, the social has been diminished; capitalism remains'.[57]

The empirical picture of public procurement 'in action' resonates strongly with Giddens' and Sennett's accounts of social change. Although the mere fact that the prison was put out to tender undoubtedly had some influence, there is also evidence from Birmingham that the manner in which the public procurement rules are in some cases operated tend to globalise, fragment and contractualise relationships. Outsourcing public services can be seen as both a symptom and a driver of late modernity. HMP Birmingham was transformed through the competitive tendering exercise from being a locally staffed, locally cultured prison within a national, relational public service structure to being a prison managed by a global company, G4S, through a relationship structured by a contract outside of the national public service structure. To that extent, public procurement can be seen as part of Giddens' account of late modern institutional restructuring. In so far as the empirical procurement 'reality' can be seen to have been caused, or at least shaped, by the procurement rules, this is in many ways only to revalidate (through a different theoretical lens) Kunzlik and other's theses that the public procurement rules are vehicles (albeit imperfect—see section III(A), above) of neoliberalism. It may nevertheless be useful to think about public procurement within the broader complementary sociological framework that Giddens provides, since this draws our attention to how public procurement might relate to other phenomena (and their regulation) that restructure social relationships at an institutional level.

The principal added benefit of infusing neoliberal accounts of the procurement rules with some sociological theory is that sociology attempts to 'bridge the gap' between the institutional and individual dimensions of change. Unlike neoliberalism, which does not shed light upon the individual impacts of its approach to institutions, Giddens and Sennett explicitly reflect upon the nature of changes on both planes. As Giddens argues in *Modernity and Self-Identity*, 'Modernity must be understood on an institutional level; yet the transmutations introduced by modern institutions interlace in a direct way with individual life and therefore with the self'. He argues, as does Sennett, that one of the distinctive features of modernity (and new capitalism) is the increasing interconnection between

[57] R Sennett, *The Culture of the New Capitalism* (New Haven CT/London, Yale University Press, 2006) 82.

the two 'extremes' of extensionality (the external) and intentionality (the internal). Modernity and the new capitalism have caused a new relationship of increased interaction to be struck between globalising influences and personal spheres. Such a sociological narrative is able to accommodate and explain at least some of the significant social impacts that occurred at HMP Birmingham as a consequence of the competitive tendering exercise, in ways that neoliberalism cannot. A fuller picture thus emerges: a picture that explores both the micro and the macro; a picture that posits public procurement processes as socially precarious and corrosive: commodifying, de-professionalising, fragmenting and isolating. This picture, which highlights the 'social costs' of (neoliberal) procurement exercises, seems more empirically persuasive and inclusive (on the Birmingham data at least). It may also be more valuable than relying upon only neoliberalism in thinking about how those for whom this social picture is cause for concern might seek to shape procurement law and policy. This is considered further in the concluding section that follows.

V. CONCLUSIONS

This chapter has sought to add a new empirical dimension to recent debates about the purposes of the public procurement rules and the balance between Member State discretion and EU power in procurement processes and decision-making. On the basis of data from an ethnographic study of the operation of the public procurement rules at HMP Birmingham, I have argued that doctrinal analyses of public procurement regulation as a neoliberal construct are simultaneously both an overstatement and an understatement of the reality of how the rules operate in practice. Neoliberalism is an ideological overstatement as compared to empirical data from the national procurement level because procurement exercises are not in practice 'efficient' or straightforward. Rather, they are costly, protracted and politicised. Moreover, even in the absence of a strong national horizontal procurement policy agenda, non-commercial interests were influential and narrowed bidder discretion through, for example, mandated compliance with 'Fair Deal'. These empirical findings might suggest that the efforts of those who seek to highlight or enlarge the scope for national autonomy within the public procurement framework might be better directed by looking beyond further reform proposals to engage more directly with procurement practitioners and commissioners. The use of horizontal procurement policies may already be more widespread in practice than is realised, particularly if England and Wales is taken as representative of a jurisdiction with little appetite for pursuing horizontal policies in its official procurement policy.

On the other hand, I have also argued in this chapter that neoliberalism is also too 'thin' as an ideological description of the procurement rules in practice, in the sense that it fails to capture the lived experience of competition at a local level. I have suggested that it would be helpful to draw upon some sociological theory, particularly the work of Giddens and Sennett, since it offers a richer conceptual language and an account of the social world that encompasses both national institutional and local individual experiences of procurement in practice. There was strong resonance between the local Birmingham data and the three 'social deficits' that Sennett has described as arising from the new capitalism. The power of this narrative and the light it might shed upon the capacity and social sustainability of competitive tendering exercises (particularly as mechanisms to reform public services) merit further attention in research to inform procurement policy and any future reform of the procurement rules. Data from both the national and local procurement levels during the Birmingham competition suggest that there may be 'good' reasons (social, economic and political) to source public services outside of the public procurement framework. These data make a valuable contribution to, for example, debates about the extent to which public services (or services of general interest) ought to be subject to the EU's internal market rules. Empirical methods are essential to 'uncovering' such insight and drawing more widely upon scholarship from other disciplines, through interdisciplinary collaboration, will help to better understand the full range of the public procurement rules' effects. Public procurement law is often presented as technical and dry but an empirical approach points to exciting possibilities for interdisciplinary engagement and the potential to position the field as a microcosm for important and contentious sociological, economic, political and legal debates.

3

The Legal Framework for New Economic Governance and its Implications for Wage Policy Learning

SAMUEL DAHAN

Abstract

This chapter examines the implications of the new European economic governance framework from a policy-learning point of view. It is argued that a new form of EU learning influence has emerged in the wake of the EMU legal and institutional crisis. The author takes the view that an inherent asymmetry in the EMU, namely the presence of a unified monetary policy without a commensurate coordination of social policy and wage-setting mechanisms, contributed to the development of the crisis. The latent consequences of this flaw—diverging (wage) growth and cost competitiveness—were brought into full view when the global financial crisis struck. In response, new wage governance instruments were established in order to exert learning pressure on wage development and wage-setting systems in the EU. The substantive orientation of this new framework is examined with an eye to determining whether it qualifies as a learning process under which wage and spending cuts supplant the role of currency depreciation as a means of addressing external economic shocks and competitiveness gaps. Finally, drawing on recent findings concerning the workings of the 'European Semester', the chapter assesses whether the new economic governance reforms are already generating learning outcomes at the domestic level.

I. INTRODUCTION

THE ONSET OF the financial crisis in the Eurozone has seen the emergence of a new economic governance architecture, one under which stabilisation of the single currency requires the introduction of stricter national economic and social policy coordination.[1] This new model comprises several elements including the Fiscal Compact,[2] the so-called Six-Pack,[3] the Euro Plus Pact (EPP)[4] and the European Semester, among others. The first two—the Fiscal Compact and the Six-Pack—aim to promote a pan-European fiscal and wage policy process by strengthening the Stability and Growth Pact (SGP) enforcement mechanisms and establishing a new 'macroeconomic imbalance procedure' (MIP). The third element, the EPP, addresses areas that fall strictly within national competence with respect to law-making powers but that may be the subject of mutual benchmarking and learning processes. Finally, at the core of the new model is the European Semester, through which the Commission, the Council and the European Council set priorities for the Union. This six-month process brings together the new arrangements for economic governance: the SGP, the MIP, the EPP, the Fiscal Compact, the Europe 2020 Strategy and the Integrated Economic and Employment Guidelines.

These developments raise several substantive questions, as they give the EU significant leverage to interfere in fiscal, social and even wage policies.[5] A first set of questions concerns legal and institutional causes of the crisis and more specifically how the new economic governance attempts to address the EMU's institutional flaws. This chapter takes the view that the institutional failure was the embedding of a unified monetary policy without a commensurate coordination of economic and social policy. In particular, it is argued that economic and social learning within the SGP and the Open Method of Coordination (OMC) was distorted by excessive emphasis on price stability. The latent consequences of these flaws were brought into full view when the global financial crisis struck. In particular, the Eurozone was vulnerable mainly for two reasons: First, the EU had no mechanism for dealing with the crisis more effectively. Secondly, there was a lack of

[1] S Deakin and R Rogowski, 'Reflexive Labour Law, Capabilities, and the Future of Social Europe' in R Rogowski and others (eds), *Transforming European Employment Policy: Labour Market Transitions and the Promotion of Capability* (Cheltenham, Edward Elgar Publishing, 2011).

[2] The term 'Fiscal Compact' refers to the fiscal part of the Treaty on Stability, Coordination and Governance in the Economic and Monetary Union (TSCG). The TSCG is intended to further strengthen fiscal discipline by introducing more automatic sanctions and stricter surveillance and to reinforce the coordination of economic policies.

[3] These are Regulation (EU) No 1173/2011 of 16 November 2011 ([2011] OJ L306/1); Regulation (EU) No 1174/2011 of 16 November 2011 ([2011] OJ L306/8); Regulation (EU) No 1175/2011 of 16 November 2011 amending Council Regulation (EC) No 1466/97 ([2011] OJ L306/12); Regulation (EU) No 1176/2011 of 16 November 2011 ([2011] OJ L306/25); Council Regulation (EU) No 1177/2011 of 8 November 2011 amending Regulation (EC) No 1467/97 on ([2011] OJ L306/33); and Council Directive 2011/85/EU ([2011] OJ L306/41).

[4] See Conclusions of the Heads of State or Government of the Euro Area, 'A Pact for the Euro. Stronger Economic Policy Coordination for Competitiveness and Convergence', 11 March 2011.

[5] D Chalmers, 'The European Redistributive State and a European Law of Struggle' (2012) 18 *European Law Journal* 667.

real convergence between the core and the periphery, leading to diverging growth paths. This bifurcation was exacerbated by the 'one-size-fits-all' ECB interest-rate policy; distorted fiscal policy; and the lack of an integrated social policy or common approach to wage determination.[6]

A second set of questions relates to the substantive orientation of the social and economic governance process. It is argued that the euro crisis response has created learning opportunities for economic and fiscal integration, at the same time signalling the 'marginalization of social policy at EU level and an increase in the use of internal market law and monetary policy as catalysts for deregulation'.[7] Social policy is meant to become a flexible instrument under conditions of stricter fiscal control in the same way that wage and spending cuts supplant the role of currency devaluation as a means of addressing external economic shocks and competitiveness gaps.

A third set of questions concerns the learning impact of the new economic governance reforms on wage developments and wage-setting at the domestic level. This analysis will draw on learning models, as these can help to cultivate a deeper understanding of whether social and wage policy governance is subordinated to economic and fiscal discipline objectives. This chapter identifies three types of learning outcomes: single-loop, which takes the form of a minor procedural adjustment; double-loop, which makes an adjustment but also reflects on whether the rules themselves should be changed; and triple-loop, which considers how the rules should be changed but also reflects on the paradigm underlying those rules.[8] This chapter focuses on the evidence from the workings of the European Semester, which suggests single- and double-loop changes in the form of adjustments in labour and wage standards.

The analysis will draw on the analytical framework of Radaelli[9] and Di Maggio[10] to assess the new legal framework for economic (specifically wage) governance and the extent to which it attempts to address the EMU flaws (Section II). Furthermore, it will discuss the substantive orientation of the new wage instruments for wage governance (Section III). Finally, drawing

[6] S Deakin, F Wilkinson and C Didry, 'Marchés du Travail, Crise Financière et Réforme: Projet d'Agenda pour une Politique du Travail' (2012) 182 *L'Homme et la Société* 25; A Callinicos, *Bonfire of Illusions: The Twin Crises of the Liberal World* (Cambridge, Polity Press, 2013) 23.

[7] Deakin and Rogowski, n 1 above at 249.

[8] This classification is drawn from the previous work of C Argyris and PA Hall. See C Argyris, 'Single-Loop and Double-Loop Models in Research on Decision Making' (1976) 21 *Administrative Science Quarterly* 363–75; PA Hall, 'Policy Paradigms, Social Learning, and the State: The Case of Economic Policymaking in Britain' (1993) 25 *Comparative Politics* 275, 284.

[9] F Gilardi and C Radaelli, 'Governance and Learning' in D Levi-Faur (ed), *The Oxford Handbook of Governance* (Oxford, Oxford University Press, 2012).

[10] WW Powell and PJ DiMaggio (eds), *The New Institutionalism in Organizational Analysis* (Chicago IL, University of Chicago Press, 1991).

on recent qualitative evidence, it will assess the learning intensity and outcomes produced by this new wage-governance process at the domestic level (Section IV).[11]

II. ADDRESSING EMU FLAWS THROUGH WAGE COORDINATION

Until the economic crisis of 2008, the EU had been limited to making non-binding recommendations on national wage and labour market policies as part of employment guidelines. However, the Union has since engaged in an innovative governance model that combines fiscal austerity with far-reaching reforms in the field of wage and collective bargaining in the hope of solving what seems to be a competitiveness problem.[12] Indeed, the euro crisis is regarded not only as a problem of fiscal profligacy, but also as a problem of competitiveness that can only be solved through greater labour law flexibility and lower labour costs.

A. EMU Institutional Asymmetry: Lack of Wage Coordination and the Development of the Crisis

The EMU project has been built as a multi-layered process combining both social and economic aspects, although the social dimension is said to have played a secondary role.[13] Specifically, the EMU legal framework is characterised by an asymmetric model of governance in which a fully centralised monetary policy is not combined with a supranational decision-making process in the fields of economic and social policy. Since Maastricht, Member States have retained control of the means to the ends regarding economic policy in that the Union and the Member States have shared competence over fiscal policy. In particular, the SGP has imposed strict fiscal criteria[14] in order to enable the European Central Bank (ECB) to achieve its objective of

[11] I Sanderson, 'Evaluation, Policy Learning and Evidence-based Policy Making' (2002) 80 *Public Administration* 1–22; PJ May, 'Policy Learning and Failure' (1992) 12 *Journal of Public Policy* 331–354.

[12] E Angelini, A Dieppe and B Pierluigi, 'Learning about Wage and Price Mark-ups in Euro Area Countries' (ECB, February 2013).

[13] The new Social Chapter of the EC Treaty, as amended by the Treaties of Amsterdam and Nice (Art 136 EC, now Art 151 TFEU), incorporates the Agreement on Social Policy. The new Social Chapter of the EC Treaty, as amended by the Treaties of Amsterdam and Nice (Arts 136 ff EC, now Arts 151 ff TFEU), incorporates the Agreement on Social Policy; P Pochet and B Vanhercke, *Social Challenges of Economic and Monetary Union* (Berlin, Peter Lang, 1998) 68.

[14] Art 3a of the Maastricht Treaty (Art 119 TFEU).

price stability.[15] As for social and wage policy, however, Maastricht has not introduced any form of pan-European social policy that could counterbalance the pressure exerted by financial and monetary constraints.

It is only with the Amsterdam Treaty of 1997 and the Lisbon Strategy of 2000 that new modes of governance and learning such as the OMC were introduced as a means of addressing EMU asymmetry. However, it was argued at the time that weak non-binding models would be unable to resist the pressures stemming from the EMU. Moreover, it was claimed that learning instruments were distorted by the economic rationale behind the Maastricht convergence criteria. Thus, for most proponents of Social Europe, the main driving force of the OMC was Maastricht, and the true objective of the Lisbon Strategy was not to achieve more social policy learning but to achieve labour and fiscal convergence, which is to say budgetary discipline and downward wage convergence.[16]

Recent findings on the operation of the Social OMC and the European Employment Strategy (EES) have demonstrated that none of these dire predictions has been realised. Even though policy learning has not been easily observable, we have found evidence of single- and double-loop learning resulting from OMC cycles. Most researchers agree that adjustments of domestic settings are not always apparent and that we have to look beneath the legal surface for a better understanding of the various learning scenarios. Most changes do not take the form of triple-loop learning and yet they are no less relevant than direct legislative changes. Instead, most changes show signs of single/double-loop learning in early stages of the policy-making process. The type of influence the OMC exerts is discursive or cognitive, involving mostly single-loop cognitive shifts.[17]

In spite of these positive results, the institutional asymmetry of the EMU—embedding a unified monetary policy; with fiscal policy distorted through an excessive emphasis on price stability; and without sufficient coordination of economic and social policy—is said to have contributed to the development of the euro crisis.

First, the 'one-size-fits-all' ECB interest-rate policy[18] reflected average conditions in the Eurozone and could not be adapted to specific national

[15] M Herdegen, 'Price Stability and Budgetary Restraints in the Economic and Monetary Union: Law as the Guardian of Economic Wisdom' (1998) 35 *Common Market Law Review* 9–32.

[16] S Deakin and H Reed, 'The Contested Meaning of Labour Market Flexibility: Economic Theory and the Discourse of European Integration' (Centre for Business Research, University of Cambridge 2000) ESRC Working Papers.

[17] M Büchs, D Friedrich and P Pochet, 'Surface Integration' in J Zeitlin and L Magnusson (eds), *The Open Method of Co-ordination in Action: The European Employment and Social Inclusion Strategies* (PIE-Peter Lang, 2005).

[18] TI Palley, 'Europe's Crisis without End: The Consequences of Neoliberalism' (2013) 32 *Contributions to Political Economy* 29–50; S Deakin, 'Social Policy Will Be Critical to a Sustainable EMU', *Social Europe Journal*, 18 June 2013.

conditions. As a result, instead of fostering learning, the euro encouraged diverging growth paths and differential inflation rates. Indeed, the real interest rate—the nominal interest rate set by the ECB, minus country-specific inflation rates—became lower in countries with high inflation and higher in countries with low inflation. On the one hand, for countries with below-average economic growth and inflation rates, the interest rates were too high, consequently depressing weak economies even further. For instance, Germany was the main victim of this procyclical-learning model. While nominal interest rates converged, inflation rates remained low (Figure 4). As a result, interest rates in Germany became the highest in the Eurozone and growth remained lower than in almost all EMU member economies (Figures 5 and 6). On the other hand, for countries with above-average inflation rates, the nominal interest-rate policy was too accommodating because the ECB target was lower than the actual national inflation rate. The real interest rate became extremely low or even dropped into negative territory in the so-called periphery or debtor countries, consequently feeding high economic growth (Figure 6).[19] In sum, the one-size-fits-all monetary policy amplified already-existing divergences and contributed to the creation of two-speed growth models.[20]

Against this background, there have been significant divergences between countries in the driving force of growth. On the one hand, the sudden fall of nominal interest rates (Figure 6) to German levels fed into credit-financed domestic demand in high-inflation 'periphery' countries. This growth model was highly dependent on an expansion of private credit and on increasing asset prices in the market for commercial and residential investment.[21] It has become the key source of demand growth in Britain, Ireland and some continental European countries such as Spain, Greece and parts of Eastern Europe where household debt has increased dramatically in the last decade (Table 4). These countries have provided the main source of growth (and wage) inflation since the introduction of the euro and have typically run substantial account deficits. On the other hand, low-inflation countries (creditors or core economies) have followed policies of export-led growth that are dependent on targeted investment in capital goods, public support for training and labour force upgrading, and wage moderation. These countries did not experience a significant rise in household incomes, thanks to wage restraint and lower growth (Figure 6 and Table 3). However, their

[19] H Enderlein, 'Break it, Don't Fix it!' (2004) 42 *Journal of Common Market Studies* 1039–46.

[20] Space constraints prevent us from presenting an exhaustive analysis of the EMU's flaws and how they contributed to the euro crisis. B Hancké, 'Worlds Apart? Labour Unions, Wages and Monetary Integration in Continental Europe' (Institute for Advanced Studies, 2012), IHS Political Science.

[21] To a lesser extent in Portugal. See A Afonso and RM Sousa, 'Assessing Long-Term Fiscal Developments: Evidence From Portugal' (2010) 18 *Applied Economics Letters* 1–5.

competitiveness did improve, whereas the periphery, unable to counter wage inflationary pressure, lost competitiveness at the same time.

Beside monetary policy, the SGP price stability emphasis[22] may have facilitated diverging growth within the EMU in that neither the formal criteria of Maastricht nor the financial markets foresaw or corrected these developments. Indeed, the SGP only achieved formal convergence without fostering real learning, mainly because it had focused on deficit and debt figures that resulted in a high degree of apparent convergence. As a result, all Eurozone members besides Greece (and to a lesser extent Portugal) were in compliance with the Maastricht criteria at the onset of the crisis. Moreover, several Member States that had incurred soaring budget deficits after 2007, including Ireland, Portugal and Spain, had surpluses as well as national debt levels at historic lows (Tables 1 and 2).[23] However, beneath this formal compliance with Maastricht there was a lack of real convergence,[24] partly because the convergence criteria paid no attention to non-fiscal real variables such as the validity of exchange; to prevailing current account deficits and surpluses; or to the differences in inflation rates across the Eurozone.

Finally, the uniform ECB policy and the distorted SGP do not fully account for the problem of diverging (wage) growth paths. The decentralised approach to wage determination also made the EMU vulnerable in that it exacerbated the ECB's inflationary pressures and the divergence of the growth paths between the core and the periphery. On the one hand, high finance-led growth in the periphery was accompanied by fuelling (wage) inflation, thanks to the ECB interest rate but also to the ineffectiveness of wage-setting mechanisms. Wages grew faster than productivity and national wage-setting arrangements had little leverage to mitigate the inflationary pressures coming from the ECB.[25] On the other hand, the unnecessarily restrictive monetary policy imposed on low-inflation economies was accompanied by strong wage-moderation mechanisms, thereby worsening the deflationary pressures on these economies.[26] This pro-cyclical dynamic

[22] Ibid.

[23] They even ran budget surpluses for much of the five-year period (2000–2007), and their average deficits were smaller than those of Germany from 2002 to 2005.

[24] S Deakin, 'Euro Crisis and Labour Law', 5 February 2013; TI Palley, 'Europe's Crisis without End: The Consequences of Neoliberalism' (2013) 32 *Contributions to Political Economy* 29–50.

[25] S Deakin, 'Euro Crisis and Labour Law', 5 February 2013; B Hancké, 'Worlds Apart? Labour Unions, Wages and Monetary Integration in Continental Europe' (Institute for Advanced Studies, 2012), IHS Political Science.

[26] B Hancké, 'Worlds Apart? Labour Unions, Wages and Monetary Integration in Continental Europe' (Institute for Advanced Studies, 2012), IHS Political Science; FW Scharpf, 'Monetary Union, Fiscal Crisis and the Preemption of Democracy' (Max Planck Institute for the Study of Societies, May 2011), MPIfG Discussion Paper.

eventually catapulted the competitiveness of Germany and the periphery onto diverging paths (Table 3 and Figures 5 and 6).

As a result, instead of fostering learning and convergence as expected when the euro was introduced, the EMU's asymmetric design has only intensified intra-EMU wage and cost competitiveness divergence, which has in turn translated into 'destabilising macroeconomic imbalances' (Figure 4). On the one hand, the periphery has become highly dependent on an expansion of private credit and asset prices in the market for commercial and residential investments (Table 4). On the other hand, the core countries have followed policies of export-led growth that were dependent on targeted investment in capital goods, public support for training, labour force upgrading, and, most importantly, strong wage-setting systems (Table 3).

While changes in the current account balances of trading nations are not an indication of economic rigidity,[27] the Commission has nevertheless come to interpret the current crisis as being two-fold: both a debt crisis and a competitiveness crisis. First, although fiscal profligacy was only problematic in Greece (and, to a lesser extent, Portugal), it has been argued that the SGP did not impose sufficient discipline on public budgets (Tables 1 and 2). As a result, strong austerity policies must be pursued by deficit countries. These policies usually take the form of spending cuts but also include demands for wage cuts and the freezing of public sector wages.

Secondly, the Union makes the argument that intra-EMU current account imbalances are the result of diverging price competitiveness, that is to say, uneven development of Unit Labour Cost (ULC).[28] For the Commission, high labour costs have made products and services uncompetitive in the single market while also imposing pressures on national budgets. This has produced a vicious circle: government expenditures rise because they import too much, while productivity and export growth weaken (Figure 5). In a nutshell, the Commission's explanation goes as follows: Wage increases in the periphery led to an increase in ULC, which in turn resulted in competitiveness loss and therefore trade deficits.[29] At the same time, wage repression in the core countries (particularly Germany) led to a decrease

[27] They simply reflect inter-temporal savings and consumption and the investment preferences of private enterprises, households and governments, see M Obstfeld and K Rogoff, 'The Intertemporal Approach to the Current Account' in *Handbook of International Economics*, vol 3 (Amsterdam, Elsevier, 1995).

[28] See Regulation (EU) No 1176/2011 ([2011] OJ L306/25). Lack of fiscal discipline has also been an important component of the debate on the causes of the crisis but this chapter only focuses on the competitiveness debate.

[29] S Dahan, 'Social and Employment Policy Learning in the Context of the Euro Crisis: From Coordinated to Disciplinary Learning' (University of Cambridge, 2013) ch 4, for more details on the development of macroeconomic imbalances; T Schulten and T Müller, 'A New European Interventionism? The Impact of the New European Economic Governance on Wages and Collective Bargaining' in D Natali and B Vanhercke (eds), *Social Developments in the European Union 2012* (ETUI and OSE, 2013).

in ULC, which translated into greater competitiveness and current account surpluses.

Before the creation of the euro, deficit countries would have solved their competitiveness problems through currency devaluation or domestic cost reduction.[30] Low competitiveness countries would have undergone a real depreciation and deflated their general price levels in relative terms to regain competitiveness, making domestic products cheaper than foreign products. However, the legal framework of the EMU leaves little flexibility for Member States to respond to competitiveness crises through currency devaluation. Competitiveness must be restored though 'internal devaluation policy', namely by reducing labour cost, the 'functional substitute to currency devaluation'.[31] Furthermore, it seems that the corollary of internal devaluation policy is the removal of institutional rigidities in the labour market—particularly wage-setting rigidities—in order to facilitate wage alignment with productivity growth.[32] Indeed, it is a commonly held view that rigid wage-setting structures may prevent wage adjustment even though evidence shows that wage divergence has been significant in countries with weak bargaining structures.

Maastricht's asymmetric model nevertheless does not offer such a deflationary alternative, as the EU has no legal competency in the area of wage policy (Article 153(2) TFEU). For this reason, the new economic governance package, through the framework of the European Semester, had to engage in an innovative learning process in the form of a new procedure for wage coordination, one that could partially overcome the structural flaws of Maastricht.

B. The Legal Basis for Reinforced Wage Governance

A new system of economic coordination emerged in 2010 with the adoption of the 'Europe 2020' Strategy,[33] which established the new 'European Semester', an annual integrated cycle of policy coordination which has brought wage policy within the scope of the economic governance framework of the EU. The six-month Semester is described as the 'coordination of

[30] RA Mundell, 'A Theory of Optimum Currency Areas' (1961) 51 *The American Economic Review* 657–65.

[31] K Armingeon and L Baccaro, 'Political Economy of the Sovereign Debt Crisis: The Limits of Internal Devaluation' (2012) 41 *Industrial Law Journal* 254–75.

[32] This trend is well exemplified in the list of 'employment friendly' reforms discussed in the European Commission Report 'Labour Market Developments in Europe 2012', European Economy 5/2013, p 56.

[33] The successor of the Lisbon Strategy mentioned above.

coordination'[34] insofar as it brings together both economic and social policies with the aim of enhancing consistency among coordination mechanisms.

The Semester relies on three main pillars: a growth-based strategy,[35] fiscal surveillance and macroeconomic surveillance (the focus of this study). First, Europe 2020—the successor of Lisbon 2000—is based on enhanced socio-economic policy coordination, and is organised according to three priorities, which are expected to be mutually reinforcing: smart growth, sustainable growth and inclusive growth. Secondly, the so-called Six-Pack[36] and Two-Pack regulations were adopted in order to strengthen fiscal surveillance. In the same vein, the 'fiscal compact'—the fiscal part of the TSCG—constitutionalises budgetary rigour, discipline and surveillance. These new regulations bring about fundamental changes in both the preventive rules and the corrective measures previously specified by the SGP. Finally, the macroeconomic pillar, which also finds its legal basis in the Six-Pack, aims at ensuring a stable macroeconomic environment and employment creation through the MIP for the early detection of macroeconomic imbalances based on a 'scoreboard' of economic indicators, including wage policy. Moreover, macroeconomic surveillance is further reinforced through the EPP, a soft-law instrument that calls for commitments to monitor benchmark trends in unit labour costs and to ensure that wages increase only in line with productivity. While formally acknowledging the autonomy of Member States with respect to wage setting, the pact also includes a commitment to reviewing wage-setting mechanisms, in particular the degree to which bargaining is centralised and the effects of wage-indexation mechanisms.

All of these new economic governance measures have been incorporated into the European Semester. The process begins each year in November with the publication of the Annual Growth Survey (AGS), a policy document that identifies priorities and objectives for the EU and its Member States with the aim of ensuring that their policies align with the SGP and Europe 2020 Strategy. The Alert Mechanism Report, issued by the Commission at the same time, identifies Member States for In-Depth Reviews (IDRs) under the MIP, the conclusions of which are reported annually in March. At the same time, the European Council endorses annual EU and national-level priorities, provides guidelines for action, and reflects on the implementation of the previous cycle. In the spring the Member States draft their Stability and Convergence Programmes (SCPs) as part of the preventive

[34] K Armstrong, 'The Lisbon Agenda and Europe 2020: From the Governance of Coordination to the Coordination of Governance' in P Copeland, D Papadimitriou (eds), *The EU's Lisbon Strategy: Evaluating Success, Understanding Failure* (Basingstoke, Palgrave Macmillan, 2012) 208–28.

[35] European Council 'Presidency Conclusions, EUCO 7/10, Brussels', 25–26 March 2010.

[36] This is a set of six items of legislation—five Regulations and one Directive—intended to make governance more rigorous.

arm of the SGP and Fiscal Compact.[37] At the same time they draft their National Reform Programmes (NRPs), taking into account the objectives of Europe 2020, the AGS and the EPP. These programmes are submitted to the Commission in April. In May or June, the Commission assesses these programmes and provides a single integrated set of country-specific recommendations (CSRs) that are formally adopted by the Council and endorsed by the European Council in June.

III. SUBSTANTIVE ORIENTATION OF THE EUROPEAN SEMESTER: INSTITUTIONALISING A LEARNING PROCESS FOR INTERNAL DEVALUATION?

'Direct interventionism' in the field of wage policy takes different forms.[38] The most obvious is direct financial aid in exchange for domestic reforms, as in the case of certain countries receiving aid from the 'Troika'—the European Commission, the European Central Bank and the International Monetary Fund—so long as they commit themselves to far-reaching changes in wage policy. However, a new form of direct interventionism is emerging within the context of the European Semester. What could not be achieved—wage convergence—through the EMU self-regulation is now implemented through learning pressure exerted by the European Semester. Indeed, the combination of substantive guidelines and hard economic sanctions afforded by this new economic governance model (mainly via the MIP and the EPP) allows the Commission to exert pressure on many aspects of labour systems, including both wage development and wage-setting mechanisms.

A. From Downward Wage Adjustment to Wage Rebalancing?

Within the framework of the European Semester, the MIP monitors macroeconomic developments of EU countries in the light of pre-set learning targets, namely a macroeconomic scoreboard of indicators.[39] These economic figures comprise indicators belonging to all economic policy areas, including those that are exclusive national competences such as wage policy. On the basis of this monitoring process, the Commission makes policy recommendations on wages as part of the European Semester Integrated CSRs.

[37] The corrective arms of the SGP and Macroeconomic Imbalance Procedure are not included in the European Semester since these procedures are always initiated solely on an ad hoc basis.

[38] 'A New European Interventionism? The Impact of the New European Economic Governance on Wages and Collective Bargaining', n 29 above.

[39] Commission, 'Scoreboard for the Surveillance of Macroeconomic Imbalances'.

Member States that fail to comply with the recommendations risk financial sanction. More specifically, the Commission may trigger the correction mechanism for any nominal increases that exceed nine per cent over the period of the last three years, or 12 per cent for non-Eurozone members.[40] This model merely exerts a downward learning pressure on European wages. It places an overemphasis on upward wage dynamics while downplaying the problems of stagnation and wage restraint that led to the imbalances in the first place. Along these lines, the EPP expressly defines wages as a key economic adjustment variable to overcome economic imbalances and foster competitiveness. Therefore, the Pact, along with the MIP, calls for tight surveillance of wages and wage-setting mechanisms at the European level.[41]

Since the competitive wage improvements of one country are to a large extent the competitive losses of other EU countries, this distorted coordination process seems to encourage a wage race to the bottom. It is, however, important to investigate evidence from the European Semester (mainly 2011–14 CSRs) to assess whether this new wage coordination process merely exerts a downward pressure on national wages, or whether it encourages a wage rebalancing dynamic instead.

The former solution seems to be well illustrated in the European Semesters of 2011 and 2012 insofar as the CSRs expressly encouraged wage moderation for 12 Member States. While these recommendations were non-binding, in most cases they called for a moderate wage increase. However, in the case of Sweden the CSR recommended an extension of the low wage sector, and in Germany it suggested a re-alignment of wages with productivity (which is to say, higher wage growth).

As for 2013 and 2014, wage recommendations highlight a stronger rebalancing process through which deficit countries are encouraged to reduce their labour costs, whereas surplus countries are encouraged to boost wage growth. On the one hand, CSRs for Belgium, France, Slovenia and Finland, while different in their content, all suggest a downward adjustment of wage levels to lower levels of productivity growth. In the cases of Belgium and Finland, the Commission stresses that productivity still lags behind growth, but nevertheless acknowledges that 'Research and Innovation' in both countries have proved useful in mitigating the weakening of international competitiveness. On the other hand, the Commission mentions that wage growth has been weak in the United Kingdom without suggesting any rebalancing. As for Germany, CSRs suggest a wages increase insofar as wage growth still lags behind (high) productivity. According to the Commission, this would help to sustain demand and exert a positive spill-over onto deficit

[40] According to the ECB's price stability objective the threshold would be 6% and not 9%, which is considered too generous.

[41] 'A Pact for the Euro', n 4 above.

countries. It is, however, important to note that Germany was exempted from the MIP even though it has contributed to the development of macroeconomic imbalances.[42] The IDR of 2013 confirms this dynamic with its complete exclusion from the report of Germany, the country with the most serious imbalances in absolute terms. At the same time, countries such as Belgium and France, whose wage and ULC developments have been in line with the ECB's objectives, were accused of having excessive wage growth (Table 5).

In 2014, wage moderation is only recommended for Belgium and Italy (where the situation deteriorated in 2013). In fact, while CSRs for Belgium acknowledge that competitiveness loss is less problematic, there is still room for aligning wages with productivity. Furthermore, the Commission stresses that the cost of labour is still too high in Belgium (and also in France). They both must take further action to lower social security contributions since the tax burden on labour is too high, reducing firms' profitability. As for low-wage countries such as the United Kingdom, the Commission expresses concern regarding lower-than-expected growth resulting from wage constraints that were curtailing private consumption and hindering investment. For Germany, the CSRs seem to welcome the plan to introduce a general minimum wage while stressing that real wage growth slowed down in 2013.

Based on this evidence drawn from the CSRs, one can hardly argue that the European Semester favours a wage-dumping process. On the contrary, the European Semester has evolved from a downward process to a more progressive wage rebalancing process. Indeed, while the downward pressure exerted on deficit countries is quite significant, the CSRs also acknowledge that Germany's 'very high surplus' is problematic,[43] although not as problematic as the 'large deficits' of the periphery. While this pattern of attitude is a positive sign, it seems that the Commission implicitly regards Germany as the correct wage benchmark and encourages other countries, and particularly the periphery, to learn from the German wage repression experience in order to regain competitiveness.

B. Pegging Wages to Productivity through Wage-Setting Dismantling: A Paradoxical Solution

This new coordination model has also materialised via another channel: wage-setting systems dismantling. Indeed, the Commission urges the

[42] Germany's wage cost stayed close to 2% in the 2000s, and fell in 2005. While wages have grown dynamically in the past years, they are still below their 2000 levels.

[43] European Commission, 'Macroeconomic Imbalances Germany 2014', European Economy. Occasional Papers 174. March 2014. Brussels.

periphery to reform national wage-setting systems, which is instrumental in influencing ULC and thus price competitiveness.[44]

Wage-setting frameworks may be either highly centralised, taking place at the national level (as in Slovenia); semi-centralised, taking place at the level of sectors or regions (as in Spain); or highly decentralised, taking place at the company level (as in the UK). The Commission acknowledges that there is no evidence to support a superior wage-setting model.[45] However, the EU Semester (specifically the CSRs related to the EPP and the MIP) seems to be enmeshed in a self-contradictory dynamic insofar as it puts forward far-reaching demands aimed at the decentralisation of collective bargaining. Indeed, while there is little evidence to support this strategy, the Commission argues that the degree of centralisation may affect the way in which wages can reflect productivity.[46]

This 'decentralisation' trend is increasingly evident in the legal framework for economic governance. The EPP, for instance, explicitly states that wage-setting mechanisms, and notably the degree of centralisation in the bargaining process, should be adjusted in line with productivity developments. As part of the EU Semester, the Commission has made use of its new power of influence to issue CSRs (2011–14) on wage-bargaining decentralisation in Belgium, Spain and Italy.[47] For instance, in Italy and Spain, the CSRs suggest a prioritising of collective agreements at company level and the ability for companies to opt out (Table 5).

Public sector wage-setting is not excluded from this 'downward' trend. Wages have to be maintained below a certain ceiling in order to consolidate public budgets, but, more importantly, to play a signalling role for other sectors. A key argument is that wage inflation in the periphery has been particularly problematic in the public sector, notably because it had spill-over effects into the exposed sector.[48] As a result, one of the first measures imposed by the Troika in connection with economic adjustment programmes was to cut wages in the public sector or at least freeze them. The most-affected country was Greece, where the various wage cuts added up to about 30 per cent. Cuts in Italy, Ireland, Portugal, Spain and Latvia varied between 5 per cent and 10 per cent. However, besides financial aid programmes, the CSRs from 2011–14 have not called for a public-sector wage freeze.

[44] European Commission, 'Action for Stability, Growth and Jobs' COM(2012) 299; Commission, 'Country-specific Recommendations 2012' (*EU 2020*, 16 April 2013).

[45] European Commission, 'Wage Setting Systems and Wage Developments' (European Commission, 2013).

[46] See T Aidt and Z Tzannatos, 'Trade Unions, Collective Bargaining and Macroeconomic Performance: A Review' (2008) 39 *Industrial Relations Journal* 258–95.

[47] COM(2013) 750.

[48] Johnston and Hancké, n 20 above.

Along these lines, minimum wages also have to be maintained below a certain floor because they are seen as playing a signalling role in other sectors. If fixed at too-high levels, they may harm the employment prospects of lower productivity workers (as their costs may be driven above their productivity levels) and young workers (as their productivity may fall short of the minimum wage). There is no clear evidence to support this claim, but minimum wages also constitute an important component of this trend in both the Troika programmes and the Commission's recommendations. For instance, in Ireland, the statutory minimum wage was cut by one euro per hour, a drop of 12 per cent, at the beginning of 2011. In Portugal, the statutory minimum wage was frozen. Furthermore, several countries outside the Troika programmes, notably France and Slovenia, received recommendations to control minimum wage growth in order to ensure competitiveness (CSRs 2011–14). In the long term, we believe that most EU countries might be affected by this trend as they all have some form of minimum wage floor that is either fixed centrally and determined by legislation or collectively agreed by social partners.

In the same vein, wage indexation is also seen as problematic in a monetary union in that it makes adjustments more difficult.[49] Indeed, according to the one view, indexation can create a wage-price spiral and is thus likely to make any nominal shock lasting, especially since wage cost is one of the major channels of adjustment. Furthermore, indexation makes wages more rigid and therefore less adaptable to productivity. While the Commission admits that wage indexation can be an effective means of preserving the purchasing power of wages, it advocates a flexible model that could offer adequate adjustment capacity.[50] As a result, significant pressure has been exerted to reform indexation systems. For instance, trade unions in Spain suspended their wage indexation clauses in collective agreements in 2010 and are in the process of a 'gradual de-indexation', with several enterprise-level collective agreements replacing indexation (clauses) with productivity clauses. As for Cyprus,[51] the Troika bailout also imposed a radical reform of its wage indexation system, the 'Cost of Living Adjustment' (COLA). The financial programme includes, among other things, a lower frequency of adjustment, a mechanism that imposes 'automatic suspension and derogation procedures during adverse economic conditions', and a move from full to partial indexation. Other Member States, such as Belgium,

[49] European Commission, 'Wage Setting Systems and Wage Developments' (European Commission, 2013): ec.europa.eu/europe2020/pdf/themes/26_wage_settings.pdf, accessed 14 August 2013.

[50] See AGS for 2012 and 2013. With the Cyprus precedent, the Commission has a new benchmark that could exert a significant learning pressure in the near future.

[51] Malta did not receive any CSRs regarding its indexation system in 2014.

Luxembourg and Malta, which are not under the Troika programme, are also under pressure to reform their indexation models. In its CSRs for 2011–14, the Commission calls for more flexible indexation mechanisms capable of adjusting to productivity.

These reforms seem to be at odds with relevant findings on the causes of macroeconomic imbalances. This deregulatory solution is taking shape in the periphery as if wage inflation were caused by centralised wage settings or wage-indexation mechanisms, but empirical data discussed above have shown that wage-setting structures in the periphery were already weak and decentralised prior to the crisis.[52] Wage inflation was not caused by excessive centralisation of wage-setting mechanisms, but rather by the absence of wage coordination mechanisms.[53] Indeed, strong wage-setting systems have proved to be an effective means of wage control for surplus countries. Furthermore, excessive wage inflation has not been problematic in countries that link inflation to wage increases. In Belgium, for instance, wage developments in unit wage costs have closely followed the two per cent line, a line corresponding to the ECB's price stability target of 'below but close to 2% inflation'.[54] As such, indexation would seem to be fully compatible with the EMU, especially when it is part of a coordinated bargaining system that takes into account the price stability objective of the ECB.

However, in spite of this evidence, the crisis has not yet drawn sufficient positive lessons from the successful wage-setting arrangements of the core economies. While the Union should be applauded for attempting to rebalance the institutional framework of the EMU through the strengthening of wage coordination at the EU level, at the same time it has been exerting pressure to weaken the existing wage-setting mechanisms of the periphery as well as of the core economies. In sum, the crisis has only triggered a partial learning process whereby the Union questions the EMU's asymmetric design and particularly the lack of a common approach on wage coordination, flaws which contributed to the development of the crisis. However, all signs point to the likelihood that the Union may have to draw positive lessons from successful wage-setting arrangements in order to address EMU flaws.

IV. LEARNING INTENSITY OF THE EUROPEAN SEMESTER: EARLY EVIDENCE ON NATIONAL WAGE MODERATION AND WAGE-SETTING

Any attempt to theorise the learning impact of the European Semester on wage policy faces several challenges. First, the diversity of processes

[52] Johnston and Hancké, n 20 above, at 601–22.

[53] Ibid.

[54] R Janssen, 'Indexation of Wages: A Message from the Troika to Belgium, Luxemburg and Malta', *Social Europe Journal*, 9 April 2013.

(financial aid programmes, the MIP, the EPP), their relative infancy, the frequency of procedural changes and the horizontal and vertical complexity of the process make theorisation of the data an extremely cumbersome task. Secondly, there are methodological difficulties in assessing the causal relation of a learning process deprived of genuinely binding power. Thirdly, much of the debate on the European Semester suffers from a serious empirical deficit, relying on evidence based mainly on official sources. Moreover, it is often difficult to disconnect the European Semester's influence on national policy from the influence of other domestic factors that may play a greater role in the transformation of wage policy systems.

In spite of these barriers, the learning effect of the emerging normative framework on EU wages is already evident. The full scope of the emerging changes is straightforward in those countries under direct pressure from the Troika, but a learning process is already underway in the rest of Europe. Early data show that the European Semester may contribute to an innovative dynamic that is not linked to regulatory change; rather, they concern 'single/double-loop learning' in early stages of the policy-making process. The type of influence the European Semester exerts is discursive or cognitive, involving mostly single-loop *cognitive shifts*. In some instances, however, learning goes beyond single-loop to assume a more complex form through *agenda (re)framing* or *direct policy shift*. Accordingly, the following sub-sections will discuss the different types of learning outcomes taking place in the field of wage developments and wage-setting systems.

A. Progressive Wage Rebalancing

Evidence shows that both the crisis and Member States' responses to it have triggered a new wage policy-learning pattern. Indeed, the divergences accumulated in the post-EMU period have given way to a new convergence pattern. While the introduction of the euro triggered an asymmetric wage-learning pattern, with an upward development of nominal wages in the periphery and a downward dynamic in the core economies, this pattern has been completely reversed since 2010. Evidence shows that recent wage developments have moved in the direction of supporting the adjustment of external macroeconomic imbalances.[55] As shown in Figures 7 and 8, a rebalancing process has taken place across the EU. On the one hand, the periphery has already started to show a pattern of sharp decline in ULC as a result of productivity increases and wage moderation.[56] On the other hand,

[55] European Commission, n 50 above.
[56] In 2013, nominal compensation fell only in Greece, Portugal, Spain and Slovenia.

the core economies have experienced a moderate wage increase in order to outpace the wages and ULCs in those countries.[57]

It is worth noting that between 2010 and 2014, nominal wages, and to a greater extent real wages, declined in 18 of 27 EU countries (Figures 8 and 9).[58] In its 2013 report on labour market developments, the Commission stresses that consumption wages—a significant variable for consumers in that it helps to measure purchasing power—have decreased in 16 EU countries. The Commission also acknowledges that on average, productivity grew significantly faster than real compensation, thus confirming the downward wage adjustment behind this rebalancing pattern.[59] Along these lines, large improvements in cost competitiveness have been recorded in the periphery (particularly Ireland, Greece, Spain, Lithuania and Portugal) thanks to the depreciation of their ULCs.

While this trend mostly reflects market forces, it may also have been facilitated by the reforms implemented in countries under a Troika programme and, to a lesser extent, by the pressure exerted by the first CSRs. Although it is difficult to assume a learning link between the CSRs and the outcome (wage developments), the wage rebalancing process described above provides examples of both single- and double-loop learning.

One form of single-loop influence triggered by the CSRs is *ideational adjustment*.[60] For instance, while there is no evidence of a discernible impact of the CSRs in France and Germany, the European Semester may have heightened awareness of certain concepts, for instance that wage developments must reflect productivity and support demand. Indeed, the recent upward wage path in Germany illustrates this cognitive shift, even though it may not be solely the result of the CSRs. Small changes are made to domestic wage policies in order to improve routines without challenging established paradigms and underlying beliefs on what wage formation should become in Germany. To borrow Argyris' analogy, the CSRs act as a thermostat by making constant minor adjustments to regulate procedures and national reforms.

In contrast, the periphery has engaged in a deeper double-loop learning process, one taking the form of a *reframing* of the domestic agenda. Indeed, the European Semester seems to have placed the issue of wage moderation

[57] Mainly Germany, but also Sweden, France, Belgium and Poland. In 2013, Eurozone countries—Belgium, Finland, Austria, Estonia and Germany—recorded increases above 2.5%. Outside the Eurozone, Bulgaria, Romania and Hungary recorded high growth rates while Denmark and the Czech Republic recorded the most moderate growth rates.

[58] T Müller and M Bernaciak, 'Impact of the Crisis on Wages and Collective Bargaining across Europe' ETUI Conference: *Getting Europe back to work—alternatives to austerity*, 6 November 2013.

[59] Commission, n 50 above, 42.

[60] M Lopez-Santana, 'The Domestic Implications of Soft Law: Framing and Transmitting Changes in Employment Policy' (2006) 13 *Journal of European Public Policy* 481–99.

on the agenda through the CSRs. While there might be a tenuous link between wage developments and CSRs, most countries that received CSRs on wage moderation have experienced a significant nominal wage decline (Figure 7 and Table 5). These learning outcomes may be seen as examples of double-loop learning in the sense that domestic actors are evaluating their priorities in a new light as a result of the influences of the CSRs. Firstly, by *framing* a set of specific guidelines, the CSRs have established that idea X, for example lack of wage convergence, is a common challenge for the EMU and consequently national decision-makers should also see X as a problem and take action to solve it.

B. Learning Evidence on Wage-Setting Mechanisms

Since the onset of the crisis in 2008, wage-setting Member States have been under pressure to reform their bargaining systems. Indeed, it seems that the crisis has triggered significant changes in wage-formation regimes. For instance, recent evidence suggests that changes in the main bargaining levels at which wages are determined have been considerable in 12 countries. More specifically, the dominant trend was decentralisation, from the cross-sector level towards the sector or company level.[61] Similarly, statutory minimum wages were subject to significant changes in 10 countries. While some countries of the periphery have imposed wage cuts and wage freezes, and abolished their tripartite bodies, others have increased sectoral-minimum wages (Germany). Finally, wage-indexation systems were not spared by this process (besides Malta). For instance, Belgium has changed the method of calculation to temper the effect of the crisis, while Cyprus has introduced a temporary exemption for companies facing hardship (Table 6).[62]

In light of these data, it seems that most extensive changes have taken place in countries that underwent a Troika programme, although wage-setting reforms have also been prompted in other countries to a lesser extent. In line with the 2014 Eurofound findings,[63] it is possible to classify these substantive changes into three groups according to their learning intensity (Table 7). A first category of countries has engaged in single-loop learning insofar as their wage-formation systems have only witnessed minor adjustments or no changes at all. A second group of countries[64] has engaged in a double-loop learning process in that they have only experienced some

[61] Except for Belgium and Finland, which have headed towards more centralisation. Eurofound, *Changes to wage-setting mechanism in the Context of the Crisis and the EU's New Governance Regime* (Dublin, 2014).

[62] Ibid, 15.

[63] Above, n 62.

[64] Croatia, Italy, Hungary and Slovenia: seen 62 above, 19.

changes, mainly driven by domestic forces, and to a lesser extent by the European Semester. Finally, a third group, those who received financial assistance, has clearly engaged in a triple-loop learning process insofar as change is characterised by a radical shift in the 'hierarchy of goals and set of instruments employed to guide policy'.[65] Indeed, Memorandum of Understanding (MoU) requirements have resulted in significant weakening of national bargaining systems, although bargaining instruments in the periphery were already weak and unable to adjust to market conditions (Table 8). While changes have taken various forms (eg collective bargaining decentralisation and suspension of wage indexation), the common denominator is that they have significantly remoulded the wage systems in those countries.

The European Semester has played a limited role in the third group. However, it may have exerted some learning influence in the first two groups. Indeed, the impact of the European Semester on wage setting can hardly be evaluated on the basis of the direct implementation of the CSRs into national rules. Such direct transfers are rare, given the operational closure of the national political and administrative arenas. Adjustments and transformations in wage settings are not necessarily linked to CSRs; one must look beyond the legal surface for a better understanding of various learning scenarios.[66] To this end, differentiating between single- and double-loop learning once again proves useful in analysing the magnitude and source of the transfer of new knowledge on wage formation.

First, empirical data show that, as part of the European Semester, new ideas on wage settings have been downloaded at the domestic level. For instance, evidence from the 2013 and 2014 NRPs and the EPP commitments of 2011 highlights that new concepts—aligning wage formation to productivity and monitoring wage-indexation mechanisms and public sector wages—have entered national discourse in the majority of Member States.

Secondly, the CSRs' influence may qualify as second-loop learning insofar as it facilitates *identification* of new knowledge based on the discovery of new problems. Once a new problem is identified, it may be integrated into the domestic agenda such that governments will be likely to address it and formulate possible courses of action. For instance, the MIP and the EPP have enhanced 'mutual awareness of policies, practices and problems in other Member States', creating the possibility of *questioning one's own national policy instruments and rules*. More specifically, as part of the European Semester, several Member States seem to recognise that their

[65] Ibid, 284.

[66] M Büchs, D Friedrich and P Pochet, 'Surface Integration' in J Zeitlin and L Magnusson (eds), *The Open Method of Co-ordination in Action: The European Employment and Social Inclusion Strategies* (PIE-Peter Lang, 2005).

wage indexation is problematic in a monetary union in that it makes adjustments more difficult to make. In Belgium, while the government has decided to retain the indexation mechanism, it has introduced changes that mitigate its impact. Along these lines, the new governance instruments on wage setting may produce direct policy change, a more concrete form of second-loop learning. While this occurs rarely, there are a few instances in which the CSRs have significantly affected domestic wage formation. Recent data on the last European Semesters show that in some cases (eg Spain and Bulgaria)[67] CSRs have been accepted and implemented.

It is, however, important to stress that in most cases changes will not come about in an obvious way and will not affect the domestic legal framework directly. Similarly to the OMC experience, CSR outcomes should be assessed in individual Member States based on relative achievements via gradual 'progression', and not solely according to immediate effects. Caution is needed given the scarcity of empirical evidence on the impact of the European Semester and the fact that 'direct change' may be driven by domestic variables. For instance, the implementation of the CSRs in Spain coincided with the election in 2011 of a government already committed to introducing wage-setting changes.[68] Furthermore, in the 11 countries that received CSRs on wages, while substantive changes that occurred are relatively consistent with the CSRs (especially in Italy, Spain and Bulgaria) early empirical data suggest that these changes have been driven mainly by domestic factors.[69] In fact, most substantive changes are somewhat inconsistent with the CSRs, as in Belgium, Cyprus, Malta and Luxembourg (concerning indexation) or Slovenia (regarding minimum wage). In other countries, the CSRs had no apparent effect (Germany or France).

C. A Path-Dependent Wage-Governance Process

Learning about policies at the level of decision-makers is not sufficient to mobilise change.[70] Member States do not react directly to external influences. Policy pressures and more particularly CSR targets are mediated and filtered through national institutions. National policy-makers may be open to discussing best practices and successful foreign models, but are unlikely to accept blind commitments to processes and policies in areas as politically salient and sensitive as wage formation and developments. It is thus necessary to take account of the relative autonomy, inertia, and path-dependent

[67] Eurofound, n 62 above, 30.
[68] Ibid.
[69] Ibid, 41.
[70] CJ Bennett and M Howlett, 'The Lessons of Learning: Reconciling Theories of Policy Learning and Policy Change' (1992) 25 *Policy Sciences* 275–94.

trajectories of national institutions as well as actors' powers and interests in order to investigate the policy impact of learning instruments. Citi and Rhodes assert that 'different degrees of policy convergence are the result of incentive and preference structures that, from a national point of view, make the transfer of policies rational'.[71]

Accordingly, while it is recognised that the CSRs have exerted some single- and double-loop learning influences on wage systems, the transformation of wage policies is a path-dependent process mainly driven or hindered by domestic variables. CSRs therefore either contribute to or contradict those domestic transformations that are already taking place.

There are several domestic factors that may play a role in the transformation of wage policies in the EU. First, economic factors play a crucial role in the wage learning process. For instance, the fact that the crisis did not have a major impact on domestic activity, and hence on wage setting, in Austria, the Czech Republic, the Netherlands and Norway, may explain why these countries have undergone very limited changes. Furthermore, according to a recent qualitative study,[72] macro and microeconomic considerations also play an instrumental role in the development of wage formation at the domestic level. On the one hand, a primary macroeconomic consideration in the transformation of wage indexation and minimum wage setting is moderating or constraining wage costs. For instance, macroeconomic factors have also played a significant role in countries where minimum wage-setting mechanisms have been strengthened (Croatia, Slovenia, and Slovakia) and where it has been weakened (Cyprus, Greece, Ireland, and Portugal). In the former group, the objective was to sustain or stimulate demand; in the latter, it was to constrain wage costs. On the other hand, microeconomic factors, for instance the capacity of wage-setting instruments to accommodate companies under competitive circumstances, have played a prominent role in the decentralisation of collective bargaining. In all these cases, while national governments have exercised the most influence, CSRs have also had a certain degree of influence (especially regarding wage indexation).[73]

Furthermore, micro and macroeconomic considerations also help us to understand why some countries have not reformed their wage-setting systems. On the one hand, several countries have not seen the need to reform their wage-setting systems insofar as they are sufficiently effective in adjusting to changing economic conditions. On the other hand, three countries seem to regard their collective bargaining as playing a marginal role in moderating wage growth (Latvia, Lithuania and Poland).

[71] M Citi and M Rhodes, 'New Modes of Governance in the EU: Common Objectives versus National Preferences', January 2007, European Governance Papers (EUROGOV) 21.

[72] Eurofound, n 62 above.

[73] Eurofound, n 62 above.

A second variable concerns the types of *welfare state* regime.[74] In principle, the degree of fit or misfit between a country's welfare state regime and the nature of the EU pressure—direct or indirect, economic or normative—may have a decisive impact on explaining policy responses.[75] Thus, a Member State with an extensive social protection system (for example France, where the CSRs have had almost no apparent impact) may consider the CSRs a threat, while a Member State with a more fragmented system might regard the CSRs as an opportunity to improve its system. However, this does not hold true for every Member State with extensive social protections; in fact, Italy and Spain have embraced the CSR reforms as an opportunity to restructure their systems.

In keeping with this, *social groups* compete to shape responses to the crisis and more specifically to define how wage setting can contribute to absorbing the economic shock.[76] Analyses of how they interact and leverage pressure provide valuable insight into the learning influence resulting from EU policies. In particular, organised labour in both the public and the private sectors may be in a position to mobilise opposition to wage adjustment measures. One might therefore expect an inverse correlation between the level of unionisation and the likelihood of adopting orthodox stabilisation and structural adjustment measures.[77] One might also expect governments relying heavily on working-class support to be more likely to tolerate inflation experiments with heterodox policies[78] and block the adjustment, since the cost of such reforms is more likely to fall on their core constituents.[79] For instance, this may explain how social partners in Malta were able to resist international pressure.

In short, we acknowledge that the frame of reference of EU wage policy is being progressively affected by the Troika's influence, but also by the European Semester. In fact, evidence from the first cycles of the European Semester suggests that it has also produced a significant reframing and opening of national discourse. At the same time, however, it is a highly path-dependent process which merely adds a layer to the ongoing domestic

[74] G Esping-Andersen, 'The Three Worlds of Welfare Capitalism' in C Pierson and FG Castles (eds), *The Welfare State Reader* (Cambridge, Polity Press, 1990).

[75] Empirical study conducted by Lopez Santana on the OMC illustrates well this claim. See M Lopez-Santana, 'The Domestic Implications of Soft Law: Framing and Transmitting Changes in Employment Policy' (2006) 13 *Journal of European Public Policy* 481–99; M Lopez-Santana, 'Soft Europeanisation? How the Soft Pressure from Above Affects the Bottom (Differently): The Belgian, Spanish and Swedish Experiences' (European University Institute 2007), EUI Working Paper.

[76] J Ikenberry, D Lake and M Mastandano, *The State and American Foreign Economic Diplomacy* (Ithaca NY, Cornell University Press, 1988).

[77] S Haggard and R Kaufman, *The Politics of Stabilisation and Structural Adjustment* (Chicago IL, University of Chicago Press, 1989).

[78] DA Hibbs, 'Political Parties and Macroeconomic Policy' (1977) 71 *The American Political Science Review* 1467–87.

[79] PR Agénor, 'The Labor Market and Economic Adjustment', June 1996, IMF Staff Papers.

debate. The relationship between the European Semester and Member States is based on reciprocity: European policies are filtered, mediated and reshaped according to national context. It is a two-way interaction rather than a one-way causal impact; untangling the independent causal influence of the CSRs presents formidable challenges of interpretation.

V. CONCLUSION

This chapter assessed the new economic governance framework from a learning point of view. Findings show that the crisis response has substantive implications for wage policy-learning in Europe. Specifically, it investigated the substantive orientation of the new economic governance framework and particularly whether the Union has institutionalised a learning process for internal devaluation.

Evidence shows that the new economic governance framework, which is still in its infancy, has already produced first- and second-loop impacts. On the one hand, the new economic governance impetus has already prompted a progressive wage rebalancing process, with upward adjustment in the core economies and downward adjustment in the periphery. On the other hand, the new impetus on wage setting has also produced first- and second-loop changes in the form of a weakening of collective bargaining and minimum wage setting and indexation.

While the new economic governance framework should be applauded for attempting to coordinate wage policies, the weakening of wage systems does not seem to align with the genuine causes of the crisis. Excessive wage growth is a symptom of deeper legal flaws within the structure of the EMU. In fact, the crisis originated in financial sector indiscipline and diverging wage growth, which resulted partly from the absence of efficient wage-setting systems at the EU level.[80] Evidence shows that early euro-area growth relied mainly on the pro-cyclical ECB interest rate, resulting in diverging and harmful growth paths. In this model, economic growth in the periphery was sustained by finance-led policies, which in turn depended on housing-price inflation and stock-exchange bubbles. At the same time the core economies, in which consumer borrowing was lower, pursued export-led growth and wage moderation (thanks to their efficient wage-setting systems).[81] As argued by Joseph Stiglitz, such instability is as much, if not more, the result of the behaviour of countries with trade surpluses in that they impose costs with unsustainable consequences for others.

[80] M Wolf, *Fixing Global Finance* (JHU, 2010).

[81] While the problem is not confined to the EMU, there is a broad consensus that this growth model was exacerbated by EMU flaws.

Given this evidence, it will be interesting to see whether the framework of the ongoing deepening of the social dimension of the EMU of 2 October 2013 will establish a different trend.[82] While it is too early to draw definitive conclusions regarding the future of EU wage policy, this new framework currently seems unlikely to attain its objective of mitigating the social cost of the macroeconomic adjustment process. For instance, the new framework establishes relevant social and employment monitoring systems, but it does not address the issue of excessive wage moderation in the periphery; and while the framework stresses the role of social partners, the CSRs urge more decentralised wage bargaining. A combined economic and legal argument may be valuable in further exploring the need for the introduction and development of robust and effective wage-setting mechanisms at the EU level.

[82] European Commission, 'Strengthening the Social Dimension of the Economic and Monetary Union' COM(2013) 690provisoire;

ANNEX: FIGURES & TABLES

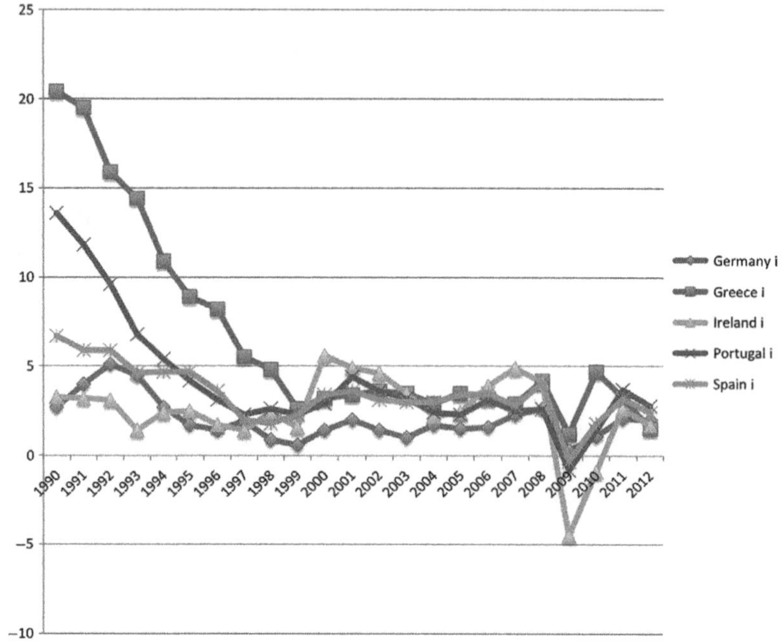

Figure 1: Consumer Price Inflation
Source: OECD

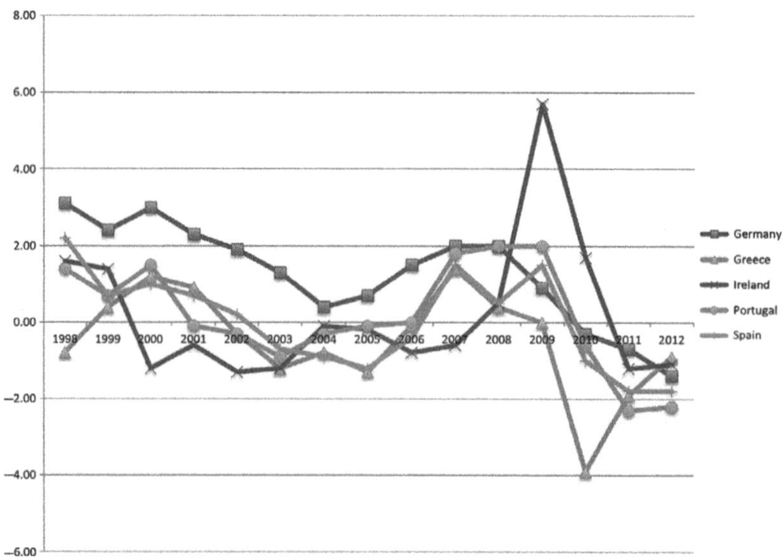

Figure 2: Real Interest Rates
Source: OECD

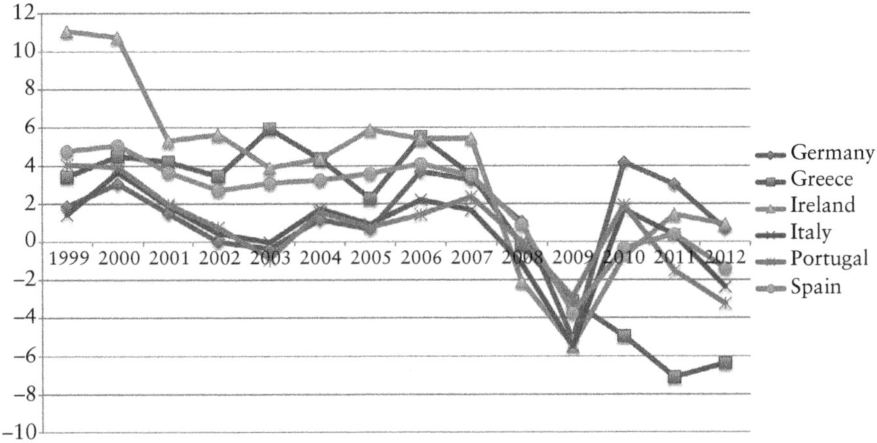

Figure 3: Gross Domestic Product (GDP): Annual Growth Rates in Percentage
Source: OECD

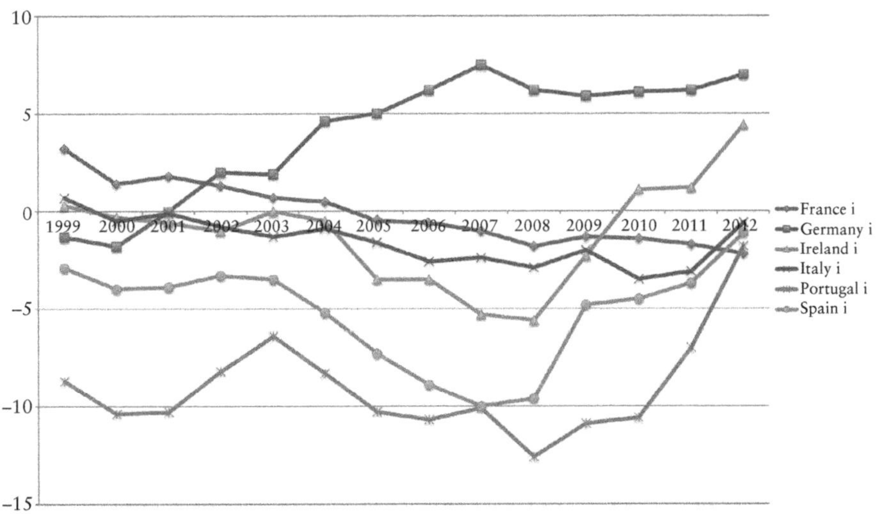

Figure 4: Current Account % of GDP
Source: OECD

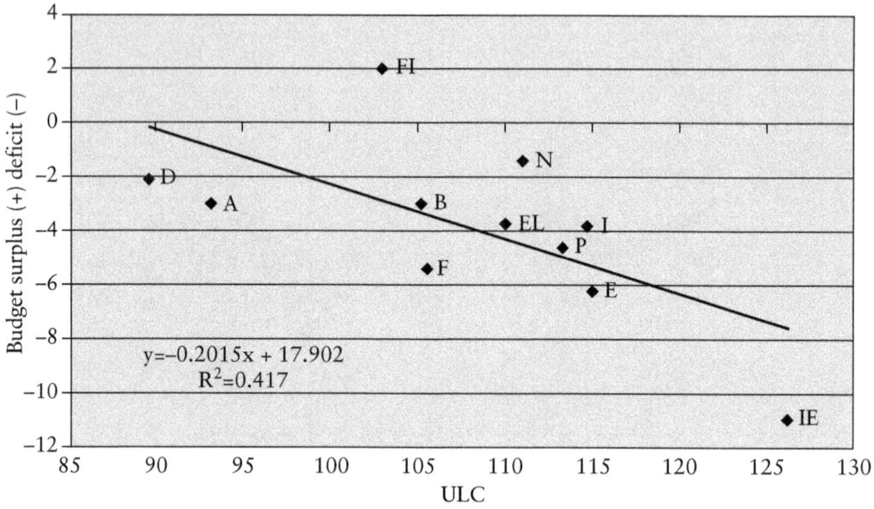

Figure 5: Correlation between Current Account and ULC
Source: European Commission, AMECO database

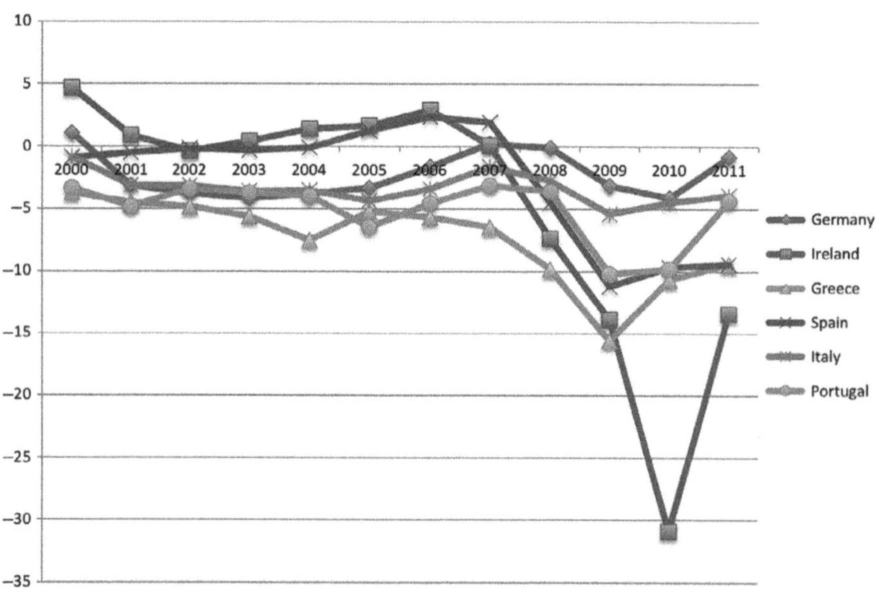

Figure 6: Relative Unit Labour Costs (1999–2008) and Budget Surplus (+), Deficit (–)
Source: Ameco

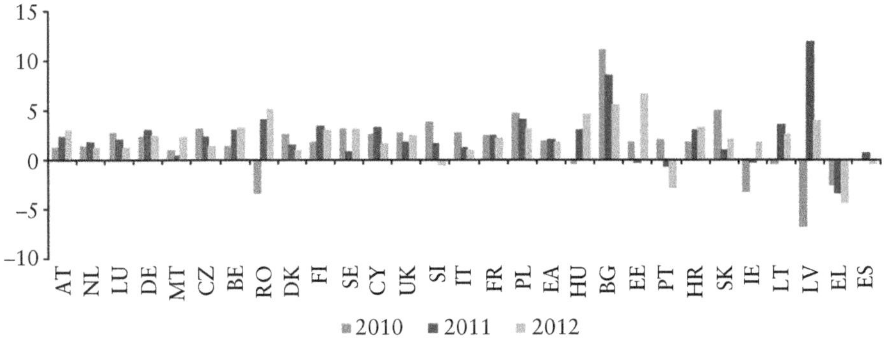

Figure 7: Nominal Compensation per Employee 2009–2012
Source: DG ECFIN, AMECO database

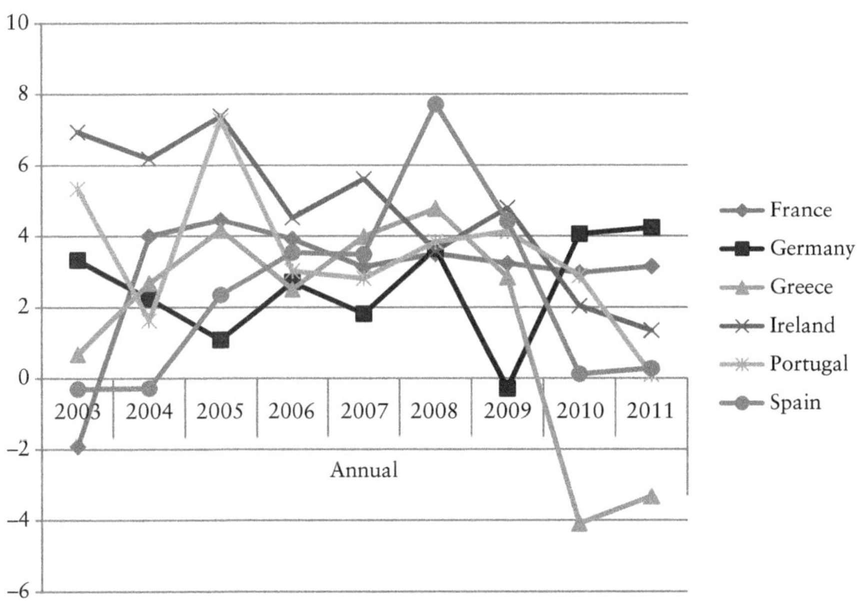

Figure 8: Nominal Compensation per Employee (Annual Growth Rate)
Source: OECD

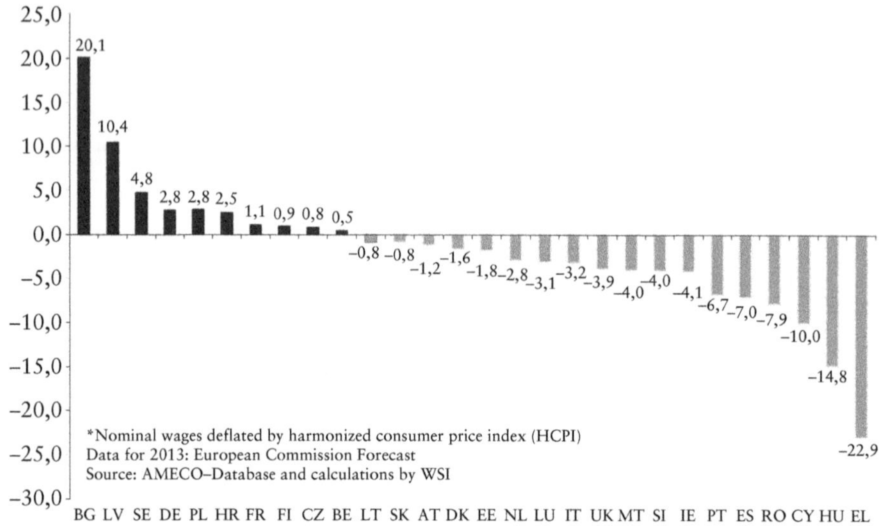

Figure 9: Real Wages Development across the EU 2010–2013
Source: T Müller and M Bernaciak

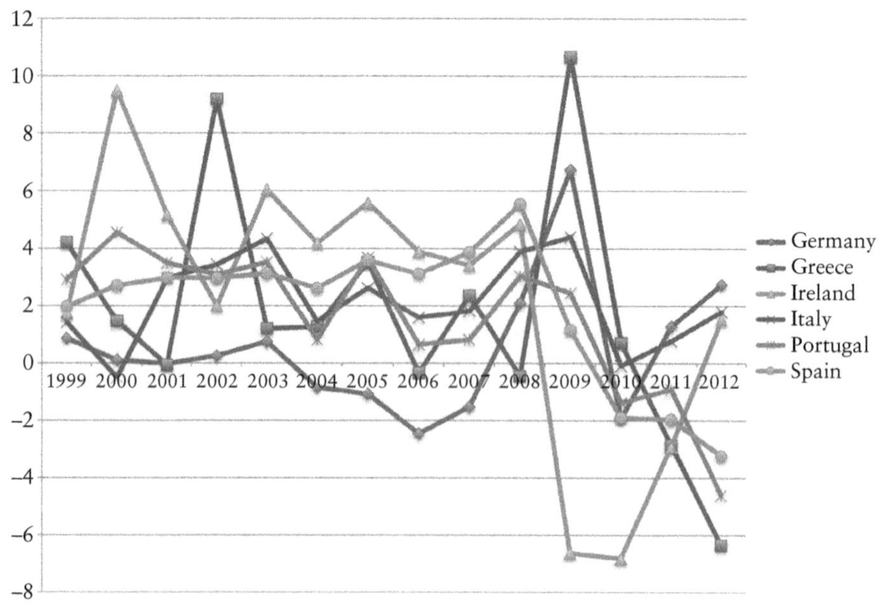

Figure 10: Unit Labour Cost
Source: OECD

Table 1: Budget Deficit/GDP (%)

	2006	*2007*	*2008*	*2009*	*2010*	*2011*	*2012*
France	-2.4	-2.7	-3.3	-7.6	-7.1	-5.7	-4.5
Germany	-1.7	0.2	-0.1	-3.2	-4.3	-1.2	-1.1
Greece	-6.0	-6.8	-9.9	-15.8	-10.8	-9.0	-7.0
Italy	-3.4	-1.6	-2.7	-5.4	-4.5	-3.6	-1.6
Portugal	-4.1	-3.2	-3.7	-10.2	-9.8	-5.9	-4.5
Spain	2.4	1.9	-4.5	-11.2	-9.3	-6.2	-4.4
Euro area (15 countries)	-1.4	-0.7	-2.1	-6.4	-6.3	-4.0	-2.9

Source: OECD

Table 2: Public Debt/GDP (%) and Change in Debt in 2007–2012 (%–points)

	2006	*2007*	*2008*	*2009*	*2010*	*2011*	*2012*
France	71.2	73.0	79.3	90.8	95.2	98.6	102.4
Germany	69.8	65.6	69.7	77.4	87.1	86.9	87.3
Greece	116.9	115.0	118.1	133.5	149.1	165.1	181.2
Ireland	29.2	28.7	49.6	71.1	98.5	112.6	118.8
Italy	116.9	112.1	114.7	127.1	126.1	127.7	128.1
Portugal	77.6	75.4	80.7	93.3	103.6	111.9	121.9
Spain	46.2	42.3	47.7	62.9	67.1	74.1	77.2
Euro area (15 countries)	74.7	71.8	77.0	87.6	92.9	95.6	97.9

Source: OECD

Table 3: Wage Restraint under ERM and EMU

Wage restraint is the change in nominal wage growth minus the change in labour productivity. A negative outcome indicates wage *restraint*; a positive outcome indicates wage *excess*.

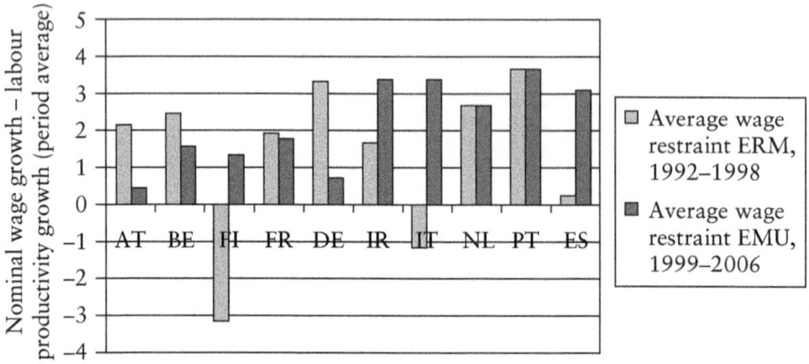

Source: Nominal wage growth data from AMECO and labour productivity growth data from OECD. Calculation by Hancke and Johnston 2009[1].

Table 4: Increase in Household Debt (in % GDP) 2000–2004 and 2000–2008

Export-led	*2000–2004*	*2000–2008*	Finance-led	*2000–2004*	*2000–2008*
Germany	–2.74	–11.34	Greece	18.26	-------
Austria	7.05	7.21	Spain	22.01	32.53
Netherlands	24.35	29.1	Portugal	14.08	21.31
			Italy	13.05	18.09
			Ireland	35.07	61.72

Source: Eurostat[2]

[1] Johnston and Hancké, n 20 above.

[2] While household debt is falling in Germany and moderately increasing in Austria, it is dramatically increasing in the Southern periphery, with all countries well above the Euro (12) area average. In the Netherlands household debt increases rapidly as well, though not as fast as in Ireland and Spain.

Table 5: Country-specific Recommendations 2011–2014 on Wage Growth and Wage Setting

CSRs 2011 and 2012				
Wage Rebalancing		**Wage-Setting Restructuring**		
Wage Moderation	Wage Increase	Decentralisation of Wage Bargaining	Wage Indexation	Minimum Wage Settings
BG, FI, IT, SL	GE	BG, SP, IT	BG, LU, MT, SP	FR, SL

Source: Country-specific Recommendations 2011, 2012

CSRs 2013				
Wage Rebalancing		**Wage-Setting Restructuring**		
Wage Moderation	Wage Increase	Decentralisation of Wage Bargaining	Wage Indexation	Minimum Wage Settings
BG, FR, SL, IT	GE	BG, SP, IT	BG, LU, MT, SP	FR, SL

Source: Country-specific Recommendations 2013

CSRs 2014				
Wage Rebalancing		**Wage-Setting Restructuring**		
Wage Moderation	Wage Increase	Decentralisation of Wage Bargaining	Wage Indexation	Minimum Wage Settings
BE	GE	SP	BG, LU, SP	FR, SL

Source: Country-specific Recommendations 2014

Table 6: Post-crisis Wage-setting Changes

Degree of Centralisation	
Centralised	AT, BG, CY, EL, ES, FR, IE, IT, RO, SI
Decentralised	BE, FI
Horizontal coordination across bargaining units	AT, ES, HU, IE, RO, SE, SK

Minimum Wage-setting and Indexation Regimes	
Minimum wage	CY, DE, EL, ES, HR, HU, IE, PL, PT, SI, SK
Indexation	BE, CY, ES, IT, LU

Source: Eurofound & EIRO 2014

Table 7: Learning Intensity and Outcomes

Learning Loop	*Single-Loop*	*Second-Loop*	*Triple-Loop*
Outcomes	*Minor policy adjustment:* fixing problem while 'following the rules'	*Change of policies and instruments:* changing the rules, fixing problems through a new view point	*Radical shift paradigm or hierarchy of goals:* changing the rules and questioning beliefs and perceptions

Table 8: Wage Rebalancing and Wage-Setting Learning Process

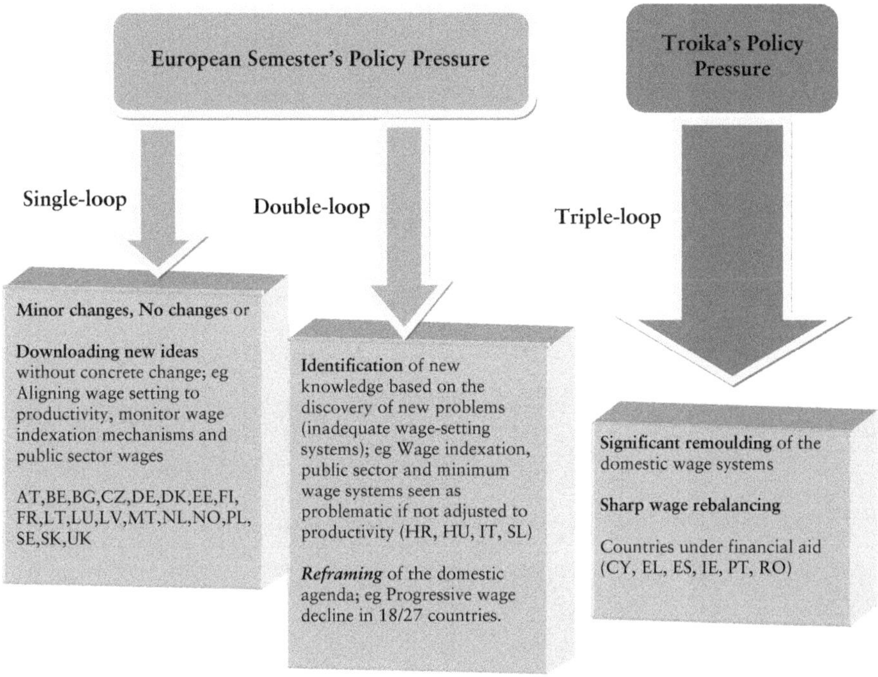

Source: Eurofound 2014

4

Clinical Trials Abroad: The Marketable Ethics, Weak Protections and Vulnerable Subjects of EU Law

MARK L FLEAR*

Abstract

This chapter explores how the EU is a largely overlooked exporter of normative power through its facilitation and use of clinical trials data produced abroad for the marketing of safe pharmaceuticals at home; a move that helps to foster the growing resort to pharmaceuticals as a fix for public health problems. This is made possible by the EU's (de)selection of international ethical frameworks in preference to the international technical standards it co-authors with other global regulators. Clinical trials abroad underscore how ethics are contingent and revisable in light of market needs, producing weak protections for the vulnerable subjects of EU law. I argue that these components and effects of the regime are ultimately about that which undergirds, shapes and directs regulatory design. That is, I point to the use, infiltration, perpetuation and extension of market-oriented ideas, values and rationalities into formally non-market domains like biomedical knowledge production and public health. I explain how these are central to efforts at producing and legitimating the EU, its related imagined socio-political order based on a more innovative, profitable and competitive pharmaceutical sector in order to foster economic growth, jobs and prosperity, and with them the project of European integration. 'Bioethics as risk' is highlighted as a way to reshape and redirect the regulatory regime in ways that are more consistent with the spirit and letter of the ethical standards (and through them the human rights) the EU claims to uphold.

I. INTRODUCTION

CLINICAL TRIALS ARE increasingly being carried out abroad as they are 'off-shored'[1] from the European Union (EU) and wider global North towards the global South. The performance of

[1] A Petryna, 'Clinical Trials Offshored: On Private Sector Science and Public Health' (2007) 2 *BioSocieties* 21. Also see A Petryna, *When Experiments Travel* (Princeton NJ, Princeton University Press, 2009).

clinical trials abroad offers several benefits and possibilities to an industry dominated by so-called 'big pharma',[2] which enjoyed a boom period in the 1990s but is now struggling to deliver sufficient numbers of new 'block-buster drugs'. Those benefits include lower costs and populations whose epidemiology makes them especially useful in order to demonstrate the quality, safety and efficacy of new drugs, and so to more easily justify the marketing of and turn to pharmaceuticals in the global North.[3] This forms part of a wider resort to pharmaceuticals as a weapon in the fight against public health problems and in shaping what are regarded as problems in the first place. This so-called 'pharmaceuticalisation'[4] is also part of the increasing shift of attention and distribution of scarce public resources towards treatment and other technological fixes (especially for problems that can be more easily if not properly tackled in that way), and away from risk-based strategies of prevention and health promotion.[5] In short, pharmaceuticalisation might produce a distraction of attention away from the socio-economic and political conditions and inequities producing public health problems in the first place.[6] The (mis)uses of pharmaceuticals and clinical trials also highlight concerns over, inter alia, the lack of research into the diseases producing the greatest mortality and morbidity worldwide and the global barriers to accessing essential medicines and sharing the benefits of globalised research.

Hitherto there has been a relative dearth of attention to these matters in law and regulation studies[7] as compared to medicine and bioethics, anthropology, critical theory, science and technology studies (STS) and sociology. Extant analyses correctly emphasise the alignment of regulation

[2] B Goldacre, *Big Pharma* (London, Harper Perennial, 2009).

[3] All noted in the (business) media, for example: A Jack, 'A New Lease of Life? The Ethics of Offshoring Clinical Trials', *Financial Times*, 28 January 2008; N Singer, 'Outsourcing of Drug Trials Is Faulted', *New York Times*, 18 February 2009.

[4] J Abraham, 'Evolving Sociological Analyses of "Pharmaceuticalisation": A Response to Williams, Martin and Gabe' (2011) 33 *Sociology of Health & Illness* 726; J Biehl, 'Pharmaceuticalisation: AIDS Treatment and Global Health Politics' (2007) 80 *Anthropological Quarterly* 1083; SJ Williams, J Gabe and P Davis, 'The Sociology of Pharmaceuticals: Progress and Prospects' (2008) 30 *Sociology of Health & Illness* 813; SJ Williams, P Martin and J Gabe, 'Evolving Sociological Analyses of "Pharmaceuticalisation": A Reply to Abraham' (2011) 33 *Sociology of Health & Illness* 729; SJ Williams, P Martin and J Gabe, 'The Pharmaceuticalisation of Society? A Framework for Analysis' (2011) 33 *Sociology of Health & Illness* 710.

[5] Pharmaceuticalisation is arguably especially apparent in contexts of rare but potentially high impact medical emergencies like global pandemics in which vaccines and medicines are stockpiled in preparedness planning for surge capacity and distribution by triage. There is a notable trend in non-emergency contexts too: S Boseley and others, 'Antidepressant use on the rise in rich countries, OECD finds', *The Guardian*, 20 November 2013.

[6] SE Bell and AE Figert, 'Medicalisation and Pharmaceuticalisation at the Intersections: Looking Backward, Sideways and Forward' (2012) 75 *Social Science & Medicine* 775.

[7] With some notable exceptions, such as E Jackson, *Law and the Regulation of Medicines* (Oxford, Hart Publishing, 2012).

to corporate interests and the way in which that explains the outsourcing of clinical trials and pharmaceuticalisation. As regards clinical trials abroad there is a focus on standard issues in research ethics. Debate revolves around, inter alia: the dubious relations between (usually privately funded) researchers and trial participants; the limited protection of the latter through their informed consent to participation; access to an (in)adequate standard of care during the trial; and the difficulties of ensuring access to post-trial benefits for trial participants drawn from often highly distressed social, economic and political circumstances. I argue that the problem is ultimately about that which undergirds, shapes and directs that regulatory design. That is, I point to the use, infiltration, perpetuation and extension of market-oriented ideas, values and rationalities into wider and formally non-market domains, like biomedical knowledge production and public health, and how they are central to efforts at producing and legitimating formally accountable actors, their related imagined socio-political orders and projects of rule.

I use the European Union—and the centrality of market rationality to its socio-political order and project of rule—as the case study through which to advance this argument. Law and regulation studies analyses in this area have focused on the national level, while in the cognate disciplines noted above much of the attention has been on the United States (US) regime and its imbrication with global patent law and technical standards on pharmaceuticals, in producing and sustaining the outsourcing of clinical trials and pharmaceuticalisation. The importance of the EU as an actor in itself as well as its relations with those other sites in ways that produce and sustain the overall picture has been largely overlooked.[8] Clinical trials *abroad* also underscore important (and related) features and effects of the EU's project of rule aimed at European integration.

Specifically, the EU is an exporter of normative power through the production of data abroad that is not merely an adjunct to, but is increasingly central to speeding up, authorisations for the marketing of safe drugs in its internal market.[9] This chapter underlines that risk-based regulation as part of an attempt to produce a European socio-political order based on a more innovative, profitable and competitive pharmaceutical sector in order to foster economic growth, jobs and prosperity through the marketing of safe pharmaceuticals. As part of that the EU has a key role as a global regulator

[8] Further analysis could bring out how the underpinning norms that shape EU law go above or beyond those which characterise national frameworks, whether those of the EU's Member States or of the US. This chapter is concerned with highlighting the norms, orientation and importance of the EU's regime—rather than a more comparative study.

[9] Black's definition of regulation is 'the intentional use of authority to affect behaviour of a different party according to set standards, involving instruments of information-gathering and behaviour modification' (J Black, 'Critical Reflections on Regulation' (2002) 27 *Australian Journal of Legal Philosophy* 1).

in international technical standard setting for pharmaceuticals, international ethical standards for research on human subjects, and in shaping the broader global regulatory environment and organisation of the global economy.[10]

In this setting, international ethical standards are (de)selected by the EU, sometimes prompting their reworking in an effort to ensure continued relevance to regulatory aims. In that way, those very standards are made marketable, as well as, of course, the pharmaceuticals produced in compliance with them. More than that, the EU's facilitation, procurement and use of clinical trials data produced abroad also has external effects.[11] The market-friendly ethics provide weak protections for trial subjects; through the protections the vulnerability of those enrolled in trials (now subjects of EU law) is marginalised and effectively erased. This in turn works to support the continued and growing use of the data produced through those trials for market authorisation and corporate profitability, while limiting the EU's responsibilities and accountabilities to safety matters (such as adverse reactions to medicines), to the exclusion of others (such as the distortions in public health governance facilitated by the pharmaceutical regulatory regime). These key normative dimensions are obscured and de-politicised by its construction through imbricating legal, scientific, technical and ethical discourses.

In meeting the chapter's aims, in the next section I expand on these introductory comments to elaborate on the perspective for the subsequent analysis, which is fashioned by combining insights gleaned from medicine and bioethics, anthropology, critical theory, STS and sociology with law and regulation studies. In doing so I address a related aim of this chapter: to encourage the growing discourse between those disciplines seen in other areas.[12] From there I go on to consider how EU law on clinical trials is situated within the EU's broader overarching governance architecture and aligned to market authorisation. After which, through a series of related and to some extent overlapping points—the use of data from trials carried out abroad; informed consent; designing trial protocols; the role of

[10] See, relatedly: J Scott, 'Extraterritoriality and Territorial Extension in EU Law' (2014) 61 *American Journal of Comparative Law* 87.

[11] Cf E Cloatre, *Pills for the Poorest. An Exploration of TRIPS and Access to Medication in Sub-Saharan Africa* (Basingstoke, Palgrave Macmillan, 2013).

[12] See: J Abraham and H Lawton-Smith (eds), *Regulation of the Pharmaceutical Industry* (Basingstoke, Palgrave, 2003); J Aronson, *Genetic Witness: Science, Law, and Controversy in the Making of DNA Profiling* (Piscataway, Rutgers University Press, 2007); E Cloatre and MD Pickersgill (eds), *Knowledge, Technology and Law* (London, Routledge, 2014); A Daemmrich, *Pharmacopolitics: Drug Regulation in the United States and Germany* (Chapel Hill NC, University of North Carolina Press, 2006); R Hindmarsh and B Prainsack (eds), *Genetic Subjects: Global Governance of Forensic DNA Profiling and Databasing* (Cambridge, Cambridge University Press, 2010); S Jasanoff (ed), *Reframing Rights: Bioconstitutionalism in the Genetic Age* (Cambridge MA, MIT Press, 2011).

placebos in that regard; and the relationship between clinical trials abroad, global access to medicines and EU trade policy—I underline how trials are embedded within, and reflective of, that architecture, related to the global regulatory environment, and ultimately the EU's imagined socio-political order and project of rule. In the final section I will reflect on the implications of the growing dissemination of market interests into the organisation of formally non-market policy domains like public health. In particular, I will point to the importance of attending to that which underpins, shapes and directs regulation as part of a strategy to impel its redesign.

II. CONCEPTUAL APPROACH

My starting point for conceptualising EU law's role in supporting the pharmaceuticalisation of responses to public health problems and the implications for its vulnerable subjects comes from critical theory, especially that influenced by Foucault. He described how security relates to markets; a point that is, of course, of central importance to the internal market, which is at the core of the EU's wider efforts at producing its socio-political order and project of rule. The internal market is defined by Article 26(2) TFEU as 'an area without internal frontiers in which the free movement of goods, persons, services and capital is ensured in accordance with the provisions of the Treaties'.[13] Pharmaceuticals fall within the free movement of goods.[14]

Foucault explained how, within liberalism, markets are the instantiation of freedom understood as 'the possibility of movement, change of place, and processes of circulation of both people and things'.[15] Security is about responding 'to a reality [ie, markets] in such a way that ...[it] cancels out the reality to which it responds—... regulates it'.[16] Regulating the dangers, risks and uncertainties attendant to the circulation of pharmaccuticals (other things and people), while facilitating their benefits, is a core concern of law and regulation studies—including in relation to public health.[17] Risk regulation is likewise a central concern of the EU, particularly following high-profile regulatory failures such as the BSE[18] crisis of the 1990s. These led to a proliferation of debate as to what 'regulation'—in cases of scientific

[13] The establishment of the internal market is required by Art 3(3) as amended TEU.

[14] Arts 28–36 TFEU. Pharmaceuticals are goods for these purposes ie, 'products which can be valued in money and which are capable, as such, of forming the subject of commercial transactions' (Case 7/68 *Commission v Italy (Art Treasures case)* [1968] ECR 423).

[15] M Foucault, *Security, Territory, Population: Lectures at the Collège de France, 1977–1978* (Basingstoke, Palgrave Macmillan, 2007) 48–49.

[16] Ibid, 47.

[17] R Brownsword, *Rights, Regulation and the Technological Revolution* (Oxford, Oxford University Press, 2008).

[18] That is, bovine spongiform encephalopathy.

risk and uncertainty—should look like, and how it should be implemented.[19] Throughout this chapter I examine how the EU is a particular example of the transformation and integration of law and regulation within what Foucault termed governmentality. The latter includes discourses, techniques and elements, including law and ethics, in order to regulate everyday life.[20]

Moreover, I bring out how EU governance is making use of, and being (re)organised by and within, neoliberal political rationality,[21] which increasingly fuses governmentality with technical reason and means–end, or instrumental, market rationality. In this way EU law and its pharmaceuticals regime can be understood as part of a broader neoliberal technology (an assemblage of components) that functions to optimise the circulation of people and things (pharmaceuticals, and clinical trials data as the basis for their marketing) and which tackles the attendant dangers through risk regulation (with clinical trials data being central to the safety of pharmaceuticals). The dissemination of neoliberalism is also part of efforts to produce self-managing and sovereign subjects through the (re)configuration of relationships between power and responsibility, governance and the governed, knowledge and power, and sovereignty and territoriality, in order to optimise life.[22]

Even as governance itself is presented as limited power is actually extended through these (re)configurations. Particularly important for this chapter are the ways in which the EU's normative power extends beyond the territory where it is constituted (the EU) to govern practices of biomedical knowledge production (clinical trials) abroad, but so as to generate that which is usable (data) for its domestic purposes (authorisation of pharmaceuticals for circulation and consumption in the internal market). Those purposes are in turn tied to, underpinned by and directed at meeting broader aims found within the overarching architecture of EU governance through the improved competitiveness of EU industry; consequential economic growth; an optimised internal market through innovative pharmaceuticals; and the positioning of the EU as a key global regulator. Resonating with Foucault's work, a core contribution of STS, which is increasingly influential

[19] For discussion, see: M Everson and E Vos, 'The Scientification of Politics and the Politicisation of Science' in M Everson and E Vos (eds), *Uncertain Risks Regulated* (Abingdon, Routledge-Cavendish, 2009).

[20] M Foucault, *Power, Essential Works of Foucault 1954–1984, vol 3* (London, Penguin, 2002), especially 'Governmentality'. Cf W Walters and JH Haahr, *Governing Europe: Discourse, Governmentality and European Integration* (Abingdon, Routledge, 2006).

[21] What Rose et al describe as 'a way of doing things that [is] oriented to specific objectives and that [reflects] on itself in characteristic ways': N Rose, P O'Malley and M Valverde, 'Governmentality' (2006) 2 *Annual Review of Law Society and Science* 83, 84.

[22] A Ong, *Neoliberalism as Exception: Mutations in Citizenship and Sovereignty* (Durham NC, Duke University Press, 2006) 3. See also: M Dean, *Governmentality: Power and Rule in Modern Society* (London, Sage, 1999); R Flynn, 'Health and Risk' in G Mythen and S Walklate (eds), *Beyond the Risk Society* (Maidenhead, Open University Press, 2006).

in law and regulation studies,[23] is showing how science and technology, including the knowledge (data) and products (pharmaceuticals) discussed in this chapter, are 'incorporated into practices of state-making, or of governance more broadly'.[24] In short, pharmaceuticals and the clinical trials data that authorise their marketing, are increasingly important as part of attempts to produce the EU's identity and as part of its narrative about itself as a socio-political order and project of rule that is founded upon and oriented towards market optimisation.[25]

The people enfolded into the pharmaceutical regime and whom it affects highlight the exportation and circulation of the EU's normative power beyond its territory as well as the (re)configuration between governance and the governed. As part of the latter, research subjects are more than part of risk society.[26] Indeed, recognised in various and diverse disciplines, perhaps especially sociology and anthropology, these subjects come to know themselves and relate to others through the prism of biomedical knowledge and therapeutic options.[27] The 'governed' therefore extends beyond those in possession of formal EU citizenship,[28] to include research subjects as part of a broader range of citizens,[29] individuals with the capacity to demand and contest decisions in relation to their lives, so-called biopolitics.[30]

However, the norms, values and socio-political imaginaries and links to projects of rule reflected in and underpinning regulation, are obscured by its framing of health issues as matters of risk necessitating technological solutions (in this case pharmaceuticals). This framing de-politicises and naturalises the EU's regulation and its attendant pitfalls and failures, such as those related to the distribution of post-trial benefits and the implications for the

[23] K Yeung and M Dixon-Woods, 'Design-based Regulation and Patient Safety: A Regulatory Studies Perspective' (2010) 71 *Social Science & Medicine* 613.

[24] S Jasanoff, 'The Idiom of Co-production' in S Jasanoff (ed), *States of Knowledge* (London, Routledge, 2004) 3.

[25] W Brown, *Regulating Aversion* (Princeton NJ, Princeton University Press, 2006) 15; S Jasanoff, *Designs on Nature* (Princeton NJ, Princeton University Press, 2005) 5–6.

[26] U Beck, *Risk Society: Towards a New Modernity* (London, Sage, 1986); U Beck, *World at Risk* (Cambridge, Polity Press, 2009); A Giddens, 'Risk Society: The Context of British Politics' in J Franklin (ed), *The Politics of Risk Society* (Cambridge, Polity Press, 1998).

[27] Such as: 'moral pioneers' in R Rapp, *Testing Women, Testing the Fetus: The Social Impact of Amniocentesis in America* (London, Routledge, 2000); 'biological citizens' in N Rose and C Novas, 'Biological Citizenship' in A Ong and S Collier (eds), *Global Assemblages: Technology, Politics, and Ethics as Anthropological Problems* (Oxford, Blackwell, 2005), cf J Biehl, *Will to Live: AIDS Therapies and the Politics of Survival* (Princeton NJ, Princeton University Press, 2007); 'therapeutic citizens' in V-K Nguyen, 'Antiretroviral Globalism, Biopolitics, and Therapeutic Citizenship' in A Ong and SJ Collier (eds), *Global Assemblages* (Oxford, Blackwell, 2005).

[28] Arts 18–25 TFEU.

[29] It also includes eg, those whose treatments are not the focus of trials or who do not have access to comprehensive data on trial results (discussed below) and therefore cannot make informed decisions on treatment options.

[30] Originating in Foucault's work, this term has been widely discussed. See further: T Lemke, *Biopolitics* (London, New York University Press, 2011).

research subjects of clinical trials. Abetting this are the individualisation and responsibilisation crystallised in risk's focus on self-management,[31] itself supported by the figuration of the sovereign and autonomous subject in law and human rights, and the focus on the individual in ethical protections (discussed in the next section). As the basis for the marketing of pharmaceuticals on the internal market, clinical trials data are part of efforts to render the EU auditable and inspectable. A key aspect of this is the distribution and delimitation of responsibilities and accountabilities in the event of failure (such as harms caused by adverse reactions to medicines), and the management of public expectations and perceptions in order to maintain the '*production* of legitimacy in the face of these perceptions' (emphasis added).[32]

A key function of clinical trials data, then, is the legitimation of the EU's integration project and its regulatory interventions through the availability of safe pharmaceuticals, but in ways that obscure normative effects for those enrolled in trials as well as the wider resort to pharmaceuticals in the fight against public health problems.[33] Legitimation is particularly salient to the EU given its ongoing problems in maintaining public confidence and legitimacy.[34] These include the high-profile regulatory failures noted above, as well as wider concerns about the EU's democratic credentials and the justice of its institutional response to the ongoing economic and financial crisis threatening the Eurozone (and de-stabilising the wider EU).

III. RISK, MARKET AUTHORISATION AND CLINICAL TRIALS

A. Innovation and Public Health in the EU

Under Article 6 of the Treaty on the Functioning of the European Union (TFEU) health is an area of supporting and complementary competence where EU action can provide added value. Article 168 (TFEU), the legal

[31] This tendency is apparent in relation to, say, new diagnostic technologies, which make possible certain discourses on risk for those trying to determine their individual risk of cancer (A Robertson, 'Biotechnology, Political Rationality and Discourses on Health Risk' (2001) 5 *Health* 293). More generally see: GC Gray, 'The Responsibilisation Strategy of Health and Safety: Neo-liberalism and the Reconfiguration of Individual Responsibility for Risk' (2009) 49 *British Journal of Criminology* 326.

[32] M Power, *Organized Uncertainty* (Oxford, Oxford University Press, 2007) 21.

[33] A Petryna and A Kleinman, 'The Pharmaceutical Nexus' in A Petryna and others (eds), *Global Pharmaceuticals: Ethics, Markets, Practices* (Durham NC, Duke University Press, 2006); SR Whyte and others, *Social Lives of Medicines* (Cambridge, Cambridge University Press, 2003), especially 'Drug Vendors and Their Market: The Commodification of Health'.

[34] See further: C Scott, 'Accountability in the Regulatory State' (2000) 27 *Journal of Law and Society* 38; F Scharpf, *Governing in Europe. Effective and Democratic?* (Oxford, Oxford University Press, 1999); A Arnull and D Wincott, *Accountability and Legitimacy in the European Union* (Oxford, Oxford University Press, 2002).

basis for the adoption of legislation in the area of public health, underlines that the primary responsibility lies with the Member States (MSs), but, consistent with Article 6 TFEU, EU action is essentially limited to incentive measures (all, of course, subject to them being proportionate[35] and justified at the EU level by the principle of subsidiarity.[36]) 2007's *Together for Health: A Strategic Approach for the EU 2008–2013*[37] (*Together for Health*) notes 'the *political importance of health*'[38] and elaborates on these foundations. The strategy deals with health and not just public health, and as such it encompasses the fostering of coordination and cooperation between Member States across seemingly the full sweep of health law and policy, ranging from quality of health care; value for money of new health technologies; compensation for cases of medical malpractice liability incurred abroad; and pharmaceuticals and clinical trials. However, the EU law applicable to pharmaceuticals and clinical trials is based on Article 114 TFEU, which provides for the adoption of harmonising legislation for the establishment and functioning of the internal market. Article 114(3) requires the European Commission to take 'as a base a high level of protection' of, inter alia, health, 'taking account in particular of any new development based on scientific facts'.

The understanding of pharmaceuticals and the legislation to which they are subject must also be placed within the context of the overarching architecture of EU governance. The latter steers, underpins, shapes and directs EU law's role in facilitating the pharmaceuticalisation of responses to public health problems and produces implications for its vulnerable subjects. Most importantly, health is directly linked to economic optimisation in *Together for Health*: '[T]his Strategy reinforces the importance of health in policies such as the Lisbon Strategy for Growth and Jobs, emphasising the links between *health and economic prosperity*' (emphasis added).[39] Several key figures help to support the link between health and the economy and the former's framing by the latter, in particular that EU expenditure on health 'accounts for around 10% of GDP and almost 15% of public spending'

[35] Art 5(4) TEU.

[36] Art 5(3) TEU.

[37] European Commission, *White Paper, Together for Health: A Strategic Approach for the EU 2008–2013*, COM(2007) 630 final; European Commission, *Commission Staff Working Document Accompanying White Paper, Together for Health: A Strategic Approach for the EU 2008–2013*, SEC(2007) 1376. For an overview of initiatives, see European Commission, *Commission Staff Working Document, Report on European Governance (2003–2004)*, SEC(2004) 1153.

[38] European Commission, *Together for Health*, ibid, 2.

[39] European Commission, *Together for Health*, n 37 above, 2. On the Lisbon Strategy, see further: K Armstrong, 'Governance and Constitutionalism After Lisbon' in *JCMS Symposium: EU Governance After Lisbon* (2008) 46 *Journal of Common Market Studies* 413. The Lisbon Strategy was subsequently refocused on growth and jobs: W Kok, *Facing the Challenge: The Lisbon Strategy for Growth and Employment. Report from the High Level Group Chaired by Wim Kok* (Brussels, European Commission, 2004).

and the 'health and social sector workforce accounts for 10% of all jobs in the EU'.[40] In other words, *Together for Health* '*supports* the overall Europe 2020 strategy' (emphasis added)[41] for economic growth,[42] the most recent follow-on to the Lisbon Strategy, and although acknowledged as a 'value in itself' the overall concern with health is with it as 'a precondition for economic prosperity'.[43] Moreover, the Innovation Union,[44] one of Europe 2020's flagship initiatives, is particularly revealing in that—as one of its aims—the EU wants to 'boost and improve the competitiveness of the markets for innovative products and services that respond to the ageing challenge both at EU and global level, thus creating new opportunities for businesses'.[45] This imaginary of the EU as a market- and innovation-optimising actor is clearly beneficial for the pharmaceutical industry, which boomed through the 1990s and is now struggling. Overall, the EU's responsibility for health is not just limited by the distribution of competence with its Member States; it is also limited to being about health as a dimension of the EU's internal market.

B. The Alignment of Clinical Trials to Market Authorisation

It is against this broad normative background that the EU regulates pharmaceuticals and their marketing. Facilitating speedier approvals is in the interests of getting drugs to market, making it easier for producers to profit more quickly from their investment in research and development, which, in turn, grows a more profitable pharmaceutical sector that can invest in the pharmaceutical development pipeline or 'cycle of innovation'. The latter begins with an idea that drives basic research, leading (where successful) to non-clinical, pre-clinical, and clinical research, and from there (where successful) to marketing and subsequent surveillance (or pharmaco-vigilence) within the market.

However, there is concern that the EU is not as important as the US as a site of innovation.[46] As such speeding-up approval is an important end

[40] 'Key figures': http://ec.europa.eu/health/strategy/policy/figures/index_en.htm.

[41] 'Health strategy': http://ec.europa.eu/health/strategy/policy/index_en.htm.

[42] See, generally, 'Europe 2020': http://ec.europa.eu/europe2020/index_en.htm. Also see: European Commission, *Smart Regulation in the European Union*, COM(2010) 543 final; European Commission, *Europe 2020 Flagship Initiative Innovation Union*, COM(2010) 546 final.

[43] Ibid.

[44] 'Innovation Union': http://ec.europa.eu/research/innovation-union/index_en.cfm.

[45] 'Europe 2020', n 42 above.

[46] European Commission, *A Stronger European-Based Pharmaceutical Industry for the Benefit of the Patient—A Call for Action*, COM(2003) 383 final; European Commission, *Putting Knowledge into Practice: A Broad-based Innovation Strategy for the EU*, COM(2006) 502 final.

of regulatory design[47]—and the EU appears to be matching and perhaps even overtaking the US regulator, the Food and Drug Administration.[48] In this way, then, regulatory competition between the EU and the US provides another driver for the alignment of clinical trials to market authorisation. This series of aims and concerns point to the dissemination of market interests and rationality into regulatory design. Moreover, that design—the alignment of clinical trials to market authorisation, and their configuration within the overarching architecture of EU governance—is undergirded, shaped and directed towards the EU's efforts at producing and legitimating its imagined socio-political order and project of rule by and through the (hoped for) consequent economic optimisation.

In the EU there are several types of procedure for market authorisation.[49] The centralised procedure is compulsory for products derived from bio-technology, orphan medicinal products, and products for human use containing an active substance authorised and intended for the treatment of HIV/AIDS, cancer, neurodegenerative disorders or diabetes.[50] Products that represent a significant scientific, therapeutic or technical innovation or that benefit public health can also make use of this route to the market. Mutual recognition applies to most conventional products and means that a manufacturer can obtain market authorisation in one Member State, after which it is recognised in all others—adding competition between Member State regulators to that between the EU and the US. Finally, there is the less well used, de-centralised procedure, which allows for simultaneous approval in several Member States. Each of these requires compliance with the Directive on the Community code relating to medicinal products for human use (Community code), which mentions clinical trials data as the basis for the market authorisation of pharmaceutical treatments on the grounds of their quality, safety and efficacy,[51] rather than 'comparative therapeutic efficacy' and genuine need. Clinical trials are subject to specific

[47] And approval figures are important for communicating success and performance: 'EMA Recommends 81 Medicines for Marketing Authorisation in 2013', www.ema.europa.eu/ema/index.jsp?curl=pages/news_and_events/news/2014/01/news_detail_002006.jsp&mid=WC0b01ac058004d5c1.

[48] Comparisons between the EU and FDA include 'EMA Bests FDA in 2013 New Drug Approval Numbers': www.raps.org/focus-online/news/news-article-view/article/4519/ema-bests-fda-in-2013-new-drug-approval-numbers.aspx; LJ Howie and others, 'A Comparison of FDA and EMA Drug Approval: Implications for Drug Development and Cost of Care' (2013) *Oncology* www.cancernetwork.com/oncology-journal/comparison-fda-and-ema-drug-approval-implications-drug-development-and-cost-care#sthash.SO6MTTLW.dpuf.

[49] For an overview see 'Authorisation procedures for medicinal products': http://ec.europa.eu/health/authorisation-procedures_en.htm.

[50] Regulation 726/2004/EC laying down Community procedures for the authorisation and supervision of medicinal products for human and veterinary use and establishing the European Medicines Agency.

[51] Directive 2001/83/EC on the Community code relating to medicinal products for human use.

regulation through the Clinical Trials Directive (CTD),[52] which requires Member States to set standards for the planning, performance, reporting, and archiving of research. Member States are also required to establish systems of monitoring and inspection in relation to good clinical practice (GCP), many of which are further concretised in subsequent legislation.[53]

The very definition of clinical trials[54] highlights their alignment to the requirements for market authorisation—they are:

> any systematic study of medicinal products in human subjects whether in patients or non-patient volunteers in order to discover or verify the effects of and/or identify any adverse reaction to investigational products, and/or study their absorption, distribution, metabolism and excretion *in order to ascertain the efficacy and safety of the products* (emphasis added).[55]

In all there are four phases of clinical trials. Phase I trials use between 20–80 healthy volunteers in order to determine the tolerable dose range of a new drug. Phase II trials use between 100–300 subjects who have the disease or condition to be treated in order to evaluate efficacy and safety of the drug. Phase III trials tend to be multi-centred and might involve up to 10,000 people located in between 10–20 countries. This phase generates more safety and efficacy data. Phase IV trials are used to furnish more safety and efficacy data, but post-marketing of the drug. This phase can involve millions of people.

At phases II and III, double-blind randomised clinical trials (RCTs) are considered the 'gold standard'. The research participants included in the protocol for this type of trial tend to be those suffering from the condition that the new drug is intended to treat. RCTs involve random allocation to the control or the active arm of the study. Participants allocated to the control group are provided with either the best standard treatment for their condition or a placebo ie, an inert substance. Where the former is the control the objective might be to demonstrate superiority of the trial drug or even just non-inferiority, in other words, that it falls within a pre-selected margin of effectiveness and can be deemed not inferior to the standard treatment despite being, as Jackson puts it, 'not *too* inferior' or perhaps

[52] Directive 2001/20/EC on the approximation of the laws, regulations and administrative provisions of the Member States relating to the implementation of good clinical practice in the conduct of clinical trials on medicinal products for human use. This requires the Commission to establish principles relating to good clinical practice and detailed rules in line with those principle.

[53] Directive 2005/28/EC laying down principles and detailed guidelines for good clinical practice as regards investigational medicinal products for human use, as well as the requirements for authorisation of the manufacturing or importation of such products.

[54] For an overview of the EU approach see: http://ec.europa.eu/health/human-use/clinical-trials/index_en.htm.

[55] Directive 2001/83/EC, Annex I, Part 4.

even 'just a little bit worse'[56] (the subsequent use of the 'little bit worse' drug as the comparator in further trials can produce steadily decreasing effectiveness over time).[57] There is the possibility of producing a more striking difference between those in the control group and those given the new trial drug when a placebo is used—and that is particularly useful where the objective of the trial is not to demonstrate superiority.

As the European Medicines Agency (EMA) explains in its 'soft law' guidance (which should be followed in order to obtain a market authorisation):

> it is not necessary for the benefit-risk profile of an experimental medicine to [be] at least as favourable as the benefit-risk profile of any or all established medicines in order to receive marketing authorisation. This is appropriate as frequently more than one treatment is required per indication (some medicines suit some people better than others) and clinical trials do not definitively capture all information on benefits and risks; knowledge accumulates during a product's lifecycle.[58]

For example, having multiple, equally effective medicines available can help to tackle resistance to medication, and so a non-inferiority trial using a placebo control can be useful. Alternatively, producing a cancer drug that has fewer side effects seems useful. Importantly,

> the purpose of regulatory approval is not to determine clinical practice (over and above the act of issuing a particular licence for a medicine) and there is no limit to the number of medicines that can be licensed for any given therapeutic indication providing the benefit risk of each is favourable (emphasis added).[59]

In short, regardless of the trial phase, clinical trials need only at the bare minimum ensure that pharmaceuticals are as good as or at least no worse than existing products, albeit with a marginal or supposed benefit.

Crucially, EU law permits and legitimates the growing use of data produced *outside* the EEA by the clinical trials industry for the production and marketing of pharmaceuticals *within* the EU's internal market. This is how EU law has extra-territorial relevance, application and effects for the trial participants abroad, now subjects of EU law. Under the Community code, data produced in 'third countries' is portable and usable as part of the market authorisation application submitted by those who want to sell their pharmaceutical products within the EU (and EFTA), provided principles *equivalent* to those found in the CTD (which necessarily includes GCP), and

[56] Jackson, *Law and the Regulation of Medicines*, n 7 above, 29.

[57] More generally, see: N Cartwright, 'What is this Thing Called "Efficacy"?' in C Mantzavinos, *Philosophy of the Social Sciences: Philosophical Theory and Scientific Practice* (Cambridge, Cambridge University Press, 2009).

[58] EMA, *Reflection Paper on the Need for Active Control in Therapeutic Areas Where Use of Placebo is Deemed Ethical and One or More Established Medicines are Available*, EMA/759784/2010, 3–4.

[59] Ibid, 4.

which are found in Article 8 and Annex 1, are followed.[60] Most important is the (repeated) stress on 'the freely given *informed consent* of each trial subject'[61] in accordance with the Helsinki Declaration and ensuring that '[a]ll phases of clinical investigation ... shall be designed, implemented and reported in accordance with *good clinical practice*' (emphases added).[62]

Building on this, the EMA seeks to facilitate the portability and use of externally produced data in the EU's clinical trials and market authorisation system.[63] This includes, for example, ensuring 'verification, at the time of the evaluation of the marketing authorization application, that trials carried out in third countries have been conducted in accordance with the required GCP and ethical standards', through 'increased GCP inspection including *further extension of the GCP policy* on increasing numbers of routine inspections as part of the need for greater supervision of the *conduct and ethical standards of clinical trials performed outside the EEA*' (emphasis added).[64]

Clinical trials—especially those performed abroad—literally service the EU's risk-based regulation of pharmaceuticals and, beyond that, the wider overarching normative architecture aimed at economic optimisation. Without successful trials and the crucial data on product safety they provide as the condition for market authorisation and production, there would be no new pharmaceuticals, no market, no sales and economic optimisation through them—and no pharmaceuticalisation. Indeed, the Community code states that the 'essential aim of *any rules* governing the production, distribution and use of medicinal products must be to safeguard public health'[65]—immediately followed by the qualification that 'this objective must be attained by means which will *not hinder the development of the pharmaceutical industry or trade* in medicinal products within the Community' (emphases added).[66]

This might be read as a rejection of a zero-sum calculation pitting public health against the pharmaceutical industry and trade. However, with its legal basis in Article 114 TFEU the Community code has as its principal aim the establishment and functioning of the internal market. As such it is optimisation of the internal market, rather than public health, which is central. Despite mention of a high base of health protection for legislation

[60] Directive 2001/83, Art 8(3)(i) mentions the results of clinical trials, submitted in accordance with Annex I, as particulars and documents that 'shall' accompany an application for market authorisation.

[61] Directive 2001/83, Annex 1, Part 4, B, 1.2. Also see: Directive 2001/20, Art 2(j).

[62] Directive 2001/83, Annex 1, Part 4, B, 1.1. Also see: Directive 2001/20, Art 8.

[63] EMA, *EMEA Strategy Paper: Acceptance of Clinical Trials Conducted in Third Countries, for Evaluation in Marketing Authorisation Applications*, EMEA/228067/2008.

[64] Ibid, 1.

[65] Directive 2001/83/EC, Recital 2.

[66] Directive 2001/83/EC, Recital 3.

in Article 114(3) TFEU, through the Community code health is understood in relation to, and effectively subordinated to, the market.

Further, reflecting the narrow criteria for market authorisation and the purpose of clinical trials, the public health implications of pharmaceuticals are confined to their safety. This distracts attention away from the legal, regulatory and broader social conditions underpinning and orienting the production of scientific and technical knowledge. Far from being innovation-orientated—ie, what the EU purports to foster—decisions on the development of, and innovation in, pharmaceuticals are left to the industry. Clinical trials data—knowledge—is reduced to being about promoting a version of market optimisation that abets commercial interests in continued profitability, but without the need for significant innovation. More than that, the scientific substance of clinical trials—knowledge creation—is linked to and reoriented by its place as a key part of the risk-based cycle of innovation. In sum, the focus on safety considerations in market authorisation and clinical trials effectively shields the field of knowledge creation and innovation and the alignment of regulatory processes with commercial interests from public accountability around key questions such as what is being done, why and how, who benefits and who is hurt.[67]

C. Informed Consent

The law's limited focus is especially apparent in the reliance on and instrumentalisation of bioethical procedural guarantees for the production of data that verifies the safety, and permits the marketing, of pharmaceuticals. This is undergirded, shaped and directed at producing a European socio-political order based on a more innovative, profitable and competitive pharmaceutical sector in order to foster economic growth, jobs and prosperity through the marketing of safe pharmaceuticals. As part of that, the EU has a key role as a global regulator in international technical standard setting for pharmaceuticals, international ethical standards for research on human subjects, and in shaping the broader global regulatory environment and organisation of the global economy.

Clinical trials (and market authorisation) hinge on finding, mobilising and using subjects—and justifying their involvement in clinical trials to research ethics committees (RECs).[68] A series of human rights-related but primarily

[67] For instance, on claims about justice and access to the benefits of research see: JP Kahn and others, *Beyond Consent: Seeking Justice in Research* (Oxford, Oxford University Press, 1998).

[68] Institutional review boards in the US. See further: CL Bosk, 'Professional Ethicist Available: Logical, Secular, Friendly. Bioethics and Beyond' (1999) 128 *Daedalus* 47; CL Bosk and RG de Vries, 'Bureaucracies of Mass Deception: Institutional Review Boards and the Ethics of Ethnographic Research' (2004) 595 *Annals of the American Academy of Political and Social Science* 249; J Guillemin, 'Bioethics and the Coming of the Corporation to Medicine' in R de Vries and J Subedi (eds), *Bioethics and Society* (Upper Saddle River NJ, Prentice Hall, 1998).

ethics-based protections for research subjects exists at the international level.[69] The protections were a response to the atrocities of World War II, which prompted the Nuremberg Code.[70] The latter was made more applicable to medical research involving human subjects through the Helsinki Declaration,[71] produced by the World Medical Association (WMA) and modified many times, the last time in 2008 by the 59th WMA General Assembly. The Helsinki Declaration foregrounds the creation, refinement and advancement of scientific knowledge—the scientific enterprise[72]—as central to ethics.

Research involving human subjects must not only seek to produce generalisable knowledge, but at the same time also seek to '*improve* preventive, diagnostic and therapeutic interventions (methods, procedures and treatments)' (emphasis added)[73] in such a way that the subjects are not subordinated to the interests of society. A calculation of risk and benefit is deployed to ensure the research subject is not worse off than she would have been otherwise. Yet, such a narrow, utilitarian calculation, entailing the determination of risk proportionate to anticipated benefit is based on a degree of guesswork. This also provides scope for the instrumentalisation of the scientific enterprise for *primarily* commercial ends as it is linked to market authorisation, ie, provided the test drug is as good as or at least no worse than existing products it can be marketed.

Nevertheless, this normative background is reflected in EU law through its foregrounding of risk in the protection of the individual that is supplemented with additional and more limited assurances of compliance with international ethical standards focused around consent and GCP. Human rights, although part of the EU's constitutional architecture as general principles,[74] are largely left to be reflected in ethical standards and it is these that are used to justify enrolment of trial subjects to RECs. The CTD makes reference to 'the protection of clinical trial subjects—and in particular the weighing of risks and inconveniences with benefits'.[75] References to consent occur through the CTD,[76] and it is connected with the 'protection of human

[69] Reflecting: Universal Declaration of Human Rights, itself highly influenced by the Nuremberg Code; International Covenant on Civil and Political Rights; International Covenant on Economic, Social and Cultural Rights; Convention on the Elimination of All Forms of Discrimination against Women; Convention on the Rights of the Child.

[70] GJ Annas and MA Grodin (eds), *The Nazi Doctors and the Nuremburg Code: Human Rights in Human Experimentation* (Oxford, Oxford University Press, 1992).

[71] Declaration of Helsinki: Ethical Principles for Medical Research Involving Human Subjects, available at: www.wma.net/en/30publications/10policies/b3/17c.pdf.

[72] HM Marks, *The Progress of Experiment: Science and Therapeutic Reform in the United States, 1900-1990* (Cambridge, Cambridge University Press, 1997).

[73] Declaration of Helsinki, n 71 above, para 7.

[74] P Craig and G de Búrca, *EU Law: Text, Cases and Materials*, 5th edn (Oxford, Oxford University Press, 2013), ch 11.

[75] Directive 2001/20/EC, Art 3.

[76] Directive 2001/20/EC, Recitals 3, 4, 16, Arts 2–5.

rights and the dignity of the human being with regard to the application of biology and medicine, as for instance reflected in the 1996 version of the Helsinki Declaration'.[77] Further protections are provided in the CTD by the prohibition on the carrying out of obsolete or repetitive tests within the EU or in third countries.[78]

Moreover, a strong ethics dimension is provided in the CTD's special protection for those 'who are incapable of giving legal consent to clinical trials'.[79] This is also apparent in the EU register bringing together information on the content, commencement, and termination of clinical trials, which is subject to protections for confidentiality,[80] invoking rights to privacy. Cross-references to the Data Protection Directive[81] are embedded throughout EU clinical trials regulation. Overall, the 'clinical trial subject's protection is safeguarded through risk assessment based on the results of toxicological experiments prior to any clinical trial, screening by ethics committees and Member States' competent authorities, and rules on the protection of personal data'.[82]

In terms of GCP, the CTD also requires the Commission to establish principles of GCP and detailed rules in line with those principles.[83] GCP is:

> a set of *internationally recognised ethical and scientific quality requirements* which must be observed for designing, conducting, recording and reporting clinical trials that involve the participation of human subjects. Compliance with this good practice provides assurance that the rights, safety and well-being of trial subjects are protected, and that the results of the clinical trials are credible (emphasis added).[84]

In a delegation of tasks from the Commission, these rules are in fact established by the EMA,[85] in accordance with the International Conference on Harmonisation of Technical Requirements for Registration of

[77] Ibid, Recital 2.

[78] Directive 2001/20/EC, Recital 6.

[79] Ibid, Recitals 3 and 4. For instance, Recital 3 reads that they should be included in clinical trials only 'when there are grounds for expecting that the administering of the medicinal product would be of direct benefit to the patient, thereby outweighing the risks'.

[80] Ibid, Recital 9 and Art 11(3).

[81] Directive 95/46/EC on the protection of individuals with regard to the processing of personal data and on the free movement of such data. This includes data in health care settings, including research and development of pharmaceuticals and medical technologies more broadly. See also European Commission, *Proposal for a Regulation of the European Parliament and of the Council on the protection of individuals with regard to the processing of personal data and on the free movement of such data (General Data Protection Regulation)*, COM(2012) 11 final.

[82] Directive 2001/20/EC, Recital 2.

[83] Directive 2001/20/EC, Arts 1(3) and 8.

[84] Directive 2001/20/EC, Art 1(2).

[85] EMA, *E6: Guideline for Good Clinical Practice*, CPMP/ICH/135/95. Also see 'Inspections procedure': www.emea.europa.eu/ema/index.jsp?curl=pages/regulation/document_listing/document_listing_000140.jsp&mid=WC0b01ac05800296c6.

Pharmaceuticals for Human Use (ICH)[86] standards, which seek to avoid duplicate (and therefore ethically dubious and unnecessary) trials of new medicines and consequent inefficiency and increased costs. These standards also seek to speed up the movement of innovations through the development pipeline, by providing a unified standard for the EU, Japan and the US that facilitates the mutual acceptance of clinical data between their respective regulatory authorities—and beyond to those jurisdictions that have little or no regulatory capacity.[87] All clinical trials falling within the scope of the CTD must be designed, conducted, and reported in accordance with GCP,[88] and this again is framed in terms of risk.

GCP lays down additional requirements relating to the investigational medicinal product used in the clinical trial, detailed requirements of data collection and handling, and provisions on inspections mechanisms. GCP frames the rights of individual trial subjects as concerning their protection from risk. For instance, the first principle of GCP is that 'The rights, safety and wellbeing of the trial subjects shall prevail over the interests of science and society'.[89] The relationship between risk and markets reappears here: this Directive (and thus the detailed guidance based thereon) refers to the marketing of medicinal products as its underlying basis and highlights how risk articulates to markets.[90] Overall, the constant reference point is the aim of getting new and safe products to market so that consumers will have confidence in their quality, safety and efficacy, and in the ethics and rights dimensions of their production.

Often seen as a one-time event rather than as a continual process requiring ongoing renewal, consent also functions to protect medical researchers from claims for compensation under the law of tort.[91] This makes it, as Petryna explains, a key 'legal strategy … releasing investigators or sponsoring institutions from liability in case of adverse effects or negligence'.[92] The focus on consent can also stymie ongoing reflection on the wider social and ethical implications of biomedical labour too. Even as ethical discourse (on consent and GCP) continues to operate, those wider considerations are

[86] www.ich.org.

[87] WHO, *Effective Medicines Regulation: Ensuring Safety, Efficacy and Quality, WHO Policy Perspectives on Medicines* (Geneva, WHO, 2003).

[88] Directive 2001/20/EC, Art 1(4).

[89] Ibid, Art 2(1).

[90] Ibid, Recital 3.

[91] For instance, the standard for professional liability in English tort law is notoriously high (*Bolam v Friern Hospital Management Committee* [1957] 1 WLR 582), although it has gradually become less so (*Bolitho v City and Hackney Health Authority* [1997] 4 All ER 771). Art 3(2)(f) Directive 2001/20/EC requires 'provision has been made for insurance or indemnity to cover the liability of the investigator and sponsor' before any clinical trial is undertaken.

[92] Petryna, *When Experiments Travel*, n 1 above, 77.

effectively side-lined.[93] This implies that the regulatory focus on informed consent is too narrow, in particular because it ignores how the ability to make a fully informed choice about participation requires more. That might include an awareness of not just whether the pharmaceutical product offers advantages to patients, but also the wider purpose and social, political and economic value of the knowledge produced, matters that are arguably no more difficult—and might be easier—to convey to prospective participants.[94] But this alone is probably insufficient given that participants in phase II and III trials abroad (in particular) are incentivised by the possibility of access to health care they would not otherwise receive. As such, this suggests the need for consideration of wider factors before trials abroad can be considered ethical as well as broader reforms (discussed below).

In terms of clinical trials abroad, these more general problems around consent might be exacerbated, for instance, because it can be harder to ensure participants understand the information provided to them,[95] especially the idea of randomisation. Relatedly, there can be misunderstanding that the trial is not part of standard care[96]—part of what has been called the 'therapeutic misconception'.[97] Another problem is that the idea of consent, especially its withdrawal at any time, does not necessarily translate easily to societies in which individual autonomy is less significant than group decisions.[98] Voluntariness can also be undermined where non-participation is not an option, ie where the trial is effectively a substitute for healthcare.

In sum, consent is detached from the scientific enterprise, but it has a central role in supporting the pharmaceutical regime and in turn the EU's socio-political order. The focus on consent and GCP abstracts the research subject[99] from social context while also freighting subject with responsibility. This in turn limits the responsibilities and accountabilities of those carrying out trials: the EU as the regulator that uses the data produced in order to authorise the marketing of products on safety grounds, and the corporations who ultimately profit. In short, in general, ethics and protections are reduced to legitimating devices through their support and justification

[93] M Pickersgill, 'The Co-production of Science, Ethics, and Emotion' (2012) 37 *Science, Technology & Human Values* 579.

[94] H Jonas, 'Philosophical Reflections on Human Experimentation' (1969) 98 *Daedalus* 219.

[95] C Pace and others, 'Quality of Parental Consent in a Ugandan Malaria Study' (2005) 95 *American Journal of Public Health* 1184.

[96] N Lynöe and others, 'Obtaining Informed Consent in Bangladesh' (2001) 344 *New England Journal of Medicine* 460.

[97] PS Appelbaum and others, 'The Therapeutic Misconception: Informed Consent in Psychiatric Research' (1982) 5 *International Journal of Law and Psychiatry* 319.

[98] Nuffield Council on Bioethics, *The Ethics of Research Related Healthcare in Developing Countries* (London, NCOB, 2002) para 6.22.

[99] M-A Jacob, 'Form-Made Persons: Consent Forms as Consent's Blind Spot' (2007) 30 *Political and Legal Anthropology Review* 249. See further: M-A Jacob and A Riles, 'The New Bureaucracies of Virtue: Introduction' (2007) 30 *Political and Legal Anthropology Review* 181.

of market-oriented risk regulation, undergirded, shaped and directed at producing a more innovative, profitable and competitive pharmaceutical sector in order to foster economic growth, jobs and prosperity.

D. Designing Clinical Trials

With the costs of research and development so high, and with continued, let alone increased, corporate profitability harder to achieve, corporations are under mounting pressure to satisfy the criteria for market authorisation. I have already indicated that regulatory design provides much scope for trial protocols to be crafted so as to produce the most favourable results in order to meet the (already market-friendly) criteria for market authorisation. This is no accident given that which underpins, shapes and directs that design, ie the production and legitimation of the EU's imagined socio-political order and project of rule via the market availability of pharmaceuticals, (potential for) their innovation and a growing industry.

Skewed trial design also raises questions over the scientific quality of the data produced, which means it becomes harder to justify the trial and, therefore, the involvement of research subjects. Still, the focus of REC approval tends to be limited to ensuring informed consent and GCP.[100] This might appear to be the correct approach: delving into science risks accusations of regulatory creep. However, in this instance there is a very strong case for more engagement with science. That is because the limited range of REC work effectively provides space for trials and the evidence they furnish to be distorted by the pharmaceutical industry. Abetting this is a related shift from academic institutions towards (now dominant) contract research organisations (or CROs) in designing and carrying out clinical trials and locating compliant research subjects.[101] In other words, there is yet another way in which corporate interests—and with them market rationality—are able to shape and even compromise the gathering and production of knowledge that underpins the regulation of public health.

A particular problem is that the focus on following ethical procedures abstracts the research from social context and does not attend to the ways in which trial subjects are found, mobilised and utilised in trials so as to produce favourable risk profiles for new drugs that will ensure their market authorisation.[102] Here the *source* of clinical trials data becomes vital.

[100] For discussion see: Jackson, *Law and the Regulation of Medicines*, n 7 above, 43–47.

[101] JA Fisher, 'Co-ordinating "Ethical" Clinical Trials: The Role of Research Coordinators in the Contract Research Industry' (2006) 27 *Sociology of Health & Illness* 678. On compliant research subjects see: JA Fisher, *Medical Research for Hire: The Political Economy of Pharmaceutical Clinical Trials* (New Brunswick NJ, Rutgers University Press, 2009).

[102] S Sismondo, 'How Pharmaceutical Industry Funding Affects Trial Outcomes: Causal Structures and Responses' (2008) 66 *Social Science & Medicine* 1909.

Nguyen underlines the point: the '[t]ransnational socioeconomic inequalities, and the gradients of disease and inequity in access to health care that are associated with them, may unwittingly *produce ideal conditions for the conduct of clinical research that furthers ... the pharmaceutical industry*' (emphasis added).[103] Thus, the very vulnerability of populations and their tracking through biological indicators produced by the science of prevention, as well as other factors such as the lack of exposure of those populations to pharmaceuticals ie, because those options tend to be unavailable, makes them useful for integration as research subjects in clinical trials.

Moreover, the performance of clinical trials in the global South appears to be grafted onto the approach to medicine taken in colonial and post-colonial settings. That is, in those places medical practices have often been used as part of the apparatus of social control of subject populations in which their governance at the level of aggregates, rather than the individual, is central.[104] The latter provides the basis for exploitative behaviours, in particular because the focus in the authorisation of clinical trials on procedural matters implies there is a gap—or even a break—between ethics and empirical reality,[105] which opens the way for the revision of ethics in light of market needs.

Another concern is that the design of trials can literally be used to mask or preclude harms from arising. In this regard there is another potential use of epidemiologically convenient groups often found in the global South: since the treatment naïve populations there are more likely to demonstrate benefit from treatment this can help to mask harms or so-called 'adverse events'.[106] More widely at the input end of protocol design those most likely to benefit from treatment can be selected while those who are least likely to benefit can be excluded.[107] Those who are most likely to use the treatment (if market authorisation is granted and treatment is accessible) might also not be selected for the trial where, say, they are less likely to comply with the instructions and therefore undermine the demonstration of efficacy.[108] At the output end, any harms that arise can be put down to,

103 V-K Nguyen, 'Antiretroviral Globalism, Biopolitics, and Therapeutic Citizenship' in A Ong and SJ Collier (eds), *Global Assemblages* (Oxford, Blackwell, 2005) 139.

104 W Anderson, *The Cultivation of Whiteness: Science, Health, and Racial Destiny in Australia* (New York, Basic Books, 2003); D Arnold, *Colonising the Body: State Medicine and Epidemic Disease in Nineteenth-Century India* (Berkeley CA, University of California Press, 1993); J Biehl, *Vita: Life in a Zone of Social Abandonment* (Berkeley CA, University of California Press, 2003); M Vaughan, *Curing Their Ills: Colonial Power and African Illness* (Stanford CA, Stanford University Press, 1992).

105 Jonas, 'Philosophical Reflections', n 94 above.

106 Petryna, *When Experiments Travel*, n 1 above, 25.

107 P Farahani and others, 'Clinical Data Gap between Phase III Clinical Trials (Pre-Marketing) and Phase IV (Post-Marketing) Studies: Evaluation of Etanercept in Rheumatoid Arthritis' (2005) 12 *Canadian Journal of Clinical Pharmacology* e254.

108 VJ Burroughs, 'Racial and Ethnic Inclusiveness in Clinical Trials in Ethics and the Pharmaceutical Industry' in MA Santoro and TM Gorrie (eds), *Ethics and the Pharmaceutical Industry* (Cambridge, Cambridge University Press, 2005).

say, environmental factors. The process of (de)selection of individuals and groups for inclusion in the trial means that generalisable data might not be produced. That being so the primary aim of the clinical trial (ie, the production of generalisable knowledge) is undermined.[109]

Some other ways in which failures can be hidden or explained away—responsibility avoided and accountability frustrated—involve the pharmaceutical being tested and the means of comparison, ie, the control. For example, using an ineffective treatment,[110] or placebo, too high a dose of an existing drug in order to produce adverse events, or too low a dose of an existing drug, can all help to flatter the benefits (especially effectiveness and safety) of the pharmaceutical being trialed,[111] as can truncating the trial length in order to prevent adverse events from emerging at all. Petryna's research with trial subjects and researchers has underscored the ways in which 'protection and safety considerations are weighed against immediate health benefits or the knowledge to be gained. Ethics and method are modified to fit the local context and experimental data required'.[112]

Wider infiltration of commercial interests into knowledge dissemination underlines the ultimate use, ie, for market authorisation and profitability. For example, there is an endemic non-publication of results and under-reporting of negative results.[113] This can undermine informed consent in that there might be insufficient information provided to trial subjects on existing options and their safety, the necessity of the trial, and societal benefit that follows from dissemination of trial results and that helps to justify participation. At the same time positive results can be reported more than once, a problem that is magnified where results are picked-up again in meta-analyses. Moreover, the journals where results are published do not necessarily have in place adequate and robust systems of peer review that can ensure the scientific rigor of trials, and in any case they are often dependent on advertising by industry. This is a classic conflict of interest that ensures the scientific enterprise is effectively reduced to servicing market needs for market authorisation and, beyond that, the advertising and sale of pharmaceuticals.[114] To reflect on the implications for health care providers

[109] Petryna, n 1 above.

[110] HK Johansen and PC Gotzsche, 'Problems in the Design and Reporting of Trials of Antifungal Agents Encountered During Meta-analysis' (1999) 282 *Journal of the American Medical Association* 1752.

[111] J Safer, 'Design and Reporting Modifications in Industry-Sponsored Comparative Psychopharmacology Trials' (2002) 190 *Journal of Nervous and Mental Disease* 583.

[112] Petryna, 'Clinical Trials Offshored: On Private Sector Science and Public Health', n 1 above, 24.

[113] CW Jones and others, 'Non-publication of Large Randomised Clinical Trials: Cross Sectional Analysis' (2013) 347 *British Medical Journal* doi: dx.doi.org/10.1136/bmj.f6104.

[114] For extensive discussion see: Jackson, *Law and the Regulation of Medicines*, n 7 above, 50–56.

within the EU, these distortions skew funding decisions—and that implies a skewing in the distribution of scarce resources.

The absence of a worldwide clinical trials registry (required by the Helsinki Declaration[115]) and an EU registry (noted above), which applies only to trials carried out within the EU and focuses on ensuring approval by RECs rather than publishing and tackling the dissemination of the results (whether or not there is a successful market authorisation),[116] also supports the inadequate evidence base for market authorisation and decisions on the funding of treatment. Overall, EU law helps to maintain, and even facilitates and sanctions, the production of a skewed, incomplete and ethically dubious evidence base that eases market authorisation for pharmaceuticals that are not significant innovations and for which there is no need.

E. Using Placebos in Clinical Trials Abroad

Placebos have an important role to play in RCTs and can be central to protocol design—and as such they deserve more specific attention. Indeed, a placebo control arm can be useful, say, when used with an active control arm in order to demonstrate that a new drug and the existing drug both work, a design that improves reliability. The Community code states:

> In general, clinical trials shall be done as controlled clinical trials, and if possible, randomized; any other design shall be justified. *The treatment of the control groups will vary from case to case and also will depend on ethical considerations*; thus it may, in some instances, be more pertinent to compare the efficacy of a new medicinal product with that of an established medicinal product of proven therapeutic value rather than with the effect of a placebo (emphasis added).[117]

So placebo use can be permissible. Still, given the history of abuse, often among marginalised and vulnerable populations,[118] placebo use is subject to quite extensive regulation on GCP.[119] Commenting on offshored clinical

[115] Helsinki Declaration, n 71 above, para 19.

[116] The revision of the CTD by the new Clinical Trials Regulation (European Commission, *Proposal for a Regulation of the European Parliament and of the Council on Clinical Trials on Medicinal Products for Human Use, and Repealing Directive 2001/20/EC*, COM(2012) 369 final and to come into force in 2016) is designed to increase transparency, but it will not change the position in relation to trials carried out outside the EU. See further: European Commission, *Q&A: New Rules for Clinical Trials Conducted in the EU*, MEMO/14/254. The EMA currently only provides access to summaries of clinical trials data once the decision-making process on market authorisation has been completed, see further: 'Release of data from clinical trials', at: www.ema.europa.eu/ema/index.jsp?curl=pages/special_topics/general/general_content_000555.jsp.

[117] Directive 2001/83/EC, Annex 1, Part 4, F, 1.

[118] FD Gray, *The Tuskegee Syphilis Study* (Montgomery Al, NewSouth Press, 2013).

[119] Directive 2001/20; Directive 2005/28.

trials the (European Group on Ethics in Science and New Technologies) EGE notes:

> The use of placebos should be regulated in developing countries *in principle by the same rules* as in European countries. *Any exception must be justified*: an obvious one is when the primary goal of the clinical trial is to try to simplify or to decrease the costs of treatment for countries where the standard treatment is not available for logistic reasons or inaccessible because of the cost. It *may thus be justified to derogate from the rule of best proven treatment. The justification of using a placebo must be clearly demonstrated in the research protocol* submitted to the ethical committees and especially approved by the local committee (emphasis added).[120]

Put differently, the default (and apparently mandatory) position is to use the best proven treatment as the control *unless* there is a reason that serves to justify derogation. Treating a person who is newly diagnosed as HIV positive with a placebo instead of a new anti-retroviral drug or the best proven treatment would seem to be without justification and, therefore, unethical. But random allocation to either a new anti-retroviral drug or the best proven treatment (the active or the control arm of a study) would not leave such a person worse off than if she had not been enrolled and been given the standard treatment.

Although the EGE's guidance has only moral and advisory value, it supports the EMA's soft law guidance on the use of placebo control in clinical trials abroad, which refers to the International Ethical Guidelines for Biomedical Research Involving Human Subjects (CIOMS guidelines for short) produced by the WHO and the Council for International Organisations of Medical Sciences,[121] which are aimed at applying the Helsinki Declaration in developing countries,[122] as well as ICH guidance outlined below. But the EGE then underlines that 'clinical trial cannot be justified ethically unless it is capable of producing scientifically reliable results' and that placebo can be acceptable provided 'the rights, safety and wellbeing of the trials subjects are the most important considerations and should prevail over the interests of science and society'.[123] Moreover, 'EU Regulatory Authorities *should neither require nor accept study designs*, involving placebo or other comparator, which would not be ethically

[120] EGE, *Opinion on the Ethical Aspects of Clinical Research in Developing Countries* (Opinion No 17) para 2.10.

[121] CIOMS Guidelines 8 and 11.

[122] That is, 'given their socioeconomic circumstances, laws and regulations, and executive and administrative arrangements'. The Council's name gives the guidelines their abbreviated name of CIOMS. The guidelines have been updated twice, the last time being in 2002. See further: www.cioms.ch/publications/guidelines/guidelines_nov_2002_blurb.htm.

[123] EMA, *Reflection Paper on Ethical and GCP Aspects of Clinical Trials of Medicinal Products for Human Use Conducted Outside of the EU/EEA and Submitted in Marketing Authorisation Applications to the EU Regulatory Authorities*, EMA/121340/2011, 26.

acceptable *in* the [European Economic Area or] EEA' (emphasis added).[124] In sum, the focus is on providing justification for placebo use irrespective of the trial's location in order to prevent (a repeat of) the most egregious kinds of abuse. The need for justification does not seem to present an insurmountable difficulty: placebo use is more prevalent in industry-sponsored trials.[125]

That indicates how placebo is useful for the commercial imperative of producing data for market authorisation—and that again underlines the continuing extra-territorial relevance, application and effects of EU law, here in the creation of biomedical knowledge. Importantly, '[r]egardless of the location of the trial, all patients participating in these trials should receive *the same or a similar standard of care and comparable treatment options* as trial participants within the EEA' (emphasis added).[126] Still, this focus on similarity or comparability opens the way for placebo-controlled trials in countries that do not have access to the best EEA (or indeed global) standard of care or treatment, but where local equivalents can be said to provide 'similarity' or 'comparability'. In other words, there is scope for a double standard ie, the best treatment in the EEA and placebo elsewhere. Although this might be justifiable, for instance, where it leads to locally affordable options,[127] as the two members of the EGE mentioned above have observed, this is unlikely given TRIPS.[128] Still, the permissibility of such trials adds further reductions in costs to the other attractions attendant to carrying out clinical trials abroad (such as their populations), making them even more attractive.[129]

These examples also point to how international ethical standards are (re) aligned to regulatory processes and aims. This is also apparent through the way in which those standards are (de)selected and occasionally reworked in order to ensure their continued alignment and relevance to market authorisation, but in ways that undermines protections for research subjects and ensures their vulnerability is usable for those purposes. The most

124 Ibid.

125 B Djulbegovic and others, 'The Uncertainty Principle and Industry-Sponsored Research Research' (2000) 356 *The Lancet* 635.

126 EMA, n 124 above, 27.

127 RK Lie and others, 'The Standard of Care Debate: The Declaration of Helsinki Versus the International Consensus Option' (2004) *Journal of Medical Ethics* 190.

128 EGE, n 121 above, para 2.10.

129 M Landes, 'Can Context Justify an Ethical Double Standard for Clinical Research in Developing Countries?' (2005) 1 *Globalisation and Health* 11; U Schüklenk, 'The Standard of Care Debate: Against the Myth of an "International Consensus Opinion"' (2004) 30 *Journal of Medical Ethics* 194. One study found that 'only 16% of the trials conducted in resource-poor settings provided therapy that could be considered consistent with the best current standard of care, even when the Declaration of Helsinki required that standard'. See: D Kent and others, 'Clinical Trials in Sub-Saharan Africa and Established Standards of Care: A Systematic Review of HIV, Tuberculosis, and Malaria Trials' (2004) 292 *Journal of the American Medical Association* 237, 241.

notable example is the EU's (de)selection of international ethical standards in preference to the international technical standards it co-creates. In response to the 2000 version of the Helsinki Declaration the EMA's previous incarnation[130] noted its position that upon a 'strict interpretation ...[it] appears to rule out clinical trials that use a placebo control arm whenever authorised therapeutic methods already exist, preferring active controls'.[131]

Overall, although always legally speaking non-binding the value of the Helsinki Declaration is noted—'it remains *a vital expression* of medical ethics whose *aims* deserve unanimous support' (emphasis added)[132]—but since its content frustrated the use of placebo, which in turn threatened to undermine market authorisations, strict compliance was no longer possible. This meant the content of Helsinki lost its regulatory relevance even as support for its aims remained useful for the legitimation of the EU's regime. This position was reinforced by the stress on the ICH E10 guideline (which permits placebo use), but the EU's manoeuvring has tended to be overlooked in extant analyses; whereas the parallel move made by the US, one of the EU's ICH partners and collaborator in GCP, has been the focus.[133] In fact, the approach of the EU and US is the same in this respect: the US has actually broken with the advisory guidance offered by the Helsinki Declaration,[134] and, like the EU, preferred that of the ICH itself.

The ICH supports the EU's view that placebo use can be necessary and ethical. In sum, 'the efficacy of some new medicinal products can be satisfactorily demonstrated without the use of a placebo, [but] for others the judicious use of placebo remains essential to demonstrate their value'. Specifically, 'trials that seek to prove that a new agent and an active control have *similar efficacy* are inherently less reliable than trials that seek to prove the superiority of the new agent to a comparator, whether inactive or active' (emphasis added).[135] Increased trial sizes do not mitigate this problem. Without a placebo the only alternative is superiority trials—and these require the demonstration of increased efficacy over a currently authorised treatment. As already stressed, this is *not* required for EU market authorisation. Indeed, underscoring this, the EMA deems that a need for increased efficacy 'may be too restrictive'[136] and 'contrary to public health interest as

[130] European Medicines Evaluation Agency, which lost mention of 'evaluation' in 2009.

[131] EMEA, *EMEA/CPMP Position Statement on the Use of Placebo in Clinical Trials with Regard to the Revised Declaration of Helsinki*, EMEA/17424/01, 1.

[132] Ibid, p 1.

[133] See further: 'Good clinical practice compliance': www.ema.europa.eu/ema/index.jsp?curl=pages/regulation/general/general_content_000072.jsp.

[134] US Food and Drug Administration, 'Human Subject Protection; Foreign Clinical Studies Not Conducted Under an Investigational New Drug Application—Notice of Final Rule' see: www.regulations.gov/#!documentDetail;D=FDA-2004-N-0061-0002;oldLink=false.

[135] EMEA, n 132 above, 1.

[136] Ibid, 1–2.

there is a need for both new products and alternatives to existing medicinal products'.[137]

Although there can indeed be a need for alternative treatments, mention of this obscures how *genuine* need is not important for market authorisation purposes. Rather the focus is on product safety: new drugs need only be are as good as or at least not substantially worse than existing products. This focus facilitates the (de)selection of international ethical standards with the effective replacement of the Helsinki Declaration in preference to the international technical standards co-authored by the EU and its partners. While this serves to stimulate the subsequent (re)shaping of the former in an effort to maintain regulatory relevance,[138] the (de)selection of ethics also underlines their importance to the legitimation of the EU's market-oriented regulatory processes and with them its wider socio-political order and project of rule.

F. Clinical Trials Abroad, Access to Medicines and EU Trade Policy

Thus far I have underscored EU law's permissibility and legitimation of the growing use of data produced *outside* the EEA by the clinical trials industry for the production and marketing of pharmaceuticals *within* the EU's internal market. At first glance although the European and Developing Countries Clinical Trials Partnership (Partnership)[139] also seeks to facilitate clinical trials abroad, its purpose seems quite different from what I have considered thus far, in terms of its normative orientation, implications and its effects for those enrolled as participants. Indeed, the Partnership has the ostensible purpose of augmenting public science and policy in order to close the so-called 10/90 research gap in which only 10 per cent of global health research is spent on problems that affect 90 per cent of the global population, especially poverty-related diseases,[140] and widening access to essential medicines.

The Partnership focuses on Phase II and Phase III trials, and the establishment of GCP that is equivalent to those found in the CTD. For instance, many of the projects financed focus on the founding and functioning of RECs and the maintenance of the ICH standards for data production and use for market authorisation purposes. The Partnership has also been the subject of an EGE opinion on ethical aspects of clinical research in developing

137 Ibid, 2.

138 In 2008 the Helsinki Declaration was revised such that para 33 now clarifies and provides increased scope for placebo use and, for present purposes, EU law is arguably in-line with it.

139 www.edctp.org.

140 Global Forum for Health Research, *The 10/90 Gap in Health Research* (Geneva, GFHR, 1999).

countries.[141] Further validation of the Partnership comes through its operation within the broader guidance provided by the EMA. Still, the Partnership does not seem to contain explicit mention of protections in addition to those in the CTD. In light of the previous discussion it appears more is required in order to safeguard the specific vulnerabilities of research subjects in developing countries. That might include greater emphasis on the otherwise largely marginalised (within EU law) CIOMS guidelines.

Moreover, EU support of the Partnership through research funding should be viewed within the context of the wider drives towards innovation and its facilitation by (most recently) Europe 2020's so-called Horizon 2020 funding programme, which, as discussed above, is focused on generating economic value from research that promotes innovation in Europe.[142] In this light the Partnership arguably seems to be more about exporting and installing infrastructures and facilitating the training of research personnel outside the EU. These might be to the benefit of the wider community,[143] especially where a test drug is useful to it ie, because it is needed (a calculation that can take away from the individual's capacity to decide whether to participate).

Still, these benefits also function to perpetuate the use of the data produced for market authorisation and drives towards innovation *within* the EU's internal market. This abets objectives of augmenting corporate profitability. In the meantime, although local benefits might follow from the Partnership and wider humanitarian and philanthropic efforts aimed at widening access,[144] *global* access remains stymied by the unequal global trade system that helps to produce the vulnerability that these kinds of initiative seek to address. As (just) two members of the EGE have pointed out, clinical trials in developing countries might 'contribute to developing new treatments which can be patented in rich countries and are then *unaffordable for poor countries*, and on the other hand *the non-availability of treatment in the poorest countries is due partly to the patent costs*' (emphasis added).[145]

[141] EGE, n 120 above.

[142] European Commission, *Towards a European Research Area*, COM(2000) 6 final; European Commission, *Putting Knowledge into Practice: A Broad-based Innovation Strategy for the EU*, COM(2006) 502 final. For discussion, see: G Bache, ML Flear and TK Hervey, 'The Defining Features of the European Union's Approach to Regulating New Health Technologies' in ML Flear and others (eds), *European Law and New Health Technologies* (Oxford, Oxford University Press, 2013).

[143] EJ Emanuel, 'Addressing Exploitation: Reasonable Availability versus Fair Benefits' in JS Hawkins and EJ Emanuel (eds), *Exploitation and Developing Countries: The Ethics of Clinical Research* (Princeton NJ, Princeton University Press, 2008).

[144] Such as the World Health Organisation's essential drugs list, the Global Fund, and the Gate Foundation's support of the latter and other initiatives. For discussion see: JA Greene, 'Making Medicines Essential: The Emergent Centrality of Pharmaceuticals in Global Health' (2011) 6 *BioSocieties* 10; T Yamada, 'Global Health and the Bill & Melinda Gates Foundation' (2009) 373 *The Lancet* 2195.

[145] EGE, n 120 above, para 2.10.

In other words, the increasing use of clinical trials data produced using research subjects in the global South for the patenting, production and marketing of medicines in the global North is even more problematic in light of the EU's trade policy and the unequal and unjust global regulatory environment it perpetuates and represents.[146] The global trade system is produced and sustained in part by the EU's trade policy. Particularly important for this chapter is the way in which that policy undercuts the flexibilities on access to patent-protected medicines under the Agreement on Trade-Related Aspects of Intellectual Property Rights (TRIPS).[147] For instance, access to within-patent drugs can be provided through compulsory licensing.[148] Nevertheless, the usefulness of this flexibility is undermined by the lengthy[149] and resource intensive process for obtaining a licence,[150] and the reluctance of poorer MSs to participate in licensing for fear of being penalised by richer MSs through trade agreements (discussed below). The Doha Declaration[151] sought to reinforce the flexibility. It did so by underlining the link between pricing and patents in inhibiting access to treatment and reconfiguring trade and human rights. The latter came through the affirmation that TRIPS permits Member States to freely use patented pharmaceuticals where there is a 'national emergency or other

[146] For discussion see: SR Benatar, 'Distributive Justice and Clinical Trials in the Third World' (2001) 22 *Theoretical Medicine and Bioethics* 169; SR Benatar and PA Singer, 'A New Look at International Research Ethics' (2000) 321 *British Medical Journal* 824; P Farmer, 'Can Transnational Research Be Ethical in the Developing World?' (2002) 360 *Lancet* 1301; DJ Rothman, 'The Shame of Medical Research' (2000) 47 *New York Review of Books* 60; U Schuklenk and R Ashcroft, 'International Research Ethics' (2000) 14 *Bioethics* 158.

[147] Marrakesh Agreement Establishing the World Trade Organization, opened for signature 15 April 1994, 1867 UNTS 3, annex 1C (Agreement on Trade-Related Aspects of Intellectual Property Rights) (entered into force 1 January 1995) (TRIPS). This agreement is enforceable via the WTO's Understanding on Dispute Settlement. Least developed countries do not have to implement TRIPS until 2016. The EU and its MSs are all members as required by their membership of the World Trade Organisation. TRIPS came into force on 1 January 1995 and in signing up to it (WTO) MSs agree to recognise one single global patent that lasts 20 years and to forbid generic equivalents of the patented drug from entering the marketplace during that period. Under TRIPS it is for MSs to determine what deserves to be patented, and as such countries in the industrialised global North, ie, where the biggest producers of pharmaceuticals have their homes, are effectively able to export their patent protections.

[148] An alternative route is through so-called 'parallel importation', which occurs when a state imports a patented medicine from another state where it is available at a lower price, but without patent owner approval.

[149] For instance, Apotex spent three years struggling to obtain a licence for the use of three drugs in a combined treatment for HIV/AIDS, but eventually it was made available in Rwanda. See: SE Davies, *Global Politics of Health* (Cambridge, Polity Press, 2010) 169. Also see: M Rimmer, 'Race against Time: The Export of Essential Medicines to Rwanda' (2008) 1 *Public Health Ethics* 89.

[150] Cloatre, n 11 above.

[151] Declaration on the TRIPS Agreement and Public Health (adopted 14 November 2001) WTO Doc WT/MIN(01)/DEC/2 (Doha Declaration).

circumstances of extreme urgency'.[152] This means essential medicines can be used without liability for licensing fees when necessary for the protection of public health.[153] In other words, TRIPS Member States have what Dreyfuss terms 'wiggle room'[154] to get around patents for pharmaceuticals in circumstances of public health emergency, like HIV/AIDS,[155] and to negotiate lower prices.[156] Since this was of no benefit to countries with little or no manufacturing capacity further flexibility was added in 2003 allowing such MSs to import medicines from a foreign producer of generics.[157]

'TRIPS plus' bilateral agreements impose harsher provisions on developing countries, but in order to protect pharmaceutical industry interests.[158] One Oxfam report, *Trading Away Access to Medicines*, explains *How the European Union's Trade Agenda has Taken a Wrong Turn*.[159] Low and middle income countries, including those in Central America, Brazil, China and India are under intense pressure to sign these agreements, and their room for manoeuvre is limited because TRIPS-plus requirements are part of larger free trade agreements.[160] The EU's use of these agreements attests to the infiltration of market rationality into its governance through the subordination of the external dimension of public health to trade policy. Moreover, this points to the configuration by and alignment of those domains to the overarching architecture and the production of the EU's

[152] Article 31(b) See: M Cassier and M Correa, 'Patents Innovation and Public Health: Brazilian Public-Sector Laboratories' Experience in Copying AIDS Drugs' in *Economics of AIDS and Access to HIV/AIDS Care in Developing Countries: Issues and Challenges* (Paris, ANRS, 2003).

[153] An interpretation supported by the World Trade Organisation (WTO), 'Declaration on the TRIPs Agreement and Public Health', 9–14 November 2001), Ministerial Conference Fourth Session (WT/MIN(01)/DEC/W/2) ('Doha Declaration'), para 5(c).

[154] RC Dreyfuss, 'TRIPS and Essential Medicines: Must One Size Fit All? Making the WTO Responsive to the Global Health Crisis' in T Pogge and others (eds), *Incentives for Global Public Health: Patent Law and Access to Essential Medicines* (Cambridge, Cambridge University Press, 2010), 55.

[155] S Sell, *Private Power, Public Law: The Globalization of Intellectual Property Rights* (Cambridge, Cambridge University Press, 2003).

[156] VB Kerry and K Lee, 'TRIPS, the Doha Declaration and Paragraph 6 Decision: What are the Remaining Steps for Protecting Access to Medicines?' (2007) 3 *Global Health* 3.

[157] Implementation of Paragraph 6 of the Doha Declaration on the TRIPS Agreement and Public Health: Decision of 30 August 2003, WTO Doc WT/L/540; Amendment of the TRIPS Agreement: Decision of 6 December 2005, WTO Doc WT/L/641.

[158] A Mitchell and T Voon, 'Patents and Public Health in the WTO, FTAs and Beyond: Tension and Conflict in International Law' (2009) 43 *Journal of World Trade* 571.

[159] Such as the EU-India bilateral agreement, see further: Oxfam, *Trading Away Access to Medicines: How the European Union's Trade Agenda has taken a Wrong Turn* (Oxfam, 2009).

[160] Oxfam India, *Oxfam Urges India to Remain 'Pharmacy of the Developing World'* (Oxfam, 2010). Also see: S Ecks, 'Global Pharmaceutical Markets and Corporate Citizenship: The Case of Novartis' Anti-cancer Drug Glivec' (2008) 3 *BioSocieties* 165; A Pollock, 'Transforming the Critique of Big Pharma' (2011) 6 *BioSocieties* 106; JP Ruger and NY Ng, 'Emerging and Transitioning Countries' Role in Global Health' (2010) 3 *Saint Louis University Journal of Health Law & Policy* 253.

socio-political order and project of rule.[161] All that is even starker given the rationale for patents in low and middle income markets and their strict application via 'TRIPS-plus' agreements is undermined: 'patents are not a relevant factor or effective in stimulating R&D and bringing new products to [those] market[s]'.[162]

IV. CONCLUSION

Through the analysis in this chapter I have drawn attention to the EU as a largely overlooked actor in the regulation of pharmaceuticals and clinical trials. I have argued that concerns around pharmaceutical regulation and the controls on clinical trials can be understood and explained by that which undergirds, shapes and directs regulatory design. In that regard, I have pointed to clinical trials abroad as exemplary of the use, perpetuation and extension of market-oriented ideas, values and rationalities into biomedical knowledge-production and public health, as part of efforts at producing and legitimating the EU and its related imagined socio-political order and project of rule. Clinical trials abroad and the data they produce are situated within the EU's overarching governance architecture, which is concerned with producing a market-optimised European socio-political order based on innovation, economic growth, jobs and prosperity through the speeding up of authorisation for the marketing of safe pharmaceuticals in its internal market.

In this way the EU is an exporter of normative power through clinical trials abroad, especially as a global regulator in international technical standard setting for pharmaceuticals, international ethical standards, and in shaping the broader global regulatory environment and organisation of the global economy. Trial participants in the global South are not provided with equal protection under EU law. Rather, their very vulnerability makes them particularly useful as biomedical labour whose participation in trials is legitimated by ethics that focus on consent and GCP. These ethics have been made marketable, that is, (re)shaped in ways that make them useful for the licensing of pharmaceuticals in the EU, but such that they provide weak protections for participants. Trial participants and their wider communities might not be able to access those treatments due to the unequal global order that is being perpetuated through the EU's trade policy, which undercuts the limited openings for access available under global patent law.

Consent and GCP also freight research subjects abroad (in particular) with responsibility, even despite their often great vulnerability. At the same

[161] Cf G de Búrca and J Scott, *EU and the WTO: Legal and Constitutional Issues* (Oxford, Hart Publishing, 2001).

[162] WHO Commission on Intellectual Property Rights, 'Innovation and Public Health, Public Health Innovation and Intellectual Property Rights' (Geneva, WHO, 2006).

time this also limits the responsibility and accountability, not only of the pharmaceutical industry and those running the clinical trials, but also of the wider system of drug development, including the EU, to documentary evidence of adherence to ethical standards and product safety—or at least their supposedly rigorous pursuit. The EU, the Commission and the EMA (and its global partners) are able to avoid responsibility and accountability for this and other failures, such as related and wider public health problems and the unequal global order that are de-politicised and perpetuated.

The current regime does not deliver a competitive industry that generates optimal public benefits, such as attending to the most important health problems globally, focusing on the production of genuinely innovative new pharmaceuticals, and flowing from them, economic growth, jobs and prosperity. The marketable ethics, weak protections and vulnerable subjects of EU law are components and effects of a regime that produces 'more of the same drugs, if not a bit worse'. The comparative neglect of wider preventative (and non-pharmaceutical) public health interventions and their greater effectiveness, equity and justice as compared to the current preference for technological fixes (pharmaceuticalisation) underlines the failure of the current regime. This failure is an institutional and even existential risk ie, it can have an adverse impact on the EU's public reputation, standing and identity as an ethical and human rights friendly regulator that could undermine its legitimacy *and* project of furthering European integration. As a risk regulator, the EU is already sensitised to, and can be responsibilised by, and rendered accountable through, 'bioethics as risk'.[163] In highlighting that risk, such as in the ways discussed in this chapter, trial subjects and others—together, the EU's citizenry—could impel moves to reshape and redirect the regulatory regime in ways that are more consistent with the spirit and letter of the ethical standards (and human rights) the EU claims to uphold.

That implies revision of the criteria for market authorisation by the Commission and the EU legislature, consistent with the high level of health protection under Article 114(3) TFEU, such that they require the demonstration of 'comparative therapeutic efficacy' and genuine need for the new pharmaceutical. Clinical trials could be carried out by a new independent regulator with distance from the industry. Weight should also be accorded to improved 'therapeutic efficacy' and genuine need for the new pharmaceutical as part of the justification for clinical trials: where they are not the objective then the trial should not be justified by a REC, which means that data will not be produced and market authorisation will not follow. Similarly, consent to participation in trials should be reinforced through more emphasis on whether or not there is a genuine need and

[163] Cf the idea that rights are also a risk: T Murphy, 'Taking Revolutions Seriously: Rights, Risk and New Technologies' (2009) 16 *Maastricht Journal of European and Comparative Law* 15.

hoped for 'comparative therapeutic efficacy' for the pharmaceutical being trialed as well as whether post-trial access for trial participants and their wider communities will be stymied in the event of successful auhorisation (patents make this very likely).

The EMA should also revise its guidance on the design of trials, including the use of placebo, particularly in the global South, so that they are less open to contingent and exploitative behaviour. The design of trials and the scientific quality of the data likely to be produced are also ethical issues and should become central to the work of RECs, particularly if the issue becomes whether the trial data demonstrates *comparative* efficacy, quality and safety. The obligation for transparency in the results of clinical trials should apply to those performed *outside* the EU as well as those carried out *within* the EU. Finally, the Commission should ensure that patents for essential medicines are decoupled from the EU's trade agreements. Overall, these changes would ensure that ethics (and through them human rights) are not merely instrumental to the EU's pharmaceutical and clinical trials regime. Instead, the subjects of EU law would be better protected by the recognition of their vulnerability that is acted upon in ways that actually attend to and do not merely perpetuate inequity and injustice.

5

The EU and Environmental Multilateralism: The Case of Access and Benefit-Sharing and the Need for a Good-Faith Test

ELISA MORGERA*

Abstract

This chapter discusses the need for a good-faith test for assessing the legitimacy of ongoing and future EU initiatives aimed at contributing to the development and implementation of international environmental law. A test that is based on the international legal principle of good faith may serve to better understand when the EU is effectively supporting environmental multilateralism to the benefit of the international community, rather than seeking to unduly influence it purely for its own advantage. The test is developed mostly on the basis of EU efforts of contributing to climate change multilateralism, and is applied to a much less studied case: the adoption and implementation of the Nagoya Protocol on Access to Genetic Resources and Benefit-sharing under the Convention on Biological Diversity.

THE EUROPEAN UNION (EU) is well known for its prolific environmental law-making activities,[1] and for the multi-faceted environmental dimensions of its external relations.[2] It has also attracted scholarly attention for increasingly establishing explicit linkages

* The author is grateful to Dr Gracia Marín Durán and Professor Kati Kulovesi, as well as to the editor and an anonymous reviewer, for their invaluable suggestions on a previous draft of this article.

[1] The classic textbooks are: M Lee, *EU Environmental Law: Challenges, Change and Decision-making* (Oxford, Hart Publishing, 2014); L Kramer, *EU Environmental Law*, 7th edn (London, Sweet and Maxwell, 2011); J Jans and H Vedder, *European Environmental Law* (Gröningen, Europa Law Publishing, 2012). For an introduction, see also E Morgera, 'Environmental Law' in C Barnard and S Peers (eds), *EU Law* (Oxford, Oxford University Press, 2014) 651.

[2] E Morgera (ed), *The External Environmental Policy of the European Union: EU and International Law Perspectives* (Cambridge, Cambridge University Press, 2012).

between its internal environmental regulation and its external environmental or environment-related action.[3] This can be in great part explained by the EU's ambitious efforts to support environmental multilateralism. According to its own constitutional objectives,[4] the EU has set for itself the aim of helping develop international measures to preserve and improve the quality of the environment and the sustainable management of global natural resources;[5] and of promoting an international system based on stronger multilateral environmental cooperation and good global environmental governance, with a view to promoting multilateral solutions to common environmental problems, in particular in the framework of the United Nations.[6] To these ends the EU has put in place a diversity of approaches[7] based on complex interactions between internal regulation, sometimes with extraterritorial implications,[8] on the one hand, and unilateral and bilateral external action, on the other.[9] The lion's share of EU activity in that regard, and of academic reflection, has certainly been taken by climate change.[10]

[3] M Pallemaerts (ed), *The EU and Sustainable Development: Internal and External Dimensions* (Brussels, VUB Press, 2006); H Vedder, 'Diplomacy by Directive: an Analysis of the International Context of the Emissions Trading Directive' in M Evans and P Koutrakos (eds), *Beyond the Established Legal Orders—Policy Interconnections Between the EU and the Rest of the World* (Oxford, Hart Publishing, 2011) 105; G Marín Durán and E Morgera, *Environmental Integration in the EU's External Relations: Beyond Multilateral Dimensions* (Oxford, Hart Publishing, 2012); and, to a lesser extent, M Pallemaerts (ed), *The Aarhus Convention at Ten. Interactions and Tensions between Conventional International Law and EU Environmental Law* (Groningen, Europa Law Publishing, 2011).

[4] J Larik, 'Entrenching Global Governance: The EU's Constitutional Objectives Caught between a Sanguine World View and a Daunting Reality' in B Van Vooren, S Blockmans and J Wouters, *The EU's Role in Global Governance: The Legal Dimension* (Oxford, Oxford University Press, 2013) 7.

[5] Art 21(2)(d) TEU.

[6] Arts 21(2)(h) and 21(1), second sentence TEU, read in conjunction with Article 11 TFEU on environmental integration ('Environmental protection requirements must be integrated into the definition and implementation of the Union policies and activities, in particular with a view to promoting sustainable development'). On environmental integration in the EU, see Dhondt, *Integration of Environmental Protection into Other EC Policies* (Groningen, Europa Law Publishing, 2003) at 84; and discussion in Marín Durán and Morgera (n 3 above) ch 1.

[7] E Morgera, 'Ambition, Complexity and Legitimacy of Pursuing Mutual Supportiveness through the EU's External Environmental Action' in Van Vooren, Blockmans and Wouters (n 4 above) 194.

[8] As opposed to measures with an extraterritorial 'effect': see distinction drawn by AG Kokott with regards to EU internal measure that do not embody a concrete rule of conduct for subjects beyond the territory of the EU, but still create an indirect incentive for them: Opinion, C-366/10 *Air Transport Association of America and Others v Secretary of State for Energy and Climate Change*, 6 October 2011, paras 145–47.

[9] Marín Durán and Morgera (n 3 above) ch 7.

[10] S Oberthür and M Pallemaerts (eds), *The New Climate Policies of the European Union: Internal Legislation and Climate Diplomacy* (Brussels, VUB Press, 2010); K Kulovesi, E Morgera and M Munoz, 'Environmental Integration and the Multi-faceted International Dimensions of EU Law: Unpacking the EU's 2009 Climate and Energy Package' (2011) 48 *Common Market Law Review* 829; J Scott, 'The Multi-level Governance of Climate Change' (2011) *Carbon and Climate Law Review* 25; and E Morgera and K Kulovesi, 'The Role

These efforts are particularly interesting from an international environmental perspective, as the development and successful implementation of this area of international law is in dire need of leadership.[11] On the other hand, they have raised mounting concerns about the legitimacy and legality of EU action,[12] particularly since the 'aviation' case before the Court of Justice of the EU.[13] To a significant extent, concerns have focused on the alleged extraterritoriality and/or unilateral nature of EU measures, their potential infringement of other States' sovereignty and/or their compatibility with the law of the World Trade Organization (WTO). This contribution, however, intends to take a different angle: it seeks to assess to what extent EU measures effectively contribute to the development and implementation of international environmental law in the interest of the whole international community. In other words, this contribution is written from the viewpoint of international environmental law and general international law. To that end, WTO law will be set aside for present purposes, although the proposed assessment in part overlaps with the consideration of unilateralism under WTO law.[14] In relation to extraterritoriality, it suffices to recall that the question as to whether extraterritorial measures are allowed under WTO law has not been settled,[15] and this question may in all events not be relevant for present purposes. This is because, in the words of Joanne Scott, the EU engages in 'territorial extension' rather than extraterritorialism—that is, EU measures are aimed at enabling the EU to influence international law

of the EU in Promoting International Climate Change Standards' in S Poli et al (eds), *EU Management of Global Emergencies: Legal Framework for Combating Threats and Crises* (Brill Nijhoff, 2014) 304.

[11] E Morgera, 'Bilateralism at the Service of Community Interests? Non-judicial Enforcement of Global Public Goods in the Context of Global Environmental Law' (2012) 23 *European Journal of International Law* 743.

[12] C-366/10 *Air Transport Association of America and Others v Secretary of State for Energy and Climate Change* [2011] ECR I-13755.

[13] J Scott and L Rajamani, 'EU Climate Change Unilateralism' (2012) 23 *European Journal of International Law* 469; J Scott and L Rajamani, 'Contingent Unilateralism—International Aviation in the European Emissions Trading Scheme' in B Van Vooren, S Blockmans and J Wouters, *The EU's Role in Global Governance: The Legal Dimension* (Oxford, Oxford University Press, 2013) and K Kulovesi, '"Make Your Own Special Song, Even if Nobody Else Sings Along": International Aviation Emissions and the EU Emissions Trading Scheme' (2011) 2 *Climate Law* 535. See also L Bartels, 'The WTO Legality of the Application of the EU's Emission Trading System to Aviation' (2012) 23 *European Journal of International Law* 429.

[14] United States—Import Prohibition of Certain Shrimp and Shrimp Products, Report of the Appellate Body (adopted 6 November 1998) WT/DS58/AB/R; and United States—Import Prohibition of Certain Shrimp and Shrimp Products (Article 21.5—Malaysia), Report of the Appellate Body (adopted 21 November 2001), WT/DS58/AB/RW. For a discussion, see Kulovesi (n 13 above) and K Kulovesi, 'Addressing Sectoral Emissions outside the UN Framework Convention on Climate Change: What Roles for Multilateralism, Minilateralism and Unilateralism?' (2012) 21 *RECIEL* 193.

[15] P van den Bossche and W Zdouc, *The Law and Policy of the World Trade Organization* (Cambridge, Cambridge University Press, 2013) 551.

on the basis of internationally agreed objectives, rather than to export its own norms.[16]

Instead, two other aspects to the debate will be emphasized. First, this assessment will be grounded in the understanding that most EU *environmental* action guided by international environmental law is inevitably and inherently *global* (that is, it has implications for and it responds to developments outside EU borders).[17] In other words, EU environmental action is developed in the context of an overarching system that already provides for significant limitations to national sovereignty and sophisticated approaches to international cooperation that may justify the adoption of measures with extraterritorial implications. Secondly, it will seek to explore the extent to which the EU engages in *mini-lateralism*[18] as a path towards strengthened or more effective environmental multilateralism. This may be seen as another facet of global (environmental) law: as consensus has become increasingly difficult to reach in certain areas of multilateral (environmental) negotiations, 'more decentralised forms of implementation and more iterative and reflexive styles of policy-making' are relied upon in the further development or implementation of international (environmental) law.[19]

Against this background, the objective of this chapter is to discuss the need for a test to assess the legitimacy of ongoing and future EU initiatives aimed at contributing to the development and implementation of international environmental law that is based on good faith.[20] Such a test may serve to better understand when the EU is effectively *supporting* environmental multilateralism to the benefit of the international community, rather than seeking to *unduly influence* it purely for its own advantage. Clearly the distinction is not easily drawn in practice: relevant EU initiatives (as well as those of any other powerful global player) involve an inevitably mixed agenda that should then be evaluated on the basis of the balance achieved

[16] J Scott, 'Extraterritoriality and Territorial Extension in EU Law' (2014) 62 *American Journal of Comparative Law* 87.

[17] In other words, these efforts can be characterised by their 'global reach' (that is, being 'present across and between a range of [legal] sites and purport[ing] to cover all actors and activities relevant to its remit across the globe') and their 'global justification' ('an endorsement or commitment to a shared purpose or common political morality that may be explicitly invoked or implied'): N Walker, *The Intimations of Global Law* (forthcoming 2014), at 18. This idea is to some extent touched upon by Kokott (n 8 above) para 154.

[18] S Barrett, *Why Cooperate? The Incentives to Supply Global Public Goods* (Oxford, Oxford University Press, 2007).

[19] Walker (n 17 above) 108, making reference to the specific case of climate change and marine protection as areas 'where there is increasing failure to deliver grand settlements across significant interest divisions and across the broader set of sovereign States who assert a significant stake in these settlements', and hence a reliance on 'less unified and settled institutional structures with wider forms of participation and accountability, more decentralised forms of implementation and more iterative and reflexive styles of policy-making, so emphasis on dispersed influence and incremental policy development'.

[20] The need to resort to the notion of good faith in this connection was first underscored in Morgera and Kulovesi (n 10 above).

between the protection of the interests of the international community and the interests of the EU.[21] A possible test will be developed mostly on the basis of EU efforts contributing to climate change multilateralism, and will then be applied to a much less studied case: the adoption and implementation of the Nagoya Protocol on Access to Genetic Resources and Benefit-sharing,[22] adopted in 2010 under the Convention on Biological Diversity (CBD).[23]

I. THE EU'S KALEIDOSCOPIC TOOLKIT FOR INFLUENCING ENVIRONMENTAL MULTILATERALISM

Before discussing the need for a good-faith test and what such a test may look like, an introduction to the plethora of internal and external, legal and quasi-legal tools utilised by the EU to support and influence environmental multilateralism appears necessary to set the scene.

At the multilateral level, the EU, together with its Member States, is a powerful negotiating block in environmental negotiations.[24] In addition, the EU and its Member States make up one of the world's largest providers of funding for multilateral environmental protection initiatives and instruments.[25] This certainly provides the foundations for the EU's approach to global environmental leadership. But it has increasingly been seen as insufficient to fulfil the EU's ambition, particularly since the 2009 Copenhagen Climate Change Conference.[26] In light of limitations and challenges at the multilateral level, the EU has increasingly coupled its multilateral tools with systematic use of external relations tools of a unilateral, bilateral and inter-regional nature.

Bilateral and inter-regional trade-related instruments have thus increasingly included sophisticated clauses on environmental cooperation linked to international environmental standards.[27] In particular, the bilateral agreements

[21] See similar comments in a more general context by S Villalpando, 'The Legal Dimension of the International Community: How Community Interests are Protected in International Law' (2010) 21 *European Journal of International Law* 387, at 415 and 418–19.

[22] Convention on Biological Diversity, 5 June 1992, 1760 UNTS 79.

[23] Nagoya Protocol on Access to Genetic Resources and the Fair and Equitable Sharing of Benefits Arising from their Utilization to the Convention on Biological Diversity (2010) UN Doc UNEP/CBD/COP/10/27, in force 12 October 2014.

[24] T Delreux, *The EU as an International Environmental Negotiator* (Aldershot, Ashgate, 2011).

[25] European Commission, 'Communication on external action: thematic programme for environment and sustainable management of natural resources including energy' COM(2006) 20 final, 24.

[26] Eg, N Fujiwara, 'Reinvigorating the EU's Role in the post-Copenhagen Landscape' (2010) Climate Change, CEPS Commentaries, at: www.ceps.be/book/ reinvigorating-eu%E2%80%99s-role-post-copenhagen-landscape; J Curtin, The Copenhagen Conference: How Should the EU Respond? (Dublin, IIEA, 2010).

[27] While these agreements have different denominations and objectives, their environmental clauses are notably similar: for a discussion, Marín Durán and Morgera (n 3 above) 57–63.

concluded by the EU since 2005 ('post-Global Europe agreements')[28] have established obligations to effectively implement and enforce key multilateral environmental agreements (MEAs) in the context of trade and sustainable development. In addition, environment-specific mechanisms for cooperative monitoring and dispute resolution have been set up in that context, requiring the involvement of environmental experts and allowing also for advice to be sought from MEA Secretariats.[29] The negotiations of these agreements have been preceded by Sustainability Impact Assessments (SIAs), which contribute to identify trade-offs between the trade component of the agreement under negotiation and environmental protection in the EU and in the partner country. For present purposes, it should be pointed out that SIAs often serve to address global environmental issues or instruments.[30] For countries that have no trade agreement in place with the EU, the Union's Generalised System of Preferences unilaterally offers developing and least-developed countries trade incentives that are made conditional upon the ratification and effective implementation of key MEAs.[31]

In terms of development aid, the EU practice of integrating environmental concerns in external assistance is also increasingly targeting the implementation of key MEAs, as well as contributions to the reform of global environmental governance.[32] Notably, the Commission clarified that this has the explicit objective of *shaping* global environmental governance by the external dimensions of the EU's *own* environment and climate change policies.[33] In addition, the EU has institutionalised a plethora of policy dialogues with various individual developed and developing countries, and with various groups of third countries, for the periodic exchange of views on environmental priorities and respective negotiating positions. These exercises, which are mainly organised at the initiative of the EU, serve to develop specific action plans that also address global environmental issues,

[28] As their negotiations were launched by the Commission, '*Communication—Global Europe: Competing in the world: A contribution to the EU's Growth and Jobs Strategy*', COM(2006) 567 final of 4 October 2006. See Marín Durán and Morgera (n 3 above) 133–42, and for an insider's perspective, R Zvelc, 'Environmental integration in the EU trade policy: the examples of the GSP+, trade sustainability impact assessments and free trade agreements' in Morgera (n 2 above) 174.

[29] See Marín Durán and Morgera (n 3 above) 140.

[30] Ibid, ch 6.

[31] Ibid, ch 3. This is the 'Special Incentive Arrangement for Sustainable Development and Good Governance' in Regulation (EU) 978/2012 of 25 October 2012 applying a scheme of generalised tariff preferences and repealing Council Regulation (EC) No 732/2008, [2012] OJ L303/1, Arts 9–16 and Annex VIII. Note that Article 9(1)(b) makes reference to the condition that 'the most recent available conclusions of the monitoring bodies under those conventions ... do not identify a serious failure to effectively implement any of those conventions.'

[32] For a discussion, see Marín Durán and Morgera (n 3 above) ch 4 and G Marín Durán, 'Environmental Integration in EU Development Cooperation: Responding to International Commitments or Its Own Policy Priorities?' in Morgera (n 2 above) 204.

[33] Commission, '*Environment and natural resources thematic programme—2011–2013 strategy paper and multiannual indicative programme*', 29 October 2010, at 25.

including specific common objectives to support the successful conclusion of ongoing multilateral environmental negotiations.[34]

These external relations instruments are inter-linked in a complex and somewhat obscure manner. SIAs feed into the negotiations of bilateral agreements, but their outcomes should also be taken into account in the implementation of these agreements, particularly because some of the recommendations emerging from SIAs may be addressed through other EU external relations tools, such as financial and technical assistance.[35] The implementation of bilateral agreements is followed up on through policy dialogues, which produce action plans to attract funding on certain priority activities falling under the broad scope of the environmental cooperation clauses included in bilateral agreements.[36] The allocation of EU external funding, however, remains separate from these dialogue processes and in the vast majority of cases, also from bilateral agreements: generally it is up to the EU's own regulations on each funding instrument to set the principles and procedures for integrating environmental requirements in EU external funding, although even under these unilateral instruments there is provision for some form of dialogue with the third party concerned in relation to the allocation of funding.[37] Enhanced dialogue is, in turn, seen as an objective of the Union's external funding, as well as a means to increase the visibility of EU financial and technical assistance supporting environmental protection in partner countries. Furthermore, dialogues are expected to be informed by SIAs and ex-post SIAs, and are used by the EU to support the understanding beyond its borders of certain pieces of EU internal environmental legislation with extraterritorial implications.

These complex interactions are increasingly reflected and explicitly cross-referenced in EU internal legislation: recent pieces of EU environmental law refer or reflect the Union's multilateral negotiating positions,[38] as well as its reliance on other external relations tools supporting environmental multilateralism.[39] In parallel, the EU relies more and more on its own legislation as well as on its unilateral and bilateral external relations tools in the context of its interventions in multilateral fora. In some instances, as Joanne Scott has aptly explained, EU internal legislation (and the EU's market power) are designed to have certain extraterritorial implications and influence multilateral negotiations in an effort that combines 'structural leadership' and 'contingent unilateralism'.[40]

[34] Marín Durán and Morgera (n 3 above) ch 5.
[35] Ibid, 249.
[36] Ibid, 231.
[37] See references in n 32 above, and in particular Marín Durán and Morgera (n 3 above) 176.
[38] Vedder (n 3 above) 105.
[39] Kulovesi, Morgera and Munoz (n 10 above).
[40] Scott (n 10 above) 28 and 32.

On the face of it, through creative combinations of the above instruments, the Union has put in place three modalities to support environmental multilateralism through the development and implementation of international environmental law. First, the EU seeks to use its external action to support politically, technically and financially the implementation of *existing* multilateral environmental agreements beyond its borders, particularly in developing countries. Secondly, the EU is using its external action tools to build alliances with third countries, regions or groups of countries with a view to influencing *ongoing* international environmental negotiations. Thirdly, the EU is using these tools to make progress on environmental issues on which the international community has been unable to launch negotiations towards the development of an international legally binding agreement: in the *absence* of multilateral environmental negotiations, the EU wishes to pursue certain environmental goals with other willing countries with a view to building international consensus from the bottom up.[41] This strategy has a demonstrated potential to promptly respond to the changing multilateral landscape: EU external environmental action has switched from one of the above-outlined modalities to the other, depending on progress or lack thereof at the multilateral level.

II. CRITICISMS AND CONCERNS

While their effectiveness is difficult to prove, the EU's combined efforts to affect environmental, and particularly climate change, multilateralism have been the target of criticism. As already discussed above, legality questions have been raised with respect to the extraterritoriality of certain EU measures and their compatibility with WTO law.[42] Other concerns have also been raised from the viewpoint of legitimacy and compatibility with general international law. It has been argued, for instance, that through these efforts the EU seeks unilaterally to impose its own view of international law upon third countries.[43] This may spark unhealthy regulatory competition among other (powerful) countries equally wishing to impose their own regulatory preferences.[44] In addition, it has led to allegations about the EU's failure to respect principles of international environmental law of essential importance in North/South relations, such as the principle of common but differentiated responsibilities and respective capabilities:[45] in this connection, the EU is seen as imposing high standards that are beyond the reach of developing countries. Furthermore, it has been argued that rather

[41] Marín Durán and Morgera (n 3 above) ch 7.
[42] See references in n 13.
[43] Scott and Rajamani (n 13 above); Marín Durán (n 32 above).
[44] Kulovesi (n 14 above).
[45] Scott and Rajamani (n 13 above) 469.

than (only) contributing to environmental multilateralism, such measures also (or mainly) pursue the EU's own competitiveness agenda.[46] Finally, they have also raised human rights concerns.[47]

All of the above criticisms appear crucial to better understand the extent to which the EU supports, rather than unduly influences, environmental multilateralism. Such concerns can and should be addressed from a dual perspective. From an EU law standpoint, it appears necessary to ascertain whether and under which conditions the Union's significant resources devoted to unilateral, bilateral and inter-regional environmental action are effectively used for the pursuit of multilateral environmental objectives as required by the Treaty. From an international law standpoint, it seems necessary to consider whether these EU initiatives comply with general principles of international law.

One principle of international environmental law has already been invoked: as mentioned above, this is the case of common but differentiated responsibility.[48] The principle essentially justifies the design of different international obligations on the basis of differences in the current socio-economic situations of countries and their historical contribution to a specific environmental problem, thus 'reconcil[ing] the tensions between the need for universalism in taking action to combat global environmental problems and the need to be sensitive to individual countries' relevant circumstances' and thereby responding to concerns of legitimacy, equity and effectiveness.[49] It calls on developed countries (and may therefore justify the EU) to take the lead in addressing global environmental issues.[50] At the same time, it has resulted in the allocation of less burdensome obligations on developing countries.[51] Thus, in the context of the EU unilateral and bilateral external relations tools, it can be argued that respect for common but differentiated responsibility prevents the Union from subverting globally determined allocation of international responsibility, particularly through trade-related instruments.[52] Third, in terms of development aid,

[46] Marín Durán (n 32 above) 224–40.

[47] On these concerns, D Augenstein, 'The Human Rights Dimension of Environmental Protection in EU External Relations Post-Lisbon' in Morgera (n 2 above) 263. On limited practice specifically related to environmental rights, see E Morgera, 'The Promotion of Environmental Rights through EU Bilateral Agreements: Mapping the Field' in F Lenzerini and A Vrdoljak (eds), *International Law for Common Goods* (Oxford, Hart Publishing, 2014) 421.

[48] Scott and Rajamani (n 13 above); Morgera (n 7 above).

[49] T Honkonen, 'The Principle of Common but Differentiated Responsibility in Post-2012 Climate Negotiations' (2009) 18 *RECIEL* 257, at 259.

[50] United Nations Framework Convention on Climate Change, 4 June 1992, 1771 UNTS 107 (UNFCCC), Art 3.

[51] There are various examples in MEAs of differentiated responsibilities: the most notable is the Kyoto Protocol, which provides for quantified and time-bound obligations to mitigate climate change only for so-called 'Annex-I countries', ie developed countries.

[52] Morgera (n 11 above) 759.

the principle is usually translated in developed countries' obligations to transfer technology and 'new and additional' financial means to developing countries, to enable them to implement international environmental obligations.[53] Overall, therefore, this principle serves to ascertain whether in EU efforts to contribute to environmental multilateralism the different circumstances of developing countries are fully taken into account, and in particular whether appropriate assistance is provided to facilitate developing countries' compliance with international environmental law.

While common but differentiated responsibility certainly touches on key issues to ensure the legitimacy of EU efforts to contribute to environmental multilateralism, it may not necessarily factor in other critical questions for multilateral environmental processes. Namely, the legitimacy question also needs to take into account circumstances where at the multilateral level an impasse is reached and multilateral determinations related to common but differentiated responsibilities have not been made or are the very reason of the impasse. In these situations, the EU's reliance on unilateralism, bilateralism and minilateralism[54] needs to be assessed as a constructive and complementary path that will eventually lead to environmental multilateralism.[55]

A. A Good-faith Test

For these reasons, it is proposed that the general principle in international law of good faith provides a more rounded approach to the question at hand, for its implications in terms of duty to cooperate, duty to negotiate, a duty to perform international obligations and as a cardinal principle of treaty interpretation.[56] With regard to the duty to cooperate, good faith entails the need to show third countries individually and the international

[53] This is a common obligation across MEAs, although it is most clearly expressed in CBD Art 20(4).

[54] Morgera (n 2 above), and for a specific reply to the concerns raised by Scott and Rajamani (n 13 above) and Kulovesi (n 14 above).

[55] AG Kokott, Opinion, C-366/10 *Air Transport Association of America and Others*, 6 October 2011, paras 185–86, noted that the EU 'could not reasonably be required to give … [multilateral] bodies unlimited time in which to develop a multilateral solution'. The salience of the timing of unilateral measures is discussed by B Jansen, 'The Limits of Unilateralism from a European Perspective' (2000) 11 *European Journal of International Law* 309, at 313; and L Boisson de Chazournes, 'Unilateralism and Environmental Protection: Issues of Perception and Reality of Issues' (2000) 11 *European Journal of International Law* 315, at 332; and D Bodansky, 'What's so Bad about Unilateral Action to Protect the Environment?' (2000) 11 *European Journal of International Law* 339, at 347.

[56] Declaration on Principles of International Law concerning Friendly Relations and Co-operation among States in accordance with the Charter of the United Nations (24 October 1970) UN Doc A/RES/25/2625 and VCLT Arts 26 and 31. For an overview, see generally M Kotzur, 'Good Faith' in R Wolfrum (ed), *Max Planck Encyclopedia of International Law* (Oxford, Oxford University Press, 2012, online edition).

community as a whole that the EU respects the international legal order.[57] This means protecting reasonable interests of other States that arise from the appearances created by bilateral or minilateral efforts of the EU.[58] In other words, it implies the need for the EU to show trustworthiness and predictability[59] in how it develops and uses its unilateral, bilateral and minilateral approaches to support environmental multilateralism by taking the legitimate expectations of the other members of the international community into account.[60] Demonstrating good faith, thus, necessitates systematic respect for multilateral norms as well as reliance on multilateral institutions that are essential to the effective, objective and even-handed promotion and protection of the international community's interests.[61] It also necessitates the creation of opportunities for, and the pursuance of, genuine negotiations with other countries with a 'genuine intention to achieve a positive result'.[62] With regard to the duty to perform international obligations, good faith translates into mutual supportiveness—that is, an obligation at the interpretative level to 'disqualify solutions to tensions between competing regimes involving the subordination of one regime to the other', and at the law-making level exerting efforts to negotiate and conclude instruments that clarify the relationship between competing regimes, when interpretative reconciliation efforts have been exhausted.[63] With regard to treaty interpretation (and its implications for supporting the effective implementation of international environmental law), good faith also requires that excessive interpretations of multilateral environmental treaties will be avoided when they would allow the EU and its Member States to obtain an unfair advantage, disregard legitimate expectations, or exercise rights in a way that would be damaging to other states.[64]

On these bases, a four-pronged test of the legitimacy of EU efforts to genuinely contribute, rather than unduly influence, environmental multilateralism can be put forward.

[57] Ibid, para 4.

[58] M Virally, 'Review Essay: Good Faith in Public International Law' (1983) 77 *American Journal of International Law* 130.

[59] S Litvinoff, 'Good Faith' (1997) 71 *Tulane Law Review* 1645, 1664.

[60] Kotzur (n 56 above) para 26.

[61] B Simma, 'From Bilateralism to Community Interests in International Law' (1994) IV (250) *Recueil des Cours* 217, 319.

[62] ICJ, *Gulf of Maine case*, [1984] ICJ Rep 246, para 87.

[63] R Pavoni, 'Mutual Supportiveness as a Principle of Interpretation and Law-Making: A Watershed for the WTO-and-Competing-Regimes Debate?' (2010) 21 *European Journal of International Law* 649, particularly 661–69.

[64] M Villiger, '1969 Vienna Convention on the Law of Treaties: Forty Years After' (2009) 344 *Recueil Des Cours* 1, 1116–17.

i. Respect for the Objective of Multilateral Environmental Agreements

First, the EU's efforts should respect and clearly contribute to the realisation of the objective of the multilateral environmental agreements to which the EU and its Member States are parties and to the development or implementation of which the EU unilateral, bilateral and inter-regional measures are explicitly geared towards.[65] There is, of course, a certain room for interpretation in referring to the objective of a treaty,[66] but efforts must be made to rely on a largely shared view, as for instance documented in consensus-based soft law.[67] This is something that the EU has already done, occasionally. For instance, the EU has clearly articulated its strategy for gradually building international consensus on sustainable forest management from the bottom up: it has developed an action plan and then enacted a series of regulations to tackle this global problem in the immediate term, in the face of limited progress at the multilateral level.[68] In so doing, it has explicitly drawn on global soft-law commitments,[69] and made its efforts compatible with ongoing, albeit partial, multilateral efforts.[70]

ii. Responsiveness to Intervening Multilateral Developments

The second step in the good-faith test is assessing whether EU measures ensure *responsiveness* to intervening developments in global fora. The launch or continuation of multilateral negotiations may not be a sufficient trigger in this regard, in my view, as multilateral negotiations could be very protracted and/or of uncertain outcome, and therefore genuine environmental leadership by the EU on its own may still be needed in the meantime. On the other hand, multilateral determinations, where consensus has been reached, concerning the interpretation or preferred implementation of multilateral environmental treaties, including when they are expressed through

[65] This was first put forward in Morgera (n 7 above). Joanne Scott appears to think along the same lines in her recent piece on EU territorial extension (n 16 above), when she refers to the need to 'pursuing internationally agreed objectives rather than its own autonomous objectives ("promoting fidelity to international law")'.

[66] D Jonas and T Saunders, 'The Object and Purpose of a Treaty: Three Interpretative Methods' (2010) 43 *Vanderbilt Journal of Transnational Law* 565.

[67] In that regard, note that Principle 12 of the Rio Declaration on Environment and Development (1992) UN Doc A/CONF.151/26, vol 1, Annex 1) reads: '...Environmental measures addressing transboundary or global environmental problems should, as far as possible, be *based on international consensus*' (emphasis added).

[68] Commission, '*Forest Law Enforcement, Governance and Trade (FLEGT): Proposal for an Action Plan*' COM(2003) 251 final, 3; endorsed by the Council, '*Conclusions—Forest Law Enforcement, Governance and Trade (FLEGT)*' [2003] OJ C268/1 ('FLEGT Action Plan').

[69] Ibid, at 5; World Summit on Sustainable Development Plan of Implementation, (2002) UN Doc A/CONF.199/20, Resolution 2, para 45(c).

[70] Namely, timber species listed under Convention on International Trade in Endangered Species of Wild Fauna and Flora, 3 March 1973, 993 UNTS 243: FLEGT Action Plan, 20, 9 and 11.

soft-law instruments, should lead to a clear and prompt response from the EU. This is the case of determinations by multilateral environmental agreements' governing and compliance bodies relating to the link between financial solidarity, capacity building, and compliance.[71] The EU should thus avoid 'upsetting' multilateral determinations of common but differentiated responsibilities through bilateral or unilateral routes.[72] This is particularly relevant when the specific EU measure has extraterritorial implications.[73] In either case, EU measures can provide specific guarantees such as review clauses expressly triggered by developments at the multilateral level and inputs from third countries at the bilateral level.

The 2009 EU Climate and Energy Package, for instance, contains review clauses linked to the *outcome* of ongoing international negotiations.[74] In addition, the FLEGT initiative provides an example of EU responsiveness to changed international landscapes. As deforestation issues were increasingly addressed in the context of the negotiations on a post-2012 climate change regime under the so-called REDD-plus item[75] and eventually some *consensus* was reached in 2010 in that regard,[76] the EU proposed to use FLEGT to influence forest-related negotiations in the international climate change regime.[77] Specifically, it aimed at capitalising on agreement on key concepts related to forest governance emerging from FLEGT, as well as the lessons learnt in related multi-stakeholder processes, as concrete inputs into

[71] The idea of responsiveness was first put forward in Morgera (n 7 above) 207–8.

[72] Morgera (n 2 above).

[73] Scott (n 16 above) 116. See n 8 for an explanation of 'extraterritorial implications'.

[74] See, for example, Arts 10b(1) and 11a of Directive 2009/29/EC of the European Parliament and of the Council of 23 April 2009, amending Directive 2003/87/EC, so as to improve and extend the greenhouse gas emission allowance trading scheme of the Community ('EU ETS Directive'), [2009] OJ L140/63, and Arts 5.2, 5.3, 8 and 9 of Decision No 406/2009/EC of the European Parliament and of the Council of 23 April 2009 on the effort of Member States to reduce their greenhouse gas emissions to meet the Community's greenhouse gas emission reduction commitments up to 2020, [2009] OJ L140/136.

[75] REDD-plus means 'reducing emissions from deforestation and forest degradation, conservation of forest-carbon stocks, sustainable management of forests, and enhancement of forest-carbon stocks'. For a discussion, see H van Asselt, 'Managing the Fragmentation of International Environmental Law: Forests at the Intersection of the Climate and Biodiversity Regime' (2014) *NYU Journal of International Law and Politics*; A Savaresi, 'Reducing Emissions from Deforestation in Developing Countries under the UNFCCC. Caveats and Opportunities for Biodiversity' (2011) 21 *Yearbook of International Environmental Law* 41.

[76] Cancun Agreements, Decision adopted by the Conference of the Parties to the UN Framework Convention on Climate Change on its sixteenth session (2011) UN Doc FCCC/CP/2010/7/Add.1, 70–73.

[77] Commission, '*Proposal laying down the obligations of operators who place timber and timber products on the market*', COM(2008) 644/3 final, 5; and Agreement establishing an Association between the EU and its Member States, on the one hand, and Central America on the other, [2012] OJ L346/3, Art 20; Free Trade Agreement between the EU and its Member States, on one side, and Colombia and Peru, on the other side, [2012] OJ L354/3, Art 286; Second Revision of the Cotonou Partnership Agreement—Agreed Consolidated Text (11 March 2010), Art 32 bis.

multilateral negotiations on REDD-plus.[78] This was a particularly useful contribution to multilateralism, as negotiations on REDD-plus have proven particularly complex in ensuring mutual supportiveness between climate change mitigation objectives, on the one hand, and biodiversity conservation and respect for the rights of forest-dwelling communities on the other hand.[79] These two examples can be usefully contrasted with the decision in late 2012 to 'stop the clock' on the implementation of the inclusion of non-EU flights under the EU Emission Trading Scheme, which was linked to a desire to create a positive atmosphere for international negotiations at the International Civil Aviation Organization, rather than the intervening of an actual multilateral outcome in that regard.[80]

iii. Dialogue

The third step in the good-faith test is assessing whether there is *genuine* dialogue with third countries (and stakeholders).[81] Dialogue is an essential ingredient for genuine cooperation, within and beyond multilateral frameworks, based on the respect for sovereign equality among partner countries.[82] This is particularly important when partnering countries have differentiated responsibilities. Some examples of EU action to support multilateralism have specifically provided for such dialogue, although to differing extents.

The 2009 EU Climate and Energy Package cross-references EU bilateral external tools used for dialogue and cooperation with third countries in relation to climate funding and the expansion of the global carbon market,[83] capacity building and collaborative research,[84] joint projects with third

[78] For a more detailed discussion, see A Savaresi, 'FLEGT and REDD: Interactions between EU Bilateral Cooperation and the Development of International Law' in Morgera (n 2 above) 149.

[79] This relates to the international debate on the so-called 'safeguards' for REDD-plus concerning biodiversity and forest-dependent communities. See Environmental Council Conclusions of 20 December 2010 on the Nagoya Conference of the Parties to the CBD, where Member States and the Commission are invited to 'actively contribute to the preparation of advice on the application of relevant safeguards for biodiversity in relation to REDD+, in line with the CBD COP 10 decision, and facilitate the development and implementation of such safeguards under REDD+'. This was reflected in the EU-Africa partnership: Third EU-Africa Summit, 'Joint Africa-EU Strategy Action Plan (2011–2013)' Tripoli, 30 November 2010.

[80] Stopping the clock of ETS and aviation emissions following last week's International Civil Aviation Organisation (ICAO) Council, MEMO/12/854, 12 November 2012.

[81] Morgera (n 11 above) 765–66; and Scott (n 16 above) 117–18.

[82] P-M Dupuy, 'The Place and Role of Unilateralism in Contemporary International Law' (2000) 11 *European Journal of International Law* 19, 22–23.

[83] EU ETS Directive, Arts 10(3) and 25.

[84] Directive 2009/31/EC of the European Parliament and of the Council of 23 April 2009 on the geological storage of carbon dioxide and amending Council Directive 85/337/EEC, European Parliament and Council Directives 2000/60/EC, 2001/80/EC, 2004/35/EC, 2006/12/EC, 2008/1/EC and Regulation (EC) No 1013/2006, [2009] OJ L140/114, preambular para 7.

countries,[85] and cooperation in monitoring.[86] Other interesting examples are provided by the joint activities under the FLEGT process, which is coupled with structured stakeholder involvement in third countries. In this framework, the EU and its partner countries acted as 'co-generators of norms', jointly identifying solutions to multilateral impasses, based on their respective internal frameworks and relevant international instruments,[87] as well as joint monitoring. Voluntary Partnership Agreements (VPAs) between the EU and timber-exporting third countries are designed to be concluded to this end. They provide a reference, based on a joint evaluation by the third country and the EU of the alignment of third-country national forest law with relevant multilateral standards,[88] for the verification of the legality of harvests of timber imported into the EU. On that basis, reform of national forest law and governance structure in the third country is usually undertaken.

Dialogue may also involve relevant bodies under multilateral environmental agreements, particularly compliance committees, or relevant international organisations. Such dialogue may thus contribute to dispelling the 'danger of abuse' by individual states or groups of states based on lack of objectivity and even-handedness in the pursuit of community interests.[89] Once again the FLEGT process provides an interesting example: support is provided by an independent, specialised international organisation, namely the Food and Agriculture Organization of the UN (FAO), which is managing a global project funded by the EU to support African, Caribbean and Pacific countries in the review of their legislation and upgrading of their forest governance and law enforcement capacities.[90] FAO has a long-standing and well-respected tradition of providing expert and independent advice on the reform of national forest laws.[91]

[85] Directive 2009/28/EC of the European Parliament and of the Council of 23 April 2009 on the promotion of the use of energy from renewable sources and amending and subsequently repealing Directives 2001/77/EC and 2003/30/EC ('Renewables Directive'), [2009] OJ L140/16, Art 9(1).

[86] In relation to the biofuels sustainability criteria: Renewables Directive, Arts 18(4) and 23(2).

[87] Morgera (n 7 above).

[88] Recitals 3–4, EU-Ghana VPA, [2010] OJ L70/3 point to the multilateral instruments of reference.

[89] Morgera (n 2 above), building on Simma (n 61 above) 319.

[90] See www.fao.org/forestry/acp-flegt/en. Note that while there is no formal link between the FAO FLEGT Programme and the VPAs, FAO assistance specifically targets countries depending on 'their level of interest in the FLEGT Action Plan and in negotiating a VPA' through support for national and regional FLEGT/VPA workshops to share information, knowledge and lessons learnt, feasibility studies on VPA-related issues; and support for national multi-stakeholder committees in charge of VPA negotiations and for the participation of local stakeholders: FAO, Improving Forest Governance in Africa, the Caribbean and the Pacific (FAO, undated) 6 and 9, at: foris.fao.org/static/data/acpflegt/4087Forestgovernance_en.pdf.

[91] See FAO Legal Office, 'Legal Advisory Services: Forestry and Wildlife', at: www.fao.org/legal/advserv/forest-e.htm.

iv. Mutual Supportiveness

The fourth step in the good-faith test is assessing whether the EU measures support a holistic interpretation of relevant obligations deriving from different international treaties. In this connection, one should bear in mind that EU primary law similarly requires overall policy coherence, and specifically environmental and climate change mainstreaming,[92] as well as support for human rights in helping to develop international environmental measures.[93] Thus, both in accordance with general international law and EU primary law, the EU's contribution to environmental multilateralism needs to be based on mutual supportiveness.[94]

Clear examples of mutual supportiveness can be found in EU climate change efforts, in particular in relation to the need to ensure that climate change response measures be environmentally sustainable also from a broader environmental, including biodiversity, perspective. The sustainability criteria for the production of biofuels, under the Renewables Directive, for instance, have specifically provided for protection of land with high biodiversity value and relied on multilateral definitions to that end.[95] The support for human rights in EU climate measures, however, remains a matter for debate.[96]

III. APPLYING THE TEST: THE CASE OF THE NAGOYA PROTOCOL ON ACCESS AND BENEFIT-SHARING

This section will apply the test to a more unusual case study: the negotiations and implementation of the Nagoya Protocol on Access and Benefit-Sharing. EU efforts to influence multilateral biodiversity standard-setting will first be introduced, and then some of the specific features of the Nagoya Protocol will be illustrated.

[92] Arts 7 and 11 TFEU. Climate change mainstreaming has become an explicit Treaty requirement, based on a combined reading of Article 11 TFEU and Article 191(1), where climate change is for the first time explicitly mentioned as a result of the amendment introduced by the Lisbon Treaty.

[93] Article 21(2)(b) read in conjunction with Article 21(2)(d) and (f) TEU. For a discussion of coherence in the EU's external relations and environmental integration, see M Cremona, 'Coherence and EU External Environmental Policy' in Morgera (n 2 above) 33.

[94] Morgera (n 7 above) 207.

[95] Directive 2009/28/EC of 23 April 2009 on the promotion of the use of energy from renewable sources, [2009] OJ L 140/16, Art 17(3). For a discussion, see Kulovesi, Morgera and Muñoz (n 10 above) 877–82.

[96] Morgera (n 47 above) 435–38.

A. The EU and Multilateral Biodiversity Cooperation

The EU is party to several biodiversity-related conventions.[97] One notable exception[98] is the Convention on International Trade in Endangered Species (CITES),[99] because the latter did not originally allow membership of regional economic integration organisations, untill its Gaborone Amendment (adopted in 1983), which permits membership by regional economic integration organisations of CITES, entered into force.[100] Nonetheless, the EU has adopted unilateral and more stringent domestic legislation on trade in endangered species.[101]

International biodiversity law[102] has increasingly expanded its reach and ambition, through decisions adopted by governing bodies (Conferences of the Parties) of the above-mentioned treaties. They periodically set wide-ranging targets and guidelines that, albeit non-binding, aim to influence national legislation and practice in innovative and pervasive ways in a variety of sectors. Nowadays, international biodiversity law challenges states to adopt a holistic and people-centred approach to nature conservation, with the full participation of and respect for the rights of indigenous peoples and local communities.[103] It requires states to prevent continued biodiversity loss and thereby its implications for current and future human well-being, including the provision of food, fibre, medicines, and fresh water, the pollination of crops, the filtration of pollutants, and protection from natural disasters.[104] As it is becoming increasingly clear that biodiversity loss is accelerated by climate change, states are further expected to ensure

[97] In addition to the CBD, it is also party to the: Convention on the Conservation of Migratory Species of Wild Animals, 23 June 1979, 1651 UNTS 333; International Treaty on Plant Genetic Resources for Food and Agriculture, 3 November 2001, 2400 UNTS 303; Cartagena Protocol on Biosafety, 29 January 2000, 2226 UNTS 208.

[98] Other key biodiversity agreements to which the EU is not a party are the Convention on Wetlands of International Importance, 2 February 1971, 996 UNTS 245; and the Convention Concerning the Protection of the World Cultural and Natural Heritage, 16 November 1972, 1037 UNTS 151.

[99] Convention on International Trade in Endangered Species of Wild Fauna and Flora, 3 March 1973, 993 UNTS 243.

[100] CITES, 'Gaborone Amendment': www.cites.org/eng/disc/gaborone.shtml.

[101] Regulation (EC) No 338/97, [1997] OJ L61/1.

[102] M Bowman, P Davies and C Redgwell, *Lyster's International Wildlife Law*, 2nd edn (Cambridge, Cambridge University Press, 2010).

[103] E Morgera and E Tsioumani, 'Yesterday, Today and Tomorrow: Looking Afresh at the Convention on Biological Diversity' (2011) 21 *Yearbook of International Environmental Law* 3; and E Morgera, 'Against All Odds: The Contribution of the Convention on Biological Diversity to International Human Rights Law' in Alland et al (eds), *Unity and Diversity of International Law. Essays in Honour of Professor Pierre-Marie Dupuy* (Martinus Nijhoff, 2014) 983.

[104] In mid-2010, official scientific evidence was released, stating that the global target for reducing the rate of biodiversity loss had not been met: CBD and UNEP-World Conservation Monitoring Centre, *Global Biodiversity Outlook-3* (Montreal, Secretariat of the CBD, 2010).

biodiversity conservation and ecosystem restoration as essential tools for climate change mitigation and adaptation.[105]

In parallel with these international developments, EU biodiversity law has developed in a 'patchy' manner, resulting in a system that is complex, ambiguous and in part overlapping.[106] It remains mainly focused on 'traditional' conservation measures (protected areas and species) that developed in the late 1970s and early 1990s.[107] While it has been considered 'highly influential ...[in] affecting for the first time Member States' use of land'[108] and equipped to accommodate climate change adaptation concerns,[109] it remains 'structurally weak' and affected by poor enforcement.[110] Besides continuing difficulties in implementation, significant gaps remain in the EU regulatory framework on biodiversity, which are also acknowledged by the Commission itself, such as a lack of EU legislation on invasive alien species and on soil protection.[111] These shortcomings are considered significant also from an external relations perspective, as they undermine the credibility of the EU as a global player in multilateral biodiversity processes.[112] There is therefore nothing comparable to the comprehensive and ambitious 2009 Climate and Energy Package,[113] which has been often highlighted by the EU in the context of multilateral climate negotiations and in bilateral dialogues with third countries with a view to encouraging adoption of similar measures.[114]

While the EU is generally a vocal negotiator at the multilateral level, its efforts to contribute to biodiversity multilateralism through unilateral,

[105] Ibid, 75 and 83.

[106] N Sadeleer, 'EC Law and Biodiversity' in R Macrory (ed), *Reflections on 30 Years of EU Environmental Law—a High Level Protection?* (Groningen, Europa Law Publishing, 2005) 351, 368–69.

[107] Notably, the Birds and Habitats Directives: Directive 2009/147/EC on the conservation of wild birds, [2010] OJ L20/7 (codified version) and Directive 92/43/EEC on the conservation of natural habitats and of wild fauna and flora, [1992] OJ L206/7.

[108] J Holder and M Lee, *Environmental Protection, Law and Policy* (Cambridge, Cambridge University Press, 2007) 627.

[109] A Trouwborst, 'Conserving European Biodiversity in a Changing Climate: The Bern Convention, the European Union Birds and Habitats Directives and the Adaptation of Nature to Climate Change' (2011) 20 *RECIEL* 62.

[110] Kramer (n 1 above) 196; and European Parliament, Resolution on the implementation of EU legislation aiming at the conservation of biodiversity (2009/2108(INI)), 21 September 2010.

[111] Commission, 'Communication—Our Life Insurance, Our Natural Capital: An EU Biodiversity Strategy to 2020' COM(2011) 244, 6–7 ('2020 Biodiversity Strategy'); and endorsement by Council, 'Conclusions—EU Biodiversity Strategy to 2020', 23 June 2011.

[112] The EU 2020 headline target reads: 'halting the loss of biodiversity and the degradation of ecosystem services in the EU by 2020, and restoring them in so far as feasible, while stepping up the EU contribution to averting global biodiversity loss' (COM(2011) 244 (n 111 above), 2).

[113] For comprehensive analysis, see Kulovesi, Morgera and Muñoz (n 10 above).

[114] Eg, UNFCCC, Views related to carbon dioxide capture and storage in geological formations as a possible mitigation technology, Submission from Parties (2010) UN Doc FCCC/SBSTA/2010/MISC.2, 32–42.

bilateral and inter-regional measures have so far been exerted in an ad hoc fashion,[115] particularly when compared with similar efforts in the area of climate change.[116] While the EU has prominently mainstreamed climate change into the unilateral and bilateral tools of its external relations, with specific climate change cooperation clauses in recent bilateral/inter-regional agreements,[117] specific references to biodiversity cooperation can be found only in some inter-regional and bilateral treaties, such as Partnership and Cooperation Agreements between the EU and countries from the Commonwealth of Independent States.[118] Furthermore, the trade and sustainable development chapters of certain post-Global Europe agreements limit themselves to supporting the implementation of the Convention on Biological Diversity, its Biosafety Protocol and the Convention on International Trade in Endangered Species.[119] Only in two notable exceptions[120] is the protection of traditional knowledge of indigenous peoples and local communities identified as an area for cooperation.

Traditional knowledge refers to knowledge, innovations and practices of indigenous and local communities embodying traditional lifestyles relevant for the conservation and sustainable use of biodiversity, according to the CBD.[121] Cooperation on traditional knowledge sits at the intersection between international biodiversity law and the protection of human rights: it would thus appear as an ideal area in which the EU can pursue its external relations goals of supporting human rights, and fostering the

[115] E Morgera, 'The Trajectory of EU Biodiversity Cooperation: Supporting Environmental Multilateralism through EU External Action' in Morgera (n 2 above) 235.

[116] K Kulovesi, 'Climate Change in EU External Relations: Please Follow My Example (or I Might Force You to)' in Morgera (n 2 above) 115.

[117] Eg Free Trade Agreement between the EU and its Member States, of the first part, and Colombia and Peru, of the other, [2012] OJ L354/3 (COPE FTA), Art 63; Free Trade Agreement between the European Union and its Member States, of the first part, and the Republic of Korea, of the other part, [2011] OJ L127/4 (South Korea FTA), Art 13.5(3).

[118] Which feature the same, detailed article on cooperation on the conservation of biodiversity, protected areas and the sustainable use and management of biological resources: eg, Partnership and Cooperation Agreement between the European Communities and their Member States, of the one part, and the Republic of Armenia, of the other part, [1999] OJ L239/3, Art 55(2).

[119] COPE FTA, Art 267(2)(b) and 270(2); South Korea FTA, Art 13.11.

[120] Economic Partnership Agreement between the CARIFORUM States, of the one part, and the European Community and its Member States, of the other [2008] OJ L289/3 (EU-CARIFORUM EPA), Art 150(1); (COPE FTA), Art 272.

[121] CBD Article 8(j) reads: 'Each Contracting Party shall, as far as possible and as appropriate: ... Subject to its national legislation, respect, preserve and maintain knowledge, innovations and practices of indigenous and local communities embodying traditional lifestyles relevant for the conservation and sustainable use of biological diversity and promote their wider application with the approval and involvement of the holders of such knowledge, innovations and practices and encourage the equitable sharing of the benefits arising from the utilization of such knowledge, innovations and practices'.

sustainable development of developing countries, with the primary aim of eradicating poverty.[122] Following the adoption of the Nagoya Protocol,[123] the significant implications from a human rights perspective of the protection of traditional knowledge in the biodiversity context have become more evident.[124]

Policy dialogues have also served to review the outcomes of ongoing multilateral negotiations sessions, to discuss and better understand respective negotiating positions, and in the case of the most cooperative partners (Africa, Mexico and Japan, for instance) formally commit to prepare joint negotiating positions, including in the case of the Nagoya Protocol.[125] But the EU has not institutionalised biodiversity-specific cooperation and dialogue initiatives in a way comparable to the Global Climate Change Alliance.[126]

With regards to external funding, the Commission concluded in 2011 that 'biodiversity is … a relatively low priority for EU external aid, as it gets less than 1/50 of EU and Member States' total annual development aid budgets'.[127] This is certainly in stark contrast with the significant financial and technical assistance targeted by the EU to various issues related to ongoing multilateral climate negotiations, such as the reform of the Kyoto Protocol's Clean Development Mechanism (CDM), adaptation, low-emissions development strategies and new market mechanisms.[128] The Commission thus proposed increased emphasis for the period 2011–13 on the protection of biodiversity and ecosystems in its thematic funding, including in relation to access and benefit-sharing (ABS).[129]

As emerges from this brief overview of internal, as well as bilateral and inter-regional external relations instruments adopted by the EU in relation to biodiversity, the adoption of the Nagoya Protocol represents a significant

[122] Art 21(b) and (d) TEU.

[123] For a discussion of the Nagoya Protocol from an EU perspective, see M Buck and C Hamilton, 'The Nagoya Protocol on Access to Genetic Resources and the Fair and Equitable Sharing of Benefits Arising from their Utilisation to the Convention on Biological Diversity' (2011) 20 *RECIEL* 47.

[124] A Savaresi, 'The International Human Rights Law Implications of the Nagoya Protocol' in E Morgera, M Buck and E Tsioumani (eds), *The 2010 Nagoya Protocol on Access and Benefit-sharing in Perspective: Implications for International Law and Implementation Challenges* (Leiden/Boston MA, Martinus Nijhoff, 2013) 53; and E Morgera, E Tsioumani and M Buck, *Unraveling the Nagoya Protocol: A Commentary on the 2010 Protocol on Access and Benefit-sharing to the Convention on Biological Diversity* (Leiden/Boston MA, Brill Nijhoff, 2014).

[125] 18th Japan-EU Summit, 'Joint Press Statement' (9454/09 (Presse 113) 2009) para 15.

[126] See: www.gcca.eu. For a discussion, Marín Durán and Morgera (n 3 above) 229.

[127] Commission, 'Impact Assessment Accompanying the Communication—Our Life Insurance, Our Natural Capital: an EU Biodiversity Strategy to 2020', SEC(2011) 540, 16.

[128] Commission, 'Environment and Natural Resources Thematic Programme—2011–2013 Strategy Paper and Multiannual Indicative Programme' (ENRTP Strategy 2011–13), 29 October 2010, 9 and 13.

[129] ENRTP Strategy 2011–2013, 7, 17 and 23.

opportunity for the EU to step up its efforts to contribute to environmental multilateralism in as far as biodiversity cooperation is concerned.

B. A Primer on the Nagoya Protocol: Opportunities for the EU and Risks Arising from Vested Interests

The Nagoya Protocol on Access and Benefit-Sharing is an innovative environmental treaty that has significantly developed the international biodiversity regime. It details new international obligations to ensure equity between countries that provide access to genetic resources and traditional knowledge, and countries that use them for commercial research and development (R&D) purposes.[130] The Protocol envisages a *bilateral*[131] inter-state arrangement for sharing with the country providing genetic resources the monetary and non-monetary benefits arising from R&D conducted by the country that sought access to these resources. In the specific context of these transactions, benefit-sharing is expected to operationalise equity in relation to the uneven natural distribution of genetic resources across different countries and the unevenly distributed capacities to develop these resources. It thus aims at striking a fair balance between the claims of a user country (and of its individual users) to obtain vital and unique material for scientific research and to protect resulting inventions that require considerable risk, time and effort in being developed, on the one hand, and the rights of provider countries (and of their indigenous peoples and local communities) to obtain equitable rewards for the genetic resources and traditional knowledge that they have conserved, on the other.[132] The continued political tension between the two sides (access and benefit-sharing respectively) of the transnational relation of exchange regulated by the Protocol, however, has led to compromise language and frequent interpretative ambiguities in the Protocol.

Nonetheless, the Nagoya Protocol is notable for spelling out the rights of indigenous peoples and local communities to their traditional knowledge and to genetic resources held by them.[133] The Protocol requires state parties to take the appropriate measures to ensure that these genetic resources and traditional knowledge are accessed with the prior informed consent

130 Morgera, Tsioumani and Buck (n 124 above) on Article 1, 48–52.

131 Although note the possibility for a multilateral benefit-sharing mechanism to be established under Nagoya Protocol, Article 10: see Morgera, Tsioumani and Buck (n 124 above) 197–208.

132 Francesco Francioni, *Genetic Resources, Biotechnology and Human Rights: The International Legal Framework*, Working Paper (Florence, European University Institute, 2006): cadmus.eui.eu/handle/1814/6070, at 20–21.

133 Morgera, Tsioumani and Buck (n 124 above), 382–84.

(or approval and involvement) of indigenous and local communities.[134] It also requires that benefits arising from the utilisation of these resources and knowledge are shared in a fair and equitable way and on mutually agreed terms with them.[135] Other relevant obligations are of a procedural nature and reflect both the recognition of communities' customary laws and procedures by domestic legal systems and the establishment of mechanisms to facilitate implementation of ABS-related regulations with regard to traditional knowledge.[136] In addition, parties to the Nagoya Protocol are to proactively support communities' implementation of national ABS regulations, by empowering and preparing them to develop ABS arrangements.[137] The implementation of all these provisions will be particularly challenging, in developed and developing countries alike,[138] thus providing a fertile ground for cooperation both on legislative development and on institutional and stakeholder capacity-building. As already highlighted, this in principle provides a golden opportunity for the EU to pursue its objectives related to human rights and sustainable development in its external relations.

Another novel and challenging aspect of the Protocol is compliance, which fundamentally rests on bilateral cooperation between provider and user countries. The Protocol requires parties to take 'appropriate, effective and proportionate legislative, administrative or policy measures' to ensure that genetic resources and traditional knowledge utilised within their jurisdiction have been accessed in accordance with the legislation and requirements of the party that provided them.[139] This provision makes national legislation of both the provider and the user country indispensable for implementing the Nagoya Protocol's requirements. Implementation of such provisions would require the establishment of some kind of mechanism in countries with users in their jurisdiction that would ensure that these users receive information on, and respect, the legislation of the countries that have provided the genetic resources or traditional knowledge. Parties have thus to ensure inter-operability[140] among their respective domestic measures on ABS, compliance, as well as inter-operability with compliance-related multilateral tools established by the Protocol, namely an

[134] Nagoya Protocol, Arts 6(2) and 7. Morgera, Tsioumani and Buck (n 124 above) 145–56 and 170–77.

[135] Nagoya Protocol, Art 5(1)–(2) and (5). Morgera, Tsioumani and Buck (n 124 above) 117–30.

[136] Nagoya Protocol, Art 12. Morgera, Tsioumani and Buck (n 124 above) 216–28.

[137] Nagoya Protocol, Arts 21–22. Morgera, Tsioumani and Buck (n 124 above) 301–13.

[138] See the review of implementation challenges in different regions in Part II of Morgera, Buck and Tsioumani (n 124 above).

[139] Nagoya Protocol, Arts 15 and 16. Morgera, Tsioumani and Buck (n 124 above) 249–70.

[140] T Young, 'An international cooperation perspective on the Implementation of the Nagoya Protocol' in Morgera, Buck and Tsioumani (n 124 above) 451.

international clearing-house,[141] an internationally recognised certificate of compliance,[142] and multilateral compliance mechanisms and procedures.[143] This provides in principle an ideal background for the EU to further experiment in the co-generation of norms with third countries in support of environmental multilateralism. It would be particularly useful in identifying specific and inter-operable mechanisms for the implementation of the Nagoya Protocol, which—due to unresolved issues between the access and benefit-sharing sides of its negotiations—leaves considerable discretion at the national level.

Overall, the implementation of the Protocol entails complex and creative links between different areas of international law, such as (but not limited to) international environmental and human rights law (which are key priorities for EU external relations), a dynamic web of national laws of provider and user countries[144] and contractual arrangements between private parties feeding into a system of internationally recognised certificates, and the respect for the customary laws of local and indigenous communities at all these regulatory levels.[145] In the face of this complexity, genuine cooperation is needed among parties to the Protocol at the bilateral, regional and multilateral levels.[146] This multi-level cooperative effort, however, may be in conflict with the vested interests of user countries interested in obtaining access to the genetic resources and traditional knowledge found in developing provider countries.

Such vested interests may likely play out when user countries such as EU Member States legislate to implement the Nagoya Protocol, as there is a risk that the open-ended or unclear provisions of the Protocol are interpreted to unduly favour European biotech interests rather than the international community's interest in effective implementation of the Protocol. Good faith[147] is therefore key to interpreting and implementing the Nagoya Protocol when developing EU and its Member States' own frameworks on benefit-sharing,[148] access,[149] and on ensuring individual users' compliance[150] with a view to ensuring inter-operability. These measures are to be *reasonably*

[141] Nagoya Protocol, Art 14. Morgera, Tsioumani and Buck (n 124 above) 237–48.

[142] Nagoya Protocol, Art 17(3)–(4). Morgera, Tsioumani and Buck (n 124 above) 279–82.

[143] Nagoya Protocol Art 30. Morgera, Tsioumani and Buck (n 124 above) 346–62.

[144] Although CBD developed-country parties have mostly characterised themselves as user countries and developing ones as provider countries, '[p]arties that are countries of origin of genetic resources may be both users and providers and that parties that have acquired these genetic resources in accordance with the Convention on Biological Diversity may also be both users and providers' (CBD Decision VII/19 D, Recital 16).

[145] S Vermeylen, 'The Nagoya Protocol and Customary Law: The Paradox of Narratives in the Law' (2013) 9 *Law Environment and Development Journal* 185.

[146] See generally Young (n 140 above).

[147] Morgera, Tsioumani and Buck (n 124 above) 377–81.

[148] Morgera, Tsioumani and Buck (n 124 above) 110–35.

[149] Nagoya Protocol, Arts 6–7.

[150] Nagoya Protocol, Arts 15–16.

appropriate in embodying Parties' *best possible efforts* to reach the objective of the Protocol—the fair and equitable benefit-sharing among states and towards indigenous peoples and local communities, with a view to contributing to the conservation and sustainable use of biodiversity.[151]

Vested interests may also play out when user countries act as providers of financial and technological assistance,[152] as well as capacity-building[153] that are badly needed by developing provider countries. User countries could use such assistance to create conditions in provider countries that unduly favour the access side of the exchange. Specific approaches to funding, capacity-building, and technology transfer may unduly favour the interests of user countries when provider countries find themselves dependent on external support or are offered ready-made solutions that may not respond to their particular circumstances. Good faith is thus critical in assessing whether the EU and its Member States' implementation of their solidarity obligations is in the interest of the international community in the effective implementation of the Protocol (on the basis of respect for provider countries' exercise of their national sovereignty over their genetic resources and on the human rights of indigenous peoples and local communities), or in their own interest to ensure predictability and expediency for their own users.

In addition, vested interests may undermine the bilateral cooperation that is needed for the detection and follow-up in user countries of possible breaches of provider countries' domestic measures implementing the Protocol.[154] User countries may create unnecessary obstacles or devote insufficient resources to the detection of violators in their jurisdictions, rather than effectively responding to the expectations and reasonable requests from other parties. Good faith efforts are thus required in the establishment of effective administrative control systems and the exercise of an appropriate level of vigilance in enforcement[155]—by relying on all tools provided to that end by the Protocol at the multilateral and national

[151] Note that the EU argued in the negotiations of the Protocol that 'access' should have been included on an equal footing with 'benefit-sharing' in the objective of the Protocol: EU proposal to this end in Report of the first part of the ninth meeting of the CBD Working Group on Access and Benefit-sharing, (2010) UN Doc UNEP/CBD/WG-ABS/9/3, p 19.

[152] Nagoya Protocol, Arts 23 and 25. Morgera, Tsioumani and Buck (n 124 above) 314–21 and 325–32.

[153] Ibid, Art 22.

[154] Ibid, Arts 15–16. Morgera, Tsioumani and Buck (n 124 above), 249–70.

[155] ICJ, *Case concerning Pulp Mills on the River Uruguay (Argentina v Uruguay)* [2010] ICJ Rep 14, para 197 ('*Pulp Mills* case'); ITLOS, *Responsibilities and obligations of States sponsoring persons and entities with respect to activities in the Area (Request for Advisory Opinion submitted to the Seabed Disputes Chamber)*, Advisory Opinion (1 February 2011), [2011] *ITLOS Rep* 10, paras 115–16 ('*Sea Bed* Advisory Opinion').

levels[156]—as well as in the context of bilateral cooperation in addressing alleged cases of users' non-compliance with provider countries' laws.[157]

It can be preliminarily concluded that the delicate balance of international obligations enshrined in the Nagoya Protocol creates for the EU both opportunities to contribute to effective environmental multilateralism, and risks[158] that unilateral and bilateral initiatives tainted by vested interests may undermine the partnership between user and provider countries that is essential for the implementation and further development[159] of the Protocol.

C. Applying the Good-Faith Test to the EU's Contribution to the Development and Implementation of the Nagoya Protocol

The Nagoya Protocol, therefore, provides ideal ground to apply the proposed good-faith test. To that end, this section will first discuss the role of the EU in the negotiations of the Nagoya Protocol, and then examine the EU's efforts in implementing the Protocol, considering the fact that the EU represents half of the utilisation of genetic resources to be regulated under the Protocol.[160] In particular, attention will be drawn to the European Commission's proposal[161] on how to implement the Protocol at EU level, which reveals specific views about the Protocol that had already emerged during the negotiations, which were for a great part led by the Commission.[162] The shortcomings in the Commission proposal identified by the European Parliament[163] and NGOs[164] will be drawn upon to apply

156 This is particularly the case of the obligation to establish 'effective' checkpoints: Nagoya Protocol, Art 17(1)–(2); and Morgera, Tsioumani and Buck (n 124 above), 274–78.

157 Nagoya Protocol, Arts 15(3) and 16(3).

158 Morgera (n 2 above).

159 Several issues under the Nagoya Protocol have not yet been fully resolved and in some cases the Protocol itself calls for further multilateral negotiations: for example, the determination of the need for and modalities of a global multilateral benefit-sharing mechanism (Art 10) and the establishment of the compliance procedures and mechanisms (Art 30).

160 This is due to the non-participation of the US: see S Oberthür and F Rabitz, 'The Role of the European Union in the Nagoya Protocol Negotiations: Self-interested Bridge Building' in S Oberthür and K Rosendal (eds), *Global Governance of Genetic Resources: Access and Benefit Sharing After the Nagoya Protocol* (London, Routledge, 2013) 79.

161 European Commission, Proposal for a Regulation of the European Parliament and of the Council on Access to Genetic Resources and the Fair and Equitable Sharing of Benefits Arising from their Utilization in the Union, COM(2012) 576 ('Commission proposal').

162 Oberthür and F Rabitz (n 160 above), 90–91.

163 Amendments adopted by the European Parliament on 12 December 2013 on the proposal for a regulation of the European Parliament and of the Council on Access to Genetic Resources and the Fair and Equitable Sharing of Benefits Arising from their Utilization in the Union ('European Parliament amendments').

164 Natural Justice and Berne Declaration, 'Access or Utilization—What Triggers User Obligations? A Comment on the Draft Proposal of the European Commission on the Implementation of the Nagoya Protocol on Access and Benefit-sharing' (2013): http://naturaljustice.

the good-faith test to these initial implementation efforts, as well as to provide an assessment of the final text of the Regulation.[165]

According to research conducted by Oberthür and Rabitz, the EU was certainly a key actor in the negotiations of the Nagoya Protocol, and has effectively enabled final agreement on its text,[166] by ensuring that a significant portion of the global biotech industry is going to be subject to a new international instrument. In so doing, the EU 'achieved most of its political objectives'.[167] This was particularly significant at the end of 2010 given that less than one year earlier the EU had failed in its leadership efforts at the Copenhagen Climate Change Conference.[168] That being said, the EU is not considered a global environmental leader in the case of the Nagoya Protocol, as 'its policy objectives were not in line with 'recognised collective international goals' and its position was 'quite conservative' and displaying 'little ambition'.[169] Rather, the EU engaged in what has been termed 'self-interested bridge building': with the US not participating in the negotiations, the EU, representing the second-largest industry in the global biotech sector, was seen as protecting biotech interests and fending off developing countries' efforts to make more substantive progress towards benefit-sharing,[170] which is one of the three objectives of the Convention on Biological Diversity.

As the prompt ratification of the Protocol is considered essential for the EU 'to continue to lead international biodiversity policy',[171] the European Commission moved quickly to develop proposed legislation to implement the Protocol. The proposal, however, equally quickly became the target of criticism from civil society and the European Parliament. In many respects the sticking points can be seen as an expression of the EU's disregard of its commitment to supporting environmental multilateralism. This is particularly significant, as the draft regulation has been seen as a 'de facto global standard',[172] giving not only the EU an opportunity to take the lead in the

org/wp-content/uploads/pdf/Submission-EU-ABS-Regulation.pdf; and United Nations University (UNU), Natural Justice and Berne Declaration, 'The Ambiguous March to Equity: A Commentary on the Limitations of the European Union Regulation on Access and Benefit-sharing' (2014): www.evb.ch/fileadmin/files/documents/Biodiversitaet/KORR_The_Ambiguous_March_to_Equity.pdf.

165 Regulation (EU) No 511/2014 of the European Parliament and the Council of 16 April 2014 on compliance measures for users from the Nagoya Protocol on Access to Genetic Resources and the Fair and Equitable Sharing of Benefits Arising from their Utilization in the Union, [2014] OJ L150/59—('Final Regulation')—which entered into force on 9 June 2014 and applies after the Nagoya Protocol itself entered into force.

166 Oberthur and Rabitz (n 160 above) 84–85.

167 Ibid, 79.

168 Ibid, 80.

169 Ibid.

170 Ibid, 84.

171 2020 Biodiversity Strategy (n 111 above), 7.

172 G Burton and E Evans-Illidge, 'Emerging R & D Law: The Nagoya Protocol and Its Implications for Researchers' (2014) 9 *ACS Chemical Biology* 588, 589.

Protocol implementation, but also to impose a certain interpretation of the open-ended provisions of the Protocol. The shortcomings of the Regulation will thus be analysed against the proposed good-faith test.

i. Respect for the Objective of Multilateral Environmental Agreements

First of all, the draft regulation proposed by the Commission had the objective to minimise risk that illegally obtained genetic resources and traditional knowledge are used in the Union and to *support* fair and equitable benefit-sharing upon mutually agreed terms (MAT).[173] The draft regulation's objective thus appeared not only more modest than the objective of the Nagoya Protocol, but also qualified it significantly. The objective of the Protocol is unambiguous in requiring the *achievement* of fair and equitable benefit-sharing.[174] In addition the objective of the Protocol is not qualified by reference to MAT, which are private-law contracts.[175] Furthermore, the Protocol stressed in its objective and in several of its provisions the need to ensure that access and benefit-sharing contribute to conservation and sustainable use of biodiversity[176]—an aspect that was completely omitted in the Commission's proposal.[177] In framing the objective of the draft regulation in that way, the Commission thus seemed to give more prominence than intended in the Protocol to contractual freedom and so de-emphasise the responsibility of its Member States to exercise due diligence in ensuring that their private operators effectively share benefits. It is true that the Nagoya Protocol does not contain an explicit determination of or mechanism to assess the extent to which benefit-sharing is indeed fair and equitable in the context of specific ABS transactions. But nothing prevents individual parties from establishing substantive rules on the content of MAT in their domestic ABS frameworks, as regards fair and equitable benefit-sharing.[178] The EU could thus have taken a bolder approach in pursuing the objective of the Protocol, including in light of relevant international human rights law implications of obligations concerning equitable benefit-sharing arising from the use of genetic resources held by indigenous peoples and local communities and their traditional knowledge.[179] These departures from a good-faith interpretation of the objective of the Protocol

[173] Commission proposal, draft preambular paras 8, 28. Compare with European Parliament amendment 35; and final text of the Regulation, preambular para 35.

[174] Morgera, Tsioumani and Buck (n 124 above) 49–52.

[175] MAT are instead referred to in the operative provision on benefit-sharing of the Nagoya Protocol: Article 5. For a discussion on the role of MAT in the Nagoya Protocol, see Morgera, Tsioumani and Buck (n 124 above) 131–32.

[176] Nagoya Protocol, Art 1.

[177] But an omission that was promptly underlined by the European Parliament amendment 24, and has been remedied in the Final Regulation preambular paras 9, 22 and 32 and Art 1.

[178] Morgera, Tsioumani and Buck (n 124 above) 376.

[179] See also European Parliament amendments 8 and 14–15.

have to a great extent been remedied in the final version of the Regulation, which rather makes reference to *achieving* the benefit-sharing objective of the Protocol,[180] as well as reiterating other relevant preambular references in the Protocol on the expected contribution of benefit-sharing to poverty reduction, biodiversity conservation and sustainable use.[181] The remaining reference to benefit-sharing in accordance with MAT is linked to the need for effective implementation.[182]

Two other problematic aspects of the draft regulation relate to the effective pursuance of the objective of the Protocol. One concerned the temporal scope: this was one of the most contentious issues in the negotiations of the Protocol, as many genetic resources have already been accessed before the entry into force of the Protocol. The Commission proposed, and the final text of the Regulation confirms, the explicit exclusion from the ambit of application of the EU Regulation of new ex-situ access from collections or third party transfers if the original transfer occurred before the entry into force of the Nagoya Protocol.[183] This, however, is not a point that is clearly or explicitly addressed in the Protocol, so the Commission is advancing a unilateral interpretation to the advantage of its own biotech companies, instead of supporting future determinations at the multilateral level.[184] This unilateral approach has the practical result of significantly limiting the amount of benefits to be shared under the Protocol, arguably 'undermining [its] spirit'.[185]

The second problem is the light-touch approach to state due diligence in achieving the objective of the Protocol. The draft regulation proposed by the Commission placed 'strangely light' administrative burdens upon Member States,[186] limiting the establishment of checkpoints required by the Nagoya Protocol to a case-by-case verification of users' declaration when receiving research funding or at the final stage of product development.[187] Checkpoints under the Nagoya Protocol have the responsibility to monitor the utilisation[188] of genetic resources, in order to support the possible detection

[180] Final Regulation, preambular paras 32 and 35.

[181] Final Regulation, preambular paras 7, 32 and 35, and Art 1.

[182] Final Regulation, preambular para 9.

[183] Commission proposal, draft art 2 (and Final Regulation, Art 2). See European Parliament amendment 21.

[184] Clarifications in this regard could be achieved in the context of negotiations on the Nagoya Protocol Art 10 (n 159 above). For a more in-depth discussion of open questions on the temporal scope of the Protocol, see Morgera, Tsioumani and Buck (n 124 above) 77–80.

[185] UNU, Natural Justice and Berne Declaration (n 164 above), 6–7; and Natural Justice and Berne Declaration (n 164 above), 3 noting that the interpretation is debatable and relying on V Koester, 'The Nagoya Protocol on ABS: Ratification by the EU and its Member States and Implementation Challenges' (Rskilde University, Study 3/12, 2012).

[186] UNU, Natural Justice and Berne Declaration (n 164 above), 8.

[187] Commission proposal draft art 7. UNU, Natural Justice and Berne Declaration (n 164 above), 8.

[188] Nagoya Protocol Art 2(c). See Morgera, Tsioumani and Buck (n 124 above) 274–76.

of users' violations of domestic ABS frameworks in other countries and to ensure the realisation of the benefit-sharing objective of the Protocol. The general assumption in favour of users' due diligence unless proven to the contrary that transpires from the Regulation, instead, combined with the 'outsourcing' of monitoring responsibilities to 'trusted collections' and 'user-driven remedial action' in case of violations,[189] may not be able to meet a good-faith reading of the due diligence requirements embodied in the Protocol. These comprise the need for all reasonably appropriate domestic measures embodying Parties' best possible efforts to reach the objective of the Protocol through the establishment of administrative control systems to effectively monitor activities and the exercise of an appropriate level of vigilance in enforcement. According to general international law, due diligence in this context would rather entail the exercise by states of effective administrative control over private operators,[190] so that reliance on private users' due diligence[191] and voluntary, industry-led instruments,[192] would be merely additional, but not an alternative, to states' due diligence. Overall, it appears unlikely that the *minimalist* approach proposed by the Commission,[193] which has been generally retained in the final text of the Regulation,[194] can be considered effective in achieving the objective of Article 17 of the Protocol and ultimately effectively contributing to the Protocol's objective.

ii. Responsiveness to Intervening Multilateral Developments

Another troubling aspect in the (proposed and final) Regulation when seen from a multilateralism perspective is the definition of traditional knowledge, which once again is made subject to contractual negotiations among private parties.[195] This provision is problematic because while the Protocol

[189] UNU, Natural Justice and Berne Declaration (n 164 above), 8 referring to Commission proposal, draft arts 4–6. See also European Parliament amendments 55 (proposing deletion of the draft provision on Union trusted collections), 60–61 and 63 (significantly strengthening the provision on checkpoints) and 62 (proposing deletion of the draft provision on users' best practices).

[190] *Pulp Mills* case, para 197; *Sea Bed* Advisory Opinion, paras 115–16.

[191] Commission proposal, draft art 4(1).

[192] The EU draft regulation would encourage users' associations to seek recognition of a combination of procedures, tools or mechanisms (eg, on the deployment of data-sharing tools for tracking) developed for the purpose of implementing their obligations under the regulation as 'best practice', by subjecting users implementing such recognised best practice to less intense compliance checks (Commission proposal, draft Arts 8–9).

[193] Commission proposal, draft preambular Recital 14 noted the need for 'only minimum features of due diligence' due to the diversity of users; the European Parliament proposed to delete this reference: amendment 14, which has disappeared from the Final Regulation.

[194] Final Regulation, Arts 4–10.

[195] Traditional knowledge is defined as that 'held by indigenous and local communities that is relevant for the use of genetic resources and *that is as such described in the mutually agreed terms* applying to the use of genetic resources': Commission proposal, draft art 3(8).

does not provide a definition of traditional knowledge, said definition is likely to be worked out multilaterally either under the Protocol or the CBD, or in parallel negotiations under the World Intellectual Property Organization (WIPO).[196] The EU approach therefore does not appear to support the development of a multilateral definition nor to propose an alternative that may constructively contribute to such multilateral efforts. It rather chooses to leave private parties with conflicting interests to find on an *ad hoc* basis a solution that may or may not be in line with the Protocol objective.

Furthermore, no review clause expressly triggered by other relevant multilateral developments had been inserted in the Commission's proposal,[197] even if several open questions are subject to further multilateral negotiations.[198] Instead, the European Parliament not only noted the need for the EU to 'act in a proactive manner' in relation to ongoing negotiations supporting the objective of the Protocol,[199] but also the need for 5-year reviews 'in light of developments in other relevant international organisations' with regard to traditional knowledge.[200] The final text of the Regulation provides for an initial assessment of implementation by the Commission in 2018,[201] and thereafter a 10-year review that will also take into account 'developments in other relevant international organisations'.[202] These, however, seem unduly long time-spans, if one considers the fervent and multi-faceted intergovernmental negotiations that have been ongoing even before the Protocol's entry into force and that will likely continue in the near future. While this approach does not send the right message in terms of responsiveness to multilateral developments, it remains true that should the EU commit itself to an international legally binding instrument (for instance, under WIPO), it would still be required to change the Regulation regardless of the trigger clause. In the case of the ongoing negotiations under the Nagoya Protocol, however, consensus-based solutions to open questions will be rather embodied in formally non-binding decisions, which may nevertheless be interpreted as 'subsequent practice in the application of the treaty which establishes the agreement of the parties regarding its interpretation.'[203] So a manifestation

See comments by UNU, Natural Justice and Berne Declaration, 10 and European Parliament amendment 8. The Final Regulation makes reference to the relevant provision of the CBD (preambular para 5), but otherwise retains the reference to MAT without any mention of relevant international human rights standards (preambular para 20 and Art 3(7)).

196 Morgera, Tsioumani and Buck (n 124 above) 24–30.

197 Commission proposal, draft art 16(3), which provided for a review every 10 years.

198 Which will be addressed on a periodic basis by the governing body of the Protocol: Nagoya Protocol Art 26, and comments by Morgera, Tsioumani and Buck (n 124 above) 333–36.

199 European Parliament amendment 31.

200 European Parliament amendment 76.

201 Final Regulation, Art 16(2).

202 Final Regulation, Art 16(3).

203 Vienna Convention on the Law of Treaties, Art 31(3)(b).

of willingness to take those expressions of shared interpretation on the part of the EU in the form of a trigger clause is an important indication of good-faith support for environmental multilateralism.

iii. Dialogue

Contrary to recent EU legislation on climate change, the draft regulation on the Nagoya Protocol proposed by the Commission did not contain references to the use of bilateral external relations tools to support implementation of the Protocol.[204] It only provided a minimal and non-committal preambular reference whereby 'in order to take into account the inherently international character of ABS activities, the Commission should also consider whether cooperation with third countries or regions should support an effective application of the system created to implement the Protocol'.[205] It then established a general obligation for Member States' national authorities to cooperate with administrative authorities in third countries to ensure compliance.[206] This limited approach is particularly striking, as there is much scope and need for bilateral approaches to support the multilateral process for the implementation of the Protocol.[207] In fact, the European Parliament proposed supporting regional cooperation on benefit-sharing arrangements concerning transboundary genetic resources and traditional knowledge[208]—as provided by the Nagoya Protocol[209]—and support to research and development in third countries.[210] Neither was included, however, in the final text of the Regulation. The final Regulation only adds to the obligation to cooperate with third-country authorities in compliance matters, that 'special consideration shall be given to [compliance] concerns raised by provider countries'.[211] It remains to be ascertained in the practice of the EU's relations with third countries whether dialogue will be pursued systematically to ensure inter-operability in the setting up of domestic and regional ABS frameworks, and effective cooperation in relation to compliance.

In addition, the Commission proposal did not contain any reference to possible dialogue with relevant international organisations. Instead the European Parliament underscored the need to involve relevant international organisations and representatives of indigenous and local communities

[204] European Parliament amendment 66.
[205] Commission proposal, preambular para 25; and Final Regulation, preambular para 31.
[206] Commission proposal, draft art 12(1).
[207] On the usefulness of bilateral approaches to support the implementation of the Nagoya Protocol, see Young (n 140) 496–98.
[208] European Parliament amendment 73.
[209] Nagoya Protocol Art 11; Morgera, Tsioumani and Buck (n 124 above) 209–15.
[210] European Parliament amendment 73.
[211] Final Regulation, Art 9(3)(b).

in the cooperation concerning implementation among Member States' national authorities, the Commission and third countries, as well as in a EU-level Consultation Forum.[212] The European Parliament also proposed mandating the Commission to seek arrangements with the European Patent Office and WIPO to ensure compliance with the Protocol in the context of patent applications.[213] None of these proposals can be found in the final text of the Regulation, which limits itself to calling for the inclusion of 'other interested parties' in the Consultation Forum focusing on issues related the implementation of the Regulation.[214] It remains to be ascertained in the practice of the EU whether relevant international organisations and representatives of indigenous and local communities will be involved in implementation.

iv. Mutual Supportiveness

It has already been noted with regard to the objective of the Protocol, that the EU could have taken a bolder approach in light of relevant international human rights law. In effect, the EU does not seem to have seized other opportunities offered by the Protocol to realise its own objective to ensure the respect for human rights in its external relations, and in so doing ensuring mutual supportiveness between international environmental and human rights law. The definition of traditional knowledge under the Regulation (discussed above) further proves this point. By making the definition subject to contractual negotiations among private parties, the EU opens the door for interpretations at the contractual level that may go against international human rights involved. In other words, the EU could have rather built upon the duty of states to protect indigenous peoples' rights also when granting permits to private parties relating to indigenous peoples' resources.[215] Such duty includes the obligation to provide business with clarity on the right of indigenous peoples in that regard, including when indigenous peoples do not have a state-recognised title to the resources affected.[216] As user countries and home states of transnational biotech corporations operating in

[212] European Parliament amendment 66 and 75.

[213] European Parliament amendment 68.

[214] Final Regulation, Art 15.

[215] ILO Convention No 169, Art 15(1); Inter-American Commission on Human Rights, *Maya Indigenous Community of the Toledo District v Belize, Merits, Case No 12.053* (IACHR, 12 October 2004) 194–95; and, more generally, Inter-American Commission on Human Rights, 'Indigenous and Tribal Peoples' Rights over Their Ancestral Lands and Natural Resources. Norms and Jurisprudence of the Inter-American Human Rights System' (2010) 35 *American Indian Law Review* 386.

[216] Follow-up report of the Special Rapporteur on the rights of indigenous peoples (2012) UN Doc A/HRC/21/47, paras 32–35; and Report of the Special Rapporteur on the rights of indigenous peoples, James Anaya—Extractive industries and indigenous peoples (2013) UN Doc A/HRC/24/41, paras 26–40.

territories used or inhabited by indigenous peoples,[217] EU Member States are expected under international human rights law to consider ways to ensure that indigenous peoples affected by the operations of their biotech multinationals abroad have access to effective remedies,[218] taking into account the specificities of indigenous peoples and ensuring that any barriers in this regard are addressed and removed.[219]

Overall, the draft regulation and in significant part also the final text of the Regulation reveal the half-hearted intention of the EU to support biodiversity multilateralism in relation to benefit-sharing. Even if on the face of it the Regulation aims to implement international environmental law in a timely fashion, it remains doubtful whether the legitimate concerns raised both by the European Parliament and international civil society have been taken on board in the final text of the Regulation. In effect, the Regulation appears poorly equipped to respond to the changing multilateral landscape and to lay the foundations for mutual supportiveness between international biodiversity and human rights law. In addition, it does not lay the ground for engaging in genuine dialogue with third countries or relevant international organisations to ensure that the implementation of the Protocol in the EU contributes to effective biodiversity cooperation in the interest of the international community.

IV. CONCLUSIONS

The Nagoya Protocol provides an unsettling case study with regard to the EU's ambition to pursue environmental multilateralism. It proves the need for a good-faith test to ensure that the EU not only effectively complies with its own constitutional obligations, but also with basic tenets of general international law in supporting environmental multilateralism to the benefit of the international community, rather than unduly influencing it to its own advantage. Given the variety of approaches in EU external and internal environmental action, and the importance of the EU as a global actor, bilateral or inter-regional partner and/or unilateral decision-maker that can utilise access to its significant market as leverage, further studies appear necessary to assess EU's initiatives in different areas of environmental law against their alignment to the objectives of environmental treaties, their responsiveness to the changing multilateral landscape, their reliance on genuine dialogue with third countries and relevant international organisations, and their mutual supportiveness with other relevant international regimes, particularly in the area of human rights. These aspects can provide useful pointers to assess whether genuine efforts are put in place by the

[217] Ibid, para 55(a).
[218] Ibid, para 55(j).
[219] Ibid, para 37.

EU to ensure good faith in the interpretation of multilateral environmental agreements and in their implementation through the duty of cooperation. From an international environmental law perspective, this remains a vital question even when EU measures do not necessarily raise obvious extraterritoriality or unilateralism concerns.

6

The Role of Private Enforcement within EU Competition Law

NIAMH DUNNE*

Abstract

Private enforcement is an increasingly prominent element of EU competition law. The forthcoming Directive on damages actions aims to strengthen and, to a degree, harmonise procedures for private competition litigation, while recent case law of the Court of Justice reaffirms the centrality of the right to claim compensation for losses stemming from breach of the competition rules. Moreover, this right has been presented as an essentially unitary one, whereby any victim of any type of competition infringement has, in principle, the right to claim damages. This chapter reviews the evolving framework, and considers, specifically, the role for private enforcement within the overall system of EU competition law. Taking into account the Commission's efforts to facilitate and increase private enforcement, the emerging EU public enforcement framework, as well as the substantive EU competition rules more generally, this chapter argues that, contrary to the rhetoric, private enforcement is a mechanism best adapted, and arguably most appropriate, for use only in the context of hard-core cartels. It is further suggested that the gap between rhetoric and reality is not problematic as such, yet difficulties may arise insofar as these divergences conflict with the principle of effectiveness.

I. INTRODUCTION

IT IS FIRMLY established that the competition rules contained in the Treaty on the Functioning of the European Union (TFEU) constitute, in the terminology of the Court of Justice, 'a matter of public policy'.[1] In the past decade, and in tandem with a renewed approach to public

* Many thanks to Kenneth Armstrong, Angus Johnston and Okeoghene Odudu for their helpful comments on earlier versions of this chapter. All remaining errors are the author's own.

[1] Joined Cases C-295 to 297/04 *Vincenzo Manfredi v Lloyd Adriatico Assicurazioni SpA etc*, EU:C:2006:461, para 31.

enforcement—including high-profile investigations pursuant to both Articles 101[2] and 102 TFEU[3]—the EU Courts and the European Commission have sought to establish and encourage a 'culture' of private enforcement of EU competition law.[4] These efforts gathered momentum more recently, following a number of (somewhat controversial) rulings that firmly underline the centrality of the right of private action,[5] plus the Commission's continuing endeavours to increase the number of damages actions at national level. These culminated in a formal proposal for a Directive on this issue, published in June 2013, which has since been making its way, slowly but surely, through the EU legislative procedures. This chapter considers the evolving role of private enforcement within the framework of EU competition law, in light of these developments and the broader competition context.

Private enforcement refers to the decentralised application of the competition rules by individuals through private litigation before Member State courts, typically seeking damages. It provides an alternative to public enforcement, which involves the top-down application of competition law by the EU or Member State competition authorities against infringing parties.[6] While the wider corpus of competition law comprises a broad spectrum of rules—governing, inter alia, merger control[7] and state aid[8]—the question of private enforcement relates only to what are described by the Commission as the 'antitrust' provisions, contained in Articles 101 and 102 TFEU.[9] Unlike the merger control rules, which incorporate a distinct Commission enforcement structure as a substantive element of the pre-notification framework,

[2] For example, the recent fine of €1.7 billion imposed on banks participating in cartels to fix the LIBOR and EURIBOR benchmark interest rates: see European Commission Press Release IP/13/1208, 'Antitrust: Commission fines banks €1.71 billion for participating in cartels in the interest rate derivatives industry', published 4 December 2013 (no decision yet published).

[3] Including cases against technology giants Microsoft (confirmed in T-201/04 *Microsoft Corp v Commission*, EU:T:2007:289) and Intel (confirmed in T-286/09 *Intel Corp v European Commission*, EU:T:2014:547).

[4] European Commission, White Paper on Damages actions for breach of the EC antitrust rules (COM(2008) 165 final), published 2 April 2008 ('White Paper') p 3.

[5] Namely, Case C-360/09 *Pfleiderer AG v Bundeskartellamt*, EU:C:2011:389; Case C-199/11 *Europese Gemeenschap v Otis NV and Others*, EU:C:2012:2390; Case C-536/11 *Bundeswettbewerbsbehörde v Donau Chemie AG and Others*, EU:C:2013:366; and Case C-557/12 *Kone AG and Others v BB Infrastruktur AG*, EU:C:2014:1317.

[6] See also European Commission, *Staff Working Paper. Annex to the Green Paper on Damages actions for breach of the EC antitrust rules* (SEC(2005) 1732), published 19 December 2005 ('Staff Working Paper (Green Paper)') para 2.

[7] Council Regulation (EC) No 139/2004 of 20 January 2004 on the control of concentrations between undertakings ([2004] OJ L24/1, 29.1.2004).

[8] See Articles 107–109 TFEU.

[9] Confirmed by, inter alia, the Commission's *Proposal for a Directive of the European Parliament and of the Council on certain rules governing actions for damages under national law for infringements of the competition law provisions of the Member States and of the European Union* (COM(2013) 404 final), published 11 June 2013 ('Proposal for Damages Directive') p 2.

Articles 101 and 102 TFEU impose freestanding prohibitions on certain forms of anticompetitive behaviour that are enforceable, publicly, by the Commission or national competition authorities (NCAs), *and* privately, by individuals that have suffered losses. The orthodoxy within EU law, moreover, is to view public and private enforcement as 'complementary'[10] and, essentially, mutually reinforcing.[11]

Yet the reality of private enforcement in Europe is rather more complex. Certain recent cases on access to information relating to follow-on actions in cartel cases challenge the assumption of 'peaceful co-existence' between public and private enforcement mechanisms, potentially necessitating EU-level legislative action to clarify and balance difficult competing interests. Additionally, the EU lags far behind the United States in relation to the proportion of private actions pursued, while the legal procedures and remedies available in many Member States remain deeply unfavourable. These two issues—clarifying the accommodation of public and private enforcement, and strengthening national procedures for private competition litigation—comprise the subject of the Commission's proposed Directive on damages actions.[12]

Moreover, whilst the EU competition rules (or at least the 'antitrust' provisions) are presented as an essentially uniform construct for the purposes of private enforcement, the practical reality is that the right of private action is—or will be—perhaps most appropriate, and certainly most readily exercisable, in the context of hard-core cartel violations, contrary to Article 101 TFEU. By contrast, breaches of Article 102 TFEU, alongside vertical and non-cartel horizontal breaches of Article 101 TFEU, appear to fall largely outside the private enforcement framework envisaged by the proposed Directive. A number of reasons as to why this is or should be the case can be discerned, including: the less favourable treatment of such offences under the legislative reforms; the increased use of the commitment decision procedure in non-cartel cases, which deprives claimants of a binding statement of breach for follow-on litigation; and the comparatively expansive nature of many EU competition doctrines outside the cartel context, which may render such provisions inappropriate for private enforcement. A differentiated approach to enforcement across differing competition infringements is not problematic per se, yet difficulties may arise insofar as these divergences conflict with the principle of effectiveness, an issue explored below.

[10] Proposal for Damages Directive, p 3.

[11] See eg European Commission, *Communication from the Commission on quantifying harm in actions for damages based on breaches of Article 101 or 102 of the Treaty on the Functioning of the European Union* ([2013] OJ C167/19, 13.6.2013) ('Communication on quantifying harm'), paras 1–2.

[12] Proposal for Damages Directive, n 9 above, pp 2–3.

This chapter aims to explore the evolution of the role of private enforcement within EU competition law, and the prospects for its future development. It is structured as follows. Section II considers various general conceptualisations of competition infringements as, alternatively: public offences, private offences or market failures. These differing conceptions of the nature and purpose of the competition law prohibitions serve to inform contrasting visions of how, by whom and to what end these rules should be enforced. Section III offers an overview of the evolution of private enforcement within the EU to date, including the intended reforms of the proposed Directive on damages actions. Section IV provides an analysis of the role that private enforcement plays currently, and may play in the future, within the overall framework of EU competition enforcement. Drawing evidence from the proposed Directive on damages, from the existing public enforcement structures for competition law within the EU and, more obliquely, from the substantive content of the EU competition rules, it will be argued that, contrary to the rhetoric of the EU courts and the Commission, private enforcement is a remedial option that is designed primarily for application in the context of hard-core cartels contrary to Article 101 TFEU. Section V assesses the impact of the emerging dichotomous approach to competition enforcement within the EU. A brief conclusion is provided in Section VI.

II. CONCEPTUALISING COMPETITION LAW: PUBLIC, PRIVATE AND MARKET FAILURE APPROACHES

We begin by considering the assumed nature and purpose of the antitrust prohibitions within Articles 101 and 102 TFEU. The relatively open-textured structure of these provisions creates scope for divergences about the optimal role for competition law within the larger scheme of market regulation. The rhetoric of 'public policy',[13] moreover, leaves open the question of *which* public interests, as such, the rules are intended to protect. The varying conceptualisations of competition law that can be discerned—as, alternatively, a mechanism by which to address public offences, private offences or market failures—are significant insofar as such overarching ideas have tended to inform the design of the relevant enforcement framework, and even the underlying substantive rules. This may include determination of the appropriate enforcer; the requisite legal standards for intervention; and the type of remedies or penalties to be imposed. As Crane has argued convincingly, institutions really matter in the antitrust arena, particularly in relation to enforcement.[14]

[13] See n 1 above.

[14] See DA Crane, *The Institutional Structure of Antitrust Enforcement* (New York, Oxford University Press, 2011) 128; cf WPJ Wils, 'The Relationship between Public Antitrust Enforcement and Private Actions for Damages' (2009) 32 *World Competition* 3, 23–25.

First, and perhaps most prominently, the EU competition rules can be construed as embodying a 'public wrong', as against society as a whole. The economic case against monopoly points to the allocative inefficiency, deadweight loss and welfare-dissipating rent-seeking behaviour that tend to result.[15] Thus, it can be argued that all consumers suffer where there is an overall diminution in market competition, due to the generally higher prices, lower output, and/or decreased innovation or product choice that typically follows.[16] The 'moral' case against antitrust infringements focuses on the exploitation of consumers and/or equivalence to theft.[17] Former Competition Commissioner Neelie Kroes, for example, suggested that, 'when [the EU] break up cartels, it is to stop money being stolen from customers' pockets'.[18] By conceiving of competition violations as 'wrongs', moreover, the focus is upon the infringing behaviour of the monopolising firm(s) and not merely the harm suffered.

Unsurprisingly, a 'public wrong' conception of competition law mandates a public response to breach. Public enforcement demonstrates the societal interest in maintaining competitive markets by punishing infringements, thereby deterring future anticompetitive behaviour. Public enforcement at EU level is undertaken by the Directorate-General for Competition of the European Commission, pursuant to an administrative sanctioning procedure under Regulation 1/2003[19] with full merits review available before the Court of Justice of the European Union (CJEU).[20] Although Article 7(1) of Regulation 1/2003 provides for the possibility of proportionate behavioural or structural remedies in response to breach of Articles 101 or 102 TFEU,[21] the usual sanctions are (often very large) fines pursuant

[15] See M Motta, *Competition Policy* (Cambridge, Cambridge University Press, 2004) 41–45.

[16] Although, of course, certain producers may see an increase in their individual welfare: see Motta, *Competition Policy*, ibid, 43.

[17] See eg P Whelan, 'Cartel Criminalization and the Challenge of "Moral Wrongfulness"' (2013) 33 *Oxford Journal of Legal Studies* 535; Wils, 'Public Antitrust Enforcement and Private Actions for Damages', n 14 above, 7; GJ Werden, 'Sanctioning Cartel Activity: Let the Punishment Fit the Crime' (2009) 5 *European Competition Journal* 19; and writing specifically in the US context, JB Kirkwood and RH Lande, 'The Fundamental Goal of Antitrust: Protecting Consumers, Not Increasing Efficiency' (2008) 84 *Notre Dame Law Review* 191, 196 and 202. cf C Parker, 'Economic Rationalities of Governance and Ambiguity in the Criminalization of Cartels' (2012) 52 *British Journal of Criminology* 974, who argued forcefully that the sole concerns of antitrust are economic, not moral.

[18] See Neelie Kroes, *Taking Competition Seriously—Antitrust Reform in Europe* SPEECH/05/157, Speech to the International Bar Association/European Commission Conference 'Antitrust Reform in Europe: A Year in Practice', Brussels, 10 March 2005.

[19] Council Regulation (EC) No 1/2003 of 16 December 2002 on the implementation of the rules on competition laid down in Articles 81 and 82 of the Treaty ([2003] OJ L1/1, 4.1.2003) ('Regulation 1/2003').

[20] See, on this point, *Otis*, n 5 above, paras 56–64.

[21] Structural remedies can be imposed only where only be imposed where there is no 'equally effective' behavioural remedies or where the behavioural remedy would be 'more burdensome' for the defendant undertaking.

to Article 23(2)(a).[22] Regulation 1/2003 states expressly that Commission decisions to impose fines for antitrust violations 'shall not be of a criminal law nature'.[23] Nonetheless, the increasingly high level of fines has resulted in a growing recognition that this practice falls within the 'criminal sphere' for the purposes of the fair trial protections of Article 6 of the European Convention on Human Rights, albeit outside the 'hard core' of criminal law.[24] The theft analogy finds further expression in some Member States, which impose criminal penalties for participation in certain infringements, particularly cartels.[25] Firmly established in the context of cartel enforcement in the United States,[26] the prospect of criminalisation is controversial within certain Member States, however, while 'teething problems' with implementation have been encountered in others.[27] Regulation 1/2003 additionally requires NCAs to enforce Articles 101 and 102 TFEU alongside national competition provisions where the anticompetitive conduct at issue affects inter-state trade.[28] A wider array of sanctions may be available at the national level, such as the use of director disqualification orders.[29]

Secondly, and of particular relevance for this chapter, the competition rules can be construed as embodying a 'private wrong' against specific individuals. As noted, in economic terms monopoly tends to result in allocative inefficiency, but it may augment productive efficiency through a transfer of wealth from consumers to producers.[30] Thus, the effective outcome of a competition law breach may be to disadvantage *specific* consumers (or, perhaps, competitors or other market actors) to the benefit of the infringing undertaking(s); to continue Commissioner Kroes' analogy, these are the *actual* pockets from which the cartelists have stolen. The rationale for private enforcement of competition law is to empower individual consumers that have suffered distinct and quantifiable harms attributable directly to an antitrust breach—for example, an inflated contract price following

[22] See also the Commission's current Guidelines on the method of setting fines imposed pursuant to Article 23(2)(a) of Regulation 1/2003 ([2006] OJ C210/2, 1.09.2006).

[23] Article 23(5), Regulation 1/2003.

[24] See Opinion of Advocate General Sharpston in Case C-272/09 P *KME Germany AG, KME France SAS and KME Italy SpA v European Commission*, EU:C:2011:63, paras 63–67.

[25] See eg the UK's Enterprise Act 2002, s 188, and Ireland's Competition Act 2002, ss 6–7. For a thoughtful consideration of the potential for criminalisation at the EU level, see WPJ Wils, 'Is Criminalisation of EU Competition Law the Answer?' (2005) 28 *World Competition* 117.

[26] See Werden, 'Sanctioning Cartel Activity', n 17 above, 19–22.

[27] See eg Wils, 'Is Criminalisation the Answer?', n 25 above; C Beaton-Wells and A Ezrachi (eds), *Criminalising Cartels* (Oxford, Hart Publishing, 2011); and M Furse, *The Criminal Law of Competition in the UK and in the US: Failure and Success* (Cheltenham, Edward Elgar Publishing, 2012).

[28] Article 3(1), Regulation 1/2003.

[29] See eg Office of Fair Trading, *Director Disqualification Orders in Competition Cases: An OFT Guidance Document* (2010), and A Stephan, 'Disqualification Orders for Directors Involved in Cartels' (2011) 6 *Journal for European Competition Law & Practice* 529.

[30] See E Gelhorn, 'An Introduction to Antitrust Economics' (1975) 2 *Duke Law Journal* 34.

bid-rigging of a tender—to obtain compensation for their losses. Private enforcement thus reflects more of an obligations-based approach: offending firms must make good the actual losses incurred by individual victims, a requirement that prioritises reparation over punishment.[31] Plaintiffs in private antitrust litigation predominantly seek monetary damages as compensation for pecuniary losses suffered,[32] although, more unusually, plaintiffs may seek more interventionist remedial measures, such as an injunction to end an abusive refusal to supply.

As noted, to date private enforcement of competition law remains (ostensibly, at least) under-developed within the EU, and it is this absence that the Commission sought to address with its proposal for a Directive on damages actions. By contrast, the United States is unique among established competition jurisdictions insofar as levels of private enforcement greatly exceed public enforcement: more than 90 per cent of antitrust suits are brought by private plaintiffs.[33] The framework for private antitrust enforcement within the US is particularly plaintiff-friendly; this includes use of jury trials; generous discovery rules; the availability of opt-out class actions; treble damages; and one-way fee-shifting.[34] Yet trenchant criticisms of the inefficiencies of the US approach have been advanced,—sceptics include the European Parliament[35]—while the negative impact that suspicion regarding the excesses of private enforcement has had on the development of the substantive US antitrust rules is well recognised, an issue considered below. In crafting its final legislative proposals, the Commission thus deliberately aimed to develop a 'genuinely European approach',[36] abandoning some of the more far-reaching 'American'-style procedural devices—such as multiple damages or class actions—considered in its initial consultation.[37]

Compliance with EU competition law is thus ensured through a combination of public and private enforcement[38]—'the two pillars of enforcement of EC antitrust rules'[39]—a complementary duality that is encouraged to improve the effectiveness of competition law.[40] According to the Commission, the objective of public enforcement, premised upon the use of administrative

[31] See RH Lande, 'Benefits of Private Enforcement: Empirical Background' in AA Foer and JW Cuneo (eds), *The International Handbook of Private Enforcement of Competition Law* (Cheltenham, Edward Elgar Publishing, 2010) 9.

[32] See eg Communication on quantifying harm, n 11 above.

[33] See Lande, 'Benefits of Private Enforcement', n 31 above, 4; and Crane, *Institutional Structure* (2011), n 14 above, 163.

[34] 15 USC §15.

[35] European Parliament resolution of 26 March 2009 on the White Paper on Damages for breach of the EC antitrust rules (2008/2154(INI)) ('EP Resolution on White Paper'), at Recital (I).

[36] White Paper, p 3.

[37] See generally AP Komninos, 'The Road to the Commission's White Paper for Damages Actions: Where We Came From' (2008) 4 *Competition Policy International* 81.

[38] Proposal for Directive on Damages, n 9 above, p 2.

[39] Staff Working Paper (Green Paper), n 6 above, para 3.

[40] See eg White Paper, n 4 above, p 3.

fines, is deterrence. This encompasses both *specific* deterrence, by sanctioning the undertaking concerned, and *general* deterrence, by deterring other undertakings from breaching the competition rules.[41] The primary objective of private enforcement, the Commission maintains, is compensation: that is, to 'repair the harm' caused by the breach.[42] Nonetheless, benefits of deterrence and greater competition law compliance are also envisaged as a result.[43] Whilst the latter goal has been borne out to an extent by the US experience,[44] Advocate General Jääskinen has questioned the additional value of private litigation as an *enforcement* mechanism within EU competition law, given the very different legal frameworks available for damages actions in most Member States. He has thus suggested that antitrust plaintiffs in the EU are, instead, 'simply seeking legal protection of a private law claim-right rather than enforcing a public policy'.[45]

Beyond this conventional two-pronged approach, which balances public fines with private damages, a third conception of the competition rules conceives of these prohibitions in more obviously regulatory terms, as, in effect, a means by which to correct market failures. The classic definition of 'market failure' points to 'the failure of a more or less idealized system of price-market institutions to sustain "desirable" activities or to estop "undesirable" activities'.[46] The economic rationale for a market failure or regulatory approach to competition law is, again, the overall suboptimal market structures or outcomes that tend to follow from antitrust violations. Unlike the public wrong approach, however, the focus of this third conceptualisation is less upon the *fault* of the infringing firm(s) and more upon the overall *harm* to the market that results. For this reason, public enforcement is likely to be most appropriate; not only does society as a whole benefit from the improved market environment, but also relatively few individuals are likely to have sufficient incentives to bring private actions that aim at more general market improvements. The primary aim of such enforcement is, however, to restructure the market for greater competition going forward rather than to punish the infringer(s) and/or compensate any victims.

Claims and criticisms of competition law as a regulatory enterprise are more common, and more controversial, in the US than the EU. Many US commentators have identified a (contentious) shift within antitrust

[41] Communication on quantifying harm, n 11 above, para 1.

[42] Communication on quantifying harm, n 11 above, para 2; contrast the more expansive range of objectives canvassed by R Nazzini and A Nikpay, 'Private Actions in EC Competition Law' (2008) 4 *Competition Policy International* 107.

[43] Communication on quantifying harm, n 11 above, para 2. See also *Donau Chemie and others*, n 5 above, para 23.

[44] Lande, 'Benefits of Private Enforcement', n 31 above.

[45] Opinion of Advocate General Jääskinen in Case C-536/11 *Bundeswettbewerbsbehörde v Donau Chemie and others*, EU:C:2013:67, para 48.

[46] FM Bator, 'The Anatomy of Market Failure' (1958) 72 *Quarterly Journal of Economics* 351, 351.

enforcement over time, from an adversarial-judicial to a technocratic-administrative model.[47] By contrast, the argument that EU competition law is regulatory in nature was perhaps more compelling several decades ago. Historically, the content and enforcement structure of EU competition law were more closely aligned to the regulatory paradigm than US antitrust.[48] The EU rules were applied primarily under a tightly centralised public enforcement system administered by the Commission, with distinct quasi-regulatory undertones;[49] many earlier competition cases were criticised as unduly intrusive and, effectively, regulatory in their approach to market supervision; and EU competition law incorporates a discrete single-market objective which may necessitate a departure from efficiency considerations in some instances.[50] Regulation 1/2003 has 'modernised' EU competition enforcement,[51] however, while recent years have seen the adoption of a 'more economic approach' by the Commission,[52] thus departing from the conventional quasi-regulatory model in both procedural and substantive terms.

Nonetheless, Article 9 of Regulation 1/2003 introduced the increasingly important commitment procedure, which has, arguably, re-established a distinct regulatory flavour within a sub-section of EU competition enforcement.[53]

[47] See eg ML Weiner, 'Antitrust and the Rise of the Regulatory Consent Decree' (1995) 10 *Antitrust* 4; AD Melamed, 'Antitrust: The New Regulation' (1995) 10 *Antitrust* 1; S Weber Waller, 'Prosecution by Regulation: The Changing Nature of Antitrust Enforcement' (1998) 77 *Oregon Law Review* 1383; RA Epstein, *Antitrust Consent Decrees in Theory and Practice: Why Less is More* (Washington, AEI Press, 2007); A Devlin, 'Antitrust as Regulation' (2012) 49 *San Diego Law Review* 823; and DH Ginsburg and JD Wright, 'Antitrust Settlements: The Culture of Consent' in N Charbit, E Ramundo, A Chehtova and A Slater (eds), *William E. Kovacic: An Antitrust Tribute Liber Amicorum, Vol I* (New York, Institute of Competition Law, 2013).

[48] See eg DJ Gerber, 'Private enforcement of competition law: a comparative perspective' in TMJ Möllers and A Heinemann, *The Enforcement of Competition Law in Europe* (Cambridge, Cambridge University Press, 2007) 446.

[49] In particular, under the original enforcement framework of Regulation 17 of 1962 ([1962] OJ 13/204, 21.2.1962), any agreement that might breach (the precursor to) Article 101(1) TFEU yet which could be exempted under Article 101(3) TFEU had to be notified to the Commission for pre-approval.

[50] See, most notably, the decision in C-501/06 P *GlaxoSmithKline Services and others v Commission*, EU:C:2009:610.

[51] See European Commission, *White Paper on Modernisation of the Rules Implementing Articles 85 and 86 of the EC Treaty*, COM(99) 101 final, published 28 April 1999; and A Schaub, 'Modernization of EC Competition Law: Reform of Regulation No. 17' (1999) 23 *Fordham International Law Journal* 752.

[52] See European Commission, *A proactive Competition Policy for a Competitive Europe*, published 20 April 2004 (COM(2004) 293) 7; also *Guidelines on the application of Article 81(3) of the Treaty* ([2004] OJ C101/97, 27.4.2004), and European Commission, *Guidance on the Commission's enforcement priorities in applying Article 82 of the EC Treaty to abusive exclusionary conduct by dominant undertakings* ([2009] OJ C 45/7, 24.2.2009) ('Enforcement Priorities for Article 82 EC').

[53] See, generally, N Dunne, 'Commitment Decisions in EU Competition Law' (2014) 10 *Journal of Competition Law & Economics* 399.

The Commission[54] is empowered by Article 9 to conclude competition investigations on the basis of legally binding commitments from defendant undertaking(s) to modify their behaviour or structure to meet competition concerns. Commitment decisions require a finding that there are no longer grounds for action insofar as the market failure has been remedied prospectively, but 'without concluding whether or not there has been or still is an infringement'.[55] Settling firms also avoid the high fines that typically accompany Article 7 infringement decisions. In this regard, Regulation 1/2003 clarifies that commitment decisions are 'not appropriate' where the Commission intends to impose a fine, which means, in practice, that hard-core cartels cases are excluded.[56] Nonetheless, a significant proportion of Commission investigations that have reached the decision stage within the past decade have been concluded under Article 9.

Commitment decisions are inescapably regulatory in nature, incorporating many characteristics—such as administrative enforcement, an ex ante focus, frequent application of quasi-regulatory case theories and the use of regulatory remedies—typically identified as elements of the regulatory shift within antitrust. This is reflected, moreover, in the characterisation of the Article 9 procedure within the enforcement framework. In contrast to the rationales of deterrence and compensation, the Commission has expressly acknowledged the distinct purpose of commitment decisions, namely, 'to preserve effective competition and to obtain faster changes in the market for the future'.[57] The CJEU, for its part, recognises the procedural economy and effectiveness advantages of commitment decisions, and accepts that the 'give-and-take' nature of the procedure may persuade undertakings to offer greater concessions to avoid a finding of liability.[58] The onerous nature of the commitments made by certain settling undertakings in recent years[59]

[54] Pursuant to Article 5 of Regulation 1/2003, NCAs are also empowered to accept commitments to conclude investigations; see also H Schweitzer, 'Commitment Decisions: An Overview of EU and National Case Law' (2012) 48150 *e-Competition Bulletin*: www.concurrences.com/english/bulletin/special-issues/commitments-decisions/.

[55] Recital (13) of Regulation 1/2003.

[56] See European Commission, *Notice on best practices for the conduct of proceedings concerning Articles 101 and 102 TFEU* ([2001] OJ C 308/6, 20.10.2001) para 116.

[57] See European Commission, *Commission Staff Working Paper accompanying the Communication from the Commission to the European Parliament and Council: Report on the functioning of Regulation 1/2003* (SEC(2009) 574 final), published 29 April 2009 ('Report on Regulation 1/2003') para 94.

[58] See Case C-441/07 P *European Commission v Alrosa*, EU:C:2010:377, especially paras 35 and 48; also T-342/11 *Confederación Española de Empresarios de Estaciones de Servicio (CEEES) v Commission*, EU:T:2014:60, especially paras 54–55.

[59] See, eg, divestiture of business units in several energy commitments decisions, including Commission Decision of 18 March 2009 in Case COMP/39.402—*RWE Gas Foreclosure* ([2009] OJ (C 133) 10); Commission Decision of 29 September 2010 in Case COMP/39.315—*ENI* ([2010] OJ (C 352) 8); and Commission Decision of 26 November 2008 in Case COMP/39.388—*Germany Electricity Wholesale Market* and Case COMP/39.389—*German Electricity Balancing Market* ([2009] OJ (C 36) 8).

may, plausibly, increase the deterrent power—both specific and general—of EU competition enforcement, in addition to solving existing market failures. Nonetheless, the Commission's increasing use of the Article 9 procedure has potentially negative implications for the compensatory rationale, insofar as commitment decisions include no binding statement of breach for the purposes of follow-on litigation, an issue explored further below.

This threefold categorisation—of public wrongs, private wrongs and market failures—offers a basic account of the nature, and thus the roles, of the competition prohibitions discernible within contemporary EU law. This approach is neither exhaustive nor mutually exclusive. Possible additional or alternative conceptualisations include, for example, the role of competition law as a mechanism to achieve single market interpenetration or to rebalance economic power within society—although one might, arguably, assimilate either viewpoint quite readily within the broader public wrong or market failure viewpoints. Overlaps can, moreover, arise in practice. It has been suggested, for instance, that public enforcement might incorporate a compensatory component,[60] or that greater use be made of behavioural or structural remedies within the conventional Article 7 infringement procedure, thus incorporating quasi-regulatory components within the conventional public wrong framework.[61] Nonetheless, these differing interpretations remain significant insofar as they generate differing implications for the scope and application of these provisions.

As we have seen, the public wrong and market failure conceptions of competition law favour a public enforcement model, whereas the private wrong conception suggests that an individual suffering loss is best placed to enforce the rules to recover compensation. Private individuals tend to be motivated (quite reasonably) by narrow private interests, whereas public enforcers are typically viewed as motivated by broader social concerns.[62] This suggests, potentially, the need for more stringent legal standards

[60] See, eg C Canenbley and T Steinvorth, 'Effective Enforcement of Competition Law: Is there a Solution to the Conflict between Leniency Programmes and Private Damages Actions?' (2011) 2 *Journal of European Competition Law & Practice* 315, 324–26; and A Ezrachi and M Ioannidou, 'Public Compensation as a Complementary Mechanism to Damages Actions: From Policy Justifications to Formal Implementation' (2012) 3 *Journal of European Competition Law & Practice* 536. An example of this approach in practice, albeit in somewhat unusual circumstances, is the infringement decision of the UK's Office of Fair Trading in Case CE/2890–03 *Exchange of information on future fees by certain independent fee-paying schools*, of 20 November 2006. Here, the defendant schools agreed, inter alia, to make ex gratia payments to support an educational trust fund for the benefit of pupils who attended the schools during academic years in respect of which fee information had been exchanged in breach of the Competition Act 1998.

[61] See F Wagner-Von Papp, 'Best and Even Better Practices in Commitment Procedures after *Alrosa*: The Dangers of Abandoning the "Struggle for Competition Law"' (2012) 49 *Common Market Law Review* 929, 931 and 965.

[62] See Wils, 'Public Antitrust Enforcement and Private Actions for Damages', n 14 above, 6 and 9.

for intervention in cases of private enforcement. Since a market failure approach focuses on remedying existing competition problems rather than attributing fault for breaking the law, moreover, one might argue that less demanding standards are merited than where fault is to be attributed. In terms of consequences for breach, a public wrong conception typically merits a retrospective penalty with sufficient punitive and (potentially prospective) deterrent force; a public wrong conception requires again retrospective—and typically monetary—reparation for loss; whereas a market failure approach necessitates prospective behavioural or structural market changes to alleviate existing problems. These distinctions are relevant insofar as the basis for enforcement in each instance is a *single* set of competition rules; yet the manner in which these rules are applied, and may subsequently evolve, can differ significantly depending upon the perceived role that the rules play within the overall legal framework.

III. THE EVOLUTION OF PRIVATE ENFORCEMENT WITHIN THE EU

We turn now to consider, specifically, the private wrong conception of competition law, and its evolution within EU law. The emergence and development of the right of private action under EU competition law can be traced according to two distinct strands: the foundational pronouncements of the CJEU, and the administrative efforts of the Commission to embed and bolster this right at national level.

A. Establishing a Right to Damages: The Role of the Court of Justice

The direct effect of (now) Articles 101(1) and 102 TFEU has long been established, with the corollary that these provisions confer rights upon individuals that national courts must '*safeguard*'.[63] It was not until the decision in *Courage v Crehan*[64] in 2001, however, that the Court of Justice confirmed the existence of a distinct right to claim damages before national courts for breach of EU competition law, albeit formulated within the constraints of the doctrine of national procedural autonomy. Thus, EU law—and in particular, the principle of the effectiveness of competition law—requires that individuals must be able to claim compensation for losses incurred as a result of infringements of Articles 101 or 102 TFEU,[65] where

[63] Case 127/73 *Belgische Radio en Televisie v SV SABAM and NV Fonior (BRT (I))*, EU:C:1974:6, para 16. Regulation 1/2003 rendered Article 101 TFEU directly effective in its entirety.

[64] Case C-453/99 *Courage Ltd v Bernard Crehan* and *Bernard Crehan v Courage Ltd v Others*, EU:C:2001:465.

[65] *Courage*, ibid, para 26.

a causal link between the harm suffered and the competition infringement can be established.[66] The existence of such a right, the Court argued, 'strengthens the working of the [EU] competition rules and discourages agreements or practices, which are frequently covert, which are liable to restrict or distort competition', so that, 'actions for damages before the national courts can make a significant contribution to the maintenance of effective competition',[67] a point of view that it has reiterated continually.[68]

In its subsequent *Manfredi* judgment, the Court confirmed that the right to damages extends not only to actual loss (*damnum emergens*) but also to any loss of profit (*lucrum cessans*), plus interest.[69] In this regard, the Court made reference to the *Marshall (II)* judgment, in which it articulated a requirement of 'full compensation' for harm suffered as a result of breach of EU law.[70] The right to claim compensation from undertakings that infringe the competition rules even extends, as a matter of principle, to losses due to 'umbrella pricing,' that is, where competitors *outside* the cartel raise their prices as a result of diminished competition within the overall market.[71] The now 'settled'[72] nature of the right to damages for competition infringements has, moreover, been confirmed by a number of recent decisions of the Court of Justice, including its *Pfleiderer*, *Otis*, *Donau Chemie* and *Kone* preliminary rulings.

Yet, in the absence of harmonised EU law governing application of the right to damages, the judicial procedures and remedies by which this right is realised at national level are determined by Member States—the principle of national procedural autonomy—with the proviso that the relevant domestic rules must respect the principles of effectiveness and equivalence.[73] An interesting, and unresolved question arises as to whether the *Courage* judgment articulated a freestanding right to damages against infringing private parties analogous to *Francovich*[74] claims for state liability, or merely reflects a more detailed exposition of the general rule that national courts must provide effective protection for rights derived from EU law.[75] In principle,

[66] *Manfredi*, n 1 above, at para 63.

[67] *Courage*, n 64 above, para 27.

[68] See eg *Manfredi*, n 1 above, para 91; *Pfleiderer*, para 29; *Otis*, para 42; *Donau Chemie*, para 23; and *Kone*, para 23 (all n 5 above).

[69] *Manfredi*, para 61.

[70] *Manfredi*, para 97, citing Case C-271/91 *Marshall v Southampton and South West Hampshire Area Health Authority*, EU:C:1993:335, para 31. See also *Donau Chemie*, para 24.

[71] *Kone*, paras 33–34.

[72] *Pfleiderer*, para 28.

[73] *Courage*, n 64 above, para 29; reiterated more recently in *Pfleiderer*, para 30, and *Donau Chemie*, para 25.

[74] Joined Cases C-6/90 and 9/90 *Francovich and Bonifaci and Others v Italian Republic*, EU:C:1991:428.

[75] Compare eg A Albors-Llorens, '*Courage v Crehan*: Judicial Activism or Consistent Approach?' (2002) 61 *Cambridge Law Journal* 38, 41; Möllers and Heinemann, *Enforcement*, n 48 above, 424–25; W van Gerven, 'Private Enforcement of EC Competition Rules in the

EU law does not require the creation of new remedies within national legal systems to ensure realisation of directly effective rights at Member State level,[76] and it is clear that *Courage* did not establish a generally applicable rule of liability in damages for private parties that breach directly effective rights granted by EU law. Nonetheless, although *Francovich* was referenced in *Courage* only in support of the fundamental principle of direct effect,[77] more recently the Court of Justice has drawn an oblique analogy between these strands of case law,[78] while Advocate General Kokott has highlighted the inherent similar of liability under both *Francovich* and *Courage*, insofar as they have in common a 'direct anchoring in European Union law … notwithstanding all the conceptual differences which may otherwise exist between those instruments'.[79] From this perspective, the existence of claims to compensation for infringements of Articles 101 or 102 is a matter of EU law, although rules and procedures for enforcing such claims continue to be dictated by national law.[80]

The potential limitations of a necessary reliance upon *national* frameworks to apply rights derived from EU law were seen in several rulings on access to material for the purposes of follow-on litigation. In *Pfleiderer*, concerning access to the administrative case-file of the German competition authority, the Court of Justice refused to articulate a general EU law principle prohibiting access to material provided under a leniency programme, despite urging from the Commission to exempt at least 'corporate statements' from disclosure.[81] Instead, such requests must be assessed on a case-by-case basis, with a weighing of the respective interests of disclosure to facilitate private enforcement and protection of the integrity of leniency programmes.[82] The *Pfleiderer* judgment created much controversy, and faced criticism that it endangered the effectiveness of various leniency

ECJ—*Courage v Crehan* and the Way Ahead' in J Basedow (ed), *Private Enforcement of EC Competition Law* (The Hague, Kluwer Law International, 2007) 28; K Havu, 'Horizontal Liability for Damages in EU Law—the Changing Relationship of EU and National Law' (2012) 18 *European Law Journal* 407; and C Cauffman, 'The European Commission Proposal for a Directive on Antitrust Damages: A First Assessment' (2013) *Maastricht European Private Law Institute Working Paper No 2013/13*, para 3.1. For a more general discussion of the spillover effects between EU law and national private law, see A Johnston, 'Instances and Analysis of Feedback in the Loop-flow between EC Law and National Private law: Some Tentative Insights for Comparative and European Community Lawyers' in O Remien (ed), *Schuldrechtsmodernisierung und Europäisches Vertragsrecht* (Tübingen, Mohr Siebeck, 2007).

[76] See eg Case C-432/05 *Unibet (London) Ltd and Unibet (International) Ltd v Justitiekanslern*, EU:C:2007:163, paras 40–41.

[77] *Courage*, n 64 above, para 19.

[78] *Donau Chemie*, n 5 above, para 20.

[79] See Opinion of Advocate General Kokott in Case C-557/12 *Kone AG and Others*, EU:C:2014:45, para 24.

[80] See Opinion of Advocate General Kokott in *Kone*, para 23.

[81] Opinion of Advocate General Mazák in Case C-360/09 *Pfleiderer AG v Bundeskartellamt*, EU:C:2010:782, para 17.

[82] *Pfleiderer*, ibid, paras 30–31.

programmes for cartel conduct that exist at EU and Member State levels. This approach was nonetheless confirmed in *Donau Chemie*, where the Court held that a national rule requiring the consent of *all* parties for disclosure of material relating to judicial proceedings before the Austrian cartel courts breached EU law, insofar as it precluded the case-by-case balancing exercise mandated by *Pfleiderer*.[83] Whilst acknowledging the practical importance of leniency programmes for the detection and prosecution of cartels,[84] the Court in *Donau Chemie* maintained that an absolute bar on disclosure 'renders nugatory the right to compensation' where plaintiffs have no other means of obtaining evidence.[85] In its most recent consideration of this question in *EnBW*, however, the Court appears to have taken a somewhat narrower view.[86] It clarified that the *Pfleiderer* principle mandates access only in cases of absolute 'necessity';[87] in the instant case, where the applicant had merely claimed to be 'utterly dependent' on access without further establishing an absence of alternative means by which to acquire necessary evidence, this high threshold was not met.[88]

The introduction of Article 19(1) of the Treaty on European Union (TEU) alongside the elevation of the Charter of Fundamental Rights following the Lisbon Treaty introduced the language of effective judicial protection—guaranteed by Article 47 of the Charter—into the private enforcement debate.[89] On the one hand, the right to damages is said to constitute, or at least to assist in realising, effective protection against adverse effects of any antitrust breach.[90] On the other, questions have been raised regarding the compatibility of the Commission's administrative fining procedures with the requirements of Article 47.[91] This issue is of relevance in the context of private enforcement insofar as Article 16(1) of Regulation 1/2003 prohibits national courts from taking decisions 'running counter' to decisions taken, or contemplated, by the Commission in relation to the application of Articles 101 and 102 TFEU. This means, in practice, that a Commission decision finding breach pursuant to Article 7 of Regulation 1/2003 constitutes conclusive proof of a competition law infringement for the purposes of follow-on litigation.[92] In the curious case of *Otis*, in which

[83] *Donau Chemie*, paras 43–49.

[84] *Donau Chemie*, paras 33 and 42.

[85] *Donau Chemie*, para 32.

[86] Case C-365/12 P *European Commission v EnNW Energie Baden-Württemberg AG*, EU:C:2014:112.

[87] *EnBW*, paras 106–108.

[88] *EnBW*, para 132.

[89] See eg Opinion of Advocate General Mazák in Case C-360/09 *Pfleiderer*, EU:C:2010:782; *Otis*, n 5 above, paras 45–48; and *Donau Chemie*, para 24.

[90] *Donau Chemie*, para 24.

[91] See eg IS Forrester, 'Due Process in EC Competition Cases: A Distinguished Institution with Flawed Procedures' (2009) 34 *European Law Review* 817.

[92] *Otis*, n 5 above, paras 50–54.

the Commission sought to bring follow-on litigation premised upon its own *Elevators and Escalators* cartel decision[93] for private losses incurred by the EU institutions, the Court of Justice held that the Commission's administrative procedures are compliant with Article 47 of the Charter due to the availability of full merits review by the Union Courts on issues of law and facts, including unlimited jurisdiction in respect of the amount of the fine under Article 31 of Regulation 1/2003.[94] Nonetheless, a degree of scepticism about the appropriateness of the Commission's procedures remains.[95]

B. Developing the Right to Damages: The Role of the European Commission

In tandem with the Court's pronouncements regarding the availability and importance of private enforcement, the Commission engaged in complementary efforts to render this abstract right a concrete reality at Member State level. First, in 2005 the Commission issued a Green Paper on damages actions (which it reads broadly to include restitutionary claims), which was intended to identify existing obstacles to damages claims and to outline options for potential action.[96] Significant existing problems were identified, insofar as there was, according to the Commission, both 'total underdevelopment' in terms of actions before national courts for damages, and an 'astonishing diversity' of available approaches between Member States.[97] The Green Paper accordingly presented, and sought comments on, a broad range of options for reform, covering a wide spectrum of issues including: access to evidence; the use of infringement decisions to establish breach; the relationship between fault and liability; defining and calculating damages; the passing-on defence and indirect purchaser standing; class actions, albeit formulated less provocatively as 'collective actions'; costs; conflicts of law; and limitation periods. Although the Commission acknowledged that plaintiffs may prefer remedies other than damages in private enforcement actions—such as injunctions, or contract voidness under Article 101(2) TFEU—the Green Paper, without explanation, focused solely on monetary

[93] Commission Decision of 21 February 2007 in Case COMP/E-1/38.823—*Elevators and Escalators* (summary at [2008] OJ C 75/19, 26.3.2008).

[94] *Otis*, n 5 above, para 63.

[95] Compare eg R Nazzini, 'Administrative Enforcement, Judicial Review and Fundamental Rights in EU Competition Law: A Comparative Contextual-Functionalist Perspective' (2012) 49 *Common Market Law Review* 971; and WPJ Wils, 'The Compatibility With Fundamental Rights of the EU Antitrust Enforcement System in which the European Commission acts both as Investigator and as First-Instance Decision Maker' (2014) 37 *World Competition* 5.

[96] European Commission, Green paper on Damages actions for breach of the EC antitrust rules COM(2005) 672 final ('Green Paper') p 4.

[97] Staff Working Paper (Green Paper), n 6 above, para 29.

compensation,[98] an approach continued in its subsequent work. This article will, accordingly, also concentrate on damages actions as the predominant mechanism of private competition enforcement, although we will revisit briefly the argument that alternative remedies may be more effective or appropriate below.

Responses to the 2005 consultation were broadly positive, although certain more far-reaching options proposed by the Commission met with considerable resistance from some stakeholders.[99] Building on this work, the Commission issued a White Paper in 2008, setting out a series of definite proposals to secure full compensation through effective redress mechanisms.[100] These included: opt-in collective actions; standing for indirect purchasers; minimum levels of disclosure inter partes; extending the binding effect of infringement decisions to final decisions taken by NCAs; and making available the passing on defence, as well as specific rules on fault, limitation periods and protection of leniency material, where relevant. Notably, the Commission was of the view that,

> in line with the requirement set out by the Court of Justice that any victim of antitrust infringements must be able to exercise his right to compensation effectively, the issues addressed in the White Paper concern, in principle, all categories of victim, all types of breach of Articles [101 and 102 TFEU] and all sectors of the economy (emphasis omitted).[101]

Accordingly, at this stage the Commission took a largely undifferentiated approach to private enforcement, conceiving of it as a universally available mechanism by which to secure redress for all varieties of breach of either Article 101 or 102 TFEU. This viewpoint was, moreover, supported by the facts of the *Courage* case itself, which, unlike subsequent private enforcement cases before the CJEU, concerned a vertical supply agreement rather than a secret cartel.

Both the Green Paper[102] and the White Paper[103] received the qualified approval of the European Parliament, and, following consultation on proposals made in the White Paper, the Commission proceeded with the preparation of a draft Directive incorporating many of its suggestions.

[98] Staff Working Paper (Green Paper), n 6 above, paras 16–17.

[99] Discussed in European Commission, *Staff Working Paper accompanying the White Paper on Damages actions for breach of the EC antitrust rules* (COM(2008) 165 final), published 2 April 2008.

[100] White Paper, n 4 above, p 3.

[101] White Paper, n 4 above, p 3.

[102] European Parliament resolution of 25 April 2007 on the Green Paper on Damages for breach of the EC antitrust rules (2006/2207(INI)). Note Recital 32, however, stating that the European Parliament: '[e]mphasises that Parliament should play a co-legislative role in the field of competition law'.

[103] European Parliament resolution of 26 March 2009 on the White Paper on Damages for breach of the EC antitrust rules (2008/2154(INI)) ('EP Resolution on White Paper').

Shortly before the draft was due to be published in 2009, however, it was leaked in Brussels, and quickly withdrawn. Controversy centred upon two issues: the inclusion of a de facto opt-out collective action provision, contra the White Paper approach; and the Commission's proposal to use (now) Article 103 TFEU—which excludes the Parliament from the decision-making process—as legal basis, an affront that apparently angered the EU legislature.[104] Thus the Commission was forced to abandon, at least temporarily, its plans for legislation. Work continued at Commission level nonetheless, and in June 2013 it released a three-part package of measures to facilitate and encourage private actions at the national level.

First, the concept of collective redress, framed in generally applicable terms, was an issue viewed particularly favourably by the European Parliament;[105] accordingly, this was an area upon which the Commission focused, working alongside the Directorates-General for Justice and for Consumer Protection.[106] Following consultation and a public hearing,[107] the Commission in June 2013 issued a Recommendation advising (but *not* requiring) Member States to enact collective redress systems at national level, which should follow the same basic principles throughout the EU.[108] Although competition law is highlighted as an area where collective redress mechanisms are 'of value', the principles espoused in the Recommendation are intended to apply 'horizontally and equally' in any area where collective claims for violations of EU law are relevant.[109]

Secondly, the need to provide assistance on the complex issue of quantification of antitrust damages had been recognised for some time.[110]

[104] See P Boylan, 'Draft Damages Directive: Off the Agenda for Now', *Practical Law*, published on 28 October 2009, available at: uk.practicallaw.com/8-500-5687?service=competition; MA Sittenreich, 'The Rocky Path for Private Directors General: Procedure, Politics, and the Uncertain Future of EU Antitrust Damages Actions' (2012) 78 *Fordham Law Review* 2701, 2723; and G Barling, 'Collective Redress for Breach of Competition Law—A Case for Reform?' (2011) 10 *Competition Law Journal* 5, 15.

[105] See EP Resolution on White Paper, n 103 above, Recitals 3–6. On this issue, see generally V Pinotti and D Stepina, 'Antitrust Class Actions in the European Union: Latest Developments and the Need for a Uniform Regime' (2011) 2 *Journal of European Competition Law & Practice* 24.

[106] See eg European Commission, *Towards a Coherent European Approach to Collective Redress: Next Steps. Joint information note by Vice-President Reding, Vice-President Almunia and Commissioner Dalli* (SEC(2010) 1192), published 5 October 2010.

[107] European Commission, *Staff Working Document Public Consultation: Towards a Coherent European Approach to Collective Redress* (SEC(2011) 173 final), published 4 February 2011.

[108] European Commission, *Recommendation of 11 June 2013 on common principles for injunctive and compensatory collective redress mechanisms in the Member States concerning violations of rights granted under Union Law* ([2013] OJ L201/60, 26.7. 2013), in particular paras 1–2.

[109] Ibid, Recital (7).

[110] See eg Green Paper, n 96 above, p 7; White Paper, n 4 above, p 7; EP Resolution on White Paper, n 103 above, Recital (17).

The Commission accordingly published a non-binding 'Practical Guide'[111] to quantification of harm in competition cases, in order to assist national courts in this regard. Emphasising the principle of 'full compensation' from *Manfredi* as its starting point,[112] the Guide provides an overview of applicable analytical methods and techniques, followed by a closer assessment of the potential application of these tools to cases of anti-competitive overcharge or exclusion. Explicitly non-binding and non-exhaustive,[113] the Guide moreover urges national courts to accept a degree of imprecision and uncertainty in their approach to quantification of harm, reflecting the unavoidable technical limitations and ambiguities inherent in this task.[114]

Thirdly, and most significantly, the Commission published a (revised) proposal for a Directive on damages actions.[115] As a preliminary point, it must be noted that the utility of harmonisation in this area has not been an unquestioned proposition. Some commentators have challenged, fundamentally, the underlying assumption either that harmonisation is practically possible,[116] or that the existing state of private enforcement in Europe is such to necessitate action, insofar as the Commission may overstate under-enforcement by failing to take into account the impact of settlements.[117] Nonetheless, the Commission remained convinced of both the value and necessity of legislative intervention. The draft Directive pursues dual objectives: to address the perceived threat to public enforcement posed by the permissive *Pfleiderer* approach to disclosure; and to strengthen private enforcement at the national level to secure full compensation.[118] Notably, the legal bases are two-pronged: Article 103 TFEU, insofar as it aims to give effect to the principles set out in Article 101 and 102 TFEU; and Article 114

[111] European Commission, *Staff Working Document. Practical Guide Quantifying Harm in Actions for Damages Based on Breaches of Article 101 or 102 TFEU of the Treaty on the Functioning of the European Union* (SWD(2013) 205), published 11 June 2013 ('Staff Working Document on Quantifying Harm'); see also Communication on quantifying harm, n 11 above, para 10.

[112] Communication on quantifying harm, n 11 above, para 6.

[113] Staff Working Document on Quantifying Harm, n 111 above, paras 7 and 10.

[114] Staff Working Document on Quantifying Harm, para 17.

[115] Proposal for Damages Directive, n 9 above.

[116] See eg the views of P Pohlmann, 'Private Losses in European Competition Law: Public or Private Enforcement' in R Schulze (ed), *Compensation of Private Loses: The Evolution of Torts in European Business Law* (Munich, Sellier European Law Publishers, 2011) 161–62; and R Stürmer, 'Duties of Discolsure and Burden of Proof in the Private Enforcement of European Competition Law' in J Basedow (ed), *Private Enforcement of EC Competition Law* (The Netherlands, Kluwer Law International, 2007) 170, both pre-dating the current proposal.

[117] See J Kortmann and R Wesseling, 'Two Concerns Regarding the European Draft Directive on Antitrust Damages Actions' (August 2013) *CPI Antitrust Chronicle* 3–5. Other practitioners point to a 'spontaneous harmonization' occurring as a result: see A Komninos, 'Private Enforcement: An Overview of EU and National Case Law' (March 2012) *e-Competitions Special Issue No 44442*, www.concurrences.com.

[118] Proposal for Damages Directive, n 9 above, in particular draft Article 1, p 30.

TFEU, insofar as the Directive aims to create a 'more level playing field' for competition enforcement throughout the EU.[119] On this latter point, the Commission notes that many elements of the proposal apply equally to EU and national competition rules, thus making use of Article 114 TFEU unavoidable.[120] From a strategic perspective, Article 114 TFEU also utilises the perhaps more politically palatable ordinary co-decision legislative procedure.[121] The proposal received preliminary Council approval in December 2013, subject to minor amendments; a final compromise text, incorporating these and other amendments, was approved by the European Parliament in April 2014 (somewhat at the 11th hour before elections the following month); while formal approval by the Council is expected later in 2014.

Given the potentially significant impact at national level, the individual provisions of the draft Directive, together with relevant amendments made during the course of the legislative processes, merit scrutiny. The Directive begins, in Chapter I, by setting out its dual objectives, by restating the principles of full compensation alongside those of effectiveness and equivalence, and by providing certain technical definitions. Its provisions then address a series of issues that tend to arise in private enforcement, and which have been identified by the Commission's preceding work as presenting a barrier to effective redress in some or all Member States. Notably, however, the Directive does not attempt to establish a comprehensive harmonised framework for private enforcement at the national level, and several problematic areas, identified in previous work, remain untouched by its provisions.[122] Moreover, the recitals to the compromise text emphasise that disparities between national procedures for damages actions that are not subject to harmonisation should be accepted to the extent that these are nonetheless compliant with EU law.[123]

Chapter II addresses disclosure of evidence, and has undergone considerable redrafting during the legislative process. The Commission's proposal was to require Member States to empower national courts to order (proportionate) disclosure where a claimant established 'plausible grounds' for suspecting that a competition breach has caused harm, whether the evidence was held by the defendant(s) or third parties. Reflecting the

[119] Proposal for a Directive, Explanatory Memorandum, p 8.

[120] Proposal for a Directive, Explanatory Memorandum, p 10.

[121] In this regard, see the comments (and veiled warnings to the European Parliament) of Vice-President Almunia in his speech to the College of Europe GCLC annual conference, 'Antitrust damages in EU law and policy', SPEECH/13/887, delivered 7 November 2013.

[122] The proposed Directive has thus been criticised as comprising, at first glance, 'a random selection of minimum procedural requirements that lack coherence or structure': see A Howard, 'Too little, too late? The European Commission's Legislative Proposals on Anti-Trust Damages Actions' (2013) 4 *Journal of European Competition Law & Practice* 455, 456.

[123] Recital 11, Revised Draft Directive.

difficulties of harmonising disclosure requirements across Member States that lack existing equivalent procedures, however, the compromise text appears to raise the bar for access by requiring applicants to provide a reasoned justification to support the plausibility of their claims. It thus emphasises that only 'relevant' evidence is subject to the disclosure requirement and, at least in the recitals, indicates a degree of suspicion in respect of requests relating to categories of evidence rather than specified pieces of evidence.[124] Indeed, the revised recitals now state explicitly that '[p]articular attention should be paid to preventing fishing expeditions'.[125] Both the initial proposal and the compromise text would, moreover, impose an absolute bar on disclosure of leniency statements or settlement submissions, and would allow disclosure of material prepared specifically for the proceedings of a competition authority—whether by natural or legal persons or the authority itself—only after proceedings have been closed or a decision taken. Accordingly, the Directive seeks to the temper the potentially negative implications of the *Pfleiderer* and *Donau Chemie* decisions—its revised language echoes that of *EnBW* to this extent[126]—while protecting the integrity of on-going competition investigations. While the compatibility of an absolute bar on disclosure with the holdings of the Court of Justice in those cases has been questioned,[127] arguably these decisions were premised expressly on the *absence* of relevant Union harmonised rules.[128] Limitations are also placed on reuse of information obtained through access to the file of national competition authorities, and Member States will be obliged to provide penalties, to be imposed by national courts, for failure to comply with disclosure requirements or abuse of disclosure rights.

Chapter III addresses a more heterogeneous range of issues. The Directive would extend the binding effect of final infringement decisions, afforded to the Commission by Article 16(1) of Regulation 1/2003, to decisions taken by NCAs and review courts. The compromise text departs from the Commission's initial proposal by restricting *cross-border* binding effect, meaning that decisions taken in other Member States must have effect only as prima facie evidence, but not conclusive proof, of breach.[129] A minimum limitation period of five years for damages actions would be established; limitation periods should not run until the cause of action is known, and

[124] Recital 15, Revised Draft Directive.

[125] Recital 21, Revised Draft Directive.

[126] See eg Recitals 19–21, Revised Draft Directive.

[127] See C Kersting, 'Removing the Tension between Public and Private Enforcement: Disclosure and Privileges for Successful Leniency Applicants' (2014) 5 *Journal of European Competition Law & Practice* 2; and Cauffman, 'The European Commission Proposal', n 75 above, at section 4.

[128] See *Pfleiderer*, paras 23–24, and *Donau Chemie*, paras 25–27.

[129] See Council of the European Union Document 2013/0185(COD)—03.12.2013 Debate in Council.

would be suspended for related proceedings by competition authorities. The draft Directive also provides for joint and several liability and contribution where two or more undertakings infringe the competition rules through 'joint behaviour'. For a successful leniency applicant, the rules on joint and several liability apply only to its direct or indirect purchasers, although leniency recipients will continue to be liable to other injured parties as a fall-back where full compensation cannot be obtained from other undertakings. The compromise text also adds an additional exception for small and medium-sized enterprises, which can avoid joint and several liability where this would seriously jeopardise the economic viability of the undertaking, provided that the firm did not play a leadership role in the infringement nor is a recidivist.

Chapter IV tackles the contentious issues of the 'passing-on' defence, namely where a claimant has passed on to its own customers the entirety or part of an overcharge resulting from the competition infringement. Member States will be obliged to make available the passing-on defence to defendants, and claims by indirect purchasers are thus envisaged, although such claimants bear the burden of proving the existence and scope of the overcharge. EU law will, accordingly, adopt a markedly different approach from the US antitrust regime, which prohibits use of the passing-on defence, and hence bars indirect claims, in the interests of simplicity.[130] Under the Directive, an indirect purchaser is 'deemed' to establish a passing-on by establishing an infringement, a resulting overcharge for the direct purchaser, and that the claimant subsequently purchased the affected goods or services, although this presumption remains rebuttable by the defendant. National courts must take 'due account' of other actions for damages and judgments relating to the same infringement but brought by claimants at different levels in the supply chain. Finally, the compromise text of the Directive instructs the Commission to issue guidelines for national courts on estimation of the extent of passing-on in indirect purchaser cases.

The Directive concludes, in Chapters V and VI, by establishing a rebuttable presumption of harm in cartel cases, coupled with a requirement that national courts are empowered to estimate the amount of harm where it is practically impossible or excessively difficult to quantify this precisely. It thus echoes the realism of the Practical Guide on quantification of harm in this regard. There are, additionally, several provisions on consensual dispute resolution, including standstill requirements for limitation periods and on-going related damages actions. The Directive includes final provisions on review (rendered considerably more prescriptive in the compromise text), transposition and entry into force.

[130] *Hanover Shoe, Inc v United Shoe Machinery Corp*, 392 US 481 (1968), and *Illinois Brick Co v Illinois*, 431 US 720 (1977); see also F Richmond, 'Pursuing Effective Remedies in Private Competition Actions' [2013] *Competition Law Journal* 192, 197–98.

Certain acknowledged limitations within the existing provisions for private enforcement at Member State level remain unaltered by the proposed Directive, however. Most notably, the draft contains no provisions relating to collective claims, a previously divisive issue.[131] Whilst the proposal would not rule out an individual Member State choosing to permit antitrust class actions, for instance, it does not require the availability of these procedural devices as a matter of EU law, although further legislative activity on collective redress generally may follow the Commission's Recommendation.[132] Yet the undoubtedly pragmatic decision to address collective actions only in the form of a non-obligatory recommendation to Member States may limit the actual effectiveness of the reforms, given the practical utility of combined claims[133] and the recognition that existing levels of private enforcement are highest in Member States that currently allow collective action in some form.[134] In addition, the draft contains no provisions addressing a range of issues raised in earlier consultations, including: causation; costs; the availability of multiple or punitive damages; the necessity or otherwise of fault requirements; conflict of laws; and the need for and use of expert evidence. The assistance offered by the Practical Guide on damages assessment is, moreover, non-binding in nature, and unlikely to provide a consistent solution to recurring problems such as causation, remoteness or consequential losses.[135] For these reasons, amongst others, reactions to the Commission's proposals amongst both commentators[136] and Member States[137] were mixed, and prospects for success once the Directive has been transposed remain somewhat uncertain. It is clear, nonetheless, that private enforcement is a topic that remains very firmly on the agenda at both EU and Member State levels at present.

[131] See text accompanying n 104 above.

[132] See n 108 above.

[133] In defence of class actions in this context, see Barling, 'Collective Redress', n 104 above, and EM Iacobucci, 'Cartel Class Actions and Immunity Programmes' (2013) 1 *Journal of Antitrust Enforcement* 272.

[134] Kortmann and Wesseling, 'Two Concerns Regarding the European Draft Directive, n 117 above, 3. The authors nonetheless approve of the horizontal approach to collective redress (ibid). In favour of a sector-specific approach to collective action in the antitrust field, see P Buccirossi and M Carpagnano, 'Is it Time for the European Union to Legislate in the Field of Collective Redress in Antitrust (and how)?' (2012) 4 *Journal of European Competition Law & Practice* 3, 9.

[135] See Howard, 'Too Little, Too Late?', n 122 above, 459.

[136] See eg FP Maier-Rigaud, 'Toward a European Directive on Damages Actions' (2014) 10 *Journal of Competition Law & Economics* 341, and Kersting, 'Removing the Tension between Public and Private Enforcement', 127 above.

[137] See Kortmann and Wesseling, 'Two Concerns Regarding the European Draft Directive', n 117 above, 2.

IV. THE ROLE OF PRIVATE ENFORCEMENT WITHIN THE EU COMPETITION LAW FRAMEWORK

Having considered the right of private action—past, present and future developments—at a technical level, we step back to reassess the role of the private enforcement within the overall framework, both procedural and substantive, of EU competition law. Our starting point is the unitary notion of competition law as a single public policy, with a complementary, and essentially symbiotic, relationship between public and private enforcement mechanisms. Yet the reality of competition enforcement within the EU today, and looking towards the future, departs significantly from this plenary rhetoric. The potential implications of this divergence are considered in the next section.

In terms of public enforcement, distinctions between different *types* of antitrust violations tend to be drawn with respect to the severity of the infringement, but not so much as to the preliminary question of breach as such. The orthodox approach to enforcing Articles 101 and 102 TFEU at EU level is to view these provisions, and the many permutations by which each might be breached, in largely unitary terms.[138] The Article 7 (infringement decisions) and Article 9 (commitment decisions) procedures under Regulation 1/2003 are applicable in both Article 101 and 102 TFEU cases. Although the proviso that commitment decisions are inapplicable where the Commission intends to impose a fine means that hard-core cartels contrary to Article 101 TFEU are excluded,[139] the procedure has been applied in numerous non-cartel Article 101 cases, encompassing both vertical[140] *and* horizontal[141] agreements, and, conversely, the Commission has invoked the proviso against settlement in the context of Article 102 TFEU, rejecting proffered commitments in favour of an infringement decision and fine.[142] In its *Alrosa* ruling, the Court of Justice, too, spoke generically in terms of 'the competition rules laid down in the EC Treaty'[143] and 'an infringement of competition law'[144] when discussing the distinction between the Article 7

[138] Indeed, in a number of instances the Commission and EU Courts have drawn express parallels between the substantive content and application of Articles 101 and 102 TFEU: see eg Commission Decision of 21 December 1988 in Cases IV/30.979 and 31.394—*Decca Navigator System* ([1989] OJ L43/27, 15.2.89); Case T-51/89 *Tetra Pak Rausing SA v Commission*, EU:T:1999:41; and Joined Cases C-395 and 396/96 P *Compagnie Maritime Belge v Commission*, EU:C:2000:132.

[139] See n 56 above.

[140] See eg Commission Decision of 12 April 2006 in Case COMP/B-1/38.348—*Repsol CPP* (summary at [2006] OJ L176/104, 30.6.2006).

[141] See eg Commission Decision of 8 December 2010 in Case COMP/39.398—*VISA MIF* (summary at [2011] OJ C79/8, 12.3.2011).

[142] Commission Decision of 22 June 2011 in Case COMP/39.525—*Telekomunikacja Polska*, at 12 (summary at [2011] OJ C324/7, 9.11.2011).

[143] *Alrosa*, n 58 above, para 35.

[144] *Alrosa*, para 48.

and Article 9 procedures. Nonetheless, both the Court and the Commission accept that certain types of antitrust infringements—particularly hard-core cartels—tend to be more 'harmful' to competition than others, and thus require, for example, a higher fine as a result.[145] Accordingly, the perceived gravity of an infringement tends to inform the severity and urgency of the public enforcement response, although it does not, in itself, affect the compatibility or otherwise of conduct with competition law.

By contrast, both the CJEU and the Commission have adopted an essentially all-embracing approach to the right to claim damages in private litigation for breach of the competition rules.[146] While the Court has not addressed directly the application of the *Courage* right to damages in the context of a violation of Article 102 TFEU, the tenor of its judgments on private enforcement suggest that, in principle, this right adheres to *any* violation of Articles 101 or 102 TFEU. This expansive approach was discernible even within the decision in *Courage* itself, in which the Court considered breach of Article 101 TFEU but formulated the right to damages more broadly in term of, inter alia, 'loss caused ... by conduct liable to restrict or distort competition'.[147] This generous formulation utilises the wording of Article 101 TFEU but, it is submitted, is broad enough similarly to encompass the prohibitions of Article 102 TFEU. This wording has been, moreover, repeated in recent decisions concerning alleged cartel violations,[148] in which the Court has continued to rule in much broader terms, making reference, inter alia, to Articles 101 and 102 TFEU together,[149] and the generic notion of 'the EU competition rules'.[150] In *Manfredi*, the Court stated explicitly that both 'Articles [101 and 102 TFEU] are a matter of public policy';[151] the breadth of this statement is noticeable given that *Manfredi* involved an alleged cartel, and the Court supported its holding by reference to the *Eco-Swiss* decision, on the relationship between EU competition law and arbitration, which held only that Article 101 TFEU constitutes a matter of public policy.[152] Yet that judgment, once again, stopped short of declaring expressly that the right to damages extends to breaches of Article 102 TFEU. For its part, the Commission interprets the pronouncements of the Court of Justice as establishing a right to damages applicable to breaches of both Articles 101 and 102 TFEU, and this orthodoxy was reflected in the

145 See eg European Commission, *Guidelines on the method of setting fines imposed pursuant to Article 23(2)(a) of Regulation No 1/2003* ([2006] OJ C210/2, 1.9.2006) paras 19–26.

146 See also Havu, 'Horizontal Liability for Damages', n 75 above, 416–17.

147 *Courage*, n 64 above, para 26.

148 *Pfleiderer*, paras 28–29; *Otis*, para 41; *Donau Chemie*, para 21 (all n 5 above).

149 *Pfleiderer*, paras 19 and 25.

150 *Otis*, para 42.

151 *Manfredi*, n 1 above, para 31.

152 Case C-126/97 *Eco Swiss China Time Ltd v Benetton International NV*, EU:C:1999:269, paras 36–39.

first Article of its initial proposal for a Directive,[153] although this language has been altered to a more basic reference to 'infringement of competition law' in the compromise text. Furthermore, the Commission's legislative proposals drew no distinction, in terms of liability, between different types of antitrust infringements, focusing instead on the more objective issues of breach, causation and harm.

In terms of practical application, however, the rhetoric of universality with respect to private enforcement is difficult to support. Specifically, the Commission's proposal on damages actions appears to be intended, whether deliberately or unconsciously, to facilitate private enforcement primarily in the context of hard-core cartels. This institutional preference is, moreover, reinforced if its proposals are viewed in light of the existing EU competition framework, at both a substantive and procedural level. Three aspects of this overarching framework—which suggest that private enforcement is intended, or at least most suited, primarily for application in the context of losses attributable to secret cartels—will be discussed. These are the enforcement framework envisaged by the forthcoming Directive on damages actions; the broader enforcement framework at EU level balancing infringement decisions and commitment decisions; and the nature of the existing substantive competition rules in some areas.

A. The Proposals of the Directive

The Directive does not aim to achieve the comprehensive harmonisation of national rules and procedures for private enforcement. Given the non-exhaustive nature of its coverage, there is, inevitably, some picking and choosing between issues addressed. What is noticeable, however, is the particular—and arguably disproportionate, if the rhetoric of universality is to be respected—emphasis that has been placed on issues that arise with greatest frequency, or even exclusively, in the context of cartel actions. As a consequence, the Directive will serve to facilitate private enforcement to the greatest extent only in this area. Whilst it would be injudicious to conclude, simply by virtue of the skewed coverage of the proposal, that non-cartel private enforcement is disfavoured, the approach at least suggests that cartel cases are viewed as a clear priority for private enforcement, *additionally* to their prioritisation within public enforcement.

First, a significant number of provisions of the forthcoming Directive will apply, or address issues that arise, only in cartel cases. The rebuttable presumption of harm applicable only to cartel infringements is the most

[153] The original draft Article 1(1) began: 'This Directive sets out certain rules necessary to ensure that anyone who has suffered harm caused by an infringement of Article 101 or 102 of the Treaty or national competition law, can effectively exercise the right to full compensation'.

obvious example here, which will have the practical effect of privileging claimants in cartel cases in comparison with non-cartel antitrust claimants. A number of other provisions seek to address the relationship between private enforcement and public leniency programmes, again an issue that is only of relevance in the context of cartel litigation. This includes the absolute bar on disclosure of leniency statements, and the limited application of the rules on joint and several liability with respect to undertakings granted immunity under a leniency programme. These provisions, at first glance, would appear to limit the opportunity for private redress in the cartel context. Nonetheless, the purpose of the reforms is to clarify the relationship between public leniency programmes and private enforcement, providing safeguards for the former so as to ensure that cartels continue to be uncovered, thus facilitating follow-on litigation. The protections granted are relatively narrow, so that, for example, pre-existing information is excluded from the definition of leniency statements, while the exception from joint and several liability is disapplied where claimants are unable to obtain full compensation from the other cartelists. These provisions are, moreover, effectively of benefit only to leniency applicants, and not to all cartel participants.

Secondly, a number of other proposed reforms are likely to be of greatest assistance in the context of cartel litigation. These include the provisions clarifying application of the passing-on defence and standing for indirect purchasers;[154] and the rules on joint and several liability, which foresee multiple defendants that infringe competition law though 'joint behaviour'. Under the Commission's initial proposal, the absolute bar on disclosure of 'settlement submissions' applied only in relation to Article 101 TFEU, and the Commission appeared to have in mind its own settlement procedure for cartel cases,[155] or national analogues. While the compromise text broadens the definition to acknowledgements of participation in *any* infringement of competition law to enable use of a simplified or expedited procedure, for reasons discussed further in the next section this is likely, in practice, to relate overwhelmingly to cartel cases. A bar on disclosure in such circumstances is likely to encourage greater use of settlement procedures, and thus can be justified on the basis that it facilitates the expeditious arrival at a cartel infringement decision. Finally, the greater availability of disclosure

[154] Supporting the argument that the passing-on defence arises primarily or exclusively in the context of cartel cases, see eg M Hellwig, 'Private Damage Claims and the Passing-On Defence in Horizontal Price-Fixing Cases—An Economist's Perspective' in J Basedow (ed), *Private Enforcement of EC Competition Law* (The Netherlands, Kluwer Law International, 2007); WH van Boom, 'The Law of Damages and Competition Law: Bien étonnés de se trouver ensemble?' in R Schulze (ed), *Compensation of Private Loses: The Evolution of Torts in European Business Law* (Munich, Sellier European Law Publishers, 2011) 166; and van Gerven, 'Private Enforcement of EU Competition Rules', n 75 above, at fn 33.

[155] See n 165 below.

mechanisms will, arguably, be of greatest utility in the context of secret cartels, where the informational asymmetry between claimants and defendants is perceived to be most acute.

Perhaps most telling is the approach taken in the Commission's Practical Guide on quantification of harm. Mirroring both the established case law and the approach of the Directive, the guidance takes as its starting point the need to ensure 'full compensation' for losses incurred because an antitrust infringement. It emphasises the inherent imprecision of this task, and notes the consequent need for a degree of latitude from national courts.[156] Rather pointedly, however, the Practical Guide appears ready to abandon the conventional full compensation standard when it comes to anti-competitive behaviour resulting in market foreclosure, as opposed to a simple overcharge. Thus, the Guide suggests that,

> foreclosed competitors may decide to seek damages only in relation to the costs borne in order to enter the market rather than the whole of the profits foregone. This approach can be more straightforward than claiming competition for loss of profits as it only involves quantifying the sunk costs incurred by the claimants.[157]

Examples of such sunk costs may include expenditure on marketing or infrastructure expansion rendered worthless as a result of the anti-competitive practice.[158] This restrictive approach is significant, for our purposes, insofar as cartel cases do not, typically, involve claims of foreclosure (unless, for example, the anti-competitive behaviour comprises a collective boycott[159]), whereas exclusionary effects are common in Article 102 TFEU cases[160] and many non-cartel Article 101 TFEU cases.[161] Moreover, no explanation is given as to why straightforwardness of assessment is prioritised over the effectiveness of the competition rules in this instance. Accordingly, the Guide appears, at least indirectly, to favour certain types of antitrust injury—most typically associated with cartel behaviour—over other forms in its approach, despite the express statements of the Court of Justice that

[156] See n 111 above and accompanying text.

[157] Practical Guide, n 111 above, para 203. See also the fuller explication of this restrictive approach at para 192.

[158] ibid, para 192.

[159] See eg Case C-68/12 *Protimonopolný úrad Slovenskej republiky v Slovenská sporiteľňa as*, EU:C:2013:71.

[160] See eg Enforcement Priorities for Article 82 EC, in which the Commission describes its priorities for application of Article 102 TFEU solely in terms of exclusionary conduct resulting in 'anticompetitive foreclosure' (see eg paras 19 and 23). While the possibility that exploitative conduct may also breach Article 102 TFEU is acknowledged (para 7), the Commission provides no guidance on the potential application of Article 102 in such circumstances, suggesting, at the very least, that such forms of abuse are a lesser priority, if not entirely discounted.

[161] See eg European Commission, *Guidelines on Vertical Restraints* ([2010] OJ C130/1, 19.5.2010) ('Guidelines on Vertical Restraints'), and European Commission, *Guidelines on the applicability of Article 101 of the Treaty on the Functioning of the European Union to horizontal co-operation agreements* ([2011] OJ C11/1, 14.1.2011).

all forms of loss caused by competition breaches are recoverable as a matter of EU law.

Finally, it is worth noting that the Impact Assessment accompanying the proposed Directive considers only the effects and costs of hard-core cartels, and not of other forms of antitrust violations, across the EU.[162] In this regard, it followed the approach of an external Impact Study commissioned to accompany the White Paper in 2007.[163] Whilst the choice to focus only on cartel costs does not deny the costs that may arise from other type of violation, it does, once again, point to a notable prioritisation of the detrimental impact, and the consequent need for adequate private enforcement mechanisms, in the cartel context.

B. The Emerging EU Public Enforcement Framework

The second consideration is the impact of the emerging dichotomous framework for public enforcement of EU competition law. Article 16(1) of Regulation 1/2003 facilitates private follow-on enforcement at the national level by requiring domestic courts to treat Commission decisions finding breach of competition law as, effectively, conclusive proof of the existence of the infringement. A claimant seeking damages in follow-on litigation need therefore only prove harm, and a causal link between breach and those losses. The proposed Directive would extend such binding effect to infringement decisions taken by NCAs, further assisting private damages actions.

This synergetic relationship between public and private enforcement depends upon a conclusive finding of breach at the public enforcement stage, however. In the context of competition enforcement by the Commission, this requires an infringement decision under Article 7 of Regulation 1/2003. Such decisions are routinely used against secret cartels, for which the Commission refuses to apply its commitment procedure,[164] and are typically accompanied by high fines. Although a settlement procedure for cartel cases was introduced in 2008,[165] settling cartelists are nonetheless required to 'acknowledge their participation in a cartel violating Article [101 TFEU]

[162] European Commission, *Impact Assessment: Damages actions for breach of the EU antitrust rules* (SWD(2013) 203 final), published 11 June 2013 ('Impact Assessment') paras 64–65.

[163] See Report for the European Commission, 'Making antitrust damages actions more effective in the EU: welfare impact and potential scenarios', Final Report (Contract DG COMP/2006/A3/012), published 21 December 2007.

[164] See n 56 above.

[165] See Commission Regulation (EC) No 622/2008 of 30 June 2008 amending Regulation (EC) No 773/2004, as regarding the conduct of settlement procedures in cartel cases ([2008] OJ C171/3, 1.7.2008) and European Commission, *Notice on the conduct of settlement procedures in view of the adoption of Decisions pursuant to Article 7 and Article 23 of Council Regulation (EC) No 1/2003 in cartel cases* ([2008] OJ C167/1, 2.7.2008).

and their liability in respect of such participation',[166] and the Commission continues to use Article 7 decisions as the means by which to sanction cartels under this procedure. (Cartelists receive a 10 per cent reduction in fine as an incentive for settlement.) Moreover, enforcement against cartels is the declared 'top priority' for competition policy by the Commission, underlining the perceived seriousness of this category of infringements in particular.[167] As a result, Commission enforcement practice in the area of secret cartels has created a rich, and growing, body of binding precedent for the purposes of follow-on actions.[168]

By contrast, as discussed in section II above, a significant—and growing—number of Article 102 TFEU and non-cartel Article 101 TFEU decisions at EU level are now concluded via the Commission's settlement procedure under Article 9 of Regulation 1/2003. Article 9 decisions impose binding commitments on settling undertakings, with potentially serious penalties for non-compliance.[169] Crucially, however, commitment decisions do not contain definitive findings regarding the existence of antitrust infringement in such circumstances, and so cannot be used as binding proof of breach in follow-on litigation. While the choice of the Commission to opt for an Article 9 compromise instead of a formal infringement decision under Article 7 does not appear to preclude national courts from finding breach in similar circumstances,[170] private litigants pursing stand-alone (rather than follow-on) damages actions face the often difficult threshold task of establishing actual infringement of Articles 101 or 102 TFEU prior to issues of causation and loss. The use of commitment decisions in relation to novel or controversial forms of anti-competitive harm[171] might be seen as particularly unhelpful in this respect. Despite the Commission's suggestion that its practice under Article 9 should be treated as a 'model' or 'guidance' regarding the requirements of EU competition law,[172] commitment decisions

[166] Regulation (EC) No 622/2008, Recital (2).

[167] See eg Speech of Joaquín Almunia, Vice President of the European Commission responsible for Competition Policy, *Cartels: the priority in competition enforcement*, delivered at the 15th International Conference on Competition: A Spotlight on Cartel Prosecution, Berlin on 14 April 2011 (SPEECH/11/268).

[168] Indeed, two recent cases before the Union courts—*EnBW* and *Otis*—also had their origins in efforts to bring follow-on actions premised upon Commission infringement decisions.

[169] See eg Commission Decision of 6 March 2013 on non-compliance with commitments in Case COMP/39.530—*Microsoft (Tying)* (summary at [2013] OJ C120/15, 26.4.2013).

[170] See, to similar effect on the question of whether NCAs can subsequently adopt findings of breach, the approach of the General Court in Case T-342/11 *CEEES*, n 58 above, para 66, and Report on Regulation 1/2003, para 107.

[171] For example, 'patent ambush,' applied in Commission Decision of 9 December 2009 in Case COMP/38.636—*RAMBUS* (summary at [2010] OJ C30/17, 6.2.2010), or strategic under-investment resulting in a constructive refusal to supply, as in Commission Decision of 29 September 2010 in Case COMP/39.315—*ENI* ([2010] OJ C352/8).

[172] Report on Regulation 1/2003, para 109.

fail to provide litigants with binding precedent regarding the *actual* parameters of the law, with limited prospects for judicial review before the Union courts to clarify the law subsequently. These difficulties for litigants are compounded by the typical complexities of the causation and loss inquiries, particularly in non-cartel cases. The Commission's Impact Assessment on the draft Directive, for example, acknowledged that the higher detection rate for non-cartel (and thus, usually, non-secret) antitrust infringements is more than offset by the significantly lower rate of successful damages actions, given the difficulties that claimants often suffer in establishing anti-competitive effects.[173]

The outcome of this two-pronged approach to public enforcement at EU level is, perhaps unwittingly, to facilitate and essentially to favour private enforcement in the context of cartels, whereas private enforcement remains ostensibly available but receives little or no assistance in the context of non-cartel offences. Returning to the differing conceptions of the nature and purpose competition law from section II above, it can be seen that, while the aims of enforcement against cartels are to punish cartelists and compensate victims, in the context of non-cartel enforcement the emphasis is placed upon resolving market failures rather than imposing punishment or providing compensation. This significant divergence has, perhaps surprisingly, been largely overlooked in the case law and the Commission's work on damages actions to date. Although coordination of the relationship between public and private enforcement is an express aims of the Directive, both the Court and Commission have been largely concerned with the extent to which private enforcement might undermine public enforcement efforts, and not vice versa. Yet, the Commission's pragmatic choice to prioritise infringement decisions only against cartels, and to prefer consensual settlement under Article 9 to resolve competition problems in non-cartel cases (albeit at the expense of a formal finding of breach), is likely to have a significant knock-on effect upon the development of private enforcement at the national level. Stand-alone actions under EU competition law have, quite simply, very limited prospects for success, particularly given the significant differences in terms of legal culture and the procedural frameworks for private enforcement that will continue to exist between the US and most Member State legal systems even when the Directive is enacted and implemented at Member State level.[174] The comparative absence of binding findings of breach upon which to base private action thus compounds the difficulties for non-cartel claimants, who, as discussed, will also find themselves disadvantaged in comparison with cartel claimants under the harmonising reforms.

[173] Impact Assessment, para 66.

[174] See van Gerven, 'Private Enforcement of EU Competition Rules', n 75 above, 24–25; and Wils, 'Public Antitrust Enforcement and Private Actions for Damages', n 14 above, 15.

It should be noted that NCAs remain free to choose between enforcement mechanisms as they see fit,[175] and so are not bound to adopt the Commission's dichotomous approach on this issue. It is foreseeable, however, that many NCAs are likely to follow a broadly similar pattern in this regard,[176] further reinforcing the difficulties for private litigants in non-cartel cases.

C. The Substantive EU Rules

Finally, it is instructive to consider the procedural mechanisms available for enforcement of EU competition law in light of the general tenor and substantive content of these rules. While there is no suggestion from either the Court or the Commission that this issue has informed the development of private enforcement to date, there is an inescapable link between the content of legal rules and their appropriate enforcement framework. Moreover, a comparative assessment of the impact of private enforcement on evolution of the substantive content of US antitrust rules demonstrates the interlinked nature of these elements, and particularly, the potentially negative implications of the former for the content of the competition rules.

As discussed in section II, the different mechanisms available for enforcing the EU competition rules are, typically, motivated by differing public interest concerns, and seek to achieve differing ends. Despite these divergent conceptions of what, effectively, competition law is about, the content of the prohibitions to be enforced remains the same, regardless of whether the enforcement action is brought by a public agency or private individual, and regardless of whether the remedy sought is monetary (fines or damages) or requires prospective structural or behavioural changes by the defendant(s). The US experience suggests, nonetheless, that the procedural mechanisms available for enforcement of the antitrust rules can have a significant impact upon the actual substantive content and requirements of the law. As noted, enforcement by public agencies in the (ostensible) public interest is likely to be viewed with less scepticism, and therefore afforded greater deference, than private enforcement that aims to further purely private interests. It is widely acknowledged, by contrast, that the predominant role of private antitrust litigation within the US system has, in more recent decades, led courts to adopt particularly narrow interpretations of the substantive

[175] Although Article 5 of Regulation 1/2003 does at least require that NCAs should have the power to both impose fines and accept commitments to conclude cases when applying Article 101 and 102 TFEU.

[176] See eg Schweitzer, 'Commitment Decisions: An Overview' n 54 above.

requirements of antitrust law outside the cartel context.[177] In so doing, the Supreme Court has been explicit about the extent to which 'institutional concerns'[178]—in particular, the risk of meritless private litigation that may ultimately, and entirely counterproductively, 'chill' competition—have, for better or worse, informed this increasingly restrictive approach.[179] Significant, and what are likely to be enduring, differences in the institutional structures of enforcement within the US and the EU mean that the full implications of the US experience cannot be immediately transposed to the EU context.[180] Nonetheless, it is worthwhile giving consideration as to how and why the lessons of the US retrenchment in terms of antitrust doctrine may provide some explanation, or at least an implicit rationalisation, for the emerging dichotomous approach within private enforcement in the EU.[181]

At a doctrinal level, little separates the US and EU rules with respect to the prohibition of hard-core cartels: secret price-fixing and market-sharing constitute per se violations of §1 of the Sherman Act,[182] and restrictions of competition by object under Article 101(1) TFEU for which efficiency justifications under Article 101(3) TFEU are rarely if ever accepted.[183] Once in the realms of non-cartel restraints and anti-competitive unilateral conduct, however, significant jurisprudential divergences emerge. Minimum resale price maintenance (RPM) is assessed under the relatively permissive 'rule of reason' standard by US antitrust,[184] for example, whereas EU law treats minimum RPM as a hard-core restriction for the purposes of the block exemption on vertical agreements, and thus prohibited by Article 101(1) TFEU unless efficiency justifications under Article 101(3)

[177] See eg WE Kovacic, 'The Intellectual DNA of Modern US Competition Law for Dominant Firm Conduct: The Chicago/Harvard Double Helix' [2007] *Columbia Business Law Review* 1; O Odudu, 'Developing Private Enforcement in the EU: Lessons from the Roberts Court' (2008) 53 *Antitrust Bulletin* 873; DI Baker, 'Private and Public Enforcement: Complements, Substitutes and Conflicts—A Global Perspective' in A Ezrachi (ed), *Research Handbook on International Competition Law* (Cheltenham, Edward Elgar Publishers, 2012) 245, and DA Crane, 'Antitrust and the Judicial Virtues' [2013] *Columbia Business Law Review* 1, especially 8–14.

[178] *Pacific Bell Telephone Co, d/b/a AT&T California et al v linkLine Communications, Inc, et al*, 129 S Ct 1109 (2009).

[179] See eg *Matsushita Electric Industrial Co v Zenith Radio Corp*, 475 US 574 (1986); *Brooke Group Ltd v Brown & Williamson Tobacco Corp*, 509 US 209 (1993); *Credit Suisse Securities (USA), LLC, et al v Billing et al*, 127 S Ct 2383 (2007); and *linkLine Communications*, n 178 above.

[180] Gerber, n 48 above, 452.

[181] See also, in this regard, Odudu, n 177 above.

[182] See eg *US v Trenton Potteries Co*, 273 US 392 (1927) and *US v Socony-Vacuum Oil Co*, 310 US 150 (1940).

[183] See European Commission, Guidelines on the application of Article 81(3) of the Treaty ([2004] OJ C101/97, 27.4.2004), para 46, and the approach in eg Joined Cases C-204/00 P etc, *Aalborg Portland A/S and others v Commission*, EU:C:2004:6.

[184] *Leegin Creative Leather Products, Inc v PSKS, Inc*, 551 US 877 (2007).

can be established.[185] Neither margin squeeze[186] nor excessive pricing[187] is accepted as a theory of antitrust harm under §2 of the Sherman Act, whereas both may violate Article 102 TFEU.[188] The possibility of recoupment is a necessary element to establish predatory pricing under US antitrust,[189] but not under EU law.[190] Fidelity-inducing rebates violate Article 102 TFEU, but are rarely problematic under §2 of the Sherman Act.[191] Moreover, the controversial 'refusal to deal' doctrine is accepted, cautiously, within EU law,[192] whereas its status in US antitrust following the *Trinko* decision seems doubtful.[193] While, of course, the US and EU competition rules correspond on many points—see, for example, recent cases on pay-to-delay agreements in both jurisdictions[194]—the divergences with respect to non-cartel conduct are remarkable, even in the context of the 'more economic' approach to EU competition enforcement in the past decade.[195]

Viewing the considerably more demanding requirements of EU competition law against the backdrop of the Commission's efforts to increase private enforcement of these rules, two contentious, and linked, issues arise. The first is the appropriateness of damages actions by self-interested

[185] See Commission Regulation (EU) No 330/2010 of 20 April 2010 on the application of Article 101(3) of the Treaty on the Functioning of the European Union to categories of vertical agreements and concerted practice ([2010] OJ L102/1, 23.4.2010), Article 4(a), and Guidelines on Vertical Restraints, paras 223–29. The status of maximum RPM as an object restriction was established in Case 161/84 *Pronuptia de Paris GmbH v Pronuptia de Paris Irmgard Schillgallis*, EU:C:1986:41.

[186] *linkLine Communications*, n 178 above.

[187] *Berkey Photo, Inc v Eastman Kodak Co*, 603 F 2d 263 (2d Cir 1979), 297; and *Trinko*, n 193 above, 407.

[188] On margin squeeze, see Case C-280/08 P *Deutsche Telekom v European Commission*, EU:C:2010:603, and Case C-52/09 *Konkurrensverket v TeliaSonera Scerige AB*, EU:C:2011:83; on excessive pricing, see Case 27/76 *United Brands Company and United Brands Continentaal BV v Commission*, EU:C:1978:22, and a recent application of this theory by the Commission, in the context of commitment proceedings, in its Decision of 15 November 2011 in Case COMP 39.592—*Standard & Poor's* ([2012] OJ C31/8, 4.2.2012).

[189] *Brooke Group*; confirmed and applied to monopsony purchasing in *Weyerhaeuser Company v Ross-Simmons Hardwood Lumber Company*, 549 US 312 (2007).

[190] Case C-202/07 P *France Télécom SA v Commission*, EU:C:2009:214; contrast the approach urged by Advocate General Mazák in his Opinion, EU:C:2008:520, particularly paras 68–78, who argued that recoupment should be required as a matter of both law and policy.

[191] Contrast the approaches of the Federal Trade Commission in *In the Matter of Intel Corporation*, Docket No 9341, Decision and Order of 29 October 2010 and the European Commission in its infringement Decision of 13 May 2009 in Case COMP/C-3/37.990—*Intel* ([2009] OJ C227/13, 22.9.2009).

[192] See Case C-7/97 *Oscar Bronner GmbH v Mediaprint Zeitungs*, EU:C:1998:569, and Enforcement Priorities for Article 82 EC, paras 75–90.

[193] *Verizon Communications, Inc v Law Office of Curtis V Trinko*, 540 US 398 (2004).

[194] See European Commission Press Releases IP/13/563 'Antitrust: Commission fines Lundbeck and other pharma companies for delaying market entry of generic medicines', published 19 June 2013 (decision not yet published), and the US Supreme Court decision in *FTC v Activis, Inc*, Docket No 12-416, judgment of 7 June 2013.

[195] See n 52 above.

'private attorneys-general' to enforce these comparatively broad and, in some instances, disputed prohibitions. Whereas we may, to a greater or less extent, trust the Commission to exercise its enforcement discretion to pursue only behaviour that results in an overall diminution in consumer welfare, private litigants typically (and not unreasonably) have only their own self-interest in mind. So, for example, while the Commission has stated categorically that, in its competition enforcement capacity, it 'is not and does not wish to act as a price regulator',[196] and thus takes few excessive price cases as a result,[197] private litigants cannot be expected to demonstrate such restraint. Although, for the reasons discussed above, such actions are likely to be stand-alone and thus face an uphill battle to success, national courts are nonetheless bound, at least formally, by the expansive pronouncements of the Court of Justice. Moreover, the risk that even failed litigation may 'chill' innovative, pro-competitive behaviour has been a serious concern in the US context, while the wasted costs of unmeritorious litigation can themselves be seen as a form of rent-seeking. The comparatively demanding, and thus onerous, scope of the EU competition rules outside the cartel context therefore raises the question as to whether private enforcement of these powerful, and thus potentially counterproductive, provisions is desirable.

The second, to an extent inverse, issue is the possible impact of private enforcement on the future development of these rules. While they are not without critics—*amici curiae* in the *linkLine* case, for example, warned of 'the Potemkin village of managed competition' that would follow from adopting the perceived European approach of protecting competitors rather than consumers[198]—others defend the more expansive coverage of Article 102 TFEU and the non-cartel provisions of Article 101 TFEU by reference to the effectiveness of antitrust supervision and the enhanced ability of the EU rules to address competition problems that harm consumers.[199] The danger is, however, that as private enforcement increases within the EU, the same public policy concerns that motivated US courts to restrict the ambit of the competition rules to avoid apparently abusive litigation may come

[196] *XXXVIIth Report on Competition Policy* (1997), 77.

[197] See eg Rejection Decision of 23 July 2004 in Case COMP/A.36.568/D3—*Scandlines Sverige AB v Port of Helsingborg*; cf Commission Decision of 15 November 2011 in Case COMP/39.592—*Standard & Poor's* summary at [2012] OJ C31/8, 4.2.2012).

[198] See Brief of *Amici Curiae* Professor and Scholars in Law and Economics in Support of the Petitioners in *Pacific Bell Telephone Co, d/b/a AT&T California et al v linkLine Communications, Inc, et al*, subsequently published as JG Sidak, 'Abolishing the Price Squeeze as a Theory of Antitrust Liability' (2008) 4 *Journal of Competition Law & Economics* 279, 295. This frequent criticism is explored, and to an extent debunked, by F Wagner-von Papp, 'Rhetoric and Reality: You Protect Competitors, We Protect Competition—Except When We Protect Competitors' in N Petit and E Ramundo (eds), *William E Kovacic: An Antitrust Tribute Liber Amicorum, vol II* (New York, Institute of Competition Law, 2014).

[199] Contrast the approach of Sidak, 'Abolishing the Price Squeeze' with eg A Heimler, 'Is Margin Squeeze and Antitrust or a Regulatory Violation?' (2010) 6 *Journal of Competition Law & Economics* 879.

to the fore. This may occur at EU level, as the Union courts reinterpret the competition provisions to provide more limited protections, or, more probably, at national level, as domestic courts seek the narrowest interpretation available within the confines of EU law obligations. It is therefore conceivable—though not inevitable—that, although private enforcement may increase the extent and protectiveness of competition law supervision overall, it may result in a diminution in protection in certain areas where the risk of unmeritorious or abusive litigation is particularly acute.

It is apparent that, outside secret cartels, something of a 'give and take' relationship exists between, on the one hand, the substantive coverage of the antitrust rules including standards for intervention, and, on the other, the enforcement context including the identity of the enforcer and remedies available. This tension is illustrated clearly by recent efforts, in the US, to reinvigorate the scope and application of §5 of the Federal Trade Commission Act, which declares unlawful '[u]nfair methods of competition in or affecting commerce'.[200] Conventionally, §5 has been interpreted and applied by the Federal Trade Commission (FTC) as essentially coterminous with the ordinary antitrust rules contained in the Sherman and Clayton Acts, despite earlier Supreme Court precedent giving the provision a considerably wider scope.[201] In view of the increasingly narrow coverage of these ordinary rules as noted above, however, many commentators have advocated a reimagining of §5 to match its expansive wording, so as to catch, for example, oligopoly behaviour or incipient breaches such as invitations to collude.[202] Notably, advocates of this approach emphasise that §5 is enforceable only by the FTC and only prospectively through 'cease and desist' orders pertaining to future behaviour. Accordingly, to the extent that reimagining §5 would expand the coverage of the antitrust rules, the direction of these developments would be informed by the 'institutional comparative advantage'[203] of the FTC as an expert agency acting in the public interest, and the effects of any expanded coverage would not extend to assist private litigants seeking treble damages. As a result, the proposed

[200] Now 15 USC §45.

[201] See eg *FTC v Cement Institute et al*, 333 US 683 (1948); *FTC v Brown Show Co*, 384 US 316 (1966) and *FTC v Sperry & Hutchinson Co*, 405 US 233 (1972).

[202] See eg H Hovenkamp, *Federal Antitrust Policy: The Law of Competition and its Practice* (St Paul, West Publishing, 2011), 647; E Elhauge, *United States Antitrust Law and Economics* (New York, Foundation Press, 2008) 549; RH Lande, 'Revitalizing Section 5 of the FTC Act Using "Consumer Choice" Analysis' (2009) 8(3) *Antitrust Source*, February 2009; WE Kovacic and M Winerman, 'Competition Policy and the Application of Section 5 of the Federal Trade Commission Act' (2012) 76 *Antitrust Law Journal* 929; and M Ohlhausen, 'Section 5 of the Federal Trade Commission Act: Principles of Navigation' (2014) 2 *Journal of Antitrust Enforcement* 1.

[203] Kovacic and Winerman, 'Competition Policy and the Application of Section 5', n 202 above, 947.

benefits would be maximised, while the risk of negative consequences would be minimised.[204]

Of particular interest, for our purposes, is the well-recognised possibility that expanding §5 would be to bring this area of US antitrust closer to the EU rules, by, for example, expanding the coverage to address conduct that would constitute an abuse of dominance under Article 102 TFEU but which fails to satisfy the 'market share' threshold or falls outside the established categories of monopolisation under §2 of the Sherman Act.[205] Expansion of §5 might also bridge the gap between §1 of the Sherman Act and Article 101 TFEU, by avoiding the sharp per se/rule of reason dichotomy.[206] Crucially, however, the acceptability of this expansion towards the perceived 'European' approach is similarly contingent upon the public enforcement context of the §5 provisions. As Hovenkamp has thus argued, 'more aggressive substantive rules are appropriate [only] when remedies are limited and the rules cannot be enforced by private parties'.[207]

Reinvigorating §5 is a controversial prospect in any event.[208] This comparative example does illustrate clearly, however, the unavoidable interrelationship between the substantive content and enforcement mechanisms of antitrust. As the European Commission seeks to expand access to and use of private enforcement mechanisms at the national level, it should thus be aware of the possible impact of these changes upon the existing balance between procedural and substantive aspects of EU competition law. Moreover, it is noteworthy that controversy regarding the claimed excesses of EU (and formerly US) competition law has concentrated on non-cartel provisions.[209] This realisation thus provides at least oblique support for the contention that private enforcement is most appropriate in the cartel context.

[204] See also Hovenkamp, *Federal Antitrust Policy*, n 202 above, 200.

[205] See eg Kovacic and Winerman, 'Competition Policy and the Application of Section 5', n 202 above, 930; and AA Foer, 'Section 5 as a Bridge towards Convergence' (February 2009) 8(3) *Antitrust Source*, 2–3.

[206] Foer, 'Section 5 as a Bridge', 7.

[207] Hovenkamp, *Federal Antitrust Policy*, n 202 above, 488.

[208] Compare the views of eg Kovacic and Winerman, 'Competition Policy and the Application of Section 5'; Ohlhausen, 'Principles of Navigation', both n 202 above; J Sims, 'Section 5 Guidelines: Josh Wright as the New King of Corinth?' *CPI Antitrust Chronicle*, September 2013, with the particularly trenchant criticisms of current Federal Trade Commissioner Joshua Wright: see Statement of Commissioner Joshua D Wright, *Proposed Policy Statement Regarding Unfair Methods of Competition Under Section 5 of the Federal Trade Commission Act*, published 19 June 2013.

[209] Even Robert Bork, famous scourge of antitrust over-expansiveness, accepted that price-fixing and market-sharing cartels ought to be per se illegal under antitrust: see RH Bork, *The Antitrust Paradox* (New York, Free Press, 1973), particularly ch 13.

V. ANALYSIS

The preceding section has contended—on the basis of the harmonisation efforts of the Directive on damages, the emerging dichotomous framework for public enforcement, and even the comparatively demanding nature of the non-cartel provisions of EU competition law—that private enforcement is likely to be realised successfully, and arguably is appropriate, only in the context of secret cartels. This leads to a disjunction, of sorts, between the rhetoric of the Union courts and the Commission, and the practical reality of private enforcement as it may develop at Member State level. What this section seeks to explore is whether this gap between rhetoric and reality is problematic and, if so, why.

First, it should be acknowledged that the Court of Justice has never stated expressly that Article 102 TFEU falls within the *Courage* right to damages, although the *Courage* case itself demonstrates that non-cartel breaches of Article 101 TFEU are included. Nonetheless, accepting the orthodoxy that all 'antitrust' violations may, in principle, generate a right to damages for losses resulting, the divergence might still plausibly be explained as simply a matter of words, reflecting an idealised hope that may, eventually, come to describe reality. Somewhat cynically, one might point to other areas of EU law where a chasm exists between the statements of the Court of Justice and the practical reality at Member State level, such as citizenship, where the Court's heroic contention that 'Union citizenship is destined to be the fundamental status of nationals of the Member States'[210] remains far from accurate at present. Furthermore, antitrust is an area of EU law with a distinct commercial flavour, in which much if not most private litigation is likely to be brought by firms against firms, often with long-standing commercial relations already in place. Given this context, it may be churlish or misguided to fixate upon the formal pronouncements of the Court, or the policy prescriptions of the Commission, without acknowledging innate obstacles that exist—including those stemming from the irrationalities of human or corporate behaviour—to realising these aims in practice.

Accordingly, it might be suggested that, although damages claims must be *available* in principle in respect of all potential breaches of Articles 101 or 102 TFEU, it is not the case that private enforcement will be an *appropriate* response to every breach of the EU competition rules. In particular, for behaviour that is less unequivocally anti-competitive than a secret cartel and thus not so obviously prohibited, and in circumstances where the claimed harm is more inherently speculative and thus possibly dubious, private enforcement is a relatively blunt instrument. Legitimate but difficult-to-prove

[210] See Case C-184/99 *Rudy Grzelczyk v Centre public d'aide sociale d'Ottignies-Louvain-la-Neuve*, EU:C:2001:458, para 31; reaffirmed in Case C-34/09 *Gerardo Ruiz Zambrano v Office national de l'emploi (ONEm)*, EU:C:2011:124, para 41.

cases may be dismissed while less meritorious claims may, by chance, succeed. On this view, damages actions are simply a less effective tool for enforcement within certain areas of competition law. To say that private damages actions are thus 'disfavoured' in such cases is merely to acknowledge their limitations, and to suggest that more appropriate enforcement instruments may be available. It was noted above that the Commission chose, in its initial Green Paper, to focus exclusively on damages claims as the means of private enforcement;[211] however, victims of on-going antitrust infringements may well prefer an alternative remedy—such as an injunction mandating supply or the modification of exclusionary contract terms—which restores competition for the future instead of merely compensating for its loss. This is more likely to be the case, furthermore, outside the cartel context, particularly in response to continuing exclusionary conduct. Indeed, the range of remedial options might extend beyond application of the competition rules as such, to include, for example, sector-specific regulation to address on-going structural problems within a market.[212] In line with the *Courage* case law, damages actions therefore make a 'significant contribution to the maintenance of effective competition' within the EU, but the degree and value of the contribution that is realisable in practice varies according to the type of harm and broader enforcement context.

Yet, the plausibility of this explanation depends, to an extent, on what we actually mean by 'effectiveness' here. This may, in turn, depend upon the otherwise esoteric question, considered briefly above, as to whether *Courage* merely clarified that national rules for enforcing the directly effective antitrust prohibitions must provide for the possibility of a *claim for damages* under domestic law; or rather, whether it established an EU law *right to claim damages* for breaches of Articles 101 or 102 TFEU, similar to the approach in *Francovich*, yet enforceable via national procedures and remedies. The significance, if any, of this relatively fine distinction turns upon the degree of pro-active support required—from Member States, and perhaps also the Commission—to realise the effective exercise of the right to compensation in practice. Generally speaking, the principle of effectiveness, in the context of national procedural autonomy, requires that domestic procedural rules governing actions for protecting an individual's rights conferred by Union law must not render practically impossible or excessively

[211] See n 98 above.

[212] In relation to payment card interchange fees, for example, the Commission proposes to supplement its antitrust enforcement efforts—see eg Commission Decision of 19 December 2007 in Case COMP/34.579—*MasterCard* (summary at [2009] OJ C264/8, 6.11.2009) and Commission Decision of 8 December 2010 in Case COMP/39.398—*VISA MIF* (summary at [2011] OJ C79/8, 12.3.2011)—with a sector-specific regulation: see European Commission, *Proposal for a Regulation of the European parliament and of the Council on interchange fees for card-based payment systems* (COM(2013) 550 final), published 24 July 2013.

difficult the exercise of such rights.[213] Effectiveness is now treated as an aspect of the broader principle of effective judicial protection,[214] contained in Article 19(1) TFEU and Article 47 of the Charter, the latter of which provides, inter alia, that '[e]veryone whose rights and freedoms guaranteed by the law of the Union are violated has the right to an effective remedy before a tribunal'.[215]

Accepting that EU law merely requires the availability of compensation as a matter of national law where breach of the competition rules results in loss, then, arguably, all that is demanded by the principle of effectiveness is a negative obligation that domestic procedural requirements for accessing compensation in such circumstances—such as rules on standing, or time-limits—must not restrict unduly the right of litigants to claim damages. In any event, EU law does not mandate that national courts must accept as valid in substance any claim based on EU competition law, but, instead, merely that the national courts must provide appropriate protection for rights derived from EU law where breach, loss and causation can be established to the relevant standard. From this viewpoint, the fact that non-cartel private actions are unlikely to succeed because, in substance, the necessary elements for a successful claim for compensation under *Courage* will rarely be made out on the facts should not infringe the effectiveness principle as such. As Advocate General Kokott reiterated recently, there is a significant distinction between the availability in principle of compensation for breach of EU competition law, and a successful claim for compensation in response to a specific breach.[216]

Yet, insofar as the *Courage* decision established a distinct right under EU law to claim damages where competition infringements cause harm, the principle of effectiveness may require more than a *theoretical possibility* of obtaining compensation outside the cartel context. It may, instead, require appropriate action to ensure that the right to claim damages as such is *realisable in practice*, without distinction by reference to the type of antitrust breach at issue. Support for this more intensive and substantive understanding of effectiveness in this context can be found, most readily, in the cases of *Pfleiderer* and *Donau Chemie* on access to documents held by public bodies. Here, the Court held that national procedural rules would violate EU law to the extent that those rules unduly restricted access to evidence necessary to maintain a successful claim for damages for losses resulting from breach of the EU competition rules. This suggests that EU law requires not only the *availability* of compensation for such losses, but, additionally, that Member States are obliged, more proactively, to *facilitate*

213 *Unibet*, n 76 above, para 43.
214 *Unibet*, n 76 above, paras 42–43.
215 Article 47(1), Charter of Fundamental Rights of the European Union.
216 Opinion of AG Kokott in *Kone*, n 79 above, para 69.

such claims. Indeed, the Court in *Donau Chemie* spoke, quite forcefully, in terms of an 'obligation to compensate' in such circumstances.[217]

Further evidence that EU law may require more of Member States is found in the Commission's initial proposal for the Directive, specifically the portion dealing with subsidiarity and the need for the proposed legislation. Here, the Commission noted that, although the right to damages is theoretically available throughout the EU, few Member States have provided 'on their own initiative, for an effective framework for compensation'.[218] The Commission thus talked in terms, not merely of providing a right to compensation in appropriate cases, but rather of 'enabling antitrust damages actions';[219] in discussing the need for harmonisation, it also distinguished between the disparate experiences at Member State level with respect to claims for compensation for antitrust breaches, and the actual 'entitlement to damages guaranteed by EU law'.[220] Moreover, the final compromise text of the Directive contains, in Article 2(1), a reference to the right of an individual harmed by infringements of competition law 'to claim and *to obtain* full compensation'. The significant wording in italics was not included in the original proposal, although the impact of this amendment may be tempered slightly by alteration of the wording of Article 1(1) from a 'right to full compensation' to a 'right to claim full compensation'. The viewpoint of Advocate General Kokott is again of relevance here: she has suggested that Article 19(1) TEU and Article 47 of the Charter 'require Member States to provide, within the field of application of EU competition law, remedies sufficient to ensure *adequate* legal protection' (emphasis added).[221]

From this perspective, the apparent two-speed approach to private enforcement—which distinguishes between cartel and non-cartel infringements—is problematic insofar as it suggests that the requirements of this more demanding understanding of effectiveness may not be met outside the cartel context. Specifically, to the extent that *Courage* and its later manifestations require Member States to enable, and not merely to make available, claims for damages where loss results from competition infringements, it is arguable that the emerging laissez-faire approach to non-cartel private action may be insufficient to discharge this increased burden. As already stated, EU law defers to national courts in terms of determining whether a private plaintiff has established the requisite elements to the requisite standard to permit recovery for losses stemming from breach of EU law rights. Nonetheless, it is difficult to maintain both that the right to compensation under *Courage* is of universal application and that current practice respects

[217] *Donau Chemie*, para 47.
[218] Proposal for Damages Directive, n 9 above, p 11.
[219] Ibid.
[220] Ibid.
[221] Opinion of AG Kokott in *Kone*, n 79 above, para 70.

the principle of effectiveness, given that, without reference to the merits of any individual case, certain *types* of antitrust infringements face much higher (and perhaps insurmountable) barriers to recovery of damages.

Of course, the principle of state liability under *Francovich* does not itself amount to an unfettered entitlement to compensation for breaches of EU law. Here, too, the principle of national procedural autonomy means that claims derived from EU law are administered through the domestic procedural framework. Moreover, taking account of the often politically-sensitive context of national activities leading to claimed infringements, the CJEU in *Brasserie de pêcheur* clarified that only 'sufficiently serious' breaches of EU law would generate such liability.[222] This means, in circumstances where the Member State had a degree of discretion, that it must have 'manifestly and gravely disregarded the limits on its discretion'.[223] No such restriction was articulated in respect of the right to damages for competition infringements under *Courage*, although the Court of Justice suggested that factors such as the relative bargaining power of the parties might be relevant.[224] Nonetheless, an interesting parallel can be discerned between the 'sufficiently serious' criterion for the purposes of state liability, and the previous approach to characterising competition violations under the 1998 Guidelines on the method of setting fines, which divided infringements into three categories: minor, serious and very serious. The Guidelines stated that the third category would comprise 'horizontal restrictions such as price cartels and market-sharing quotas' or other 'clear-cut' competition abuses, whereas less blatantly anti-competitive non-cartel horizontal or vertical practices would fall under the first two categories only.[225] Given the prioritisation of cartel infringements in the context of private competition enforcement, the similarity between the language of a 'sufficiently serious' breach and a 'very serious infringement' might suggest an implicit threshold in terms of gravity to generate liability under *Courage*. Formally, however, the 1998 Guidelines applied only to the administrative fining practices of the Commission, and were subsequently replaced with updated guidelines that abandon the threefold categorisation of competition infringements.[226]

Finally, a curious incidental consequence of the favouring of cartel plaintiffs within the developing framework for private enforcement is that it may, perhaps inadvertently, go some way towards countering a common criticism of EU competition law: namely that it protects competitors rather than competition as such. The marked focus, evinced in particular in the

[222] Case C-46/93 *Brasserie du pêcheur v Bundesrepublik Deutschland*, EU:C:1996:79, para 51.
[223] Ibid, para 55.
[224] *Courage*, n 64 above, para 32.
[225] Guidelines on the method of setting fines imposed pursuant to Article 15(2) of Regulation No 17 and Article 65(5) of the ECSC Treaty ([1998] OJ C9/3, 14.1.98), Section 1A.
[226] See n 22 above.

Commission's Practical Guide on quantification of harm, on overcharges and negative impact upon the vertical value chain was considered above[227] and has been discussed by other commentators.[228] By contrast, the potential significance of injury resulting from market foreclosure, for example, has been largely downplayed in this guidance, suggesting diminished importance or relevance. Since the latter would tend to affect rivals most acutely, whereas the former is likely to harm direct and indirect customers of the defendant, in terms of recovery in private competition enforcement actions, the developing legal framework would appear to privilege customers—whom we might construe, broadly, as beneficiaries of competition—over competitors. This distinction is not absolute, of course, so that a cartel may aim at market foreclosure, or an exclusionary strategy by a dominant firm may involve overcharging for essential inputs, for example. Nonetheless, there would appear to be a prioritisation of compensation of customers who have suffered loss as a result of diminished competition rather than competitors who have seen their profits drop as a result of anti-competitive conduct by rivals. While this distinction may be applauded by sceptics and potentially even reformers of EU competition law, the extent to which it is desirable and defensible is again linked to the discussion of effectiveness above, as well as the broader issue of the appropriate role(s) of competition law within the EU.

VI. CONCLUSIONS

The enforcement of Articles 101 and 102 TFEU—these key instruments of EU 'public policy'—has undergone significant, perhaps seismic, changes in the past few decades in both substantive and procedural terms. As this chapter has sought to demonstrate, the role of private enforcement of the EU competition rules, primarily by means of antitrust damages actions, has grown continually in terms of visibility and perceived importance, and will, moreover, receive a significant boost with enactment of the long-anticipated Directive on damages actions. The Directive aims, broadly, to strengthen and, in part, to harmonise what is at present a fairly impressionistic and uneven landscape of differing rules and procedures for private damages actions across the various Member States. Yet, even after its enactment, and assuming successful and reasonably convergent transposition—not, indeed, a given—the extent to which the Directive will actually bolster and align mechanisms for private enforcement throughout the EU remains uncertain. Moreover, as has been argued here, it is likely that the full impact of these efforts will be felt only with respect to victims of cartel infringements. This

[227] See nn 157–161 and accompanying text above.
[228] Maier-Rigaud, 'Toward a European Directive', n 136 above.

further reinforces the existing dichotomy between cartels, which apparently constitute the top priority for both public and private enforcement in the EU, on the one hand, and other violations of Articles 101 and 102 TFEU, which are, increasingly, subject to more regulatory consensual forms of enforcement, particularly the commitment procedure pursuant to Article 9 of Regulation 1/2003, on the other.

The practical implications of this divergence may be no more than a reaffirmation of the truism that some antitrust damages actions are more readily convincing, or conversely more speculative, than others. But the evolving role of private enforcement within the overall framework of EU competition law raises some interesting and as yet largely unresolved questions, particularly with respect to the threefold categorisation of 'concepts' of competition infringements—as public wrongs, private wrongs, and market failures—considered in section II above. Within a system where exceptionally high public fines for very serious antitrust violations, particularly hard-core cartels, are routine, it is legitimate to question whether an additional layer of potentially equally high financial penalties, this time levied by private parties with the support of national courts, is equitable. Of course, few would have sympathy for deliberate cartelists who, ultimately, come out the worse for their anti-competitive bargains. Yet the interaction between public and private remedies in this instance may become problematic. This is particularly the case insofar as the 'full compensation' standard, coupled with indirect purchaser standing, appears to be fully complementary, at least in formal legal terms, with the prior imposition of high punitive fines that are, similarly, calculated roughly on the assumed impact of the cartel and, thus, arguably already incorporating a disgorgement component. It is notable that, within the US where antitrust damages actions are far more prevalent, public fines are typically levied at a much lower level (albeit criminal sanctions are much more common). One might ask whether the cumulative effect of public and private enforcement in the EU has the potential to over-penalise even very serious antitrust infringements such as cartels—at least to the extent, perhaps more of a danger in theory than practice, that full compensation is realised over and above high public fines. This possibility is undesirable, moreover, regardless of whether one views cartelisation as an instance of moral turpitude or simply an economically inefficient phenomenon.[229]

Another potential impact, taking account of the contours of the emerging framework for public enforcement at EU level discussed in section IV.B above, may be further to incentivise greater use of the commitment procedure in non-cartel cases, thus somewhat reducing defendant undertakings' potential exposure to follow-on liability. While this continued

[229] See n 17 above.

shift might bring its own benefits in terms of procedural economy, it would, nonetheless, result in further cleavage between cartel and non-cartel competition violations in enforcement terms. Whereas the former would remain squarely within the public and private wrong conceptualisations, non-cartel offences are, under the Article 9 procedure, increasingly treated as regulatory issues where the optimal punishment remedy is not monetary in nature, but rather involves behavioural or structural changes. To this extent, the already romantic notion of EU competition law as a largely unitary instrument of public policy may become even more untenable, as differentiation in enforcement leads to very different outcomes and suggests very different conceptualisations of the various forms of potential breach.

As for the nature of private enforcement itself within the EU system, section V above explored the open question as to whether the 'right' to damages, as such, is a specific requirement of EU law or, rather, merely a particular manifestation of the more deferential principle of national procedural autonomy. The answer is perhaps of greater interest to academics than litigants, although, as was argued above, it may have some impact upon the permissibility under EU law of the emerging differentiated enforcement structure. The increasingly entrenched role for private enforcement within (at least a subset of) the EU competition framework is obvious. Yet what remains to be resolved is whether and how, as private damages actions grow in practical and not merely theoretical importance, this will affect the existing balance between differing enforcement mechanisms and conceptions of competition law's role within the EU.

7

Tax Law and the Internal Market: A Critique of the Principle of Mutual Recognition

JULIAN GHOSH[1]

Abstract

The principle of mutual recognition tests a potential breach of internal market treaty provisions and restricts the scope for a Member State to justify a breach by reference to what happens, or has happened, in a different Member State. The principle of mutual recognition is a distinct principle to that of non-discrimination and does not apply by reference to the functional equivalence of Member States' regulatory regimes. Mutual recognition has been developed by the Court of Justice of the European Union (CJEU) as a distinct principle (perhaps a general principle) of EU Law, quite separate to the settled principles of non-discrimination and prohibition of obstacles to market access. The principle of mutual recognition entrenches a neo-functionalist model of the Union project and acts as an accelerant to the harmonisation of the domestic regimes of Member States which are subject to its application, in areas where harmonisation is realistically possible. In areas where harmonisation is not realistically possible, the application of the internal market by reference to the principle of mutual recognition sets aside non-internal-market-compliant Member States' regulatory provisions, leaving an unsatisfactory space in these regulatory regimes. However, the principle of mutual recognition is, in the light of the application of the principles of non-discrimination and the prohibition of obstacles to market access, quite unnecessary and operates to frustrate legal certainty and the legitimate expectations of the Member States.

[1] I am grateful to Professor Catherine Barnard, Trinity College, Cambridge, Professor Kenneth Armstrong, Sidney Sussex College, Cambridge and to Professor Derrick Wyatt QC, St Edmund Hall, Oxford for their comments on a draft of this chapter. I am also immensely grateful to Professor Stephen Weatherill, Somerville College, Oxford, for an early sight of his article which is a coruscating (and entertaining) attack on the principle of mutual recognition: 'Why there is no "principle of mutual recognition" in EU law (and why that matters to consumer lawyers)' (now published as chapter 19 of *Varieties of European Economic Law and Regulation* (Springer International Publishing, 2014) 401). Any errors are mine.

I. INTRODUCTION

SINCE THE COURT of Justice of the European Union's (CJEU) decision in *Cassis de Dijon*,[2] mutual recognition has been described as the 'core' of the CJEU's strategy of achieving market integration.[3] The notion generally appears in the context of the free movement of goods.[4] However, in the case law of the CJEU concerning the direct taxation regimes of Member States, the principle has been extended to Article 49 (freedom of establishment) and to Article 63 (free movement of capital). As is made clear below, there is no reason in principle why the CJEU's reasoning does not also apply to the internal market provisions as a whole.[5] The principle of mutual recognition has generally attracted supportive comment.[6] But it will be argued that the application of the principle of mutual recognition is unnecessary and unwelcome.

In the context of the free movement of goods, 'mutual recognition' entails the presumption that goods lawfully manufactured in one Member State (a 'host Member State') should be capable of being marketed and sold in any other Member State (a 'home Member State'). Indeed, this is seemingly

[2] Case 120/78 *Rewe-Zentrale AG v Bundesmonopolverwaltung für Branntwein* [1979] ECR 649 ('*Cassis de Dijon*').

[3] P Craig and G De Búrca, *EU Law: Text Cases and Materials*, 5th edn (Oxford, Oxford University Press, 2011) 595.

[4] See Commission Communication 3 October 1980 [1980] OJ C256/2 ('the 1980 Communication'): 'Any product imported from another Member State must in principle be admitted to the territory of the importing Member State if it has been lawfully produced, that is, conforms to the rules and processes of manufacture that are customarily and traditionally accepted in the exporting country, and marketed in the territory of the latter ... Only under very strict conditions does the Court accept exceptions to this principle'; '*Completing the Internal Market*' COM(85) 310, 14 June 1985: 'The general principle should be approved that, if a product is lawfully manufactured and marketed in one Member State, there is no reason why it should not be sold freely throughout the [Union]' (para 58); see also Commission Communication '*Mutual Recognition in the Context of the Follow-up to the Action Plan for the Single Market*', June 1999.

[5] This chapter describes the provisions within TFEU, Articles 28–33 (Free Movement of Goods, Common Customs Union), Articles 34–37 (Free Movement of Goods—Prohibition of Quantitative Restrictions), Articles 45–48 (Free Movement of Workers), Articles 49–55 (Freedom of Establishment), Articles 56–62 (Freedom to Provide Services) and Articles 63–66 (Free Movement of Capital and Payments) collectively as the 'internal market provisions'.

[6] KA Armstrong, 'Mutual Recognition' in C Barnard (ed), *The Law of the Single European Market—Unpacking the Premises* (Oxford, Hart Publishing, 2002) 225; MP Maduro, 'So Close and Yet So Far: The Paradoxes of Mutual Recognition' (2007) 14 *Journal of European Public Policy* 814; K Nicolaïdis, 'Trusting the Poles? Constructing Europe Through Mutual Recognition' (2007) 14 *Journal of European Public Policy* 682; J Pelkmans, 'Mutual Recognition in Goods. On Promises and Disillusions' (2007) 14 *Journal of European Public Policy* 699; SK Schmidt, 'Mutual Recognition as a New Mode of Governance' (2007) 14 *Journal of European Public Policy* 667; see also FKP Schioppa (ed), *The Principle of Mutual Recognition in the European Integration Process* (Basingstoke, MacMillan, 2005). For a recent treatment of the notion, see C Janssens, *The Principle of Mutual Recognition in EU Law* (Oxford, Oxford University Press, 2013).

orthodoxy.[7] This chapter uses the notion in this sense: 'mutual recognition' is a judicial technique used by the CJEU,[8] whereby the (conceptually distinct) questions of whether the internal market provisions are breached, whether such breach is justified and whether any such justification is proportionate, in scrutinising the domestic laws of any one particular Member State, are answered by what happens in a *different* Member State. In other words, 'mutual recognition' is a principle which requires scrutiny not only of the application of the internal market provisions to a particular Member State but the interaction of that Member State's laws under scrutiny with those of another. It is as well to make clear that mutual recognition is not used in the sense of any assessment of the functional equivalence of the respective regulatory regimes of a host Member State or a home Member State which, as is made clear below, is an exercise in the application of the principle of non-discrimination, not that of mutual recognition.

This chapter will set out the framework of the Treaties, within which the principle of mutual recognition has been developed, and examine the case law of the CJEU which has articulated and extended the principle. The chapter pays particular attention to the direct taxation case law of the CJEU, as this case law not only serves as a conduit through which the principle has been significantly extended but also provides a vivid illustration of how the principle of mutual recognition operates as an accelerant to the harmonisation of those Member States' domestic regimes which are subject to the internal market provisions. This examination of the CJEU's case law will illustrate that the principle of mutual recognition is conceptually redundant, in the light of the general principles of non-discrimination and the prohibition of market access obstacles. The analysis of the case law will further demonstrate the extent to which mutual recognition frustrates legal certainty and the legitimate expectations of Member States subject to its application.

II. THE TREATY CONTEXT OF THE INTERNAL MARKET: FOUR PROPOSITIONS

As the principle of mutual recognition is deployed by the CJEU in its application of the internal market provisions, it is as well to set out the framework of the Treaties within which the internal market provisions are set. It is this framework which must ultimately determine the legitimacy and

[7] Craig and de Búrca, *EU Law*, n 3 above, 596.

[8] As opposed to legislative obligations imposed on Member States to recognise, say, qualifications of other Member States, which might (but need not) have the same policy rationale as the notion of 'mutual recognition' developed by the CJEU but bear quite a different analysis as regards its application and legitimacy, which is outside the scope of this chapter.

coherence of the principle of mutual recognition. This context can be set out in a series of short propositions.[9]

A. The TEU and TFEU Articulate a Neo-functionalist Integrationist Agenda

The terms of the TEU and TFEU make this clear *per adventure*. Article 3(3) TEU promotes 'economic, social and territorial cohesion'. This is supplemented by the Loyalty Clause in Article 4(3) TEU and the duty of Member States to co-ordinate economic policies in Article 5(1) TFEU. The Common Customs Union established by Articles 28–32 TFEU is accompanied by an absolute prohibition on quantitative restrictions in Articles 34–36 TFEU, subject to the provisos in Article 37 TFEU. Despite the shared competence as between the Union and Member States in relation to the internal market established by Article 4(2)(a) TFEU, measures designed to secure the establishment and functioning of the internal market are left to the Union alone to implement in Article 26(1) TFEU. So far as these areas are concerned, this model leaves no room for competitive federalism, whereby jurisdictions within a union (here the Member States of the European Union) are entitled to retain particular regimes distinct from that of other jurisdictions within that union, so as to compete for inwards investment by reference to the respective attractions of these differing regimes. The integration process is one

> whereby political actors [here Member States] in several distinct national settings are persuaded to shift their loyalties, expectations and political activities towards a new centre, whose institutions possess or demand jurisdiction over the pre-existing national states [leading to an] end-result of a process of political integration [which] is expected to lead to a new political community, super-imposed over the pre-existing ones.[10]

And Article 115 TFEU, by permitting the Union to legislate in areas such as direct taxation, in order to achieve market integration,[11] means that such areas are also subject to an ultimate objective of harmonisation (so that, in the context of direct taxation, there is an ultimate objective of tax harmonisation).[12] Of course, regulatory diversity of Member States'

[9] Some of which may be controversial but which in the writer's view, ought not to be; debate on these propositions shall have to take place elsewhere.

[10] EB Haas, *The Uniting of Europe*, 2nd edn (Stanford CA, Stanford University Press, 1968) 16; and see W Wessels, A Maurer and J Mittag (eds), *Fifteen into One? The European Union and its Member States* (Manchester, Manchester University Press, 2003) 10.

[11] Albeit, in the context of fiscal provisions, that qualified majority voting does not apply.

[12] The Union has legislated in three contexts in the field of direct taxation: see Council Directive 2011/96/EU on the common system of taxation applicable in the case of parent companies and subsidiaries of different Member States [2011] OJ L345/8 ('the Parent-Subsidiary Directive') concerning distributions paid by subsidiary companies to their parent companies; Council Directive 90/435/EEC on the common system of taxation applicable in the case of

regimes is preserved until and unless harmonisation is achieved. That is obvious. And minimalist harmonising measures might leave room for Member State diversity. But to the extent (either as a matter of scope or as to the level of detail of any harmonising legislation) that the Treaties have a harmonisation objective which is achieved by detailed internal market-compliant legislation, that objective and such legislation leave no room for Member State regulatory diversity.

B. The Internal Market Provisions are Purely Destructive and Negative Integrationist in their Nature

This is clear from the text of the internal market provisions, which are couched in terms of the prohibition of restrictions,[13] and the abolition of discrimination.[14] The internal market provisions are applied to remove existing obstacles to the Union-wide movement of the factors of production, by treating such obstacles as a breach of the Treaties (hence the use of the term 'destructive'). The internal market provisions are wholly unconcerned with informing the content of the regime which will govern the internal market, once established (which must be achieved by the Union institution or Member State with the appropriate competence).[15]

parent companies and subsidiaries of different Member States [1990] OJ L225/6 ('the Mergers Directive') concerning intra-Union cross-border mergers; and Council Directive 2003/49/EC on a common system of taxation applicable to interest and royalty payments made between associated companies of different Member States [2003] OJ L157/49 ('the Interest Directive') on interest and loyalty payments made between associated companies, cross-border within the Union. And see the observations of the CJEU in Case C-250/95 *Futura Participations SA v Administration des Contributions* [1997] ECR I-2471 ('*Futura*') at para 33, where the CJEU clearly contemplates the harmonisation of Member States' domestic tax rules: '*As yet*, no provision has been made for harmonising domestic rules relating to the termination of the basis of assessment to direct taxes' (emphasis added). See also Case C-374/04 *Test Claimants in Class IV of ACT Group Litigation v Inland Revenue Commissioners* [2006] ECR I-11673 ('*Class IV ACT*'), para 52. Put another way, the objective of the internal market is 'to unite national markets in a single market having the characteristics of a domestic market' (Case 207/83 *Commission of the European Communities v United Kingdom* [1985] ECR 1201, para 17 of the judgment of the Court) with an absence of 'disparities between the laws of the Member States ... liable to create or maintain distorted conditions of competition' (Case C-300/89 *Commission of the European Communities v Council of the European Communities* [1991] ECR I-2867 ('*Titanium Dioxide*'), para 15 of the judgment of the Court).

[13] TFEU Articles 34 (imports) and 35 (exports). Article 49.1 (establishment), 56.1 (services), 63 (capital and payments).

[14] TFEU Article 45 (workers).

[15] This terminology appears in a number of works; see, for example, T Heller and J Pelkmans, 'The Federal Economy: Law and Economic Integration and the Positive State: The USA and Europe Compared in an Economic Perspective' in M Cappelletti, M Seccombe and J Weiler (eds), *Integration through Law: Europe and the American Federal Experience* (New York, Walter de Gruyter, 1986) 90, 324 et seq, discussed in AJM Jimenez, *Towards Corporate Tax Harmonisation in the European Community: An Institutional and Procedural Analysis* (London, Kluwer Law International, 1999) 2–3.

C. The Common Rationale of the Internal Market Provisions Means that the Test for Breach, Justification and Proportionality Should be Common to All of Them

The common treaty basis and rationale of the internal market provisions (see Article 3(3) TEU and Articles 4(2)(a) and 26 TFEU) demonstrates that all of the internal market provisions should be subject to the same principles of construction and subject to the same overall limitations of scope and application, as regards the test for breach, justification and proportionality.[16]

D. Breach, Justification and Proportionality: Distinct Concepts

It is trite that, in scrutinising a Member State's domestic laws to assess whether such laws are compliant with the internal market provisions, the CJEU ascertains, first, whether there has been prima facie breach of one or more of the internal market provisions; secondly if so,[17] whether that breach can be justified,[18] and thirdly proportionality, whereby a 'justifying' provision, which legitimately breaches the internal market provisions is

[16] This should be an uncontroversial proposition, given their common treaty and policy archaeology, was expressly recognised by the CJEU: see Case C-19/92 *Kraus v Land Baden-Wurttemberg* [1993] ECR I-1663, para 29 of the judgment of the Court (citing previous case law); Case C-107/94 *PH Asscher v Staatssecretaris van Financiën* [1996] ECR I-3089, para 29 of the judgment of the Court and Case C-311/97 *Royal Bank of Scotland Plc v Greece* ECR I-2651, para 20 of the judgment of the Court. For academic acknowledgment that the internal markets should have a common test for breach justification and proportionality, see JB Cruz, *Between Competition and Free Movement: The Economic Constitutional Law of the European Community* (Oxford, Hart Publishing, 2002) 91–98. However, as is made clear below, the application of the principle of mutual recognition has led to a fundamental inconsistency in the CJEU's application of the internal market provisions, certainly as between Arts 34 and 35 (goods) on the one hand and Art 56 (services) on the other.

[17] The distinction between there being no breach and a breach which might be justified is critical, since only in the latter case is proportionality engaged: see, for example, the discussion of *Futura* below.

[18] Whether by reference to an express proviso in the internal market provisions themselves or by reference to the 'mandatory requirements', whereby the domestic Member State provision which seeks the protection of the mandatory requirements must pursue an objective which is compatible with the Treaties, since it is only then that the provision (and the objective which it pursues) may take precedence over the internal market objective of the free movement of the factors of production throughout the Union: Cases C-60/84 and C-61/84 *Cinetheque SA v Federation Nationale des Cinémas Francais* [1985] ECR 2065, paragraph 23 of the judgment of the Court; Case C-362/88 *GB-INNO-BM NV v Confederation du Commerce Luxembourgeoise* [1990] ECR I-667, paras 15 and 19; *Futura*, para 26. Put another way, the breach of the internal market provisions was to have as its explanation the pursuit of another legitimate Treaty objective, for example, to help large families to create employment (Case C-209/01 *Schilling v Finanzamt Nurnberg Süd* [2003] ECR I-13389, paragraph 40), or to purport research and development (Case C-39/04 *Laboratoires Fournier SA v Direction des Verifications Nationales et Internationales* [2005] ECR I-2057).

'necessary' to achieve that other TEU/TFEU-compliant aim.[19] The reason for setting out what is well-trodden ground in this section of the chapter is two-fold. First, it makes it clear that the settled principles of non-discrimination and the prohibition against market access impediments are adequate and sufficient grounds to permit the CJEU to ascertain whether Member States' regulatory regimes breach the internal market provisions, with no need to appeal to a principle of mutual recognition. Secondly, this section of the chapter provides a framework which makes it clear that the principle of mutual recognition has been applied by the CJEU at each stage of the breach-justification-proportionality exercise (so that the conceptual objections to its application at each of these stages might be separately addressed).

So far as breach is concerned, it is tolerably clear that there are two separate grounds for breach. First, in relation to market participation conditions of a particular Member State (a 'host Member State'), in whose market a non-host Member State national wishes to compete, such conditions should not be discriminatory, either directly or indirectly. Thus, comparable situations should not be treated differently (or different situations treated in the same way).[20] Discrimination may be overt ('direct'), in that a domestic provision may expressly treat nationals and non-nationals, in objectively similar circumstances, differently, to the disadvantage of the non-national; or discrimination may be covert, or 'indirect' in that, although the criteria of application of a particular provision do not expressly include nationality, they has the effect (whatever the intention may have been) that non-nationals are treated less favourably than nationals. The difference between direct and indirect discrimination is not academic. Direct discrimination can be justified only under the express provisos to the internal market provisions, whereas indirect discrimination may be justified by reference to the 'mandatory

[19] Case C-204/90 *Bachmann v Belgium* [1992] ECR I-249, para 27. 'Necessary' means 'indispensable': Case C-118/96 *Safir v Skattemyndigheten i Dalarnas Lan* [1998] ECR I-1897, para 33. It is worthwhile noting that the notion of 'proportionality', in this context, is very different to that expressed in Art 5 of TEU. In Art 5 of TEU, the notion of 'proportionality' provides that legislation (whether at Union level or at Member State level) should not go beyond what is necessary to achieve a Union-compliant objective. 'Proportionality' in the context of a 'justified' Member State domestic provision which prima facie breaches the internal market provisions, plays a very different role indeed. Here, proportionality effectively gives precedence to the internal market objective, in any competition with the other Union-compliant objective pursued by a Member State, whose pursuit of that latter objective causes breach of the internal market provisions. The notion that a provision must be 'necessary' or 'indispensable' to achieve that latter objective (be it helping large families, research and development, or other objectives specified in the TEU/TFEU) means that it is the internal market which takes precedence in any such competition.

[20] Opinion of the Advocate-General in Cases 117/76 and 16/77 *Albert Ruckdeschel & Co v Hauptzollamt Hamburg-St Annen* [1977] ECR 1753 at 1778. Prohibited discrimination extends to such treatment on grounds of nationality, age etc.

requirements'.[21] This seemingly obvious observation is important when assessing the role of 'mutual recognition' in the context of whether the internal market provisions have been breached (see below).[22]

Quite separately from the notion of market participation conditions and the principle of non-discrimination, the internal market provisions may be breached by the domestic laws of a particular Member State, in circumstances where the application of a principle of non-discrimination is unintelligible. There are circumstances in which Member States' domestic provisions may create obstacles and impediments to intra-Union movement of the factors of production but which do not involve comparable situations. Examples are particularly plentiful in the field of direct taxation. So, in relation to a complaint that the requirement to obtain Treasury consents for an English-incorporated company to move its 'seat' from the United Kingdom to the Netherlands, constituted an illegitimate restriction on the company's freedom of establishment, under Article 49 TFEU, the CJEU observed that:

> Even though [the internal market provisions] are directed mainly to ensuring that foreign nationals and companies are treated in the host Member State in the same way as nationals of that State, they also prohibit the Member State of origin from hindering the establishment in another Member State of one of its nationals or of a company incorporated under its legislation ... [T]he rights guaranteed by [Article 49] would be rendered meaningless if the Member State of origin could prohibit the undertakings from leaving in order to establish themselves in another Member State.[23]

There is no 'similar' or 'comparable' circumstance to the company which wished to move its 'seat' from the United Kingdom to the Netherlands, to which a discrimination analysis could be applied. Companies which did not wish to leave the United Kingdom are self-evidently in different circumstances, as are companies already established in the Netherlands. But a hindrance, on the part of a 'Member State of origin' ('a home Member State') upon that home Member State's nationals is nevertheless a clear breach of the internal market provisions, albeit clearly distinct from a breach founded on discrimination. The distinction was also expressly recognised in *Bosman*

[21] Case C-264/96 *ICI Plc v Colmer* [1998] ECR I-4695, para 28 of the Advocate-General's Opinion.

[22] The question of the appropriate comparator for cases of alleged discrimination, that is, whether the comparison is also to be made between the nationals of the Member State under scrutiny ('the host Member State') and the non-host Member State-national, or whether comparisons may legitimately be made between two host Member State-nationals, or two non-host Member State-nationals are outside the scope of this chapter. For an assessment of this question, see J Ghosh, *Principles of the Internal Market and Direct Taxation* (Oxford, Key Haven, 2007) 69–73.

[23] Case 81/87 *R v HM Treasury and IRC, ex parte Daily Mail and General Trust Plc* [1988] ECR 5483 ('*Daily Mail*'), para 16 of the judgment of the Court.

(Case C-415/93),[24] paragraphs 94, 100, 103, where restrictions imposed by UEFA on the transfer of players, cross-border, within the Union, was held to constitute an 'obstacle' to the free movement of workers, on the basis that the transfer rules affected access to employment markets, cross-border, and were thus 'capable of impeding freedom of movement for the workers', without reference to 'discrimination' at all. For further examples in the field of direct taxation, analogous to *Daily Mail*, where no 'comparable' situation existed but nevertheless Member States' direct taxation provisions constituted illegitimate restrictions on the freedom of establishment, see *De Lasteyrie* (Case C-9/02)[25] and *N* (Case C-470/04)[26] (home Member State tax charges on a deemed disposal of assets by reason of emigration alone). The principle is founded on the notion of market access:

> Provisions which, even though they are applicable without distinction, preclude or deter a national of a Member State from leaving his country of origin in order to exercise his right of freedom of movement ... constitute an obstacle to that freedom. However, in order to be capable of constituting such an obstacle, they must affect the access of workers to the labour market.[27]

Thus the 'restriction' or 'market access' approach applies in circumstances (usually in relation to home Member State restrictions) which affect access to the internal market, within the Union, outside the borders of the home Member State.[28]

The distinct grounds for breach of the internal market provisions, discrimination on the one hand and the market access principle on the other, are not, in any conceptual sense, in competition. They occupy mutually exclusive sets of circumstances: discrimination in relation to host State market participation conditions; and the market access principle in relation to (usually) home State impediments to leaving a home State to access other parts of the internal market within the Union.[29] As it happens, the text of

[24] Case C-415/93 *Union Royale Belge des Sociétés de Football Association (ASBL) v Bosman* [1995] ECR I-4921.

[25] Case C-9/02 *De Lasteyrie du Saillant v Ministère de l'Économie, des Finances et de l'Industrie* [2004] ECR I-2409.

[26] Case C-470/04 *N v Inspecteur van de Belastingdienst Oost/Kantoor Almelo* [2006] ECR I-7409.

[27] Case C-190/98 *Graf v Filzmoser Maschinenbau GmbH* [2000] ECR I-493, at paragraph 23 of the judgment (see also para 32 of the Opinion of the Advocate-General). In *Graf*, the absence of a right to be paid compensation, for leaving an employment without cause, in circumstances where host Member State-nationals did not receive such compensation either (so that the relevant host Member State provision was not discriminatory, directly, or indirectly) did not constitute such an obstacle.

[28] This market access is clearly particularly pertinent in relation to the freedom to provide services under Article 56: see Case C-384/93 *Alpine Investments BV v Minister van Financien* [1995] ECR I-1141; *Safir*, n 19 above, paragraph 23 of the judgment of the Court.

[29] Although this view may be controversial: see C Barnard and S Deakin, 'Market Access and Regulatory Competition' in C Barnard and J Scott (eds), *The Law of the Single European Market—Unpacking the Premises* (Oxford, Hart Publishing, 2002) 204–13.

the internal market provision distinguishes between prohibited 'restrictions' on the one hand and prohibited 'discrimination' on the other, thus supporting the analysis that prohibited 'discrimination' and 'restrictions' which impede 'market access' occupy different respective territories.[30] Having said all of that, the CJEU has adopted a test for breach for all of the internal market provisions which is wider than either that of non-discrimination or market access: '[rules] ... capable of hindering, directly or indirectly, actually or potentially, intra-[Union][31] trade' constitute such breach ('the *Dassonville* formulation'). The *Dassonville* formulation of the test for breach encompasses Member State domestic provisions which are either discriminatory or present a market access obstacle, since either might 'hinder' intra-Union trade.[32] And since the *Dassonville* formulation for breach is wider than either a test predicated on the principle of non-discrimination or on the prohibition of market access obstacles, it follows that there is no need for the CJEU to develop a separate principle of mutual recognition to widen the test for breach; the principles of non-discrimination and market access, as wrapped up in the wide *Dassonville* formulation, provide an adequate test to ascertain breach.

This brief summary of the internal market provisions also illustrates that there are three distinct areas (breach, justification for breach and proportionality) in which the CJEU might (and indeed has) applied the principle of mutual recognition, each of which repays analysis.

[30] See, for example, Art 49 (freedom of establishment) which prohibits 'restrictions on the freedom of establishment' in Art 49, first paragraph and (separately) specifically 'includes' 'the right to take up and pursue activities ... under the conditions laid down [by a host Member State] for its own nationals' (Art 49, second paragraph); Art 56 (freedom to provide services) prohibits 'restrictions on the freedom to provide services' whereas Art 57 expressly confers the right, on a person providing a service, to 'temporarily pursue its activity in [another] Member State with the services provided, under the same conditions as are imposed by that State on its own nationals'. And Art 63 (free movement of capital) prohibits restrictions on the movement of capital, whereas Art 65(3) (certain express derogations to Member States, permitting restrictions on the free movement of capital and payments) expressly distinguishes between discrimination and restrictions by providing that 'the measures and procedures [constituting permitted derogations to Article 63] shall not constitute a means of arbitrary discrimination *or* a disguised restriction on the free movement of capital and payments' (emphasis added).

[31] Case 8/74 *Procureur du Roi v Dassonville* [1974] ECR 837, para 5 ('*Dassonville*').

[32] See Ghosh, *Principles of the Internal Market*, ch 4 for an analysis of the CJEU's approach in both its tax and non-tax case law which, for a while, at least until Case C-98/01 *Commission of the European Communities v United Kingdom* [2003] ECR I-4641 ('*Special Share*'), did successfully distinguish between discrimination and obstacles to market access as separate grounds for breach but then reverted to the *Dassonville* formulation in the '*Special Share*' action.

III. MUTUAL RECOGNITION: CASSIS DE DIJON

Having set out the background of the internal market provisions in the Treaties, we can now turn to the development, by the CJEU, of the principle of 'mutual recognition' to see how the CJEU has developed mutual recognition as a distinct ground for breach, and has done so by seemingly elevating mutual recognition to a general principle of EU Law.

The principle of mutual recognition was first articulated in *Cassis de Dijon*, where the CJEU held that a minimum (25 per cent) alcohol content for spirits, required as a matter of German law, was an 'obstacle' to the free movement of goods.[33] Thus the Court decided that the provisions of Article 34 TFEU were breached. That the requirement for minimum alcohol content, which prohibited the marketing and sale of the French fruit liquor within Germany, constituted an 'obstacle' was seemingly accepted by the CJEU without discussion (see paragraph 8). Thus the CJEU concentrated its attention on whether that breach was justified by an appeal by the host Member State, Germany, to public health or consumer protection (see paragraphs 9–13). The answer, according to the CJEU, was 'No'. The critical passage in its judgment is found at paragraph 14:

> It is clear ... that the requirements relating to the minimum alcohol content of alcoholic beverages do not serve a purpose which is in the general interest and as such to take precedence over the requirement of the free movement of goods, which constitutes one of the fundamental rules of the [Union].
>
> In practice the principal effect of requirements of this nature is to promote alcoholic beverages having a high alcohol content by excluding from the national market products of other Member States which do not answer that description.
>
> It therefore appears that the unilateral requirement imposed by the rules of a Member State of a minimum alcohol content for the purposes of the sale of alcoholic beverages constitutes an obstacle to trade which is incompatible with the provisions of Article [34] of the [TFEU].

Pausing there, in the first two sub-paragraphs of paragraph 14, the CJEU, having held that the minimum alcohol content requirement imposed by Germany was an illegitimate quantitative restriction under Article 34 TFEU, quite simply rejects any argument that the minimum alcohol requirement served either the purposes of public health or consumer protection (indeed any purpose which was 'in the general interest') but rather, as it observes in the second sub-paragraph of paragraph 14, 'the principal effect ... is to promote alcoholic beverages having a high alcohol content', by excluding low-alcohol drinks from Germany's market.

[33] Para 8 of the judgment of the Court.

In other words, Germany's minimum alcohol content did not have any public health or consumer protection purpose and was, to boot, indirectly discriminatory, since Germany's market participation conditions operated to the disadvantage of non-German producers of alcoholic beverages, who produced low-alcohol drinks, whereas their German national competitors, who produced high-alcohol drinks were left with the marketplace to themselves.

This analysis, in the first two sub-paragraphs of paragraph 14, is all that the applicant required to succeed in having Germany's minimum alcohol requirement set aside (so as to permit the French fruit liquor to be lawfully marketed within Germany). *Cassis de Dijon* was no different, in truth, to a case like *Humblot*,[34] where the CJEU held that a French special car tax, imposed on cars with an engine power exceeding 16cv was prohibited discriminatory internal taxation, within TFEU, Article 110(1). The CJEU held that French-made cars generally had an engine power of 16cv or less (and thus escaped the special tax), so that the French special tax was far more likely to be fixed on non-French cars (and was thus indirectly discriminatory).[35] The approach of the CJEU in *Humblot* and the approach of the CJEU in *Cassis de Dijon*, in the first two sub-paragraphs of paragraph 14 of its judgment in the latter, are indistinguishable.[36] In *Humblot* the French special tax had an indirectly discriminatory effect, since it affected non-French-made cars to a far greater extent; and in *Cassis de Dijon* the minimum alcohol requirement had an equally discriminatory effect, on non-German producers of alcoholic beverages, who produced beverages with an alcohol content of less than 25 per cent.

But the CJEU, in the third sub-paragraph of paragraph 14 in its judgment in *Cassis de Dijon*, went on to observe that:

> There is *therefore* no valid reason why, provided that they have been lawfully produced and marketed in one of the Member States, alcoholic beverages should not be introduced into any other Member State; the sale of such products may not be subject to a legal prohibition on the marketing of beverages with an alcohol content lower than the limits set by the national rules (emphasis added).

There are several observations to be made on this critical passage in the CJEU's judgment in *Cassis de Dijon*.

First, it is unnecessary: as observed above, the applicant in *Cassis de Dijon* would have succeeded on the CJEU finding that the minimum alcohol content was an 'obstacle', which had an indirectly discriminatory effect and which could not be justified. There was no need for the CJEU to

[34] Case 112/84 *Humblot v Directeur des Services Fiscaux* [1987] ECR 1367.

[35] See paras 13–17 of the judgment of the Court.

[36] That *Cassis de Dijon* concerned TFEU Art 34 and *Humblot* concerned TFEU Art 110(1) is irrelevant; both analyses are predicated on the application of a standard notion of indirect discrimination on the part of a host Member State.

appeal to any observation that the relevant low-alcohol beverage had been lawfully produced and marketed in another Member State. Put another way, if the principles of non-discrimination and the prohibition of market access obstacles operate in an orthodox manner, it is very difficult indeed to see what work there is left to do for the principle of mutual recognition in articulating the grounds for breach of the internal market provisions.

Secondly, the CJEU's observation in the third sub-paragraph is a non sequitur. At paragraph 14 of its judgment, the Court is considering, not the question of breach (as to whether the minimum alcohol content requirement was an 'obstacle'; that had been decided by the time the Court had reached paragraph 8 of its judgment) but the question of justification and Germany's appeal to public health and consumer protection as good reasons which justified the free movement of goods. But the Court's ruling that the minimum alcohol requirement did not serve either of those purposes, which rejection was expressly articulated by the Court, has nothing to do with its observation that the relevant beverage was lawfully manufactured and marketed in another Member State (the '*therefore*' articulated by the CJEU makes no sense). And neither could the Court possibly be said to have been suggesting that because the relevant beverages had been 'lawfully produced and marketed in [another] Member State', that they should somehow be presumed to have passed scrutiny to ensure that they did not offend public health or consumer protection considerations. *Cassis de Dijon* was

> not ... an example of the [CJEU] looking for substantive functional equivalences between Home State and Host State rules by engaging in a comparative exercise and then concluding that the duplication of equivalent rules was unnecessary and disproportionate ... Rather, the necessity and proportionality of the German rule was assessed simply by examining the rule on its own and considering whether [Germany] had succeeded in justifying its regulatory approach.[37]

So, at least on its terms, the CJEU's observations as to 'mutual recognition' in *Cassis de Dijon* should not have led to any suggestion that there was an emergence of some new principle of mutual recognition at all. Indeed, given the archaeology of the CJEU's judgment, as examined in this chapter, the CJEU's observation is simply reinforcing its rejection of Germany's appeal to public health and consumer protection (as to why there is no 'valid reason' why the relevant beverages should not be marketed and sold in Germany) and the observation that they had, after all, been lawfully been produced and marketed in another Member State can either be dismissed as mere judicial rhetoric or, in fact, affording host Member States additional protection, in that beverages which had *not* been lawfully produced and marketed within the Union could not expect the assistance of the internal

[37] KA Armstrong, 'Mutual Recognition', n 6 above, 234–35.

market provisions (including Articles 34 and 35) in attacking the market participation conditions of a particular Member State.

However, the notion of 'mutual recognition' was enthusiastically seized upon by the Commission and became a cornerstone of its strategy to achieve market integration.[38]

Furthermore, it is now clear that the CJEU considers that not only is the notion of 'mutual recognition' a 'principle' (indeed seemingly a general principle[39]) but one which, at least in the context of the free movement of goods and Article 34 TFEU in particular, has (at least rhetorically) the same significance as the principle of non-discrimination. In *Commission v Italy* ('*Italian Trailers*')[40] the CJEU held that Italy breached Article 34 TFEU by prohibiting the marketing and manufacture of motorcycles which were capable of towing vehicles (thus impeding the cross-border marketing of vehicles manufactured outside Italy which were specifically designed to be towed by motorcycles and nothing else). The CJEU[41] addressed the question of breach (whether the relevant rules were 'capable of hindering, directly or indirectly, actually or potentially, intra-[Union] trade' and observed (at paragraph 34) that:

> It is also apparent from settled case-law that [Article 34] reflects the obligation to respect *the principles of non-discrimination and of mutual recognition* of products lawfully manufactured and marketed in other Member States, as well as the principle of ensuring free access of [Union] products to national markets (emphasis added).

The CJEU cited *Cassis de Dijon* as authority for its observations at paragraph 34. The CJEU went on to observe, at paragraph 35, that:

> Obstacles to the free movement of goods which are the consequence of applying, to goods coming from other Member States where they are lawfully manufactured and marketed, rules that lay down requirements to be met by such goods constitute measures of equivalent effect to quantitative restrictions.

[38] See the Commission Communications referred to above. Certainly the 1980 Commission Communication's observation that 'the principles derived by [the CJEU in Cassis de Dijon] imply that a Member State may not in principle prohibit the sale in its territory of a product lawfully produced and marketed in another Member State ... [because] [w]here a product "suitably and satisfactorily" fulfills the legitimate objective of a Member State's own rules (public safety, protection of the consumer or the environment etc), the importing country cannot justify prohibiting its sale by claiming that the way it fulfils the objective is different from that imposed on domestic products ... [and] in such a case, an absolute prohibition could not be considered "necessary" to satisfy a mandatory requirement' cannot be taken legitimately from para 14 of the CJEU's judgment in *Cassis de Dijon*.

[39] *Commission v Italy (Italian Trailers)* was a direct action case raised under Art 258 TFEU. Thus there was no *actual* home Member State of manufacture of trailers whose sale within Italy was impeded, which the CJEU could consider in its judgment. It follows that an appeal by the CJEU to mutual recognition can only be intelligibly made if the notion is indeed a general principle.

[40] Case C-110/05 *Commission of the European Communities v Italy* [2009] ECR I-519.

[41] At para 33.

The CJEU, in *Italian Trailers*, quite unlike in *Cassis de Dijon*, was addressing the question of breach (not justification). And 'mutual recognition' was considered by the CJEU expressly to be a ground for breach and a ground which amounted to a 'principle' (and as a matter of the rhetoric of the CJEU, equivalent in status to that of the general principle of non-discrimination at that). Thus mutual recognition serves as a separate ground of breach (elevated to a general principle) to that of (direct or indirect) discrimination, so far as market participations in a host Member State are concerned.[42] The language employed by the CJEU makes it clear that mutual recognition is not a synonym for either market access or discrimination as a ground on which to establish breach. In particular, the express distinction made by the CJEU between '*non-discrimination*' and '*mutual recognition*' makes it clear that the CJEU did not consider mutual recognition as addressing the question of any sort of functional equivalence of home Member State and host Member State regulatory regimes. Any such exercise would simply be an application of the principle of non-discrimination (functional equivalence puts the goods in the same situation, which makes any host Member State disadvantage imposed on goods arriving from their home Member State an impermissible discriminatory burden) with there being no need for an appeal to 'mutual recognition' terminology. More fundamentally, the CJEU's notion of mutual recognition cannot be predicated on the functional equivalence of host Member State and home Member State regulatory regimes, since at no stage did the CJEU assess any such functional equivalence in its appeal to mutual recognition (indeed, since *Italian Trailers* was a direct action raised by the Commission, it is difficult to see how any such assessment could have been made, as there were no actual home Member State regulatory regimes to assess).

That mutual recognition serves to establish a distinct ground for breach (as opposed to testing justification or proportionality) was reiterated by the CJEU in *Aklagaren v Mickelsson* ('*Mickelsson*').[43] The prohibition of personal watercraft on public waterways was held to be in breach of Article 34 TFEU, on the same formulation as that employed by the CJEU in *Italian Trailers*, namely, that such a restriction impeded the sale and marketing in the host Member State (Sweden) of personal watercraft lawfully manufactured and sold in other Member States, thus breaching the principles of both non-discrimination and mutual recognition (see paragraph 24).[44]

[42] As it happens, the prohibition on motorcycles towing trailers was held to be justified on public safety grounds and also to be proportionate: see paras 59 et seq.

[43] Case C-142/05 *Aklagaren v Mickelsson* [2009] ECR I-4273.

[44] Again, the prima facie breach was justified (see paras 31–43), although the matter was remitted to the National Court for a conclusive finding on such justifications (see para 41).

Similarly, in *ANETT*,[45] a prohibition on the direct import of tobacco products from other Member States was held to be in breach of Article 34 TFEU and the CJEU reiterated the formulation that the breach occurred by reason of the separate principles of non-discrimination and mutual recognition. Again *Cassis de Dijon* was cited as authority for these observations.[46] And again, there was no assessment of any functional equivalence of host Member State and home Member State regimes, to suggest that mutual recognition was simply a synonym for an application of the principle of non-discrimination.

IV. CRITICISMS OF THE PRINCIPLE

Having settled that the CJEU considers the notion of mutual recognition as a distinct ground for breach of the internal market provisions concerning the free movement of goods (seemingly on the footing that mutual recognition is properly elevated to the status of a general principle of Union Law),[47] the following criticisms may be made of the CJEU's development of this principle. The criticisms gain strength when, as is made clear below, it is appreciated that this principle has been extended beyond the scope of the free movement of goods in Articles 34 and 35 TFEU to that of establishment and the free movement of capital (and at all three levels of the application of the internal market provisions, that is, breach, justification and proportionality).

First, as has already been observed, in *Cassis de Dijon* itself (and more generally) the very notion of 'mutual recognition' is unnecessary. If the market participation conditions of a host Member State are directly or indirectly discriminatory, or present a non-discriminatory obstacle (imposed by a home Member State) to market access vis-à-vis the host Member State, that is sufficient to engage Article 34, Article 35 and the internal market provisions generally, whichever freedom is relied upon. And if the relevant provision is not directly or indirectly discriminatory, and (separately) does not present a 'market access' obstacle, there is no legitimate reason to engage the internal market provisions (whether through the internal market provisions, or through the surrogate of general principles) at all. There is, in such a case, quite simply, no breach of the internal market provisions (because the relevant Member State provisions, not being discriminatory, or impeding market access, are not frustrating the internal market objective). Examples of the application of the principle of mutual recognition which

[45] Case C-456/10 *Asociacion Nacional de Expendedores de Tabaco y Timbre (ANETT) v Administracion del Estado* [2012] 2 CMLR 45.

[46] In *ANETT*, the quantitative restrictions were not justified: see paras 50–56.

[47] And if the principle is indeed a general principle of Union Law, it presumably constitutes a *sufficient* ground for breach of TFEU Arts 34 and 35.

lead to the CJEU establishing breach of the internal market provisions where there would otherwise have been no breach are given below, in the section of this chapter dealing with the direct taxation case law of the CJEU.

To be sure, the notion of 'mutual recognition' applied as a distinct general principle, serves as an accelerant to harmonisation, in cases where harmonising measures indeed fill the space left by the application of the internal market provisions.[48] If the principle of mutual recognition applies in addition to the dual principles of market access and non-discrimination, which adequately frame the grounds for breach of the internal market provisions, mutual recognition can serve only to increase the strength of the negative integrationist process of the internal market provisions by creating additional space (or space at a faster rate) for harmonised, Union-wide legislation to be enacted than would otherwise have been created (especially given the width of the *Dassonville* formulation for breach, quite apart from the application of the principle of mutual recognition). This then makes the presence of political will of the Union and Member States to enact internal market-compliant provisions to fill that space vital. And in the absence of such political will, the unfilled-space must either be left unfilled (which is unlikely), or attract the enactment of Member State provisions which have their regulatory objectives compromised by (often) a grudging objective to secure a minimalist compliance with the internal market provisions.[49] It has already been observed above that the current model of the Treaties leaves no room for competitive federalism, or regulatory diversity to the extent that harmonising measures provide detailed prescriptive rules. The negative integrationist rule of the internal market provisions paves the way

[48] This is a better description of the principle of mutual recognition than any sort of description of a 'conflict resolution' rule which settles a fight between the respective regulatory regimes of host Member States and home Member States. It is not a question of the settlement of any conflict but rather the answer to the question of which factors are relevant to ascertain breach, justification and proportionality in relation to the internal market provisions. This in turn depends on the correct analysis of the nature and perspective of these provisions.

[49] For example, the United Kingdom's 'transfer pricing' regime, which adjusts artificial pricing amongst connected persons, was, in the light of Case C-168/01 *Bosal Holding BV v Staatssecretaris van Financien* [2003] ECR I-9409, extended from its application to only cross-border transactions to intra-United Kingdom transactions, resulting in additional tax-compliance costs (to ensure that the transactions' consideration process was properly valued) for the relevant parties, in circumstances in which the tax take for the United Kingdom remained exactly the same (since any under or over-pricing by one party within the United Kingdom would result in a greater taxable profit for either the purchaser (in the case of under-pricing by the seller) or the seller (in the case of the over-pricing by the purchaser). The United Kingdom imposed these additional compliance cost by means of a primitive extension of a regime designed to counter cross-border tax avoidance as the simplest means of securing compliance with the internal market provisions, rather than engaging in a commitment to a common consolidated tax base within the Union, which was designed (on a Union-wide basis) to counter tax-driven manipulation of the pricing-connected party transactions (which would be less effective within a common consolidated tax base in any event, for the reasons given above), without attracting unnecessary compliance costs.

for a harmonised, Union-wide, set of rules. It is simply not the case that the application of a principle of 'mutual recognition' creates a 'competitive process among the different national rules [so that] the choice of producers of where to produce and of consumers of what to buy will determine the "best rules"'.[50] Mutual recognition is not an alternative mechanism to legislative harmonisation to achieve market integration. Mutual recognition (and all of the other principles which are applied once the internal market provisions are engaged) applies the destructive, negative integrationist provisions on the internal market so as to leave a space which is to be filled by harmonised legislation. Put another way, the form of 'mutual recognition' adopted by the CJEU in *Italian Trailers*, *Mickelsson* and *ANETT* does not permit the host Member State regime to survive the application of the principle of mutual recognition so as to be in competition with other Member States' regulatory regimes at all. The effect is to allow the home Member State (where the relevant goods are lawfully manufactured) to export its (less restrictive) regulatory regime to the host Member State which wishes to prohibit their marketing and sale within its borders, albeit subject to the proportionate application of potential justifications which cure prima facie breach, which arises precisely because the host Member State's regulatory regime is more restrictive than that of the home Member State of manufacture. There is not so much a 'horizontal transfer of sovereignty' by the host Member State to the home Member State—whereby the host Member State must trust the regulatory regime of the home Member State[51]—as a step towards the neo-functionalist integrative process—whereby space in the host Member State's regime[52] is created by the application of the principle of mutual recognition. This space demands to be filled by appropriate Union legislation (if harmonisation is not realistically possible in that area, this space will remain unfilled) that is more aptly described as an (inevitable) 'vertical' transfer of sovereignty, since the space must be filled by internal market-compliant legislation (whether enacted at Union or Member State level), which satisfies the harmonisation objective of the Treaties.

Secondly, the application of the principle of mutual recognition, whereby breach of the internal market provisions by one Member State may be triggered by the content of the regulatory regime of another Member State (which will govern what is lawfully produced and marketed in the latter)

[50] Cf MP Maduro, *We the Court, the European Court of Justice and the European Economic Constitution* (Oxford, Hart Publishing, 1998) 132. See also C Barnard and S Deakin, '*Market Access and Regulatory Competition*' 202–4.

[51] Cf MP Maduro, 'So Close and Yet So Far: The Paradoxes of Mutual Recognition', n 6 above.

[52] Or that of a home Member State, where the application of mutual recognition cannot be viewed as any sort of conflict between a host Member State and a home Member State at all (see below in relation to the discussion of Case C-446/03 *Marks & Spencer Plc v Halsey (Inspector of Taxes)* [2005] ECR I-1083 ('*Marks & Spencer*')).

is inconsistent with the CJEU's general approach in relation to justification for a prima facie breach of the internal market provisions.[53] The CJEU has (unsurprisingly) held that a suspected breach of a directive by one Member State does not justify a breach of Article 35 TFEU by another. So the United Kingdom could not justify a breach of Article 35 TFEU (the refusal to grant a licence for the export of live sheep to Spain) by reason of a suspicion that Spain was not correctly implementing a Council Directive as to the method of slaughtering the sheep, once they had arrived in Spain.[54] This was on the basis that Member States were prohibited from taking unilateral action to counteract breaches of Union law by other Member States (in other words, 'self-help' remedies are not available to Member States to cure breaches of Union law by other Member States).[55] Furthermore, a breach of the internal market provisions by a particular Member State cannot be cured by the conferral of 'countervailing advantages'. So, for example, where the CJEU held it to be discriminatory for France to fail to confer a particular tax credit on the French branch of a non-French tax resident company, where French tax resident companies with French resident parent companies would have obtained that tax credit, breach of Article 49 TFEU could not be justified by an appeal to other tax advantages conferred on the French branch of the non-French tax resident company.[56]

If breach of its Union obligations by one Member State cannot cure a breach of the internal market provisions by another Member State, it should follow that the application of a particular regulatory regime of one Member State should not be relevant in testing whether or not a breach has occurred in another Member State. And if breach of the internal market provisions cannot be cured by countervailing advantages conferred by the Member State under scrutiny, a fortiori it should follow that what happens in another Member State should not be relevant to the question of whether or not a particular Member State has breached the internal market provisions. It is difficult to see a principled position where one might accept the former proposition but not the latter.

These are not trivial points. They illustrate the perspective of the internal market provisions. Negative integrationist provisions, such as the internal market provisions, which set aside non-Union-compliant Member States'

[53] It should be remembered that the CJEU's observations in *Cassis de Dijon* related to justifications, not to breach.

[54] Council Directive 74/577/EEC on stunning of animals before slaughter [1974] OJ L316/10.

[55] Case 5/94 *R v Minister of Agriculture, Food & Fisheries ex parte Hedley Lomas (Ireland) Ltd* [1996] ECR I-2553, paras 20–21 of the judgment of the Court.

[56] Case 270/83 *Commission of the European Communities v France* [1986] ECR 273 ('*Avoir Fiscal*'), para 20; see also Case C-175/88 *Biehl v Administration des Contributions du Grand-Duché de Luxembourg* [1990] ECR I-1779, para 16; Case C-330/91 *R v Inland Revenue Commissioners, ex parte Commerzbank* [1993] ECR I-4017, para 18.

domestic regimes are properly applied on a country-by-country basis, since the resulting space to be occupied by (harmonised) Union-wide legislation requires a self-evident combination of political will and Member State cooperation. To accelerate the process, by the application of the principle of mutual recognition creates space at a rate which is much faster than, at least potentially, Member States can gather up both political will and engage in appropriate cooperation.

V. DIRECT TAXATION: A CASE STUDY ON MUTUAL RECOGNITION

It will not have escaped attention that the cases referred to so far have concerned the application of mutual recognition only to the free movement of goods (and Articles 34 and 35 TFEU). It is also true that the Court has been reluctant to extend the principle of mutual recognition in relation to Article 56 (freedom to provide services). So restrictions on the level of fees lawyers may charge in Italy could not be challenged on the basis that a less restrictive regime applied elsewhere in the Union.[57] It is impossible to reconcile the enthusiasm of the CJEU in applying the principle of mutual recognition to the free movement of goods with its ambivalence in relation to its application for the free movement of services.[58] Thus the undesirability[59] of the extension of the mutual recognition principle is given expression only at the expense of an equally undesirable inconsistency in the CJEU's approach to the application of the freedoms (and in the context of what the CJEU seems to have articulated as a general principle).

[57] Case C-565/08 *Commission of the European Communities v Italy* [2011] 3 CMLR 1 ('*Italian Lawyers' Fees*'), para 49 of the judgment of the Court; see also Case C-518/06 *Commission of the European Communities v Italy* [2009] ECR I-3491, para 63.

[58] Indeed it is difficult to reconcile the CJEU's application of mutual recognition to its decision in Cases C-267/91 and C-268/91 *Criminal Proceedings against Keck and Mithouard* [1993] ECR I-6097, where the CJEU narrowed the test for breach of Art 34 by holding that non-discriminatory selling restrictions (in relation to pricing of goods) did not impede access to the host Member State's market place (see paras 15–17) if goods were lawfully marketed in the home Member State free from such pricing restrictions. In *Italian Trailers*, Member States made submissions that the CJEU's approach in *Keck* meant that the non-discriminatory prohibition on the sale of trailers in Italy was protected from an accusation of breach of Art 34 by *Keck* (see para 22). The CJEU simply did not meet this point at all, merely citing paras 16–17 of its judgment in *Keck* as an instance of the CJEU's acknowledgment of the principle of mutual recognition (which is wrong: paras 15–17 in *Keck* merely acknowledge that the relevant goods were marketed lawfully in Member States other than France, without any formulation of a principle of mutual recognition): see paras 33–37. *Italian Trailers* is only reconcilable with *Keck* if the CJEU's approach in Keck is restricted in its application to 'selling arrangements' which do not fix on the nature of the goods under scrutiny, as opposed to the market participation conditions which frame the regime in which such goods are sold (permitted pricing arrangements, permitted hours of trading etc), none of which was addressed by the CJEU in *Italian Trailers*.

[59] It is fair to say that the CJEU did not at all try to reconcile its approach in *Italian Lawyers' Fees* to *Italian Trailers/Mickelsson/ANNETT*.

It is in the direct taxation[60] case law of the CJEU that we can see the extension of the principle of mutual recognition at its most stark.[61] The principle has been applied in relation to breach, justification and proportionality. And it is this case law which reveals the principle to be an unwelcome one.

Looking first at breach, a primitive application of the principle of mutual recognition was made by the CJEU in *Futura*.[62] The CJEU had to consider whether the obligation of a non-Luxembourg tax resident company to keep accounts for its Luxembourg branch was a breach of Article 49 TFEU. The CJEU held that it was, on the basis that the additional Luxembourg requirement to keep accounts to that of the home Member State (here, France) infringed Article 49.[63] The CJEU seems to have applied a test of discrimination; 'the imposition of such a condition ... specifically affects companies or firms having their seats in another Member State ... [and is therefore] prohibited by [TFEU Article 49]'.[64] But this type of 'cumulative discrimination', whereby the effect of a host Member State's market participation conditions and their compliance with the internal market provisions, is assessed by the home Member State's regulatory regime, not only assumes congruence as to the form and content of that regime (here the form and content of the type of accounts which must be kept in France) but again effectively exports the home Member State's regulatory regime to that of the host Member State, without any scrutiny of the nature of the home Member State's regime. And if the requirement is not discriminatory, looking at the participants within the host Member State's market place, and does not present an obstacle to market access (which it should not, since the obligation to keep accounts only arises once market participation commences),[65] the CJEU should have found that there was no breach of the internal market provisions. *Futura* is an example (wherein lies its importance) of the principle of mutual recognition establishing breach where otherwise breach would not have occurred. And to the extent that mutual recognition leads to an over-wide test for

[60] Meaning the taxation of persons, on their income and capital profits, as opposed to 'indirect taxation' imposed on transactions, such as Value Added Tax.

[61] Unfortunately, this case law has received relatively little attention. Neither *Futura*—discussed below as an important example of the application of the principle to establish breach in the context of Art 49 in relation to a host Member State non-discriminatory, non-market-access-impeding provision—nor the cross-border dividend case law mentioned below, are mentioned at all in C Janssen's, *The Principle of Mutual Recognition in EU Law*, while *Marks & Spencer*, which raises severe conceptual problems in its application of mutual recognition, is relegated to a footnote (at p 39, fn 163) as an example of a home Member State regime being set aside (although as observed below, it is not apt to discuss *Marks & Spencer* in terms of a 'home Member State' and a 'host Member State' analysis.

[62] *Futura Participations SA v Administration des Contributions* [1997] ECR I-2471.

[63] Paras 25–26.

[64] Para 26.

[65] Thus making the obligation to keep accounts a fortiori *Graf* in its compliance with the internal market provisions.

breach, it is unwelcome. The principle goes from being merely redundant to fixing obligations on Member States which are not contemplated by the internal market provisions.[66]

The notion of mutual recognition was further applied by the CJEU in relation to Article 63 TFEU, in the context of cross-border dividend payments, although not at first.

In *Verkooijen*,[67] Article 63 TFEU was breached by reason of a Netherlands income tax exemption for dividends, available for dividends paid by Netherlands-established companies to Netherlands residents, not being extended to dividends paid by non-Netherlands resident companies outside the scope of Netherlands tax. The CJEU established breach in *Verkooijen* without reference to mutual recognition, holding that the 'restriction' on capital movements[68] was on the basis that it had the effect 'of dissuading nationals of a Member State residing in the Netherlands from investing their capital in companies which have their seat in another Member State'.[69] The CJEU also observed that the provision had a restrictive effect as regards companies established in other Member States, in that it was an obstacle for the investee companies to raising capital in the Netherlands, since the dividends they paid to the Netherlands residents were less favourably treated than dividends distributed by a Netherlands resident company.[70] Nationality discrimination and mutual recognition (the two principles used, together, in the *Italian Trailers/Mickelsson/ANETT* trilogy) were not mentioned at all. The CJEU simply did not articulate the breach of Article 63 as one of the breaches of the principle of equality of treatment.

The CJEU's approach changed however in *Lenz*,[71] and was replicated in *Manninen*.[72] In *Lenz*, the question for the CJEU was whether it was a breach of Article 63 TFEU for Austria to confer an option for Austrian tax resident recipients of dividends from Austrian-established companies, to have those dividends taxed at either a flat rate of 25 per cent or one-half

[66] The CJEU recognised that Luxembourg was entitled to police its tax regime to cross-check losses claimed for Luxembourg tax purposes with accounting losses (paras 31–35: 'effective fiscal supervision' is a legitimate justification) but held that the rights of the Luxembourg tax authorities to make enquiries under the Mutual Assistance Directive (Council Directive 77/799 concerning mutual assistance by the competent authorities of the Member States in the field of direct taxation [1977] OJ L336/15) meant that the requirement to keep Luxembourg accounts in respect of the Luxembourg branch was not proportionate (paras 36–42).

[67] Case C-35/98 *Staatssecretaris van Financien v Verkooijen* [2000] ECR I-4071 ('*Verkooijen*').

[68] Para 36.

[69] Para 34.

[70] Para 35.

[71] Case C-315/02 *Anneliese Lenz v Finanzlandestirektion für Tirol* [2004] ECR I-7063 ('*Lenz*').

[72] Case C-319/02 *Proceedings Brought by Manninen* [2004] ECR I-7477 ('*Manninen*').

of the ordinary income tax rate but to subject dividends received from non-Austrian-established companies to the full rate of ordinary income tax. The CJEU could quite easily have held that the answer was 'Yes' on the same approach as it used in *Verkooijen* (without any appeal to mutual recognition) and indeed the CJEU observed that the relevant Austrian tax legislation had 'the effect of deterring taxpayers living in Austria from investing their capital in companies established in another Member State' and also 'produced a restrictive effect in relation to companies established in other Member States, in as much as it constitutes an obstacle to their raising capital in Austria'.[73] However, in addressing submissions by various Member States on Articles 65(1)(a)—Article 63 TFEU is without prejudice to the right of Member States to apply fiscal provisions which 'distinguish between taxpayers who are not in the same situation with regard to their place of residence or with regard to the place where their capital is invested'[74]—the CJEU observed that the lower tax rate applied to dividends received by Austrian residents from Austrian-established companies was to alleviate effective economic double taxation. Dividends could only be paid out of taxed profits. Dividends received by Austrian resident shareholders therefore would be taxed twice, once in the hands of the company to Austrian corporation tax and again in the hands of the recipient shareholders, to Austrian income tax—albeit that the profits were taxable in the hands of the paying company in their capacity as taxable business receipts, whereas the dividends were taxable in the shareholders' hands as taxable dividends.[75] The conclusion to which the CJEU might (indeed ought) to arrive was that Article 65(3) TFEU expressly provides that any Member State provision which seeks the disapplication of Article 63 TFEU under Article 65(1)(a) must not 'constitute a means of arbitrary discrimination or a disguised restriction on the free movement of capital and payments as defined in Article 63'. In *Lenz*, investors in Austrian tax resident companies were not in a comparable situation to investors in non-Austrian tax resident companies, looking at their respective repositories of invested capital. So it is true to say that Article 65(1)(a) was engaged. But the restriction of the favourable income tax rates did constitute an obstacle for investor and investee alike in contributing and raising capital cross-border, thus engaging Article 65(3), which removed the protection of Article 65(1)(a).[76] In other words any breach, by applying the appropriate tests, of the internal market provisions (here the free movement of capital and payments provisions in

[73] *Lenz*, n 71 above, paras 20–21.

[74] Since Art 65(1)(a) disapplies Art 63, the question is one of breach, rather than one of justification to cure prima facie breach.

[75] See *Lenz*, n 71 above, paras 31 and 32.

[76] By removing the dis-application of Art 63.

Article 63) could not be cured by an appeal to Article 65(1)(a).[77] However the CJEU, instead, observed that:

> shareholders who are fully taxable in Austria and receive revenue from capital from a company established in another Member State are ... *in a situation comparable with that of shareholders who are likewise fully taxable in Austria but receive revenue from capital from the company established in Austria*[78] (emphasis added).

It was that 'comparability' which meant that, according to the CJEU,

> the Austrian tax legislation which [imposes favourable tax rates] [on] revenue from [Austrian-established] capital ... does not relate to a difference in situation within the meaning of [Article 65(1)(a)] between revenue from capital of Austrian origin and revenue from capital originating in another Member State.[79]

In other words, taxation in any Member State amounts to taxation in Austria, in the hands of a company which pays dividends. Hence shareholders who receive dividends from companies taxed in Member States other than Austria are in a 'comparable' situation to that of Austrian shareholders who receive dividends from Austrian resident companies and are subject to prohibited discrimination if the favourable tax rates which apply to Austrian dividends are not extended to non-Austrian dividends.

The CJEU replicated this approach in *Manninen*. A Finnish tax resident shareholder complained that, whereas dividends received from Finnish-established companies obtained a tax credit (to alleviate economic double taxation, in the same way as in *Lenz*), dividends from non-Finnish companies did not, in circumstances in which the relevant Finnish tax legislation was 'designed to prevent double taxation of company profits by granting to a shareholder who receives dividends a tax advantage linked to the taking into account of the corporation tax due from the company distributing the dividends'.[80] Again, the CJEU could have (and should have) adopted the approach it applied in *Verkooijen* and simply observed that Article 63 was indeed breached by reason of the restriction on investors who chose to invest in non-Finnish-established companies, given the less favourable tax treatment on dividends, as compared to an investment in Finnish-established companies

[77] The mandatory common construction of all of the internal market provisions demand that the same approach to breach, justification and proportionality apply to all of the freedoms (see above) which means, in turn, that the terms of Art 65(1) must be seen as a mere quantification of the case law which relates to justification and proportionality in relation to the free movement of goods, the free movement of workers, the freedom of establishment and the freedom to provide services (hence the terms of Art 65(3)). This approach does not make Art 65(1)(a) redundant. Rather it recognises the need for common construction of the freedoms and allows the CJEU's case-law on the other freedoms to inform the application of Art 65(1)(a).

[78] *Lenz*, n 71 above, para 32.

[79] Para 33.

[80] *Manninen*, n 72 above, para 33.

(and the consequent obstacle to non-Finnish-established companies raising capital from Finnish investors). And in relation to Article 65(1)(a), the CJEU should have rejected any submissions on its application by reference to Article 65(3), as set out above. But, as in *Lenz*, the CJEU embarked on a consideration of the comparability of circumstances as between a Finnish investor who invested in a Finnish-established company, and a Finnish investor who invested in a non-Finnish-established company.[81] The CJEU observed that:

> Those dividends distributed by a company established in Finland and those paid by a company established in Sweden are, apart from the tax credit, capable of being subjected to double taxation. In both cases, the revenue is first subject to corporation tax and then—insofar as it is distributed in the form of dividends—to income tax in the hands of the beneficiaries ... Where a person fully taxable in Finland invests capital in a company established in Sweden, there is thus no way of escaping double taxation of the profits distributed by the company in which the investment is made. In the face of a tax rule which takes account of the corporation tax owed by a company in order to prevent double taxation of the profits distributed, shareholders who are fully taxable in Finland find themselves in a comparable situation, whether they receive dividends from a company established in that Member State or from a company established in Sweden.[82]

The CJEU thus concluded that:

> The Finnish tax legislation makes the grant of the tax credits subject to the condition that the dividends be distributed by companies established in Finland, while shareholders fully taxable in Finland find themselves in a comparable situation, whether they receive dividends from companies established in that Member State or from companies established in other Member States.[83]

The CJEU, in *Lenz* and *Manninen*, thus adopted the principle of mutual recognition in the context of Article 63 in the free movement of capital. Moreover, it did so unnecessarily (since the application of Article 65(3) would have disposed of the issue) and unthinkingly (demonstrated by the CJEU's failure to even consider Article 65(3) and its application in the light of the case law on market access and non-discrimination). The burden of the CJEU's approach in *Lenz* and *Manninen* was that corporation tax paid by a company resident in one Member State equates to corporation tax paid by a company in all Member States. That is why shareholders who receive dividends in a home Member State are entitled to the same favourable tax treatment as in relation to dividends received from home Member

[81] Although Art 65(1)(a) was not mentioned in the CJEU's judgment in *Manninen*, it is clear that the CJEU had Article 65(1)(a) in mind, since the CJEU addressed the investors' comparability of circumstances where the investors 'might differ according to the place where they invested their capital': para 34.

[82] Paras 35–36.

[83] Para 37.

State-established companies. In the same way that goods which are lawfully manufactured and marketed in one Member State ought, according to *Italian Trailers/Mickelsson/ANETT* to be lawfully marketed in all other Member States, tax paid by a company in one Member State should be recognised as tax paid by that company in all other Member States, for the purpose of applying the internal market provisions (in this context, Article 63).

The criticisms of the CJEU's approach in *Futura*, *Lenz* and *Manninen*[84] mirror those which this chapter makes in relation to the principle of mutual recognition, as it has been developed in the context of the free movement of goods.[85]

First, as in *Cassis de Dijon*, the appeal, by the CJEU, to comparability of circumstances or situations in *Lenz* and *Manninen* was, quite simply, unnecessary (and see the discussion above in relation to *Futura* where mutual recognition led to a finding of breach which was illegitimate, in relation to a non-discriminatory provision which did not present a market access obstacle either). The restriction of favourable tax treatment to home Member State dividends was a restriction on the free movement of capital (whether viewed from the shareholders' perspective, or that of the company, as observed by the CJEU in *Verkooijen*).

Secondly, the role of the principle of mutual recognition (here the home Member State having to recognise a tax charge of another Member State, on a particular person, that is, a company which makes profits and pays dividends, which imposes an obligation to confer tax advantages on a different person, that is, the recipient of those dividends) is not a mere theoretical acceleration of the fructification of the internal market. The setting aside of the Member State's tax regime on the grounds of 'discrimination' leaves, as has already been observed above, a space, here relating to the taxation of dividends, which will not be filled for a considerable time by harmonised

[84] The CJEU's approach to mutual recognition in this direct taxation case law is exactly the same as that applied in relation to the free movement of goods in *Italian Trailers, Mickelsson* and *ANNETT* (effect of the regulatory regime in one Member State must be recognised in any application of the internal market provisions to another Member State).

[85] Incidentally, there is no criticism made by the writer (at all) based on the observation that, of course, there is no 'economic double taxation' as regards the home Member State in which the recipient shareholder resides. Of course, it is true to say that, so far as Austria was concerned, there is not economic double taxation of the company (which was established outside Austria) and therefore no double (Austrian) taxation of the amount distributed to the Austrian tax resident shareholder. The same is true in *Manninen*. Finland had not taxed the Swedish-established company and therefore there was no Finnish double taxation of the dividend, once received in the hands of the Finnish resident shareholder. Although the relevant home Member State (respectively, Austria in *Lenz* and Finland in *Manninen*) would have a perfectly sensible complaint as a matter of orthodoxy international tax law, these cases are simple examples of orthodox fiscal considerations yielding to the objectives of the internal market (discriminatory market participation conditions and obstacles to the free movement of the factors of production must be set aside and in the case of any conflict the direct effect and supremacy of European Union law trumps all competing considerations).

Union-wide fiscal legislation, since there is no evidence of any political will of any Member State to engage in cooperation with other Member States to enact a Union-wide harmonised tax regime (quite apart from the observation that Article 115 requires unanimity for any such project). The result is a risk that Member States will be incentivised, to avoid accusations of internal market non-compliance, to be uniformly miserly in their tax regimes, rather than to extend favourable tax treatment to home Member State and non-home Member State dividends alike.

There is a quite separate objection to the application of mutual recognition in areas which have no realistic prospect of harmonisation. In such cases, the application of the internal market provisions (whether by reference to the principles of market access or non-discrimination on the one hand or mutual recognition on the other) damages Member State regulatory regimes by setting non-internal market compliant provisions aside, leaving only a space not likely to be filled with appropriate Union legislation. The application of the principle of mutual recognition, when the very principle itself is, for the reasons given in this chapter, unnecessary, in such areas may lead to frustrating the Union Project altogether, to the extent that Member States' reactions may be to enact (albeit non-discriminatory) provisions which serve revenue-protection aims, rather than free movement objectives.

Put another way, in each of *Futura*, *Lenz* and *Manninen*, an objection to the application of the mutual recognition principle might be dismissed as a mere practical complaint (that there is insufficient political will to enact a Union-wide, harmonised tax regime). Such a response would be unworldly (put at its lowest). But the 'practical' complaint, if this is what it is, runs deeper. It may well be that Member States have similar tax systems, in which notions of tax residence[86] and source[87] are considered the sufficient connecting factors to permit a jurisdiction to tax a particular person.[88] Even this is questionable, with (now) 28 Member States. But, more relevantly, the actual tax charge on a company, on its taxable profits, may have little or nothing to do with the nominal tax rate imposed by a particular tax system. The combination of tax reliefs, the interaction of foreign taxes on a company's foreign profits (if any) and tax credits for foreign taxes paid by its foreign subsidiaries, quite apart from any network of Double Tax Treaties concluded by the company's home Member State, mean that the actual tax paid by a particular company may have no relationship at all to the nominal rate of corporation tax set by that company's home Member

[86] Whereas some combination of connecting factors, both physical, such as location and legal, such as, for companies, the place of incorporation.

[87] The location of profits.

[88] Orthodoxy is that a tax resident person is taxed on his worldwide profits, whereas a non-resident person is only taxed on those profits located ('sourced') in the taxing State: see Ghosh, *Principles of the Internal Market and Direct Taxation* Chapter 1.

State. Thus it is not at all obvious that the recipient of a dividend from a company established in the same Member State as the recipient is in a 'comparable' situation to the recipient of a dividend established in another Member State.[89] Thus even if (which is not the case) the CJEU had based its application of mutual recognition on a notion of functional equivalence of Member States' regulatory regimes (here of direct taxation systems), such an approach would not justify the application of mutual recognition in *Futura*, *Lenz* or *Manninen*.

The extension of the principle of mutual recognition was made even worse by the CJEU's approach in *Marks & Spencer Plc v Halsey*, where the CJEU applied the principle to justification and to proportionality (in the latter case in an almost completely unintelligible manner). In *Marks & Spencer* the CJEU was faced with the United Kingdom's group relief rules, which permitted United Kingdom-established (tax resident) companies to surrender trading losses against otherwise taxable profits of other United Kingdom tax resident companies, in the same 'group'.[90] A United Kingdom resident parent company (*Marks & Spencer Plc*) held certain (indirect) subsidiaries, established and tax resident (solely) in France, Germany and Belgium. The subsidiaries all made losses. The United Kingdom group relief rules prohibited the set-off of the foreign subsidiaries' losses against the United Kingdom tax resident parent company's profits. The United Kingdom parent company raised an action against the United Kingdom, based on Article 49 TFEU on the basis that the inability to make use of the foreign subsidiaries' losses infringed its right of establishment (in France, Germany and Belgium). The CJEU held that there was prima facie breach but that breach was both justified and proportionate. The latter conclusions were based on an application of the principle of mutual recognition which raises severe conceptual problems.

So far as breach was concerned, the Court held that the absence of group relief for the losses of the non-UK tax resident subsidiaries against the profits

[89] It is no answer to say that, of course, even two home Member State companies may have different tax profiles depending on the availability of reliefs under the home State's own tax regime. That is, of course, true. And two home State tax resident companies may be in very different circumstances as regards their subsidiaries (one may have no subsidiaries, the other may have many subsidiaries, some of which are foreign, some of which are not, which may, in turn, effect the actual tax charge on those companies). But the network of Double Tax Treaties concluded by both jurisdictions, and their terms, which are dependent on negotiations, on any view, may be very different indeed. And the home Member State in which the recipient of any dividend is resident may or may not have its own Double Tax Treaty with the state in which the dividend-paying company is tax resident, adding yet another layer of complexity and driving a further wedge between the 'comparability' of the situations between the recipient of a dividend who is resident in the same Member State as the paying company and his counterpart, where the paying company is tax resident in another Member State jurisdiction.

[90] Broadly, at the material times, defined as companies which had a direct or indirect 75% shareholder relationship either as parent and subsidiary companies or as 'sister' companies: Income and Corporation Taxes Act 1988, ss 402 and 413(3).

of the UK tax resident parent was indeed prima facie breach of Article 49.[91] However, the Court went on to hold that the cumulative effect ('taken together')[92] of three justificatory factors cured the prima facie breach of Article 49 TFEU. First, the asymmetry of a circumstance where a Member State (here the United Kingdom) does not tax a particular person (here the non-United Kingdom tax resident subsidiaries) but is required to relieve its losses was a distortion of the 'allocation of the power to impose taxes'.[93] Secondly, the prospect of double loss relief (that is, the prospect of the loss-making company using its losses twice, once in the country of the tax residence of the loss-maker and again in the country of the profit-making group member, here the United Kingdom)[94] was also a cure for such prima facie breach. And thirdly the possibility of 'tax avoidance', that is, the setting off of losses of a subsidiary in a low tax jurisdiction against the profits of a group member in a high tax jurisdiction,[95] justified such breach.

Pausing there, the notion of 'double loss relief' and of 'tax avoidance' in *Marks and Spencer* as justifications which might cure prima facie breach are both applications of (some form of) the principle of mutual recognition. In both cases, whether or not the United Kingdom's group relief provisions may continue to be properly applied (because the prima facie breach is cured by the cumulative effect of these two justifications) depends on the tax regime of another jurisdiction (the home Member State of tax residence of the subsidiary who has the losses which it wishes to surrender against the profits of the United Kingdom tax resident company), implicitly treating the two tax regimes as comparable and effectively exporting tax regime of the home Member State of the loss-making subsidiary as a relevant factor in the application of the tax regime of the Member State of the profit making company (here the United Kingdom) to ensure internal market compliance. Both of these formulations of justification are open to conceptual criticism.

First, in relation to 'double loss relief', the very question of 'double loss relief' was a problem of the CJEU's own making. If the CJEU had found that the prohibition against a company, which was completely outside the scope of the United Kingdom's tax regime, setting its losses against the profits of a company within the United Kingdom's tax regime was no breach of Article 49 TFEU at all,[96] the question of 'double loss relief' simply would not have arisen.

[91] Case C-446/03 *Marks & Spencer Plc v Halsey (Inspector of Taxes)* [2005] ECR I-1083, para 40.

[92] Para 51.

[93] Paras 45–46.

[94] Para 48.

[95] Para 49.

[96] A recognition that Art 49 was simply not engaged by reason of prohibiting loss-relief in respect of companies wholly outside the United Kingdom's tax net (since there was no exercise of jurisdiction over these companies by the United Kingdom at all) should have led to

Secondly, in relation to 'tax avoidance', the CJEU's formulation of 'tax avoidance' is a radical and erroneous departure from previous articulations of that notion. In *Cadbury Schweppes Plc v IRC*[97] the Court expressly held that the establishment by a United Kingdom parent company of a subsidiary in Ireland, merely so that the subsidiary might be taxed at 10 per cent (the relevant Irish corporation tax rate), rather than the (then) United Kingdom corporation tax rate of 30 per cent, was not in any sense 'tax avoidance' or an 'abuse of right'. The 10 per cent Irish tax rate was a Union-compliant (non-State Aid) tax rate to which the United Kingdom could not object. The United Kingdom thus could not impose anti-avoidance[98] provisions (which dissuaded United Kingdom tax resident companies from establishing subsidiaries in low tax jurisdictions) to the profits of those Irish tax resident subsidiaries; otherwise Article 49 (freedom of establishment) would be breached.[99] But if Article 49 TFEU is properly engaged because a company established in one Member State wishes to access the tax rates on another Member State, in relation to the taxation of the profits of that subsidiary, it is a very odd proposition indeed that the relief of the losses of that subsidiary (albeit established in a low tax jurisdiction) against the profits of its parent company,[100] which happens to be resident in a high tax jurisdiction, constitutes illegitimate 'tax avoidance' which justifies a, prima facie, breach of Article 49 TFEU. Again, the principle of mutual recognition (the recognition and relevance of the tax rate of one jurisdiction affecting the compliance, or otherwise, of another Member State's obligations as regards the internal market provisions) is unwelcome.

In *Marks & Spencer* the application of the principle of mutual recognition, whereby justification for breach, as respects one Member State, is dependent on what happens in another Member State[101] gives a very

the conclusion that the negative integrationist internal market provisions were not engaged, as negative integration is predicated on an illegitimate exercise of jurisdiction. By requiring the United Kingdom to, at least potentially, allow cross-border group relief, the CJEU effectively turned the internal market profits into tools of positive integration, which is conceptually wrong in principle. This aspect of the CJEU's decision in *Marks & Spencer* and why it was wrong is discussed in Ghosh, *Principles of the Internal Market and Direct Taxation*, ch 3.

[97] Case C-196/04 *Cadbury Schweppes Plc v Inland Revenue Commissioners* [2006] ECR I-7995 ('*Cadbury Schweppes*').

[98] The 'Controlled Foreign Companies' regime, which penalised the establishment of subsidiaries in low-tax jurisdictions.

[99] And thus require justification, subject to the application of the principle of proportionality.

[100] Or indeed any other 'group' company.

[101] It is inapt to analyse *Marks & Spencer* as any sort of conflict between a 'home Member State' (the United Kingdom) and a host Member State (the jurisdictions of the loss-making subsidiaries), since the tax regimes of the subsidiaries' respective jurisdictions (France, Belgium, Germany) were not the subject of scrutiny at all. There was no conflict of tax regimes analogous to the free movement of goods case law in *Cassis de Dijon* and *Italian Trailers/Mickelsson/ANNETT*, where the less restrictive regime of the home Member State of export could indeed be seen to be in conflict with the host Member State which prohibited their sale.

different dynamic to that which operates in relation to mutual recognition in the context of the free movement of goods. In *Italian Trailers*, *Mickelsson* and *ANETT*, what was at stake was whether the regulatory regime of the exporting Member State meant that the relevant goods were prima facie to be lawfully marketed in the host Member State. But the mandatory requirements (and indeed the express provisos) permit the host Member State to exclude the relevant goods nonetheless (so, in *Italian Trailers*, the motorcycles were ultimately legitimately prohibited, although that meant that the free movement of the trailers they were designed to pull was restricted and in *Mickelsson*, the personal watercraft were legitimately banned in Sweden on public safety grounds). In *Marks & Spencer*, however, the justifications which apply mutual recognition, double loss relief and 'tax avoidance' are predicated on the content of the Home State in which the loss-making company is established (and tax resident), which regimes may change (thereby either conferring or removing justification for breach). Changes to the usability of losses in the home Member State of a loss-making company may mean that 'double loss relief' may appear or disappear, whereas changes to a Member State's corporation tax rate may mean that the justification of 'tax avoidance' may arise (if the loss-making company's Member State decreases corporation tax rates) or vanish (if those tax rates are raised). It is not conducive to legal certainty, or to a Member State's legitimate expectations, that notions of justifications for breach of the internal market provisions are dependent on factors outside its control.

Similar comments apply in relation to the approach of the CJEU to proportionality in *Marks & Spencer*. The CJEU held that the restriction of loss relief to losses of subsidiaries within the home Member State tax jurisdiction was proportionate unless the loss-making subsidiaries outside the home Member State tax jurisdiction had 'exhausted' the 'possibilities' of loss relief in its State of residence (whether against its own profits, or against the profits of a third party which acquired the loss-making subsidiary in the subsidiary's state of residence).[102] The CJEU's reasoning was conceptually confused. The CJEU acknowledged that the justifications had to be proportionate, that is, they could not go beyond what was 'necessary' to attain the objectives they pursued, in order to cure a prima facie breach.[103] But even laying aside the objections in principle to the justifications themselves, neither of the conditions imposed by the Court to test proportionality (exhaustion of loss relief in the home Member State of the subsidiary and used by third parties in that home Member State)[104] can be said to be 'necessary' to the achievement of any of the justifications accepted by the Court in *Marks & Spencer*. Certainly, it is difficult to see

[102] *Marks & Spencer*, n 91 above, paragraph 55.
[103] Para 53.
[104] Para 55.

why loss relief for a subsidiary in its home Member State is at all relevant (let alone 'necessary') to preserve the 'balanced allocation of the power to impose taxes', or to prevent 'double loss relief' (since double loss relief only arises if a subsidiary has indeed utilised its losses). And neither can the exhaustion of the prospect of relief in the loss-making subsidiary's home Member State be said to be 'necessary' to prevent 'tax avoidance' in the *Marks & Spencer* sense, that is, the prospect of the group relief of losses in a low tax jurisdiction against the profits of a company established in a high tax jurisdiction.

Indeed this notion of 'contingent proportionality', which, in turn, results in a 'contingent justification', draws the repetition of an earlier criticism. It is orthodoxy that a Member State cannot cure a discriminatory breach against a non-national by reference to a countervailing advantage conferred on the non-national. And, as observed above, it should follow that a Member State in breach of the internal market provisions should not be able to cure that breach by reference to the regime of another Member State. And it follows that breach should not appear and disappear (because either justification or proportionality appears or disappears) in relation to the profit-making company's home Member State depending on the current tax regime (and any amendment to that regime) of the home State of another person, namely the loss-making company. In holding the profit-making company's home State (in *Marks & Spencer*, the United Kingdom) to be in contingent breach of Article 49, depending on the availability of loss relief in the subsidiaries' respective home States (France, Belgium and Germany), the CJEU has effectively made a countervailing advantage (loss relief in the respect of the subsidiary's home Member State) a justification, and (worse) the subsidiary's home Member State's tax regime a trigger for breach, in both cases where the subsidiar's home State's tax regime is a matter wholly outside the control and jurisdiction of the profit-making company's Home State. This offends legal certainty and legitimate expectation from the perspective of the Member States under scrutiny as to their compliance with the internal market provisions. The CJEU's analysis in *Marks & Spencer* has given rise to quite a mess.

VI. CONCLUSION

The application of the principle of mutual recognition to the internal market provisions is orthodoxy certainly in relation to the free movement of goods and, it seems, in relation to the freedom of establishment and the free movement of capital, at least in the context of the CJEU's direct taxation case law. The CJEU has applied mutual recognition to test breach, justification for breach and proportionality. In every case, it is conceptually unnecessary to the application of the internal market provisions, in the light of the developed principles of the prohibition of market access and of the prohibition against discrimination. The CJEU has never assessed the respective regulatory regimes of host Member States and home Member States so as to render mutual recognition a species of the principle of non-discrimination. But if a particular Member State provision neither impedes market access, nor is discriminatory, the CJEU has no need (and no legitimacy) to appeal to a distinct principle of mutual recognition. This observation is intensified in the light the *Dassonville* formulation for breach, which is wider than both the principles of non-discrimination and the prohibition of market access obstacles. The principle of mutual recognition acts as an accelerant to harmonisation (applying the internal market provisions so as to set aside Member States' regulatory provisions by holding there to be breach, or lack of justification, or an absence of proportionality) in contexts where harmonisation is readily available. Mutual recognition also subjects Member States' regulatory regimes to a harmonisation objective in areas where harmonisation may not be readily achievable, which, in turn, leaves a space in Member States' regulatory regimes which may remain (damagingly) unfilled for some time. In the context of the direct taxation case law, it has given rise to severe conceptual problems (frustrating legal certainty and the legitimate expectations of Member States, whose liability under the internal market provisions become contingent on what happens in another Member State, in relation to matters outside their control) which, for this writer, do not admit of any ready or easy answer. If the CJEU were to abandon the principle, in the context of a judicial technique,[105] it would, quite literally, not be missed.

[105] There can be no objection to Member States incurring obligations under a legislatively recognised mutual recognition principle, as in the context of qualifications etc. That is a wholly separate and different conversation.

8

Consumer Protection in EU Residential Mortgage Markets: Common EU Rules on Mortgage Credit in the Mortgage Credit Directive

TATJANA JOSIPOVIĆ[1]

Abstract

For many years now, there has been an attempt in the European Union to create a common legal framework for mortgage credit contracts and cross-border activities in the mortgage financial sector. One of the greatest challenges has been the establishment of a corresponding level of consumer protection in EU residential mortgage markets. This issue has become particularly important at the time of financial crisis. Consumers are increasingly exposed to the risk of losing their homes because of failing to fulfil, in due time, their obligations arising from mortgage loans, and thus losing confidence in the EU financial sector. Therefore, the European Union has intensified its efforts to improve consumers' ability to inform themselves of the potential risks when entering into mortgage loans and mortgaging their real property. On 4 February 2014 the EU adopted the new rules on mortgage credits in the Mortgage Credit Directive. The main objective of the Directive is to increase the protection of consumers in EU mortgage markets from the risks of defaults and foreclosures. A higher level of protection must be ensured by consumers' increased information capacity related to mortgage credits, as well as by developing a responsible mortgage lending practice across the EU. The Mortgage Credit Directive is also aimed at contributing to the gradual establishment of a single internal market for mortgage credits. In this chapter, the author analyses previous and current attempts by the EU to establish a uniform

[1] This chapter is a revised version of a seminar paper given on 12 February 2014 on the occasion of the Lent Term Seminar Programme organised by the Centre for European Legal Studies, University of Cambridge. I would like to thank Professor Kenneth Armstrong, Director of the Centre for his kind invitation, and Dr Jens M Scherpe, University Senior Lecturer, for the recommendation to participate in the seminar.

market of mortgage loans, and assesses the possible impact of the Mortgage Credit Directive on the protection of consumers in the market of mortgage credits and on the development of cross-border activities in the mortgage financial sector. Special emphasis is placed on the possible impact of the new EU rules on mortgages on national protection measures aimed at consumer protection at the time of financial crisis. The transposition of the Mortgage Credit Directive will undoubtedly contribute to a higher level of consumer protection when consumers enter into home loan contracts. However, the question arises whether, because of different levels of harmonisation of some rules laid down in the Directive, its implementation will actually contribute to an increase in cross-border home loans. The possibility for Member States to opt for increased consumer protection in some aspects of credit agreements when implementing the Directive, or the existence of different options for the exercise of individual rights that they may use cannot bring about an integration of mortgage credit markets.

I. INTRODUCTION

THE EFFICIENT FUNCTIONING of the residential immovable property market is highly important for economic wealth and social progress, both at the level of individual Member States and at the level of the entire European Union. Only a well-developed residential immovable property market with properly balanced protection of the interests of all participants can contribute to economic and social welfare. The establishment of well-balanced protection of all participants is particularly sensitive in the residential mortgage credit market where it is very important to balance various rights and interests: economic interests and the functioning of financial institutions on the one hand, and the human rights and social and economic interests of debtors (consumers) on the other. The problems connected with the establishment of balanced protection of all these rights and interests have in the past few years mostly arisen from the global financial crisis. The most recent statistics of 2013 in the residential mortgage market have shown that because of the financial crisis, in some EU Member States, these markets are developing at a different pace. In some, a modest increase in residential lending has recently been observed, while in others the impact of the crisis on the residential mortgage market is still negative.[2] This is most probably only one of the reasons why, at this point, there is no integrated residential mortgage market at the European level.

There are currently 28 different frameworks for mortgages and 28 different legal frameworks for residential mortgage credits in the EU. Each of these national residential mortgage markets functions separately and

[2] See the data published in: EMF HYPOSTAT 2013, www.hypo.org/Content/Default.asp?PageID=524.

independently, and development is primarily affected by specific national economic, social and cultural circumstances, as well as by the particularities of national legislation that regulates residential mortgage credits, consumer protection and other areas. The national legislation of EU Member States differs extensively, not only in the regulation of mortgage and other security rights on immovables, but also in the regulation of mortgage credit agreements. There are also differences in the types of security rights on immovables (mortgage, hypothec, fiduciary transfer of ownership, retention of title, etc),[3] conditions for the establishment of security rights, the enforcement of security rights, the rights and obligations of mortgagors and mortgagees, the publicity of land registers, the flexibility of security rights (ie, dispositions with secured claims and security rights), and the connection between secured claims and security rights (accessory/non-accessory mortgage).[4]

Regarding mortgage credit agreements, there are many differences in national legislation when it comes to early repayment rules (conditions for early repayment, the compensation regime for creditors), the method and formula for the calculation of annual percentage rates, property valuation, the enforcement of mortgage credits, consumer protection rules, etc.[5] As a result, there are no developed primary and secondary pan-European mortgage credit markets. Cross-border activities in the mortgage financial sector in the EU internal market are in principle conducted by setting up branches or subsidiaries in the territory of another Member State. In the long run, this actually means that mortgage financial services are provided for under

[3] Conceptual differences in individual security rights on immovables mostly ensue from the fact that some are typical of common law systems (ie mortgage), and some of civil (continental) law systems (ie hypothec). The most important differences are reflected in the legal effects of the establishment of security rights on immovables (conveyance of the mortgagor's title to the mortgagee, the establishment of an unlimited real right in favour of the mortgagee, conditional/fiduciary transfer of ownership to the mortgagee). For more, see S van Erp, 'A secure start for the development of European property law' in *Sicherungsrechte an Immobilien in Europa*, ed M Hinteregger and T Borić (Vienna, Lit Verlag GmbH & Co KG, 2009) 5; M Hinnteregger, 'Die Immobiliensicherheit in Europa—eine rechtvergleichende Skizze' in *Sicherungsrechte an Immobilien in Europa*, ibid, 42; V Sagaert, 'Harmonization of Security Rights on Immoveables: An Ongoing Story' in *Towards a European Civil Code*, ed A Hartkamp, M Hesselink, E Hondius, C Mak and E du Perron (Kluwer Law International BV, 2011) 1046–48.

[4] See eg the results of the comparative research of the legal regulation of mortgage in Europe published in verband deutscher pfandbriefbanken, Round Table 'Flexibility, Security and Efficiency of Security Rights Over Immovable Property in Europe', Schaubilder ENGLISH (Stand Bd III, 3. Erweiterte Auflage, Berlin 2012—Übersetzung gem Bd 50 vdp-Schriftenreihe) at: www.pfandbrief.de/cms/_internet.nsf/tindex/de_de_rtall.htm.

[5] See eg the results of the comparative research published in the White Paper on the Integration of EU Mortgage Credit Markets, ANNEX 3 (2007): ec.europa.eu/internal_market/finservices-retail/home-loans/integration_en.htm#whitepaper. See MB Aalbers, 'The Globalisation and Europeanisation of Mortgage Markets' (2009) 33 *International Journal of Urban and Regional Research* 400.

the law of the host Member State.[6] Only exceptionally are cross-border mortgage credit agreements concluded.[7]

In such a disintegrated residential mortgage credit market, we may justifiably wonder how to achieve greater integration of the market at the EU level in order to contribute to cross-border activities in residential mortgage lending and efficient and better protection of individual rights and interests. For many years now, there has been an attempt in the EU to create a common legal framework for mortgage credit contracts and cross-border activities in the mortgage financial sector. One of the greatest challenges has been the establishment of a corresponding level of consumer protection in the EU residential mortgage markets. This issue has become particularly important at the time of financial crisis. Consumers are increasingly exposed to the risk of losing their homes because of failing to fulfil, in due time, their obligations arising from mortgage loans, and thus losing confidence in the EU financial sector.

It ensues from past activities in the EU market integration of the mortgage financial sector that discussions and actions connected with the integration of mortgage credit markets have mostly been directed at the provision of optimal levels of simplicity, flexibility, legal security, transparency, consumer protection, the protection of SMEs and creditors.[8] Two possible options to achieve these goals, and to create an internal market for mortgage loans, have thus emerged: the introduction of common rules on EU mortgages, ie, the introduction of a common pan-European security right on immovable

[6] Cross-border provision of financial services is thus based on the TFEU rules on the freedom of movement of capital (Arts 63–66 TFEU), freedom of movement of services (Arts 56–62 TFEU) and freedom of establishment (Arts 49–55 TFEU).

[7] In such cases, a special problem can be the application of separate rules on the applicable law for mortgage agreements and credit agreements. When a credit agreement is entered into in a Member State and the immovable property securing the repayment of the credit is located in another Member State, the law applicable to a mortgage agreement, or to a credit agreement, may be different. A mortgage agreement as a contract relating to the right *in rem* in immovable property is governed by the law of the country where the property is situated (Art 4(1)(c) Rome I Regulation). This rule applies even in the case where a consumer concludes a mortgage agreement with a financial institution (Art 6(4)(c) Rome I Regulation). On the other hand, the applicable law for credit agreements is determined under the rules of the Rome I Regulation on freedom of choice (Art 3) and on the applicable law in the absence of choice (Art 4), or, in the case of consumers' credit agreements, under the rules referred to in Art 6 of the Rome I Regulation. (See Ch König, 'The creation of an internal market for mortgage loans: A never ending story?' (2013) 2 *European Policy Analysis*). Every foreign investor who secures his loan with an immovable in another Member State must, therefore, acquaint himself with its national legal system in order to adjust (if this is even possible) the conditions of his loan and its security to a different legal framework from the one in his country. This is usually very time consuming and costly. In situations of a single or occasional cross-border provision of services, it is often also not commercially cost-effective. For more on consumer protection in the Rome I Regulation see Christophe Bisping, 'Consumer Protection and Overriding Mandatory Rules in the Rome I Regulation' in *European Consumer Protection*, ed J Devenny and M Kenny (Cambridge University Press, 2012) 239–56.

[8] For more, see under Sections II. and III.

property (Euromortgage/Eurohypothek) and/or the creation of common rules on mortgage credit agreements. Both of these approaches to integration call for answers to numerous questions concerning the choice of an optimal legal instrument for integration, the determination of personal and substantive areas of harmonisation, and the determination of the optimal level of cogent EU norms in the area of mortgage credit agreements. A crucial dilemma is whether to unify or merely to harmonise (adjust) the rules on mortgage and mortgage credit agreements; whether to carry out adjustment by minimum or maximum harmonisation, or whether to conduct full or targeted harmonisation. In terms of the personal and substantive area of harmonisation, a dilemma arises about whether harmonisation should encompass all mortgage credits or only consumer mortgage credits, cross-border and/or only domestic mortgage credits, all mortgage credits, or only residential (home) mortgage credits. There is a question, after all, about whether all aspects of mortgage credit agreements should be harmonised, or only some of them. There are still ongoing discussions on many of these questions. However, in the area of the protection of consumers in the mortgage credit market, the EU has already adopted some concrete measures.

In this chapter, the author analyses possible options for the integration of the EU internal mortgage credit market. In the first section of the chapter, some ideas, projects, possibilities and perspectives for the introduction of a common model of security rights at the European level (*Eurohypothek*) are presented. In the second section, an analysis is made of EU initiatives to integrate the mortgage credit markets resulting in the adoption of the Mortgage Credit Directive 2014/17/EU (MCD)[9] on 4 February 2014. This Directive sets out the current position of EU institutions on how, to what extent and in which segments it is necessary to integrate mortgage credit markets at the level of the EU and to establish common EU rules on mortgage credit agreements. The objectives of the Mortgage Credit Directive are analysed, as well as the level and scope of harmonisation. Finally, a possible transposition of the Mortgage Credit Directive for the protection of consumers in the mortgage credit market is assessed, and for the subsequent process and dynamics of EU market integration in the mortgage financial sector. The transposition of the Mortgage Credit Directive will undoubtedly contribute to a higher level of consumer protection when consumers enter into home loan contracts. However, the question arises whether, because of the different levels of harmonisation of some rules laid down in the Directive, its implementation will in fact contribute to an increase in cross-border home loans. The possibility for Member States to opt for increased consumer protection in some aspects of credit agreements when implementing

[9] Directive 2014/17/EU of the European Parliament and of the Council of 4 February 2014 on credit agreements for consumers relating to residential immovable property and amending Directive 2008/48/EC and 2013/36/EU and Regulation (EU) No 1093/2010 [2014] OJ L60/34.

the Directive, or for different options to exist whereby consumers may exercise individual consumer rights, cannot bring about an integration of mortgage credit markets.

II. 'EUROMORTGAGE/*EUROHYPOTHEK*' AS A MODEL FOR THE INTEGRATION OF THE MORTGAGE CREDIT MARKET

In the European Union, discussions on the introduction of a common pan-European security right on immovable property as collateral for securing loans started from as early as the mid-1960s. At different levels, academic, professional (within the framework of banking and notary public associations) and institutional (involving the competent bodies of the EU), various projects, research activities and discussions were organised and European legal documents were drafted, aiming to find an optimal model for a European system of securing claims by mortgages. Analyses, research activities and discussions on these issues resulted in different answers and proposals concerning ways to develop a common European mortgage credit market.[10] Despite the existing differences, all the initiatives were based on the same idea: an efficient common European mortgage credit market could best be established by the introduction of a new and special European model of securing loans by mortgage, the so-called *Eurohypothek* or Euromortgage. This would be a security right on immovables existing in parallel with 28 national legislative schemes regulating security rights on immovable property. The Euromortgage would be a security right on immovable property governed by separate rules uniformly applied in all Member States. These rules on the Euromortgage and its legal nature, acquisition, disposition, protection, settlement and on the legal relations between a mortgagor and a mortgagee would apply regardless of where the encumbered immovable property was located. This specific European model of a security right on immovables would have to be designed in such a way as to represent a flexible instrument of security for both creditors and debtors, whereby all parties ought to be provided with the corresponding legal protection both in their mutual relations and in their relations with third persons. An appropriate balance in the realisation of their interests and possible conflicts should also be ensured.

The model should not provide an efficient security right only for creditors. The Euromortgage should not only be an instrument for securing claims but also an instrument by which the value of immovables is efficiently mobilised in the common European market and in legal transactions other than

[10] For more, see Sagaert (n 3 above) 1054–62; van Erp (n 3 above), studies and reports on the integration of EU mortgage markets by expert groups established by the European Commission at: http://ec.europa.eu/internal_market/finservices-retail/credit/mortgage/index_en.htm#maincontentSec3.

credit contracts comprising various financial transactions. Therefore, all the proposals for the introduction of the Euromortgage, although they differ with regard to the regulation of individual aspects of this legal institution, in principle define its basic features in the same way. The Euromortgage should cumulatively fulfil the following conditions: it should be (a) a non-accessory right whose establishment and existence should not be conditioned by the existence of a valid claim secured by it;[11] (b) a registered right acquired by an entry in the corresponding register, where such an entry fulfils the requirement of publicity towards any third persons and offers the possibility of its being used against any third persons; (c) a right incorporated in securities.

However, there are differences among individual projects dealing with the introduction of the Euromortgage in terms of the extent to which and how some of the mentioned features should be manifested in the regulation of the Euromortgage. These differences largely arise from the fact that, in some projects, various models of lien, already existing in individual legal orders, have been used for the regulation of the Euromortgage. In the current practice and because of their features, they have proven to be successful instruments for securing claims. The two basic models used in the proposals for the regulation of the Euromortgage have been the German *Grundschuld* and the Swiss *Schuldbrief*. Both these instruments are characterised by the fact that, in a particular way but with a different theoretical explanation, they unify all three features highlighted above as necessary for the efficiency of the Euromortgage in the European market of mortgage credits and for its flexibility in the financial market.

One of the first initiatives for the introduction of a common pan-European mortgage was the 'Segré Report' of 1966.[12] The European Commission organised a task force led by Professor Claudio Segré which developed an extensive report entitled 'Development of the European Capital Market' (the Segré Report) dealing with the problems ensuing from the liberalisation of the circulation of capital and the implications of

[11] The accessoriness or non-accessoriness of the security right on immovables depends on the legal nature of the relationship/connection between the secured claim and the security right. Accessory security rights are characterised by a strong legal connection between the security right and the security claim. The emergence, existence, termination and the exercise of a security right depend on the existence of a valid and enforceable secured claim. When it comes to non-accessory security rights, a security right exists regardless of a secured claim. A non-accessory security right may be disposed of independently of a secured claim. A person other than the holder of a secured claim may be the holder of a non-accessory security right. Therefore, non-accessory security rights are considered to be more flexible in legal transactions. For more on the types or effects of accessoriness, see OM Stöcker and R Stürner, *Flexibility, Security and Efficiency of Security Rights over Real Property in Europe vol III* (Berlin, Verband deutcher Pfandbriefbanken, 2010) 44.

[12] *The Development of a European Capital Market*, Report of a Group of experts appointed by the EEC Commission, Brussels, November, 1966 (Segré Report): http://ec.europa.eu/economy_finance/emu_history/documentation/chapter1/19661130en382develeurocapitm_a.pdf.

the establishment of an integrated capital market.[13] Among other things, harmonisation of the national legislation of the Member States on security rights on immovables was proposed. The German *Briefgrundschuld* was recommended, ie non-accessory liens on immovables incorporated in securities (*Grundschuldbrief*).[14] The task force was of the opinion that such a model for the real property security of claims could instigate the integration of the capital market among the Members States. It could, at the same time, play a particularly important role when it comes to housing loans because it is a cheaper and more flexible instrument of security than an accessory mortgage.[15,16] The Segré Report was followed by the proposal of the Union of Latin Notaries where, for the first time, the name Euromortgage was given to a single European model of security rights on immovables.[17] In its Report of 22 May 1987,[18] the Union of Latin Notaries officially proposed the introduction of a single real property security on immovables—the Euromortgage. According to the Report, it was meant to exist in parallel with other security rights on immovable property already existing in some Member States and it would be regulated on the model of the Swiss *Schuldbrief*.[19] The Euromortgage would be defined as a non-accessory security right on immovable property[20] whose application would eliminate/remove the barriers to the cross-border establishment of security rights on immovables. It was emphasised that the Euromortgage should be an optional security right provided for in European law which would exist along with the national security rights on immovables. It was believed that such a 'European' security right would remove legal, economic and

[13] For more, see O Stöcker, *Die Eurohypothek* (Berlin, Duncker & Humblot, 1992) 216, 217.

[14] See Stöcker (n 13 above) 216, 217; S Kircher, *Grundpfandrechte in Europa* (Berlin, Duncker und Humblot, 2004) 442.

[15] See Stöcker (n 13 above) 217.

[16] The accessoriness of security rights means the following: a security right only exists if a secured claim also exists (accessoriness of origin); the scope of a security right is determined by the amount of the secured claim (accessoriness of scope); the holder of the security claim (creditor) is always the holder of the security right (accessoriness of competency); a security right terminates with the extinguishment of the secured claim (accessoriness of extinguishment); a security right can be enforced only if the secured claim is capable of enforcement (accessoriness of enforcement). These types of accessoriness are taken over from Stöcker, Stürner (n 11 above) 44.

[17] Since then, *Eurohypothec* started to be used as a common name for all other proposals for a universal European real property security instrument on immovables and even in EU documents where the possibility of its introduction was considered.

[18] A shortened version of the Report with the proposals was published in the German language in HG Wehrens, 'Der schweizer Schuldbrief und die deutsche Briefgrundschuld—Ein rechtvergleich als Basis für eine zukünftige Eurohypothek' (1988) 7 *Ősterreichische Notaritars Zeitung* 181–91; HG Wehrens, 'Überlegungen zu einer Eurohypothek' (1992) 14 *Wertpapier-Mitteilungen WM Zeitschrift für Wirtschafts- und Bankrecht* 557–96.

[19] The regulation of *Eurohypothec* on the model of the Swiss *Schuldbrief* is explained by the fact that the Swiss *Grundschuld* as a non-accessory security right is even more flexible as a security instrument than the German *Grundschuld*. See Stöcker (n 13 above) 229; Wehrens, 'Überlegungen zu einer Eurohypothek' (n 18 above) 560.

[20] See Wehrens, 'Überlegungen zu einer Eurohypothek' (n 18 above) 560; HG Wehrens, 'Das Grundbuch als Finanzierungsinstrument' (1993) *Notariatszeitung* 69, 70.

practical deficiencies of strictly accessory security rights in the national legal orders of Member States.[21]

A more concrete determination of the Euromortgage was laid down in the 'Basic Guidelines for the Eurohypothec' of 2005.[22] These Guidelines represent a kind of 'model law' where all important aspects of the legal regulation of the Euromortgage were provided for. They constitute the most concrete and developed model of the Euromortgage[23] that describes its basic features and the principles on which it is based, as well as its establishment, publication, disposition, termination, the protection of trust and the right of settlement against the value of immovables, and its position in bankruptcy proceedings and its implementation in the national legal orders of Member States. Both the German and Swiss models had an impact on the proposed model of the Euromortgage, so that individual solutions were the result of the unification of some elements of the German *Grundschuld* and the Swiss *Schuldbrief* as the best practices in credit transactions. The Euromortgage is again defined as a non-accessory security right entitling its holder to the settlement of a specified pecuniary amount against the value of the immovable (Article 2.1). In the Guidelines, non-accessoriness is emphasised as the most important feature of the Euromortgage (Articles 12, 2.1). It is expressly laid down that the establishment, transfer and existence of the Euromortgage and the exercise of the right to settlement do not depend on the existence of a secured claim (Article 3.4). However, the separation of the Euromortgage from the secured claim is bridged with a so-called security agreement establishing a contractual connection between the secured claim and the security right, and a specific fiduciary relation between the owner of the immovable and the creditor.[24] In addition, according to the

[21] See Wehrens, 'Der schweizer Schuldbrief' (n 18 above) 181; Wehrens, 'Überlegungen zu einer Eurohypothek' (n 18 above) 559; Kircher (n 14 above) 483; O Stöcker, 'The Eurohypothek' in *The Future of European Property Law*, ed S van Erp, A Salomons, B Akkermans (Munich, Sellier European Law Publishers, 2012) 75.

[22] See Agnieszka Drewicz-Tułodziecka (ed), *Basic Guidelines for a Eurohypothec: Outcome of the Eurohypothec Workshop, November 2004/April 2005* (Warsaw, Mortgage Credit Foundation, 2005). The Guidelines are developed in cooperation with experts gathered in a research group called 'The Eurohypothec: A Common Mortgage for Europe', members of the subgroup 'Collateral' working within the 'Forum Group on Mortgage Credit' established by the European Commission, a representative of the European Land Information Service/EULIS and experts from various Member States gathered around the project 'Real Property Law and Procedure in the European Union' at the European University Institute in Florence.

[23] G Watt, 'The Eurohypothec and the English Mortgage' (2006) 2 *Maastricht Journal of European and Comparative Law* 175; Stöcker, 'The Eurohypothek' (n 21 above) 73, 74; S Nasarre-Aznar, 'The need for the integration of the mortgage market' in *Europe, The Future of European Property Law*, ed S van Erp, A Salomons and B Akkermans (Munich, Sellier European Law Publishers, 2012) 96–98.

[24] The security agreement stipulates under what conditions the holder of the Eurohypothec may keep and enforce the Eurohypothec (Arts 2.2, 4.1, 4.2). If the creditor exercises his rights under the Eurohypothec contrary to this agreement, the owner of the immovable is entitled to the compensation of damage (Art 4.3).

Guidelines, the Euromortgage is a registered security right (Article 3.2) and it can also be designated as a certified (letter) right (Article 3.3).

Despite these concrete initiatives for the legal regulation of the Euromortgage, so far no concrete measures have been adopted at the EU level for the introduction of the Euromortgage as a European optional security right. There are several reasons for this. One is undoubtedly the existence of limited EU competences for the introduction of the Euromortgage. There is no doubt that the mortgage credit market is part of the financial market and that the TFEU provisions on free movement of capital apply accordingly.[25] However, it is questionable whether, on the basis of EU competences for the adoption of approximation measures for the establishment and functioning of the internal market (Article 114 TFEU) and according to the principles of subsidiarity and proportionality (Article 5 TEU), the EU is really competent for the harmonisation of security rights on immovable property. It is also questionable whether all the prerequisites referred to in Article 352 of the TFEU could have been fulfilled so that the EU could possibly provide for the Euromortgage as an optional instrument which would exist as the 29th regime in parallel with 28 national legal regimes regulating security rights on immovables.[26] The reactions of Member States, financial institutions, associations of consumers and others regarding the need and justification for the Euromortgage have also been different and mostly very restrained. The European Commission incorporated the issues of justification of the Euromortgage in the 'Green Paper—Mortgage Credit in the EU'[27] of 2005. In discussion on this Green Paper—Mortgage Credit in the EU,[28] only a small number of those involved supported the idea of the introduction of the Euromortgage as a separate parallel security right on immovables (21 per cent of financial institutions, 31 per cent of Member States and 16 per cent of other participants). Those who supported the idea of

[25] See eg Case C-222/97 *Trummer v Mayer* [1999] ECR I-1661.

[26] Art 345 TFEU is very important for the harmonisation of security rights on immovables as a segment of property law. It states that 'The Treaties shall in no way prejudice the rules in Member States governing the system of property ownership'. In literature, viewpoints can be found that this provision does not exclude the whole of property law from the impact of European law. It is also emphasised that Art 352 TFEU may be a suitable legal basis for future optional instruments on EU property law. See E Ramaekers, *European Union Property Law* (Cambridge, Intersentia, 2013) 140, 220–23.

[27] Green Paper on Mortgage Credit in the EU (COM(2005) 0327) of 19 July 2005, final.

[28] In the Green Paper on Mortgage Credit in the EU, the Commission highlighted the question of regulation of security rights to secure loans as one of the key issues for the integration of the mortgage credit market. It referred to the recommendations for the introduction of the Eurohypothec (eg Basic Guidelines for the Eurohypothec) as a special optional non-accessory security right to be applied in the whole EU. It is characterised by increased flexibility and it would exist as a separate security right in parallel with the national regulations for mortgages. However, being aware of the complexity of the issue, particularly because it overlaps with many other legal areas such as substantive law and the law of obligations, the EC initiated consultations on the necessity and appropriateness of introducing the Eurohypothec.

introducing the Euromortgage believed that its flexibility could increase competitiveness, reduce interest and create better conditions for consumer credits. On the necessity to introduce the Euromortgage, participants in the discussion emphasised the need for further examination of the model, particularly with regard to its impact both on national legal regulations and on other legal areas (bankruptcy law, enforcement law, registration of immovables and others) and on the benefit for the protection of consumers. When it comes to the most important problem connected with the Euromortgage—its non-accessoriness—positions were also divided. While some were opposed to the abandonment of accessoriness to protect debtors, others advocated a more detailed elaboration of the idea of non-accessoriness. There were also those who, by referring to the positive experience in their national legislation, supported the idea of non-accessoriness of the Euromortgage.[29] Such reservations regarding the introduction of the Euromortgage, as well as increased problems in financing mortgage credits resulting from the financial crisis, contributed even more to the subsequent minimising of the Euromortgage as a model for the integration of mortgage credit markets.[30] Thus, the White Paper on the 'Integration of EU Mortgage Credit Markets' of 2007[31] no longer dealt with the problems of the introduction of the Euromortgage.[32] It only focused on defining measures to protect consumers in mortgage credit markets at the time of global financial crisis. For all these reasons, the question of introducing the Euromortgage as a model for the integration of mortgage credit markets remained open and was shifted to become only a subject of academic discussion.

III. COMMON EU RULES ON MORTGAGE CREDIT—A NEW APPROACH TO THE INTEGRATION OF MORTGAGE CREDIT MARKETS

EU initiatives in the area of mortgage credits have been mostly directed towards the protection of consumers in mortgage credit markets. Although it is clear from all EU initiatives aimed at the integration of mortgage credit markets that they are directed at creating a functional internal market for mortgage credits, facilitating their funding and increasing product

[29] For more, see 'Feedback on the Consultation on the Green Paper on Mortgage Credit 2006', 23 May 2006 MARKT/H3JR D(2006): http://ec.europa.eu/internal_market/finservices-retail/archive/mortgage_en.htm; AJM Steven, 'Accessoriness and Security over Land' (2009) 13 *Edinburgh Law Review* 421.

[30] See S van Erp, B Akkermans, 'European Union Property Law European Union Private Law, ed Ch Twigg-Flesner (Cambridge, Cambridge University Press, 2010) 181.

[31] White Paper on the Integration of EU Mortgage Credit Markets, 18 December 2007 [SEC/2007) 1683, SEC(2007) 1684] (COM/2007/0807 final). For more see S Nasarre-Aznar (n 23 above) 90, 91.

[32] The *Eurohypothec* is mentioned only in one of the annexes (Annex Three 'Impact Assessment of Specific Issues') as one of the models which could facilitate the cross-border transfer of mortgage loan portfolios (169).

diversity, the most significant emphasis is placed on improving consumer confidence and facilitating mobility to establish a single mortgage credits market. This was already obvious in the Commission Recommendation on pre-contractual information to be given to consumers by lenders offering home loans (2001),[33] resulting in the European agreement on a voluntary code on pre-contractual information for home loans.[34] Ever since 2003, the Commission has intensified its research on the level of integration of mortgage credit markets and the obstacles to their further integration which have blocked their development in order to determine the possible advantages of further integrating mortgage credit markets within the European financial market. Three different expert groups were organised and a number of studies developed dealing with the problems of mortgage credit markets[35] This resulted in the issuance of the Green Paper 'Mortgage Credit in the EU' (2005) in which the Commission presented its positions regarding possible interventions in the European mortgage credit markets. The European Parliament adopted its Resolution on Mortgage Credits in the EU (2006)[36] and subsequently the Commission published its White Paper on the Integration of EU Mortgage Credit Markets (2007). It ensues from all these documents issued by the Commission that the crucial question in the European mortgage credit markets is the protection of consumers. It is precisely the protection of consumers and their trust in mortgage credit markets which can be the main integrative element for the establishment of a single mortgage credit market. Therefore, the following issues were highlighted in the White Paper as the most important: improving the quality and comparability of information; promoting responsible lending and borrowing; rules on early repayment; the development of valuation standards; the transparency and reliability of land registers; and improving the efficiency of foreclosure procedures.[37] The Euromortgage is no longer referred to as a possible solution for integration. In short, the European institutions, when it comes to the further integration of mortgage credit markets, aim at the creation of common rules on mortgage credit agreements to ensure the greater protection of consumers founded on the principles of responsible borrowing and responsible lending as key factors of intensified cross-border

[33] Commission Recommendation of 1 March 2001 on pre-contractual information to be given to consumer by lenders offering home loans [2001] OJ L69/25.

[34] Agreement on the Code of Conduct and Register of Institutions adhering to the European Code are published at: http://ec.auropa.eu/internal_market/finservices-retail/home-loans/code_en.htm. For more on the implementation of the Code see HJ Dübel and M Rothemund, 'A New Mortgage Credit Regime for Europe—Setting the Rights Priorities' (2011) *Center for European Policy Studies/European Credit Research Institute*, EPS Special Report (www.ceps.eu/book/new-mortgage-credit-regime-europe-setting-right-priorities) 37–41.

[35] See expert group studies and reports on the integration of EU mortgage markets at: http://ec.europa.eu/internal_market/finservices-retail/archive/mortgage_en.htm.

[36] 2006/2012(INI): www.europarl.europa.eu.

[37] See White Paper on the Integration of EU Mortgage Credit Markets (n 31 above).

activities in the mortgage financial sector. This concept was adopted in the Mortgage Credit Directive of 4 February 2014, by which consumer protection at the European level is ensured when entering into residential mortgage credit agreements.

A. The Mortgage Credit Directive—Harmonisation of Consumer Mortgage Residential Credit Agreements

The Mortgage Credit Directive (MCD)[38] is the first adopted measure of the European Union which specifically provides for particular aspects of mortgage credit agreements.[39,40] The Directive is the result of several years of discussions on the 'Proposal for a Directive on credit agreements relating to residential property' of 2011.[41] It entered into force on 20 March 2014 and the Member States are bound to transpose it in their national legislation before 21 March 2016. The final adoption of the Mortgage Credit Directive was largely supported by the fact that 'the financial crisis had shown that irresponsible behaviour by market participants could undermine the foundations of the financial system, leading to a lack of confidence among all parties, in particular consumers, and potentially severe social and economic consequences'.[42] The existing problems that consumers had with loan credit agreements resulted in the final text of the MCD differing significantly from the Commission's first 'Proposal for a Directive on the freedom of establishment and the free supply of services in the field of mortgage credit' of 1985[43] and thus also from the Commission's 'Proposal for a Directive on credit agreements relating to residential property' of 2011.[44] In its proposal for the Directive of 1985, the Commission proposed to regulate only the issues connected with the exercise of the right to establishment and the right to provide services. In the proposal for the Directive of 2011, the emphasis was put on the protection of consumers in the cases of credit agreements relating to residential immovable property and certain aspects

38 See n 9 above.

39 This Directive was adopted on the basis of Art 114 TFEU which constitutes the basis for the harmonisation of consumer protection in Member States in the context of the completion of the internal market (Art 169(2)(a) TFEU).

40 For more on previous attempts of the Commission to regulate EU mortgage credit markets see Ch König (n 7 above) 3, 4.

41 The proposal for a Directive of the European Parliament and of the Council on credit agreements relating to residential property (text with EEA relevance), COM(2011) 0142 final—COD(2011) 0062.

42 The quotation taken from Recital (3) of the Preamble to the Mortgage Credit Directive.

43 Proposal for a Directive on the freedom of establishment and the free supply of services in the field of mortgage credit, Brussels, 7.2.1985, COM(84) 730 final (http://aei.pitt.edu/8826).

44 Proposal for a Directive of the European Parliament and of the Council on credit agreements relating to residential property, Brussels, 31.3.2011, COM(2011) 142 final (http://eur-lex.europa.eu/legal-content/EN/TXT/?uri=CELEX:52011PC0142).

of the prudential and supervisory requirements for credit intermediaries and creditors. In the proposal of the Directive of 2011, the emphasis was placed on consumer protection regarding pre-contractual information, the calculation of the annual percentage rate of charge, and early repayment.[45] However, in comparison with the proposed text, the final text of the MCD was much more extensive and detailed in the regulation of individual consumer rights. In the course of the discussion in the European Parliament, almost every provision in the proposal was amended and expanded[46] and special emphasis was placed precisely on the need to protect consumers from over-indebtedness with home loans and on the establishment of a system to promote sustainable lending and borrowing.[47] This is why numerous provisions on the financial education of consumers, on the protection of consumers from tying and bundling practices, and on a standardised information sheet for pre-contractual information, foreign currency loans, arrears and foreclosures and the like were added. In addition, many provisions in the proposal were amended to ensure greater consumer protection (eg early repayment, general information, adequate explanations, etc).

The MCD was adopted on the basis of Article 114 TFEU providing for the procedure of launching measures for the approximation of laws important for the establishment and functioning of the internal market. The reason for choosing Article 114 TFEU as the basis for the MCD was actually the only possible solution, because on the basis of that Article, the EU was authorised to adopt measures by which, in the context of the completion of the internal market, the economic interests of consumers were ensured (Article 169(2)(a) TFEU). The goals of the harmonisation to be achieved on the basis of Article 114 TFEU (the establishment and the functioning of the internal market) also determined the areas of harmonisation in the MCD. Therefore, the MCD harmonises only particular aspects of credit agreements relating to residential immovable property. For example, specific aspects of security rights on residential immovable property are not the subjects of harmonisation, although they may be of great importance for consumer protection. Likewise, specific aspects of consumer protection in foreclosure proceedings which, in cases of delayed payment, lead to the repossession of residential immovables are not the subjects of harmonisation, although they are one of the most frequent problems concerning consumer protection and home loans, particularly in the Member States affected by the financial crisis.

[45] See Arts 9, 12, 18 of the Proposal/2011.

[46] See the Amendments adopted by the European Parliament on 10 September 2013 on the proposal for a directive of the European Parliament and of the Council on credit agreements relating to residential property (COM(2011) 0142—C7-0085/2011—COD(2011) 0062): www.europarl.europa.eu/sides/getDoc.do?type=TA&reference=P7-TA-2013-0341&language=EN&ring=A7-2012-0202.

[47] See, eg p 3, 6 MCD – Text adopted by European Parliament (n 42 above).

i. The Main Objectives of the Directive

The main objectives of the Directive can be summarised as follows: (a) establishment of a high level of consumer protection; (b) prevention of irresponsible lending and borrowing, of unaffordable loans, and of defaults and foreclosures; (c) establishment of a high level of professionalism among creditors and credit intermediaries; (d) introduction of a passport regime for credit intermediaries; (e) establishment of an efficient and competitive single market for the benefit of consumers, creditors and credit intermediaries; and (f) promotion of financial stability on the internal market. In this respect, the Directive is a specific complement to the Consumer Credit Directive (CCD),[48] by which the laws, regulations and administrative provisions of the Member States covering consumer credit have been harmonised. Both directives supplement each other, widening the framework for consumer protection on the EU financial market and establishing a harmonised protective mechanism for various types of consumer credit agreements.[49,50] The Consumer Credit Directive generally applies to credit agreements (Article 2(1) CCD).[51] Due to the fact that the CCD does not apply to credit agreements secured by mortgage (Article 2(2)(a) CCD), the aim of the MCD is precisely the harmonisation of consumer mortgage residential credit agreements at the level of the European Union. For the most part, the MCD provides for the harmonisation of the same aspects of consumer credit agreements following the basic structure of the CCD, but taking into consideration particular characteristics of residential credit agreements and the very specific consumer protection needs of such agreements.

In order to meet these objectives, the scope of application of the MCD is determined in such a way that its application also encompasses so-called

[48] Directive 2008/48/EC of the European Parliament and of the Council of 23 April 2008 on credit agreements for consumers and repealing Council Directive 87/102/EEC [2008] OJ L133/66–92.

[49] Cf points 19, 20 of the Preamble to the Directive.

[50] In order to ensure harmonised protection of consumers in taking consumer loans, residential mortgage credits and home loans, there are various links (in individual articles of the Mortgage Credit Directive) between the CCD and MCD. Eg, in some of its articles, the MCD refers to the appropriate application of the CCD. Thus, the MCD, in Art 4 which outlines some definitions for the purpose of this Directive, only refers to the definitions given in the CCD, such as the definitions of 'consumer', 'total amount of credit', 'total amount payable by the consumer', 'borrowing rate', 'durable medium' (Art 4, points (1), (12), (14), (16), (18) MCD). On the other hand, the MCD in some cases leaves an option to Member States not to apply some provisions of the MCD to some credit agreements but only under the condition that they apply the provisions of the CCD (Art 3(3)(a), (e) MCD).

[51] The exceptions from the scope of application of the CCD are expressly laid down in Art 2(2) CCD. However, the MCD has expressly broadened the scope of application of the CCD regardless of these exceptions. Art 46 MCD expressly supplements the CCD by widening the scope of application also to unsecured credit agreements whose purpose is the renovation of residential movable property involving a total amount of credit exceeding €75,000.

'home loans', ie agreements relating to residential immovable property regardless of whether they are secured by a real security right on immovable property. The scope of application of the MCD covers, on the one hand, consumer credit agreements[52] secured by a real security right on residential immovable property, ie agreements secured by mortgage or another comparable security commonly used in a Member State, or by a right related to residential immovable property (Article 3(1)(a)). On the other hand, the Directive applies to credit agreements whose purpose is to acquire or retain property rights in land or in an existing or projected building (Article 3(1)(b)) and regardless of the fact that they are not protected by security on immovable property.[53] The scope of application encompasses only consumer[54] residential property agreements, irrespective of whether cross-border or domestic credit agreements are at issue. The Directive does not distinguish in any way the legal regulation of credit in immovable property agreements protected by security depending on whether the charged property is located in the state where the consumer resides or in another state.

Regarding consumer protection in credit agreements, it is irrelevant whether a mortgage agreement is made as a cross-border or a domestic agreement. For the Directive to apply it is decisive that a credit agreement relates solely and predominantly to residential immovable property, for such property is charged by a real security right either because the purpose of the credit agreement is the acquisition or retention of a property right in land or in an existing or projected building.[55] Other consumer credit agreements that relate to immovable property without any residential purpose are not covered by the Directive.[56] It is obvious that the main aim of the Directive is to establish common standards of consumer protection for credit agreements most frequently taken by consumers to ensure their elementary existential need for acquiring a home and satisfying their housing needs.

[52] For the purposes of the Directive, 'credit agreement' means an agreement whereby a creditor grants or promises to grant, to a consumer, a credit falling within the scope of the Directive (Art 3) in the form of a deferred payment, loan or other similar financial accommodation (Art 4(3) MCD).

[53] Credit agreements excluded from the scope of application of the Directive are expressly specified in Art 4(2) MCD.

[54] For the purposes of the Directive, 'consumer' is defined as in Art 3(a) CCD (Art 4(1) MCD). According to the MCD, 'consumer' is considered to be a natural person who, in transactions covered by the Directive, is acting for the purposes which are outside his trade, business or profession. 'Creditor' means a natural or legal person who grants or promises to grant credit falling within the scope of the Directive (Art 3) in the course of his trade, business or profession (Art 4(2) MCD).

[55] Cf Recital 13 of the Preamble to the Directive.

[56] The Member States may, however, extend the scope of application of the Directive also to credit agreements related to other forms of immovable property (recital 13 of the Preamble).

In order to establish a common framework of consumer protection, various levels of harmonisation of individual aspects of credit agreements relating to residential immovable property are envisaged, from the minimum to the targeted maximum, or to optional harmonisation. In principle, the adjustment of individual aspects of credit agreements regulated in the Directive is based on minimum harmonisation (Article 2(1) MCD). Therefore, the Member States may keep or transpose into their national legislation more stringent provisions in order to protect consumers. Maximum harmonisation is envisaged only for two aspects of credit agreements (so-called targeted maximum harmonisation) with regard to standard pre-contractual information (Articles 2(2), 14(4), Annex II) and to the standard for the calculation of the annual percentage rate of charge (Articles 2(2), 17(1) (5), (7), (8), Annex I). As for these rules, the Member States may neither keep nor introduce any rules different from those prescribed in the Directive, but are bound to establish the level of protection laid down in the Directive. Indeed, many provisions of the Directive leave the possibility for the Member States to use the option of not applying some articles on specified consumer mortgage credit agreements to allow, or provide, some specific practice or obligations for the parties to the agreement (so-called optional harmonisation).[57] At the same time, for all the provisions of the Directive, its imperative nature is expressly prescribed (Article 41). In order to ensure the optimum protection of consumers, the provisions on consumer protection incorporated in the national law by the transposition of this Directive must be compulsory (*ius cogens*). In their credit agreements, consumers may not waive the rights conferred on them (Article 41(a) MCD), and the parties, by entering into other types of credit agreements, may not avoid the application of the provisions implementing the Directive (Article 41(b) MCD).

The measures whose implementation in the national legislation should lead to an efficient and competitive single market for consumer mortgage residential credit agreements are different in their content. The Directive contains a series of measures providing for requirements for the establishment and supervision of credit intermediaries and appointed representatives.[58] The aim of their implementation is to introduce a so-called passport regime for credit intermediaries to ensure a high level of professionalism when making cross-border credit agreements and a simpler and safer cross-border provision of financial services (Articles 7–9, 22, 29–34). Most measures relate to the harmonisation of the national rules on credit agreements, particularly concerning creditors' pre-contractual obligations, some contractual elements, the rights of consumers when paying their credit commitments, and

[57] Compare, eg Arts 3(3); 7(5); 11(1); 12(2), (3), (4); 14(6); 16(2); 22(4), (5); 23(2), (5); 25(2), (3), (5); 27(2); 28(2), (3).

[58] Cf Arts 29–35 MCD.

the like. The goal of these measures is to prevent irresponsible lending and borrowing and defaults and foreclosures detrimental to consumers. Some of these measures must be implemented from as early as the pre-contractual phase, ie before entering into credit agreements, and some are implemented for the duration of credit agreements in order to make it easier for consumers to meet their obligations in a timely and proper manner. These will be considered in turn.

ii. Measures for the Prevention of Irresponsible Lending and Borrowing

According to the MCD, consumer protection in the pre-contractual phase is based on various measures, the common aim of which is to prevent irresponsible lending and borrowing, ie to prevent consumers from assuming unaffordable credit obligations which at the end of the day may lead to residential immovable property foreclosures. All these measures must ensure, both for consumers and for creditors, the making of informed and responsible decisions on whether to conclude a credit agreement, who to conclude it with and under what conditions. Such informed consumer decisions regarding the making of credit agreements are facilitated by measures which provide clearer and general information and which standardise the method of calculating the annual percentage of charge (APRC). Measures important for a creditor's decision on whether to enter into a credit agreement are those that will ensure an objective and regular assessment of the creditworthiness of the consumer in order to establish, in the pre-contractual phase, the consumer's real capacity to regularly meet his or her credit commitments.

iii. Clearer and General Information for Consumers

Clearer and better information for consumers in the pre-contractual phase is provided for in the Directive through various measures, from binding the Member States to promote measures for the financial education of consumers (Article 6 MCD), defining the principles for the conducting of business of creditors, credit intermediaries and appointed representatives (Articles 7, 8, 9 MCD),[59] to the obligation of providing information to consumers in various phases of the conclusion of the credit agreement (Articles 10–16 MCD). The Directive expressly lays down the rules on creditors' obligations in terms of standard information in advertising, general information

[59] The principles for conducting business must include the obligation to act honestly, fairly, transparently and professionally, to organise sound and effective risk management, to act in the consumer's best interest, to provide information free of charge to consumers, to have an appropriate level of knowledge and competence, the obligation for advertising to be fair, clear and not misleading, and the prohibition of tying practices. See Ch König (n 7 above) 4.

about credit agreements, information concerning intermediaries and representatives, and the obligations of providing adequate explanations and advice to consumers.[60]

When the pre-contractual obligations of providing information are at issue, a central place in the Directive is given to the creditor's obligation to provide the consumer with personalised pre-contractual information in the form of European Standardised Information Sheet (ESIS) (Article 14 MCD) the model for which is given in Annex II of the Directive. With full standardisation of personalised pre-contractual information, consumers are offered a comparison between the existing credit possibilities available on the market and are thus able to make an assessment of their implications in order to make an informed decision about whether to conclude a credit agreement. Special standardisation of personalised pre-contractual information at the level of the EU is emphasised in the rules binding Member States to transpose the rules on the ESIS (Article 14(2), Annex II) into their national legislation without any variations (maximum harmonisation, Article 2(2) MCD). The obligation of maximum harmonisation refers only to the rules on the use of a standard form.

Other rules on personalised pre-contractual information are subject to either minimum or optional harmonisation. For example, rules on the time period during which the consumer will have sufficient time to make an informed decision are subject to minimal harmonisation. The Directive prescribes that such a period will last at least seven days (Article 14(6) MCD). This means that Member States may determine a longer period for making an informed decision. They thus have an option to decide whether this period of time will be a period of reflection before the conclusion of the agreement, a period for exercising the right of withdrawal, or a combination of the two (Article 16(6) MCD). It actually depends on Member States whether or not a consumer who concludes a credit agreement will be entitled to the right of withdrawal.[61] In such a way, the Directive has made an exception compared to previous consumer directives where consumers were given the right of withdrawal as a separate right after the conclusion of a consumer agreement.

The regulation of the time available as a period of reflection prior to the conclusion of an agreement protects the consumer in a different way because he is granted such a period of time for making an informed decision before entering into an agreement. This is why there is a special option in the Directive if a Member State decides to regulate such time as a period of reflection. To increase consumer protection, a Member State may then provide that consumers may not accept an offer for a period not exceeding

[60] See Ch König (n 7 above) 6.
[61] See Ch König (n 7 above) 5.

the first 10 days of the reflection period (Article 14(6) MCD). In such a way, the protection existing in other consumer contracts where consumers may exercise their right to withdrawal is moved into the pre-contractual phase. Protection is offered in such a way that the conclusion of an agreement is actually prevented until all the relevant information in the form of a standard information sheet has been obtained.

All the rules laid down in the MCD regarding information and practices prior to the conclusion of a credit agreement undoubtedly make it possible for the consumer to make an informed decision on whether to enter into a credit agreement, with whom, and what kind of credit agreement this is going to be. Pre-contractual information to make an informed decision on entering into an agreement is one of the key pillars of consumer protection in the EU. In this particular sector, consumer protection is constantly increasing. Specific obligations regarding information are introduced in the phase of advertising and offering general information. Maximum harmonisation is envisaged for the rules on the pre-contractual provision of necessary information. Special forms for such information are being standardised and the lists of those that are compulsory are extended. The MCD follows all the trends already existing in the previous consumer contracts directives[62] and in particular those contained in the Directive on Consumer Rights of 2011,[63] where the obligation of pre-contractual information was raised to the level of a general rule for all consumer contracts (Article 5), while for distance and off-premises contracts there is a special list of pre-contractual information requirements as a maximum harmonisation rule (Article 6).[64] Compared with the rules on pre-contractual information for distance and off-premises contracts laid down in the Directive on Consumer Rights (Article 6), the MCD provides for the content of pre-contractual information in an even more complex manner.[65] In the very text of the MCD, not all information that must be given to a consumer is listed (as in the Directive on Consumer Rights, Article 6(1)), but the obligatory list of pre-contractual personalised information is derived from the European Standardised Information Sheet (ESIS). All these pieces of information are

[62] See eg Consumer Credit Directive (n 48 above), or Directive 2008/122/EC of the European Parliament and of the Council of 14 January 2009 on the protection of consumers in respect of certain aspects of timeshare, long-term holiday product, resale and exchange contracts [2009] OJ L33/10.

[63] Directive 2011/83/EU of the European Parliament and of the Council of 25 October 2011 on consumer rights, amending Council Directive 93/13/EEC and Directive 1999/44/EC of the European Parliament and of the Council and repealing Council Directive 85/577/EEC and Directive 97/7/EC of the European Parliament and of the Council [2011] OJ L304/64.

[64] The obligation of pre-contractual information does not apply to consumer contracts exempted from the area of application of the Directive on Consumer Rights (Art 3(2)) or for distance and off-premises contracts in the case of which pre-contractual requirements are particularly provided for in this Directive (Art 6).

[65] Comp Annex II MCD.

adjusted to the particular data of the parties and their obligations arising from the loan credit agreements (amount and currency of the loan, the borrower's rights, interest rate, other costs, the number of payments, etc) and they must offer a complete picture of the borrower's rights and obligations, and all financial and legal consequences for the borrower in the case of the non-fulfilment of obligations. A standardised form in which information is provided contributes to better understanding. However, despite such a clear presentation of information in the ESIS, it is questionable whether one can expect the average consumer to be able to read and understand all the information contained on the information sheet and to make an informed decision whether to enter into a credit loan agreement. The complexity and amount of data may ultimately discourage consumers from entering into such agreements, and, what is even worse, this may result in contracts being concluded without the necessary understanding of the conditions of taking loans. Therefore, a particularly important provision is the one contained in Article 16 MCD on adequate explanations. The MCD lays down that Member States must ensure that the creditor, credit intermediaries and appointed representatives must provide adequate explanations to the consumer, such as those about the essential characteristics and specific effects of the credit, including the consequences of default in payment (Article 16 MCD). Such additional explanations, if the consumer asks for them, may lead to informed decisions being made on the loan which satisfies the consumer's needs and his or her financial situation.

iv. Standardised Calculation of Annual Percentage Rate of Charge (APRC)

A particularly important measure for the prevention of irresponsible borrowing is full and timely information for consumers of the total cost of credit throughout its duration. Very important is the information on the annual percentage rate of charge (APRC) and the method of its calculation. Therefore, the Mortgage Credit Directive, like the Consumer Credit Directive, prescribes a standardised calculation of the annual percentage rate of charge (Article 17).[66] In order for the consumer to be fully informed about the method of calculation and the total amount of his debt ahead of time, the Directive lays down a mathematical formula (Annex I) for the calculation of the APRC. It is expressly prescribed that the calculation must be based on the assumption that the credit agreement is to remain valid for the period agreed (Article 17(3)) and what costs must be included in the total cost of credit (Article 17(2)). The rules set forth in the Directive on the method of calculation of the annual percentage rate of charge

[66] See Ch König (n 7 above) 7.

(Article 17(1)–(5), (7), (8)) are the rules subject to maximum harmonisation (Article 2(2) MCD). Member States are not allowed to provide a different method of calculation of the interest rate and the total cost of credit in their national regulations and they may not allow consumers to waive the rights conferred on them ensuing from the rules on the calculation of the interest rate (Article 41 MCD). After the Directive has been transposed into national law, creditors will be bound to calculate interest rates only by using the formula and the method prescribed in the Directive. In such a way, legal security, certainty, transparency and product comparability will be established in credit agreements relating to residential immovable property.[67] The possibility of using different methods of calculation of interest rates and altering them for the duration of the credit agreement will be excluded.

v. Obligation to Assess the Creditworthiness of the Consumer

The creditor's obligation to verify the creditworthiness of the consumer before concluding a credit agreement is specifically regulated in the MCD as a measure by which irresponsible lending is prevented. When transposing the Directive in their national legislation, Member States must establish separate rules by which they bind creditors to make a thorough assessment of the consumer's creditworthiness (Articles 18–21 MCD). This is an essential condition on the part of creditors to be able to make informed decisions whether to enter into a credit agreement with a particular consumer. The basic criterion for such a decision will be an impartial, objective, independent and documented valuation of all factors important to verify the prospect of the consumer meeting his obligations under the credit agreement (Article 18(1) MCD). The Directive expressly provides that such assessment of creditworthiness will not rely predominantly on the fact that the value of the charged immovable property is higher than the amount of the credit (Article 18(3)) but that other reliable standards have also been taken into account for the valuation of the immovable property, such as the consumer's income, expenses and other financial and economic circumstances. However, particular importance in the Directive is given to the valuation of residential immovable property that will be encumbered by mortgage (Article 19). Creditors must use reliable standards for property valuation, and the appraisers who carry it out must be professionally competent and independent of the credit underwriting process.

The basic condition for a detailed and objective assessment of the creditworthiness of the consumer is the possession of all information relevant for the assessment. The sources of information specified in the Directive come

[67] See HJ Dübel and M Rothemund (n 34 above) 3.

from all relevant internal and external sources, including the information provided to the creditor by the consumer, an intermediary, or appointed representative. They include access to databases used in all Member States for the assessment of creditworthiness (Articles 20, 21 MCD). Therefore, Member States must expressly provide for the consumer's obligation to submit, in the pre-contractual phase, all the information and evidence that creditors specify as essential for the appropriate assessment of creditworthiness. Regarding access to databases, Member States must provide access to the databases used for the assessment of creditworthiness to all creditors from all Member States, regardless of whether they are operated by public or private registers.

The assessment results determine the creditor's actions with regard to the credit application. If the creditor finds that the consumer will not be able to fulfil his obligations under the credit agreement, he must reject the credit application.[68] When transposing the Directive, Member States must establish separate rules providing for such a creditor's obligation. The mere fact that the consumer has given insufficient data to the creditor may not be the basis for the termination of the credit agreement, but Member States may prescribe that termination is allowed if the consumer knowingly withholds or falsifies information (Article 20(3) MCD).

The assessment of the creditworthiness of the consumer is by all means one of the very important conditions for an informed decision on whether the creditor will accept or refuse a credit application. The MCD very broadly determines the sources which help the creditor to acquire all the relevant information on the creditworthiness of the consumer (Article 20). These are not only the information given to the creditor by the consumer him or herself, but also the information from different public and private databases used in individual Member States to assess the creditworthiness of consumers and to monitor the observance by consumers of credit obligations. However, we must not forget that these are the consumer's personal data that need to be protected. The MCD does not contain any special provisions on the liability of the creditor for the use of the consumer's personal data from a database. The only thing that is provided for in the MCD is that the provisions on the access and disclosure of a database and the verification of consumer information are without prejudice to Directive 95/46/EC on the protection of individuals with regard to the processing of personal data and on the free movement of such data (Articles 20(5), 21(3) MCD). In other words, the protection of the consumer's personal data should be provided by the measures of the Member States for the implementation of Directive 95/47/EC. Taking into consideration the specific characteristics of

[68] The creditor would not be in a position to subsequently cancel or alter the credit agreement because of irregular assessment, unless the consumer consciously withholds or falsifies information (Art 18(4) MCD).

the data kept in various credit registers, more efficient consumer protection would require the special organisation of personal data protection in the process of assessing the creditworthiness of consumers This is of particular importance because, according to the MCD, consumers' data on their creditworthiness may also be used in cross-border credit agreements.

B. Measures for the Prevention of Defaults and Foreclosures

The protection of the consumer for the duration of the credit agreement is primarily directed at ensuring the conditions necessary for the regular, timely and complete fulfilment of credit obligations, particularly in situations where, after the conclusion of the credit agreement, particular circumstances occur which have a negative impact on the possibility to fulfil credit obligations. In principle, these are alternative measures by which consumers are assisted when they have difficulty in fulfilling their credit obligations. On the one hand, some of these alternative measures are regulated in individual Member States with the help of dispositive norms of the law of obligations, and the parties may incorporate them in their credit agreement. On the other, the incorporation of these measures in the credit agreement is expressly prohibited in other Member States of the EU. Indeed, the aim is to provide for greater protection of the consumer/debtor, although in the end, this makes his or her position even more difficult if he or she is unable to fulfil the obligations arising from the loan.[69] The current Directive lays down common standards for some of these alternative measures, and if these standards are observed, consumers are allowed to make use of these measures. In the Directive, particularly important measures for the prevention of defaults and foreclosures are specific consumer rights in the case of foreign currency loans, such as the right to early repayment, the right to agree on the transfer of the charged residential immovable property, or the right to the proceeds from the sale to repay the credit, as well as the measures for forbearance before and during the foreclosure proceedings.

i. Foreign Currency Loans

Entering into credit agreements relating to residential immovable property in foreign currency loans is a very common practice in some Member States. The biggest problem with such loans is the protection of consumers against the exchange rate risk which significantly increases credit obligations and

[69] See below under III.B.iii on contracting the right to agree the transfer of charged property to repay the credit.

ultimately leads to the consumer's insolvency.[70] Because of such changed circumstances, protection of consumers is possible by the application of the general rules of the law of obligations. It is also possible to agree that some protection clauses be entered in the loan agreement in accordance with the national law. In practice, such national measures do not provide sufficient consumer protection, partly because of specific conditions for their realisation, and partly because of the insufficient level of information on the part of consumers. In order to harmonise the rules on the protection of consumers against exchange rate risks, the Directive binds Member States to expressly provide for the regulatory framework of consumer protection when concluding foreign currency loans (Article 23).

This commitment to protect consumers against exchange rate risks is resolved in the Directive in a very specific way. The basic right that consumers must have when taking foreign currency loans is the right to convert the credit agreement into an alternative currency,[71] or the right to make other arrangements to limit the exchange rate risk (Article 23(1) MCD).[72] The concrete regulation of consumer protection within the framework established in the Directive is left to individual Member States. They may recognise both options or only one of them. They may also regulate these rights in such a way that they allow *creditors* to specify whether the consumer is left with both choices, or with only one of them (Article 23(2) MCD). In the case of the option of 'other arrangements to limit the exchange rate risk', Member States are completely free to choose and regulate such arrangements. The Directive only prescribes that the purpose of such arrangements must be to limit the exchange rate risk, and the rules on the imperative nature of the Directive (Article 41) provide that the consumer may not waive these rights.

Consumers' rights aimed at limiting exchange rate risks are extremely important for the prevention of consumer over-indebtedness, arrears and foreclosures. Various problems arising in practice due to changes in exchange rates have resulted in situations where in some Member States

[70] The Commission's proposal for a Directive on credit agreements relating to residential property of 2011 did not provide for the protection of consumers when taking foreign currency loans. Special rules on consumer protection have been incorporated in the Directive as an amendment by the European Parliament.

[71] An alternative currency is either the currency in which the consumer primarily receives income or holds assets from which the credit is to be repaid, or the currency of the Member State in which the consumer was either resident at the time the credit agreement was concluded, or in which he is currently resident (Art 23(2) MCD). In the case of the conversion of a credit agreement into an alternative currency, the exchange rate at which the conversion is carried out is the market exchange rate applicable on the day of the application for conversion, unless otherwise specified in the credit agreement (Art 23(3) MCD).

[72] The basic condition for the realisation of the right by which the consumer is protected against an exchange rate risk is his being well informed about the risk. In line with this requirement, the Directive puts an obligation on Member States to bind creditors to warn consumers of the changes of the exchange rate at least where the value of the total amount payable by the consumer varies by more than 20% (Art 23(4) MCD).

special measures have been taken to prevent over-indebtedness.[73] The efficiency of the measures referred to in Article 23 MCD primarily depends on how they are implemented at the national level in different Member States. Article 23 leaves Member States with very broad possibilities regarding consumer protection, as well as different options. Some of them have not even been sufficiently defined in the MCD. For example, the MCD does not define in any way and does not give any examples of which 'other arrangements' would be appropriate for consumer protection, apart from the conversion of loans into an alternative currency. Moreover, the MCD leaves it to Member States to allow creditors to determine the possibilities available to consumers to protect themselves from currency rate changes (Article 23(1)). Finally, Member States are given the possibility to additionally regulate foreign currency loans under the condition that these regulations do not apply retroactively (Article 23(3) MCD). This can certainly not solve the problem of the already existing over-indebtedness of consumers on the basis of existing housing loans resulting from current foreign exchange differences. Such an approach in the regulation of a very important consumer right when it comes to foreign currency contracts appears insufficiently concrete to ensure, at the national level, appropriate consumer protection from changes in foreign currency rates. The final result of consumer protection at the national level will thus largely depend on how individual Member States balance the protection of consumers' interests on the one hand, and that of creditors on the other. In a very specific way, the MCD opens up possibilities for giving a certain kind of precedence to creditors' interests if the possibility of deciding whether these possibilities referred to in the MCD, or only some of them, are available to consumers.

ii. The Right to Early Repayment

A special measure of consumer protection in the execution of credit agreements laid down in the Directive is the recognition of the consumer's right to early repayment of the loan with a reduction consisting of the interest and the costs for the remaining duration of the contract (Article 25). In their national legislation, Member States must regulate the right to early repayment, ie the right to discharge fully or partially their credit obligations prior to the expiry of the credit agreement (Article 25(1) MCD) as a special consumer right in credit agreements relating to residential immovable

[73] Eg, in December 2013, the Republic of Croatia, shortly after having become a full Member State of the EU (1 July 2013), amended the Consumer Credit Act (2009), by which the Consumer Credit Directive was implemented with the provision on the protection of consumers from changes in exchange rates. The Croatian Consumer Foreign Currency Housing Loans Act lays down a maximum amount of variable rate credit if the exchange rate changes by 20% or more. There is also a provision binding creditors to offer the conversion of loans into the domestic currency (Art 11(a)).

property.[74] The exercise of this right must not be subject to any sanctions. However, the regulation of all other conditions and modalities for the realisation of the right to early repayment continues to be left to Member States. For example, Member States may provide that the creditor is entitled to fair and objective compensation, which must not exceed the financial loss caused by early repayment of the loan. Member States may also provide restrictions, special conditions and time limitations under which the right may be exercised, as well as different treatment depending on the type of the borrowing rate or on the moment the consumer exercises the right to early repayment, and the like.

As with consumer protection involving foreign currency loans, the regulation of the right to early repayment at the national level leads to large differences which may have a strong impact on the level of consumer protection. The legal regulation of early repayment depends on how every individual Member State assesses the optimum level of the protection offered to consumers, or whether the right to early repayment has certain conditions and limitations, and whether the creditor, in such situations, is entitled to direct and objective compensation (Article 25(3) MCD). Indeed, the MCD provides that the compensation to be given to the creditor should not exceed the creditor's financial loss. However, the question still remains about whether, by prescribing such additional conditions for exercising the right to early repayment, consumers are discouraged from exercising their rights. In order to achieve better consumer protection, it would be much better for the MCD to contain a legal framework within which the right to early repayment may be exercised. It now seems that the right to early repayment is only declared as one of the consumer rights in credit agreements, but the circumstances still do not exist for the harmonisation of that right at the EU level.

iii. The Right to Agree on the Transfer of Charged Residential Immovable Property to Repay the Credit

One of the oldest traditional measures of consumer protection is the prohibition imposed on the parties to contract in advance that the charged real property will be transferred to the creditor's ownership if the debtor does not pay the debt in due time, and that in such a way the secured claim will be settled (the so-called *lex commissoria*). Such a clause is prohibited to protect the debtor as the weaker party to a mortgage agreement, and to prevent creditors from insisting that such a clause be entered in the mortgage agreement. Therefore, many national laws prohibit the incorporation

[74] The so-called 'pre-payment option' is considered as a measure ensuring financial and physical mobility of European consumers. See HJ Dübel and M Rothemund (n 34 above) 4, 60.

of such clauses before the repayment is due. Upon maturity, the possible transfer of ownership of the charged immovable to the creditor instead of the repayment of the loan is governed by the rules on the so-called *datio in solutum*.[75] Because of the financial crisis and the inability to make regular and timely payments arising from credit agreements relating to residential immovable property, the approach to the problem of the repayment of loans by transferring ownership of the charged immovable has become more liberal. In some cases, particularly when residential immovable property is at issue, it is believed that regulation of the right to free a debtor of his credit obligations by way of transferring the ownership of the charged immovable to the creditor may be more beneficial for the consumer than if enforcement proceedings for the repayment of the loan are conducted against him.[76]

Such a liberal approach to the possibility of contracting the transfer of ownership of an immovable as a substitute for the repayment of the credit is also laid down in the MCD. The Directive binds Member States not to prevent an express agreement that transferring the charged immovable to the creditor, or the proceeds from the sale, are sufficient to repay the credit (Article 28(4) MCD). In other words, the consumer and the creditor may expressly contract that by transferring the ownership of the residential immovable property to the creditor, all obligations from a credit agreement are deemed to have been met. The Directive does not say that the Member States must make it possible for the consumer to make a unilateral statement to free himself of his credit obligations by transferring the ownership of a charged immovable to the creditor, but only that they must allow for the possibility to contract a clause on the transfer of ownership based on the mutual consent of both the consumer and the creditor. It is not clear from the provisions of the Directive whether such an express agreement is allowed only after the credit obligations have matured, ie in the phase of foreclosure, or whether it would be possible to make such an agreement in advance, before the maturity of the credit obligations. The obligation of Member States to allow such an express agreement on the transfer of the charged residential immovable property to repay the credit is provided in the Directive on Arrears and Foreclosures, which leads to the conclusion that at least at the stage of enforcement it should be possible to expressly contract the transfer of the ownership of a charged immovable instead of repaying the credit. However, because Article 28 of the Directive is a provision

[75] For more, see in the 'Study on the Means to Protect Consumers in Financial Difficulty: Personal Bankruptcy, Datio in Solutum of Mortgages, and Restrictions on Debt Collection Abusive Practices'. Final Report prepared by London Economics (2012) 106–54, 201–18: http://ec.europa.eu/internal_market/finservices-retail/docs/fsug/papers/debt_solutions_report_en.pdf.

[76] See the 'Study on the Means to Protect Consumers in Financial Difficulty' (n 75 above) 204–13, 218.

of minimum harmonisation, it seems that Member States may broaden such consumer protection to include the time prior to the maturity of the credit obligations.

iv. Measures Before the Foreclosure Procedure

The Directive binds Member States to take particular measures to prevent the foreclosure procedure for the payment of claims arising from credit agreements, ie by which the position of consumers in foreclosure proceedings will be alleviated as much as possible (Article 28 MCD). The Directive obliges Member States to adopt measures to encourage creditors to exercise reasonable forbearance before the foreclosure proceedings. The selection of appropriate measures to ensure considerate creditor action is left to the discretion of individual Member States. Every Member State must lay down whether a creditor is entitled to charges because of the consumer's default. In that case, only the charges necessary to compensate for the creditor's costs may be sought. Regarding the foreclosure proceedings to sell residential immovable property, the Directive obliges Member States to adopt measures by which the best price for the charged immovable can be achieved in the foreclosure proceedings. When the creditor still has not been fully compensated in the foreclosure proceedings, Member States must adopt special measures to make it easier for the consumer to pay the remaining debts also after the sale. However, the Directive does not expressly lay down what measures should be introduced at the national level in order to achieve all these goals in the foreclosure proceedings. Therefore, the measures and their content, as well as their realisation, primarily depend on how the foreclosure proceedings are regulated in a Member State and by which instruments within the foreclosure proceedings debtors are normally protected. If the existing measures do not provide efficient protection of consumers in the foreclosure proceedings,[77] in order to act in conformity with the obligations

[77] A very important aspect of the protection of a consumer whose residential immovable property is sold in foreclosure proceedings for the repayment of debts arising from a credit agreement is the legal instrument (eg legal action, complaint, appeal, or an interim measure) by which the consumer in foreclosure proceedings may exercise the protection of his rights, challenge the validity of a credit agreement, unfair contract terms, etc. All these instruments must be regulated in such a way that they offer the consumer efficient protection of his rights. See eg Case C-415/11 *Mohamed Aziz v Caixa d Estalvis de Catalunya, Tarragona i Manresa (Catalunyacaixa)* [2013] ECR nyr. This case concerns the interpretation of the principle of the efficiency of interim relief in mortgage enforcement proceedings for the payment of a claim arising from a consumer mortgage credit agreement. For more on the meaning of the principle of efficient consumer protection when dealing with unfair contract terms, see in N Reich, *General Principles of EU Civil Law* (Cambridge, Intersentia, 2014) 89–129; J König, *Der Äquivalenz- und Effektivitätgtundsatz in der Rechtsprechung des Europäischen Gerichtshofs* (Nomos, 2011) 205–11; P Rott, 'The Court of Justice's Principle of Effectiveness and its Unforeseeable Impact on Private Law Relationships' in *The Involvement of EU Law in Private Law Relationships*, ed D Leczykiewicz and S Weatherill (Oxford, Hart Publishing, 2013) 181–98.

in the Directive, it will be necessary to introduce some new measures for consumer protection. The Directive does not specify these measures and it does not even lay down the criteria to be followed by Member States when assessing the existing measures and introducing new ones to alleviate the position of consumers as debtors.

IV. CONCLUSION

Once the Mortgage Credit Directive is transposed into the national legislation of Member States, it will undoubtedly contribute to the greater protection of consumers when they conclude credit agreements relating to residential immovable property, both in the pre-contractual phase and in the phase of fulfilling their credit obligations.[78] This Directive declares high standards in terms of consumers being well-informed and thus being able to make informed decisions when entering into credit agreements. In the phase of the fulfilment of their credit obligations, consumers are offered a number of different measures to facilitate the fulfilment of such obligations and to minimise potential credit risks. It is to be expected that the realisation of these measures will have a positive impact on consumer trust in the housing loans market. In that sense, the Mortgage Credit Directive is by all means a step forward in the process of establishing a single market for residential mortgage credits.

However, it was been argued here that the implementation of the Directive will open many new questions regarding consumer protection when taking home loans. First of all, a question remains about whether the implementation of the Directive will really contribute to an increase in cross-border home loans. It is also uncertain to what extent the implementation of the Directive will really contribute to a more transparent, legally secure and competitive single market of loans relating to residential immovable property. It seems that even after the implementation of the Directive, a great diversity of national rules on mortgages and residential mortgage credit agreements will continue to exist, which may discourage consumers from the cross-border conclusion of credit agreements. The Directive harmonises only some aspects of credit agreements relating to residential immovable property. Minimal harmonisation is what is mostly foreseen. Even where minimum harmonisation is envisaged, the Directive leaves it to Member States to choose from various options offered as a compromise, or specific possibilities for the regulation of individual rights of the parties to credit agreements. In some cases, it is left to Member States to allow creditors to choose which proposed options they want to offer to consumers. Therefore, it seems that even after the transposition of the Directive, significant differences in the national regulation of credit agreements relating to

[78] See Ch König (n 7 above) 13.

residential immovable property will remain. This will be reflected in different levels of consumer protection in the national markets of Member States.

It is also uncertain whether the implementation of the Directive will provide the level of consumer protection needed when consumers take home loans because of the high level of over-indebtedness of consumers resulting from the economic crisis. A question also arises as to whether the implementation of the Directive can contribute to solving the problems that consumers who have already taken home loans face and against whom foreclosure proceedings have already started. Although the Directive contains a series of measures aimed at better consumer protection when consumers take home loans, most of them are set forth in a very general way. This may lead to problems when they are made concrete and when they are implemented at the national level. In the end, it may make the accomplishment of the main goals of the Directive more difficult. Efficient consumer protection when consumers enter into credit agreements relating to residential immovable property at the EU level requires a different approach to harmonisation—an approach where individual consumer rights and the conditions for their realisation are regulated in a more concrete way, and the scope of maximum harmonisation is also extended to other aspects of the contract rather than being limited only to pre-contractual information and the calculation of the APRC. Because of the present need to protect consumers from over-indebtedness, it is not enough to determine generally consumer rights and other measures to be taken to protect them. Likewise, it is not sufficient to bind Member States to adopt measures encouraging creditors to act with reasonable forbearance towards consumers, or measures to facilitate repayment in order to protect consumers. Better protection of consumers as the weaker contractual party could certainly be achieved by concrete and clear rules governing their rights when entering into credit agreements, and possibly also by the extension of consumer protection at least to some aspects of contracts establishing security rights regarding credit claims. In the MCD, only some consumer rights in credit agreements are regulated. This Directive does not provide for any aspect of consumer protection in agreements establishing mortgage or other security rights, although most frequently, in the cases of non-payment, forceful collection is carried out against the mortgaged immovable. The consequences of irresponsible borrowing and lending can best be seen in proceedings for the forced sale of mortgaged immovables, because very often these proceedings end with the repossession of the residential immovable in favour of creditors or third persons. Therefore, the MCD can only be considered as the first serious step in taking the necessary measures for efficient consumer protection on mortgage credit markets. More efficient and complete protection will only be achieved when individual consumer rights arising from credit agreements and mortgage agreements are more thoroughly provided for and when a higher level of harmonisation of the rules is achieved at the level of the entire European Union.

9

The Impact of the European Union Current Crisis on Law, Policy and Society

ANCA D CHIRITA*

Abstract

This chapter aims to understand the general nature of the current economic crisis from a socio-legal, economic, ideological and political perspective and to analyse the complexity of the multiple causes which have led to this crisis. The impact of the crisis on different areas of law is also considered, especially on banking, securities, contract, competition and corporate law. Furthermore, the article aims to criticise law in action and the management of the crisis through political decision-making (state intrusiveness), that is, the various responses and reactions to the crisis and the effectiveness of the measures implemented by policy-makers and enforcers. In particular, this article questions the constitutional legitimacy of the TBTF (Too-Big-to-Fail) theory as a predominant doctrine and criterion of state intervention in the economy. The chapter carries out a multi-layered analysis that covers aspects of economic, social, and political governance. It also draws insights from micro-economics—looking at how economic agents have affected individuals such as consumers—and from macroeconomics—looking at how state intervention in the economy has impacted upon taxpayers and considering the economic and social costs of the crisis. Finally, it approaches the crisis from the perspective of political economy by looking through the lenses of ideology and policy and by reflecting on the role of neoliberalism today.

I. INTRODUCTION

THE PURPOSE OF this chapter is to understand the general nature of the current crisis (banking, financial, debt, currency, constitutional, political) from a socio-legal, economic, ideological and political

* This chapter is based on the CELS Seminar in the University of Cambridge, 16 October 2013, and a Pre-sessional Lecture on 'Competition, Financial Markets and the Economic Crisis', Josephine Butler College, Durham, 11 September 2013. I would like to thank Dr Albertina Albors-Llorens, Dr Markus Gehring, Dr Folarin Akinbami, and Professor Kenneth Armstrong for extremely helpful comments and insightful discussions.

perspective and to analyse the complexity of the multiple causes which led to it. Interdisciplinary areas of law in which the crisis has manifested itself will be highlighted throughout this chapter, in particular financial, banking, securities, contract, competition and corporate law. Finally, the chapter aims to criticise the legal response and the management of the crisis through political decision-making (state intrusiveness), that is, the various responses and reactions to the crisis and the effectiveness of the measures implemented by policy-makers and enforcers, and to question the constitutional legitimacy of the TBTF (Too-Big-to-Fail) theory as a predominant doctrine and criterion of state intervention in the economy.

The methodology of this chapter is interdisciplinary and encompasses law, economics, and politics. A multi-layered level of economic, social, and political governance is envisaged through insights from microeconomics, by looking at how economic agents have affected individuals such as consumers; from macroeconomics, by looking at how state intervention in the economy has impacted upon taxpayers and the economic and social costs of the crisis; and from political economy by looking through the lenses of ideology and policy and reflecting on the role of neoliberalism today.

The heavy reliance on the TBTF doctrine became an EU 'Too Big to Crash' theme amid fears of an eventual repeat of the 1929 Wall Street Crash, which to date has been avoided by all possible means of political intervention. Unfortunately, competition law could be seen as the scapegoat of this unprecedented restructuring of the banking and financial markets through the use of generous state aid to benefit inefficient financial game players. This last recognition leads us to question the adequacy of measures of profit-seeking capitalism.

The structure of this chapter is as follows. After a brief introduction, Section II questions the nature of the crisis and its origins. It explains both the micro and the macroeconomic level of intervention in times of crisis, and it highlights the need to address the failures of both public and private economic actors. Section III digs deeper into the roots of the crisis and generally classifies the major disturbing causes playing a role in the current crisis. In turn, Section IV focuses on one particular cause of the problem, namely the behavioural exploitation of consumers by bankers and states through the use of a low interest rate stimulus. It critically engages with the EU high unemployment rate and challenges its austerity policies. Section V contrasts the existing convergence criteria for harmonious EU economic development across Member States with the current economic outlook and challenges the critical and apparent legitimacy of bailouts. The lack of democratic legitimacy of the latter is exacerbated by the social and economic costs of the EU crisis, which are the subject of Section VI. In particular the main categories of state aid will be explored here, as well as the political and the institutional dimension of the crisis. Section VII will explain the widespread financial derivative contracts which are the object of the recent investigations conducted by the European Commission (EC). These investigations culminated with record fines, which will be discussed in greater detail in Section VIII. Finally, Section IX engages with the neoliberal ideology and challenges it as a social model of economic governance. Looking back at previous positions on social and corporate responsibility, employment, and capital mobility, the chapter is able to identify an overarching critical edge to the current scenario, in the form of the financialisation of global markets.

II. ON THE NATURE AND ORIGIN OF THE CRISIS

The nature of the current crisis has been determined by the sectors of the economy which are most affected by economic failures. As large financial institutions such as commercial, investment or securities banks and other major corporations have experienced a large number of defaults, this has first been recognised as a banking crisis.[1] However, a greater risk to affect and spread the banking crisis to other financial institutions has made it systemic. Before the crisis, banks experienced longer periods of credit expansion, which had also led to a rise of real estate and equity prices, above the gross domestic product (GDP). On the negative side, the credit boom reached a peak and burst into a price 'bubble', ie house prices fell below outstanding balances on home mortgages. Thus, a sovereign debt crisis then emerged as defaults on payments of debt obligations became the rule, which called for the restructuring of the banking sector. This process meant offering debtors less favourable terms than the expected capital gains.

One cannot fully understand the nature of the crisis without questioning first its origins. The global crisis emerged first in the US subprime market,[2] which generated losses during summer 2007 to mid-2008. Hundreds of billions of dollars in bad mortgage loans initially set at bargain rates[3] were reset at market rates so that when housing prices started to fall, owners defaulted on their payments. This was followed by the bail-out of Bear Stearns; the nationalisation of mortgage agencies Fannie Mae and Freddie

[1] See, eg, CM Reinhart and KS Rogoff, *This Time is Different: Eight Centuries of Financial Folly* (Princeton NJ, Princeton University Press, 2009); J de Haan, S Oosterloo and D Schoenmaker, *Financial Markets and Institutions: A European Perspective*, 2nd edn (Cambridge, Cambridge University Press, 2012); S Valdez and P Molyneux, *An Introduction to Global Financial Markets*, 7th edn (Basingstoke, Palgrave Macmillian, 2013).

[2] See M Jarsulic, 'The Origins of the US Financial Crisis of 2007: How a House-Price Bubble, a Credit Bubble, and Regulatory Failure Caused the Greatest Economic Disaster since the Great Depression' in MH Wolfson and GA Epstein (eds), *The Handbook of the Political Economy of Financial Crisis* (Oxford, Oxford University Press, 2013) 30; P Krugman and R Wells, *Macroeconomics*, 3rd edn (New York, Worth's Publishers, 2013) 432.

[3] Interest rates were extremely low due to large capital flows from abroad to the US economy, the US Federal Reserve, and low inflation. See, eg, Jarsulic, n 2 above.

Mac; and the Lehman Brothers' bankruptcy in September 2008. Until late October of that year, a global loss of confidence created a systemic risk of collapse.

The recession manifested itself through sharp increases in budget deficits and slow economic recovery. In addition, the limits of the Stability and Growth Pact of 1997[4] were breached. After September 2008, European Union (EU) rescue policies focused on restoring the liquidity of banks and guarantees, while the ECB (European Central Bank) and national central banks outside the euro adjusted the provision of liquidity and cut interest rates.[5] The Recovery Plan provided a discretionary fiscal stimulus of €200 billion, which was used for budgetary expansion rather than to 'boost demand and stimulate confidence'.[6] A Financial Stabilisation Mechanism provided Member States with another €500 billion. Not until mid-March 2009, were there any signs of stabilisation.[7]

Unique due to its geo-political architecture, the EU crisis revealed that it is not solely private economic actors who can default on their contractual obligations. Member States such as Greece failed to keep up with their borrowing costs. Furthermore, the political pursuits of monetary union and its single currency highlighted the complexity of the crisis at the microeconomic level. At the macroeconomic level, there was also a risk that Member States which maintained fixed exchange rates could also experience a currency crisis where the value of the national currency fell suddenly as a result of a loss of confidence followed by speculative attacks.[8]

The events in Greece led the EU to reconsider both the political and the constitutional dimension of the sovereign debts crisis. In May 2010, the EU set a precedent by granting a total of €80 billion to Greece.[9] In this context, the solidarity with Greece's economic failure triggered a political crisis fuelled with heated legal arguments. In particular, solidarity is pre-empted by Article 125(1) TFEU itself, which rules out state bail-outs[10] when it says

[4] See R Guttman and D Plihon, 'Whither the Euro? History and Crisis of Europe's Single-Currency Project' in Wolfson and Epstein, n 2 above, 368.

[5] See, eg, C Quigley, 'Review of the Temporary State Aid Rules Adopted in the Context of the Financial and Economic Crisis' (2012) 3 *Journal of European Competition Law & Practice* 237; see generally C Quigley and AM Collins, *EC State Aid Law and Policy* (Oxford, Hart Publishing, 2003).

[6] Ibid.

[7] See, eg, positive signs are noted in 'Towards a Genuine Economic and Monetary Union', available at: www.consilium.europa.eu/uedocs/cms_data/docs/pressdata/en/ec/134069.pdf.

[8] In 1999 several MS attempted to stabilise their exchange rates through the Exchange Rate Mechanism, see generally P Arestis and M Sawyer, 'Can the Euro Survive after the European Crisis?' in Arestis and Sawyer (eds), *The Euro Crisis* (Basingstoke, Palgrave Macmillian, 2012).

[9] E Chiti and PG Teixeira, 'The Constitutional Implications of the European Responses to the Financial and Public Debt Crisis' (2013) 50 *Common Market Law Review* 686; Guttman, n 4 above, 372 reported €750 bn.

[10] M Ruffert, 'The European Debt Crisis and European Union Law' (2011) 48 *Common Market Law Review* 1785.

that both the EU and its Member States shall not be liable for or assume commitments of central governments. A constitutional crisis emerged which suggested Greece's possible exit from the Eurozone. The precarious situation of sovereign debts transformed this crisis into a euro currency crisis amid speculations over Greece's economy. This was the first major test of both economic and, foremost, social European integration, which revealed the perils of free capital markets, liberalisation, and a single currency based on institutional foundations which were not capable of sharing the economic costs of major economic imbalances. In the absence of a fiscal union, the Founding Treaties proposed an Economic and Monetary Union subject to strict convergence criteria, which will be analysed in Section V.

In a nutshell, the crisis has highlighted the existing economic disparities in terms of economic development across the EU. Thus, some Member States became economically and socially responsible for other Member States' inefficiency. Likewise, the financialisation of capital services worldwide has triggered the responsibility of various economic actors, institutions, and the wider society. It has raised the question of who is primarily responsible for the crisis. This is not easy to answer either before or after judging the roots of the crisis, which follows in the next section.

III. ON THE ROOTS OF THE CRISIS: WHAT WENT WRONG?

The vast literature on the economic crisis abounds in suggestions of what went wrong before and after the crisis. Thus failures appear first as poor economic governance because the state employs ineffective means of correlating and/or correcting macroeconomic indicators which later affect individual decision-making. For example, some of the convergence criteria which Member States are required to fulfil prior to joining the Eurozone emerge first as economic indicators which went wrong, such as public deficit and spending, GDP, or interest rates. Valdez and Molyneux[11] have identified the following major macroeconomic imbalances: (i) large and persistent current account deficits following previous surpluses due to capital flows from emerging to rich industrial economies; (ii) a long period of low real interest rates fuelled by deflationary concerns; (iii) a credit boom for home mortgage lending which put up the housing prices before the crisis by more than 30 per cent; (iv) low interest rates that encouraged consumer spending and persuaded banks to take on more risk in various long-term contracts.

Among the leading variables indicating a financial crisis are rising defaults and government deficits, the rapid growth of credit and money supply,

[11] See n 1 above.

declining GDP etc.[12] This simplified picture has to be explored in greater depth to identify what went wrong with private and public actors, including Member States, law in action, policy-makers, and policy influencers.[13]

(i) What went wrong with public economic actors? Access to credit was easy, with too much money made available through a lax monetary policy, ie lowering interest rates. Through the transformation of investment banks into holding companies the shadow banking system acquired access to governmental funding.[14] Finally, banks which took high risks were bailed out and this encouraged them to indulge in more risk-taking.

(ii) What went wrong with private economic actors? Individual economic actors (consumers, borrowers, lenders) underestimated the economic cost and engaged in highly speculative contracts (eg variable mortgage rates, and loan insurance contracts).[15] In other words, consumers failed to be aware of risks to themselves and soon, complexity was mistaken for sophistication, with consumers assuming that their investments were safe. Corporate managers also failed to evaluate risks before entering into complex transactions, such as securitisation and credit default swaps, which will be detailed in Section VII.

In sum, the collective solidarity of banks had been oriented towards hazardous risk-taking,[16] market indiscipline, and market abuse. Managers increased returns by boosting excessive leverage, ie, the return on equity as the major indicator of a firm's performance.[17] In essence, the ownership of capital was financed by debts.[18] The net income generated to shareholders

[12] E Tymoigne, 'Financial fragility' in J Toporowski and J Michell (eds), *Handbook of Critical Issues in Finance* (Cheltenham, Edward Elgar, 2012) 102.

[13] For existing classifications see, eg, RM Lastra and GE Wood, 'The Crisis of 2007–2009: Nature, Causes, and Reactions' (2010) 13 *Journal of International Economic Law* 531; 537; L Garicano and R Lastra, 'Towards a New Architecture for Financial Stability: Seven Principles' (2010) 13 *Journal of International Economic Law* 597.

[14] E Avgouleas, 'The global financial crisis, behavioural finance and financial regulation: in search of a new orthodoxy' (2009) 9 *Journal of Corporate Law Studies* 121. The US abolished the Glass-Steagall Act 1933. On information asymmetries and 'moral' hazard problems see, eg, O Kessler and B Wilhelm, 'Financialization and the Three Utopias of Shadow Banking' (2013) 17 *Comp and Change* 251; on government failure, see ME Stucke, 'Lessons from the Financial Crisis' (2011) 77 *Antitrust Law Journal* 314.

[15] F Möslein, 'The focus of regulatory reforms in Europe after the global financial crisis: from corporate to contract governance' in W Sun, J Stewart and D Pollard (eds), *Corporate Governance and the Global Financial Crisis: International Perspectives* (Cambridge, Cambridge University Press, 2011) 286.

[16] Banks and firms were taking on extensive risk; therefore, managers were given incentives so as to generate higher returns for shareholders. On collective moral hazard see, eg, E Farhi and J Tirole, 'Collective Moral Hazard, Maturity Mismatch and Systemic Bailouts' (2012) 102 *American Economics Review* 60.

[17] The 2009 *Report of the OECD Steering Group on Corporate Governance* (24 February 2010) identified excessive remuneration, risk management, board practices and the exercise of shareholder rights as main problematic areas of corporate governance.

[18] Profits had to be paid to bond holders and other creditors plus a competitive return to equity owners see, eg, Kregel, 'Political Economy Approaches to Financial Crisis: Hyman Minsky's Financial Fragility Hypothesis' in Sun et al (eds), *Corporate Governance and the Global Financial Crisis* n 15 above, 237.

created the bonus culture, while compensation schemes encouraged short-run risk-taking.

(iii) What went wrong with policy? Macroeconomic policy registered numerous failures through relaxed credit, followed by an industrial restructuring of banks through the application of the TBTF doctrine of state intervention in the economy. The lack of regulation in the banking sector—including investment, insurance, securities, and lending[19]—combined with a less interventionist approach to mergers of large financial institutions, meant that these became TBTF and 'Too-Big-to-Supervise'.[20] As banks were allowed to merge, they escaped competition scrutiny[21] but were encouraged to compete. The latter aspect exacerbated risk-taking through improper disclosure requirements put in place to uncover banks' speculative pursuits.[22] In 2012, the EC finally activated its competition policy, which helped to block a mega-merger between Deusche Börse and the New York Stock Exchange[23] in the market for financial derivatives. Many believed that the unaccomplished economic, monetary, and fiscal integration of Member States was another culprit, as was the absence of a central authority dealing with the crisis.

(iv) What went wrong with law in action? There was inadequate regulation of special contracts in the banking, financial and securities sector; an excessive use of securitisation as a financial innovation to engineer debts 'cleansing'; excessive sophistication of commercial contracts;[24] and a lack of codes of honest business practice or models of contracts in place for consumers.[25] As banks became increasingly sophisticated, their innovative products were not priced accurately. It was impossible to assess the hazard due to innovative securitised products. In this context, 'soft' law[26] used in

[19] See for the US JW Markham, 'Lessons for Competition Law from the Economic Crisis: The Prospect for Antitrust Responses to the "Too-Big-to-Fail" Phenomenon' (2011) 16 *Fordham Journal of Corporate & Financial Law* 263.

[20] Stucke, n 14 above, 319; on rising bank concentration see, eg, FM Scherer, 'Financial Mergers and their Consequences', *Harvard Kennedy School of Government Research Working Paper* 19/2013.

[21] See, eg, D Zimmer and L Rengier, 'Entflechtung, Fusionskontrolle oder Sonderregulierung für systemrelevante Banken? Ansätze zur Lösung des "Too-big-to-fail" Problems' (2010) 8 *Zeitschrift für Wettbewerbsrecht* 105, who proposed a specific merger control, including a 'decartelisation' of banks.

[22] X Vives, 'Competition policy in banking' (2011) *Oxford Review of Economic Policy* 27, 487.

[23] COMP/M6166 *Deutsche Börse/NYSE Euronext* [2011] OJ C199.

[24] L Buchheit, 'We Made it Too Complicated' (2008) 27 *International Financial Law Review* 24, who highlighted the complexity of modern financial instruments as the 'big culprit' of the crisis.

[25] C Brummer, *Soft Law and the Global Financial System: Rule Making in the 21st Century* (Cambridge, Cambridge University Press, 2012) 223.

[26] C Brummer, 'Why Soft Law Dominates International Finance-And Not Trade' (2010) 13 *Journal of International Economic Law* 623; retrospectively see, eg, AF Lowenfeld, 'The International Monetary System: A Look Back Over Seven Decades' (2010) 13 *Journal of*

the framework of state aid policy, turned competition law into a major tool for the restructuring of the banking industry.

(v) What went wrong with EU institutions? As regards institutional responses to the crisis, on 12 November 2008, the EC proposed tighter rules for credit rating agencies; on 29 April 2009, it presented a draft directive on hedge funds and private equity;[27] on 23 September 2009, the EC proposed a legislative package for EU financial macro supervision[28] (Systemic Risk Board) and micro-prudential supervision (Banking Authority, Securities and Market Authority, and Insurance and Occupational Pensions Authority); in October 2010, the EC discussed a tax on financial transactions; in March 2011, it drafted rules on mortgage lending. Finally, in June 2011, the EC unveiled million-euro fines for rule-breaking bankers.

(vi) What went wrong with influencing views? This refers to the views of leading academic and economic experts who influenced policy-making and on whom policy-makers later relied to reshape economic and social governance and/or manage the crisis. There was a fervent reliance on faulty neo-classical economic theories[29] and liberal ideologies,[30] an over-reliance on mathematical risk models which failed to adequately predict and mitigate corporate risk,[31] and scientific interpretations.[32]

(vii) A knock-on effect of the limits of knowledge? This is attributed to the narrow focus of competition law[33] and the lack of interdisciplinary understanding, not only of law with other sciences, such as economics or

International Economic Law 575; JP Trachtman, 'The International Law of Financial Crisis: Spillovers, Subsidiarity, Fragmentation and Cooperation' (2010) 13 *Journal of International Economic Law* 719; G Hufbauer and DD Xie, 'Financial Stability and Monetary Policy: Need for International Surveillance' (2010) 13 *Journal of International Economic Law* 939.

[27] Source: EurActiv, 'Financial Regulation: The EU's agenda', 1 April 2009, available at: www.euractiv.com/euro-finance-regulation-eus-agenda-linksdossier-188497.

[28] Critically on the Basel Committee's 'Core Principles for Effective Banking Supervision', see Brummer, n 26 above, 225.

[29] ME Stucke, 'Teaching Antitrust After the Financial Crisis' (2013) 8 *Journal of Business & Technology Law* 209, suggesting that behavioural economics is now 'mainstream'; J Crotty, 'The Realism of Assumptions does Matter: Why Keynes-Minsky Theory Must Replace Efficient Market Theory as the Guide to Financial Regulation Policy' in Wolfson and Epstein (eds), n 2 above, 134.

[30] See RA Posner, *A Failure of Capitalism: The Crisis of '08 and the Descent into Depression* (Cambridge MA, Harvard University Press, 2009) 235. Posner identified one of the causes of the crisis as laissez-faire liberalism.

[31] F Akinbami, 'Is meta-regulation all it's cracked up to be? The case of UK financial regulation' (2013) 14 *Journal of Banking Regulation* 16, 20.

[32] Especially trust in the superiority of mathematics, game theory and modelling over rigorous disciplines such as law, political science, psychology, sociology and history.

[33] Markham, n 19 above, 265.

sociology,[34] but among different areas of law like competition, contract, finance, banking and corporate law.[35] This led Westbrook to explain:

> [D]erivatives are contracts; corporations ... are creatures of law. Economics, however, has always aspired to be a natural science, and so has considered the social as if it were natural. This fundamental ontological error has led to fanciful pricing models, as if we could model the movements of legal instruments like we model the movements of the stars.[36]

In other words, the practical inability of macroeconomics to test its predictions empirically has played a major role in this crisis.[37] Statistics and the reliance on macroeconomic models by central banks have proven to be useful. For example, econometrics has demonstrated how a series of macroeconomic measures, specifically those targeting active employment policies, impact upon individuals. Nevertheless, these tools remain limited and have proven to be grossly inadequate in practice.[38]

What conclusions can be drawn from the above? It is necessary to identify both the plethora of causes which have contributed to this crisis and the means of correcting the resulting negative effects. A preliminary balance of these causes would include the institutional problems of leading public authorities—which ought to have prevented and managed the crisis (eg governments, regulators)—the legal problems regarding the economics of special contracts which imply a speculative risk and the application of non-interventionist competition supervision at a microeconomic level. Furthermore, an inadequate macro supervision of shadow banking, and the influence of schools of economics/economists on crisis management also played an important role. Given the complexity of this crisis, it is difficult to identify *one* major root of the crisis; rather, multiple causes have led to major negative events.

[34] See the insightful contributions of I Lianos, 'Judging' Economists: Economic Expertise in Competition Law Litigation: A European View' in I Kokkoris and I Lianos (eds), *The Reform of EC Competition Law: New Challenges* (Kluwer Law International, 2010) 185; I Lianos and C Genakos, 'Econometric Evidence in EU Competition Law: An Empirical and Theoretical Analysis' CLES Research Paper 06/2012.

[35] See, eg, T Cottier, 'Challenges Ahead in International Economic Law' (2009) 12 *Journal of International Economic Law* 3, on the failures of a 'strictly disciplinary tradition' of fragmentation and specialisation.

[36] D Westbrook, *Out of Crisis: Rethinking our Financial Markets* (Boulder CO, Paradigm Publishing, 2009).

[37] G Kirchgässner, 'Die Krise der Wirtschaft: Auch eine Krise der Wirtschaftwissenschaften?' (2009) 10 *Perspektiven der Wirtschaftspolitik* 447, 452: '*Dies ist ein Preis, den wir dafür zahlen müssen, dass wir zumindest im Bereich der Makroökonomik—keine experimentelle Wissenschaft sind: makroökonomische Experimente sind nie kontrolliert and sollten auch sehr zurückhaltend eingesetzt werden, da sie dann, wenn sie schief gehen, enorme gesellschaftliche Kosten haben können*'. Thus one can disagree with the last paragraph since macroeconomic policies have always been tested on mankind and citizens have paid the social and economic costs of policy failure.

[38] Ibid.

As it is possible that a certain cause is the effect and vice versa, the first scenario is pitched at a microeconomic level. The next section aims to investigate what has happened in the subprime mortgage lending market and then goes on to question the perceived influence of certain schools of economics/economists to verify their plausibility if applied to the current crisis. The following problem–question scenario builds upon all of the above insights into the roots of the crisis.

IV. ON THE INTERPLAY OF MICRO WITH MACROECONOMICS IN THE SUBPRIME[39] MORTGAGE LENDING MARKET

At a microeconomic level, consumers borrowed more on terms which were favourable in the short term, but the long-term effect was building up a bubble due to a lack of economic foresight and human irrationality. A variable interest rate inducement coupled with myopia over any eventual job loss reveals an unconscionable moral hazard. It is believed that banks intentionally exploited consumers by taking advantage of their well-known decision-making biases,[40] namely, a tendency to ignore the long-term costs of complex transactions, while opting for a variable interest rate, or a limited experience with commercial transactions.[41] The relevance of consumer law here is the potential to find the behavioural exploitation of consumers as a form of deceptive conduct, such as a lender's omission of terms and conditions. It is a well-established principle that offering incomplete information to consumers about the costs of their transaction, through false statements or omissions, will give rise to contractual misrepresentation, which, in turn, if it is based on intentional behaviour, becomes fraudulent.[42]

Unfortunately, the existing consumer protection and available remedies have not been adequate tools for antitrust intervention due to an artificial separation of the consumer from competition laws.[43] The drawback is therefore leaving behavioural economics to consumer protection laws which address information asymmetries for borrowers who are being

[39] Posner, n 30 above, 23 suggested 'subprime' as a euphemism for mortgage loans to people at high risk of default.

[40] See also F Akinbami, 'Retail Products and the Global Financial Crisis', available on SSRN.

[41] M Huffman and D Heidtke, 'Behavioural Exploitation Antitrust in Consumer Subprime Mortgage Lending' (2012) 3 *William & Mary Policy Review* 77, available on SSRN.

[42] For a disposition to fraud, see MR Darby and E Karni, 'Free competition and the optimal amount of fraud' (1973) 16 *Journal of Law and Economics* 67; F Akinbami, 'Financial services and consumer protection after the crisis' (2011) 29 *International Journal of Bank Marketing* 134, 137.

[43] See especially NW Averitt and R Lande, 'Using the "Consumer Choice" Approach to Antitrust Law' (2007) 74 *Antitrust Law Journal* 175; A Albors-Llorens, 'Competition and Consumer Law in the EU: Evolution and Convergence' (2014) 33 *Yearbook of European Law* 1.

misled through lenders' business marketing strategies. Reliable credit information is believed to correct information asymmetries[44] through an effective credit reporting mechanism. Recently, the hypothesis that lenders are more likely to share credit information when entry barriers are high and the threat of competition is low has been rejected empirically due to burdensome administrative costs.[45] Banks with larger market shares earn higher monopoly rents on their borrower information than do banks with a smaller market share. Furthermore, higher entry barriers are associated with lower transparency in credit reporting.[46]

The above picture needs to further explore the macroeconomic level. Hayek's theory of trade cycle is worth highlighting. He argued that interest rates below the 'natural' rate lead banks to expand their lending in a manner which is unsustainable.[47] This, in turn, leads inevitably to a crisis, since businesses are misled into believing that more resources are available than is really the case.[48] According to his theory, it is then government action or misinformation by the central bank which 'awakes' the crisis through the banking system. In essence, the past reaction to such governmental stimulus was an impulsive entrepreneurial spirit towards excessive lending with dramatic effects on the real economy. Banks were attracted to sub-prime mortgage lending by higher interest rates of 2 per cent above fixed prime lending.[49] For consumers, mortgage financing became attractive; for example, a buyer could pay £350,000 with a 90 per cent mortgage, and three years later, the house price had increased to £500,000.

A serious analysis of the cause–effect–result phenomenon shows that but for the low interest rates, consumers would not have mortgaged, bankers would not have assumed risky lending, and everybody would have been happy. The shortcoming of the cause–effect platitude is that it is precisely the inherent risk and its hazardous multiplication that is the real cause which has resulted in the default bubble. Since the maintenance of a low interest rate is a macroeconomic state policy, one could argue that it was the widespread reliance on this policy which created this mess. The interest-rate-effect in macroeconomics postulates that a rising price level pushes up

[44] A Padilla and M Pagano, 'Sharing default information as a borrower discipline device' (2000) 44 *European Economic Review* 1951–80.

[45] M Bruhn, S Farazi and M Kanz, 'Bank Competition, Concentration, and Credit Reporting', The World Bank Development Research Group, Finance and Private Sector Development Team, *Policy Research Working Paper* 64422/2013, 5.

[46] Ibid, 16.

[47] FA Hayek, *Prices and Production* (London, Routledge, 1931).

[48] RCB Miller, 'The Austrians and the Crisis' (2009) 29 *Economic Affairs* 27, 28.

[49] On the existing link between the use of aggressive mortgage lending and house price volatility see, eg, A Pavlov and S Wachter, 'Subprime Lending and House Price Volatility', *University of Pennsylvania Institute for Law and Economics Research Paper* no 08/2008.

the interest rate, which in turn, lowers consumption and new investments in plant and equipment.[50]

In conclusion, it would be naive to assume that a mortgage multiplier could eventually create a crisis of such proportions. There are other trading exchanges which operated much in the same way or even worse and which will be explained in Section VII. In contrast, others have argued that under the influence of neoliberalism, the economy 'benefited' from an explosion of public and private credit.[51]

Another belief is that a recession is able to destructively correct the errors of a boom. In other words, bad businesses will collapse, which explains the rescue mechanisms put in place by the EC. In contrast to the previous credit boom period, interest rates have to be higher to collect through deposit savings the monies needed for the liquidity of banks which are due to collapse. This view has been contradicted more recently, because the liquidity problems were created 'by the unexpected decline in the value of financial assets and by the consequent reduction of inter-bank lending'.[52]

The level of interest rates is said to depend upon the depth of the recession.[53] Anecdotal evidence of the promised triple-dip recession proves how interest rates for savings have not been tripled, much to our own economic loss. In contrast, Member States were able to borrow at historically low interest rates.[54] Following the Austrian School of Economics' advice, Member States failed to raise interest rates significantly.[55] Rather, the EU simulated a destructive recession and restructured banks through recapitalisation, the difference this time being that the resources which allowed this to happen have flown directly from EU taxpayers to hazardous risk-takers. Nevertheless, irrespective of whether the process of restructuring itself should not have been implemented effectively, the real worry turns on whether this sacrifice is actually worth anything?

Furthermore, the reverse of not encouraging government spending for fear of any taxation mismatch or of a pervasive inflationist course seems equally odd, as it results in austerity, which promotes job cuts and raises unemployment levels. Unfortunately, the austerity obsession has delivered economic failure, social poverty, migration and unprecedented levels of unemployment. This will be documented in Section V. Now, to return

[50] SL Slavin, *Macroeconomics*, 9th edn (Boston MA, McGraw-Hill, 2009) 257.

[51] J O'Connor, 'Marxism and the Three Movements of Neoliberalism' (2010) 36 *Critical Sociology* 704.

[52] A Heimler and F Jenny, 'The limitations of European Union control of state aid' (2012) 28 *Oxford Review of Economic Policy* 347, 363.

[53] Ibid, 31.

[54] G Grahl, 'The Subordination of European Finance' (2011) 15 *Comp and Change* 31, 43 noting in particular Japan (0.96%), Germany (2.40%), US (2.56%), France (2.86%), UK (3%).

[55] Ibid.

to Hayek's prescription of 'flexible' wages, ie, cutting wages to minimise unemployment and combat inflation, the latter being currently low at 1.7 per cent, it is worth revealing that global population[56] is more than three times higher than 1.8 billion, as it was in the 1920s. This makes one particularly circumspect of creative ideas of 'full' employment in real terms[57] as applied to a different historical level in society's development. In the EU, the last total population revealed by Eurostat in 2012 was 503.7 million, not counting 4.2 million Croatians. As nearly 26.2 million unemployed citizens account for 10.8 per cent of the active work force, it means that we have an active population of 235.8 million but only 212.22 million employed citizens.

In conclusion, the EU has just 41.7 per cent of its total population in full employment. This dramatic unemployment situation comes just after what we could call a Failed Financialisation of Big Banks, and proves that what Stiglitz has already suggested about macroeconomic multipliers is true,[58] namely that, assessed retrospectively, the process of EU restructuring of banks, with its overly generous stimulus package, has failed to generate either jobs or any extra GDP.[59] Fortunately, the EU unemployment rate does not exceed the 200 million estimate of the International Labour Organization as a global crisis unemployment figure.[60] Finally, macroeconomics suggests that only an unemployment rate of 20 per cent triggers a depression.[61]

Another cause of the fragile growth lies in the more restrictive and austere macroeconomic policies that are necessary to achieve the economic and monetary union.[62] Nevertheless, Austrian economics offer one excellent tip: if undertaken, bank recapitalisation and state control is most likely to be unsuccessful. This is true in the EU when one confronts the bleak industry predictions available so far and the high unemployment rate.

[56] Currently estimated at approximately 7 billion.

[57] On the rejection of 'full' employment see L von Mises, *Human Action* (New Haven CT, Yale University Press, 1949).

[58] J Stiglitz, 'The global crisis, social protection and jobs' (2009) 148 *International Labour Review* 4.

[59] See, eg, J Bivens and H Shierholz, 'The Great Recession's Impact on Jobs, Wages, and Incomes' in Wolfson and Epstein (eds), n 2 above, 61.

[60] T Clarke, 'Corporate governance causes of the global financial crisis' in Sun et al (eds), *Corporate Governance and the Global Financial Crisis* n 15 above, 43.

[61] Slavin, n 50 above, 218.

[62] See, eg, Grahl, n 54 above, 34; J Stiglitz, 'Towards a Better Measure of Well-being' in *Financial Times*, 13 September 2009.

It is argued here that Stiglitz's assertion that the rejection of the Keynesian theory of employment[63]—which promoted rigid wages—[64] formed the basis of the many post-Keynesian doctrines and undermined job protection and labour rights[65] was accurate. In macroeconomics, a 5 per cent unemployment rate means that the economy attains full employment.[66] The misconstruction of employment theory, with a strong emphasis on its 'utopian' vision of full employment, can be justified by the distrust of wage competition, which even if it could achieve labour flexibility, does so at the expense of worsening workers' conditions. According to Keynes, lowering wages would lower workers' incomes and reduce further spending on goods.[67] This makes Keynesian theory socially human. Thus Keynes believed that capitalism has a natural tendency to cut employment[68] but falling interest rates, prices, and wages are insufficient to stimulate investment and consumption[69] as a way out of the recession.[70] In other words, without government intervention, the economy does not move toward full employment.

Unfortunately many Keynesian policies implemented in the 1950s and 1960s were inappropriately addressing deflation after it had ceased to represent a major threat.[71] Therefore, Minsky's financial fragility theory postulated that the trade cycle reacts to endogenous shocks, such as a change in monetary policy by the central bank (eg increasing interest rates to slow the economy for fear of inflation, or a supra-production crisis where markets are saturated with cars, electronics etc)[72] and that a deficient aggregate demand triggers a stagnant unemployment situation, which could eventually attain Keynesian full employment through monetary and fiscal policy.[73] If nothing else works, another option suggested by Austrian

[63] See Keynes' letter to TS Elliot in DE Moggridge (eds), *The Collected Writings of John Maynard Keynes: Activities 1940–1946. Shaping the Post-War World: Employment and Commodities* vol 27 (London, Macmillan, 1980) 384: 'the full employment policy by means of investment is only one particular application of an intellectual theorem. You can produce the result just as well as by consuming more or working less ... How you mix up the three ingredients of a cure is a matter of taste and experience, ie of morals and knowledge'.

[64] See JM Keynes, 'The General Theory of Employment' (1937) 51 *Quarterly Journal of Economics*, 209; Keynes, *The General Theory of Employment, Interest and Money* (London, Macmillan, 1973), also available at: www.isn.ethz.ch.

[65] Ibid, 9.

[66] Slavin, n 50 above, 258.

[67] Ibid, 262.

[68] Kirchgässner, n 37 above, 462.

[69] On government spending, Keynes argued: 'quantity is more relevant than quality. Even if the government employed some people to dig holes and others to fill up those holes' see, eg, Slavin, n 55 above, 368.

[70] Ibid, 268.

[71] Tymoigne, n 12 above, 100.

[72] Macroeconomics describes the saturation of markets through the innovation theory where economic downturn continues until a new innovation takes hold. Another endogenous theory focuses on psychological factors whereas optimism triggers investments in plants, more jobs and consumer spending.

[73] Kregel, n 18 above, 237.

economics is to promote competition in currency exchange. Obviously, this did not work well for the Eurozone countries, which could not devalue their national currencies.[74]

Finally, as a last resort, tax is viewed with much scepticism.[75] Granting temporary facilities to individuals contributes to raising the level of savings deposits, which, in turn, actively stimulates consumption. However, direct tax helps little if it targets only those consumer goods that are to be produced in the long run and imports. Since 50 per cent of the lower taxed goods account for only 2.8 per cent of revenues, while the upper 5 per cent account for 63.5 per cent, and because the marginal consumption rate falls as earnings increase, then adjusting the private consumption deficit through direct taxation is thus possible for the category of lower income taxation. As government spending was feared to become inflationary,[76] spending has remained static, whereas taxation has served to increase reliance on consumption taxes, such as VAT and payroll taxes, and to diminish corporate tax.[77] In conclusion, trying to fix a crisis through taxation is nothing but a vicious circle.

In conclusion, all these insights reveal how unhelpful economic policies or economists' predictions[78] are; how the crisis has destroyed them one after another, thereby shaking our society in the search for social justice, the rule of law, and a new order; and how this crisis managed to exacerbate its social and economic costs instead of fixing the economy.

V. ON THE MACROECONOMICS OF THE EURO CRISIS

Before looking to the current economic outlook, it is useful to re-call the macroeconomic legal framework which has been instrumental for setting out the overall performance criteria in the EU. Article 119(2) TFEU refers to a single currency, namely the euro, monetary policy, and exchange-rate policy. Its primary objective is to maintain price stability and to support the general economic policies in the Union, in accordance with the 'principle of an open market economy with free competition'. This principle means that at a microeconomic level, free competition will be complemented by macroeconomic policy. The primary objective of price stability is also mentioned

[74] Another suggestion has been to create a mechanism by which Member States with a current account deficit could devalue in real terms and other Member States with a surplus could revalue.

[75] Kirchgässner, n 37 above, 462.

[76] Karl Otto Pohl, former president of the German Bundesbank once said: 'Inflation is like toothpaste. Once it is out of the tube, it is hard to get it back again'. Hyperinflation happened in Germany after World War I when prices rose 10% an hour: see, eg, Slavin, n 50 above, 240.

[77] OECD 1998, *Economic Outlook*, Paris, June 1998 which shows how corporate tax rate fell by 10.3% compared to 12.4% which corresponds to the fall of the average top marginal income.

[78] LJ Peter, *Peter's Quotations*: 'An economist is an expert who will know tomorrow why the things he predicted yesterday didn't happen today'.

under Article 105 of the Protocol on the European System of Central Banks (ESCB). According to Article 119(3), macroeconomic policy shall comply with the following guiding principles: stable prices, sound public finances and monetary conditions, and a sustainable balance of payments. Article 140(1) TFEU sets out the Maastricht convergence criteria for the accession of Member States to the single currency. Unfortunately, these nominal terms are tight. They mandate that the EC and the ECB report to the Council on the progress made by the Member States regarding the achievement of economic and monetary union, with a view to the achievement of a high degree of sustainable convergence. The economic criteria refer respectively to the 'achievement, sustainability, observance and durability' of:

(i) a high degree of price stability, by looking at the inflation rate of the three best performing Member States;[79]
(ii) the sustainability of the government financial position, by looking at the public deficit;
(iii) normal fluctuation margins provided for by the exchange-rate mechanism without devaluing against the euro;
(iv) convergence achieved by the Member States with derogation and its participation in the exchange-rate mechanism being reflected in the long-term interest-rate levels.

In conclusion, the above criteria refer to various nominal values, such as an inflation lower than 1.5 per cent; exchange rates within the range of 15 per cent; long-term interest rates no more than 2 per cent higher than the arithmetic coverage of the similar 10-year government bond yields in the three Member States with the lowest HICP inflation; a budgetary deficit lower than 3 per cent GDP; and a government public debt criterion lower than 60 per cent. While these criteria aim to establish financial responsibility, they fail to include unemployment targets. Only in the last paragraph of Article 140 TFEU, is it spelled out that the monitoring reports 'shall also take account of … an examination of the development of unit labour costs and other price indices'.

Current Economic Outlook

EU Real GDP Growth	−4.2% (2009)	0.1% (2013)
EU Unemployment	9.6% (2010)	10.8% (12% euro area) (2014)
EU Government debt	78.7% (2009)	86.8% (92.7% euro area) (2014)
	highest in Greece 171.8%, Italy 132.9% and Portugal 128.7%	

Source: *Eurostat*[80]

[79] It will be inferred from a rate of inflation which is close to that of the three best performing Member State.

[80] Source: EU Commission, Towards More Responsibility and Competitiveness in the European Financial Sector, 2012.

The current economic situation reveals interesting insights into the state of the economy. Inflation has generally been higher than 2 per cent. According to the latest Eurostat figures,[81] the annual *inflation* rate in the Eurozone area was 1.6 per cent in July 2013 compared to 2.4 per cent a year earlier. The annual inflation rate in the EU was 1.7 per cent in July 2013.[82] Therefore, a country with a relatively low (high) inflation rate has a relatively high (low) real interest rate. However, monetary policy has been operated in a perverse manner, with low real rates being applied where inflation is relatively high. This contradicts the presumption that high inflation is met by high real rates of interest to dampen demand. Many economists agree that compared with the Bank of England and the US Federal Reserve, which have reduced aggressive interest rates, the ECB has adopted a stricter approach. In April 2011, interest rates reached 1.25 per cent. Apart from the existing large current account imbalances between the EMU Member States, there are also substantial differences in terms of changes in unit labour costs.

Again, unemployment rose to 26.2 million in January 2013, which accounts for 10.8 per cent of the active population[83] and 11.9 per cent of the active population in the euro area (19 million). Furthermore, long-term unemployment reached another historical high[84] in the third quarter at 11.2 million, which is 86 per cent higher than four years earlier. Another aspect worth highlighting is that youth unemployment reached its peak in January 2013 with 23.6 per cent of active youths.[85] Immigration was 20.7 million in January 2012 and migration was 13.6 million.[86] In addition, 25.7 per cent of people aged between 55 and 64 were living in poverty and social exclusion,[87] while the lowest average monthly salary was just 393 euros (Bulgaria).[88] In 24 Member States, the likelihood of finding a job was lower in the third quarter of 2012 than four years before.[89] And this is not all. Major planned cuts in the industry sectors cast rather a bleak shadow over the overall economy. For example, in the banking sector, Commerzbank is implementing a global restructuring plan targeting between 4000 and 6000 job losses by 2016; in the airline sector, Iberia is cutting 19 per cent of its entire workforce (3807 employees) and Air Berlin another

[81] Eurostat, euro indicators, press release 123/2013, 16 August 2013.

[82] The largest increase to the euro area ('Eurozone') annual inflation is said to come from fruit, vegetables and tobacco.

[83] European Commission, 'EU Employment and Social Situation' (2013) *Quarterly Review* 5. Other high unemployment rates were recorded in Bulgaria (–4.9%), Cyprus (–4.8%) and Spain (–4.5%).

[84] Ibid, 6.

[85] The youth unemployment rate ranges from 15% or more in Austria, Denmark, Germany and the Netherlands to 55% or more in Greece and Spain. Highest unemployment rates were registered in Greece (–6.5%) and Portugal (–4.3%).

[86] Ibid, 15.

[87] Ibid, 24.

[88] Ibid, 28.

[89] Ibid, 30.

900 by 2014,[90] while the manufacturing sector lost 36,964 jobs last year, and financial intermediation 19,585. The worst prognosis is in the construction industry, and wholesale and retail trade as a result of significant reductions in terms of output, added value, and employment.[91]

A. The 'Efficiency' Justification against Bail-outs of Inefficient Banks or States

So how was it then legally possible to instrument the bail-outs of banks? Article 119 TFEU makes it clear that the adoption of an economic policy which is based on the 'close coordination' of Member States' economic policies has to be in accordance with the principle of an open market economy with free competition. It must be added that competition law rarely accepts a failing-firm-defence on the grounds of its poor economic performance, that is, inefficiency. In this respect Article 120 TFEU mandates that economic policies ought to follow the same principle, 'favouring an efficient allocation of resources'. Furthermore, Article 123(1) TFEU contains an imperative prohibition of

> [o]verdraft facilities or any other type of credit facility with the European Central Bank or with the central banks of the Member States ... in favour of Union institutions, bodies, offices or agencies, central governments, regional, local or other public authorities, other bodies governed by public law, or public undertakings of Member States,

as well as 'the purchase directly from them by the European Central Bank or national central banks of debt instruments'. One cannot possibly comment more on the legally binding hierarchy and 'constitutional' ranking of the above provisions, which clearly eliminate the possibility of granting bailouts on the basis of inefficiency, be it at state or TBTF level, without basically undermining the rule of law and transforming the spirit of free competition into coercive freedom, the meaning of which will be revealed in the end Section IX.

Another critical argument is that competition intervention in favour of TBTF banks has been implemented through substantial crisis communication in the form of soft law. It has been argued elsewhere that state aid communications bear no legally binding force.[92] Thus, they are administrative provisions which offer guidance on how to deal with the restructuring or capitalisation of banks. Therefore, a higher hierarchical and constitutionally

[90] Ibid, 66.
[91] Ibid, 58.
[92] See, eg, T Doleys, 'Managing State Aid in a Time of Crisis: Commission Crisis Communications and the Financial Sector Bailout' (2012) 34 *Journal of European Integration* 549.

accepted rescue provision is Article 107(3)(b) TFEU on state aid to 'remedy a serious disturbance in the economy of a Member State'. This has closed the academic debate over the primacy of 'hard' over 'soft' law.[93] The latter could be called an administrative measure which has binding force. No legal act or decision whatsoever would otherwise be enacted if it were to be disregarded. Furthermore, if it were legally valid that soft law communications are not binding on EU courts, this would be instrumental, on the one hand, for states to claim disgorgement of profits for cashed bail-outs of banks engaged in fraudulent pursuits and, on the other hand, for EU citizens to claim fair compensation through taxation. It would be legitimate for them to pay lower taxes until the almost 40 per cent of the GDP in bail-outs was credited on their payroll accounts.

In conclusion, the apparent legitimacy of state bail-outs is in the treaty; the implementation of banks bailouts is in administrative law communications.

VI. ON THE SOCIAL COSTS OF THE CRISIS

After the apparent legitimacy has just been discussed above, it is worth checking the actual economic cost involved in bail-outs. This begs the following question: how much state aid was really needed and why? Insights into how state aid gradually progressed reveal that between 2002 and 2007, the amount of state aid decreased by 2 per cent annually and ranged within 0.5 per cent of the GDP,[94] followed in 2008 by a nearly fourfold increase to 2.2 per cent of the GDP. Between 2008 and 2009, the figure of €3.632 billion, the equivalent of 29 per cent GDP, signalled an alarming shift of perspective when everybody started to see red. Even ad hoc state aid in favour of individual financial institutions amounted to €587 billion (9 per cent GDP).[95] Germany, the UK and France, which make up 60 per cent of the EU banking sector, received 60 per cent of the total amount of state aid granted.[96] A total of 215 financial institutions received some form of aid, but 114 received toxic asset support relief.[97] Between 2008 and 2011, the EC approved a shocking €4.5 trillion of state aid, that is, nearly

[93] See the insightful contributions on soft law of O Stefan, *Soft law in court: competition law, state aid and the Court of Justice of the European Union* (Kluwer Law International, 2013); 'Hybridity before the court: a hard look at soft law in the EU competition and state aid case law' (2012) 37 *European Law Review* 49.

[94] P Nicolaides, 'State aid' in I Kokkoris and R Olivares-Caminal (eds), *Antitrust Law amidst Financial Crisis* (Cambridge, Cambridge University Press, 2010).

[95] B Lyons and M Zhu, 'Compensating Competitors or Restoring Competition? EU Regulation of State Aid for Banks during the Financial Crisis' (2013) 13 *Journal of Industrial Competition & Trade* 47.

[96] Quigley, n 5 above, 240.

[97] Ibid.

36.7 per cent of the GDP.[98] This makes the entire GDP worth €12.26 trillion.[99] Minus the bail-outs, the remaining €7.76 trillion was nearly approaching another Great Depression as macroeconomics suggests that at extremely low levels of real GDP, when output is €3 trillion, the economy is in a depression.[100]

The economic costs estimated for the UK economy post-intervention amount to nearly £40 billion of lost output.[101] Other macroeconomic crisis mechanisms, such as the Stabilisation Mechanism, allow the EC to raise up to €60 billion as financial assistance to Member States experiencing financial difficulties. The Financial Stability Facility has been set up to issue debt securities guarantees of up to €444 billion.[102] Therefore it does not make us feel any better to know that in 2009, the US bail-out amounted to US$8 trillion,[103] that is $30,000 per citizen, $650 billion of GDP income, 5.5 million jobs etc.[104] Recent figures contradict a 2009 estimate by the International Monetary Fund of US$11.9 trillion as the total cost of the global crisis.[105]

It is by no means controversial to say that banks were being favoured before the current crisis hit. Banks were immune from competition intervention and allowed to merge, which is another fact that is statistically documented. Between 1997 and 2007, the number of EU banks declined by 29 per cent compared to 22 per cent in the US.[106] Bank concentration levels remain relatively high post-crisis, while recent research contradicts the economic assumption that concentration levels should necessarily translate into high market shares.[107] Against the shortcoming of immunity to competition agency scrutiny,[108] it does not follow that banks did not compete against each other. Another telling fact is that it is precisely tougher competition that has increased the risk-taking incentives of banks and pushed them

[98] Source: DG COMP at: ec.europa/competition/recovery/financial_sector.html. See, eg, J Pisani-Ferry and A Sapir, 'EU banking policies' (2010) *Economic Policy* 358, who reported that by the end of August 2009 state aid measures amounted to 44% GDP.

[99] See http://epp.eurostat.ec.europa.eu/portal/page/portal/eurostat/home/.

[100] Slavin, n 50 above, 262.

[101] Several economists argued that countries facing insolvency should default as quickly as possible to allow a substantial debt restructuring aimed at restoring sustainable debt levels. The UK government spent $856 billion to support the crisis in 2008 see, eg, Clarke, n 60 above, 44.

[102] Source: European Commission, MEMO/12/413, Brussels 6 June 2012.

[103] Thus Moseley reported US$700 billion for US banks bailouts see, eg, F Moseley, 'The Bailout of the 'Too-Big-to-Fail' Banks: Never Again' in Wolfson and Epstein (eds), n 2 above, 645.

[104] See, eg, R Macdonald, 'The Nature and Effects of the 2007–2010 Crisis and Ways to Resolve it' in MacDonald, *Genesis of the Financial Crisis* (London, Palgrave Macmillan, 2012).

[105] See especially Sun, et al (eds), n 15 above.

[106] Vives, n 22 above, 482.

[107] Scherer, n 20 above, 10.

[108] For example, the US Dodd-Frank Act of July 2010 prohibited any merger or acquisition which results in a combined market share of more than 10% of domestic deposits. This Act aims to protect the American taxpayer by ending bail-outs and consumers from abusive financial services practices.

to pursue risky portfolios.[109] Shareholders have designed compensation contracts to insure managers against failure and incentivise risk-taking. Therefore, keeping this numeracy exercise in mind is essential when questioning how state aid has been spent on banks which will be detailed next.

A. Main Categories of Crisis State Aid

So far the EU has offered €2,738 billion in guarantee schemes, €231 billion in the form of recapitalisation, and €76 billion in liquidity measures and asset relief. The first €26 billion bail-out went to the German IKB and Sachsen LB, which had been exposed to asset-backed securities in the US subprime market. This was followed by the UK bail-out of Northern Rock, late 2007 and early 2008. Northern Rock (fifth largest mortgage bank with a 9.7 per cent market share)[110] received £20 billion in a guarantee scheme and £25 billion liquidity facility from the Bank of England. There is disagreement over whether Northern Rock was a systemically important bank, since it did not trigger problems elsewhere in the banking system.[111] While the intervention did not allow this to happen, it created a UK precedent of intervention on the basis of TBTF. It is useful to recall here that the ECB identified some 46 systemically important banks which account for 68 per cent of EU banking.[112] This can only be the result of allowing mega-mergers to go ahead[113] and the monopoly power of banks on business lending.[114]

WestLB, Fortis and Dexia followed. The *Irish Daily* offered €400 billion as a guarantee scheme to cover retail, commercial, and interbank deposits. Royal Bank of Scotland received £45 billion to ensure its survival because the bank failed to maintain adequate liquidity and was involved in a risky financial strategy.[115]

The reaction of the EU Commission to the crisis was to issue an administrative act, the *Banking communication*,[116] following which it received

[109] Vives, n 22 above, 485.

[110] Lyons and Zhu, n 95 above, 49.

[111] Ibid, 51.

[112] European Central Bank (2006 and 2008), 'EU Banking Structures', Frankfurt am Main.

[113] See Stucke, n 14 above, 318 who points at the post-merger consolidated assets of $751 bn; Markham, n 19 above, 291 pinpointing that between 1980 and 1999, the number of commercial banks declined from 15000 to just 9000; HA Shelanski, 'Enforcing Competition During an Economic Crisis' (2010/2011) 77 *Antitrust Law Journal* 238.

[114] MH Wolfson, 'An Institutional Theory of Financial Crisis', n 2 above, 183.

[115] Akinbami, n 31 above, 23.

[116] Communication from the Commission—The Application of State Aid Rules to Measures Taken in Relation to Financial Institutions in the Context of the Current Global Financial Crisis, [2008] OJ C270/8, departs from its predecessor EC Guidelines on State Aid for Rescuing and Restructuring Firms in Difficulty, [2004] OJ C244/2. The latter allowed the EC to distinguish among guarantees, recapitalizations, impaired assets measures, as aid modalities, and their recipient, distressed firms. The Banking Communication made possible

notifications for guarantee schemes, recapitalisation, and other interventions of up to €2 trillion.[117] This aid was insufficient to restore market confidence as bank balance sheets continued to erode. The ECB intervened through liquidity operations. The EC's disagreement with French institutions over 'preventive recapitalization' caused alarm bells to ring in that there were some serious doubts over whether €10.5 billion[118] was, indeed, offered to TBTF banks. In this context, the EC issued its *Recapitalisation communication*,[119] which provided guidance on the pricing of capital injections. It distinguished between 'distressed' and 'fundamentally sound' banks.[120] The former were required to pay higher coupon rates.

Following German plans to create a series of special purpose vehicles (SPV) and a heated debate over assets pricing, the EC issued its *Impaired assets communication*[121] to handle toxic assets. Asset relief in the form of asset purchase has meant that MS would buy the impaired asset portfolio at a fixed price, but higher than the market price. On the basis of toxic asset guarantees, MS have practically taken over a share of the default risk and losses.[122] The conditions for granting such aids required full disclosure of the assets; sharing the cost between MS, shareholders and creditors, and coordination among them; and restructuring distressed banks.[123] The German scheme allowed financial institutions to transfer structured securities to a SPV for a period of 20 years and bear the full risk of losses.

Another *Restructuring communication*[124] targeted banks with unsustainable business models. Banks were required to demonstrate their own strategies to achieve long-term viability without state aid under adverse economic conditions, known as a bank 'stress' test.[125] The restructuring of banks began with Commerzbank,[126] which was required to divest itself of its investment banking and real estate and accepted a short-term

the authorisation of state aid in the form of guarantees, capital, asset relief or liquidity on a non-discriminatory basis, for a limited time and scope see, eg, Quigley, n 5 above, 239.

[117] Doleys, n 92 above, 556.

[118] Ibid, 558.

[119] Communication from the Commission—The Recapitalisation of Financial Institutions in the Current Financial Crisis: Limitation of Aid to the Minimum Necessary and Safeguards against Undue Distortions of Competition, [2009] OJ C10/2.

[120] See T Franchoo and M Pollard, 'The Application of European Competition Law in the Financial Services Sector' (2012) *Journal of European Community Law & Policy*.

[121] Communication from the Commission on the Treatment of Impaired Assets in the Community Banking Sector, [2009] OJ C72/01.

[122] Quigley, n 5 above, 239.

[123] Ibid.

[124] Commission Communication, The return to viability and the assessment of restructuring measures in the financial sector in the current crisis under the State aid rules, [2009] OJ C195/9.

[125] Quigley, n 5 above, 239.

[126] Commerzbank case (State aid No N 625/2008); see, eg Heimler and Jenny (n 52 above, 364) criticisms on the imposition by the Commission of limitations on managers' compensation and severance packages.

ban on acquisitions.[127] Other restructured banks included RBS, Lloyds, Anglo-Irish Bank, Fortis, Dexia, Bayern LB, HSH Nordbank, IKB, WestLB, ING and ABN Amro. Lloyds TSB/HBOS, as a result of a rescue merger with HBOS,[128] received £17 billion state recapitalisation in 2009,[129] with £260 billion of toxic assets temporarily insured.[130] Lloyds was the second largest bank with 24 per cent market share in gross mortgage lending, while HSBC had 13 per cent.[131] As a result of its acquisition of HBOS, Lloyds and RBS were required to divest a 5 per cent market share to a new market entrant and achieve a £181 billion reduction of assets by 31 December 2014.[132]

As Lyons and Zhu have rightfully commented, the above 'zombie' banks 'withdraw lending as they rebuild their own capital, to the detriment of lending to the non-financial sector',[133] thereby contributing to the current recession. Another excellent point to make is the need to reform any banking system that 'privatises' shareholders' profits and 'socialises' losses through bail-outs of inefficient or poor economic performance.[134] The EU intervention in the banking sector, on the basis of its flawed TBTF doctrine of state intervention in the economy, has transferred the economic responsibility of inefficient corporations to the social responsibility of individual taxpayers.[135]

✓ **TBTF Banks[136]**

- rescue aids: Hypo Real Estate Holding, Commerzbank, WestLB;
- restructuring: Sachsen LB, IKB, WestLB, Landesbank Baden Württemberg, Sparkasse KölnBonn, Hypo Real Estate, HSH Nordbank, NordLB, Bayern LB;

[127] Doleys, n 92 above, 561.

[128] Prior to its takeover, HBOS was collapsing because of its high-risk lending practices and excessive use of leverage. See P Marsden and I Kokkoris, 'The Role of Competition and State Aid Policy in Financial and Monetary Law' (2010) 13 *Journal of International Economic Law* 889.

[129] Figures are slightly contradicted by R Tomasic, 'The failure of corporate governance and the limits of law: British banks and the global financial crisis' in Sun et al (eds), *Corporate Governance and the Global Financial Crisis* n 15 above, 59, relying on the House of Commons Treasury Committee, 'Banking Crisis: Dealing with the Failure of the UK Banks: Seventh Report of Session 2008–09', London, 519.

[130] The UK government has recently sold part of its 43.5% equity ownership.

[131] Vives, n 22 above, 493. However, Lloyds was not allowed to take over Abbey in 2001.

[132] Quigley, n 5 above, 245; see also Marsden and Kokkoris, n 128 above, 877.

[133] Lyons and Zhu, n 95 above, 45.

[134] Ibid, 47.

[135] See FM Scherer, 'A Perplexed Economists Confronts "Too Big to Fail"' (2010) 7 *European Journal of Comparative Economics* 267.

[136] For an overview of decisions and ongoing in-depth investigations in the context of the financial crisis see European Commission, Brussels, 20 December 2012, available at: http://europa.eu/rapid/press-release_MEMO-12-1018_en.htm.

- WestLB €3 billion capital injections, €11 billion impaired assets of which €3.4 billion.[137]
- Anglo Irish Bank €29.3 billion
- Irish Nationwide Building Society (INBS) €5.4 billion;
- Hypo Real Estate €9.95 billion in capital injections, €145 billion in guarantees and €20 billion in asset relief;
- ING €17 billion
- Fortis Bank €11.2 billion

One cannot reflect on the above famous bail-outs without formulating the following question: what did these banks have in common? The answer is a very fragile funding model supported by a risky loan portfolio and the fact that, in their rescue, the EC did not come up with a pertinent 'counterfactual'[138] scenario of what would have happened if they had been allowed to fail. Fortis[139] is yet another example of bank rescue due to excessive risk-taking as a result of its participation in the ABN AMRO merger.[140] Competition authorities ought to be prudent when accepting the failing-firm-defence for under-performing, inefficient, and poorly managed firms.[141] While Member States may block a merger in order to protect a 'legitimate interest', such as financial stability in the domestic market, the US Department of Justice cannot review a merger for systemic risk.[142] Thus competition authorities have been ill-equipped to assess the systemic risk which eroded the legitimacy of the TBTF doctrine of intervention. The latter helped inefficient banks to remain 'viable' on the market.[143] Fortunately, the EC has realised its defective implementation since it has later called for a 'sound' restructuring plan for banks before capitalisations or taking any other asset protection measures.[144] This new move follows early indications that the EC is going to 'toughen' its state aid to failing banks.[145] The major criticism of the TBTF doctrine remains, however, its having been endorsed by EU policy-makers as a 'way out' of the crisis.

In conclusion, the above developments in administering state aid have changed the whole structure of the EU banking sector in a way which has

[137] The state aid was said to be incompatible with the restructuring communication as it exceeded the real economic value of this bank's assets.

[138] See also Lyons and Zhu, n 95 above, 54 on WestLB.

[139] On Fortis case see, eg, Pisani-Ferry and Sapir, n 98 above, 354.

[140] On unsustainable business models see, eg, Lyons and Zhu, n 95 above, 58.

[141] See, eg, Marsden and Kokkoris, n 128 above, 881.

[142] Stucke, n 14 above, 322.

[143] See also Heimler and Jenny, n 52 above, 358, both of whom are critical on restructuring aid being offered to 'inefficient firms to remain active in the market'.

[144] EC, 'State aid: Commission adapts crisis rules for banks', IP/13/672, Brussels, 10 July 2013.

[145] Bloomberg, J Brunsden and E Duarte, 'EU to Toughen Creditor-Loss Rules at Failing Banks', 8 July 2013, at: www.bloomberg.com/news/print/2013-07-08, reported that the EU has spent €1.7 trillion on the basis of the TBTF doctrine.

substantially departed from the traditional prevention of distortions of competition. The next question to ask, therefore, is not whether competition enforcers have not been prepared to undertake this mission—because, obviously, they were not—but to ask how much state aid has been taken away from the overall prospects of economic growth in terms of GDP and weighted against, as mentioned earlier, the rising unemployment in the EU and the passing on of social costs through taxation. Finally, this revolutionary change of perspective makes competition law and policy the scapegoat of a New Banks Deal. Its story of success for banks and failure for citizens has been possible on the basis of the Union's democratic deficits, since its citizens have no say in the next election of the President or of the College of Commissioners, both of which have been instrumental in matters of competition policy.[146] This point uncovers an existing institutional crisis; for example, the EC's plans to create an agency to rescue or shut failed banks by 2015 against the significant backdrop of not having an EU banking union until January 2014.[147] The latter aspect pinpoints the politics of the crisis. Recent research suggests that, for a number of reasons, electoral competition is likely to constrain the abuse of public resources in the form of bail-outs.[148] This is fully evidenced in the following criticism by a member of Socialists and Democrats (Elisa Ferreira) who said: 'We need to stop casino banking, break the link between public finance and failing banks, and ensure sustainable financing of the real economy to encourage growth'. As Wibbels rightfully put it when investigating the constitutional dimension of crisis bail-outs,[149] the above statement based on 'competitive politics' encourages what one commentator would famously call in competition a way of 'publicly distancing oneself'[150] from the culprit of bail-outs. Electoral competition should actively discourage zombie banks from looking at the welfare state as their lender of last resort.

Briefly, what this bitter crisis has taught us, so far, is that structural changes happen during a crisis whenever state intervention is insufficiently backed up by constitutional and institutional safeguarding mechanisms, since it is easier to abuse the rule of law on the basis of predicted, imminent economic downturn.

[146] In contrast, architectural differences did not allow the US antitrust enforcers to administer bail-outs through means of antitrust policy see, eg, American Antitrust Institute, Remarks of Bert Foer, 'Competition Policy and "Too Big" Banks in the European Union and the United States', 27 June 2013.

[147] Source: EurActiv, 'New banking authority pits Commission against Berlin', 11 July 2013 available at: www.euractiv.com/euro-finance/new-banking-resolution-authority-news-529225.

[148] E Wibbels, 'Bailouts, Budget, and Leviathans: Comparative Federalism and Lessons from the Early United States' (2003) 36 *Comparative Political Studies* 486.

[149] Ibid, 487.

[150] To quote David Bailey's excellent article on 'Publicly Distancing Oneself from a Cartel' (2008) 31 *World Comparative Law & Economics Review* 177.

VII. ON EMERGING ANTI-COMPETITIVE PRACTICES RELATED TO THE TBTF DOCTRINE

Recent antitrust investigations have dealt with innovative and highly sophisticated financial contracts, such as securitisation, credit default swaps (CDS) or repos, which have affected both businesses and consumers.[151] Therefore, this section will first detail how financial contracts operate before explaining their relevance for the purpose of recent investigations.

It was estimated that the total value of financial derivative contracts was US$596 trillion, that is, eight times the size of the real global economy,[152] with a growth rate of 32 per cent per annum since 1990.[153] An excellent definition of derivatives is offered by Braithwaite.[154] Derivatives are 'bilateral contracts where the rights and obligations of the parties reference an underlying asset, benchmark, index or other variable'. *Over-the-counter derivatives* were estimated at US$707 trillion,[155] that is nine times the world GDP in 2010.[156] An estimate of 65 million derivatives is used, for example, to hedge interest rates and credit risk, minimise tax liabilities, or speculate on currencies, etc.[157] Hedging itself implies a transfer of risk assets.[158]

Credit default swaps (CDSs) are financial derivative contracts designed to transfer the risk of credit default on debt obligations.[159] The classic example is a CDS where A and B decide on a notional sum. A agrees to pay B a fixed interest rate on that sum (periodic payment) while B agrees to pay a variable rate in return. As a result, B, who has a variable rate income but a fixed rate debt, can swap income streams with counterparties.[160] In practice, CDS are used by investors as a Special Purpose Vehicle (SPV) to hedge assets against default risks and assess debtors' creditworthiness. *Securitisation* is a highly sophisticated process of pooling high-risk debt assets from mortgage loans, credit cards and so on, which were sold to

[151] See the Commission's 'new' mission: 'Competition law should ensure that credit institutions and other financial service providers do not behave in a manner that hampers the efficient functioning of the internal market', available at: http://ec.europa.eu/competition/sectors/financial_services/capital_markets.html.

[152] See generally n 15 above, 9.

[153] T Clarke, 'Corporate governance causes of the global financial crisis' in Sun et al (eds), *Corporate Governance and the Global Financial Crisis* n 15 above, 31.

[154] JP Braithwaite, 'Standard Form Contracts as Transnational Law: Evidence from the Derivatives Markets' (2012) 75 *Modern Law Review* 783.

[155] Ibid, 785, 789. Five firms dominate the EU and US OTC derivatives market, see Scherer, n 20 above, 14.

[156] GA Epstein and P Habbard, 'Speculation and Sovereign Debt: An Insidious Interaction', in *The Handbook of the Political Economy of Financial Crisis,* n 2 above, 328.

[157] Ibid.

[158] P Lysandrou, 'Hedge funds', in P Lysandrou, 'Hedge funds', in *Handbook of Critical Issues in Finance,* n 12 above, 145.

[159] See, eg, Brummer, n 26 above, 212.

[160] Ibid, 784.

a SPV in return for securities.[161] Put simply, this process makes sure that risks associated with loans are shifted away from the original lenders to investors. First, the originator (O) applies for a mortgage loan; then the SPV buys O's mortgage to guarantee the remoteness of the cash flows in return for securities which are purchased by investors (I). The cash received from I pays O's loan. Basically, any interest rate or currency risk associated with the pooling of such assets is hedged[162] using a variety of credit swap transactions. Credit rating agencies[163] have played a key role in boosting the attractiveness of such securitised assets by assigning a credit rating for securities issued via the SPV. Investors have been overly reliant on ratings.

Previously, the EC has issued guidance on how to calculate the pricing of capital injections to 'rescue' CDSs.[164] Later, the EC sent a statement of objections (SO) to 13 investment banks, which have acted as intermediaries in the market for credit derivatives.[165] Another investigation into CDSs targets the International Swaps and Derivatives Association involved in the over-the-counter (OTC) trading of derivatives.[166] Preliminary indications suggest that the association may have been involved in a coordinated effort of investment banks to 'delay or prevent exchanges' from entering the credit derivatives business.

Finally, a *repo* is a collaterised loan where the seller agrees to sell securities at a discount (haircut) to the buyer (lender).[167] Lenders are rich institutional investors, like pension funds and mutual funds, which need a liquid but relatively safe place to invest cash. Repo is a generic name for repurchase agreements and sell/buy-backs, namely, A sells an asset to B at price X. A also commits itself to repurchase the asset from a third party, C, at price

[161] See also BJ Keys, TK Mukherjee, A Seru and V Vig, 'Did Securitization Lead to Lax Screening? Evidence from Subprime Loans' (2010) 125 *Quarterly Journal of Economics* 307; S Krishnan, 'Securitization', in *Handbook of Critical Issues in Finance*, n 12 above, 290.

[162] Hedge funds are collective investments with a wide range of objectives, strategies, styles, techniques and assets, normally open to selected institutions.

[163] For example, Standard & Poor's, Moody's and Fitch.

[164] Source: Communication from the Commission on the application of State aid rules to support measures in favour of banks in the context of the financial crisis, [2011] OJ C356/02. The guarantee fee should be the sum of a basic fee, a risk-based fee and a risk metric composed using the following formula: the guarantee fee=40bp x (1+ (1/2 x A/B) + (1/2 x C/D)), where A is the beneficiary's median five-year senior CDS spread; B is the median iTraxx Europe Senior Financials five-year index; C is the median five-year senior CDS spread of all Member States; D is the median five-year senior CDS spread of the Member State granting the guarantees. In other words, the risk profile in recapitalisation state aid is measured through the media five-year senior debt CDS spread.

[165] EC, IP/13/630, Brussels, 1 July 2013. The 13 banks are Merrill Lynch, Barclays, Bear Stearns, Paribas, Citygroup, Credit Suisse, Deutsche Bank, Goldman Sachs, HSBC, Morgan, Morgan Stanley, RBS, UBS and ISDA.

[166] EC, IP/13/286, Brussels, 26 March 2013.

[167] JS Taub, 'What We Don't Talk About When We Talk About Banking', n 2 above, 457.

Y in the near future or on demand.[168] In other words, in the event that A defaults, B can sell it to C to offset its loss. Despite being labelled as the sale and repurchase of securities, repo is economically a 'secured deposit' having as its purpose the borrowing and lending of cash.

In conclusion, all of the above financial contracts are characterised by an oligopoly pricing power, asymmetric information, and unequal bargaining power.[169] The proliferation of these contractual instruments demonstrates the value of Minsky's classification of 'financial fragility'[170] as (i) hedge finance, which amounts to liability obligations to be paid with the net cash flows from routine transactions; (ii) speculative finance, where cash reserves are insufficient and require borrowing funds or selling less-liquid assets; and (iii) Ponzi finance, where there will never be enough cash to meet outstanding financial obligations.[171] Due to a failure to obtain additional financing, Ponzi firms have had to sell their assets, which created Fisher's 'price deflation'[172] for the firms' assets.

VIII. ON THE MANIPULATION OF INTEREST RATES DERIVATIVES: YET ANOTHER ANTI-COMPETITIVE PRACTICE?

LIBOR is a reference index sponsored by the British Banking Association used to calculate short-term interest rates on a range of financial derivative contracts.[173] Its daily submission indicates what each bank estimates is their cost of unsecured borrowing from another bank. Competition authorities worldwide (EC, the UK, the US, Canada and Japan) alleged that the Contributor Panel Banks exchanged information to undervalue daily submissions and that brokers colluded to manipulate LIBOR to raise the profits from certain derivatives. In other words, under competitive conditions, banks would submit their valuation independently to move away from forms of artificial collusion. In the US *USD LIBOR* scandal,[174] antitrust damage claims were rejected on the grounds of failure to prove conspiracy and restraint of trade, lack of antitrust standing and impossibility of recovery on the basis of the 'indirect purchaser rule'.[175] The US

[168] See EC, Directorate-General for Internal Policies, Policy Department Economic and Scientific Policy, Economic and Monetary Affairs, 'Note on Shadow Banking-Minimum Haircuts on Collateral' 2013, 56.

[169] Crotty, n 29 above, 153.

[170] Kregel, n 18 above, 160.

[171] See Tymoigne, n 12 above, 99.

[172] I Fisher, 'The debt-deflation theory of great depressions' (1933) 1 *Econometrica* 337.

[173] Source: CNN MONEY, A Petroff, 'Libor moving to NYSE Euronext', available at: http://money.cnn.com/2013/07/09/investing/libor-nyse-uk. See C Lim, 'Libor, Strategy, and International Cartel Investigations' (2013) *Journal of European Competition Law & Policy*.

[174] See PDS Phillip and RP Girnys, 'No Antitrust Injury in Libor Rate-Setting?—What Happened to Effects?' (2012) *Comparative Policy International* 3.

[175] Established in *Illinois Brick Co v Illinois* 431 US 720 (1977).

court ruled that there cannot be damage recovery without showing that the actual loss stems from a reduction of competition or that any harm is the result of the defendant's behaviour.[176] This interpretation endorses the traditional approach to antitrust harm, which requires proof of a resulting restriction of competition in the market for interbank loans. Since LIBOR displays only information about 'prevailing rates', the court went on to say that LIBOR quotations, even in the event that they were set artificially, did not correspond to the actual interest rate charged for interbank loans. This legal reasoning lacks a great deal of pragmatism, since the authors of this innovative anti-competitive practice are banks which have unfortunately been excluded from antitrust scrutiny. This fact also justifies the Court's reservation. Semantically different from the economics of collusion, the manipulation of exchange rates is one of the means used to deceive the bank panel and implement fraud.

Recent investigations have enquired whether the submitting banks intentionally undervalued LIBOR submissions, whether traders at banks and hedge funds tried to influence the rate to speculate on interest rate derivatives, and whether traders employed within Contributor Panel Banks received information about rates, either directly or through intermediaries, such as inter-dealer brokers. The heated question has turned to whether LIBOR should be assimilated into anti-competitive practices such as price-fixing and be criminalised, as are cartels.[177] Exchange rate manipulation has been unknown as an anti-competitive practice, while the banking sector has been practically excluded from any competition intervention against what is known as collusion by brokers/bank panels against consumers to fix the market price artificially. For example, Barclays[178] submitted low US$ LIBOR as a result of management instructions, which began in late August 2007. The EC and the UK Financial Services Authority investigated Barclays' alleged infringements between traders and rate-setters for the Euro Interbank Offer Rate (EURIBOR) in particular through mis-selling interest rate swaps to small businesses, ie low-cost protection against rising interest rates.[179] In practice, information asymmetries between informed

[176] Following a ruling by Judge Naomi Reice Buchwald of the US District Court for the Southern District of New York.

[177] A Stephan, 'Should Libor-Rigging be treated like Price Fixing?' at: http://competitionpolicy.wordpress.com/2012/07/11/should-libor-rigging-be-treated-like-price-fixing; extremely interesting on crisis cartels, see A Stephan, 'Price Fixing in Crisis: Implications of an Economic Downturn for Cartels and Enforcement' (2012) 35 *World Comparative Law & Economics Review* 511.

[178] According to the Financial Ombudsman Service, it is 'UK's most complained about bank'.

[179] Source: *The Guardian* at: www.guardian.co.uk/business/2013/feb/05/barclays-1-billion-mis-selling-compensation-bill.

contract holders and ordinary investors result in price inefficiency,[180] with clear evidence that the share prices of banks were artificially altered by the short selling of derivatives. Specifically, a manipulator sells the shares of a company short and then spreads negative rumours about the company's prospects.[181] This has led to calls for another EU proposal introducing bans on naked short selling if the price of a financial instrument falls by a significant amount in a single day.[182]

The above recent investigations and the record fine of £1.7 billion for the Euro interest rate derivatives cartel operated by Barclays, Deutsche Bank, RBS and Société Générale and for the Yen interest rate derivatives cartel run by USB, RBS, Deutsche Bank, JPMorgan and Citygroup,[183] demonstrate the determination of antitrust enforcers and policy-makers[184] to treat sophisticated financial derivative contracts as anti-competitive practices. This is yet another indication that the TBTF[185] doctrine is being constantly eroded.[186]

IX. END OF STORY: END OF CRISIS?

Finally, it is not possible to understand the dimension of the current crisis without a proper critique of the role neoliberalism has played. It is known

180 B Clarke, 'Where was the "market for corporate control" when we needed it?' in Sun et al (eds), *Corporate Governance and the Global Financial Crisis*, n 15 above, 77.

181 Ibid, 78.

182 See EU Regulation no 236/2012 on Short Selling and certain aspects of credit default swaps, [2012] OJ L86/1.

183 See EC, Press release IP/13/1208, Brussels, 4 December 2013; EC, Case AT39861, *Yen Interest Rate Derivatives*, not available yet. Further SOs were sent to Credit Agricole, HSBC and JPMorgan for suspected participation in Euro interest rate derivatives cartel, see EC, IP/14/572, Brussels, 20 May 2014, and to ICAP for its suspected participation in yen interest rate derivatives cartels, see EC, IP/14/656, Brussels, 10 June 2014.

184 See an encouraging prospect by Chancellor George Osborne, available at: www.guardian.co.uk/business/2013/feb/04/george-osborne-investment-banks-warning; www.guardian.co.uk/business/video/2013/feb/04/george-osborne-banking-reforms-video.

185 D Bush, 'Too Big to Fail: The Role of Antitrust in Distressed Industries' (2010) 77 *Antitrust Law Journal* 277; A Mateus, '"Too Big to Fail": Banking Regulatory Reform and What Still Needs to be Done' (2011) 7 *Comparative Policy International* 22; JW Markham, 'Lessons for Competition Law from the Economic Crisis: The Prospect for Antitrust Responses to the "Too Big to Fail" Phenomenon' (2011) 16 *Fordham Journal of Corporate & Financial Law* 261. The concept of TBTF was first applied in 1914 by Treasury Secretary, William Gibbs McAdoo, to rescue the municipal government of New York City.

186 Against TBTF see, eg, LH Rockwell: 'Don't Bail Them Out', 10 September 2008: 'What should have happened in 1929 is precisely what should happen now ... The government should completely remove itself from the course of action and let the market re-evaluate resource values', available at: http://mises.org/daily/3104; F Shostak, 'The Rescue Package Will Delay the Recovery', 29 September 2008: 'The government package is not going to rescue the economy, but it will rescue activities that the economy cannot afford and that consumers do not want. It will sustain waste and promote inefficiency', at: http://mises.org/daily/3131.

that neoliberalism called for the deregulation of financial markets[187] in the first instance and for a weak state.[188] Neoliberalism departs fundamentally from ordoliberal ideas of individual freedom as coerced by the state, or as Bonefeld put it,[189] this 'ordered freedom' positions itself somewhere between collectivism and laissez-faire liberalism, as a true guardian of markets. As the ordoliberal ideology emerged from attempts to address the problems created by the economic crisis in the 1920s, it has led to a different model of liberal governance, which is generally distrustful of markets. In other words, ordoliberalism was originally packaged as a hybrid product which has prided itself on being sympathetic (a '*humane*' economy)[190] to the sociological effects of industrialisation and market competition on workers. However, Rüstow contradicts the human economy at least for 'unionised' workers who threaten the 'weak' state.[191] His ideas hold water as regards pressure groups, such as lobbyists, monopolists or even oligopolists. For Eucken, in contrast, the 'well-being of capitalism' is almost synonymous with being competitive, risk-taking and self-responsible.[192] In other words, it is inconceivable that where the entrepreneurial spirit fails in practice, society should take on the responsibility for such a failure. This is precisely the rather hidden message of the 'social market economy' according to Bonefeld,[193] namely, a social policy that ensures that individuals act as self-responsible entrepreneurs. Applied to our crisis scenario, the big players of speculative games will have to agree to demonstrate social and corporate responsibility if, as Vanberg put it,[194] such players 'systematically' perform poorly. Reflecting on the social and economic cost of the EU crisis through bail-outs this principle has failed in the EU.

For Röpke, the challenge of capitalism lay in the measure of state intervention, ie a 'crisis of interventionism'.[195] This is also true for the EU crisis. Academics agree on one vital point: the real disaster did not happen because banks started to fail, but because the EU and its Member States rescued

[187] On the US deregulation of swaps markets see M Greenberger, 'Derivatives in the Crisis and Financial Reform', in Krugman and Wells, *Macroeconomics*, n 2 above, 473, through the Commodity Futures Modernization Act of 2010 which removed OTC derivatives transactions from exchange trading and clearing requirements.

[188] See, eg, W Bonefeld, 'Freedom and the Strong State: On German Ordoliberalism' (2012) 17 *New Political Economy* 635.

[189] Ibid, 639.

[190] A Rüstow, 'General Social Laws of the Economic Disintegration and Possibilities of Reconstruction' in *Afterword to Röpke, W International Economic Disintegration* (London, W Hodge, 1942); W Röpke, *A Human Economy* (Wilmington Delaware, ISI Books) 1998.

[191] Rüstow, 276.

[192] W Eucken, 'Staatliche Strukturwandlungen und die Krise des Kapitalismus' (1932) 36 *Weltwirtschaftliches Archiv* 297.

[193] Bonefeld, n 188 above, 647.

[194] V Vanberg, '"Ordungstheorie" as Constitutional Economics, The German Conception of a "Social Market Economy"' (1988) 39 *ORDO* 26.

[195] W Röpke, *Crisis and Cycles* (London, W Hodge, 1936) 160.

precisely those national champions of poor performance and, in the case of toxic assets, of fraud.

The final question after the assessment of law in action and neoliberal policy, as has been implemented in real life, is to challenge the ideological foundations of neoliberalism as a proper model of social and economic governance. It is recognised that no social change can take place without shaking the economic ideology and the politics underpinning such ideology. Neoliberalism has been portrayed as 'the ascendancy of financial capital over industrial capital in the pursuit of profit'.[196] Capitalism survived several generalised recessions (1974–75 and 1980–82) with high unemployment, a collapse in investment, and high inflation.[197] As has previously been explained in Section IV, because of the lost battle over the achievement of Keynesian 'full employment', this idealistic goal[198] has had to surrender to austere monetary policies to combat inflation. This influenced policy-makers to re-configure their focus on labour rigidities, market imperfections and distortions and to call for aggressive competition for both workers and capital.[199] As O'Connor suggested, 'coercive' competition replaced the 'socialisation' of economic activity by embedding at its foundation ideas of state rationalisation, market contestability, and mobility. How were these three ingredients implemented? Contestability of markets called for the prohibition of discrimination and eradication of market barriers to ensure a level playing field which would, in turn, guarantee labour mobility so as to enable capital to be relocated profitably elsewhere and to facilitate workers' wage flexibility, ie cheaper labour.[200] In contrast, the Keynesian vision stands out for higher wages and extensive social protection.[201]

According to O'Connor, neoliberalism re-established unemployment in the early 1980s so as to curb welfare benefits and collective bargaining agreements which was followed by the complete liberalisation of capital markets.[202] Capital mobility enabled governments to finance their fiscal deficits, by putting upward pressure on the exchange rate and domestic taxation.[203] Ultimately, due to fierce competition among capital owners,

[196] G Duménil and D Lévy, *Capital Resurgent: Roots of the Neoliberal Revolution* (Cambridge MA, Harvard University Press, 2004).

[197] See, eg, O'Connor, n 51 above, 694.

[198] See, eg, HM Oliver, 'German Neoliberalism' (1960) 74 *Quarterly Journal of Economics* 128 on the use of Keynesian measures to combat unemployment regarded as 'foolish' by German neoliberals.

[199] Ibid, 695.

[200] Ibid, 696.

[201] Ibid, 697; see also J O'Connor, *From Welfare Rights to Welfare Fights: Neoliberalism and the Retrenchment of Social Provision* (Mimeo MA, University of Massachusetts, Amherst, 2002).

[202] OECD, 'Open Markets Matter', Paris, 1998.

[203] P Genschel, 'Globalization and the welfare state: a retrospective' (2004) 11 *Journal of European Public Policy* 619, 623.

financialisation pushed down credit rates and risk premiums.[204] Others argued that financialisation contributed to a sluggish overall performance based on consumption and export-oriented growth models.[205]

Regrettably, this re-configuration of influence has essentially led to a weakening of the social and economic position of labour. Perhaps, one of the most pervasive drivers of neoliberalism lies primarily in its ambition to achieve the global financialisation of markets. This architectural configuration is plausible since the idea of economic integration has been the fundamental principle of an internal market: where individuals' migration is achieved through free movement, and mobility has served this purpose as a cheaper source of labour which boosts capital profits through workers' flexibility; the free movement of capital has achieved financialisation and the free movement of goods has succeeded in opening up markets through active competition.

As alluded to earlier in Section V.(A), under Article 119 TFEU, the idea of 'free competition' disguises the neoliberal idea of 'coercive competition' rather than of 'ordered freedom' since its macroeconomic foundations, which endorse explicitly an efficient use of Union resources by its Member States, bear much of the neoliberal austerity imprint in the convergence criteria rather than the 'human' ordoliberal ideology previously formulated. This is revealed by another position supported by German neoliberalism[206] which argued that monetary policy should 'complement' monopoly policy to maintain the rule of law established by the ordoliberal concept of 'ordered' constitutional freedom. Thus, on the one hand, at a microeconomic level, this 'order' will safeguard individual economic rights, such as free enterprise or the freedom of contract, except when this promotes monopolies and, on the other hand, at a macroeconomic level, the rule of law will safeguard price stability, output, the distribution of income and the allocation of resources. Since the breakdown of Bretton Woods, the 'macroeconomics trilemma'[207] of open markets with free competition has favoured floating exchange rates without capital control to the detriment of other objectives of monetary policy.[208] In times of crisis coercive forms of competition dictated the EU's macroeconomic policy of restructuring banking and dominated the free competition paradigm at microeconomic level.

In conclusion, while the architectural representations of coercive freedom have not been entirely in the negative in terms of achieved impact on the economy and society as a whole—for example, one cannot deny certain

[204] Ibid.

[205] See E Stockhammer, 'Financialization', in Sun et al (eds), *Corporate Governance and the Global Financial Crisis*, n 15 above, 124.

[206] Oliver, n 198 above, 144.

[207] Attributed to P Krugman, 'The return of depression economics' (1999) 78 *Foreign Affairs* 56.

[208] G Cozzi, 'Capital controls', in Sun et al (eds), n 15 above, 27.

positive benefits of free movement of EU citizens[209]—the Achilles' heel of the above freedoms is currently *financialisation* being used as a means to misappropriate the human capital to uncover corporate responsibility for speculative pursuits.[210] Furthermore, the social costs of this full-blown financial crisis have shown that the speculative gains of this kind have not been short-termism.[211] Rather, those in pursuit of speculation of profits have embraced in the long run the mature cost of a financial servicing industry which was even highly respected as a successful driver of capitalism until its 'Big Fail' finally spread across the globe. Finally, the remaking of capitalism would not have been possible without active deregulation, a previous lack of competition intervention in the banking sector and an aggressive competitive culture. On a positive note remain, however, the recent derivative cartels investigated and fined by the EC. These recent developments infuse EU taxpayers, who must bear the costs of previous bail-outs, with optimism for the future, and demonstrate a much welcome change of perspective on financial derivatives.

[209] On the other hand, O'Connor, n 51 above, 704, reminds us that 'even elite migrant workers are more likely to sell their labour power at a lower price and work in poor conditions', much of which is experienced in real life. Generally on fundamental freedoms see C Barnard, *The Substantive Law of the EU: The Four Freedoms*, 3rd edn (Oxford, Oxford University Press, 2010).

[210] Before the breakdown of Bretton Woods in 1971 it is said that only 10% of foreign exchange transactions were purely speculative.

[211] See also O'Connor, n 51 above, 702.

10

How Has the EU Protected Depositors in the Financial Crisis?

NIALL J LENIHAN[1]

Abstract

This chapter addresses the question of how the EU has protected depositors in the financial crisis. The chapter will discuss (1) the impact in Europe of the US system for the protection of depositors, (2) the important changes made to the EU Deposit Guarantee Schemes Directive, first in 2009 in response to the 2007 deposit run on Northern Rock, and then again in 2014 in response to the financial crisis, (3) the decision of the EFTA Court regarding the scope of Iceland's obligations under the EU Deposit Guarantee Schemes Directive, following the collapse of the Icelandic banking system in 2008, and (4) the introduction of a powerful depositor preference rule throughout the EU, in response to the resolution of the Cypriot banking system in 2013. This chapter argues that the EU has responded to the impact of the financial crisis on bank depositors by enhancing the legal protections available to depositors.

I. INTRODUCTION

How has the EU protected depositors in the financial crisis? This question will be addressed in several stages.

First, this chapter will discuss the unexpected deposit run on Northern Rock, which occurred in the UK in September 2007, and the lessons drawn from that experience, not so much in the UK, as in the wider EU. Secondly, it will briefly explain some of the features of the US system for the protection

[1] Any views expressed in this chapter are those of the author, and may not be attributed to the European Central Bank (ECB). The author wishes to thank (in alphabetical order) Margarita Anastasiou, Legal Counsel, ECB Legal Services, Dr Phoebus Athanassiou, Senior Legal Counsel, and Prof Dr Hans-Georg Kamann, WilmerHale, for their comments. The author also wishes to thank the following colleagues in the ECB Legal Services for their input on specific references to certain legal source materials referenced in the chapter: Marcis Apinis, Elena Bodea, Erika Csongrádi, Maria da Graca Peres, Pascale Duparc Portier, Paul Hoyer, Asimina Koutsoukou, Esther Martínez de Bustos, and Anne Schillmöller.

of depositors, primarily through the Federal Deposit Insurance Corporation (FDIC), which has provided some inspiration for recent depositor protection reforms in Europe. Thirdly, the important changes that were made to the EU Deposit Guarantee Schemes Directive in 2009, in response to the Northern Rock case, and the financial crisis generally, will then be outlined. Fourthly, the collapse of the Icelandic banking system in 2008, and the legal ramifications of the failure of the Icelandic authorities to protect the depositors of the Netherlands and UK Icesave branches of Landsbanki, will be discussed. In particular, the chapter will consider the decision of the EFTA Court regarding the scope of Iceland's obligations, as a member of the European Economic Area (EEA), under the EU Deposit Guarantee Schemes Directive, which is a Directive having EEA-wide relevance. Fifthly, the further reforms to the EU Deposit Guarantee Schemes Directive in 2014, which are required to be implemented in 2015, will be explained. Sixthly, the bank resolution law reforms made since the start of the crisis in an increasing number of EU Member States, and most recently at the EU level, in order to grant public authorities the necessary powers to restructure their banking sectors, will be outlined. The chapter will focus, in particular, on those elements which are designed to protect depositors. Seventhly, the restructuring and resolution of the Cypriot banking system in 2013 will be discussed, with a particular focus on how depositors at the two main Cypriot banks were affected. Eighthly, the chapter will explain how the EU has responded to the Cypriot banking crisis by introducing a powerful depositor preference rule throughout the EU. Finally, it will conclude by attempting to answer the question: 'How Has the EU Protected Depositors in the Financial Crisis?' The central thesis in this chapter is that the EU has responded to the impact of the financial crisis on bank depositors in a number of EU Member States by considerably enhancing the legal protections available to depositors. These law reforms should serve to reinforce the confidence of depositors in the European financial system.

II. NORTHERN ROCK DEPOSIT RUN (2007)

In September 2007 TV viewers in the UK and, indeed, around the world witnessed what seemed to be an old-fashioned depositor bank run on Northern Rock.[2] Northern Rock was a mortgage lender which had expanded its operations by heavily financing itself on the interbank and capital markets, while passing on its mortgage loans through the mortgage securitisation market. Northern Rock's funding sources dried up during

[2] See RM Lastra, 'Northern Rock, UK bank insolvency and cross-border bank insolvency' (2008) 9 *Journal of Banking Regulation* 165, 166.

the subprime mortgage crisis, forcing it to turn to the Bank of England for liquidity support.[3]

The chronology of events immediately preceding the so-called 'run on the Rock' was that on the evening of Thursday 13 September 2007 the BBC carried a news story revealing that Northern Rock was turning to the Bank of England for emergency liquidity support, in the Bank's role as lender-of-last-resort.[4] The Bank's role in this respect was set out in a tripartite Memorandum of Understanding between the Treasury, the Bank and the former Financial Services Authority (FSA), which recognised that, in exceptional circumstances, there may be a need for an operation which goes beyond the Bank's published framework for operations in the money market. Such a support operation was expected to happen very rarely, and would normally only be undertaken in the case of a genuine threat to the stability of the financial system to avoid a serious disturbance in the UK economy. Ultimate responsibility for authorisation of such support operations in exceptional circumstances rested with the Chancellor of the Exchequer.[5]

On the morning of Friday 14 September 2007 it was announced that the Chancellor of the Exchequer had authorised the Bank of England to provide a liquidity support facility against appropriate collateral and at an interest rate premium, pursuant to the Bank's role as lender-of-last-resort. The FSA judged Northern Rock to be solvent, facing liquidity problems only.[6] Somewhat surprisingly, this announcement, which should have inspired confidence, triggered the UK's first bank run since 1866, with customers queuing in large numbers outside Northern Rock branches to withdraw their savings deposits on Friday 14 and Monday 17 September. The queues were brought to a halt on Tuesday 18 September, after an announcement by the Chancellor that the Government would guarantee all deposits held at Northern Rock.[7]

[3] See RA Eisenbeis and GG Kaufman, 'Lessons from the Demise of the UK's Northern Rock and the U.S.'s Countrywide and Indymac' in F Bruni and DT Llewellyn (eds), *The Failure of Northern Rock: A Multi-Dimensional Case Study* (Vienna, SUERF—The European Money and Finance Forum, 2009) 75–76; M Onado, 'Northern Rock: Just the Tip of the Iceberg' in F Bruni and DT Llewellyn (eds), above, at 101–6.

[4] See British Broadcasting Corporation, *Timeline: Northern Rock bank crisis*, available at: http://news.bbc.co.uk/2/hi/business/7007076.stm.

[5] See Memorandum of Understanding Between HM Treasury, the Bank of England and the Financial Services Authority, para 14, available at: www.bankofengland.co.uk/about/Documents/legislation/news/mo.pdf.

[6] See Bank of England, *News Release—Liquidity Support Facility for Northern Rock plc, Tripartite Statement by HM Treasury, Bank of England and Financial Services Authority,* 14 September 2007, available at: www.bankofengland.co.uk/archive/Pages/digitalcontent/historicpubs/news/2007/090.aspx.

[7] See British Broadcasting Corporation, *Northern Rock deposits guaranteed*, 17 September 2007, available at: http://news.bbc.co.uk/2/hi/business/6999615.stm; RM Lastra, above n 2, at 166.

Many commentators have asked the question: Why did the depositors run from Northern Rock, especially considering that the comparable failure of the US mortgage lender, Countrywide, did not trigger a similar response? One important conclusion was that there were structural flaws in the UK deposit insurance system. Under the then-prevailing deposit insurance regime, the Financial Services Compensation Scheme covered 100 per cent of the first £2,000, and 90 per cent of the next £33,000.[8] This meant, for example, that a depositor with, say, £12,000 stood to lose £1,000. This system, known as co-insurance, was based on the idea that it would give depositors an incentive to monitor the performance of the banks in which they placed their deposits, providing a source of market discipline by demanding higher rates or withdrawing their deposits if they perceived the bank to be too risky. The lesson drawn from the run on Northern Rock was that co-insurance is a flawed concept. Depositors are not interested in losing *any* of their money, and will withdraw their funds if *any* of their savings are at risk.[9]

Other perceived shortcomings were the relatively low level of the deposit guarantee, and the perception that pay-outs by the deposit guarantee scheme take too long to materialise.[10] More broadly, there was a perception that depositors also needed to be protected through the introduction of resolution powers comparable to those in the US, authorising the public authorities to transfer good assets, together with deposit and other key liabilities, out of a distressed bank to a healthy third party purchaser, or to a publicly owned bridge bank pending sale to a third party purchaser. Following such a transfer of business, residual assets and non-critical liabilities could be left behind in a rump entity to be wound down under normal insolvency procedures. Banks are not like ordinary companies, but are custodians of society's savings deposits. It is therefore important that public authorities have these kinds of powers allowing banks to be restructured and resolved, and their deposits to be ring-fenced through administrative procedures. Such a resolution process avoids leaving banks to the vagaries of a judicially administered corporate insolvency regime.[11] As we shall see, the lessons drawn from the run on

[8] See House of Commons Treasury Committee, *The run on the Rock*, Fifth Report of Session 2007–08, HC 56-I, 26 January 2008, para 221, available at: www.publications.parliament/pa/cm200708/cmselect/cmtreasy/56/5609.htm.

[9] See DT Llewellyn, 'The Northern Rock Crisis: A Multi-Dimensional Problem' in F Bruni and DT Llewellyn (eds), above n 3, at 21, 28; DG Mayes and G Wood, 'The Northern Rock Crisis in the UK' in F Bruni and DT Llewellyn (eds), above n 3, at 37; P Hamalainen, 'Fallout from the Credit Squeeze and Northern Rock Crises: Incentives, Transparency and Implications for the Role of Market Discipline' in F Bruni and DT Llewellyn (eds), above n 3, at 53–54; RA Eisenbeis and GG Kaufman, above n 3, at 81.

[10] See DT Llewellyn, above n 9, at 28; DG Mayes and G Wood, above n 9, at 38; P Hamalainen, above n 9, at 54; RA Eisenbeis and GG Kaufman, above n 3, at 81–83.

[11] See DT Llewellyn, above n 9, at 28–29; DG Mayes and G Wood, above n 9, at 41–43; RA Eisenbeis and GG Kaufman, above n 9, at 83–84; RM Lastra, above n 2, at 169–73.

Northern Rock heavily influenced subsequent EU law reform initiatives to reinforce the protection of depositors.

III. US DEPOSITOR PROTECTION ARRANGEMENTS

Before describing the EU regulatory response to the run on Northern Rock, it is worthwhile noting that a number of the features seen as lacking in Europe at the outset of the financial crisis have been present in the US bank regulatory architecture for some time.

Before the financial crisis that began with the collapse of Lehman Brothers in 2008 the standard maximum deposit insurance amount of the US Federal Deposit Insurance Corporation (FDIC) was US$100,000, without any co-insurance feature. Following the collapse of Lehman Brothers this amount was temporarily, and subsequently permanently, raised to US$250,000.[12] The FDIC is required to make payments of insured deposits as soon as possible after the failure of an insured depository institution.[13] The FDIC states that in most cases the FDIC makes insured funds available to depositors quickly, usually on the first business day after the bank is closed.[14]

In addition to these deposit insurance arrangements, the US has also had a depositor preference rule since 1993.[15] A depositor preference rule is an insolvency law rule which ranks depositors ahead of general unsecured creditors in the insolvency of a bank. Internationally, such a rule has existed in a number of G20 countries for many years.[16] However, depositor preference rules have, until the recent financial crisis, been almost entirely absent in EU Member States. In those countries where there is a depositor preference rule a depositor will typically enjoy, in the event of a bank failure, a priority claim against the assets of the insolvent bank, separately from whatever additional protection the depositor enjoys under the deposit insurance scheme.[17] A depositor preference rule thus has the effect of preserving the bank's assets for the benefit of its depositors in the event

[12] 12 USC § 1821(a)(1)(A), (E); see also Federal Deposit Insurance Corporation, Press Releases: 'Basic FDIC Insurance Coverage Permanently Increased to $250,000 Per Depositor', 21 July 2010, available at: www.fdic.gov/news/news/press/2010/pr10161.html; Federal Deposit Insurance Corporation, Press Releases: 'Emergency Economic Stabilization Act of 2008 Temporarily Increases Basic FDIC Insurance Coverage from $100,000 to $250,000 Per Depositor', 7 October 2008, available at: www.fic.gov/news/news/press/2008/pr08093.html; RA Eisenbeis and GG Kaufman, above n 3, at 81.

[13] 12 USC § 1821(f)(1).

[14] See FDIC Consumer News, *Get a Good Night's Sleep: Rest Assured—Your Money Is Safe in an FDIC-Insured Account*, Summer 2008, available at: search.fdic.gov.

[15] See generally JA Marino and RL Bennett, 'The Consequences of National Depositor Preference' (1999) 12 *FDIC Banking Review* 19–38.

[16] See Clifford Chance, *Depositor Preference Issues*, September 2011, available at: www.cliffordchance.com/briefings/2011/09/depositor_preferenceissues.html.

[17] Ibid.

of the bank's insolvency. In general, under the US depositor preference rule, in the liquidation of a failed insured depository institution a preference is granted by law to any domestic deposit liability of the institution ahead of any other general or senior liability of the institution.[18] The US depositor preference rule thus protects deposit liabilities without making any distinction between insured and uninsured deposit liabilities. However, it does not cover foreign deposits payable at offices located outside the US.[19]

The FDIC has also long had general resolution powers, as a receiver and/or conservator of a failing bank, to organise a new or a bridge depository institution, to merge an insured depository institution with another insured depository institution, or to require the transfer of any asset or liability—including deposits—to a healthy third party purchaser in a purchase and assumption transaction, or to a bridge institution.[20] As will become clear below, these legal protections of depositors in the US have provided some of the inspiration for the depositor protection law reforms which have been introduced in the EU in response to the financial crisis.

IV. AMENDMENTS TO EU DEPOSIT GUARANTEE SCHEMES DIRECTIVE (2009)

At EU level many of the structural flaws identified in the Northern Rock case were contained in the then-prevailing EU Deposit Guarantee Schemes Directive, which dates from 1994.[21] Under the Directive EU Member States were required to have a deposit guarantee scheme under which the aggregate deposits of each depositor were to be generally covered up to €20,000 (or ECU 20,000 prior to the introduction of the euro in 1999).[22] A co-insurance element was built into this number, so that Member States had an option to limit the guarantee to 90 per cent of the deposits.[23] Deposit guarantee schemes were required to be in a position to pay duly verified claims by depositors within three months of the deposits becoming unavailable.[24] In wholly exceptional circumstances, the Directive allowed the three-month time limit for pay-outs to be extended for two further three-month periods.[25] This meant that it was theoretically possible that the deposit guarantee scheme would not pay out to the depositor for up to nine months.

[18] 12 USC §§ 1813(l)(5)(A) and 1821(d)(11)(A).

[19] 12 USC § 1813(l)(5)(A); see JA Marino and RL Bennett, above n 15 at 20–21.

[20] See generally 12 USC §§ 1821, 1823.

[21] Directive 94/19/EC of the European Parliament and of the Council of 30 May 1994 on deposit-guarantee schemes, [1994] OJ L135/5.

[22] Ibid, Arts 3(1), 7(1).

[23] Ibid, Art 7(4).

[24] Ibid, Art 10(1).

[25] Ibid, Art 10(2).

In response to the Northern Rock case and the financial crisis generally the EU amended the Deposit Guarantee Schemes Directive in a number of important respects in 2009.[26] First, the minimum coverage level was increased from €20,000, initially to €50,000 by mid-2009, and then to €100,000 by the end of 2010.[27] The European Commission estimated that the new €100,000 minimum coverage level would cover 90 per cent of deposits in the EU, compared to 65 per cent under the old regime.[28] Secondly, the co-insurance option was eliminated.[29] Thirdly, the three-month pay-out delay, extendable to nine months, was reduced to 20 working days, extendible in exceptional circumstances by a further 10 working days.[30]

V. ICESAVE DECISION OF EFTA COURT (2013)

The judgment of the EFTA Court in the *Icesave* case[31] is an important case shedding light on the scope of protection under the 1994 Deposit Guarantee Schemes Directive in a cross-border context, in this case involving one Member State of the European Economic Area (Iceland) and two EU Member States (the Netherlands and UK). The background to this case was the collapse of the three main banks in Iceland in October 2008, during the turmoil in the international financial system following the collapse of Lehman Brothers in the United States. The collapse triggered a restructuring of the entire Icelandic banking system.[32]

The case concerned one of the three Icelandic banks, Landsbanki. Availing itself of the single passport to provide banking services throughout the European Economic Area (EEA), of which Iceland is a Member State, Landsbanki had opened branches in the Netherlands and UK, providing online savings accounts under the brand name 'Icesave'. The Icesave accounts offered competitive rates that drew in substantial deposits.[33] As a member of the EEA, Iceland had implemented the 1994 Deposit Guarantee Schemes Directive into Icelandic law.[34] Under the Directive national deposit

[26] See Directive 2009/14/EC of the European Parliament and of the Council of 11 March 2009 amending Directive 94/19/EC on deposit-guarantee schemes as regards the coverage level and the pay-out delay, [2009] OJ L68/3.

[27] Ibid, Art 1(3)(a).

[28] See European Commission, Proposal for a Directive of the European Parliament and of the Council amending Directive 94/19/EC on Deposit Guarantee Schemes as regards the coverage level and the pay-out delay, COM(2008) 0661 final—COD(2008) 0199, Explanatory Memorandum, para 5.3.

[29] See Directive 2009/14/EC of the European Parliament and of the Council of 11 March 2009 amending Directive 94/19/EC on deposit-guarantee schemes as regards the coverage level and the pay-out delay, [2009] OJ L68/3, Art 1(3)(c).

[30] Ibid, Art 1(6).

[31] Case E-16/11 *EFTA Surveillance Authority v Iceland* [2013] EFTA Court Report 4.

[32] Ibid, paras 28–54.

[33] Ibid, para 27.

[34] Ibid, para 26.

guarantee schemes were required to cover the deposits at branches set up by credit institutions in other Member States.[35] This meant that the Icelandic Deposit Guarantee Scheme was responsible for the coverage of the Icesave deposits in the Netherlands and UK.[36]

The Icelandic scheme had, in accordance with the Directive, a lower minimum coverage level than the UK and the Netherlands schemes.[37] In these circumstances, where the level of cover in the host Member States—meaning the Netherlands and UK—is higher than the level of cover in the home Member State—Iceland—the Directive required the host Member States to ensure that the branch may voluntarily join the local deposit guarantee scheme in order to supplement the guarantee which the branch depositors already enjoy by virtue of the scheme in the home Member State.[38] Landsbanki had availed of this option to participate in the Netherlands and UK schemes, in order to enjoy supplementary coverage for the excess over and above the lower Icelandic coverage level.[39]

Upon the collapse of Landsbanki the Icelandic authorties, acting pursuant to emergency legislation, transferred the domestic Icelandic deposits of Landsbanki to a new bank, called New Landsbanki.[40] The UK Government froze Landbanki's UK assets, and the Dutch courts appointed an administrator for Landsbanki's branch in the Netherlands.[41] In late 2008 the UK Government paid out the full value of Landsbanki's retail deposits, while the Netherlands Government paid out all deposits up to a 100,000 euro limit. The Netherlands and UK Governments then submitted claims against the Icelandic deposit guarantee scheme, which were not honoured.[42] The EFTA Surveillance Authority, which is responsible for ensuring Iceland's compliance with its obligations under the EEA Treaty, then instituted legal proceedings before the EFTA Court against Iceland. It was alleged that Iceland had breached its obligations under the 1994 Deposit Guarantee Schemes Directive for failing to compensate the depositors at the Icesave branches in the Netherlands and UK. The EFTA Surveillance Authority was supported by the European Commission, and by the Netherlands and UK Governments.[43]

The EFTA Court, which has jurisdiction with regard to EFTA states which are parties to the EEA Agreement (including Iceland, Liechtenstein

[35] Directive 94/19/EC of the European Parliament and of the Council of 30 May 1994 on deposit-guarantee schemes, [1994] OJ L135/5, Art 4(1).

[36] Case E-16/11 *EFTA Surveillance Authority v Iceland* [2013] EFTA Court Report 4, para 29.

[37] Ibid, para 30.

[38] Directive 94/19/EC of the European Parliament and of the Council of 30 May 1994 on deposit-guarantee schemes, [1994] OJ L135/5, Art 4(2).

[39] Case E-16/11 *EFTA Surveillance Authority v Iceland* [2013] EFTA Court Report 4, para 30.

[40] Ibid, paras 33–34, 36, 38.

[41] Ibid, paras 37, 39.

[42] Ibid, paras 42, 49–50, 55.

[43] Ibid, paras 61, 64, 66, 68, 70.

and Norway),[44] held that the 1994 Directive does not envisage that Iceland itself had to ensure payments to depositors in the Icesave branches in the Netherlands and UK in a systemic crisis of the magnitude experienced in Iceland. Iceland's obligation under the Directive was limited to ensuring that a deposit guarantee scheme was introduced, that an effective framework was in place and that the necessary domestic legislation was adopted for these purposes. However, there was no legal duty on the part of the Icelandic authorities to ensure compensation if the deposit guarantee scheme was unable to cope with its obligations in the event of a systemic crisis.[45] In reaching this conclusion the Court pointed to wording in the 1994 Directive that contemplated the failure of individual banks only, and not a systemic bank failure of the magnitude experienced in Iceland.[46]

The Court also drew attention to the 1994 Directive's Preamble, which envisions that the cost of financing deposit guarantee schemes must be borne in principle by credit institutions, and not by Member States. The Court stated that the provision of private funding to enable the guarantee scheme to cover deposits in a systemic crisis up to the maximum coverage level would undermine the Directive's objective of not jeopardising the stability of the banking system itself. Accordingly, the Court reasoned that the cost of the guarantee scheme must not be too onerous for the member credit institutions.[47] The Court pointed to the concept of 'moral hazard' in economic literature, which the Court found reflected in the Preamble's statement that it would not be appropriate to impose a level of protection which might have the effect of encouraging the unsound management of credit institutions. Based on this, the Court suggested that moral hazard would occur in the case of state funding, serving to immunise a deposit guarantee scheme from the costs which have, in principle, to be borne by its members.[48]

The Court also mentioned the 1994 Directive's provision according to which depositors must have the possibility to bring an action against the relevant deposit guarantee scheme for non-payment. The Court noted that the Directive does not envisage an action against the state in these circumstances.[49] The Court's ruling could be interpreted as holding that Iceland fulfilled all its obligations under the 1994 Directive simply by transposing the Directive into Icelandic law and setting up a deposit guarantee scheme,

[44] See Agreement between the EFTA States on the establishment of a Surveillance Authority and a Court of Justice, [1994] OJ L344/3, Part IV, as amended.

[45] Case E-16/11 *EFTA Surveillance Authority v Iceland* [2013] EFTA Court Report 4, paras 117–85.

[46] Ibid, paras 150–53.

[47] Ibid, paras 154–58.

[48] Ibid, paras 167–68 (citing JE Stiglitz, 'Risk, Incentives and Insurance: The Pure Theory of Moral Hazard' (1983) 8/26 *The Geneva Papers on Risk and Insurance* 4 at 6).

[49] Ibid, para 160.

without any regard to whether the compensation of depositors is, in fact, ensured in line with the presumed objective of the Directive. On this basis, it could be argued that the ruling renders ineffective the Directive's basic objective to provide coverage to depositors when their deposits become unavailable. The Court stated that depositors will not necessarily remain unprotected, as they may benefit from the activities of supervisors, central banks and governments.[50] However, this may overlook the important signalling effect of a deposit guarantee system in its own right, and also the necessary confidence which EEA States must have in each other's systems in order that the single passport to provide banking services across the EEA can function properly.

It may be that this decision is of limited precedential value. While decisions of the EFTA Court are persuasive for the European Court of Justice,[51] the EFTA Court expressly noted that its judgment was based on the Directive as it stood in 2008, before the improved depositor protections under the 2009 amendments.[52] In particular, the Court noted that the obligation to ensure a minimum coverage level under the wording of the pre-2009 Directive was that of the national deposit guarantee scheme, whereas following the 2009 amendments the Member States themselves were obliged to ensure the new, increased minimum coverage level for depositors. The Court left open the question of whether this obligation of the Member States to ensure a certain level of coverage is limited to a banking crisis of a certain size.[53] Against this backdrop, it is unclear to what extent the EFTA Court ruling in the *Icesave* case is still relevant in a situation where a national deposit guarantee scheme in the EU is unable to cope with its obligations in a systemic crisis.

VI. NEW RECAST DEPOSIT GUARANTEE SCHEMES DIRECTIVE (2014)

The EU has moved to further strengthen the EU deposit guarantee system. In April 2014 a revised Deposit Guarantee Schemes Directive was adopted by the EU Council and European Parliament.[54] One of the key drivers

[50] Ibid, para 161.

[51] See P Athanassiou, 'The Icesave ruling: legally justified discriminatory treatment?' (2013) 3 *Journal of International Banking and Financial Law* 141; M Hanten and M Plaschke, 'EU law impact on depositor protection in the financial crisis: Icesave' (2014) 51 *Common Market Law Review* 295, 297–98.

[52] Case E-16/11 *EFTA Surveillance Authority v Iceland* [2013] EFTA Court Report 4, para 124.

[53] Ibid, paras 136–41; see also P Athanassiou, above n 51, at 141.

[54] See Directive 2014/49/EU of the European Parliament and of the Council of 16 April 2014 on deposit guarantee schemes (recast), [2014] OJ L173/149.

behind this reform was that in the financial crisis uncoordinated increases in coverage across the EU have in some cases led to depositors transferring money to credit institutions in countries where deposit guarantees were higher. Such uncoordinated increases have drained liquidity from credit institutions in times of stress. In times of stability it is possible that different coverage leads to depositors choosing the highest deposit protection rather than the deposit product best suited to them. It is possible that such different coverage results in competitive distortions in the EU internal banking market. The EU therefore considered it necessary to ensure a harmonised level of deposit protection by all recognised deposit guarantee schemes, regardless of where the deposits are located in the EU.[55]

An important feature of the new Directive is that, unlike the existing Directive, it is *not* based on the principle of minimum harmonisation. Rather, with a view to eliminating competitive distortions in the internal market, the new Directive provides a uniform level of protection at €100,000 for each depositor throughout the EU.[56] This coverage level will be reviewed periodically by the Commission, at least once every five years.[57] The introduction of a fixed coverage set at €100,000 has put some Member States in the difficult situation of having to lower their coverage level, with the risk of undermining depositor confidence. Therefore, Member States whose current coverage levels range between €100,000 and €300,000 have an option to apply their higher coverage level until the end of 2018.[58]

The new Directive reduces the repayment period to a period of seven working days.[59] In order to facilitate the transition to this shorter period, Member States have an option to reduce the repayment period gradually during a transitional period, first of all to 20 working days by the end of 2018, then to 15 working days by the end of 2020, to 10 working days by the end of 2023, finally reaching the seven working day target in 2024.[60] However, in this case, if Member States opt for a transitional regime, the deposit guarantee scheme must ensure that depositors have access within five business days to an appropriate amount to cover the cost of living.[61] The new Directive introduces requirements for depositors to be informed about their coverage and the responsible deposit guarantee scheme on their

55 Ibid, Recital 19.
56 Ibid, Recitals 19–21 and Art 6(1).
57 Ibid, Art 6(6).
58 Ibid, Recital 23 and Art 19(4).
59 Ibid, Art 8(1).
60 Ibid, Art 8(2).
61 Ibid, Art 8(4).

account statements, when opening new accounts, and through the website maintained by the scheme.[62]

In order to ensure that depositors throughout the EU enjoy a similar level of protection, the new Directive harmonises the financing of deposit guarantee schemes with a uniform, ex ante financial target level for all schemes.[63] In particular, Member States are generally required to ensure that, no later than 10 years after the Directive enters into force, the available financial means of the scheme reaches a target level of 0.8 per cent of its members' covered deposits.[64] Up to 30 per cent of these 'available financial means' may comprise collateralised payment commitments.[65] Member States have an option to apply a lower target level of not less than 0.5 per cent of covered deposits, provided two conditions are satisfied. First, it should be unlikely that a significant share of the scheme's resources will be used to protect depositors. Secondly, the relevant banking sector should be highly concentrated with a large quantity of assets held by a small number of credit institutions or banking groups which are likely, in case of failure, to be subject to resolution proceedings.[66]

If the available financial means of the scheme are insufficient to repay depositors, members may be required to pay extraordinary contributions, unless these contributions would jeopardise the liquidity or solvency of the credit institution.[67] The deposit guarantee scheme must also have in place adequate alternative funding arrangements to obtain short-term funding to meet claims.[68] The new Directive also authorises deposit guarantee schemes to grant loans for up to five years to other schemes under certain conditions, up to a limit of 0.5 per cent of covered deposits of the borrowing scheme, provided that the borrowing scheme has already made recourse to extraordinary contributions from the scheme's members.[69] The new Directive makes it clear that depositors at branches set up by credit institutions in another Member State are to be repaid by the scheme in the host Member State on behalf of the scheme in the home Member State where the credit institution is incorporated.[70] The new Directive is required to be implemented within one year, by May 2015.[71]

[62] Ibid, Art 16 and Annex I.
[63] Ibid, Recital 27.
[64] Ibid, Art 10(2).
[65] Ibid, Art 10(3).
[66] Ibid, Art 10(6).
[67] Ibid, Art 10(8).
[68] Ibid, Art 10(9).
[69] Ibid, Art 12(1).
[70] Ibid, Art 14(1)–(2).
[71] Ibid, Art 20(1).

VII. NATIONAL AND EU BANK RESOLUTION LAW REFORMS (2009–2014)

An area where there have been significant developments affecting depositor protection in the EU has been that of bank recovery and resolution. It is argued that because banks are so critical to the stability of the financial system and the economy generally, it is important that when they fail, or are likely to fail, they can be restructured through an administrative process known as a resolution. Resolution is a stable alternative to a judicially administered insolvency process. The latter is more suited to ordinary companies, but not banks, where it is of critical importance to maintain depositor confidence through the continuity of critical banking functions.[72] In a resolution process the responsible public authorities are given various tools and powers, for example the power to authorise the transfer of deposits and good assets out of a failing bank to a healthy third party purchaser or to a publicly chartered temporary bridge bank until a suitable purchaser has been identified.[73]

In recent years an increasing number of EU Member States have, in response to the financial crisis, adopted resolution laws authorising public authorities—typically central banks, supervisors or special-purpose resolution authorities—to exercise these kinds of powers. Resolution legislation has now been adopted in many Member States, including the UK,[74] Germany,[75] France,[76] the Netherlands,[77] and all of the euro area Member States which have undergone EU and/or IMF programmes—

[72] See generally Basel Committee on Banking Supervision, Report and Recommendations of the Cross-border Bank Resolution Group, September 2009, available at: www.bis.org/publ; Financial Stability Board, Key Attributes of Effective Resolution Regimes for Financial Institutions, October 2011, available at: www.financialstabilityboard.org/publications; BJ Attinger, 'Crisis Management and Bank Resolution: Quo Vadis Europe?' (2011) 13 *ECB Legal Working Paper Series*, available at: www.ecb.europa.eu/pub; EH Hüpkes, *The Legal Aspects of Bank Insolvency: A Comparative Analysis of Western Europe, the United States and Canada* (The Hague, Kluwer Law International, 2000) 7–30.

[73] Ibid.

[74] Banking Act 2009, ch 1.

[75] Kreditinstitute-Reorganisationsgesetz vom 9. Dezember 2010 (BGBl I S 1900), das durch Artikel 2 Absatz 75 des Gesetzes vom 22. Dezember 2011 (BGBl I S 3044) geändert worden ist (Credit Institution Reorganization Act, 2011).

[76] Loi n° 2013-672 du 26 juillet 2013 de séparation et de régulation des activités bancaires (Law n° 2013-672 relating to the separation and regulation of banking activities), JORF n° 0173 du 27 juillet 2013, p 12530.

[77] Wet bijzondere maatregelen financiële ondernemingen, 2012 (Financial Institutions (Special Measures) Act 2012).

Cyprus,[78] Greece,[79] Ireland,[80] Portugal[81] and Spain.[82] A Bank Recovery and Resolution Directive was finalised by the EU in May 2014.[83] This will ensure that resolution authorities throughout the EU will enjoy a comparable tool-kit of resolution powers which can potentially be applied to cross-border banking and financial groups experiencing difficulties. This tool-kit includes sale of business and bridge institution tools, facilitating the transfer of deposits and good assets to third party purchasers and bridge banks.[84] The Directive introduces a number of safeguards to ensure compliance with private property and other human rights protections under the Charter of Fundamental Rights of the European Union and the European Convention for the Protection of Human Rights and Fundamental Freedoms, most notably that no creditor may incur greater losses than would have been incurred if the credit institution had been wound up under normal insolvency proceedings, to be assessed in accordance with independent valuation procedures.[85]

Concerning the treatment of deposits, the Directive takes care to ensure that deposits covered by the Deposit Guarantee Schemes Directive are excluded from the scope of the new bail-in tool, which allows the principal amount of bank claims to be reduced or converted into equity.[86] Also, in

[78] Ο περί Εξυγίανσης Πιστωτικών και Άλλων Ιδρυμάτων Νόμος, 17(Ι)/2013 (The Resolution of Credit and Other Institutions Law of 2013, Law 17(I)/2013).

[79] Νόμος 4021/2011 «Ενισχυμένα μέτρα εποπτείας και εξυγίανσης των πιστωτικών ιδρυμάτων—Ρύθμιση θεμάτων χρηματοπιστωτικού χαρακτήρα—Κύρωση της Σύμβασης—Πλαίσιο του Ευρωπαικού Ταμείου Χρηματοπιστωτικής Σταθερότητας και των τροποποιήσεών της και άλλες διατάξεις», ΦΕΚ Α 218/3.10.2011) (Law 4021/2011 'Enhanced banking supervision and bank resolution measures—Regulation of financial sector issues—Ratification of the EFSF Framework Agreement and of its amendments and other provisions', Government Gazette of the Hellenic Republic vol A 218/3.10.2011); Νόμος 3601/2007 «Ανάληψη και άσκηση δραστηριοτήτων από τα πιστωτικά ιδρύματα, επάρκεια ιδίων κεφαλαίων των πιστωτικών ιδρυμάτων και των επιχειρήσεων παροχής επενδυτικών υπηρεσιών και λοιπές διατάξεις», ΦΕΚ Α 178/1.8.2007 (Law 4021/2011 amended Law 3601/2007 'Taking up and pursuit of the business of credit institutions, capital adequacy of credit institutions and investment firms, and other provisions' (Banking Law), Government Gazette of the Hellenic Republic vol A 178/1.8.2007).

[80] Credit Institutions (Stabilisation) Act, No 36 (2010), as amended; Central Bank and Credit Institutions (Resolution) Act, No 27 (2011).

[81] Decreto-Lei nº 31-A/2012 (DR, I Série, nº 30, de 10 de fevereiro de 2012) (Decree-Law nº 31-A/2012 (DR nº 30, Series I, of 10 February 2012).

[82] Ley 9/2012, de 14 de noviembre de 2012, de reestructuración y resolución de entidades de crédito (BOE 15-11-2012) (Law 9/2012, of 14 November 2012, on the restructuring and resolution of credit institutions).

[83] See Directive 2014/59/EU of the European Parliament and of the Council of 15 May 2014 establishing a framework for the recovery and resolution of credit institutions and investment firms and amending Council Directive 82/891/EEC, and Directives 2001/24/EC, 2002/47/EC, 2005/56/EC, 2007/36/EC, 2011/35/EU, 2012/30/EU and 2013/36/EU, and Regulations (EU) No 1093/2010 and (EU) No 648/2012, of the European Parliament and of the Council, [2014] OJ L173/190.

[84] Ibid, Arts 38–41.

[85] Ibid, Recitals 50–51, Arts 34(1)(g), 73–75.

[86] Ibid, Art 44(2)(a).

exceptional circumstances, where the bail-in tool is applied, the resolution authority may exclude or partially exclude certain liabilities from the application of the write-down or conversion powers where the exclusion is strictly necessary and proportionate to avoid giving rise to widespread contagion, in particular as regards deposits held by natural persons and micro, small and medium sized enterprises.[87]

More broadly, the Bank Recovery and Resolution Directive clarifies that one of the main objectives of resolution is to protect depositors covered by the Deposit Guarantee Schemes Directive, such that resolution authorities, when applying the resolution tools and exercising the resolution powers, must have regard to this objective, and choose the tools and powers that best achieve this objective.[88] Similarly, the general principles governing resolution action include the principle that depositors covered by the Deposit Guarantee Schemes Directive are fully protected.[89]

As part of the project for a banking union in the euro area, a proposed Regulation establishing a Single Resolution Mechanism and a Single Bank Resolution Fund is in the process of being finalised, which contains comparable provisions relating to the protection of depositors.[90] The protection of depositors is being further enhanced through the adoption of resolution legislation at both the national and the EU levels. One of the key objectives of this legislation is to protect depositors by making it easier for authorities to transfer deposits held at a failing bank to healthy third party purchasers or bridge banks.

VIII. CYPRIOT CRISIS: UNINSURED DEPOSIT BAIL-IN AND RESOLUTION (2013)

One of the more significant events affecting depositors during the financial crisis in Europe has been the Cypriot authorities' bail-in of uninsured deposits, and the restructuring and resolution of the two leading Cypriot banks, Bank of Cyprus and Cyprus Popular Bank (also known as Laiki Bank).

The rapid expansion of the Cypriot banking sector since 2005 had led to the build-up of significant vulnerabilities. Banks were attracting substantial non-resident deposits, encouraging increased bank lending, in turn fuelling a real estate bubble. Bank of Cyprus and Laiki Bank engaged in substantial

[87] Ibid, Art 44(3)(c).

[88] Ibid, Art 31.

[89] Ibid, Art 34(1)(h).

[90] See Regulation (EU) No 806/2014 of the European Parliament and of the Council of 15 July 2014 establishing uniform rules and a uniform procedure for the resolution of credit institutions and certain investment firms in the framework of a Single Resolution Mechanism and a Single Resolution Fund and amending Regulation (EU) No 1093/2010, [2014] OJ L225/1.

expansion in Greece, leaving their loan portfolios exposed to the deteriorating macro economic conditions there. Finally, investments in Greek government bonds led to heavy losses in the Greek sovereign debt restructuring in 2012. By March 2013 Bank of Cyprus and Laiki Bank had additional capital needs of approximately €10 billion.[91] In addition to these problems at the Bank of Cyprus and Laiki Bank, the Cypriot Government was facing a total net financing gap of €10 billion until the end of the first quarter of 2016.[92]

On 16 March 2013 the Eurogroup (euro area Finance Ministers) politically agreed with the Cypriot authorities on a reduced financial assistance envelope of up to €10 billion only, in order to allow Cyprus' public debt to remain on a sustainable path. Initially, the Eurogroup and the Cypriot authorities agreed that Cyprus would limit the size of the financial assistance package by, inter alia, introducing a one-off 'stability' levy applicable to both resident and non-resident depositors in all Cypriot banks, to be levied at the rate of 6.75 per cent for deposits up to €100,000 and 9.9 per cent for higher deposits.[93] The imposition of a levy on insured deposits was heavily criticised across Europe as circumventing the Deposit Guarantee Schemes Directive and undermining the single banking market in the EU, creating incentives for depositors to move savings from one country to another.[94] On 18 March the one-off stability levy on depositors was rejected by the Cypriot House of Representatives, leading to the declaration by the Central Bank of Cyprus of a bank holiday, extended until 28 March, due to bank-run fears.[95] On 18 March the President of the Eurogroup emphasised that the Eurogroup continues to be of the view that small depositors should be treated differently from large depositors and reaffirmed the importance of fully guaranteeing deposits below €100,000.[96]

The Cypriot authorities proceeded to undertake an extensive restructuring and resolution of Bank of Cyprus and Laiki Bank, respectively. On 22 March, the Cypriot House of Representatives adopted the Resolution of Credit and Other Institutions Law of 2013 which, inter alia, authorised the

[91] See European Commission, The Economic Adjustment Programme for Cyprus (2013) *Occasional Papers 149* 11–16, 31–34, 38, 42.

[92] Ibid, at 54–57.

[93] See Eurogroup Statement on Cyprus, 16 March 2013, available at: http://eurozone.europa.eu/newsroom/news/2013.

[94] See, eg, S Bowles, Chair, European Parliament Economic & Monetary Affairs Committee, 'The Cyprus Bailout Deal is a Disaster for EU Rules and Single Market Principles', 16 March 2013, available at: http://sharonbowles.org.uk/en/article/2013; see also M Draghi, President of the ECB, Introduction to the ECB Press Conference (with Q&A), 4 April 2013, available at: www.ecb.europa.eu/press/pressconf/2013.

[95] See European Commission, The Economic Adjustment Programme for Cyprus (2013) *Occasional Papers 149*, 39.

[96] Statement by the Eurogroup President on Cyprus, 18 March 2013, available at: www.eurozone.europa.eu/newsroom/news/2013.

Central Bank of Cyprus to reduce, by decree, the principal amount of or convert into equity ('bail-in') the debts of a credit institution under a resolution procedure, with the exception of insured deposits up to the €100,000 limit.[97] On 25 March, following the presentation by the Cypriot authorities of their policy plans, the Eurogroup politically agreed with the Cypriot authorities on the plans for the restructuring of the financial sector, which would specifically safeguard all deposits below €100,000, but with uninsured depositors at Bank of Cyprus and Laiki Bank contributing to losses.[98]

Acting under the Resolution of Credit and Other Institutions Law of 2013, the Central Bank of Cyprus adopted a series of decrees restructuring and resolving Bank of Cyprus and Laiki Bank. The restructuring and resolution process was accomplished in three main steps. First, by way of purchase and assumption transactions, both banks were required to transfer the substantial deposit books and loan portfolios of their Greek branches to a third party purchaser in Greece, Piraeus Bank.[99] Secondly, in a separate purchase and assumption transaction, Laiki Bank was required to transfer all deposits of up to €100,000, together with certain other deposits above that level, its secured loans from the Central Bank of Cyprus, and most of its assets, to the Bank of Cyprus, receiving in return shares in the Bank of Cyprus. Many large-value, uninsured deposits were left behind in Laiki Bank, with the expectation that Laiki Bank would be liquidated in due course; Laiki Bank's remaining assets included its aforementioned shares in the Bank of Cyprus.[100] Thirdly, in order to restore the capital adequacy of

[97] Άρθρα 2 και 12(1) του περί Εξυγίανσης Πιστωτικών και Άλλων Ιδρυμάτων Νόμου, 17(I)/2013 (The Resolution of Credit and Other Institutions Law of 2013, Law 17(I)/2013, Arts 2 and 12(1)), in conjunction with the ϖερί Σύστασης και Λειτουργίας Σχεδίου Προστασίας Καταθέσεων και Εξυγίανσης Πιστωτικών και Άλλων Ιδρυμάτων Νόμος,16(I)/2013 (Law on the Establishment and Operation of the Deposit Protection and Resolution of Credit and Other Institutions Scheme of 2013, 16(I) of 2013).

[98] See Eurogroup Statement on Cyprus, 25 March 2013, available at eurozone.europa.eu/newsroom/news/2013.

[99] Το περί Πώλησης των εν Ελλάδι Εργασιών της Τράπεζας Κύπρου Δημόσιας Εταιρίας Λτδ Διάταγμα του 2013, ΕΕ. Παρ. ΙΙΙ(Ι), Αρ. 4640, 25.03.2013, σ. 745. Κ.Δ.Π. 96/2013 (The Sale of Operations in Greece of the Bank of Cyprus Public Co Ltd, Decree of 2013, *Official Gazette of the Republic of Cyprus*, 3rd Annex, Part I, Regulatory Administrative Acts Issue No 4640, 25.03.2013/ p 745, Regulatory Administrative Act No 96/2013); το περί Πώληση των εν Ελλάδι Εργασιών της Cyprus Popular Bank Public Co Ltd Διάταγμα του 2013, ΕΕ Παρ. ΙΙΙ(Ι), Αρ. 4640, 25.03.2013 σ. 749, Κ.Δ.Π. 97/2013 (The Sale of Operations in Greece of Cyprus Popular Bank Public Co Ltd, Decree of 2013, *Official Gazette of the Republic of Cyprus*, 3rd Annex, Part I, Regulatory Administrative Acts Issue No 4640,/ 25.03.2013/ p 749, Regulatory Administrative Act No 97/2013).

[100] Το περί της Πώλησης Ορισμένων Εργασιών της Cyprus Popular Bank Public Co Ltd Διάταγμα του 2013, ΕΕ Παρ ΙΙΙ(Ι), Αρ. 4645, 29.03.2013. σ. 781 Κ.Δ.Π. 104/2013 (Central Bank of Cyprus, 'Sale of Certain Operations of Cyprus Popular Bank Public Co Ltd Decree of 2013', *Official Gazette of the Republic of Cyprus*, 3rd Annex, Part I, Regulatory Administrative Acts Issue No 4645/ Friday 29 March 2013/ p 781, Regulatory Administrative Act No 104; το περί της έκδοσης Μετοχικού Κεφαλαίου της Τράπεζας Κύπρου προς Αποζημίωση της Λαϊκής Τράπεζας Διάταγμα του 2013, ΕΕ Παρ. ΙΙΙ(Ι), Αρ. 4703, 30.07.2013

Bank of Cyprus by way of a bailing-in measure, many uninsured deposits in the Bank of Cyprus, above the €100,000 limit, were subjected to a 'bail-in', whereby deposit claims were compulsorily converted into a mixture of shares and longer-term deposits.[101]

These developments have triggered litigation before the Cypriot courts. In *Christodoulou v Central Bank of Cyprus* the Cypriot Supreme Court has given guidance that the key standard governing these cases is the 'no-creditor-worse-off-than-in-insolvency' principle contained in the Resolution of Credit and Other Institutions Law of 2013.[102] The Court stated that

> it is important to stress the fundamental dimension of Article 3(2)(d) of the Law to the effect that the creditors (all creditors, including depositors) of the institution under resolution ... are not in a worse financial position due to the implementation of the resolution measures as compared to the position that they would be in if the institution was under liquidation instead. This provision, which essentially also establishes in the Law standing legal principles regarding the damage and the proof and assessment of its extent, safeguards the rights of depositors in the civil proceedings to which they are referred and demonstrates the key issue, i.e., whether a claimant has suffered more damage due to the consequences of the resolution measures than the damage which he would have suffered ... if the resolution measures had not been implemented ... The important thing is, in the final analysis, what Article 3(2)(d) of the Law has provided for ... on whether the damage suffered by the depositors is greater than that which the depositors would have suffered if

σ. 1772, Κ.Δ.Π. 279/2013 (Central Bank of Cyprus, 'Issuance of Share Capital of Bank of Cyprus for Compensation of Cyprus Popular Bank Decree of 2013', *Official Gazette of the Republic of Cyprus*, 3rd Annex, Part I, Regulatory Administrative Act 279/2013 Issue No 4703/ Tuesday 30 July 2013/ p 1772, Regulatory Administrative Act No 279.

[101] Το περί Διάσωσης με ίδια Μέσα της Τράπεζας Κύπρου Δημόσιας Εταιρείας Λτδ Διάταγμα του 2013, ΕΕ, Παρ. ΙΙΙ(Ι), Αρ. 4645, 29.03.2013, σ. 769, Κ.Δ.Π. 103/2013 (Central Bank of Cyprus, Bailing-in of Bank of Cyprus Public Company Limited Decree of 2013, *Official Gazette of the Republic of Cyprus*, 3rd Annex, Part I, Regulatory Administrative Acts Issue No 4645/ Friday 29 March 2013/ p 769, Regulatory Administrative Act No 103); το περί Διάσωσης με ίδια Μέσα της Τράπεζας Κύπρου Δημόσιας Εταιρείας Λτδ (Τροποποιητικό)(Αρ.3) Διάταγμα του 2013, ΕΕ. Παρ. ΙΙΙ(Ι), Αρ. 4703, 30.07.2013, σ. 1767, Κ.Δ.Π. 278/2013 (Central Bank of Cyprus, Bailing-in of Bank of Cyprus Public Company Limited Decree (Amended) (No 3) of 2013, *Official Gazette of the Republic of Cyprus*, 3rd Annex, Part I, Regulatory Administrative Acts Issue No 4703/ Tuesday 30 July 2013/ p 1767, Regulatory Administrative Act No 278); το περί της Επιβολής Προσωρινών Περιοριστικών Μέτρων στις Συναλλαγές της Τράπεζας Κύπρου Δημόσιας Εταιρείας Λτδ Διάταγμα του 2013, ΕΕ Παρ. ΙΙΙ(Ι), Αρ. 4702, 30.07.2013, σ. 1763, Κ.Δ.Π. 277/2013 (Minister of Finance of Cyprus, Decree under the Cypriot Enforcement of Restrictive Measures on Transactions in Case of Emergency Law of 2013, *Official Gazette of the Republic of Cyprus*, 3rd Annex, Part I, Regulatory Administrative Acts Issue No 4702/ Tuesday 30 July 2013/ p 1763, Regulatory Administrative Act No 277;) Joint Notice of the Ministry of Finance and the Central Bank of Cyprus, 30 July 2013.

[102] Απόφαση του Ανωτάτου Δικαστηρίου Κύπρου, 7 Ιουνίου 2013, Υπόθεση αρ. 551/2013 Χριστοδούλου ν. Κεντρικής Τράπεζας της Κύπρου κ.α, σ. 41-42 (Judgment of the Supreme Court of Cyprus, 7 June 2013, Case 551/2013 *Christodoulou and others v Central Bank of Cyprus and others* [2013], pp 41–42); see also J Giotaki, 'The Cypriot bail-in litigation: A First Assessment of the Ruling of the Supreme Court of Cyprus' (2013) 8 *Journal of International Banking and Financial Law* 485, 486.

> the Decrees had not been adopted and the banks had been left alone. That is, the depositors could not be in a worse situation than that, and they could not be in a better situation either—and this should be kept in mind at all times, given that it is the facts relating to the situation of the banks as of the time of adoption of the Decrees that determine the actual value of deposits at that time, with the primary consideration being that the depositors are just creditors of the bank.[103]

As we will now see, the spotlight that focused on depositors in the Cypriot crisis has triggered important developments in the area of depositor protection at the EU level.

IX. EU DEPOSITOR PREFERENCE RULE (2015)

In the immediate aftermath of the Cypriot crisis, ECB President Draghi stated that one of the lessons that could be drawn from Cyprus was the need to distinguish between depositors and bondholders in the pecking order under the proposed EU Bank Recovery and Resolution Directive. In this respect, he noted that an explicit distinction between depositors and bondholders is made by the US Federal Deposit Insurance Corporation.[104] The introduction of a depositor preference rule at EU level, at least for those deposits guaranteed under the Deposit Guarantee Schemes Directive, had already been advocated by the ECB in its opinion on the proposed Bank Recovery and Resolution Directive. In particular, the ECB stated that, from a financial stability perspective, a priority claim in respect of guaranteed deposits is supported, as it reduces the risks of bank runs.[105]

As noted previously, a depositor preference rule is a rule of insolvency law, which ranks depositors ahead of general unsecured creditors in the insolvency of a bank. A depositor preference rule thus provides separate supplementary protection to a deposit guarantee scheme. Internationally, such a rule has existed in a number of G20 countries for many years, including Australia, Switzerland and the United States.[106] However, depositor preference rules have, until recently, been almost entirely absent in EU Member States. Mainly as a result of the financial crisis, a number of EU Member States undergoing EU/IMF programmes, including Cyprus,[107]

[103] Ibid.

[104] See M Draghi, President of the ECB, Introduction to the ECB Press Conference (with Q&A), 4 April 2013, available at: www.ecb.europa.eu/press/pressconf/2013.

[105] See Opinion of the European Central Bank of 29 November 2012 on a proposal for a directive establishing a framework for recovery and resolution of credit institutions and investment firms (CON(2012) 99), [2013] OJ C39/1, para 8.2 and Amendment 11.

[106] See Clifford Chance, above n 16; G Turner, 'Depositor Protection in Australia' (2011) December Quarter *Reserve Bank of Australia Bulletin* 45, 54–55; 12 USC § 1821(d)(11)(A).

[107] Άρθρο 4(3) του περί Εξυγίανσης Πιστωτικών και Άλλων Ιδρυμάτων Νόμου του 2013, 17(I)/2013 (The Resolution of Credit and Other Institutions Law of 2013, Law 17(I)/2013, Art 4(3)).

Greece,[108] Hungary,[109] Latvia,[110] Portugal[111] and Romania,[112] have introduced depositor preference rules.

It is important to consider the precise manner in which a depositor preference rule is formulated, as the level of protection under a depositor preference rule and under a deposit insurance scheme need not be co-extensive. For example, in the US the depositor preference rule benefits domestic deposits both above and below the insurance limit. In many EU Member States which have introduced depositor preference rules to date, the depositor preference rule only benefits depositors up to the €100,000 limit covered by the deposit guarantee scheme. The Bank Recovery and Resolution Directive has established a tiered depositor preference rule at EU level which straddles both sides of the deposit guarantee limit. Member States are required to ensure that in national laws governing normal insolvency proceedings a higher priority ranking is first given to depositors up to the €100,000 coverage level under the Deposit Guarantee Schemes Directive (including deposit guarantee schemes subrogating to the rights and obligations of these depositors in insolvency). A second priority ranking, behind depositors up to the €100,000 coverage level, but ahead of ordinary, unsecured, non-preferred creditors, is then given to deposits above the €100,000 coverage level held by micro, small and medium-sized enterprises, and natural persons.[113]

[108] Άρθρα 4 (16) και 13α (4) του νόμου 3746/2009 «Ταμείο Εγγύησης Καταθέσεων και Επενδύσεων (ΤΕΚΕ), ενσωμάτωση των Οδηγιών 2005/14/ΕΚ για την υποχρεωτική ασφάλιση οχημάτων και 2005/68/ΕΚ σχετικά με τις αντασφαλίσεις και λοιπές διατάξεις», ΦΕΚ Α 27/16.2.2009 (Arts 4(16) and 13a(4) of Law 3746/2009 'Hellenic Deposit and Investment Guarantee Fund, incorporation of the Directive 2005/14/EC on insurance against civil liability in respect of the use of motor vehicles and Directive 2005/68/EC on reinsurance and other provisions', *Government Gazette of the Hellenic Republic* Vol A 27/16.2.2009).

[109] A hitelintézetekről és a pénzügyi vállalkozásokról szóló 1996. évi CXII. törvény (Law CXII of 1996 on credit institutions and financial undertakings (Magyar Közlöny 1996/109, 12.12.1996), Art 183(1), in effect until 31 December 2013), and a hitelintézetekről és a pénzügyi vállalkozásokról szóló 2013. évi CCXXXVII. törvény (Law CCXXXVII of 2013 on credit institutions and financial undertakings (Magyar Közlöny 2013/217, 23.12.2013), Art 57(1), in effect as of 1 January 2014).

[110] *Kredītiestāžu likums, LV, 163 (446)*, 24.10.1995 (Law of 5 October 1995 on credit institutions), Art 192(1).

[111] Artigo 166º_A do Decreto-Lei nº 298/92 (DR No 301, Series I-A, of 31 December), na sua última redação (Art 166-A of Decree-Law No 298/9 (DR No 301, Series I-A, of 31 December), as last amended.

[112] Ordonanţa Guvernului nr 10/2004 privind falimentul instituţiilor de credit, articolul 38 (Government Ordinance No 10/2004 on the proceedings for judicial reorganisation and bankruptcy of credit institutions, Art 38).

[113] See Directive 2014/59/EU of the European Parliament and of the Council of 15 May 2014 establishing a framework for the recovery and resolution of credit institutions and investment firms and amending Council Directive 82/891/EEC, and Directives 2001/24/EC, 2002/47/EC, 2005/56/EC, 2007/36/EC, 2011/35/EU, 2012/30/EU and 2013/36/EU, and Regulations (EU) No 1093/2010 and (EU) No 648/2012, of the European Parliament and of the Council, [2014] OJ L173/190, Art 108.

A number of points may be noted regarding this tiered depositor preference rule. Larger corporate deposits rank third in the pecking order, with equal priority alongside the senior, unsecured creditors of the bank. The Directive does not clarify what kinds of enterprises will qualify as 'micro, small and medium-sized enterprises' ranking ahead of senior unsecured creditors. Finally, the details regarding the respective ranking among preferred deposits and other preferential claims, such as tax and worker compensation claims, is left to be resolved by applicable national laws. A number of concrete ways in which a depositor preference rule benefits depositors can be mentioned. First, as noted previously, separately from whatever protection a depositor enjoys from a deposit guarantee scheme, in the event of a bank failure a depositor will have a priority claim against the assets of the insolvent bank. A depositor preference rule has the effect of preserving the bank's assets for the benefit of its depositors in the event of the bank's insolvency. Secondly, to the extent that the deposit guarantee scheme has paid out to depositors in a failed bank, the scheme inherits the preferred claims of the depositors by way of subrogation. As far as covered deposits are concerned, a depositor preference rule can therefore be seen in practice as a deposit guarantee scheme preference.[114] This protects the financial resources of the deposit guarantee scheme, for the ultimate protection of depositors. Thirdly, in the perhaps more likely event that a bank is restructured through a resolution process, and not placed into an insolvency proceeding, the existence of the depositor preference rule will have important implications. In particular, it will make it easier for the resolution authority to order the transfer of the preferred deposits to a healthy third party purchaser or bridge bank. This is because of the no-creditor-worse-off principle, which is one of the general principles governing resolution under the EU Bank Recovery and Resolution Directive.[115] Other creditors left behind in the rump entity to be wound-up following the transfer of the deposits, good assets and other key liabilities are entitled to be compensated for what they would have received if the bank—on a pre-transfer basis—had been placed into normal insolvency proceedings. If, by virtue of a depositor preference rule, the depositors would have ranked ahead of these other creditors in the insolvency of the bank, then these other creditors would have only recovered whatever value was left in the bank *after* the claims of the preferred depositors had been satisfied. This would reduce the potential compensation that could be claimed by these creditors based

[114] See Clifford Chance, above n 16.

[115] See Directive 2014/59/EU of the European Parliament and of the Council of 15 May 2014 establishing a framework for the recovery and resolution of credit institutions and investment firms and amending Council Directive 82/891/EEC, and Directives 2001/24/EC, 2002/47/EC, 2005/56/EC, 2007/36/EC, 2011/35/EU, 2012/30/EU and 2013/36/EU, and Regulations (EU) No 1093/2010 and (EU) No 648/2012, of the European Parliament and of the Council, [2014] OJ L173/190, Arts 33(1)(g), 73–75.

on the 'no-creditor-worse-off-than-in-insolvency' principle. The depositor preference therefore makes it easier for the public authorities to resolve the bank, saving the preferred depositors and key liability holders, and leaving the other creditors behind in the rump entity to be liquidated, without having to compensate them on the basis that they rank equally with the depositors.[116]

It has been suggested that a depositor preference rule comes at a price; that creditors of banks with significant deposit bases have responded to the introduction of depositor preference in the US by switching their lending from an unsecured to a secured basis. However, it will never be possible to secure more than a proportion of the liabilities of a bank, and it is likely that all banks will always have at least some significant level of senior, unsecured, non-depositor creditors. Another possible implication of a depositor preference rule is that unsecured creditors will seek to transact with non-bank entities within a banking group.[117]

Another alleged price of a depositor preference rule is that it increases a bank's cost of funding when borrowing in the capital markets, because bondholders will rank after depositors from an insolvency, and therefore also resolution, perspective.[118] Large European banking groups following the universal banking model may seek to reduce their cost of funding by segregating assets and non-deposit funding liabilities in non-bank group entities, potentially depriving depositors of any access to the assets of the remainder of the group beyond those of the deposit-taking institution.[119] The empirical evidence supporting the alleged increase in the cost of funding is not clear, based on the US experience.[120] The new depositor preference rule is to be implemented by all EU Member States from 1 January 2015.[121]

The EU has responded to the developments affecting depositors at Cypriot banks by establishing a powerful depositor preference rule throughout the EU. This depositor preference rule provides a second layer of protection, in addition to the deposit guarantee system. The depositor preference rule effectively preserves a failing bank's assets for the benefit of the preferred depositors in the bank's insolvency. The depositor preference rule also

[116] See DC Hardy, 'Bank Resolution Costs, Depositor Preference, and Asset Encumbrance' (2013) *International Monetary Fund Working Paper* WP/13/172 8, available at: www.imf.org/external/pubs/ft/wp/2013/wp13172.pdf.

[117] See Clifford Chance, above n 16.

[118] See DC Hardy, above n 116 at 8.

[119] See Clifford Chance, above n 16.

[120] See DC Hardy, above n 116 at 8–9.

[121] See Directive 2014/59/EU of the European Parliament and of the Council of 15 May 2014 establishing a framework for the recovery and resolution of credit institutions and investment firms and amending Council Directive 82/891/EEC, and Directives 2001/24/EC, 2002/47/EC, 2005/56/EC, 2007/36/EC, 2011/35/EU, 2012/30/EU and 2013/36/EU, and Regulations (EU) No 1093/2010 and (EU) No 648/2012, of the European Parliament and of the Council, [2014] OJ L173/190, Art 130(1).

makes it easier for resolution authorities to transfer preferred deposits from failing banks to healthy third party purchasers or bridge banks. As formulated, the EU depositor preference rule will favour all deposits up the €100,000 limit, and then all deposits above that limit held by natural persons or by micro, small and medium-sized enterprises. It remains to be seen how the deposits of micro, small and medium-sized enterprises will be distinguished from other corporate deposits ranking alongside senior, unsecured claims, and whether this reform will have substantial effects on the conduct of banking business, including banks' cost of funding in the capital markets. In any case, the EU has opted to place a higher priority on the protection of depositors than the funding costs of banks.

X. CONCLUSION: HOW HAS THE EU PROTECTED DEPOSITORS IN FINANCIAL CRISIS?

How has the EU protected depositors in the financial crisis? Drawing on features of the US depositor protection regime, the EU has taken important steps for the protection of depositors in the financial crisis. In response to the 2007 run on Northern Rock and the financial crisis that erupted after the 2008 collapse of Lehman Brothers, the EU strengthened the Deposit Guarantee Schemes Directive in a number of significant respects in 2009. The minimum coverage level was substantially increased, from €20,000 to €100,000. The time-limit for pay-outs to depositors was reduced from potentially as long as nine months to no more than 30 days. Co-insurance arrangements, whereby depositors might only be covered for 90 per cent of their deposits, were abolished.

Following further enhancements to the Deposit Guarantee Schemes Directive in 2014, the EU is moving towards a uniform level of coverage, set at €100,000, and a targeted seven-day pay-out period. There will be more transparency for depositors. The financing arrangements for deposit guarantee schemes will be more harmonised, ensuring a more robust level-playing field. The obligations of Member States under the Deposit Guarantee Schemes Directive are now much more focused than was the case under the 1994 Directive. Against this backdrop, it is unclear to what extent the EFTA Court ruling in the *Icesave* case—to the effect that Iceland was under no obligation under the 1994 Directive to compensate the Netherlands and UK Icesave depositors where its deposit guarantee scheme was simply unable to cope with its obligations in the systemic crisis that engulfed the entire Icelandic banking system and economy—is still relevant.

The protection of depositors is being further enhanced through the adoption of resolution legislation at both the national and the EU levels, making it easier for authorities to transfer deposits held at a failing bank to a healthy third party purchaser or a publicly chartered bridge bank. The EU has responded to the developments affecting depositors at Cypriot banks by establishing a powerful depositor preference rule, which is scheduled to come into effect throughout the EU in 2015. This depositor preference rule provides a second layer of protection, in addition to the deposit guarantee system. The depositor preference rule effectively preserves a failing bank's assets for the benefit of the preferred depositors in the event of the bank's insolvency. The depositor preference rule also makes it easier for resolution authorities to transfer preferred deposits from failing banks to healthy third party purchasers or bridge banks. As formulated, the EU depositor preference rule will favour all deposits up the €100,000 limit, and then all deposits above that limit held by natural persons or by micro, small and medium-sized enterprises. It remains to be seen how the deposits of micro, small and medium-sized enterprises will be distinguished from other corporate deposits ranking alongside senior, unsecured claims, and whether this reform will have substantial effects on the conduct of banking business, including banks' cost of funding in the capital markets. In any case, the EU has opted to place a higher priority on the protection of depositors than the funding costs of banks.

To conclude, the EU has responded to the impact of the financial crisis on bank depositors in a number of EU Member States by considerably enhancing the legal protections available to depositors. These law reforms should serve to reinforce the confidence of depositors in the European financial system.

11

The Protection of the Right to Work Through the European Convention on Human Rights

VIRGINIA MANTOUVALOU*

Abstract

The right to work was until recently under-explored in academic literature and judicial decision-making. Classified often as a social right, it was viewed as a non-justiciable entitlement. Today, as the right to work is sometimes used as a slogan in favour of deregulation of the labour market, as well as a slogan against immigration and unionisation, the analysis of the right to work as part of a labour law agenda is crucial. Against this background, this chapter examines the right to work in the European Convention on Human Rights. Even though the right to work is not explicitly protected in the ECHR, the chapter identifies in the case law of the European Court of Human Rights certain principles that underpin the right to work, which can serve as guidance in the interpretation of existing provisions of the Convention.

I. INTRODUCTION

THE VALUE OF work cannot be underestimated in today's world. Work is instrumentally valuable, as productive labour generates: goods needed for survival, like food and housing; goods needed for self-development, like education and culture; and other material goods that people wish to have in order to live a fulfilling life. In a market economy, productive labour benefits not only those who produce goods by bringing them income, but also those who purchase and consume these goods. But

* A draft of this chapter was presented at the University of Cambridge, Centre for European Legal Studies in February 2014. I am grateful to Kenneth Armstrong, Markus Gehring, the anonymous referees and all participants for excellent comments and suggestions. Thanks are also due to Hugh Collins, George Letsas, Prince Saprai and Fotis Vergis for commenting on an earlier draft.

work is not only valuable for the income that it generates. It is crucial for a person's feeling of membership in society. In addition, a job generally inspires a sense of achievement and self-esteem, as well as the esteem of the others.[1] Through work people develop relationships with others. The possibility to develop social relations, then, is another reason why most people value work. Work brings both material and non-material benefits. Given its importance, do we have a human right to work?

Until recently, the right to work was relatively under-explored in academic literature and judicial decision-making.[2] More than 30 years ago Bob Hepple published a seminal essay on the topic, which explored the meaning of a legal right to work, enforceable against the state, the employer and trade unions in English law.[3] At about the same time, James Nickel analysed the right to work as a philosophical issue, addressing in particular the objection raised in scholarship that the right to work is a social right, which is and must be treated differently to civil and political rights,[4] and Jon Elster critically examined some possible moral justifications of the right.[5] Today, during times of economic crisis and high levels of unemployment in Europe and elsewhere, the right to work has to be revisited.[6]

Against this background, in this chapter I explore the right to work in European law with a focus on the European Convention on Human Rights (ECHR or the Convention).[7] Even though the right to work is not explicitly protected in the ECHR, this chapter identifies in the case law certain principles that underpin the right to work, which can serve as guidance in the interpretation of existing provisions of the Convention. It is important

[1] For some literature on these issues, see JB Murphy, *The Moral Economy of Labour* (New Haven CT, Yale University Press, 1993); H Arendt, *The Human Condition* (Chicago IL, University of Chicago Press, 1996 [first published in 1958]) distinguishing between work and labour; R Sennett, *The Craftsman* (London, Penguin, 2009); J Shklar, *American Citizenship: The Quest for Inclusion* (Cambridge MA, Harvard University Press, 1995).

[2] For some recent literature on the right to work, see V Mantouvalou (ed), *The Right to Work—Legal and Philosophical Perspectives* (Oxford, Hart Publishing, 2014, forthcoming), cited as *The Right to Work*. See also G Mundlak, 'The Right to Work—The Value of Work' in D Barak-Erez and A Gross (eds), *Exploring Social Rights: Between Theory and Practice* (Oxford, Hart Publishing, 2007) 341; G Mundlak, 'The Right to Work: Linking Human Rights and Employment Policy' (2007) 146 *International Labour Review* 189; V Schultz, 'Life's Work' (2000) 100 *Columbia Law Review* 1881; P Harvey, 'The Right to Work and Basic Income Guarantees: Competing or Complementary Goals?' (2005) 2 *Rutgers Journal of Law and Urban Policy* 8.

[3] B Hepple, 'A Right to Work?' (1981) 10 *Industrial Law Journal* 65.

[4] J Nickel, 'Is There a Human Right to Employment?' (1978–79) X *Philosophical Quarterly* 149. On social rights, see C Gearty and V Mantouvalou, *Debating Social Rights* (Oxford, Hart Publishing, 2011).

[5] J Elster, 'Is There (or Should There Be) A Right to Work?' in A Gutmann (ed), *Democracy and the Welfare State* (Princeton NJ, Princeton University Press, 1988) 53.

[6] For an overview of problems at work in Europe, see N Countouris and M Freedland (eds), *Resocialising Europe in a Time of Crisis* (Cambridge, CUP, 2013). On the right to work, see Mantouvalou, *The Right to Work* (n 2 above).

[7] Council of Europe, Convention for the Protection of Human Rights and Fundamental Freedoms, CETS No 194.

to consider the right to work in the context of the ECHR both because the European Court of Human Rights (ECtHR or the Court) has already examined cases that address aspects of it,[8] and because in its case law the Court integrates within the scope of the Convention certain rights that have traditionally been viewed as socio-economic.[9]

The structure of the chapter is as follows: Section two introduces the debate on labour rights as human rights and places the right to work in its context. Section three explores the right to work in positive law. From this analysis, I conclude that aspects of the right to work are protected in various legal instruments. The fourth section of this chapter identifies certain normative principles that underlie the right to work, as they emerge from case law of the ECtHR. It focuses in particular on the values of dignity, non-exploitation, self-realisation and non-domination. Section five concludes.

II. THE RIGHT TO WORK AND LABOUR RIGHTS AS HUMAN RIGHTS

In recent years, academic scholars have been searching for a new framework for the idea of labour law in the context of economic globalisation, the increase of non-standard contracts of employment and the decline of union power.[10] Against this background, some authors have turned to human rights law as a new avenue for workers.[11] Human rights, incorporated in Constitutions, Bills of Rights or international treaties, seemed promising, because they are stringent normative standards that resist trade-offs with other goals, and the rights of workers, on the view of many, should be viewed and protected as such.

In addition to the proliferation of literature on labour rights as human rights, there is also scholarship that questions this move, either at a theoretical

[8] See R O'Connell, 'The Right to Work in the ECHR' [2012] *European Human Rights Law Review* 176.

[9] V Mantouvalou, 'Labour Rights in the European Convention on Human Rights: An Intellectual Justification for an Integrated Approach to Interpretation' (2013) 13 *Human Rights Law Review* 529.

[10] There is much scholarship on these issues. See, for instance, G Davidov and B Langille (eds), *The Idea of Labour Law* (Oxford, OUP, 2011); J Conaghan, RM Fischl and K Klare (eds), *Labour Law in an Era of Globalization* (Oxford, OUP, 2002).

[11] Some excellent examples include K Ewing and J Hendy, 'The Dramatic Implications of *Demir and Baykara*' (2010) 39 *Industrial Law Journal* 2; B Hepple, 'Introduction' in B Hepple (ed), *Social and Labour Rights in a Global Context* (Cambridge, CUP, 2002) 1, at 16; C Fenwick and T Novitz, 'Conclusion: Regulating to Protect Workers' Human Rights' in C Fenwick and T Novitz (eds), *Human Rights at Work: Perspectives on Law and Regulation* (Oxford, Hart Publishing, 2010) 587–88; VA Leary, 'The Paradox of Workers' Rights as Human Rights' in L Compa and S Diamond (eds), *Human Rights, Labour Rights and International Trade* (Philadelphia PA, University of Pennsylvania Press, 2003) 22; G Mundlak, 'Labor Rights and Human Rights: Why Don't the Two Tracks Meet?' (2012) 34 *Comparative Labor Law and Policy Journal* 237; L Compa, 'Solidarity and Human Rights' (2009) 18 *New Labor Forum* 38.

level or because of its implications.[12] In response to arguments made in that scholarship, in a previous article I argued that there are in fact three approaches to the question whether labour rights are human rights, which are often conflated in the literature.[13] The point can be exemplified by looking at the right to work, which is the subject of this chapter. First, there is a positivistic approach, according to which the right to work is a human right if it is explicitly mentioned in human rights documents. Public international lawyers sometimes adopt this approach.[14] Secondly, there is an instrumental approach, according to which the right to work is a human right if courts protect it as such or if civil society organisations succeed in using it strategically to promote the relevant goals. Labour lawyers are typically instrumentalists when discussing labour rights as human rights.[15] Finally, there is a normative approach, according to which a labour right is a human right, if there is a sufficiently strong justification for it at a theoretical level. On this analysis, the right to work is a human right if there are certain human interests of sufficient importance that ground it and impose duties on others.[16] In a way, this approach takes priority over the other two. If the right to work is a human right at a moral level, which can be determined by considering its justifications,[17] the real question is how to best protect it in law.

It should be acknowledged at this point that there may be risks in framing workers' rights (and the right to work) as human rights, including the empowerment of the judiciary, that may be hostile to the interests of workers.[18] Yet this chapter rests on the belief that the analysis of the right to work as a human right is important both as a genuine intellectual enquiry and as a strategic goal. After the fall of communism in Europe, it is crucial to assess the meaning of the right to work afresh, as part of a unified list of human rights. As the right to work is sometimes used as a slogan in favour of deregulation of the labour market, as well as a slogan against immigration

[12] H Collins, 'Theories of Rights as Justifications for Labour Law' in G Davidov and B Langille (eds), *The Idea of Labour Law* (Oxford, OUP, 2011) 137; K Kolben, 'Labor Rights as Human Rights?' (2010) 50 *Virginia Journal of International Law* 449; J Youngdahl, 'Solidarity First: Labor Rights Are Not the Same as Human Rights' (2009) 18 *New Labor Forum* 31.

[13] V Mantouvalou, 'Are Labour Rights Human Rights?' (2012) 3 *European Labour Law Journal* 151.

[14] For an example of the positivistic approach, see M Ssenyonjo, 'Economic, Social and Cultural Rights: An Examination of State Obligations' in S Joseph and A McBeth (eds), *Research Handbook on International Human Rights Law* (Cheltenham, Edward Elgar, 2010) 36.

[15] See the literature in nn 11–12 above.

[16] J Raz, *Morality of Freedom* (Oxford, OUP, 1986).

[17] On justifications of the right, see the literature above, nn 1, 2 and 5.

[18] H Arthurs, 'Constitutionalizing the Right of Workers to Organize, Bargain and Strike: The Sight of One Shoulder Shrugging' (2009–10) 15 *Canadian Labour and Employment Law Journal* 373; A Bogg, 'Only Fools and Horses: Some Sceptical Reflections on the Right to Work' in *The Right to Work* (n 2 above).

and unionisation, the analysis of the right to work as part of a labour law agenda is crucial.

III. THE RIGHT TO WORK IN POSITIVE LAW

The ECHR, as a traditional liberal document adopted in the aftermath of the Second World War, does not explicitly recognise the right to work. It only contains a limited number of labour rights, namely the prohibition of slavery, servitude, forced and compulsory labour,[19] and freedom of association, including the right to form and join a trade union.[20] To these, we can add the prohibition of discrimination,[21] which is not a free-standing right, but can only be violated in conjunction with some other Convention provision. Even though there is no right to work as such in the ECHR, there is case law and literature on human rights in the workplace, including protection from unfair dismissal for activities outside work,[22] health and safety at work,[23] collective labour rights,[24] religion and dismissal,[25] and protection against slavery and servitude.[26]

This chapter focuses upon the Convention.[27] However, to illustrate the extent to which the right to work enjoys legal protection, I refer to some other documents at European and international level that contain explicit references to it. It is important to note that the documents in question, to which I now turn, are generally social rights documents and do not have the binding force and effective monitoring mechanism that the ECHR enjoys.[28]

19 Art 4.

20 Art 11.

21 Art 14.

22 H Collins and V Mantouvalou, '*Redfearn v UK*: Political Association and Dismissal' (2013) 73 *Modern Law Review* 909; V Mantouvalou, 'Human Rights and Unfair Dismissal: Private Acts in Public Spaces' (2008) 71 *Modern Law Review* 912.

23 *Vilnes and Others v Norway*, App Nos 52806/09 and 22703/10, Judgment of 5 December 2013.

24 Ewing and Hendy, above n 11; N Countouris and M Freedland, 'Injunctions, Cyanamid, and the Corrosion of the Right to Strike in the UK' (2011) *European Labour Law Journal* 489.

25 H Collins, 'The Protection of Civil Liberties in the Workplace' (2006) 69 *Modern Law Review* 619; R McCrea, 'Religion in the Workplace: *Eweida and Others v United Kingdom*' (2014) 77 *Modern Law Review* 277.

26 V Mantouvalou, 'Servitude and Forced Labour in the 21st Century: The Human Rights of Domestic Workers' (2006) 35 *Industrial Law Journal* 395.

27 For further analysis of the right to work under the ESC and the EUCFR, see D Ashiagbor, 'The Right to Work', in G de Búrca, B de Witte (eds), *Social Rights in Europe* (Oxford, OUP, 2005) 241; C O'Cinneide, 'The Right to Work in International Human Rights Law in Mantouvalou, *The Right to Work*, n 2 above, for detailed analysis of the ESC and the International Covenant on Economic, Social and Cultural Rights.

28 On the monitoring mechanisms and procedures of social rights documents, see M Langford (ed), *Social Rights Jurisprudence—Emerging Trends in International and Comparative Law* (Cambridge, CUP, 2008).

The right to work is protected in the International Covenant on Economic, Social and Cultural Rights,[29] Article 6, which states in its first paragraph: 'The States Parties to the present Covenant recognize the right to work, which includes the right of everyone to the opportunity to gain his living by work which he freely chooses or accepts, and will take appropriate steps to safeguard this right'. Article 7 of the Covenant protects the right to fair and just conditions of work, and Article 8 protects trade union rights. The Committee on Economic, Social and Cultural Rights (CESCR) issues periodic reports, examines individual communications and provides authoritative interpretations of the Covenant through its General Comments.[30] It has issued General Comment 18 on the Right to Work. In this General Comment, the Committee explained that the right to work should be read holistically: Articles 6–8 are interdependent, and the right to work should be viewed as a right to decent work.[31]

The European Social Charter (ESC)[32] is the counterpart of the ECHR in the area of social rights. It is monitored by the European Committee of Social Rights through periodic reports and collective complaints.[33] The ESC includes a right to work. In Article 1 it states:

> With a view to ensuring the effective exercise of the right to work, the Contracting Parties undertake:
> 1. to accept as one of their primary aims and responsibilities the achievement and maintenance of as high and stable a level of employment as possible, with a view to the attainment of full employment;
> 2. to protect effectively the right of the worker to earn his living in an occupation freely entered upon;
> 3. to establish or maintain free employment services for all workers;
> 4. to provide or promote appropriate vocational guidance, training and rehabilitation.

Other ESC work-related rights include Article 2 on the right to just working conditions, Article 3 on health and safety at work, Article 4 on the right to fair remuneration, and Articles 5 and 6 on the right to organise and to collective bargaining.

[29] International Covenant on Economic, Social and Cultural Rights, GA Res 2200A (XXI), 21 UN GAOR Supp (No 16) at 49, UN Doc A/6316 (1966), 993 UNTS 3.

[30] See, generally, M Langford and J King, 'Committee on Economic, Social and Cultural Rights' in M Langford (ed), *Social Rights Jurisprudence* (Cambridge, CUP, 2008) 477.

[31] UN Committee on Economic, Social and Cultural Rights, General Comment No 18 (E/C.12/GC/186) February 2006, paras 7–8.

[32] Council of Europe, European Social Charter of 1961, CETS No 35; Revised European Social Charter of 1966, CETS No 163.

[33] See, generally, P Alston, 'Assessing the Strengths and Weaknesses of the European Social Charter's Supervisory Mechanism' in G de Búrca and B de Witte (eds), *Social Rights in Europe* (Oxford, OUP, 2005) 45.

The EU Charter of Fundamental Rights (EUCFR) that protects both civil and political and socio-economic rights, also contains a right to work, which has been made legally binding through the Lisbon Treaty.[34] In article 15, we find the freedom to choose an occupation and the right to engage in work:

1. Everyone has the right to engage in work and to pursue a freely chosen or accepted occupation.
2. Every citizen of the Union has the freedom to seek employment, to work, to exercise the right of establishment and to provide services in any Member State.
3. Nationals of third countries who are authorised to work in the territories of the Member States are entitled to working conditions equivalent to those of citizens of the Union.

Article 30 of the EUCFR protects against unfair dismissal, Article 31 guarantees fair working conditions and Article 32 prohibits child labour and protects young people at work. The right to work is also protected in several European national Constitutions, such as the Constitutions of Italy, Greece and France.[35]

In positive law, then, at European and international level, we find a legal right to work in documents that enjoy varying degrees of effectiveness. The right to work includes a right to access a job, which translates into a government duty to take steps towards promoting full employment, the protection from forced labour, as well as a right to fair and just working conditions. But that the right to work or some components of it are protected in positive law does not tell us much about its interpretation. Does a right to work require that the state create job opportunities for everyone? Or does it simply mean that there should be no discrimination in access to existing jobs? To what extent does it protect from unfair dismissal? Questions of this kind remain unanswered. The positivistic approach to the right to work serves as a useful starting point, but it does not address the hard questions that have been identified in the literature.

[34] See, generally, S Peers, T Hervey, J Kenner and A Ward (eds), *The EU Charter of Fundamental Rights—A Commentary* (Oxford, Hart Publishing, 2014).

[35] On the Italian approach, see M D'Antona, 'The Right to Work in the Italian Constitution and in the European Union', Centro Studi di Diritto del Lavoro Europeo 'Massimo D'Antona', Working Paper No 1/2002, available at: http://aei.pitt.edu/606/1/n1_dantona.pdf. On the French approach, see SR Olivier, 'The French Approach to the Right to Work: The Potential of a Constitutional Right in Ordinary Courts' in *The Right to Work*, n 2 above.

IV. NORMATIVE PRINCIPLES UNDERLYING THE RIGHT TO WORK IN ECHR JURISPRUDENCE

Given that a detailed overview of ECtHR case law on the right to work is provided elsewhere in the literature,[36] I do not intend to address it in similar detail here. I instead attempt to distill from the case law some interests that underpin the right to work. These are important for understanding the normative significance of the right.

The sections that follow show that even though the ECtHR does not protect the right of everyone against the state to obtain a job in order to make a living, it recognises the following important normative principles that support the right to work: First, the Court accepts that livelihood gained through work is essential for human dignity;[37] it supports a principle of non-exploitative work;[38] it underlines the importance of work for self-fulfillment;[39] and it protects the worker against the employer's domination.[40] A principle of equality and non-discrimination is also fundamental in the case law on workplace rights, but this is a topic that will not be addressed in detail in this chapter.

It should be said from the outset that the fact that we can identify the values of human dignity, non-exploitation, self-fulfillment and non-domination underlying the right to work in the ECHR does not mean that whenever these are at stake there is a violation of the Convention. Arguing otherwise could lead to an inflation of rights, which could be damaging to the values that the supporters of human rights endorse.[41] Moreover, rights are often in conflict, and even aspects of the right to work can conflict with each other.[42] For example the right of a group of workers to obtain a job may be in conflict with the existing working conditions of another group of workers. Judicial decision-making involves complex considerations and difficult trade-offs between important interests. Yet it is important to

[36] See the references above nn 17–19. See also O'Connell, above n 8; and F Dorssemont, K Lorcher and I Schomann (eds), *The European Convention on Human Rights and the Employment Relation* (Oxford, Hart Publishing, 2013).

[37] See, for instance, *Sidabras and Dziautas v Lithuania*, App Nos 55480/00 and 59330/00, Judgment of 27 July 2004, discussed below (text to n 54).

[38] See, for instance, *Siliadin v France*, App No 73316/01, Judgment of 26 July 2005, discussed below.

[39] See, for instance, *Niemietz v Germany*, App No 13710/88, Judgment of 16 December 1992, discussed below (text to nn 88–89).

[40] See, for instance, *IB v Greece*, App No 552/10, Judgment of 3 October 2013, discussed below.

[41] G Letsas, *A Theory of Interpretation of the European Convention on Human Rights* (Oxford, OUP, 2009) 126 ff. See also O O'Neill, 'The Dark Side of Human Rights' (2005) 81 *International Affairs* 427.

[42] M Freedland and N Kountouris, 'The Right to Decent Work in a European Comparative Perspective' in *The Right to Work*; A Bogg, 'Only Fools and Horses: Some Skeptical Reflections on the Right to Work' in *The Right to Work*, n 2 above.

appreciate that dignity, non-exploitation, self-fulfillment and non-domination, which are associated values, exist in the reasoning of the Court, and to explore their normative implications for the protection of the right to work.

Before moving on, a preliminary issue needs to be addressed: a traditional international lawyer may question the applicability of the Convention as a whole in the private sphere, which is where the employment relationship typically operates. Human rights law, such as the ECHR, has traditionally addressed the conduct of state authorities, rather than private individuals (employers in this case). Yet human rights law over recent years has been found to give rise to positive state obligations to regulate private conduct in several jurisdictions.[43] Positive obligations can be imposed when there is imbalance of power between private parties, and state authorities know or ought to have known that one of the private actors abused the position of power.[44] The imbalance of power between parties that requires positive intervention is very familiar in labour law, where it is used to justify unionisation or legislative intervention.[45] But the existence of positive obligations does not mean that an individual who has a claim under the Convention can turn against another individual directly. The horizontal effect of the ECHR is indirect, grounded on Article 1 of the Convention:[46] it is the state that may be liable for failing to protect individuals from abuse by other individuals. The Court has frequently ruled that human rights are applicable in the employment relationship because of lack of legislation to protect vulnerable groups or because of judicial decisions (actions of state organs) that misapplied or did not take account of Convention rights.[47]

A. Livelihood for Dignity

In considering the normative issues underlying the right to work, I will start with the most basic but fundamental function of work, namely that it provides the means by which most people earn their income. Thanks to the income generated through work, people have access to basic material conditions, such as nutrition and housing. In modern societies, it is through work that most people meet their basic needs. At the same time, the income

[43] For analysis of positive obligations under the ECHR, see A Mowbray, *The Development of Positive Obligations under the European Convention on Human Rights by the European Court of Human Rights* (Oxford, Hart Publishing, 2004).

[44] See, for instance, *Rantsev v Cyprus and Russia*, App No25965/04, Judgment of 7 January 2010.

[45] P Davies and M Freedland, *Kahn-Freund's Labour and the Law* (London, Stevens, 1983) 18.

[46] Art 1 of the ECHR provides as follows: 'The High Contracting Parties shall secure to everyone within their jurisdiction the rights and freedoms defined in Section I of this Convention'.

[47] *Wilson and Palmer v United Kingdom*, App Nos 30668/96, 30671/96 and 30678/96, Judgment of 2 July 2002; *IB v Greece*, App No 552/10; Judgment of 3 October 2013.

generated through work helps people access other benefits that they value, like arts or sports for example. Self-sufficiency reached through paid work brings satisfaction, which provision through social support does not bring. The instrumental value of work as a means of income is linked to the value of dignity. Without the income gained through work, most people are unable to live a dignified life,[48] for they will not have the essentials with which to satisfy their basic needs. Welfare-dependence, on which some unemployed people rely to satisfy their basic needs, often has a stigma attached to it.[49]

People who work are seen as citizens who make a valuable contribution to the community in which they live, and this is again linked to their dignity. Discussing American citizenship, Judith Shklar argued that the right to work is one of its central elements (together with the right to vote). 'The dignity of work and of personal achievement', Shklar said, 'and the contempt for aristocratic idleness, have since colonial times been an important part of American civic self-identification'.[50] This is true for many countries, perhaps particularly in Europe and the Western world. But it is interesting to note that Shklar presents 'work' as one of two fundamental aspects of American citizenship under the heading 'Earning' (alongside 'Voting'). Work and earning are inextricably linked on this analysis of citizenship.

The ECtHR recognises the importance of work in order to make a living. The case *Young, James and Webster v UK*,[51] in 1981, highlighted this. The case addressed 'closed shop' agreements, which are agreements between employers and trade unions, which make access to work or retention of a job conditional upon membership of specific unions. The applicants, who did not wish to be union members, claimed that these agreements violated the negative aspect of the right to organise, under article 11 of the ECHR. The Court upheld their claim, saying that compulsion to join a union with

> a threat of dismissal involving loss of livelihood is a most serious form of compulsion and, in the present instance, it was directed against persons engaged by British Rail before the introduction of any obligation to join a particular trade union.[52]

[48] On basic material conditions and the prohibition of inhuman and degrading treatment under the Convention, see, for instance, *MSS v Belgium and Greece*, App No 30696/09, Grand Chamber Judgment of 21 January 2011. See further F Tulkens, 'The Contribution of the European Convention on Human Rights to the Poverty Issue in Times of Crisis' (2013) 2 *Cyprus Human Rights Law Review* 122.

[49] See R Sennett, *Respect* (London, Penguin, 2003) ch4, 'The Shame of Dependence'.

[50] J Shklar, *American Citizenship: The Quest for Inclusion* (Cambridge MA, Harvard University Press, 1995) 1.

[51] *Young, James and Webster v United Kingdom*, App Nos 7601/76, 7806/77, Judgment of 13 August 1981.

[52] *Young, James and Webster*, ibid, para 55. This has been repeated in subsequent case law. See *Sorensen and Rasmussen v Denmark*, App Nos 52562/99 and 52620/99, Judgment of 11 January 2006.

That the applicants would lose their jobs and livelihoods, played a fundamental role in assessing the proportionality of the restriction of freedom of association. It was a significant factor that led the Court to conclude that closed shops violate the ECHR. It is interesting to note at this point that in the United States, right-to-work laws are used to outlaw closed shop arrangements. The right to work there has famously the opposite meaning to other jurisdictions.[53]

The importance of work in order to make a living has been repeated in several cases that discuss dismissal in breach of Convention rights. The landmark case *Sidabras and Dziautas v Lithuania*,[54] for example, involved the applicants' dismissal and ban from access to work in the public and many parts of the private sector, for the reason that they were former KGB members. The Court recognised that dismissal and ban from access to work created 'serious difficulties ... in terms of earning [a] living, with obvious repercussions on the enjoyment of ... private lives'.[55] It classified the claim as falling within the right to private life under Article 8 of the ECHR, and concluded that it violates Article 8, taken in conjunction with the prohibition of discrimination in Article 14. It is important to note that the Court here placed special emphasis on right to work rulings of the European Committee of Social Rights that monitors compliance with the ESC. It underlined that '[i]t attaches particular weight in this respect to the text of Article 1 § 2 of the European Social Charter and the interpretation given by the European Committee of Social Rights'.[56] This analysis of the Court is a good example of the adoption of an 'integrated approach to the interpretation' of the ECHR, which integrates civil and social rights within the scope of the Convention in the context of the right to work.[57]

The Convention does not explicitly protect salaries as such. It does not contain a provision on a right to a minimum wage[58] or a right to a decent wage. In light of the importance that the Court recognises to work in order to make a living, though, it should not come as a surprise that it has classified salaries as 'possessions'. In this way salaries may fall in the scope of

[53] See further, KVW Stone, 'A Right to Work in the United States: Historical Antecedents and Contemporary Possibilities' in *The Right to Work*, n 2 above.

[54] *Sidabras and Dziautas v Lithuania*, App Nos 55480/00 and 59330/00, Judgment of 27 July 2004. For analysis of the case, see V Mantouvalou, 'Work and Private Life: *Sidabras and Dziautas v Lithuania*' (2005) *European Law Review* 573.

[55] *Sidabras*, ibid, para 48.

[56] Ibid, para 47.

[57] Mantouvalou, above n 9.

[58] On minimum wage, see *Nerva and Others v United Kingdom*, App No 42295/98, Judgment of 24 September 2002.

Article 1 Protocol 1 of the Convention that protects the right to peaceful enjoyment of one's possessions.[59]

Income generated through work is essential not only for its role while someone is employed. It is also essential for it leads to rights to an old-age pension. The Court has examined workers' pensions in the case *Stummer v Austria*,[60] a particularly complex case (with an unfortunate outcome), which involved prison labour. The case examined the exclusion of the applicant from the Austrian state pension system, despite the fact that he had worked in the prison kitchen and bakery for long periods of time during his 28-year imprisonment. Before the ECtHR, he argued that the fact that he was not affiliated to a pension system while he performed work in prison amounted to a breach of Article 4 (forced labour). The majority of the Court accepted that 'prison work differs from the work performed by ordinary employees in many aspects. It serves the primary aim of rehabilitation and resocialisation',[61] yet it is also similar to other employees, in the sense that it should also provide for old age.[62] Despite that, the majority ruled that his exclusion from a pension was compatible with the Convention.

However, in a forceful and convincing dissenting opinion, Judge Tulkens disagreed with the view of the majority, saying that today 'prisons have gradually opened up to fundamental rights'.[63] Prison work without affiliation to an old-age pension scheme is not ordinary work, as Judge Tulkens argued. In an important passage in the dissenting opinion, it was recognised that not only is work of fundamental importance for reintegration; but also the old-age pension for work performed has a special role for human dignity. In the words of the dissenting judges,

> neither the emergency relief payments nor the social assistance can be compared to an old-age pension granted on the basis of the number of years worked and the contributions paid. The former constitute assistance, whereas the latter is a right. *The difference is significant in terms of respect for human dignity*. Social security forms an integral part of human dignity.[64]

In cases such as the above, the majority of the Court or individual judges either protected workers' income generated through work directly in

[59] See, for instance, *Evaldsson and Others v Sweden*, App No 75252/01, Judgment of 13 February 2007. See further P Herzfeld Olsson, 'Every Natural or Legal Person is Entitled to the Peaceful Enjoyment of His or Her Possessions: Article 1, Protocol 1 to the European Convention on Human Rights' in Dorssemont et al (eds) *The European Convention on Human Rights and the Employment Relation* (Oxford, Hart Publishing, 2013) 381 at 400 ff; and T Novitz, 'Labour Rights and Property Rights: Implications for (and Beyond) Redundancy Payments and Pensions?' (2012) 41 *Industrial Law Journal* 136.

[60] *Stummer v Austria*, App No 37452/02, Grand Chamber Judgment of 7 July 2011.

[61] *Stummer*, ibid, para 93.

[62] *Stummer*, ibid, para 95; dissenting opinion, para 1.

[63] Judge Tulkens, dissenting opinion, para 7.

[64] Joint partly dissenting opinion of Judges Tulkens, Kovler, Gyulumyan, Spielmann, Popovic, Malinverni and Pardalos, para 10.

the Convention, or placed emphasis on it in examining restrictions to Convention rights through a test of proportionality. Against this background, the ECtHR has endorsed the importance of earning through work for human dignity, and incorporated it in the material scope of Convention rights.

B. Non-Exploitation

A second normative concern underlying the right to work that emerges from the case law of the ECtHR is non-exploitation.[65] As was said earlier in this chapter, the CESCR General Comment on the Right to Work views decent working conditions as an essential aspect of the right to work. In this way, the right to work is not only a right to fair access to the labour market, but also a right to non-exploitative work.

The concept of exploitation is contested and has been analysed in scholarship.[66] In many writings exploitation is discussed against the background of the theory of Karl Marx. In the technical sense developed by Marx, exploitation occurs when one class of non-workers appropriates the surplus product of a class of workers.[67] On this analysis, exploitation is a condition that always exists in a capitalist society. For Marx, a right to work would probably be an oxymoron, for it would be the equivalent to a right to be exploited.[68] In a liberal society, a person exercising free will should probably be free to be exploited, if she so wishes.[69] Yet this is not what we have in mind when we talk about a human right to work. This section does not use the Marxist conception of exploitation, even though the present analysis has elements in common with the Marxist account.

For present purposes, exploitation is the abuse of a person's vulnerability, which may be due to the law or other factors, in order to make profit.[70] So this conception of exploitation has three central elements: (a) vulnerability of a worker; (b) abuse of this vulnerability that consists

[65] I develop this further in V Mantouvalou, 'The Right to Non-Exploitative Work' in *The Right to Work* (n 2 above).

[66] As a starting point, see Alan Wertheimer and Matt Zwolinski, 'Exploitation', *The Stanford Encyclopedia of Philosophy* (Spring 2013 edn), Edward N Zalta (ed), plato.stanford.edu/archives/spr2013/entries/exploitation/ See also A Wertheimer, *Exploitation* (Princeton NJ, Princeton University Press, 1996).

[67] See K Marx, *Capital—A New Abridgment* (Oxford, OUP, 1999) 183 ff. See also GA Cohen, 'Karl Marx and the Withering Away of Social Science' (1972) 1 *Philosophy and Public Affairs* 182; J Wolff, 'Marx and Exploitation' (1999) 3 *Journal of Ethics* 105.

[68] See the discussion in G Mundlak, 'The Right to Work—The Value of Work' in Barak-Erez and Gross (eds), *Exploring Social Rights* (Oxford, Hart Publishing, 2010) 341 at 345.

[69] There are limitations to this freedom. See, for instance, MJ Radin, *Contested Commodities* (Cambridge MA, Harvard University Press, 2001).

[70] This is further developed in V Mantouvalou, 'The Right to Non-Exploitative Work' in *The Right to Work* (n 2 above).

in the violation of labour rights and other human rights (c) with an aim to make a profit. Because this analysis of exploitation is based on taking advantage of someone's vulnerability, it is always a moral wrong that the law should not permit.

In the Convention, the prohibition of workers' exploitation (particularly its gravest forms) underlies Article 4, which prohibits slavery, servitude, forced and compulsory labour, and emerges in the relevant case law. Looking at the provision, the UK Supreme Court recognised that '[f]orced labour is not fully defined and may take various forms, but exploitation is at its heart'.[71]

The first case where the ECtHR ruled that there had been a violation of Article 4 because of a worker's exploitation was *Siliadin v France*.[72] In this case, the Court examined the situation of a migrant domestic worker, who lived and worked in appalling conditions. Being a minor at the time that she was brought to France from Togo, Siliadin had to work almost 15 hours a day, seven days per week. She had not chosen to work for her employers, she had no resources, was isolated, had no money to move elsewhere, and 'was entirely at [the employers'] mercy, since her papers had been confiscated and she had been promised that her immigration status would be regularised, which had never occurred'.[73] Her exploitation was such that the Court was prepared to classify it as servitude, finding for the first time in its history that there was a breach of Article 4 of the Convention.

The *Siliadin* case has been followed by more case law on domestic work[74] and sex trafficking,[75] which shows how migrant workers with restrictive visa regimes or those that are undocumented are particularly vulnerable and prone to exploitation.[76] This is not tolerated by the European human rights system. Looking at domestic servitude, in *CN v UK*, for example, the Court stressed that the authorities should not underestimate that there are both 'overt and more subtle forms of coercion', and 'many subtle ways an individual can fall under the control of another'.[77] These overt and subtle forms of coercion make migrant workers prone to exploitation, not only because of the economic imbalance that typically characterises the employment relationship, but also because of immigration rules that create what can be called 'legislative precariousness',[78] namely vulnerability created

[71] *R (on the application of Reilly and Another) v Secretary of State for Work and Pensions* [2013] UKSC 68 (30 October 2013), para 81.

[72] *Siliadin v France*, App No 73316/01, Judgment of 26 July 2005.

[73] *Siliadin*, ibid, para 126.

[74] *CN v United Kingdom*, App No 4239/08, Judgment of 13 November 2012.

[75] *Rantsev v Cyprus and Russia*, App No 25965/04, Judgment of 7 January 2010.

[76] B Anderson, 'Migration, Immigration Controls and the Fashioning of Precarious Workers' (2010) 24 *Work, Employment and Society* 300.

[77] *CN*, above n 74, para 80.

[78] V Mantouvalou, 'Human Rights for Precarious Workers: The Legislative Precariousness of Domestic Workers' (2012) 34 *Comparative Labor Law and Policy Journal* 133.

or exacerbated by law. Labour law or criminal law also create legislative precariousness, and make workers prone to exploitation.[79]

Legislative precariousness is not the only type of vulnerability that can be abused by employers. There are other types of vulnerability that stem from physical or mental characteristics of the worker, or other external reasons such as poverty. Against this background, and under Article 4, the Court has examined the issue of workers' exploitation in the context of workfare schemes. Workfare schemes are schemes that make social benefits, like a jobseeker's allowance, conditional upon acceptance of suitable work.[80] According to the Court's case law, for a form of labour to be considered forced, it must be imposed against the will of the person and under the threat of a penalty.[81] The ECtHR has said that it may be legitimate for the government to ask that someone who claims an unemployment benefit has first tried to obtain a job. When a state has a welfare system, it is entitled to set conditions on the receipt of benefits: a condition that one seeks 'generally accepted employment' is not unreasonable.[82] This is particularly so when there is a possibility to reject work that is socially unacceptable or the possibility of conscientious objection.[83] That the Court has not found that there has been a breach of Article 4 in cases that it has examined thus far does not mean that workfare schemes are never exploitative (because they lead to taking advantage of individuals' material need) and in breach of the Convention. There may be circumstances in which someone is exploited under these schemes, and can be a victim of a violation of Article 4 of the Convention.[84]

The ECHR captures aspects of the right to work that are supported by the principle of non-exploitation. The Convention does not protect against all forms of labour exploitation, particularly if we adopt a Marxist definition of the concept of exploitation.[85] This is because the Convention is a liberal document, and free-market economy is the system that is compatible

[79] On the role of labour law in creating legislative precariousness, see Mantouvalou, ibid; on the role of criminal law, see D Guilfoyle, 'Transnational Criminal Law as a Governance Strategy in the Global Labour Market: Criminalizing Migration from Below' (2010) 29 *Refugee Survey Quarterly* 185.

[80] See generally, A Paz-Fuchs, *Welfare to Work—Conditional Rights in Social Policy* (Oxford, OUP, 2008); A Paz-Fuchs, 'A Right to Work—A Duty to Work' in *The Right to Work* (n 2 above).

[81] *Van der Mussele v Belgium*, App No 1989/80, Judgment of 23 November 1983.

[82] *Schuitemaker v Netherlands*, App No 15906/08, Decision of 4 May 2010.

[83] ibid.

[84] See further, E Dermine, 'Activation Policies for the Unemployed and the International Human Rights Case Law on the Prohibition of Forced Labour' [2013] *European Journal of Human Rights* 746.

[85] On the Marxist approach towards legal rights more generally, see H Collins, *Marxism and the Law* (Oxford, OUP, 1982) 142 ff.

with it.[86] However, Article 4 in particular addresses the gravest forms of labour exploitation, and imposes on authorities positive obligations to investigate, legislate and enforce the legislation. A right to non-exploitative work can, therefore, be said to be present in case law of the ECtHR.

C. Self-Realisation

As Hugh Collins has argued, work can be an important source of self-realisation. On this analysis, self-realisation is a justification of aspects of the right to work. Collins says:

> Animals such as bees also co-operate in their relations of production, but they function like cogs in a machine, whereas human beings form social relationships through work, making choices, agreements, plans, friends, and organisations. As social animals, human beings create their society around their work relations. So we might say that human beings find meaning for their lives through work, not just from the achievements of what is produced, but also, and importantly, from the establishment of social relations with colleagues, which is also a vital part of our 'species-being'.[87]

Collins developed the value of self-realisation as a basis of the positive aspects of the right to work. Even though the Convention does not explicitly guarantee such a positive right, the value of work for self-realisation is not foreign in the case-law of the ECtHR. For example, the Court has emphasised the function of the workplace as a place where people flourish by developing social relationships. This was recognised in case law on Article 8, the right to private life. In the much-cited *Niemietz v Germany* case,[88] the Court said insightfully:

> Respect for private life must also comprise to a certain degree the right to establish and develop relationships with other human beings. There appears, furthermore, to be no reason of principle why this understanding of the notion of 'private life' should be taken to exclude activities of a professional or business nature since it is, after all, in the course of their working lives that the majority of people have a significant, if not the greatest, opportunity of developing relationships with the outside world.[89]

In *Sidabras*, having recognised that the right to private life 'secures to the individual a sphere within which he or she can freely pursue the development and fulfillment of his or her personality',[90] the Court went on to

[86] For example, the narrow formulation of the right to property in Art 1 of Protocol 1 and the prohibition of discrimination in Art 14 both suggest this.

[87] H Collins, 'Is there a Human Right to Work?' in *The Right to Work*, n 2 above.

[88] *Niemietz v Germany*, App No 13710/88, Judgment of 16 December 1992.

[89] *Niemietz*, ibid, para 29.

[90] See *Sidabras*, n 54 above, para 43.

state that the wide ban on access to employment can affect the 'ability to develop relationships with the outside world to a very significant degree'. The right to private life under Article 8 creates a space for self-development and self-fulfillment, and work is part of this space that should be protected from intrusion.[91]

A point made earlier in this contribution should be emphasised again at this stage: the fact that the Court recognises the value of self-realisation through work does not mean that individual applicants who do not have sufficient opportunities of self-realisation in the workplace can bring a successful complaint to Strasbourg. It indicates, though, that the Court may view as problematic the arbitrary exclusion of someone from work not only because it deprives the person of the opportunity to earn income, but also because it deprives him or her of the opportunity to self-realisation.

D. Non-domination

A final element emerging from Convention case law, which supports aspects of the right to work, is the principle of non-domination. For the right to work to be effectively protected, and for a worker to achieve self-realisation at work, as discussed above, she has to be protected from domination in the workplace. The power to dominate is probably most clearly expressed through the ability of the employer to dismiss the worker. According to Philip Pettit, domination exists when someone has the capacity to interfere with another person's choices on an arbitrary basis.[92] Of course, the employment relationship in general is a relationship of subordination[93] because of the economic dependence of the worker on the employer, which creates an imbalance of power. Yet if the employer can dismiss an employee 'as whim inclines him and hardly suffer embarrassment for doing so',[94] the employment relationship is not just one of subordination, but one of domination, for the employer may be able to control all aspects of the worker's life.

It should not come as a surprise that the case law that best reflects the value of non-domination involves dismissal for activities outside work. Individuals who have been dismissed from their jobs because of their personal preferences and activities outside the workplace and working time have brought claims to Strasbourg, arguing that their Convention rights are infringed. The Court has ruled that dismissal that interferes with Convention rights must be assessed for its fairness, so if a person is dismissed, there has

[91] See also *Campagnano v Italy*, App No 77955/01, Judgment of 23 March 2006.

[92] P Pettit, *Republicanism: A Theory of Freedom and Government* (Oxford, OUP, 1999) 52.

[93] Davies and Freedland, above n 45.

[94] Pettit, above n 92, 57.

to be some independent assessment of the employer's decision.[95] There is a long line of cases on dismissals that interfere with Convention rights. For example, the ECtHR has protected workers' intimate sexual life and their political views against employer interference. In *Smith and Grady v UK*,[96] it found that the applicants' discharge from the military because of their sexual orientation was in breach of the Convention. In *Schüth v Germany*,[97] the applicant, a church worker, was dismissed for having an extramarital affair, and the Court ruled that his dismissal violated his right to private life. In *Vogt v Germany*,[98] the Court found that the dismissal of the applicant, a school teacher, because of her political views, violated her freedom of expression, particularly because there was no evidence that she used her position as a teacher to indoctrinate the pupils. In *Redfearn v UK*,[99] it held that the applicant's dismissal from his job as a bus driver because of his membership of an extreme-right political party violated his freedom of association.

The problem of domination through dismissal was probably most dramatically illustrated in the case *IB v Greece*,[100] which concerned the dismissal of an HIV-positive individual, for the reason that his co-workers objected to working with him because of his status. This case highlights how the stigma that comes with the specific reason of the dismissal (HIV/AIDS)[101] has very wide implications for the person's private life, which raise issues under the Convention. The Court accepted that the stigma attached to dismissal because someone is HIV-positive is such that this dismissal falls within the ambit of his right to private life. It also placed emphasis on the uncertainty faced by the applicant in his search for a new job, namely the implications of dismissal because of positive HIV-status, which would mean that his right to access a job could be affected significantly. It held that the dismissal of IB violated the prohibition of discrimination together with the right to private life.

In jurisprudence on dismissal because of lifestyle choices and other aspects of the worker's private life, the Court has been sensitive towards the employer's power to dominate the worker. The principle of non-domination, which underlies this line of cases, supports protection from

[95] See *Redfearn v United Kingdom*, App No 47335/06, Judgment of 6 November 2012.

[96] *Smith and Grady v United Kingdom*, App Nos 33985/96, 33986/96, Judgment of 27 September 1999. See also *Lustig-Prean and Beckett v United Kingdom*, App Nos 31417/96 and 32377/96, Judgment of 27 September 1999.

[97] *Schüth v Germany*, App No1620/03, Judgment of 23 September 2010. Cf *Obst v Germany*, App No 425/03, Judgment of 23 September 2010.

[98] *Vogt v Germany*, App No 17851/91, Judgment of 2 September 1996.

[99] *Redfearn v United Kingdom*, App No 47335/06, Judgment of 6 November 2012.

[100] *IB v Greece*, App No 552/10, Judgment of 3 October 2013.

[101] On HIV/AIDS stigmatisation at work, see the ILO Recommendation Concerning HIV and AIDS and the World of Work (2010), No 200, which the ECtHR took into account in its ruling. See also *Hoffmann v South African Airways*, CCT17/00, [2000] ZACC 17.

unfair dismissal in circumstances when Convention rights are implicated and forms the basis for a right to be protected from unfair dismissal, which is a component of the right to work.

V. CONCLUSION

The ECHR does not impose duties on the state to promote full employment. Such duties might even be incompatible with a liberal human rights document. In any case, the lack of this type of duty is unsurprising, given that the Convention is a justiciable treaty that is protected through individual petition. This type of mechanism may not be appropriate for certain positive aspects of the right to work.

Yet it is important to appreciate that the ECtHR case law guarantees important principles that underlie the right to work. To return to a distinction introduced earlier, in the literature on whether labour rights are human rights, sometimes three different approaches are conflated: the positivistic, the instrumental and the normative one. From the discussion on the right to work, to a positivist,[102] we can say that even if a right is not explicitly mentioned in a specific human rights treaty, such as the ECHR, it can still be derived from the case law on other provisions through interpretation. An approach that is merely positivistic, in other words, will fail to capture in any depth the important role of judicial interpretation.[103]

In the context of judicial interpretation of the ECHR by the Court, we identified some normative principles that underlie the right to work, and which have supported aspects of it in the case law. The ideas of dignity, non-exploitation, self-fulfillment and non-domination are either openly invoked or, more often, implied in decisions of the Court. Even though these normative principles were here addressed separately, this does not mean that they are not linked. For instance, work with fear of dismissal because of private activities may be exploitative work. Exploitative work cannot be self-fulfilling. Exploitative work can also violate human dignity. But there is a value in addressing them separately and exploring their implications both in the context of a legal document and as a theoretical matter.

It is also important to re-iterate that the fact that these normative principles emerge from Convention case law does not mean that whenever they are invoked, there will always be a violation of the Convention. In fact, some aspects of the right to work are sometimes in conflict with other aspects of it,[104] and this problem will no doubt have to be addressed at

[102] See above n 14.
[103] See G Letsas, *A Theory of Interpretation of the European Convention on Human Rights*, above n 41.
[104] Freedland and Kountouris; Bogg in *The Right to Work* (n 2 above).

some point by the ECtHR.[105] Workers themselves sometimes have conflicting interests, which labour law attempts to address.[106] Some workers' rights to access a job may conflict with other workers' rights to fair working conditions. Conflicts between rights or aspects of them are not unique to the right to work. Rights are often in conflict, and the ECtHR and human rights scholars develop normative theories to address such conflicts.[107] However, exploring these normative principles is important as it highlights key interpretative values that can guide the Court's task.

To the instrumentalists then, this contribution does not suggest that the right to work as an individual human right (directly or indirectly protected) will help address all injustices at work. Labour protective legislation or associational activity through unions and other organisations are also fundamental means by which workers' rights are protected. It also does not suggest that the ECtHR alone is the appropriate forum for the protection of workers' rights. European human rights law does not and cannot address structural injustices in the workplace, such as unemployment, as Hepple rightly argued in his 1981 essay.[108] However, there may be circumstances that an individual is unfairly deprived of a job or exploited at work, in which the ECHR will give that person voice. This should not be underestimated.

[105] The Court of Justice of the EU has had to address this type of issue in the *Viking* and *Laval* line of cases. See C Barnard, '*Viking* and *Laval*: An Introduction' (2007–08) 10 *Cambridge Yearbook of European Legal Studies* 463; ACL Davies, 'One Step Forward Two Steps Back? The Viking and Laval cases in the ECJ' (2008) 37 *Industrial Law Journal* 126; T Novitz, 'A Human Rights Analysis of the *Viking* and *Laval* Judgments' (2008) 10 *Cambridge Yearbook of European Legal Studies* 541.

[106] G Mundlak, 'The Third Function of Labour Law: Distributing Labour Market Opportunities among Workers' in G Davidov and B Langille (eds), *The Idea of Labour Law* (Oxford, OUP, 2011) 315; ACL Davies, 'Identifying "Exploitative Compromises": The Role of Labour Law in Resolving Disputes Between Workers' (2012) 65 *Current Legal Problems* 269.

[107] G Letsas, 'Rescuing Proportionality' in R Cruft, SM Liao and M Renzo (eds), *Philosophical Foundations of Human Rights* (Oxford, OUP, 2014, forthcoming).

[108] Hepple, above n 3, 82–83.

Symposium

Balancing In European Law: Anatomy of Judicial Practices

LEONE NIGLIA*

THE CONTRIBUTIONS TO this *Symposium* propose a close examination of European judicial practice insofar as it involves the balancing of rights, including proportionality balancing. The focus is on free movement rights, fundamental rights and private law rights.[1] The aim is to develop an analytical understanding of the role of balancing in European judicial practice by mapping the ways in which: (a) judges deal with the many tensions between freedom of expression and free movement of goods or between human dignity and freedom to provide services;[2] (b) judges combine and/or compromise among the alternatives; (c) combinations and/or compromising acts preserve or change the measure of the balancing acts; and, the kind of substantive European law that emerges as a result of the balancing operations and related constitutional implications. The contributions consider how judicial balancing keeps encroaching upon, and transforming, legislative processes (balancing through proportionality), constitutional structures (balancing fundamental rights) and private realms (balancing private law rights) across the domestic, the European Union and the European Convention on Human Rights adjudication levels. In so doing, the contributions identify hybridisation processes in the ways

* Three of the four contributions to this *Symposium* are based on the Annual Lasok Lectures held at the *Centre for European Legal Studies* at the University of Exeter, which I have organised and chaired in my capacity as Centre Director, as respectively given in the academic years 2010–11, 2011–12 and 2013–14 by: Court of Justice of the European Union Advocate General Paolo Mengozzi; Court of Justice of the European Union Judge Alan Rosas; Professor Takis Tridimas, King's College, London. I am thankful to them for accepting my invitation to give the Lecture and for participating with their articles in the project leading to the publication of this *Symposium*. Thanks to the *Yearbook* for hosting this *Symposium*.

[1] For a stress on each set of rights see respectively below, P Mengozzi, 'The Judicial Protection of Individual Rights and the Principle of Proportionality after the Lisbon Treaty'; A Rosas, 'Balancing Fundamental Rights in EU law' and T Tridimas, 'Fundamental Rights, General Principles of EU Law, and the Charter'; L Niglia, 'Taking Private Law Rights Seriously: of Balancing and the Jurisprudence of the Court of Justice of the European Union'.

[2] Respectively CJEU cases *Schmidberger* and *Omega*: see below.

in which the principle of proportionality is judicially applied, due to the fact that it becomes blended with the principles of conferred power and of cooperation and mutual trust;[3] hierarchical, as opposed to equal, orderings among the rights being subject to balancing;[4] tensions between, on the one hand, the EU constitutional space as re-constituted as a result of the application of the Charter in a context in which 'proportionality ... has evolved to a pre-eminent balancing tool', and, on the other hand, national constitutional norms;[5] tensions, and possibilities for reconciliation, between, on the one hand, balancing private law rights understood as a 'European' practice of rights' optimisation and, on the other hand, balancing private law rights in the context of the national constitutional dimension.[6]

[3] Mengozzi, 'The Judicial Protection of Individual Rights and the Principle of Proportionality after the Lisbon Treaty' at p 339. See also Niglia, 'Taking Private Law Rights Seriously' at p 413 et seq (on balancing, rights' optimisation and hybridisation).

[4] Rosas, 'Balancing Fundamental Rights in EU Law' at p 350.

[5] Tridimas, 'Fundamental Rights, General Principles of EU Law, and the Charter' at p 392.

[6] Niglia, 'Taking Private Law Rights Seriously' at p 413 et seq. See also Mengozzi, 'The Judicial Protection of Individual Rights and the Principle of Proportionality after the Lisbon Treaty' when discussing the *DEB* case at p 340 et seq.

A

The Judicial Protection of Individual Rights and the Principle of Proportionality after the Lisbon Treaty

ADVOCATE GENERAL PAOLO MENGOZZI

Abstract

The aim of this chapter is to illustrate how the principle of proportionality as derived from the legal orders of the Member States has been incorporated in the legal order of the European Union as well as codified in the Treaties. The chapter revolves around two key arguments. It emphasises, first, that the principle of proportionality has been used as a criterion for controlling the legality of the acts of the Union and of those of the Member States when implementing Union law. Secondly, it is argued that, more recently, the same principle has been used by the Court of Justice of the European Union as a useful instrument towards ensuring an even stronger coordination with national judges.

I. INTRODUCTION

THE LEGAL ORDER of the European Union as we know it nowadays has been progressively construed on the basis of the incorporation within the Treaties instituting the Community of principles that the Court of Justice of the European Union has drawn from the legal orders of the Member States and the general principles of law. Among them the principle of proportionality is particularly relevant.

II. THE DEFINITION OF PROPORTIONALITY IN ARTICLE 5 TEU AND PROTOCOL NO 2

Compliance with the principle of proportionality is now one of the criteria on the basis of which the Union has to carry out its competences. This principle was introduced into the EC and EU Treaties by the Treaty of

Maastricht in 1992 and has been confirmed by Article 5 TEU. This article, after establishing at paragraph 1 that '[t]he use of Union competences is governed by the principles of subsidiarity and proportionality', specifies at paragraph 4, that under the latter, 'the content and form of Union action shall not exceed what is *necessary* to achieve the objectives of the Treaties' (emphasis added). The principle of subsidiarity operates in areas which do not fall within the exclusive competence of the Union. It was introduced into the Treaty in order to establish whether, and in which of those areas, the Union or a Member State may act. By contrast, the principle of proportionality presupposes the competence of the Union and aims at limiting the exercise of that competence. Since the Treaty of Amsterdam the provisions concerning the principles of proportionality and subsidiarity have been developed and refined resulting in Protocol no 2 annexed to the Lisbon Treaty.

The principle of proportionality is destined to function as a general principle of EU law. It constitutes a criterion for the determination of the legitimacy of EU acts, when these are the result of the exercise of a discretional power through which the EU legislator makes choices on the basis of complex evaluations of a political, economic and social nature. This has led the Court to exclude the possibility of replacing its own evaluation with that of the European legislator. In exercising its judicial powers, the Court has considered itself qualified only to censure the EU legislator's choices when they are disproportionate or when the inconveniences arising from them are disproportionate in comparison to the advantages that the same choices present.[1] Consequently, the Court now deems that it may only declare a disproportionate act unlawful.

III. PROPORTIONALITY AND ACTIONS FOR ANNULMENT BROUGHT BY NATURAL OR LEGAL PERSONS

Even before being 'codified' by the Treaty of Maastricht, the principle of proportionality had been applied by the Court of Justice in decisions in which, on the basis of claims by natural or legal persons, it annulled institutions' acts which were not consistent with such a principle. It considered that the principle of proportionality constitutes a general principle of Community law inferred from the legal orders of the Member States, particularly that of Germany. The Court felt entitled to apply that principle since the Treaty foresees that it has jurisdiction in actions for annulment of Union acts violating 'any rule of law relating to th[e] application [of the Treaties]'.

Significant examples of the Court of Justice considering the principle of proportionality as a general principle of Union law capable of being

[1] See R Adam and A Tizzano, *Lineamenti di diritto dell'Unione Europea*, 2nd edn (Turin, Giapichelli, 2010) 48–49.

invoked by natural and legal persons against acts of the institutions are the decisions taken in the *Consten and Grundig* cases,[2] and in the *Buitoni* case.[3]

IV. WIDENING THE SCOPE OF APPLICATION OF THE PROPORTIONALITY PRINCIPLE

The Court of Justice did not confine itself to applying the principle of proportionality with reference to actions initiated by natural and legal persons, but also applied it in cases where the Member States invoked it in order to contest the legitimacy of EU institutions' acts, maintaining that the latter had overstepped their competences. This widening of the scope of the principle of proportionality arose from the fact that the Court, after having recognised it as a rule of law under Article 263 TFEU that limits the legitimacy of acts concerning natural or legal persons, considered it as being integrated into the Union order as a general principle to which the legitimacy of all institutions' acts is subordinated, even when these acts concern Member States and other EU institutions. However, given that the achievement of a determined objective of EU interest can also be pursued by a Member State when this is requested either by the Treaty or by a Union act, the Court of Justice traditionally considers that the acts which are adopted by such a Member State in pursuing that objective are also subject to the principle of proportionality. The violation of this principle by such an act is asserted in two ways: (1) through an infringement procedure brought against the Member State which implemented the act; and (2) through a claim of such violation before a national judge, who can ask the Court of Justice, under Article 267 TFEU, if the EU law hinders the application of that act.

V. A NEW APPLICATION OF THE PROPORTIONALITY PRINCIPLE—THE *ROTTMANN* RULING

As regards the function that is traditionally attributed to the principle of proportionality—as a limit to the exercise of the competences of a Member State in pursuing an objective to which it can be bound under the Treaty or in implementing a Union act—the Court of Justice recently recognised different functions for it in the *Rottmann* ruling.

In the *Rottmann* case,[4] the Freistaat Bayern withdrew the naturalisation which, two years earlier, had been conferred on an Austrian citizen, who, because of such naturalisation, lost his Austrian citizenship. The withdrawal

[2] Joined Cases C-56 and 58/64 *Établissements Consten SàRL and Grundig-Verkaufs-GmbH v Commission of the EEC* [1966] ECR 299.

[3] Case C-122/78 *Buitoni v Fonds d'orientations* [1979] ECR 677.

[4] Case C-135/08 *Rottmann v Freistaat Bayern* [2010] ECR I-1449.

had been decided on account of deception perpetrated in the acquisition of the naturalisation. However, it had not yet become definitive due to different actions for annulment of that decision brought by the applicant, which had led to the case being brought before the federal administrative court. This court noted that, in the *Micheletti* case,[5] the Court of Justice had stated that the Member States must give relevance to the citizenship of individuals paying due regard to Union law. The German court observed that the assumption, from this statement, of the existence of an obligation to refrain from withdrawing naturalisation obtained by deception, would be to strike at the heart of the sovereign power of the Member States to define the detailed rules for the application of their own nationality law. Because of this, the federal administrative court referred the case to the Court of Justice for a preliminary ruling. It asked the Court to elucidate what it had stated in the *Micheletti* case and to clarify whether the status of Mr Rottmann being stateless and the loss of his Union citizenship, linked to the withdrawal of his German naturalisation, were compatible with European Union law. The Court of Justice admitted the request and deemed itself competent to rule, as the German decision concerned a situation which fell within the scope of Union law because of its negative effect on the right to Union citizenship attributed to a person by the Union legal order, which constitutes the fundamental status of Member States' citizens.

Passing to the substance of the CJEU decision, the Court deemed that a decision withdrawing naturalisation because of deception practised in its acquisition, adopted by Freistaat Bayern, *could* be consistent with Union law even when it entailed loss of the status of citizen of the Union for the person concerned. However, the Court of Justice considered that such a decision is not contrary to European Union law on condition that it observes the principle of proportionality. In this way it pointed out that this principle, as a general principle of Union law, can be applied as a limitation of a Member State's adoption of measures, not only when these measures are adopted to achieve an objective to which it is obliged according to Union law, but also when the same measures, even if they are brought into being in the framework of an exclusive state competence (independent of an Union obligation), have negative effect on a status and on the rights that Union law confers upon its citizens.

Furthermore, the Court refined this explanation, which is already important in itself, by offering further clarification. It took a position of apparent deference or self-restraint towards the national judge; it affirmed, nevertheless, that it is for the latter to verify whether the decision of Freistaat Bayern observed the principle of proportionality, and indicated in detail the specific elements which that judge, in so doing, has to take into account.

[5] Case C-369/90 *Micheletti v Delegación del Gobierno en Cantabria* [1992] ECR I-4239.

It identified these elements: (a) the consequences that a decision withdrawing naturalisation entails for the person concerned and for the members of his family; (b) the gravity of the offence committed; (c) the lapse of time between the naturalisation decision and the withdrawal decision; and (d) the possibility for the person concerned to recover his original nationality. Moreover, the Court specified that it is for the national court to determine whether, having regard to all these elements,

> observance of the principle of proportionality [before such a decision withdrawing naturalisation takes effect] requires the person concerned to be afforded a reasonable period of time in order to try to recover the nationality of his Member State of origin.[6]

These instructions go beyond the function which traditionally the principle of proportionality exercises with reference to the determination of the legitimacy of Community institutions' and Member States' acts of Union relevance: a function that, with reference to Member States' acts of this type, is seen as a limitation of a competence which Union law, a priori, imposes on them to carry out. On the contrary, the application of the principle of proportionality made by the Court of Justice in the *Rottmann* case, gives rise *ex novo* to an obligation which did not exist previously or is unrelated to a tradition which considered that the attribution and the withdrawal of citizenship fell within the scope of sovereignty and, therefore, was the exclusive competence of each Member State.

The consequence of this new approach of the Court is that it has determined an hybridisation of the principle of proportionality with two other principles. The first reshapes the functioning of the doctrine of conferred powers, according to which the exercise of exclusive competences of the Member States must also take place by respecting Union law and the rights that the latter attributes to individuals. The second, in my opinion more innovative, corresponds to an idea of sincere cooperation and of mutual trust. Being inspired by these three principles, the Court deemed that a Member State which means to withdraw the naturalisation of a person who had previously enjoyed the citizenship of another Member State, which he had lost because of such a naturalisation, can carry out its intention only after a sufficient lapse of time, allowing this person to try to recover his citizenship of origin. The Court did this, evidently, on the basis of the assumption that the dilatory attitude of Germany aiming to avoid the loss of a person's Union citizenship could have a corresponding attitude of attention to the condition of that same person by Austria. The above indicates that the Court of Justice does not formally deny that Member States maintain exclusive competence in allowing and withdrawing naturalisation; but nevertheless, stressing the consequences that the exercise of such a competence may have because of the loss of the Union citizenship which

[6] Case C-135/08 *Rottmann*, n 4 above, para 58.

it entails, the Court imposes its own criteria regarding how Member States, through their judges, must insure the correct exercise of such a competence. It does so to such a wide extent that that competence substantially no longer looks so exclusive.

It is evident that, even if with an iron fist in a velvet glove, this new ruling by the Court, which went further than had been expected, gave real consistency to the principle, which has been affirmed on many occasions, according to which the citizenship of the Union constitutes the fundamental status of Member States' citizens.

VI. THE '*DEB*' RULING

The position taken by the Court of Justice in the *DEB* case[7] cannot be deemed as constituting the same sort of application of the principle of proportionality as that made in the *Rottmann* case, even though it is different from previous case law. A German court referred the *DEB* case to the Court of Justice for a preliminary ruling in order to establish if a legal person, who intended to seek reparation from the German Republic for a delay in transposing an EU directive, could invoke the right of exemption from payment of the administrative charges for the proceedings, which payment is required under German law, and whether it was entitled to legal aid. That person had invoked that right with the objective of seeking the non-application of a German set of rules binding the exercise of a judicial action to the advanced payment of an administrative charge and which, in general terms, denies legal aid to a legal person who cannot provide for such an advance payment.

The Court considered that the question basically did not consist in establishing whether a legal person can qualify for legal aid from the Member State whenever intending to pursue a judicial claim seeking to establish that State's liability under Union law. Rather, according to the Court, the question consisted in asking whether the DEB's right to effective access to justice in order to proceed with that claim, without adequate justification, would be hindered by the refusal of that State's authorities to grant it legal aid. Once it had recast the question in these terms, the Court dealt with it using a procedural technique of the same type used in the *Rottmann* case: it once again left to the national court the task of deciding the case on the basis of the principle of proportionality, but, in detail, indicated the criteria to be used in applying it. It stated that the Court 'can', but one may infer that the Court really meant to say 'must',

> take into consideration the subject-matter of the litigation; whether the applicant has a reasonable prospect of success; the importance of what is at stake for the

[7] C-279/09 *DEB Deutsche Energiehandels- und Beratungsgesellschaft mbH v Germany* [2010] ECR I-13849.

> applicant in the proceedings; the complexity of the applicable law and procedure; and the applicant's capacity to represent himself effectively ... the national court may also take account of the amount of the costs of the proceedings in respect of which advance payment must be made and whether or not those costs might represent an insurmountable obstacle to access to the courts.[8]

Moreover, it added that,

> with regard more specifically to legal persons, the national court may take account of their situation ... may therefore take into consideration, inter alia, the form of the legal person in question and whether it is profit-making or non-profit-making; the financial capacity of the partners or shareholders; and the ability of those partners or shareholders to obtain the sums necessary to institute legal proceedings.[9]

However, the Court of Justice did not conceive the principle of proportionality as having the same role that it had previously conjured up in relation to the *Rottman* case. In fact, recasting, in the way indicated above, the question submitted to its attention, the Court of Justice was able to start from the idea that the German rules in question are not consistent with the duty of guaranteeing every person the right of access to justice that the Union Member States have to respect. Consequently, the Court of Justice confined the functioning of the proportionality principle to a role which Article 4 TEU and the traditional case law attribute to it: that of checking whether a behaviour, which appears inconsistent with an existing obligation, can be deemed legal because of a valid justification.

In order to affirm, as it did, that national judges, in deciding the case, must, on a substantial level, engage in applying the proportionality test in the sense indicated above, the Court started from the premise that fundamental rights were at stake in the case and that, as far as they are concerned,

> it is important, since the entry into force of the Lisbon Treaty, to take account of the Charter, which has 'the same legal value as the Treaties' pursuant to the first subparagraph of Article 6(1) TEU. Article 51(1) of the Charter states that the provisions thereof are addressed to Member States when they are implementing EU law.[10]

In the case at hand the third paragraph of Article 47 of the Charter was taken into account. It sets out that 'legal aid is to be made available "to those who lack sufficient resources"' when this is necessary to ensure effective access to justice. In his opinion in the case,[11] the Advocate General had maintained that that paragraph, at that time in the main proceedings, had no binding legal force as it presented an innovative character. The Court of Justice deemed that it was possible to bypass such an interpretation by invoking Article 47 of the Charter as a whole and by avoiding considering

[8] Ibid, para 61.
[9] Ibid, para 62.
[10] Ibid, para 30.
[11] Opinion delivered by Advocate General P Mengozzi on 2 September 2010 in Case C-279/09, para 69.

the third paragraph of the provision separately from the first and the second paragraph of the same provision (the first and the second paragraphs unequivocally codify principles which were already in force at the time of the facts of the case). The Court deemed that the three paragraphs, taken in conjunction with each other, support the right of natural and legal persons to enjoy complete and effective judicial protection of the rights conferred on them by EU law. Such a right, according to the Court of Justice, has been traditionally recognised by it and one cannot conceive that its application only began with the entry into force of the Lisbon Treaty.

In this way the Court surpassed the wording of the third paragraph which, in making reference to 'those' who lack sufficient resources, appears as if it confirms the right to legal aid for *natural and legal persons*. It deemed that that paragraph establishes a right and that the non-respect of this must *naturally* be considered as an obstacle to the access to justice that the principle of complete and effective judicial protection of the rights (granted to natural and legal persons) intends to guarantee. It is from this point of view that the Court considered that, in principle, the restraint placed by the German provisions on the possibility for legal persons to obtain legal aid constitutes a hindrance to their right to complete and effective judicial protection of the rights conferred by EU law. It was for just this reason that, given it was faced with a legal hindrance to a right traditionally conferred by EU law and simply confirmed by Article 47 of the Charter, the Court of Justice considered that the compatibility of those German provisions with EU law was subject to the proportionality test mentioned above[12] and stated:

> it is for the national court to ascertain whether the conditions for granting legal aid constitute a limitation on the right of access to the courts which undermines the very core of that right; whether they pursue a legitimate aim; and whether there is a reasonable relationship of proportionality between the means employed and the legitimate aim which is sought to achieve.[13]

[12] One can easily deduce that the position taken by the Court of Justice will provoke reactions in Germany. In that country, in fact, as the Court of Justice noted, the constitutional federal court considered that 'the granting of legal aid is a measure of social assistance which is derived from the principle of the social State and is necessary for the safeguarding of human dignity' (Case C-279/09, [2010] ECR I-13849, para 24). This is why the German constitutional court considered that legal aid can be granted to legal persons only when this is necessary for social or general purposes. However, the Court of Justice deemed that the right to receive legal aid, as it appears in Title VI (relating to justice) and not in Title IV (relating to solidarity) of the Charter, is essential in order to benefit, independently from considerations of a social nature, from effective access to justice to safeguard the rights granted by EU law. In order for the Court of Justice's reasoning to neutralise the criticisms which might come from Germany one must logically deem that also the third paragraph of Art 47, on which it is based, similarly to the first and the second paragraphs of the same article, does not show an innovative character but that it expressly specifies an idea strictly linked to the spirit in which the principle of effective judicial protection has been affirmed in the Community (now Union) order.

[13] Case C-279/09, [2010] ECR I-13849, para 60.

VII. REJECTING THE *ROTTMANN* APPROACH—THE *SAYN WITTGENSTEIN* DECISION

The fact that, in the *DEB* case, the Court of Justice applied the principle of proportionality by following the procedural technique used in the *Rottmann* case, had a particular influence on the way in which Advocate General Sharpston, in her opinion on *Sayn Wittgenstein*,[14] suggested that the Court should deal with the request for preliminary ruling in that case.

The Court was asked by the Austrian administrative supreme court to establish whether Article 21 TFEU precluded the application of legislation forbidding the use of titles of nobility. The competent administrative authorities had rectified in their records of civil status the surname of an Austrian citizen which had previously been recorded as including a title of nobility, which she had acquired and had been recognised by the German Federal Republic after her being adopted by a German citizen. In the proceedings before the Court of Justice the appellant, living in Germany, had contested the fact that the Austrian administration had proceeded with such a rectification, cancelling from her surname the title of nobility 15 years after that the same title had been recorded by the same administration. She argued that the rectification, effected under those circumstances, constituted both a hindrance to the freedom of movement from which she should benefit as a Union citizen and an interference in her private life as protected by Article 8 of the European Convention on Human Rights.

Advocate General Sharpston, in her opinion in the case, considered, inter alia, that the attribution and the acknowledgment of a surname containing a title of nobility may have been made by the German and the Austrian authorities in error as they contravene the private international law rules of both countries. However, she felt obliged to stress that the situation, unlawful because of such possible error, had been allowed by the Austrian authorities to continue for 15 years, during which it was even confirmed by the issuance of a passport and two certificates of nationality all stating the complete surname, including the title of nobility, with the consequence that the rectification with which they later proceeded, is certainly destined to cause serious inconveniences to the applicant and certainly constitutes an interference in her private life.

In line with these observations the Advocate General went on to consider whether the hindrance to the freedom of movement which she deemed to be the result of these serious inconveniences and of the interference in the applicant's private life, determined by the behaviour of the Austrian administration, could be justified. Using the procedural technique applied in the *Rottmann* case, Advocate General Sharpston (a) suggested that

[14] Opinion delivered by Advocate General Sharpston on 14 October 2010 in Case C-208/09 *Sayn-Wittgenstein v Landeshauptmann von Wien* [2010] ECR I-13693.

the Court should leave the definitive decision to the national court and (b) affirmed that the national court must decide according to the principle of proportionality, whilst clearly indicating the factors on the basis of which it must apply such a principle. In this respect she maintained that the national judges must have regard to the principle of proportionality which, with reference to the case at issue, requires them

> to take into account such factors as any legitimate expectation which the actions of their own authorities [the Austrian ones] may have led the citizen to entertain, the length of time over which the name may have been used without challenge by those authorities and the personal and professional interest which the citizen may have in maintaining the use of a previously recognised name.[15]

The Court of Justice agreed with the Advocate General's idea that the Austrian authorities' attitude towards the applicant, because of the fact that she lived in Germany and had been in the Austrian register of birth, marriages and deaths for 15 years, constituted a restriction of the freedoms granted by Article 21 TFEU to all Union citizens. However, it neither left to the national court's care the verification of the justification of such restriction, nor did it establish in detail the criteria to be used in evaluating the proportional character of the national measure which gave rise to that restriction. It simply confined itself to remarking that

a) the Austrian administration could consider the registration of the whole surname attributed to the applicant in Germany as contrary to public policy, considering that, first, the circumstances which may justify such recourse may vary from one Member State to another and from one era to another;[16] and, secondly, that the European Union respects the national identities of its Member States, which include the status of the State as a Republic and, as such, excludes the acknowledgment of any title of nobility, and
b) in the case at issue the attitude of the Austrian authorities does not result in being disproportionate with respect to the safeguarding of such a republican form, which seeks to attain the legitimate objective whilst protecting the principle of equal treatment.

The fact that the Court of Justice, in so applying the principle of proportionality, did not follow the stance adopted by the Advocate General may be explained by the fundamental character that the annulment of any title of nobility has in the Austrian constitutional order and in the circumstance that the respect of the Member States' national identities is now officially stated in Article 4(2) TEU. However, this fact can also be interpreted as a pause for reflection on the part of the Court of Justice concerning the very

15 Opinion in the case C-208/09, ibid at 'conclusion'.
16 See also Case 36/02 Omega [2004] ECR I-9609, p 31.

particular procedural technique on the basis of which, in the *Rottmann* and *DEB* cases, it applied the principle of proportionality.[17]

VIII. CONCLUSION

The way in which the Court of Justice decided the above considered three cases shows flexibility in the application of the principle of proportionality, especially as far as the preliminary ruling procedure is concerned. At the same time, in leaving a large margin of appreciation in the cases covered by Article 267 TFEU to the Member States' courts, in compliance with the principle of conferral of powers, the Court of Justice, in applying the principle of proportionality, engages with 'explaining' to those courts how to use such a margin. In this way, it tends to go beyond the rigid division of its competences and of those of the national courts and, in so doing, it applies in a particularly advanced way the principle of cooperation on which its relationship with those courts is based.

[17] On the way in which, in these two cases, the *Freystaat Bayern* and the *Bundesverwaltungsgericht* applied point by point the criteria indicated by the Court of Justice see P Mengozzi, 'Corte di giustizia, giudici nazionali e tutela dei principi fondamentali degli Stati membri' in *Il Diritto dell'Unione Europea* 3/2012, at pp 573–75 (at fns 26 and 29).

B

Balancing Fundamental Rights in EU Law

JUDGE ALLAN ROSAS

Abstract

It appears more and more often that cases brought before the European Court of Justice raise issues relating to two or more fundamental rights and the relation between them. In such situations, it is often necessary to establish a 'balance' between the fundamental rights concerned. In some cases, one of the rights involved is not a fundamental right in the strict sense but, for instance, an economic freedom (such as the free movement of goods) recognised under the basic EU Treaties. Another configuration may be a situation where, for instance, two of the fundamental rights which are at issue are to be found in the EU Charter of Fundamental Rights but only one of them appears in the European Convention on Human Rights. In such situations, one wonders what would be the relevance of Article 52(3) of the Charter of Fundamental Rights, which establishes a direct link between the Charter and the European Convention. The present contribution will look at the question of balancing of EU fundamental rights in general and also at more specific problems arising in this context, such as the two problems identified above.

I. INTRODUCTION

IT APPEARS MORE and more often that cases brought before the European Court of Justice raise issues relating to two or more fundamental rights and the relation between them. In such situations, it is often necessary to establish a 'balance' between the fundamental rights concerned. In some cases, one of the rights involved is not a fundamental right in the strict sense but, for instance, an economic freedom (such as the free movement of goods) recognised under the basic EU Treaties. Another configuration may be a situation where, for instance, two of the fundamental rights which are at issue are to be found in the EU Charter of Fundamental Rights but only one of them appears in the European Convention on Human Rights. In such situations, one wonders what would be the relevance of Article 52(3) of the Charter of Fundamental Rights, which establishes a direct link between the Charter and the European Convention. The present contribution will look at the question of balancing of EU fundamental rights in general and also at more specific problems arising in this context, such as the two problems identified above.

II. BALANCING (ECONOMIC) TREATY FREEDOMS AND FUNDAMENTAL RIGHTS

In *Schmidberger*, the European Court of Justice observed that the case raised the question of 'the need to reconcile the requirements of the protection of fundamental rights in the Union with those arising from a fundamental freedom enshrined in the Treaty'.[1] The fundamental rights in question were freedom of expression and freedom of assembly while the fundamental freedom referred to was the free movement of goods and thus a so-called economic freedom guaranteed by Union primary law. Concerning freedom of expression and freedom of assembly, the Court observed that they, unlike some other fundamental rights such as the right to life and the prohibition of torture and inhuman and degrading treatment, appeared not to be absolute but could, as recognised in paragraph 2 of Articles 10 and 11 of the European Convention on Human Rights, be subject to limitations. The Court added that in such circumstances, 'the interests involved must be weighed having regard to all the circumstances of the case in order to determine whether a fair balance was struck between those interests'.[2] The conclusion was that such a fair balance was indeed struck and that the fact that the Austrian authorities did not ban a demonstration which closed the Brenner motorway for a few days and thus restricted the free movement of goods between Austria, Germany and Italy was not incompatible with the then Articles 30 and 34 of the EC Treaty (now Articles 34 and 36 TFEU).

The *Schmidberger* case is a telling illustration of balancing, this time of balancing between a fundamental right and an economic freedom. The judgment has been criticised by some for having taken the free movement of goods as a point of departure, instead of basing the result squarely on freedom of expression and freedom of assembly. This criticism can be seen as part of a more general criticism levelled against the Court, especially in the past, for not taking fundamental rights seriously enough.[3] Without going into this debate in all its breadth, it should be noted that the approach taken in *Schmidberger*, which was a preliminary ruling case, has to be seen against the background of the questions posed by the national court.

[1] Case C-112/00 *Schmidberger* [2003] ECR I-5659, para 77.
[2] Ibid, para 81.
[3] See, eg A Rosas and L Armati, *EU Constitutional Law: An Introduction,* 2nd edn (Oxford, Hart Publishing, 2012) 55–59.

The Austrian judge was primarily interested in the question whether the restriction of the free movement of goods was compatible with Union law. That said, the Court in this case seems to have treated the two fundamental rights and the economic freedom concerned at the same level: the fundamental rights as general principles of Union law and the economic freedom as part of written primary law.[4] As both the fundamental rights and the economic freedom in question were not absolute but could be limited on certain grounds, a balance had to be struck.

A similar situation arose in *Omega*, with the difference that that case concerned the freedom to provide services under the then Article 49 of the EC Treaty (now Article 56 TFEU) and that the Court relied primarily on the right to human dignity as it was recognised under German constitutional law, accepting that this right could be invoked in the context of the derogation relating to public policy recognised in the EC Treaty, and hence that a local ban on a laser game with the object of firing on human targets could be justified on public policy grounds.[5]

In this context, mention can also be made of the case law of the Court of Justice on the right of a Member State to expel a Union citizen to another Member State. Here the issue may become one of balancing between the right of Union citizens to move and reside freely within the territory of the Member States (see Article 21 TFEU and Article 45 of the Charter of Fundamental Rights), the right to respect for private and family life (Article 7 of the Charter) and the right of a Member State to invoke grounds of public policy or public security as justification for an expulsion order.[6]

The so-called *Viking Line* case offers yet another example of a case where the European Court of Justice was faced with a tension between a fundamental right and an economic Treaty freedom.[7] The case concerned the compatibility with Union law of collective actions undertaken by a Finnish trade union and its international federation to prevent the re-flagging of a vessel from Finland to Estonia. After having established that the right to take collective action, including the right to strike, is a fundamental right forming an integral part of the general principles of Union law (see also 28 of the EU Charter of Fundamental Rights, which existed as a 'soft

[4] A Rosas, 'Fundamental Rights in the Luxembourg and Strasbourg Courts' in C Baudenbacher, P Tresselt and T Örlygsson (eds), *The EFTA Court: Ten Years On* (Oxford, Hart Publishing, 2005) 163, at 167–68.

[5] Case C-36/02 *Omega* [2004] ECR I-9609.

[6] See Arts 27 and 28 of Directive 2004/38/EC of the European Parliament and of the Council of 29 April 2004 on the right of citizens of the Union and their family members to move and reside freely within the territory of the Member States, [2004] OJ L158/77, and *corrigenda* [2004] OJ L229/35 and [2005] OJ L197/34. For an example from case law see Case C-145/09 *Tsakouridis* [2010] ECR I-11979.

[7] Case C-438/05 *The International Transport Workers' Federation and The Finnish Seamen's Union* [2007] ECR I-10779.

law' instrument at the time of the *Viking Line* judgment[8]), the Court, citing *Schmidberger* and *Omega*, went on to observe that the exercise of this fundamental right had to be 'reconciled' with the right of establishment.

The Court noted in this context that the right to collective action can be subject to restrictions and cited both Article 28 of the Charter, which provides that this right is to be protected 'in accordance with Union law and national laws and practices', and Finnish national law which also allowed for restrictions.[9] The Court recognised that restrictions on the right of establishment could be justified on the basis of the right to take collective action for the protection of workers, observing, inter alia, that the Union has 'not only an economic but also a social purpose'.[10] The Court added, however, that such restrictions could only be justified if the collective action to stop the re-flagging pursued the objective of the protection of workers and respected the principle of proportionality. *Viking Line* is also an example of a case where the task of determining whether the collective action had such an objective and whether the principle of proportionality was respected fell to a large extent on the shoulders of the national court (the Court of Appeal in England and Wales).

One can of course ask whether, and to what extent, fundamental rights and provisions of the Treaties which do not express fundamental rights should be seen as equal bedfellows. Subsequent case law—I am thinking of the famous *Kadi* case in particular[11]—and the entry into force of the EU Charter of Fundamental Rights (as part of the entry into force of the Treaty of Lisbon, on 1 December 2009) can be seen as part of a trend suggesting that at least some fundamental rights have special importance. In other words they should be given more weight than Treaty provisions which are not expressing fundamental rights. The judgment in *Kadi* and earlier case law even suggest that the basic values expressed in Article 2 of the TEU—which lists among those values respect for human dignity, freedom, democracy, equality, the rule of law and respect for human rights—prevail over the other, or at least some of the other, parts of the Treaties.[12] If that is so, conflicts or tensions between these basic values and Treaty provisions should be addressed in the context of norm hierarchy and *lex superior—lex inferior* considerations rather than as part of a balancing act. Apart from

[8] The Charter was proclaimed by the European Parliament, the Council and the Commission in December 2000, [2000] OJ C364/1. Art 6(1) of the Treaty on European Union (TEU), as amended by the Treaty of Lisbon, has made a slightly modified version of the Charter a binding part of primary law.

[9] Case C-438/05 *The International Transport Workers' Federation and The Finnish Seamen's Union*, n 7 above, paras 44-46.

[10] Ibid, para 77.

[11] Joined Cases C-402/05 P and C-415/05 P *Kadi and Al Barakaat International Foundation v Council and Commission* [2008] ECR I-6351.

[12] Rosas and Armati, n 3 above, 54–55.

such fundamental values—to cite *Kadi*, the 'very foundations of the [Union] legal order'[13]—fundamental rights should, in principle, be seen as part of primary law alongside the economic freedoms and other provisions of the Treaties. That said, fundamental rights may, because of their very nature, at least in some instances be held to be given somewhat more weight when striking a balance between them and other rules of primary law.[14]

III. BALANCING COMPETING FUNDAMENTAL RIGHTS

As far as such balancing is concerned, it is a question of reconciling fundamental rights not only with Treaty provisions, including those concerning the economic freedoms, but also with other fundamental rights. It is obvious that human rights—and if we speak of EU constitutional principles, fundamental rights—have often to be balanced against each other. Examples include the right to private and family life (Article 7 of the Charter) and the protection of personal data (Article 8), on the one hand, and freedom of expression (Article 11), on the other, and the right to private and family life and the protection of personal data, on the one hand, and the rights to good administration (Article 41) and of access to documents (Article 42), on the other. Another example could be the right to the integrity of the person (Article 3) and the right to liberty (Article 6), on the one hand, and the right of children to protection and care and the obligation of public authorities and private institutions to make the 'child's best interest' a 'primary consideration' (Article 24) on the other. As to the right to property (Article 17), tensions often arise between this right and other fundamental rights, such as workers' rights (Articles 27 to 31) and the principle of environmental protection (Article 37).[15]

These examples are not of academic interest only. Let us consider, for instance, the joined cases of *Volker und Markus Schecke and Eifert* which concerned the validity of a Union legislative act which required the publication of the names of the beneficiaries of agricultural aid and the amounts received by each beneficiary.[16] The cases raised the question of the relationship between the right to the protection of personal data (Article 8 of the Charter), which the Court noted was closely connected to the right

[13] Joined Cases C-402/05 P and C-415/05 P *Kadi and Al Barakaat International Foundation v Council and Commission*, n 11 above, para 304.

[14] Rosas and Armati, n 3 above, 55, with references to divergent opinions put forward in the literature.

[15] On the relation between property rights and other human rights see, eg A Rosas, 'Property Rights' in A Rosas and J Helgesen (eds), *The Strength of Diversity: Human Rights and Pluralist Democracy* (Dordrecht, Martinus Nijhoff Publishers, 1992) 133.

[16] Joined Cases C-92/09 and C-93/09 *Volker und Markus Schecke and Eifert* [2010] ECR I-11063.

to respect of private life (Article 7), on the one hand, and the principle of transparency on the other.

While in *Volker und Markus Schecke and Eifert* the Court did not cite the principle of transparency as a fundamental right *stricto sensu* but referred to Articles 1 and 10 of the TEU and Article 15 of the Treaty on the Functioning of the European Union (TFEU), it is obvious that the principle is of relevance for the basic values and fundamental rights referred to in Articles 2 and 6 of the TEU as well as in the Charter of Fundamental Rights, including not only fundamental rights in the strict sense but also the principles of democracy[17] and the rule of law. The Court observed that the protection of personal data is not an absolute right but must be considered in relation to its function in society[18] and that it was necessary to determine whether the Union institutions 'balanced' the interest in guaranteeing the transparency of its acts and ensuring the best use of public funds, against the interference with the right of the beneficiaries concerned to respect for their private life in general and to the protection of their personal data in particular.[19] As the institutions, as far as the publication of the names of natural persons was concerned, had not 'properly balanced' the interests involved, the legislative act was held to be invalid to this extent. On the other hand, with respect to the publication of data relating to legal persons, a 'fair balance' had been observed in the consideration taken of the respective interests at issue.[20]

Questions relating to the custody and protection of children offer another example where two or more fundamental rights may have to be balanced against each other. If the measures taken to protect the life and well-being of a child involve deprivation of his or her liberty there may be a tension between the right to liberty and security of all persons, including children (Article 6 of the Charter of Fundamental Rights) and the right of the child to protection and care, taking into account the child's best interests (Article 24 of the Charter).

In *Health Service Executive*, the Court of Justice, when assessing the procedural requirements for enforcing a decision to place a child (in this case of 17 years of age) in a secure care institution of another Member State, took into account the fact that the placement decision, taken in the interests of the child, was opposed by the child herself and thus concerned

[17] See, eg Joined Cases C-39/05 P and C-52/05 P *Sweden and Turco v Council* [2008] ECR I-4723, paras 34 and 46; Case C-28/08 P *Commission v Bavarian Lager* [2010] ECR I-6055, para 54; Joined Cases C-92/09 and C-93/09 *Volker und Markus Schecke and Eifert*, n 16 above, para 68.

[18] Joined Cases C-92/09 and C-93/09 *Volker und Markus Schecke and Eifert*, n 16 above, para 48.

[19] Ibid, para 77. See also paras 83 and 85–86.

[20] Ibid, paras 86 and 88.

her fundamental right to liberty as recognised in Article 6 of the Charter.[21] The Court concluded that in order to ensure that the system intended by the so-called Brussels II bis Regulation[22] operates properly, the use of coercion against a child in order to implement a judgment of a court of a Member State ordering her placement in a secure care institution in another Member State presupposes that the judgment has been declared to be enforceable in the latter state.[23]

A similar situation involving a possible tension between liberty and protection can be seen, for instance, in the actions to combat terrorism by imposing sanctions against suspected terrorists. In this case, however, the interest to protect concerns the population at large rather than the individual whose libertarian rights are restricted. Before the EU Courts, this constellation has concerned above all economic and financial sanctions taken by the EU legislator against persons and entities associated with terrorist activities.[24] The Courts have endeavoured to strike a balance between the right to effective judicial protection (including the right of defence) and the right to respect for property, on the one hand, and safety and security concerns, on the other.[25] It should be underlined, however, that the need to ensure safety and security and thus the effectiveness of sanctions has not been formulated in terms of fundamental rights as such, despite the fact that Article 6 of the Charter of Fundamental Rights provides for the right to not only liberty but also 'security' of person.[26] However, in the recent case of *Digital Rights Ireland*, the Court, in the context of the right to privacy and data protection observed that account must also be taken of the fact that the fight against terrorism constitutes an objective of general interest and that Article 6 of the Charter of Fundamental Rights lays down the right 'not only to liberty, but also to security'.[27]

[21] Case C-92/12 PPU *Health Service Executive v* [2012] ECR I-255.

[22] Regulation (EC) No 2201/2003 of 27 November 2003 concerning jurisdiction and the recognition and enforcement of judgments in matrimonial matters and the matters of parental responsibility, repealing Regulation (EC) No 1347/2000, [2003] OJ L338/1.

[23] Case C-92/12 PPU *Health Service Executive*, n 21 above, para 113.

[24] See, generally A Rosas, 'Counter-Terrorism and the Rule of Law: Issues of Judicial Control' in AM Salinas de Frías, KLH Samuel and ND White (eds), *Counter-Terrorism: International Law and Practice* (Oxford, Oxford University Press, 2012) 83.

[25] See, eg Joined Cases C-402/05 P and C-415/05 P *Kadi and Al Barakaat International Foundation v Council and Commission*, n 11 above, para 342; Case C-27/09 P *France v People's Mojahedin Organization of Iran* [2011] ECR I-853, para 67.

[26] Cf the case law relating to Art 9 of the International Covenant on Civil and Political Rights, M Nowak, *U.N. Covenant on Civil and Political Rights: CCPR Commentary*, 2nd revised edn (Kehl, NP Engel Publisher, 2005) 213–15. In *Delgado Paéz v Colombia*, No 195/1985, Decision of 12 July 1990, the UN Human Rights Committee held that, in order to ensure the right to security of person, states have a duty to take reasonable and appropriate measures to protect all persons under their jurisdiction.

[27] Joined Cases C-293/12 and C-594/12 *Digital Rights Ireland and Seitlinger and others*, judgment of 8 April 2014, para 42.

IV. BALANCING RIGHTS FROM DIFFERENT LEGAL INSTRUMENTS

In the *Volker und Markus Schecke and Eifert* case referred to above, the balancing which had to be performed concerned the right to privacy and the principle of transparency. While the latter principle is not formulated as a distinct human right in the Charter of Human Rights, it is, apart from being recognised in the TEU and TFEU, closely linked to fundamental rights which do appear in the Charter, such as the right to good administration recognised under Article 41 and the right of access to documents recognised under Article 42. It should be noted that the latter rights are not explicitly recognised under the European Convention on Human Rights. Such a situation—namely, that a fundamental right appears in both the EU Charter and the European Convention whereas another fundamental right is to be found in the Charter only—raises interesting questions as to the relationship between the two instruments.

It is easy to envisage cases which concern the relationship between the right to privacy and the right of access to documents, in other words a fundamental right which appears in both the Charter and the European Convention and another right which appears only in the Charter. The case of *Bavarian Lager* concerned the right of access to documents but in a situation which also affected the right to privacy and the right to the protection of personal data (Article 8 of the Charter)[28] in particular.[29] The Court of Justice referred to the 'equilibrium' which the Union legislator had intended to establish, and accepted the Commission's refusal to give access to certain documents as the applicant had not been able to demonstrate the necessity for certain personal data to be transferred and the Commission thus had 'not been able to weigh up the various interests of the parties concerned'.[30] In this case, however, there was no explicit consideration of the European Convention and, in fact, not of the Charter either, and the arguments of the parties and the reasoning of the Court centred on the relationship between two legislative acts, a regulation on the protection of personal data and one on access to documents.[31] These Regulations had been adopted before the

[28] In the European Convention on Human Rights, the right to the protection of personal data is ensured in the context of the right to respect for 'private life': see, eg P van Dijk et al (eds), *Theory and Practice of the European Convention on Human Rights*, 4th edn (Antwerp, Intersentia, 2006) 666 et seq.

[29] Case C-28/08 P *Commission v Bavarian Lager*, n 17 above.

[30] Ibid, para 78.

[31] Regulation (EC) No 45/2001 of the European Parliament and of the Council of 18 December 2000 on the protection of individuals with regard to the processing of personal data by the Community institutions and bodies and on the free movement of such data, [2001] OJ L8/1; Regulation (EC) No 1049/2001 of the European Parliament and of the Council of 30 May 2001 regarding public access to European Parliament, Council and Commission documents, [2001] L145/43.

proclamation of the Charter of Fundamental Rights as a soft law instrument and the facts of the case, an action of annulment on appeal before the Court of Justice, related to a period preceding the entry into force of the Charter as part of binding primary law.

Such cases could, of course, raise balancing questions more directly and concretely related to the relationship between the EU Charter and the European Convention. I am thinking, in particular, of Article 52(3) of the Charter, which provides that Charter rights which 'correspond' to rights guaranteed under the European Convention should be given 'the same' meaning and scope as the corresponding Convention rights.[32] At least in theory, one could imagine that the application of a particular human right, recognised under the European Convention, should, if viewed in isolation, imply a higher level of protection than the application of the same right when balanced against another right recognised under the EU Charter but not under the European Convention. Could this lead to an EU level of protection which would be less than the one guaranteed under the European Convention and would such a situation cause a problem in view of Article 52(3) of the Charter?

The problem seems more academic than real. First of all, under EU law the problem could be minimised by giving the fundamental right which corresponds to a right guaranteed by the European Convention somewhat more weight than a another fundamental right which is not be found as such in the Convention. Secondly, it should be recalled that all other than the non-derogable or absolute rights of the European Convention are subject to derogations, restrictions or limitations on various grounds, such as public safety or the protection of health.[33] Moreover, the European Court of Human Rights has developed a 'margin of appreciation' doctrine which recognises a certain national discretion in balancing the Convention rights against other interests.[34] Thus, what in the context of the EU Charter could be considered as a balancing between two fundamental rights, would be regarded as a similar balancing act in the Strasbourg system between a human right and a ground for restriction and/or the margin of appreciation recognised under the Human Rights Convention.

When, in the context of the EU legal order, judges are faced with the need for balancing between fundamental rights and other rights and freedoms protected by primary law, or between two or more fundamental rights, it

[32] See, eg Case C-400/10 PPU *McB*, judgment of 5 October 2010, [2010] ECR I-8965, para 53. See also A Rosas and H Kaila, 'L'application de la Charte des droits fondamentaux de l'Union européenne par la Cour de justice: Un premier bilan' (2011) XVI *Il Diritto dell'Unione Europea* 1, at 22–23; S Peers et al (eds), *The EU Chapter of Fundamental Rights: A Commentary* (Oxford, Hart Publishing, 2014) 1490–1503.

[33] See van Dijk et al, n 27 above, 333 et seq.

[34] See, eg HC Yourow, *The Margin of Appreciation Doctrine in the Dynamics of European Human Rights Jurisprudence* (The Hague, Martinus Nijhoff Publishers, 1996).

can be asked if there are some general criteria or signposts to guide them in their task. The answer is that it is extremely difficult, if not impossible, to lay down any clear rules in this regard. What can be done is to list some considerations which may play a role in arriving at a solution in concrete cases. The following considerations and questions may be mentioned:

- Can it be held that at least one of the fundamental rights concerned is of a 'more fundamental' nature than another fundamental right, eg if, under international human rights instruments, the former is to be seen as a non-derogable (absolute) right (such as the prohibition of torture and inhuman and degrading treatment, mentioned as an example in *Schmidberger*[35])?
- The first consideration is obviously also related to the wording and context of the fundamental rights provision in question; does the provision, for instance, provide that someone has a right 'in accordance with national laws and practices'[36] (which would suggest a wider margin of appreciation for the Member States)?
- Is there EU secondary law which can be seen as an implementation of a fundamental right and is there more far-reaching or specific legislation relating to a certain right as compared to another? Sometimes the case will be in the first place about comparing two or more legislative acts while the interpretation of the fundamental right(s) in question is of secondary importance or becomes a mere background factor.[37]
- If the balancing takes place between a fundamental right and a Treaty provision which is not recognised as expressing a fundamental right it may well be that, at least as far as some fundamental rights are concerned, they are given somewhat more weight than the relevant Treaty provision ('fundamental rights-friendly' interpretation).[38]
- Much will of course also depend on the facts of the case and its more general legal and factual context.
- If one of the EU fundamental rights corresponds to a right guaranteed by the European Convention on Human Rights, Article 52(3) of the EU Charter, as noted above, provides that the EU fundamental rights shall be given the same meaning and scope as the corresponding right guaranteed under the Convention; this may in some instances speak in favour of giving the Convention right somewhat more weight than another right not to be found as such in the Convention (although, as was explained above, this does not

[35] See at n 1 above.

[36] For an example see Art 28 of the Charter of Fundamental Rights relating to the right of collective bargaining and action and Case C-438/05 *International Transport Workers' Federation and Finnish Seamen's Union*, n 7 above, para 44.

[37] See notably Case C-28/08 P *Commission v Bavarian Lager*, n 17 above.

[38] See at n 14 above.

preclude some balancing between the two rights in the EU system and a corresponding balancing between a right and a limitation or restriction allowed under the Convention system).

V. THE EU CHARTER AND THE EUROPEAN CONVENTION ON HUMAN RIGHTS

Finally, some attention should be paid to the relation between the EU Charter and the European Convention on Human Rights more generally. Up till now, 'harmony rather than conflict' has characterised the case law of the Court of Justice and the European Court of Human rights, respectively.[39] That said, tensions between EU law and the European Convention as interpreted by the European Court of Human Rights cannot be excluded.

Apart from the specific question of balancing two or more rights recognised under the EU Charter when only one of them appears in the European Convention, to which reference was already made above, a more general problem relating to the specific characteristics of the EU and its legal order should be mentioned: The EU is not an intergovernmental organisation comparable to the United Nations or the Council of Europe but a 'federative' union of states and peoples which has the competence to enact directly applicable rules for the whole Union territory (leaving aside here various 'opt-outs' granted some Member States[40]), which in many cases imply a breaking down of borders between the Member States. The most well-known examples are the regimes relating to the internal market (which according to Article 26(2) TFEU is an 'area without internal frontiers in which the free movement of goods, persons, services and capital is ensured') and the Schengen area of freedom, security and justice (which according to Article 3(2) TEU is an 'area without internal frontiers, in which the free movement of persons is ensured in conjunction with appropriate measures with respect to external border controls, asylum, immigration and the prevention and combating of crime').

To be somewhat more concrete, EU law in these areas is to a large extent based on the principle of mutual recognition, which again is based on the assumption of mutual trust between the Member States. Thus, legislation relating to, say, the recognition of diploma, the European arrest warrant, the recognition and enforcement of judgments and the determination of the Member State responsible for examining an asylum application, is based on the idea that a Member State may have to recognise and enforce acts adopted by the courts or authorities of another Member State almost as if they had emanated from itself. Thus, a European arrest warrant has to

[39] Rosas, n 4 above.

[40] See Rosas and Armati, n 3 above, 97–110.

be enforced in another Member State unless the applicable secondary law provides for a specific ground of refusal.[41] In such situations, tensions and even conflict may well arise between EU law and the Strasbourg system. Although this problem does not strictly speaking concern the balancing of two or more fundamental rights recognised under EU law, it will be briefly considered in the following, given its obvious relevance for the question of how EU law relates to the human rights regime established under the European Convention on Human Rights. It is a question of reconciling two different legal regimes rather than of balancing two specific human or fundamental rights.

To take an example, in *NS and ME*, the Court was faced with the question of whether, under the so-called Dublin Regulation,[42] asylum seekers whose asylum application should have been examined in Greece but who had managed to enter Ireland or the United Kingdom could be sent back to Greece, despite the serious deficiencies in the asylum procedure and in the reception conditions allegedly existing in that Member State.[43] The Court held that, while under the Dublin Regulation another Member State had the right but not the obligation to transfer an asylum seeker to Greece, such a transfer could not take place if the national court deciding on the matter came to the conclusion that 'systemic deficiencies in the asylum procedure and in the reception conditions … amount to substantial grounds for believing that the asylum seeker would face a real risk of being subjected to inhuman *or* degrading treatment' in Greece.[44] This approach was in line with what the European Court of Human Rights had decided earlier the same year, in a case relating to Belgium cited by the Court of Justice in its judgment.[45]

But what if in another case, the European Court of Human Rights came to the conclusion that even a less systemic problem in an EU Member State should have led another Member State to refuse transfer? Given the threshold established by the Court of Justice for an obligation not to transfer, such decisions emanating from Strasbourg could pose a serious problem for the functioning of the EU area of freedom, security and justice, based on mutual recognition and trust and the porosity of its internal borders. EU Member States are presumed to comply with the rules, and even if they do not, other Member States are not, as a general rule, empowered to stop

[41] Council Framework Decision 2002/584/JHA of 13 June 2002 on the European arrest warrant and the surrender procedures between Member States, [2002] OJ L190/1 and Case C-399/11 *Melloui*, judgment of 26 February 2013.

[42] Council Regulation (EC) No 343/2003 of 18 February 2003 establishing the criteria and mechanisms for determining the Member State responsible for examining an asylum application lodged in one of the Member States by a third-country national, [2003] OJ L50/1.

[43] Joined Cases C-411/10 and C-493/10 *NS and ME and Others*, [2011] ECR I-865.

[44] Ibid, para 94.

[45] Ibid, para 88. See *MSS v Belgium and Greece*, ECtHR, Application No 30696/09, judgment of 21 January 2011.

abiding by the rules on the sole basis that another Member State is, in its view, failing in that respect.

A further example may serve to illustrate the point: In a recent case, the European Court of Human Rights held that an Italian court order for the return of a child wrongfully removed to Latvia amounted to a violation of Article 8 of the European Convention (respect for family life).[46] The Human Rights Court did mention the Brussels II bis Regulation of the EU[47] but seemed to pay more attention to the Hague Convention on the Civil Aspects of International Child Abduction and held that '[a] child's return cannot be ordered automatically or mechanically when the Hague Convention is applicable'.[48] Under EU law, on the other hand, the Regulation prevails over the Hague Convention[49] and there is by now fairly extensive case law of the Court of Justice on the return of wrongfully removed children which accepts practically no discretion for the courts and authorities of an EU Member State when they are asked to enforce court orders emanating from other Member States for the immediate return of the child.[50] The problem seems to have been eliminated, or at least mitigated, by the more recent judgment of the Strasbourg Court in *Povse*.[51] In this judgment, due regard is paid to the EU Brussels II bis Regulation and its requirement of a speedy return of a child unlawfully abducted.

The main problem in such situations is that for the European Court of Human Rights, EU Member States are like other Contracting Parties to the Convention, whereas for the EU legal order, and the Court of Justice as its constitutional watchdog, there is a marked difference between the internal and the external. For the Human Rights Court, Russia, Belgium and Luxembourg are all Contracting Parties with equal rights and obligations, whereas for the EU legal order Russia is a third state while Belgium and Luxembourg are integrated parts of a constitutional system.

True, the *Bosphorus* case law of the European Court of Human Rights establishes a presumption of legality if an EU Member State has simply applied EU law without being able to use any discretion.[52] This case law is based on the consideration that the EU is not a Contracting Party to the

[46] *Šneersone and Kampanella v Italy*, ECtHR, Application No 14737/09, judgment of 12 July 2011.
[47] Regulation 2201/2003, n 22 above.
[48] *Šneersone and Kampanella*, n 45 above, para 85(vi).
[49] See Art 60 of the Regulation, n 22 above.
[50] See, eg Case C-195/08 PPU *Rinau* [2008] ECR I-5271; Case C-403/09 PPU *Deticek* [2009] ECR I-12193; Case C-211/10 PPU *Povse* [2010] ECR I-6673; Case C-296/10 *Purrucker II* [2010] ECR I-11163.
[51] *Povse v Austria*; ECtHR, Application No 3890/11, Judgment of 18 June 2013.
[52] *Bosphorus Hava Yollari Turizm ve Ticaret Anonim Sirketi v Ireland*, ECtHR, Application No 45036/98, judgment of 30 June 2005. See also *Cooperatieve Producentenorganisatie van de Nederlandse Kokkelvisserij UA v The Netherlands*, ECtHR, Application No 13645/05, Decision of 20 January 2009.

European Convention on Human Rights, while a Member State may be obliged by Union law to apply Union law directly (even if it has not voted in favour or otherwise contributed to its adoption). In the case first relating to the return of a wrongfully removed child referred to above (*Šneersone and Kampanella*) the European Court of Human Rights does not seem to have taken into account the fact that Italy was merely applying the Brussels II bis Regulation and notably the special procedures provided under that Regulation for the return of wrongfully removed children[53] and thus did not consider the case under the *Bosphorus* doctrine.

Especially if the situation—including after an eventual accession of the EU to the European Convention[54]—is considered not to fall under the *Bosphorus* doctrine there is an obvious risk that Strasbourg case law could (at least indirectly) interfere with EU rules based on mutual recognition and trust in an internal market and an area of freedom, security and justice 'without internal frontiers'. Or could a possible future accession of the EU to the European Convention lead the European Court of Human Rights to recognise that the new Contracting Party (the EU) should in these matters be seen as a whole, in the same way as the existing Contracting Parties? This would mean the application of a sort of disconnection clause, implying that for certain matters the internal EU relations would not be seen in the same light as the relations between the EU and third countries? Or could it even be possible to insert in the draft accession agreement still under discussion such a disconnection clause, as used from the context of mixed agreements (agreements to which both the EU and some or all of its Member States are parties[55])?

These are questions which cannot receive a definitive answer for the time being and which, at any rate, go beyond the question of balancing EU fundamental rights, which has been the main subject of this modest contribution.

[53] See Arts 40, 42–45 of the Regulation, n 22 above.

[54] See Arts 6(2) TEU, Art 218(8) TFEU and Protocol No 8 annexed to the TEU and the TFEU and relating to Art 6(2) of the Treaty on European Union on the accession of the Union to the European Convention on the Protection of Human Rights and Fundamental Freedoms. In 2013, the negotiations between the European Commission and the Member States of the Council of Europe (including the EU Member States) produced a draft accession agreement but the compatibility of this draft with Union law is presently being considered by the European Court of Justice, in the context of the Commission's request 4 July 2013 for an Opinion.

[55] See, eg M Cremona, 'Disconnection clauses in EU Law and Practice' in C Hillion and P Koutrakos (eds), *Mixed Agreements Revisited: The EU and Its Member States in the World* (Oxford, Hart Publishing, 2010) 160.

C

Fundamental Rights, General Principles of EU Law, and the Charter

TAKIS TRIDIMAS[1]

Abstract

The purpose of this chapter is to explore selected aspects of the relationship between the general principles of EU law and the Charter of Fundamental Rights of the European Union. The chapter first looks at the expansion of fundamental rights in EU law and the importance of general principles by reference to three principles which have provided fruitful grounds for judicial activism: the right to judicial protection, the principle of non-discrimination, and the right to personal data. It then examines the sources of fundamental rights under Article 6 TEU and the relationship between Charter rights and general principles. Finally, it explores a pivotal issue in EU constitutional discourse, namely, the scope of application of the Charter and the general principles of law. The chapter concludes by observing that, far from declining in importance, the general principles of law continue to be an integral part of judicial methodology; that, following the introduction of the Charter, the CJEU applies a heightened level of judicial scrutiny; and that it favours a centralised approach opting for an autonomous interpretation of the Charter, granting it precedence over national constitutional norms, and understanding broadly its scope of application.

I. INTRODUCTION

THE PURPOSE OF this chapter is to explore selected aspects of the relationship between the general principles of EU law and the Charter of Fundamental Rights of the European Union. The chapter first looks at the expansion of fundamental rights in EU law and the importance of general principles by reference to three principles which, in

[1] This chapter is based on the Lasok Lecture 2014, given by the author at the University of Exeter on 6 March 2014.

recent years, have provided fruitful grounds for judicial activism: the right to judicial protection, the principle of non-discrimination, and the right to protection of personal data. It then examines the sources of fundamental rights under Article 6 TEU and the relationship between Charter rights and general principles. Finally, it explores a pivotal issue in EU constitutional discourse, namely, the scope of application of the Charter and the general principles of law. The chapter concludes by observing that, far from declining in importance, the general principles of law continue to be an integral part of judicial methodology; that, following the introduction of the Charter, the ECJ applies a heightened level of judicial scrutiny; and that it favours a centralised approach opting for an autonomous interpretation of the Charter, granting it precedence over national constitutional norms, and interpreting broadly its scope of application.

II. THE EXPANSION OF FUNDAMENTAL RIGHTS PROTECTION IN EU LAW

The development of fundamental rights protection in EU law has been first and foremost the product of case law. The Court's unwavering, intense commitment to the language of rights goes to the genes of European integration. Commitment to fundamental rights was seen, already at an early stage, as a force of legitimacy. It was the quid pro quo for recognising the primacy of EU law over the national constitutions.[2]

One of the most remarkable developments since the 2000s has been the expansion and deepening of the ECJ's jurisdiction on the protection of fundamental rights. Such expansion and deepening has occurred, among others, in the following ways. First, it has taken place through a broad interpretation of free movement. Since a national restriction on freedom of movement cannot be justified under the Treaties unless it respects fundamental rights, it follows that the broader the interpretation of free movement, the broader the jurisdiction of the ECJ to apply EU fundamental rights. *Carpenter*[3] and the iconoclastic judgment in *Karner*[4] provide examples of free movement and fundamental rights functioning as converging forces of integration. Secondly, the ECJ has held that fundamental rights, being an integral part of the founding treaties, can be used to mitigate rights emanating from free movement. In contrast to the first situation described

[2] See Case 11/70 *Internationale Handelsgesellschaft mbH v Einfuhr- und Vorratsstelle für Getreide und Futtermittel* [1970] ECR 1125.

[3] Case C-60/00 *Carpenter v Secretary of State for the Home Department* [2002] ECR I-6279. But see for a somewhat narrow understanding of that case: Case C-457/12 *S v Minister voor Immigratie, Integratie en Asiel,* judgment of 12 March 2014.

[4] Case C-71/02 *Herbert Karner Industrie-Auktionen GmbH v Troostwijk GmbH* [2004] ECR I-3025.

above, fundamental rights operate here as centrifugal forces. *Schmidberger*[5] and *Omega*[6] embrace the national constitutional traditions and endorse an integration model based on value diversity. The Court views national constitutional standards not as being in a competitive relationship with the economic objectives of the Union but as forming part of its polity.

Thirdly, the ECJ has deepened its jurisdiction through the increasing use of the 'outcome' approach in preliminary references. Under that approach, the ECJ reaches a conclusive result as to whether a national measure complies with EU fundamental rights, leaving no discretion to the referring court as to how to apply its ruling. This way, it provides leadership specifying a normative outcome rather than offering guidance to the national court.[7]

Finally, the Court's jurisdiction on fundamental rights has been enhanced by the Charter which, since the entry into force of the Treaty of Lisbon, has become binding. The Charter is intended to reaffirm and strengthen fundamental rights by making them more visible.[8] There is no doubt that it has increased their resonance. Since the entry into force of the Lisbon Treaty, litigation on fundamental rights has increased and the most prominent judgments delivered by the Court tend to involve such rights rather than matters of classic economic integration.

The ECJ's presence in the field of fundamental rights protection can be aptly illustrated by reference to three areas, namely the right to judicial protection, the principle of equal treatment, and the right to family life in conjunction with the right to the protection of personal data. Case law developments in those areas provide prominent examples of judicial activism and illustrate a double standard of judicial review. Whilst the ECJ is soft in reviewing the competence of the EU *ratione materiae*,[9] it is much harder in reviewing compatibility of its actions with fundamental rights.

[5] Case C-112/00 *Eugen Schmidberger, Internationale Transport und Planzüge v Austria* [2003] ECR I-5659.

[6] Case C-36/02 *Omega Spielhallen- und Automatenaufstellungs-GmbH v Oberbürgermeisterin der Bundesstadt Bonn* [2004] ECR I-9609. See also Case C-244/06 *Dynamic Medien Vertriebs GmbH v Avides Media AG* [2008] ECR I-505.

[7] For examples, of outcome cases, see *Carpenter* (n 3 above), *Schmidberger* (n 5 above), *Omega* (n 6 above), and more recently Case C-544/10 *Deutsches Weintor eG v Land Rheinland-Pfalz*, judgment of 6 September 2012; Case C-283/11 *Sky Österreich GmbH v Österreichischer Rundfunk*, judgment of 22 January 2013. In some cases, the ECJ will provide the referring court with a strong presumption leaving it to make the final determination: see eg Case C-131/12 *Google Spain SL v Agencia Española de Protección de Datos (AEPD)*, judgment of 13 May 2014, nyr, discussed below at n 65. For a detailed discussion of the 'outcome' and other approaches followed by the Court, see T Tridimas, 'Constitutional Review of Member State action: The virtues and vices of an incomplete jurisdiction' (2011) 9 *International Journal of Constitutional Law* 737.

[8] See Preamble to the Charter, Recitals 4 and 5.

[9] This is so, for example, in relation to the interpretation of Art 114 TFEU. See eg Case C-380/03 *Germany v European Parliament and Council of the European Union* [2006] ECR I-11573 *(Second Tobacco Advertisement Directive case)*; Case C-210/03 *R (on the application of Swedish Match AB) v Secretary of State for Health* [2004] ECR I-11893; For a recent case

A. Judicial Protection

Although judicial protection lies at the heart of every system which abides by the rule of law, there are specific reasons which have granted it elevated status in EU law. Judicial protection is central to the integration through law paradigm. The transition of the European Communities from an international organisation to a new form of governance was effected through the dismantling of the nation state's monopoly in granting rights. *Van Gend en Loos*[10] signalled rights creation at supra-national level thus commencing a process towards the dispersal of political power and the strengthening of the role of the judiciary. But the granting of rights presupposes the recognition of the right to judicial protection which thus becomes the starting point of that process. Furthermore, the supremacy of EU norms cannot be asserted unless individuals have access to justice. Judicial protection is thus the gateway to primacy. Additionally, it serves as a source of legitimacy. It is the quid pro quo for transferring powers to the EU institutions. In doing so, it has helped to promote the autonomy of the EU legal order and enhance the power and the role of the Court of Justice.

The importance of the right to judicial protection can best be illustrated by reference to the *Kadi* cases which provide, perhaps, the most prominent illustrations of that right in the history of the Union. In *Kadi I*[11] the ECJ was concerned with the validity of EU regulations by which the Council implemented United Nations Security Council (UNSC) resolutions imposing economic sanctions on non-state actors associated with the Al Qaeda network. The names of the persons included in the sanctions list were determined by the UN Sanction Committee. Mr Kadi and the Al Barakaat International Foundation, who were among those persons, challenged the EU regulation freezing their assets. The ECJ held that measures adopted by the EU institutions to give effect to UNSC resolutions are subject to review on grounds of respect for fundamental rights as protected by EU law. Reversing the judgment of the Court of First Instance (now the General Court), the Court adopted a dualist approach holding that, whilst it does not have power to review the lawfulness of a UNSC resolution, it does have jurisdiction to review the compatibility of measures adopted by the EU institutions to implement it. Such review does not entail any challenge to the primacy of the UNSC resolution in international law.[12] The Court upheld

where the ECJ took a broad view of agency powers, see Case C-270/12 *United Kingdom v European Parliament and Council of the European Union (ESMA case)*, judgment of 22 January 2014.

[10] Case 26/62 *NV Algemene Transport- en Expeditie Onderneming van Gend en Loos v Netherlands Inland Revenue Administration* [1963] ECR 1.

[11] Joined Cases C-402/05 P and C-415/05 P *Kadi and Al Barakaat International Foundation v European Council and Commission* [2008] ECR I-6351.

[12] *Kadi I*, ibid, paras 287–88.

the paramount nature of fundamental rights recalling its judgment in *'Les Verts'* and reiterating that neither the Member States nor the EU institutions can avoid review of the conformity of their acts with the Treaties.[13] Thus, in the Court's rationale, the primacy of the UN Charter takes place only in the sphere of international law. It does not penetrate the constitutional space of the EU and, within that space it cannot take precedence over the general principles of law of which fundamental rights form part.[14] On that basis, the Court proceeded to annul Regulation (EC) 881/2002 by which the assets of the applicants had been frozen, on the ground that the applicants' right to a hearing, the right to judicial protection, and the right to property had been infringed. The applicants had not been informed of the evidence against them, no reasons had been given for the inclusion of their names in the sanctions list, and they had not been afforded any opportunity to put their case.[15]

The judgment of the ECJ in *Kadi I*[16] is of defining constitutional importance. The Court understood the EC Treaty (now the Treaty on the Functioning of the European Union) as establishing its own constitutional space, asserted the autonomy of EC law vis-à-vis international law, and held that responses to emergencies should be handled through, rather than outside the bounds of, the EU Treaties.

Although in *Kadi I* the ECJ established the paramount nature of fundamental rights, given the complete lack of engagement by the EU authorities with process rights, the judgment was concerned solely with constitutional principle. Once the Court decided that economic sanctions were reviewable despite their UN origins, it could only find a violation, since no reasons for the decision had been given and there was no attempt to respect the rights of defence. In *Kadi II*,[17] the focus shifted onto the task of balancing conflicting interests and the intensity of review.

Following *Kadi I*, the EU institutions decided to keep Mr Kadi's name in the sanctions list but provided him with a summary of the reasons justifying his inclusion. The summary had been made available by the UN Sanctions Committee. In *Kadi II*, Mr Kadi challenged his new inclusion in the list. In its judgment, the ECJ concretised the process requirements that the EU institutions must fulfil when listing a person pursuant to a decision of the UN Sanctions Committee, and provided guidelines regarding the scope and intensity of judicial review and the handling of sensitive evidence.

[13] Case 294/83 *Parti écologiste 'Les Verts' v European Parliament* [1986] ECR 1339, para 23; *Kadi*, n 11 above, para 281.

[14] *Kadi*, n 11 above, para 308.

[15] Ibid, paras 345 et seq.

[16] Above, n 11.

[17] Joined Cases C-584/10 P, C-593/10 P and C-595/10 P *Commission and Others v Kadi (Kadi II)*, judgment of 18 July 2013, nyr.

The Court held that the EU courts must ensure the full review of the lawfulness of economic sanctions in the light of fundamental rights. Full review means that the courts will examine whether the EU institutions have complied with process requirements which include the rights of defence, the right to effective judicial protection, and the obligation to state reasons.[18] It also means that jurisdiction is not limited to examining in the abstract the cogency of reasons but also verifying whether the decision is taken on a sufficiently solid factual basis and verifying the allegations made in the statement of reasons.[19] The right to judicial protection imposes here a series of positive duties and requires an administrative and also a judicial dialogue.[20] The Court may request the EU authority to produce information or evidence.[21] *Kadi II* laid down detailed guidelines on the evidence that must be provided. In general, a decision cannot be taken on the basis of undisclosable evidence. The Court accepted that, in exceptional circumstances, overriding public security reasons may preclude disclosure of the full evidence to the person concerned. In such cases, it is for the court to verify that such reasons indeed exist and, if they do, consider possibilities such as the disclosure of a summary to the person concerned. The bottom line is that it is for the EU courts to assess whether and to what the extent the failure to disclose confidential evidence to the person concerned, and his consequential inability to submit observations, is such as to affect its probative value.[22]

The Court found justification for full review in the severe impact of sanctions and the fact that there was little protection in any alternative forum. Despite their preventive nature, sanctions impact gravely on the individuals concerned because of their scope and duration. As Sedley LJ put it, listed persons become 'effectively prisoners of the state'.[23] They also produce adverse impact because of the public opprobrium that they provoke.[24] The Court also pointed out, as a secondary reason for full review, that the delisting procedures available at UN level did not guarantee effective judicial protection. In so ruling, it was assisted by the judgment of the Strasbourg Court in *Nada*.[25] In the circumstances, the Court examined each of the reasons stated in the summary of reasoning. It found that whilst some of them were vague and did not satisfy the requirement of reasoning, others were specific but were not supported by the evidence disclosed. It thus annulled the contested regulation.

18 *Kadi II*, paras 117–18.
19 *Kadi II*, para 119.
20 See, in particular, *Kadi II*, paras 113 et seq and 120–21.
21 *Kadi II*, para 120.
22 Paras 128–29.
23 *A, K, M, Q & G v HM Treasury* [2008] EWCA Civ 1187, at para 125, and *HM Treasury v Mohammed Jabar Ahmed and others* [FC] [2010] UKSC 2.
24 *Kadi II*, n 17 above, para 132.
25 *Nada v Switzerland*, Application No 10593/08, judgment of 12 September 2012, para 211.

The judgment indicates that the Court is prepared to scrutinise the evidence and allows little margin of error to the EU authorities. In effect, the ECJ understands full review as meaning that it must apply a high standard in scrutinising the statement of reasons and that it has jurisdiction to reconstruct the decision-making process. The ECJ articulated a more persuasive account of process rights than that envisaged by the General Court[26] and, in contrast to US courts,[27] followed a model of civil libertarianism by understanding the right to judicial protection as imposing positive duties and requiring an administrative and judicial dialogue.

B. Non-discrimination

The case law on equality suggests that the general principles of law are not merely methodological tools but incorporate substantive standards of justice. The ECJ understands non-discrimination as empowering it to supplement the legislative process. Suffice it here to illustrate the principle by reference to selected cases.

In *Mangold* the ECJ elevated the prohibition of discrimination on grounds of age to a general, unwritten, principle of EU law which transcends concrete legislative outcomes and is capable of applying in horizontal situations.[28] Although this is a bold and, essentially, welcome judgment, its reasoning was 'far from compelling'.[29] The Court cited as the sources of that general principle the international instruments listed in the preamble to the Framework Directive on Equality[30] and the constitutional traditions common to the Member States. This is, however, a creative reading of those sources. The preamble to the Framework Directive refers to a number of fundamental international conventions which pertain to the principle of equality before the law and the principle of equal treatment.[31] Only one of them makes express reference to age and this is only in a specific

[26] See the judgment at the first instance which was reversed by the ECJ: Case T-85/09, *Yassin Abdullah Kadi v European Commission (Kadi II)* [2010] ECR II-5177.

[27] See *Kadi v Geithner*, US District Court for the District of Columbia, judgment of 19 March 2012.

[28] Case C-144/04 *Werner Mangold v Rüdiger Helm* [2005] ECR I-9981.

[29] See Opinion of Mazák AG in Case C-411/05 *Palacios de la Villa v Cortefiel Servicios SA* [2007] ECR I-8531, para 94 and see the criticism by Herdegen, 'General Principles of EU Law—The Methodological Challenge' in Bernitz, Nergelius, and Cardner (eds), *General Principles of EU Law in a Process of Development* (London, Kluwer Law International, 2008) 343–55.

[30] Council Directive 2000/78/EC of 7 November 2000 establishing a general framework for equal treatment in employment and occupation, [2000] OJ L303/16.

[31] Recital 4 refers to the Universal Declaration of Human Rights, the United Nations Convention on the Elimination of All Forms of Discrimination against Women, the United Nations Covenants on Civil and Political Rights and on Economic, Social and Cultural Rights, the European Convention for the Protection of Human Rights and Fundamental Freedoms, and ILO Convention No 111, which prohibits discrimination in the field of employment and occupation.

context.[32] The reference to the common constitutional traditions of the Member States appears unsubstantiated, since it is not backed by any comparative analysis of national laws or case law. In fact, the constitutions of only two Member States recognised the principle at the time of the judgment.[33] A further problem with the Court's reasoning is that the relationship between the prohibition of discrimination as a general principle of law and the Framework Directive remains unclear. Prima facie, there is an oxymoron: If the prohibition of discrimination on grounds of age is a general principle of EU law, Mr Mangold could have relied on it even in the absence of the Framework Directive. In fact, Advocate General Tizzano was not averse to that argument. The Court however went to lengths to discuss the Directive and delved into its effects before the period for its implementation had expired. The role of the Framework Directive in activating the dormant general principle of non-discrimination on grounds of age is normatively unclear and methodologically unsound. The Court treated the content of the general principle as co-terminous with the provisions of the Framework Directive. This creates a temptation to elevate a rule contained in a directive to a general principle of law and attribute to it a specific content with the benefit of hindsight, ie in the light of the provisions of the directive. There is, thus, a risk that provisions of directives would be interpreted as illustrations of pre-existing general principles and attributed the status of primary law, leading to their horizontal effect and the availability of enhanced remedies. This fusion between primary and secondary sources of law was rightly criticised by the Advocate General in *Dominguez*[34] and it appears that the ECJ heeded those dangers in subsequent case law.[35]

An equally activist approach is illustrated by *Test-Achats*.[36] Directive 2004/113 was adopted on the basis of Article 13(1) EC (now Article 19(1) TFEU) and laid down a framework for combating discrimination based on sex in access to and supply of goods and services.[37] The Directive prohibits the long-standing practice of using gender as an actuarial factor

[32] See ILO Convention No 111, Art 5(2).

[33] These were the Finnish and the Portuguese constitutions, see Lenaerts and Gutiérrez-Fons, 'The Constitutional Allocation of Powers and General Principles of EU Law' (2010) 47 *Common Market Law Review* 1629 at 1654, fn 142.

[34] Case C-282/10 *Dominguez v Centre informatique du Centre Ouest Atlantique (CICOA)*, judgment 24 January 2012.

[35] Note that, although *Mangold* was confirmed in relation to the prohibition of age discrimination in Case C-555/07 *Seda Kücükdeveci v Swedex GmbH & Co KG*, [2010] ECR I-365, the ECJ did not apply its reasoning in *Mangold* in relation to other rights in *Dominguez*, n 34 above, and Case C-176/12 *AMS v Union locale des syndicats CGT*, judgment of 15 January 2014 (discussed below). See further Case C-356/12 *Glatzel v Freistaat Bayern*, judgment of 22 May 2014, para 43.

[36] Case C-236/09 *Test-Achats v Conseil des ministers* [2011] ECR I-773.

[37] Council Directive 2004/113/EC of 13 December 2004 implementing the principle of equal treatment between men and women in the access to and supply of goods and services ([2004] OJ L373/ 37).

in calculating insurance premiums. Article 5(2) provided for an extensive derogation. It allowed Member States 'to permit proportionate differences in individuals' premiums and benefits where the use of sex is a determining factor in the assessment of risk based on relevant and accurate actuarial and statistical data'. The Court found Article 5(2) to be invalid on the ground that it allowed the derogation to persist indefinitely. It held that such a provision, which enables Member States to maintain without temporal limitation an exemption from the rule of unisex premiums and benefits, works against the achievement of the objective of equal treatment, which is the very purpose of Directive 2004/113.[38] It is therefore incompatible with Articles 21 and 23 of the Charter, which enshrine the general principle of non-discrimination and the principle of equal treatment between men and women respectively.

On the face of it, the Court intervened on procedural grounds carrying out a test of internal consistency. Allowing Member States to introduce a permanent derogation ran directly counter to the objective of the Directive, which was to implement the principle of equal treatment. It thus made for incoherent and contradictory policy-making. The Court's reasoning is based on the premise that Article 5(1) prohibits *simpliciter* the use of sex as a factor in the calculation of benefits and premiums. This is not, however, the only reading of the Directive. The purpose of Article 5(1) is to prohibit the use of sex as such a factor only where it is discriminatory, ie in cases where men and women are in a comparable situation and there is no objective justification for their difference in treatment. The effect of Article 5(2) is to delineate the limits of the prohibition of Article 5(1) by indicating that the use of unisex premiums and benefits is not required where sex is an objective factor in differentiating risk. This interpretation is supported by the preamble to the Directive.[39] For one thing, as has been noted by Watson, Article 5 of the Directive could not prohibit the use of sex as a factor in calculating benefits or premiums unless such use constituted sex discrimination: if it went beyond that, it would be ultra vires the competence of the Council under Article 19(1) TFEU.[40] For another, to prohibit the use of sex as a relevant factor even where it can objectively be linked to differential risk would amount to treating different situation in the same way which might in itself be a breach of the general principle of non-discrimination.

[38] *Test-Achats*, para 32.

[39] Recital 19 of the Preamble states as follows: 'Certain categories of risks may vary between the sexes. In some cases, sex is one but not necessarily the only determining factor in the assessment of risks insured. For contracts insuring those types of risks, Member States may decide to permit exemptions from the rule of unisex premiums and benefits, so long as they ensure that underlying actuarial and statistical date on which the calculations are based, are reliable, regularly updated and available to the public'.

[40] See P Watson, 'Equality, fundamental rights and the limits of legislative discretion: comment on Test-Achats' (2011) 36 *European Law Review* 896 at 901–2.

The Opinion of Advocate General Kokott casts a lot more light on the argument in favour of illegality. The Advocate General pointed out that, in relation to insurance products, it is much easier to implement distinctions on the basis of sex. By contrast, '[t]he correct recording and evaluation of economic and social conditions and of the habits of insured persons is much more complicated and is also more difficult to verify, particularly since those factors may be subject to changes over time'.[41] She continued that practical difficulties and reasons of convenience could not justify '[t]he use of a person's sex as a kind of *substitute criterion* for other distinguishing features'.[42] As Watson states, however, there may be another way of looking at this issue: the use of a person's sex may not be a substitute criterion but merely a conclusion drawn from an assessment of a number of factors which shows, as a result of an objective actuarial exercise, that one or the other gender is more exposed to certain kinds of risk.[43]

A notable aspect of the judgment is the way the Court treated the consequences of incompatibility. It held that Article 5(2) must be declared invalid from the expiry of an 'appropriate' transitional period which, in a rare but not unprecedented example of judicial law-making, it set as 21 December 2012.[44] It is, however, interesting that the Court did not annul the directive as a whole. Given the widespread economic repercussions of the ruling, one may entertain doubts as to whether the EU legislature would have agreed to adopt the directive if Member States were deprived of the derogation in Article 5(2). The contrast with the *Tobacco Adverting I case* on this issue is striking.[45] In that case, the Court found that certain aspects of the directive prohibiting the sponsorship and advertising of tobacco products were beyond the scope of EU competence but annulled the directive as a whole on the ground that partial annulment would entail amendment of its provisions, which was a matter for the Community legislature.[46] The intervention of the Court in *Test-Achats* amounted to such selective amendment. Its approach is all the more activist given that Directive 2004/113 regulates private law relations.

[41] Above, n 36, at para 66 of the Opinion of AG Kokott.

[42] Ibid, para 67.

[43] Watson, n 40 above, at 899. As Watson points out, if it can be proved that a particular category of persons is less likely to be exposed to a specific risk than another category within the insured group why should it be prohibited for this to be reflected in the premium paid for coverage of that risk? See Watson, n 40 above, at 904.

[44] *Test-Achats*, n 35 above, paras 33–34. Kokott AG considered as appropriate a transitional period of three years, commencing from the delivery of the judgment, which would have expired on 1 March 2014. The AG however opined that after that transitional period existing tariffs, premiums and benefits should also be re-adapted: See paras 80–81 of the Opinion.

[45] Case C-376/98 *Germany v European Parliament and Council* [2000] ECR I-8419.

[46] Ibid, para 117.

The Court's activism can further be illustrated by *Sturgeon*.[47] The case concerned the right of air passengers to compensation in the event of a flight delay under Regulation No 261/2004.[48] The Regulation seeks to protect air passengers in the event that a flight is delayed or cancelled and provides for various forms of assistance and redress. The Court interpreted it as meaning that passengers are entitled to compensation not only where a flight is cancelled, which is expressly provided in Article 5, but also where a flight is delayed despite the absence of an express provision to that effect. It came to that conclusion on the ground that, in view of the objective of the regulation which was to strengthen passenger protection, situations covered by it must be compared by reference to the type and extent of the various types of inconvenience and damage suffered by the passengers concerned. In the light of the principle of equal treatment, it would be unjustifiable to offer compensation to passengers whose flights were delayed where they suffered a similar loss to those whose flights were cancelled.

In *Test-Achat* and *Sturgeon* the Court understood equal treatment as going well beyond a negative constitutional stipulation which constrains legislative discretion. It used the principle to promote specific policy outcomes in the economic and social sphere based on the putative intentions of the legislature rather than its actual dispositions. Showing constitutional empathy, the Court sees its role as being to contribute to the realisation of substantive values.

C. Privacy and Personal Data

An area where the ECJ has been particularly active in recent times is the right to protection of personal data in combination with the right to privacy. Two cases stand out: *Digital Rights Ireland* and *Google Spain*.[49]

In *Digital Rights Ireland*[50] the Court annulled Directive 2006/24[51] which requires providers of electronic communication services to retain certain

[47] Joined Cases C-402/07 and C-432/07 *Sturgeon v Condor Flugdienst GmbH* [2009] ECR I-10923.

[48] Regulation (EC) No 261/2004 establishing common rules on compensation and assistance to passengers in the event of denied boarding and of cancellation or long delay of flights ([2004] OJ L46/1).

[49] Joined Cases C-293/12 and C-594/12 *Digital Rights Ireland v Minister for Communications, Marine and Natural Resources*, judgment of 8 April 2014; Case C-131/12 *Google Spain SL v AEPD*, judgment of 13 May 2014. For further cases involving those rights, see eg Joined Cases C-92/09 and C-93/09 *Volker und Markus Schecke GbR and Hartmut Eifert v Land Hessen* [2010] I-11063; Case C-291/12 *Schwarz v Stadt Bochum*, judgment of 17 October 2013.

[50] Joined Cases C-293/12 and C-594/12 *Digital Rights Ireland*, judgment of 8 April 2014.

[51] Directive 2006/24/EC of the European Parliament and of the Council of 15 March 2006 on the retention of data generated or processed in connection with the provision of publicly available electronic communications services or of public communications networks and amending Directive 2002/58/EC ([2006] OJ L105/ 54).

customer data in the interests of public security. The judgment is important both for its substantive outcome and the methodology followed by the Court.

The Court first established that the retention of personal data directly and specifically affected private life and therefore the rights guaranteed by Article 7 of the Charter. It also affected the right to protection of personal data as guaranteed by Article 8 of the Charter. The Court classified the interference as being wide-ranging and particularly serious.[52] As the Court noted, the fact that the data were retained and subsequently used without the subscriber or registered user being informed was likely to generate in the minds of the persons concerned the feeling that their private lives were the subject of constant surveillance.[53]

In view of the importance of electronic communications data in investigating crime, the Court accepted that the provisions of the directive were appropriate to achieve its objectives. It found, however, that the directive did not lay down clear and precise rules circumscribing the extent of interference. The retention of data did not satisfy the standard of necessity for the following reasons.

First, the breadth of coverage of the directive was too wide. It required the retention of all traffic data covering all subscribers and registered users, entailing 'an interference the fundamental rights of practically the entire European population'.[54] It affected all persons using electronic communications services and applied even to persons for whom there was no evidence capable of suggesting that their conduct might have a link, even an indirect or remote one, with serious crime.[55] Secondly, the directive did not specify substantive and procedural conditions under which national authorities could have access to the data. It thus did not lay down any objective criteria by which to determine the limits of access to data and their subsequent use.[56] Thirdly, the directive required retention of the data for a period of at least six months, without any distinction being made between the categories of data that needed to be retained on the basis of their possible usefulness or according to the persons concerned. Nor did it require that the determination of the period of retention must be based on objective criteria in order to ensure that it was limited to what was strictly necessary.[57] The Court pointed out a further mischief. The Directive did not provide for sufficient safeguards, as required by Article 8 of the Charter, to ensure effective

[52] *Digital Rights Ireland*, para 37.
[53] Ibid.
[54] Para 56.
[55] Para 58.
[56] Paras 60 and 61.
[57] Paras 63–64.

protection of the data retained against the risk of abuse and their unlawful access and use.[58]

The judgment suggests that the ECJ takes seriously the right to privacy and the right to the protection of personal data. One of the reasons which led the Court to find the interference to be disproportionate was that the directive did not provide any rules governing access to the data by the public authorities, the conditions of access and use, and the number of persons who could access them; nor did it make such access dependent on a prior review carried out by an independent body. All those conditions could be implied since, in implementing EU law, Member States must comply with EU fundamental rights standards. The Member States must therefore be considered to be under an implicit obligation to allow access to the data only subject to strict compliance with those standards. The essence of the judgment appears to be that, where the EU legislature provides for a particularly serious interference with fundamental rights, it cannot outsource their protection to the Member States. Implicit restrictions provided by national law do not suffice.

The judgment is also important for the methodology followed by the ECJ. The Court was unusually forthcoming in determining the level of judicial scrutiny that it would employ. It held that the discretion of the EU legislature may prove to be limited depending on a number of factors, including, in particular, the area concerned, the nature of the right at issue guaranteed by the Charter, the nature and seriousness of the interference, and the objective pursued by the interference.[59] Although those factors could be derived by an analysis of the case law, it is rare that the Court refers to them explicitly. In the circumstances of the case, review was strict given the important role played by the protection of personal data in the light of the fundamental right to respect for private life and the extent and seriousness of the interference caused by the directive.[60]

The Court also followed a step-by-step approach to the application of Article 52(1) of the Charter, distinguishing and examining separately the requirement that the limitation on a right must not affect its essence from the requirement of proportionality.[61] It held that although the interference with the right to private life and the right to protection of personal data was wide ranging and particularly serious, it did not affect the essence of

[58] Paras 66–68.

[59] Para 47; the ECJ referred in support to Strasbourg case law under Article 8, in particular, *S and Marper v United Kingdom*, Application Nos 30562/04 and 30566/04, § 102, ECHR 2008-V.

[60] *Digital Rights Ireland*, para 48.

[61] Art 52(1) states that any limitation on the exercise of Charter rights must fulfill the following conditions: (a) it must be provided for by law; (b) it must respect the essence of the right concerned; and (c) it must meet the requirements of proportionality, namely it must be necessary and genuinely meet objectives of general interest.

those rights. The interference with the right to private life did not affect its essence because the directive did not permit acquisition of knowledge of the content of the electronic communication as such.[62] One may conclude *a contrario* that, if the directive enabled acquisition of the knowledge of the content of an electronic communication, that would be per se a breach of the right to privacy without any need for the Court to carry out a proportionality analysis to examine possible justifications.

Similarly, there was no interference with the essence of the right to personal data because the directive required certain principles of data protection and data security to be respected. In particular, under Article 7, Member States were required to ensure that appropriate technical and organisational measures were adopted against accidental or unlawful destruction, accidental loss or alteration of the data.[63] The Court held, however, that Article 7 did not provide for sufficient safeguards to ensure effective protection of the data retained against the risk of abuse and against their unlawful access and use. The difference appears to be between complete absence of provision of safeguards and safeguards which are inadequate. In the event of a complete absence, there is interference with the very essence of the right. If the legislature provides for such safeguards but they prove to be insufficient, this amounts to disproportionate interference. This distinction is somewhat reminiscent of the test which the Court follows in determining the threshold of seriousness for the purposes of the non-contractual liability of the EU.[64] It appears to be based, however, on a quantitative rather than qualitative criterion. In truth, it is difficult to determine objectively the degree of interference that must exist to do away with the balancing act that the principle of proportionality entails.

Google Spain[65] concerned the interpretation of Directive 95/46 on the protection of individuals with regard to the processing of personal data,[66] and raised issues pertaining to the so-called right to be forgotten. The origins of the case lie in a complaint lodged by Mr Costeja González with AEPD, the Spanish Data Protection Agency, against Google. He complained that, when his name was entered into the google search engine, the results showed links to archived pages of a newspaper containing an announcement of a court-ordered property auction for the recovery of his social security debts. The AEPD upheld his complaint, requiring Google to remove his personal data. Following proceedings initiated by Google, a preliminary reference was made.

[62] *Digital Rights Ireland*, para 39.

[63] Para 40.

[64] See Joined Cases C-104/89 and C-37/90 *Mulder and Others v Council and Commission (Mulder II)* [1992] ECR I-3061.

[65] Case C-131/12 *Google Spain v AEPD*, judgment of 13 May 2014, nyr.

[66] Directive 95/46/EC on the protection of individuals with regard to the processing of personal data and on the free movement of such data, [1995] OJ L281/31.

In a bold judgment, the Court distinguished the obligations which the right to privacy and the right to protection of personal data may impose on the provider of a search engine from those that they may impose on the publisher of a website. It held that, by bringing together information about a person's private life which otherwise could not have been interconnected, a search engine facilitated a structured overview of information relating to an individual.[67] It thus made for an autonomous and intrusive interference with the rights protected by Articles 7 and 8 of the Charter. The Court held that the operator of a search engine may be obliged to remove from the list of results links to web pages published by third parties in cases where the information in question is not erased from those web pages and even when publication in itself on those pages is lawful.

The Court stated that a fair balance should be struck between the legitimate interest of internet users and the individual's fundamental rights. The Court tilted the balance in favour of privacy. It held that whilst, as a general rule, the individual's right to privacy overrides that interest of internet users, that balance may depend, in specific cases, on the nature of the information in question and its sensitivity for the individual's private life and on the interest of the public in having that information, which may vary, in particular, according to the role played by the individual in public life.[68]

The judgment establishes a qualified but extensive right to be forgotten. The Court stated, in particular, that even the processing of accurate data that was initially lawful may, in the course of time, become incompatible with the directive where those data are no longer necessary in the light of the purposes for which they were collected or processed. That is so in particular where they appear to be inadequate, irrelevant or no longer relevant, or excessive in relation to those purposes and in the light of the time that has elapsed.[69] An examination must be made in the circumstances of each case. Notably, the Court pointed out that the right to have information removed is not dependent on finding that its inclusion in the list of results causes prejudice to the individual concerned. The judgment places the burden on the search engine provider and draws the balance firmly in favour of privacy. The rights provided by Articles 7 and 8 of the Charter override, as a rule, not only the economic interest of the operator of the search engine but also the interest of the general public in finding that information upon a search relating to the individual's name. It would be otherwise only if, for reasons such as the role played by the individual in public life, the interference with his fundamental rights would be justified by the preponderant interest of the general public in having access to that information through the list of results.

[67] *Google Spain*, n 65 above, paras, 37, 80.
[68] Para 81.
[69] Para 93.

The judgment might be seen as a triumph for the individual's right to privacy but it is ripe with problems. It imposes an important economic burden on search engine providers which, no doubt, will be collectivised. Its implementation will pose huge challenges. Although it requires a balance to be drawn between the right to privacy of the individual concerned and the public's right to information, it tilts the balance too heavily in favour of the first. The judgment itself establishes a presumption in favour of privacy. Furthermore, the conflicting rights are likely to have unequal representation in practice. Whilst individuals will stand for their right to privacy, the constituency that will fight for the freedom of expression is more difficult to identify. Search engine providers do not have an obligation to enter into balancing competing interests. In some cases, at least, it will be easier for them to remove information upon request rather than stand for transparency.[70] Whilst in *Google Spain* the juxtaposition of interests was relatively straight-forward,[71] in many cases it will be much more complex. An online publication which contains adverse information about an individual in the publication of which there is no overriding public interest may also contain information about another individual which should be made available in the public interest. The solution may be to allow that information to appear as a search result selectively, ie when the name of one individual is entered but not when the name of another is entered, but it is far from clear how search engines will implement the resulting obligations. The judgment also leaves a host of issues unresolved. In particular, it is not clear whether an individual has a right of recourse only against a national supervisory body or also directly against a provider. Although this may depend on national law, a direct right of action against a provider may not be precluded.

III. ARTICLE 6 TEU: WHAT IS THE ADDED VALUE OF GENERAL PRINCIPLES?

Following the Treaty of Lisbon, Article 6 TEU recognises essentially three sources of fundamental rights: the Charter, the European Convention on Human Rights, and the constitutional traditions common to the Member

[70] The first results following the delivery of the judgment are not encouraging. On 2 July 2014, Google removed from its search engine access to a blog on the financial crisis written by the BBC's economic editor in 2007. The blog mentioned only one individual by name, a senior figure in the financial services industry who was criticised for the investment policy of Merrill Lynch in the years leading to the financial crisis. For details, see *BBC News online*, 2 July 2014, www.bbc.co.uk/news/business-28130581, accessed on 2 July 2014.

[71] In the circumstances of the case, the ECJ came very close to providing an outcome by giving a strong indication to the referring court. It held that, given the sensitivity of the information for Mr González's private life and the fact that its initial publication had taken place 16 years earlier, in principle he had the right for the link to be removed from the search.

States. The Charter is granted the same legal value as the Treaties,[72] and thus becomes part of primary EU law. Fundamental rights, as guaranteed by the European Convention and as they result from the constitutional traditions common to the Member States, are recognised as general principles of EU law.[73] Article 6, however, is less helpful than it appears on first sight. It does not provide any guidance as to the relationship among the different sources of fundamental rights. It does not differentiate between the Charter and general principles of law as to their effects. It does not draw a priority between them nor does it state that the Charter may give rise to rights but general principles may not. The ambiguity is compounded since the Charter itself is said to contain both rights and principles.[74] Also Article 6 makes reference to the general principles of EU law but does not commit itself as to their function, their status, their ranking or the criteria for their recognition. It appears that, in a spirit of deliberate but 'constructive ambiguity', the authors of the Lisbon Treaty left a host of important issues undecided, leaving them in effect in the hands of the judiciary. How then can one shed light on the relationship between the Charter and the general principles of law? One could offer the following reflections.

Following the entry into force of the Lisbon Treaty, the primary point of reference for the protection of fundamental rights should be the Charter. This is in keeping with the intentions of the Treaty authors, which granted the Charter the same value as that of the Treaties, and also the objectives of the Charter as a document which defines the values of the EU polity. Viewing the Charter as the primary source of EU fundamental rights is also more in keeping with national constitutional cultures which, bred in a civil law tradition, feel more comfortable with written lists of rights, however indeterminate, than with case law.[75]

The case law of the ECJ confirms that the Charter is now the primary point of reference.[76] The Charter's predominance, however, should be seen in context. It does not mean that fundamental rights are exhausted in the Charter. First, the interpretation of the Charter will be informed by the general principles of law. Furthermore, Article 6(3) TEU has been interpreted

[72] Art 6(1) TEU.

[73] Art 6(3) TEU. This corresponds to the pre-Lisbon version of Art 6(2) TEU, although the formulation of Art 6(3) as it currently stands is somewhat different.

[74] See Art 6(1) TEU and Art 52(5) of the Charter and the discussion below.

[75] An example of this is provided by the attitude of the German Federal Constitutional Court towards EU law. See, in particular, the post-*Mangold* judgment of the Bundesverfassungsgericht, BVERFG, 2 BvR 2661/06, 6 July 2010. For the English version, see: www.bverfg.de/entscheidungen/rs20100706_2bvr266106en.html

[76] See eg *Kadi II*, n 17 above; *Test Achats*, n 36 above; *Digital Rights Ireland*, n 49 above; *Google Spain*, n 7 above; Case C-426/11 *Alemo-Herron v Parkwood Leisure Ltd*, judgment of 18 July 2013; *Deutsches Weintor eG*, n 7 above; Case C-283/11 *Sky Österreich GmbH*, n 7 above.

as providing an independent source of rights. In *Festersen*,[77] for example, the Court held that the right of a person to move freely and choose his residence, which is guaranteed by Article 2(1) of Protocol No 4 to the ECHR, but is not provided as such in the Charter, is recognised by EU law, and applied it to support the free movement of capital.[78] *Festersen* was decided before the Charter became binding but there is no reason to suggest that the interpretation of Article 6(3) would now be different. Indeed, post-Charter, the ECJ has invoked Strasbourg case law under Article 2(1) of Protocol 4 to supplement treaty provisions on citizenship and free movement.[79] The various sources of rights provided in Article 6 are interrelated in a way which may make it difficult to ascertain the autonomous input of each source but this is not to deny that Article 6(3) can found rights which supplement the Charter. Notably, in *Glatzel* the Court held that the principle of non-discrimination, laid down in Article 21(1) of the Charter, is a particular expression of the principle of equal treatment which is a general principle of EU and is enshrined in Article 20 of the Charter.[80]

One can expect that the general principles of law will, in most cases, be used to influence and morph the interpretation of the Charter rather than establish autonomous, self-standing rights. The provisions of the Charter are so abstract and all-embracing that it is more likely that the ECJ will bring within them any emerging general principles of EU law. Keeping things under one roof makes eminent sense. The Charter itself appears to require that its provisions must be interpreted in the light of general principles of law. In particular, the Charter does not intend to restrict or adversely affect fundamental rights as recognised by Union law,[81] and therefore detract from the level of protection afforded by general principles. It must also be interpreted in harmony with the national constitutional provisions and in accordance with the Convention.[82] The treaty setting therefore provides a framework for the integration of general principles into the interpretation of the Charter. General principles have a substantive, independent input and, as stated above, the possibility exists that they

[77] Case C-370/05 *Festersen* [2007] ECR I-1129, para 36.

[78] In *Festersen* the Court held that Danish law, which required the acquirer of agricultural property to take up fixed residence in that property was a disproportionate restriction on the free movement of capital. In examining the compatibility of the requirement with the free movement of capital, the ECJ took into account the fact that it also interfered with the right to choose freely one's residence as guaranteed by the Convention. This led the Court to characterise it as particularly restrictive and follow a heightened level of review in examining its compatibility with EU law.

[79] See *Byankov*, n 114 below, para 47 referring to *Ignatov v Bulgaria* (Application No 50/02, judgment of 2 July 2009) and *Gochev v Bulgaria* (Application No 34383/03, judgment of 26 November 2009).

[80] Case C-356/12 *Glatzel v Freistaat Bayern*, judgment of 22 May 2014, para 43.

[81] See Charter, Art 53.

[82] See Charter Art 52(4).

may be relied upon as self-standing sources of rights. They also continue to have a value as underlying principles of the constitution which influence the interpretation and application of the law and provide yardsticks for determining the validity of legislation. This applies for example to the principle of protection of legitimate expectations and the principle of legal certainty, which have been used to annul EU measures or determine the scope of their application.[83] Whether, post-Lisbon, reference is made to legal certainty as a self-standing principle or, perhaps, as part of the right to judicial protection is of less importance. The essence is that, by design, Article 6 TEU recognises multiple sources of fundamental rights which are complementary and mutually reinforcing.

Beyond the Charter, the general principles of law continue to serve a number of functions. They serve to fill the *lacunae* of written law. They promote a systematic, teleological and consistent interpretation of the law rationalising polynomy and ensuring coherence.[84] They serve to promote the development of a *jus communae* even in areas which hitherto have been largely untouched by EU law, namely private and criminal law.

Finally, general principles fulfil an important methodological function. Being an integral part of ECJ methodology, they epitomise the incomplete character of the integration bargain and enable the ECJ to engage in a perpetual adjustment of constitutional imperatives. Proportionality, in particular, has developed into a universal standard of constitutionality. The methodology followed by the ECJ in interpreting the Charter is no different from its traditional methodology in applying the general principles of law. If anything, the Charter appears to have inspired a somewhat more coherent rights-based analysis and a higher standard of review.[85]

In the Charter itself the relationship between principles and rights remains uncertain. The Charter appears to draw a distinction between the two but the differences between them are not clear and, to the extent that they are, remain normatively unsatisfactory. Article 51(1) draws a distinction between rights and principles laid down in the Charter. Such a distinction is also made in Article 6(1) TEU and the Preamble to the Charter, which in fact recognises three categories, namely 'rights, freedoms and principles'.[86] The distinction is material since some provisions of the Charter apply only to rights and freedoms but not to principles.[87] Rights are to be observed

[83] See eg Case 120/86 *Mulder v Minister van Landbouw en Visserij (Mulder I)* [1988] ECR 2321; Case C-143/93 *Van eS Douane Agenten v Inspecteur der Invoerrechten en Accijnzen* [1996] ECR I-431.

[84] An example of this is the principle of abuse of right which has been recognised by the case law as a general principle of EU law. See eg Case C-321/05 *Hans Markus Kofoed v Skatteministeriet* [2007] ECR I-5795.

[85] See eg *Digital Rights Ireland* and *Google Spain*, n 49 above.

[86] See Charter, Preamble, recital 7.

[87] See Art 52(1) which circumscribes the limitations on the rights defined by the Charter.

whilst principles are to be respected.[88] It is unsatisfactory, however, that the Charter attributes legal significance to a distinction which it assumes but does not explain. Article 53(5) states as follows:

> The provisions of this Charter which contain principles may be implemented by legislative and executive acts taken by institutions, bodies, offices and agencies of the Union, and by acts of Member States when they are implementing Union law, in the exercise of their respective powers. They shall be judicially cognisable only in the interpretation of such acts and in the ruling on their legality.

According to the Explanations accompanying the Charter, the difference is that, whilst rights give rise to 'direct claims for positive action' by the Union and national authorities, principles must be implemented by legislative or executive action at Union or Member State level and become material only for the purposes of the interpretation or judicial review of such acts.[89] Although these observations go some way towards explaining the differences between principles and rights, the distinction remains elusive. First, there is no reason why articles of the Charter which incorporate principles rather than rights should be denied any interpretative value in the absence of implementing action. Indeed, the value of constitutional principles is precisely to inform the interpretation of normative rules, including those that have not been adopted specifically in order to implement them. This is the case for example with the principle of environmental protection which is proclaimed in Article 37 of the Charter.[90] Secondly, as the Explanations themselves acknowledge, articles of the Charter may incorporate elements of both principles and rights.[91] Thirdly, the normative limitations imposed on principles by Article 53(5) appear somewhat contradictory. The case law has derived rights from general, unwritten principles.[92] By virtue of Article 6(3) TEU, those principles continue to be a source of fundamental rights. The distinction drawn in the Charter therefore does not prevent the Court from ruling that a principle can give rise to enforceable rights.

[88] See Art 51(1). This is reiterated in the Explanations Relating to the Charter of Fundamental Rights, [2007] OJ C303/17/35 For the status of the explanations, see below.

[89] Explanations, ibid, p 35.

[90] Examples of provisions which lay down principles rather than rights are Arts 25 (rights of the elderly), Art 26 (integration of persons with disabilities), Art 37 (environmental protection).

[91] This is the case, for example, in relation to Arts 23 (equality between men and women), 33 (family and professional life) and 34 (social security and social assistance). Art 34 was considered in Case C-571/10 *Kamberaj Istituto per l'Edilizia sociale della Provincia autonoma di Bolzano (IPES) and Others* [2012] ECR I-0000, nyr.

[92] See eg *Mangold*, n 28 above.

IV. SCOPE OF APPLICATION OF THE CHARTER

The determination of the scope of application of the Charter is important both for practical and theoretical reasons. In practical terms, it is necessary to know in what kind of situations the Charter may be invoked. This is particularly so to the extent that its scope of application or the level of protection that it offers is broader or narrower than other sources of fundamental rights provided by national or EU law. In theoretical terms, it raises issues pertaining to the objectives and effect of the EU constitutional model and its relationship with the national constitutions. The broader the scope of application of the Charter, the more the EU asserts its own autonomous constitutional space and the more the Charter can be seen as a replacement of, rather than as a complement to, national constitutional norms.

The scope of the Charter is governed by Article 51. Article 51(2) states that the Charter does not extend the field of application of Union law beyond the powers of the Union or establish any new power or task for the Union, or modify its powers and tasks as defined by the Treaties. Thus, the Union is not transformed into a human rights organisation. The Charter does not apply unless a situation is governed by Union law by virtue of a connecting factor other than the Charter. Also, the Charter may not in itself serve as the basis for the introduction of secondary legislation. The caveat of Article 51(2) is reiterated and supplemented by Article 6(1) TEU, which states that the Charter does not extend in any way the competences of the EU.[93] The same principle is stated in a declaration accompanying the Treaty of Lisbon.[94] Such successive references reveal the sensitivity of the Charter competence dynamic and serve to allay Member State fears of Charter rights' omnipresence. In *Dereci* the Court heeded the limitation of Article 51(2) by separating the application of fundamental rights from the definition of the substantive rights emanating from EU citizenship.[95]

Nonetheless, within the ambit of EU law, there is no limitation *ratione materiae* in the scope of application of the Charter. It applies to all fields of EU policies and activities, including the Common Foreign and Security Policy, although the Court of Justice has only very limited jurisdiction to apply it in that area.[96]

[93] See Art 6(1), sub-para 2, TEU.

[94] See the declaration concerning the Charter annexed to the final act of the intergovernmental conference which adopted the Treaty of Lisbon, signed on 13 December 2007, [2008] OJ C115/337. The declaration received judicial acknowledgment in Case C-339/10 *Asparuhov Estov and Others* [2010] ECR I-11465, para 12.

[95] Case C-256/11 *Dereci v Bundesministerium für Inneres*, judgment of 15 November 2011, paras 71–72; confirmed in Case C-87/12 *Ymeraga v Ministre du Travail, de l'Emploi et de l'Immigration*, judgment of 8 May 2013.

[96] Art 24(1) TEU and 275 TFEU.

Under Article 51(1), the Charter applies with due regard to the principle of subsidiarity and has two constituencies. It is addressed to the institutions, bodies, offices and agencies of the Union. It is also addressed to the Member States 'only when they are implementing Union law'. The following sections will examine, in turn, the application of the Charter to acts of the Member States, acts of EU institutions and, finally, action by private individuals.

A. National Measures

The application of the Charter to national measures gives rise to problems. On the face of it, Article 51(1) suggests that the Charter applies to Member States only when they implement Union law. A literal understanding of that expression would make its scope of application narrower than the application of fundamental rights as developed by the ECJ. Under the case law, Member States are bound to respect fundamental rights as general principles of law not only when they implement EU law but also when they act within its scope of application, a condition which the Court has progressively interpreted more broadly.[97] The Explanations on Article 51(1) accompanying the Charter provide little help.[98] Confusingly, they refer to the judgments in *Wachauf*, *ERT* and *Karlsson* and recall that, under the case law, 'the requirement to respect fundamental rights defined in the context of the Union is only binding on the Member States when they act in the scope of Union law'.[99] This appears to suggest that Article 51 is simply a confirmation of the existing case law, and this is how it was understood by Advocate General Trstenjak in the *NS* case.[100]

This view was confirmed by the Court in *Fransson*.[101] The Swedish authorities had imposed criminal and administrative penalties on the applicant for

[97] See above, section II.

[98] See Explanations Relating to the Charter of Fundamental Rights, [2007] OJ C303/17. The explanations were originally prepared under the authority of the Praesidium of the Convention which drafted the Charter of Fundamental Rights of the European Union. They were subsequently updated under the responsibility of the Praesidium of the European Convention which drafted the aborted Constitutional Treaty. The Explanations do not as such have the status of law, however, under Art 6(1) TEU and Art 52(7) of the Charter, they must be given due regard by the EU courts and the courts of the Member States.

[99] [2007] OJ C303/17 at 32, referring to Case 5/88 *Wachauf v Bundesamt für Ernährung und Forstwirtschaft* [1989] ECR 2609; Case C-260/89 *ERT v Dimotiki Etairia Pliroforissis* [1991] ECR I-2925; Case C-309/96 *Annibaldi v Sindaco del Comune di Guidonia* [1997] ECR I-7493; Case C-292/97 *Karlsson and Others* [2000] ECR I-2737, para 37.

[100] See Joined Cases C-411/10 and C-493/10 *NS v Secretary of State for the Home Department and ME and Others v Refugee Applications Commissioner and Minister for Justice, Equality and Law Reform*, judgment of 21 December 2011, [2011] ECR I-865 at para 76 of the Opinion. This is also how it was understood by an English court: *R (Zagorski and Baze) v Secretary of State for Business, Innovation and Skills* [2011] EuLR 315.

[101] Case C-617/10 *Åklagaren v Hans Åkerberg Fransson*, judgment of 26 February 2013.

providing false information in his VAT returns. The Swedish law pursuant to which the penalties were imposed had not been adopted specifically in order to implement the VAT directive but contained the general penalties for tax evasion provided by Swedish law. The issue arose whether those penalties were in implementation of EU law. Advocate General Villalón took a narrow view of the scope of application of the Charter. He opined that the mere fact that the exercise of public authority by a national agency has its ultimate origin in EU law does not in itself suffice to establish that a situation involves the implementation of Union law. For EU fundamental right standards to apply there must be a specific interest of the EU in ensuring that the exercise of public authority accords with the interpretation of the fundamental rights of the Union.[102] The ECJ did not follow that view and held that Article 51(1) confirms the case law relating to the scope of application of the general principles.[103]

The Opinion of the Advocate General has merit. His argument was in effect that the Charter should not replace national constitutional standards and that there must be a special EU interest to dislodge the national standard of human rights protection. This contrasts with the ECJ's monist approach which promotes the establishment of a common constitutional space. Still, the Opinion is problematic. First, the criterion that he employs is uncertain. When can it be said that there is 'a specific EU interest' that justifies the application of the EU standard? The Opinion adds a layer of enquiry which cannot be applied easily and is liable to give rise to uncertainties. Secondly, the applicable standard of fundamental rights should not differ depending on whether an EU rule was implemented by national law specifically adopted in order to give it effect or national law of more general application. This would be a random distinction since in both cases the penalty is imposed to enforce the same substantive obligation. Thirdly, unlike the Opinion, the judgment ensures conformity with the scope of application of general principles. It is difficult to see why it would make sense to maintain two sets of fundamental rights sources, namely the unwritten general principles of EU law and the Charter, with differential scopes of application. If the Charter were interpreted to apply to a narrower set of national measures, that would appear to run counter to the proclamation that it is intended simply to 'reaffirm' fundamental rights as they result from the constitutional traditions and international obligations common to the Member States, the ECHR, and the case law of the ECJ.[104] Also, giving to the Charter a narrower scope of application would be likely to prove ineffective. Insofar as the Charter and the case law protect the same rights, the limitation of Article 51(1) would be spineless since, by virtue of the case

[102] See para 40 of the Opinion.

[103] *Fransson*, n 101 above, para 18.

[104] See the Preamble to the Charter, Recital 5.

law, these rights would apply to a wider category of national measures. This is countenanced by Article 53, which states that the protection afforded by the Charter may not fall below the protection guaranteed by other provisions of EU law. It is true that, insofar as the Charter might be said to incorporate rights not expressly acknowledged by the case law on general principles, such rights, by virtue of Article 51(1), would have a narrower scope of application. This, however, would lead to inconsistency and confusion and would be likely to prove unsustainable. Given that the Charter and the general principles of law draw inspiration from the same sources, it makes sense for the ECJ to understand the two as being co-extensive, ie as applying to all national measures falling within the scope of EU law.

Whilst the approach of the ECJ in *Fransson* is preferable to that of the Advocate General, by confirming that Article 51(1) reflects the existing case law, the ECJ in effect transferred all its uncertainties to the Charter. The expression 'scope of application' remains elusive. In *Fransson* itself the Court gave two reasons why the Swedish penalties fell within the scope of application of EU law.[105] First, specific provisions of the VAT directives and Article 4(3) TEU required Member States to take all appropriate measures for ensuring collection and preventing evasion. Secondly, Article 325 TFEU requires Member States to counter fraud affecting EU finances. The Court did not say whether those reasons applied cumulatively, although it appears that at least the first would by itself be sufficient to bring the national regime within the scope of EU law. More generally, any national measure, eg a penalty, which is applied in a specific instance to enforce an obligation flowing from EU law falls within the scope of the Charter even if it might not have originally been adopted in order to give effect to EU law. Its application to give effect to EU law constitutes implementation for the purposes of Article 51(1).[106]

Notably, in *Fransson*, the Court added a 'conciliation' clause. It held that, where a national court reviews the compatibility with fundamental rights of a national measure which implements EU law but does so in a situation where national action is not entirely determined by the latter, the national court remains free to apply national standards of protection, on condition that the level of protection provided for by the Charter, and the primacy, unity and effectiveness of EU law are not compromised.[107] It is,

[105] *Fransson*, n 101 above, paras 25–26.

[106] This follows also from the duty of loyalty provided in Art 4(3) TEU which has been interpreted to require Member States to impose penalties for the infringement of EU law which are effective, proportionate and dissuasive. See e.g. Case 68/88 *Commission v Greece* [1989] ECR 2965, paras 23 and 24; Joined Cases C-387/02, C-391/02 and C-403/02 *Criminal proceedings against Silvio Berlusconi, Sergio Adelchi, Marcello Dell'Utri and Others*, [2005] ECR I-3565, para 53.

[107] Fransson, n 101 above, para 29; Case C-399/11 *Melloni v Ministerio Fiscal* [2013] ECR I-0000, para 60, nyr.

however, difficult to see what is the added legal value of that clause. It does not provide a power to lower the level of fundamental rights or indeed, as *Melloni* shows,[108] to provide for a higher standard. It is a gesture of flexibility but it is questionable whether it has any hard content.

In *AMS*, decided after *Fransson*, the Court confirmed that the fundamental rights guaranteed in the legal order of the EU are applicable in all situations governed by European Union law without distinguishing among the various sources of rights provided for in Article 6 TEU.[109]

So far, the case law is guided by the express disposition that the Charter does not establish any new power for the Union.[110] In *Asparuhov Estov*[111] the applicants contested national law which prevented them from challenging a ministerial decision on town planning, on the ground that it was incompatible with Article 47 of the Charter, which guarantees the right to an effective remedy. The Court recalled that under the Charter and the settled case law, fundamental rights are binding on Member States whenever they implement European Union law. It also reiterated that the Charter does not establish any new power for the Union or modify its powers. Given that the order for reference did not contain any specific information to show that the contested ministerial decision would constitute a measure implementing European Union law 'or would be connected in any other way' with EU law, it declined jurisdiction to answer the question.[112] The same formula was used in *Vinkov*,[113] where a Bulgarian national resident in Bulgaria was fined for causing a road accident in Sofia. He challenged the unavailability of appeal under Bulgarian law as being contrary to Articles 47 and 48 of the Charter but the Court refused to answer the question for lack of connection with EU law.[114] A similar approach has been followed in other cases.[115] Those cases appear to confirm that the fact that an area falls within the potential competence of the EU, ie, within shared competence where the EU can potentially legislate, does not suffice for the Charter or general principles of law to apply. It would be otherwise if the area fell

[108] Ibid.

[109] Case C-176/12 *AMS v Union locale des syndicats CGT*, judgment of 15 January 2014, para 42.

[110] See above, Art 51(2) of the Charter and Art 6(1) TEU.

[111] Case C-339/10 *Asparuhov Estov and Others v Ministerski savet na Republika Bulgaria* [2010] ECR I-11465.

[112] Ibid, para 14.

[113] Case C-27/11 *Vinkov v Nachalnik Administrativno-nakazatelna deynost*, judgment of 7 June 2012.

[114] See ibid, para 59.

[115] See Case C-457/09 *Chartry v État belge*, order of 1 March 2011; Joined Cases C-483/11 and C-484/11 *Boncea and Others v Statul roman and Budan v Statul roman*, order of 14 December 2011; and see in relation to austerity measures: Case C-264/12 *Sindicato Nacional dos Profissionais de Seguros e Afins v Fidelidade Mundial—Companhia de Seguors SA*, order of 26 June 2014 and Case C-128/12 *Sindicato dos Bancários do Norte v BPN—Banco Português de Negócios SA*, Order of 7 March 2013.

within the exclusive competence of the EU or if the national measure in issue affected inter-state movement.[116]

In *Siragusa*,[117] the Court provided some further guidelines as to when a measure would be considered to fall within the scope of the Charter. Mr Siragusa was required to dismantle a building on the ground that it had been built in breach of an Italian law protecting cultural heritage and the landscape. The referring court raised the question whether the rigidity of Italian law was compatible with the right to property as guaranteed by the Charter, referring to the Aarhus Convention and a number of provisions of EU environmental law. None of those, however, appeared to have any link with the facts of the case or the decision of the Italian authorities ordering demolition.[118] The Court accepted that there was a connection between the proceedings and EU environmental law since protection of the landscape is an aspect of environmental protection. It held, however, that the concept of implementing Union law under Article 51 of the Charter requires 'a certain degree of connection above and beyond the matters covered being closely related or one of those matters having an indirect impact on the other'.[119] In determining whether a national measure implements EU law, the Court will take into account, among other things, the following factors: whether the measure is intended to implement a provision of EU law; the nature of that measure and whether it pursues objectives other than those covered by EU law, even if it is capable of indirectly affecting EU law; and also whether there are specific rules of EU law on the matter or capable of affecting it.[120]

Whilst there is still a considerable degree of indeterminacy, the test followed by the Court appears to be primarily objectives-based and effects-based: if national legislation pursues the same objectives as those pursued by EU law, then it will fall within the ambit of the Charter provided that the

[116] See eg Case C-249/11 *Byankov v Glaven sekretar na Ministerstvo na vatreshnite raboti*, judgment of 4 October 2012, where the Court found that national law which prohibited the applicant from leaving the national territory on the ground that he had unpaid debts to private parties was within the scope of EU law and contrary to it. The Court held that any national measure which affects inter-state movement falls within the scope of EU law irrespective of whether it is intended to implement or affect it: para 33 and Case C-434/10 *Aladzhov v Zamestnik direktor na Stolichna direktsia na vatreshnite raboti kam Ministerstvo na vatreshnite raboti* [2011] ECR I-11659, paras 31–32.

[117] Case C-206/13 *Siragusa v Regione Sicilia—Soprintendenza Beni Culturali e Ambientali di Palermo*, judgment of 6 March 2014.

[118] The national court referred to Council Decision 2005/370 approving the Aarhus Convention, Council Regulation (EC) No 1367/2006 on the application of the provisions of the Aarhus Convention on access to information, public participation in decision-making and access to justice in environmental matters to EU institutions, Directive 2003/4 on public access to environmental information, Directive 2011/92 on environmental impact assessment, Arts 3(3) TEU and 21(2)(f) TEU, and Arts 4(2)(e), 11, 114 and 191 TFEU. Cf Case C-416/10 *Križan and Others v Slovenská inšpekcia životného prostredia*, judgment of 15 January 2013, where a link with EU environmental law was established.

[119] *Siragusa*, n 117 above, para 24.

[120] Para 25.

EU objectives are sufficiently concretised. The fact that national legislation falls within the potential scope of EU shared competence does not by itself suffice to activate the application of EU standards. Also, the measure will fall within the scope of EU law if it affects EU dispositions sufficiently directly. The rationale of this approach is based on the objectives of applying EU fundamental rights. The reason for applying EU rights to national action is to ensure that those rights are not infringed in areas of EU activity, whether through action at EU level or through the implementation of EU law by the Member States.[121] The determination of the scope of application of EU law is guided by the need to avoid a situation in which the level of protection of fundamental rights varies according to the national law involved in such a way as to undermine the unity, primacy and effectiveness of EU law.[122]

Although this appears to be a neat construct, in truth, a close analysis of the judgment suggests that the criteria remain uncertain. The fact that national legislation indirectly affects EU law is not in itself sufficient to trigger the application of EU fundamental rights standards but how direct do the effects need to be? The criteria articulated leave the Court good discretion to adopt different models.

In *Siragusa*, the ECJ also reiterated that the scope of application of general principles is the same as that of the Charter. After finding that the Italian measure could not be considered to fall within the scope of application of EU law, it followed by the same token that the Court did not have jurisdiction to apply the principle of proportionality.[123]

A further case which deserves attention is *NS*.[124] There, Article 51(1) became relevant in the context of the common European Asylum System. Regulation No 343/2003[125] lays down a list of criteria for determining the Member State responsible for examining an asylum application lodged in one of the Member States. Article 3(2) states that, by way of derogation, each Member State may examine an application for asylum lodged with it even if such examination is not its responsibility under the criteria. The issue arose whether, in taking the decision to examine a claim under Article 3(2), a Member State is implementing EU law within the meaning of Article 51(1). A number of Governments argued that a decision under Article 3(2) does not fall within the scope of EU law since it involves a discretionary power the exercise of which is an expression of national sovereignty. The Court, however, did not accept that argument. Article 3(2)

[121] Para 31.

[122] Para 32.

[123] Para 35.

[124] Joined Cases C-411/10 and C-493/10 *NS v Secretary of State for the Home Department and ME and Others v Refugee Applications Commissioner and Minister for Justice, Equality and Law Reform*, judgment of 21 December 2011.

[125] Council Regulation (EC) No 343/2003 of 18 February 2003 ([2003] OJ L50/1).

granted Member States a discretionary power which formed an integral part of the Common European Asylum System provided for by EU law.[126] Furthermore, Regulation 343/2003 laid down comprehensive rules governing the legal consequences of such a decision. Thus, a Member State which decides to examine an asylum application itself becomes the Member State responsible within the meaning of Regulation No 343/2003 and must, where appropriate, inform the other Member States concerned by the asylum application.[127]

Thus, according to *NS*, the conferment of discretion on Member States makes the discretionary power subject to the normative framework of EU law and therefore not only the actual exercise of that discretion but also the decision whether to exercise it or not is reviewable on grounds of compatibility with the Charter.

B. EU Institutions

In general, the application of the Charter to EU acts of the EU institutions does not give rise to problems. An interesting issue, however, is whether the Charter may be said to apply to action undertaken under parallel international treaties concluded by Member States in the field of economic and monetary affairs. In *Pringle*,[128] the ECJ appeared to adopt a narrow interpretation. The issue raised was whether the establishment of the European Stability Mechanism (ESM) by the ESM Treaty was in breach of Article 47 of the Charter. The Court held that, since the founding Treaties did not confer any specific competence on the Union to establish the ESM, by doing so through an international treaty, the Member States were not acting within the scope of EU law.[129] The judgment, however, does not suggest that action undertaken under the ESM is beyond the reach of the Charter. The ruling is much narrower. The Court held that the general principle of effective judicial protection did not preclude either the conclusion or the ratification of the ESM Treaty by the Member States whose currency is the euro.[130]

It is submitted that action undertaken by the EU institutions pursuant to the ESM Treaty remains subject to the Charter. First, the ESM Treaty is intended to supplement the EU framework and promote the objectives of economic union and safeguard the financial stability of the euro area.[131] Both in terms of its substantive objectives and its institutional support,

[126] *NS*, n 124 above, para 66.
[127] Para 67.
[128] Case C-370/12 *Pringle v Government of Ireland*, judgment of 27 November 2012.
[129] Ibid, para 180.
[130] Ibid, para 181.
[131] See Art 12(1) of the ESM Treaty.

it is not self-standing but operates as a satellite treaty which falls within the broader project of European integration. It must therefore operate within the confines of Article 6 TEU, which, as the Court held in *Kadi I*, is all-embracing.[132] Secondly, the language of Article 51(1) of the Charter suggests that it applies to EU institutions irrespective of whether they act under EU law or under a mandate lawfully granted to them by the Member States. The extension of the Charter to institutional measures does not in any way increase the powers of the EU. Thirdly, Article 14(3) of the ESM Treaty expressly provides that the Memorandum of Understanding which details the conditions attached to the financial assistance granted to a Member State, and which is signed by the Commission, must be fully consistent with the measures of economic policy coordination provided for in the TFEU. Those, in turn, should be taken to include the constitutional standards of the Charter.

The issue whether national action undertaken by a Member State pursuant to the ESM Treaty may be reviewed in accordance with the Charter remains open. It is submitted however that, in principle, insofar as such action is required to comply with agreements or measures adopted by the EU institutions, it is implementing action that must comply with the Charter. The opposite solution would create a significant gap in the rule of law. It would result in a situation where national authorities were not bound by the same standards as the EU institutions even though they acted as agents of the latter. It would be incongruous to follow an interpretation where the EU institutions could avoid the obligation to comply with EU standards by delegating implementation to Member States.

C. Horizontal Application

A further question which arises here is this: Is it possible for the Charter to bind individuals? In *Dominguez*,[133] Advocate General Trstenjak read Article 51(1) as precluding the horizontal effect of the Charter relying on an *a contrario* argument. Since the text of the provision makes the Charter binding on the EU institutions and the Member States, it appears to exclude its binding effect vis-à-vis private parties.[134] As a further argument, the Advocate General stated that individuals cannot satisfy the legislative proviso contained in Article 52(1) of the Charter under which any limitation

[132] See *Kadi I*, n 11 above.

[133] Case C-282/10 *Dominguez v Centre informatique du Centre Ouest Atlantique (CICOA)*, judgment 24 January 2012.

[134] The Presidium Explanations accompanying the Charter state that it applies to the central authorities as well as to regional or local bodies, and to public organisations, when they are implementing Union law. See Explanations, n 88 above, at 32.

on the exercise of rights and freedoms recognised therein must be provided for by law. Finally, she added that the system of protection of fundamental rights provided for in the ECHR showed that it is not absolutely essential for fundamental rights to be directly binding on private individuals in order to guarantee reasonable protection.[135]

Despite those arguments, it is submitted that the Charter may produce at least indirect horizontal effect. Horizontality may take many forms.[136] As an instrument of primary law, the Charter has a strong interpretative force. It may thus be used for the interpretation of private obligations and state measures which affect private relations. Furthermore, courts may be required not to apply measures which regulate private relations where they offend fundamental rights. More broadly, courts, as agents of the state, are bound to uphold fundamental rights. They may therefore be bound not to give effect to private obligations which breach fundamental rights. The possibility of direct horizontality, where a private party relies directly on a Charter right against another party, also exists. Much will depend on the right invoked, the circumstances of the case, and the relationship between the parties. Some articles specifically include private parties as their addressees.[137] Even though Article 52(1) links the legitimacy of limitations on fundamental rights with the authority of the state to pass laws, this does not preclude the possibility that a private entity may breach the core element of a fundamental right or non-derogable aspects of it. Notably, in some cases such as *Mangold*, the ECJ has accepted that general principles of law may produce some kind of horizontal effect and that it would be best to grant the Charter a co-terminous scope of application of its provisions in relations between individuals. The most important question is not, perhaps, determining the addressee of a fundamental right but ascertaining whether it has a clear and precise minimum normative content which may be said to have been breached in the circumstances of the case.

The approach suggested above is consistent with the judgment in *AMS*.[138] In that case, the Court was concerned with Article 27 of the Charter which

[135] See para 84 of the Opinion, n 133 above.

[136] For an extensive discussion, see T Tridimas, 'Horizontal Effect of General Principles: Bold Rulings and Fine Distinctions' in U Bernitz, X Groussot and F Schulyok (eds), *General Principles of EU Laws and European Private Law* (London, Kluwer Law International, 2013) 213–32.

[137] See eg Art 24(2) which states that 'in all actions relating to children, whether taken by public authorities or *private institutions*, the child's best interests must be a primary consideration' (emphasis added). This provision is based on the New York Convention on the Rights of the Child signed on 20 November 1989. It was considered (but not in a horizontal situation) in Case C-648/11 *R (on the application of MA and Others) v Secretary of State for the Home Department*, judgment of 6 June 2013, nyr.

[138] Case C-176/12 *Association de médiation sociale (AMS) v Union locale des syndicats CGT*, judgment of 15 January 2014, nyr.

provides for workers' rights to consultation and information[139] and the exercise of which is governed by Directive 2002/14.[140] Article 3(1) of the Directive states that its provisions apply to undertakings employing at least 50 employees but leaves to the Member States the determination of the method for calculating the thresholds of persons employed. AMS, a French private law association, had brought proceedings against a trade union seeking to annul the appointment by the union of a workers' representative. It argued that it had fewer than 11 employees which, under the French law implementing the directive, was the threshold for the obligation to appoint staff representatives. French law excluded certain categories of employees for the purposes of calculating the threshold but, if those categories were included, AMS would have more than 50 employees, the number triggering the application of the directive. The Cour de Cassation asked whether Article 27 of the Charter could be invoked by itself or in conjunction with Directive 2002/14 in a dispute between private individuals in order to set aside a national law.

The Court held that the directive imposed a clear and precise obligation and that a national measure which excluded from the calculation of the staff numbers a specific category of employees was incompatible with it. Given, however, the status of AMS as a private law association, it was not possible for the trade union to rely on the directive against AMS. Nor could the interpretative duty imposed by *Marleasing*[141] force an interpretation consistent with the directive given the clear provisions of French law. The Court then proceeded to examine whether the trade union could rely on Article 27 of the Charter. It held that, since that article guarantees the right to consultation in the cases and under the conditions provided by EU law and national law, it could not be fully effective by itself. It did not incorporate a directly applicable rule of law.[142] The Court distinguished the case from *Kücükdeveci*[143] on the ground that the principle of non-discrimination on grounds of age at issue in that case, laid down in Article 21(1) of the Charter, was sufficient in itself to confer rights on individuals. It followed that Article 27 could not be invoked to set aside a national provision incompatible with the directive.

[139] Art 27 states as follows: 'Workers or their representatives must, at the appropriate levels, be guaranteed information and consultation in good time in the cases and under the conditions provided for by Union law and national laws and practices'.

[140] Directive 2002/14/EC of the European Parliament and of the Council of 11 March 2002 establishing a general framework for informing and consulting employees in the European Community [2002] OJ L80/29.

[141] Case C-106/89 *Marleasing SA v La Comercial Internacional de Alimentacion SA* [1990] ECR I-4135.

[142] *AMS*, n 138 above, para 46. See, to the same effect in relation to Art 26 of the Charter, Case C-356/12 *Glatzel v Freistaat Bayern*, judgment of 22 May 2014, para 78.

[143] Ibid. Case C-555/07 *Kücükdeveci v Swedex GmbH & Co KG* [2010] ECR I-365, para 46.

AMS does not exclude the horizontal effect of the Charter. The case affirms that Article 27 does not provide for a sufficiently concretised right and therefore it cannot by itself give rise to rights either in a vertical or in a horizontal situation. One might even argue that, if the Court considered that the Charter may never produce horizontal effect, it would have dismissed the arguments on that ground without entering into the discussion of direct effect. From that perspective, the Court's reasoning may be seen as an endorsement rather than a rejection of the argument that, in appropriate circumstances, the Charter, as the general principles of law, may produce at least indirect horizontality.

V. CONCLUSION

In the last decade, the ECJ has both broadened and deepened its human rights jurisdiction. In an effort to enhance the legitimacy of the Union, it seeks to provide a one-stop forum for the protection of fundamental rights. This, in turn, defines its relative position vis-à-vis Strasbourg and the national constitutional courts. The case law projects an inclusive, centralised approach to the protection of fundamental rights placing the Charter at the apex of the edifice. The Court has been particularly activist in three areas: the right to judicial protection, the principle of non-discrimination, and the right to privacy. The case law can be seen as a triumph for individual rights but, as *Google Spain* shows, it is by no means unproblematic. Despite the fact that the Charter is the primary source for the protection of fundamental rights, the general principles of law remain important, their protean nature enabling the Court to adjust outcomes in line with constitutional imperatives. The methodology of the Court remains the same. Proportionality, in particular, has evolved to a pre-eminent balancing tool, and the standard of scrutiny seems to be higher in the post-Charter era.

D

Taking Private Law Rights Seriously: Of Balancing and the Jurisprudence of the Court of Justice of the European Union

LEONE NIGLIA*

Abstract

This chapter reviews conventional understandings of the CJEU private (consumer) law jurisprudence towards overcoming the tendency to read it as if judges were just mechanically applying the relevant legislative texts (textualism). It argues that the CJEU jurisprudence revolves around the employment of balancing modes of reasoning; that it is characterised by an unresolved tension between balancing decisions that optimise rights and balancing decisions that under-optimise rights; and that scholarship should exercise vigilance, with an eye on national constitutional realms, in relation to the judges' balancing acts towards promoting awareness over the extent of rights' optimisation, rather than clinging on textualist readings that blind us as to what is really happening in the courtrooms.

I. INTRODUCTION

THIS CHAPTER ADDRESSES a rather under-researched theme in the context of the broader subject area of balancing in comparative constitutional studies: whether and to what extent the CJEU adopts balancing in private (consumer) law cases, and, if so, what kind

* Thanks to CJEU Advocate General P Mengozzi, CJEU Judge A Rosas and T Tridimas, Kings College London for conversations over the balancing theme on the occasion of the Lasok Lectures. Thanks to K Armstrong, University of Cambridge, and anonymous referees for comments on this chapter—any errors or omissions are my own. Thanks to the Carnegie Trust for the Universities of Scotland and to the Italian Ministry of Education, University and Research (MIUR) for awards supporting research and teaching activities connected to this chapter. This chapter is part of a series of essays on the state of European constitutional law; the first is 'Form and Substance in European Constitutional Law: The Social Character of Indirect Effect' (2010) 16 *European Law Journal* 439.

of balancing.[1] It contributes to a line of writings increasingly interested in balancing as a plausible explanation of the work of judges in private law in general,[2] and to episodic references to balancing as a way to explain some decisions of the CJEU in its private law case law.[3] The chapter challenges views that interpret the relevant case law as employing a subsumption type of reasoning on the basis of a mechanical application of the available legislative texts (*textualism*).[4] Whilst the point about balancing in relation to the relevant CJEU case law has been made in writings that have tended

[1] The literature on balancing is burgeoning in the constitutional law camp (for a synthesis see A Stone Sweet 'Proportionality balancing and global constitutionalism' (2008–09) 47 *Columbia Journal of Transnational Law* 1, 72–164) but less so in the private law camp. However, on balancing in private law see, in relation to the US, M Horwitz J, *The Transformation of American Law 1870–1960: The Crisis of Legal Orthodoxy* (Cambridge MA, Harvard University Press, 1992) [Volume 2]; in relation to Europe and the US, D Kennedy, 'A Transnational Genealogy of Proportionality in Private Law' in R Brownsword, H-W Micklitz, L Niglia and S Weatherill (eds), *The Foundations of European Private Law* (Oxford, Hart Publishing, 2011); in relation to Europe, N Reich, 'Balancing in private law and the imperatives of public interest' in ibid at 221.

[2] Kennedy, A Transnational Genealogy, n 1 above; Reich, 'Balancing in private law', n 1 above.

[3] MW Hesselink, 'The general principles of civil law: their nature, roles and legitimacy' in D Leczykiewicz and S Weatherill (eds), *The Involvement of EU Law in Private Law Relationships* (Oxford, Hart Publishing, 2013); S Weatherill, 'Consumer Protection under EU Law "is not absolute": *yes, but be careful!*' (2012) 2 *European Review of Contract Law* 221; W Van Gerven, 'The ECJ Case-law as a Means of Unification of Private Law?' in Hartkamp et al, *Towards a European Civil Code*, 2nd edn (Boston MA/The Hague, Kluwer Law International, 1998) 91.

[4] 'Textualism' in this chapter indicates 'subsumption' or 'rule construction' (the judicial operation of subsuming facts under rules) as opposed to 'balancing' (for this contrast in general see eg R Alexy, 'On Balancing and Subsumption: A Structural Comparison' (2003) 16 *Ratio Juris* 433). I derive the reading of the case-law under scrutiny as textualist from W Van Gerven, 'The ECJ Case-law as a Means of Unification of Private Law?' in Hartkamp et al, *Towards a European Civil Code*, 2nd edn (n 3 above) 91, at 92–93 (3rd edn, 2004) 101, at 103) ('Where the ECJ's interpretation of Treaty provisions and, even more so, of the underlying general principles is not infrequently bold, or even audacious, that is not normally the case as regards the ECJ's interpretation of specific directive provisions which is, more often than not, of a rather textual nature relating, as it usually does, to precise and often technical expressions' and calling it 'textual interpretation'; discussing textual interpretation in relation to private consumer law directives as 'no bold Treaty-related interpretation but only literally minded Directive-related interpretation': 101 et seq). Textualism is sometimes presented in conjunction with other arguments: first, the consideration that the CJEU would adopt it for respect of the competence boundaries to which private law is bound in the context of the wider EU constitutional structure (see, critically, H Collins, *The European Civil Code. The Way Forward* (Cambridge, CUP, 2007) at 56–58, commenting on *Dietzinger*, as discussed in the remainder) and, second, the implicit consideration that the CJEU would be 'protecting the consumer' to the extent that the text allows this (see H Unberath and A Johnston, 'The Double-Headed Approach of the ECJ Concerning Consumer Protection' (2007) 44 *Common Market Law Review* 1237 as discussed in the remainder). To these two arguments I return in the remainder where I also comment on a third position, closer to the balancing reading that I am proposing, adopting the interpretation that in its private consumer law case-law the CJEU would be protecting the consumer in purposive *qua* teleological mode, in the context of the broader Court's self-conscious constitutional role.

to criticise a number of key decisions of the Court,[5] this chapter proposes a more positive approach to the Court's deployment of balancing. It aims at offering a more comprehensive analysis of what modes of reasoning the Court adopts in its private law case-law (textualism and balancing), and a critical evaluation of them in relation to the extent to which the case law stands the test of really protecting individuals' rights.[6]

The chapter is structured in four sections. After identifying a framework for analysis based on the role of balancing modes of reasoning in domestic constitutional practice and theory as relevant to the resolution of disputes in the private law realm (Section II), the chapter makes intelligible the CJEU private consumer law case-law as a set of balancing decisions. Section III considers a first group of cases in which the CJEU balances in ways that fail to optimise rights. Section IV considers a second group of cases which contrast starkly with those considered in Section III for being closer to deploying balancing in ways that optimise rights. Section V puts forward the consideration that, for the whole of the CJEU case-law including the cases that optimise rights, there remains the challenge of evaluating the CJEU's measure of rights' optimisation from the vantage point of the ways in which national constitutional courts optimise rights (argument from the European plural context).

II. A FRAMEWORK FOR ANALYSIS: OF BALANCING IN DOMESTIC PRIVATE LAW

Constitutional scholars argue that balancing involves 'a head-on comparison' of each interest or factor 'with competing interests' towards their weighing,[7] as opposed to rule construction through mere subsumption.[8] The paradigmatic

[5] Raising general criticism on the role of the CJEU and national courts in private law on the basis of an understanding of European private law as having to embody the balancing of market-orientated and of social justice objectives (see 'Manifesto of the Study Group on Social Justice in European Private Law' (2004) 6 *European Law Journal* 653, at 671: warning that one should 'not rely on haphazard practice of national courts making references to the European Court of Justice, and the occasional comparisons made between national court decisions'; and placing faith in the legislature's work of balancing (at 656): 'A unified law will similarly have to strike a balance between, on the one hand, the weight attached to individual private autonomy as expressed in the idea of freedom of contract, and, on the other hand, principles which respect other equally important demands for social solidarity, which prohibit individuals from taking advantage of superior economic strength or from ignoring the claims of justified reliance upon others'.). For criticism in relation to individual CJEU cases not necessarily skeptical of balancing, see below at section III.

[6] Needless to say, the standard of 'rights optimisation' has become a conventional way in which comparative constitutional studies analyse decisions of constitutional courts towards a critical understanding of their rationality and legitimacy (see below, Section V).

[7] A Aleinikoff, 'Constitutional Law in the Age of Balancing' (1987) 96 *Yale Law Journal* 943, at 945.

[8] Alexy, 'On Balancing', n 4 above.

case, involving private law rules, is *Lüth*, concerning a conflict between constitutional rights (or, as one may also call them, principles, values, interests or goals),[9] decided by the German Federal Constitutional Court (BVerfG) through 'weighing' them (*Güterabwägung*). In *Lüth* and subsequent cases, constitutional rights are held to be values[10] (or principles)[11] that 'tend to collide' and that, as such, demand balancing for the resolution of collisions.[12] From close observation of the practices of the constitutional courts, and specifically of the BVerfG, the acknowledged originator of the adjudicatory model under consideration, Alexy has derived the following formula that tells us how constitutional judges[13] manage to rationally weigh competing values/ principles:[14] the greater the degree of non-satisfaction of, or detriment of, one principle, the greater the importance of satisfying the other.

Rights are meant to be optimisation requirements that allow the maximum of their concretisation on condition that assessment of the relative degree of non-satisfaction and importance is undertaken explicitly through rationally bound reasoning steps.[15] Alexy's formula makes intelligible the way constitutional judges operate in such situations. Judging becomes an operation at the core of which are explicit considerations as to the degree to which one right or goal is being sacrificed and, correlatively, the degree to which one can argue that it would be really important to satisfy *another* competing right or goal nevertheless. The court will end up with 'striking a balance between and among' the relevant normative considerations.[16] *Lüth*'s freedom of expression under Article 5(2) of the Basic Law (his appeal to boycotting film-making activities by the film director Harlan) was judged to be comparatively higher in importance than the related sacrifice connected to the damages inflicted on Harlan as a result of the exercise of that freedom. This balancing consideration allowed the court to exempt *Lüth* from tort liability under Article 826 BGB, which notably states that a person who, in a manner contrary to public policy, intentionally inflicts damage on another person is liable to the other person to make compensation

[9] See Alexy, 'Constitutional Rights, Balancing and Rationality' (2003) *Ratio Juris* 131.

[10] BVerfGE vol 7, 198, 201 (*Lüth*) at 205, 15 January 1958.

[11] *Lüth*, 254.

[12] *Lüth*, 210.

[13] Not only, considering that in Germany the obligation to interpret private law consistently with the Basic Law (that is, not inconsistently with it) applies to ordinary civil courts: for discussion see Matthias Ruffert, *Vorrang der Verfassung und Eigenständigkeit des Privatrechts* (Tubingen, Mohr Beck, 2001) at 65.

[14] Alexy, 'On Balancing', n 4 above, at 136.

[15] Alexy, 'Constitutional Rights' (2003) *Ratio Juris* 131, at 136 (on 'scales' involved in the balancing exercise).

[16] Aleinikoff, 'Constitutional Law', n 7 above, at 946.

for the damage. This was perceived at the time as the 'victory of freedom of speech over the vested economic interests of enterprises'.[17]

III. OF BALANCING AND THE COURT OF JUSTICE OF THE EUROPEAN UNION I—FAILING RIGHTS OPTIMISATION

This Section argues that 'balancing' makes intelligible three leading CJEU private consumer law cases (A) and that, in balancing the rights at stake in each such case, the judges of the CJEU have failed to optimise them (B).

A. Balancing in the Private Law Jurisprudence of the Court

Notably, the case law of the CJEU in the private law field is typically believed to be based on textualism,[18] that is, a subsumption type of reasoning on the basis of the available legislative texts. It is argued that the Court in such cases avoids addressing the underlying value issues, let alone balancing the relevant normative considerations, and retreats to the terrain of textualism—understood as a sub-species of what is commonly known as rule construction through 'literally minded, directive related'[19] subsumption—protecting the consumer to the extent that this is possible under the conditions of textual hermeneutics. This reconstruction offers a picture of the work of the CJEU in the private consumer law area as being in stark contrast with other EU law areas where it is widely acknowledged that the CJEU employs balancing, such as those involving economic freedom rights and fundamental rights, as discussed in the other contributions to this *Symposium*, including cases in which, as noted by Takis Tridimas in his contribution to this *Symposium*, proportionality 'has evolved to a pre-eminent balancing tool'.

A case that exemplifies the textualist reading is, according to Van Gerven, *Panagis Pafitis*,[20] in a major sub-field of European private law: European company law. Here, rather than weighing the conflicting interests of shareholders and creditors-depositors in light of considerations regarding the

[17] G Brüggemeier, 'Constitutionalisation of Private Law—The German Perspective' in T Barkhuysen and S Lindenbergh (eds), *Constitutionalisation of Private Law* (Leiden and Boston, Martinus Nijhoff, 2006), at 69.

[18] See eg Van Gerven, 'The ECJ Case-law as a Means of Unification of Private Law?' in Hartkamp et al, *Towards a European Civil Code*, 2nd edn (1998), 91, at 92–93 and 96 et seq. in the context of an argument that applies to directives in general and private (contract) law directives more specifically; H Unberath and A Johnston, 'The Double-Headed Approach of the ECJ Concerning Consumer Protection' (2007) 44 *Common Market Law Review* 1237 as discussed at n 36 below.

[19] Van Gerven, 'The ECJ Case-law', n 18 above at 100–102.

[20] Case C-441/93 *Panagis Pafitis v Trapeza Kentrikis Ellados AE* [1996] ECR I-1347.

judgement of importance and sacrifice of the relevant rights relative to each other,[21] the CJEU simply applied the text of the Second Company Directive that required the approval of the shareholders' meeting for increasing the company's capital, which, as Van Gerven argues, was clearly an impediment towards the restructuring that was required for protecting the (consumer) depositors.[22] In Van Gerven's view, '[t]he Court did not even try, as it might have done when dealing with the interpretation of Treaty provisions, to weigh the underlying and conflicting interests of shareholders and depositors against each other', arguing that

> the method of text abiding interpretation followed by the Court in that case seems typical for the Court's attitude when it is asked to interpret precise wording in directives or regulations ... in sharp contrast with some of the Court's case-law relating to the interpretation of basic Treaty provisions.[23]

Dietzinger is a paradigmatic case that (partly) confirms this conventional reading of a textually minded court with regard to the contractual law field. However, attention can be drawn to episodes of balancing that one can identify in private consumer law cases, showing that mapping the case law of the CJEU requires that one employs the 'balancing' framework of analysis alongside that of textualism. The implication of the analysis that follows is that there is no real mis-alignment between the private consumer case law of the CJEU and those other decisions discussed in this *Symposium* in which the CJEU deploys balancing, for I show that the CJEU has tended to internalise in its private consumer case law the 'private law balancing' modes of reasoning typical of the multi-national constitutional jurisprudence referred to in Section II. Three major consumer private law cases decided in relation to the Unfair Terms Directive and the Doorstep Selling Directive (now Directive on Consumer Rights) are selected with a view to re-describing them through the balancing lens and to proposing a critical reading of them in relation to the extent to which they optimise rights or otherwise (at section III.B).[24]

[21] I am translating in the balancing vocabulary adopted in this chapter the remarks of Van Gerven, 'The ECJ Case-law', n 18 above, at 93 as also partly quoted in the text, that is, that 'The Court based its decision on a textual interpretation of the Second Company directive'; and that '[t]he Court did not even try ... to weigh the underlying and conflicting interests of shareholders and depositors against each other'). For further elaboration on this point see the remainder.

[22] Ibid at 93.

[23] Ibid at 93.

[24] I am developing further an insight in scholarship whereby consumer protection in the case law of the CJEU is based on constitutional choice rather than textualism, proposing to reconstruct it in balancing mode. For scholarship pointing to the importance of what one can call a purposive orientated (teleological) mode of interpretation as making the Court's case law in the area really intelligible, see S Weatherill, 'An Ever Tighter Grip: The European Court's Pro-consumer Interpretation of the EC's Directives Affecting Contract Law' in M Andenas et al, (eds), *Liber Amicorum Guido Alpa. Private Law Beyond the National Systems* (London,

i. Balancing in *Freiburger*

A case in which the CJEU has explicitly adopted a line of reasoning that consists of balancing the interests at stake in the dispute is *Freiburger*.[25] Here a contractual clause in dispute provided for payment on the part of the buyers to take place before, as opposed to at the moment of execution of, a parking space. It was submitted that this anticipated payment reduced the price of the parking place (avoiding the need for the builder to finance the building work through use of borrowings) and that the disadvantages faced by the buyers were only limited, given a bank guarantee that ensured the return of the sum paid in the case of non-performance, defective performance or insolvency of the builder. The Court held that the term was not 'solely to the benefit of the seller', nor could one argue that it 'contained no benefit in return for the consumer'; that it was ultimately a term held to be 'fair' under the Directive on Unfair Terms because it benefitted the seller in the context of a contractual package that equally benefitted the buyers in terms of price and guarantee. The 'unfairness' of the term, argued on the basis of the disadvantage entailed in the term providing for anticipated payment—in the words of the defendants in the main proceedings, a derogation of the fundamental rule-principle 'recognized in all systems of civil law, that mutual obligations must be performed contemporaneously'—was not convincing for the Court in the circumstances. Thus, the guarantee and the price were balanced out against the contractually provided for obligation on the buyer to pay the price only after the seller's performance. Note the peculiarity of the balancing approach of the CJEU, given that the Court held that one set of interests outweighed another. As a matter of fact (at para 16), the seller's interest to receive payment in advance of its performance was held to prevail over that of the buyer to pay subsequently to the seller's performance of its obligation.

British Institute of International and Comparative Law, 2007) 1037; M Hesselink 'A Toolbox for Judges' (2011) 17 *European Law Journal* 441–69. This scholarship stresses the key role of consumer protection in constitutional terms (Weatherill, 'An Ever Tighter Grip', ibid, at 1054—Court 'ambitious, even aggressive, in pursuing its role in the field of contract law'; Court 'insists on the need for an autonomous meaning for legal concepts supplied by Community law but it *also* typically draws on the interest in consumer protection in choosing the direction of that interpretation and it *also* on occasion reaches beyond the explicit material scope of the legislation in asserting a Community content to matters in dispute, including those pertaining to matters of civil procedure'; Weatherill, 'Consumer Protection', above n 3, noting 'the long-standing and constitutionally proper assumption that the EU's legislative *acquis* shall benefit from a pro-consumer interpretation', a line of analysis that focuses on substantive aspects, as opposed to reading it all through the lens of mechanical applications of texts, and to which this chapter hopes to contribute by considering such substantive aspects in relation to the technique of balancing.

[25] Case C-237/02 *Freiburger Kommunalbauten GmbH Baugesellschaft & Co KG v Ludger Hofstetter and Ulrike Hofstetter* [2004] ECR I-3403. For a fuller critical analysis of the decision see the remainder of the chapter.

ii. Balancing in *Dietzinger*

Traces of balancing can be found in another line of cases concerning the Doorstep Selling Directive as relied upon by contractors who found themselves caught up in a problematic contractual situation involving their obligation to honour a guarantee in support of a loan, and who hoped to back out of their agreements by relying on the right of cancellation. *Dietzinger*[26] is one such case in which one can identify patterns of balancing. Here the CJEU equally adopted balancing, albeit only as obiter dicta, having then decided the case on the basis of the textualist template. Dietzinger and the Commission considered

> that Directive 85/577 applies to a contract of guarantee by virtue of the directive's aim, which is to protect those consumers who conclude a contract where, because it involved 'doorstep selling', they were unable to prepare themselves for its negotiation. Like *a purchaser*, a guarantor undertakes to perform obligations and *is even more in need of protection since he receives no consideration in exchange for his commitment* (emphasis added).[27]

Against this claim, the CJEU acknowledged the 'close link' between credit agreements and guarantees in the circumstances. As a result of the 'close link', and therefore of the consideration that the need for protecting the guarantor scores highly in terms of 'importance' relative to the related sacrifice of the interests of the bank, the Court held that one could not in principle exclude that guarantors should be given the right to cancel the contract; that is, that the interests of guarantors should outweigh those of the loan creditors (balancing). In the words of the Court:

> In view of the close link between a credit agreement and a guarantee securing its performance and the fact that the person guaranteeing repayment of a debt may either assume joint and several liability for payment of the debt or be the guarantor of its repayment, it cannot be excluded that the furnishing of a guarantee falls within the scope of the directive.[28]

This opinion did go towards meeting the concerns of the Commission and Dietzinger but—and here the case presents us with textualism—it was then ultimately decided to exclude the right of cancellation for guarantees in support of non-consumer credit, on the straightforward basis of a truly textual argument that narrows the scope of the balancing 'close link' argument, that is:

> *However*, it is apparent *from the wording of Article 1* of Directive 85/577 and from the ancillary nature of guarantees that the directive covers only a guarantee ancillary to a contract whereby, in the context of 'doorstep selling', a consumer

[26] Case C-45/96 *Bayerische Hypotheken und Wechselbank v Dietzinger* [1998] ECR I-1199.

[27] Ibid at para 12.

[28] Ibid at para 20.

> assumes obligations towards the trader with a view to obtaining goods or services from him. Furthermore, since the directive is designed to protect only consumers, a guarantee comes within the scope of the directive only where, *in accordance with the first indent of Article 2*, the guarantor has entered into a commitment for a purpose which can be regarded as unconnected with his trade or profession.
>
> The answer to the question referred to the Court must therefore be that, *on a proper construction of the first indent of Article 2 of Directive 85/577*, a contract of guarantee concluded by a natural person who *is not* acting in the course of his trade or profession does not come within the scope of the directive where it guarantees repayment of a debt contracted by another person who, for his part, *is* acting within the course of his trade or profession (emphases added).[29]

This is a case in which the Court has entered the balancing territory when acknowledging the 'close link' between credit agreements and guarantees, insofar as this substantiates the Court's view that there are substantive reasons whereby one should consider the interests of the guarantors to outweigh those of the creditors.[30] However, the decision of the Court is otherwise centred on a textualist mode of reasoning in that it explicitly subsumes the issue in dispute under Articles 1 and 2 of the relevant Directive,[31] which leads the Court to limit the right of cancellation for guarantors only to guarantees ancillary to consumer loans.[32] The decision is a hybrid of balancing (obiter dicta) and textualism.

[29] Ibid at paras 22 and 23.

[30] For more discussion on this point see the remainder of the chapter.

[31] Ibid, para 22.

[32] For the argument that the Court fails to convince in terms of substance see, eg H Collins, *The European Civil Code*, n 4 above, at 56–58 (critical on the ground that the Court follows the argument from constraints descending from the competence limitations of the EU, as opposed to arguments from coherence of policy or principle, arguing that guarantees ancillary to a commercial transaction should be covered by the Doorstep Selling Directive). The argument whereby the CJEU would adopt textualism for respect of the competence boundaries to which private law is bound in the context of the wider EU constitutional structure, cannot explain the activism of the CJEU in a case such as Case C-453/99 *Courage Ltd v Crehan* [2001] ECR I-6297 (an argument implicitly held by Collins) or Case C-481/99, *Heininger v Bayerische Hypo- und Vereinsbank AG* [2001] ECR I-9945, nor the typically creative role of the CJEU in other fields, nor the integrationist stance of the Court in consumer private law cases such as *Oceano* (n 54 below) and *Freiburger* (n 25 above), nor even the rest of the consumer private law cases that I consider in the remainder insofar as they protect the consumer under EU law—in all of these cases the CJEU takes an integrationist and/or consumer protectionist stance that indicates a Court acting as a conscious constitutional actor unrestrained by considerations regarding competence limitations. These considerations, however, should not be understood as meaning that the CJEU should act without regard for the requirements of the national constitutional realms (including those incorporated in the argument from competences): for the argument that all of the decisions of the CJEU need to be subjected to rights' optimisation tests as practised under national constitutional law see below, at Section V.

iii. Balancing in *Schulte*

A decade later, in another case involving the Doorstep Selling Directive, the Court adopted a decision similar in structure to *Dietzinger* in that it consisted of a combination of balancing and textualism. Here the Court held that the right of cancellation could apply to the position of loan-takers in relation to the credit agreement portion of the investment package (a linked contract consisting of purchase of an apartment financed by a supporting loan to be repaid by rental receipts), on the basis of obiter dicta whereby the interest of the consumer must be considered to be higher in importance than that of other party.[33] However, it held that it could *not* apply in relation to the portions of the investment contracts connected to the buying of immovable properties, on the basis of textual arguments regarding the explicit wording of the Doorstep Selling Directive that excludes from its scope immovable properties *qua* connected contracts.[34] As a result, Mr and Mrs Schulte could be freed from the credit agreement but not from the connected property obligations, which resulted in the imposition on them of the duty to repay the credit in full and with interest at the market rate at once, rather than by instalment as would have been the case had the investment deal remained in place. It should be noted that this decision ultimately worsened the position of the consumers compared to situations in which either they had not been able at all to rely on the right of cancellation (no cancellation of the investment deal) *or* they could rely on the right of cancellation with regard to the property obligation portion of the deal by avoiding any liability due to transferring back to the provider the overall risk of investment under paragraph 359(3) BGB.[35]

[33] On this point, see already Case C-481/99, *Heininger v Bayerische Hypo- und Vereinsbank AG*, [2001] ECR I-9945 (applicability of the Doorstep Selling Directive to credit agreements secured by a charge on land unlimited in time; preclusion of national legislation imposing a time limit; opposing argument on legal certainty raised by the trader, holding that the trader could have avoided the legal uncertainty by informing the consumer of the right to withdrawal), as discussed in the remainder of the chapter.

[34] Case C-350/03 *Schulte v Deutsche Bausparkasse Badenia AG* [2005] ECR I-9215 (*Schulte*) (holding that the directive cannot be interpreted in the sense that the loan-taker has a right of cancellation: at paras 75–76: 'the Directive expressly and unequivocally excludes contracts for the sale of immovable property from its scope. *While other Community directives intended to protect the interests of consumers, inter alia Directive 87/102, contain rules concerning connected contracts, the Directive contains no rule of that type and provides no basis for an assumption that such rules are implied*' (emphasis added). See also Case C-229/04 *Crailsheimer Volksbank eG v Conrads and others* [2005] ECR I-9293 (*Crailsheimer Volksbank*). For criticism see Reich, 'Balancing in private law', n 1 above

[35] For discussion see Reich, 'Balancing in private law', n 1 above; H Unberath and A Johnston, 'The Double-Headed Approach of the ECJ Concerning Consumer Protection' (2007) 44 *Common Market Law Review* 1237, at 1258 et seq (with details on 359(3) *BGB*; Terryn (2007) 44 *Common Market Law Review* 501.

B. Not Taking Private Law Rights Seriously: Failing Rights' Optimisation

Commentators have argued that the overarching objective of protecting the weak party has not been achieved in the cases considered above: denouncing the lack of protection of the guarantor of business transactions in *Dietzinger* as failing to comply with the argument from 'coherent policy or principle' requiring that individuals, under pressure in their homes to sign a guarantee, should be protected independently of the context of the transactions being guaranteed, consumer or commercial;[36] and maintaining that it is counterintuitive to worsen the position of Mr and Mrs Schulte as a result of not liberating them from the obligations related to property.[37] It is argued here that, as judges center their decisions around balancing modes of reasoning as opposed to (just) deploying textualism, we need to evaluate their work for what it is, that is, a context of balancing deliberations in which judges take on themselves the role of consciously choosing to what extent competing rights should be protected; that, in so doing, the judges must expose themselves to the public critique (including academic commentary) regarding whether or not they balance rights convincingly in terms of, to use Alexy's words, 'rights' optimization'. For at stake are conflicts among rights *qua* principles that entail values,[38] and as such ('values') they tend to conflict with each other and require balancing, with the result that any interference with them should be allowed only if proportional, which comes down to a judgement about the degree of rights' optimisation in the circumstances.[39] Also, Directives' norms such as those involved in the

[36] Contrast what one may call textual purposivism (H Unberath and A Johnston, 'The Double-Headed Approach of the ECJ Concerning Consumer Protection' (2007) 44 *Common Market Law Review* 1237—arguing, after analysing many of the relevant private consumer protection cases that 'Article 95 EC instructs the Community legislature and ultimately the Court to enforce a "high level" of consumer protection' and that '[t]he Court is, as in principle it should be, *neutral as to the policy implications of the laws it applies*. Rather it amplifies *what is given to it as Community rule*' (emphasis added))—with the more substantively purposivist and constitutionally orientated arguments about consumer protection put forward by Collins, *The European Civil Code*, n 4 above, at 56–58 that I am referring to in the text. The latter arguments expose an understanding of directives' interpretation as a tool self-consciously deployed by an activist, constitutional Court (law-maker; not policy neutral), that is, closer to the view of the case law as revolving around balancing that this chapter proposes, albeit with a focus on arguments from 'coherent policy of principle' to be implemented, rather than pointing to the role of balancing techniques. I understand the writings of Reich, 'Balancing in private law', n 1 above (discussing various consumer private law cases, including the *Schulte* saga, in a vocabulary of balancing that the author draws on the work of J Esser) and of Weatherill, 'Consumer Protection', n 3 above, as discussed in the remainder, to be the closest to the reading that I am adopting in this chapter.

[37] As discussed above. For a detailed critique of *Freiburger*, see below and L Niglia, 'The Rules Dilemma'—The Court of Justice and the Regulation of Standard Form Contracts in Europe (2006) 13 *Columbia Journal of European Law* 124.

[38] See Alexy, nn 9 and 15 above.

[39] Ibid.

case law under consideration are not just principles but *constitutional principles*, for they embody an 'order of values' constitutionally ranked. They are constitutional principles: at a minimum (form), because of their location in the realm of supranational law vis-à-vis the domestic realms of constitutional and private law; at a maximum (substance), because of their 'transferring interests' towards constituting the constitutional structure of markets.[40] At stake in the cases under scrutiny are, notably, conflicts between values such as, on the one hand, 'consumer protection' and, on the other hand, 'open market economy'.[41] This is the interpretative world that the judges have entered, I argue, and which scholarship needs to address if it is to catch up with developments on the ground and if it is to provide us with a critical platform on the basis of which to render intelligible, and evaluate, the CJEU case law in the subject area. Seen in this light, below I propose a reading that makes sense of *Dietzinger*, *Schulte* and *Freiburger* at once, arguing that the judges of the CJEU have failed to optimise rights when balancing.

i. Under-Optimisation in *Dietzinger*

In *Dietzinger* at stake is the right of cancellation as provided for in the Doorstep Selling Directive (now Directive on Consumer Rights).[42] To negate the right of the guarantor of commercial loans to cancel the guarantee in all circumstances (a right not denied to the guarantor of consumer loans) means not to allow the exercise of that right in situations in which a comparative

[40] On 'interests' (in the vocabulary of Joseph Heck) as 'transfer norms for values' see N Reich, 'Balancing', n 1 above, at 227 (explaining the work of the judge in Germany this way and drawing on the work of J Esser) and then applying this perspective for understanding key CJEU private consumer cases as involving conflicting interests.

[41] For the relevance of the values of 'consumer protection' see eg CJEU, Case C-484/08 *Caja de Ahorros y Monte de Piedad de Madrid v Asocación de Usuarios de Servicios Bancarios (Ausbanc)* [2010] ECR I-4785 at para 27: '[A]ccording to settled case-law, the system of protection introduced by the Directive is based on the idea that the consumer is in a weak position *vis-à-vis* the seller or supplier, as regards both his bargaining power and his level of knowledge. This leads to the consumer agreeing to terms drawn up in advance by the seller or supplier without being able to influence the content of those terms' (Directive on Unfair Terms interpreted as implicating the requirement of protecting the consumer in 'settled case-law'); and, commenting on *Ausbanc* and identifying the contending set of constitutional values, that is, 'the general principles of EU law, such as open market economy, competition and the fundamental freedoms', see N Reich, 'Balancing in private law and the imperatives of public interest' in Brownsword, Micklitz, Niglia and Weatherill (eds), *The Foundations of European Private Law*, n 1 above, at 240.

[42] Directive 2011/83/EU of the European Parliament and of the Council of 25 October 2011 on consumer rights, amending Council Directive 93/13/EEC and Directive 1999/44/EC of the European Parliament and of the Council and repealing Council Directive 85/577/EEC and Directive 97/7/EC of the European Parliament and of the Council ([2011] OJ L304/64), which fully harmonises the areas of pre-contractual information to be given to consumers, the consumer's right of withdrawal in distance and off-premises contracts, as well as certain aspects of delivery of goods and passing of risk.

assessment of the relative importance of the relevant rights (commercial loans' guarantors' rights versus banks' rights) would suggest otherwise. And it is counterintuitive to protect the guarantor of consumer loans but not that of commercial loans, as the CJEU has ultimately done through its textualist mode of interpretation. Since, an assessment of the relative worth of the conflicting rights in terms of their degrees of importance and of sacrifice must entail acknowledgement of the weak position of the guarantor regardless of whether they guarantee a commercial or a consumer loan. This emerges from the passages of the Court's decision that uphold the 'argument from close link', as discussed above; for, to 'translate' that argument in the vocabulary of rights' optimisation, to the greater sacrifice on the part of the bank of the right to cash in the guarantee corresponds the right of the guarantor to cancel the guarantee as proportionally higher in importance than the sacrifice of the right of the counterparty. This the Court held in relation to guarantees in support of commercial loans, before moving on and denying protection for the guarantor of commercial loans on mere textualist grounds. To say it otherwise: if one were to hold that the guarantor's right is not 'important' enough to deserve protection, relative to the degree of sacrifice of the right of the bank to cash in the guarantee ancillary to business loans, then one can certainly not argue otherwise in relation to guarantors of consumer loans, for guarantors are, substantively speaking, in the same weak position relative to the bank whatever the purpose (commercial or not) for which the loan that they support has been taken up—as correctly argued by the Commission and Mr Dietzinger in their submission before the CJEU. The Court's ultimate disregard for the interest of the guarantor of commercial loans such as Mr Dietzinger is untenable, for guarantors' rights should have been taken seriously whatever the nature of the loan being guaranteed. From this vantage point, the arguments put forward by the Commission and Mr Dietzinger are fully justified in the light of an ad hoc balancing assessment: to say it in the vocabulary of comparative constitutional studies which notably contrast *definitional* balancing—'one interest outweighing another'; placing 'the interests on a set of scales and rul[ing] the way the scales tip')—with ad hoc balancing ('the relative weights of the interests'). [43] Not to mention

[43] I draw on, and adapt to the European cases under considerations, Aleinikoff's synthesis of balancing based on the US experience (see Aleinikoff, 'Constitutional Law', n 7 above), according to whom *definitional* balancing means cases in which the court 'talks about one interest outweighing another' and 'places the interests on a set of scales and rules the way the scales tip' (at 946 and at 949, the example being that of 'constitutional standards requiring "compelling" or "important" ... interests') as opposed to *ad hoc* balancing which means instead cases in which the court 'speaks of "striking a balance" between or among competing interests', the 'image' being 'one of balanced scales with constitutional doctrine calibrated according to the relative weights of the interests', that is, interests are always subject to balancing and never taken to outweigh other interests in all circumstances (at 946 and at 958). For the purpose of this chapter, Alexy's law of balancing is taken to overlap with *ad hoc*

that the Court should have engaged with further possible circumstances in relation to which implementing the balancing exercise might have meant qualifying the application of the right of cancellation further—similarly to what domestic constitutional courts do.[44] For example, the remarkable *Bürgschaft* decision of the German Constitutional Court (on guarantees) of October 1993 *did* differentiate between contractual situations depending on the risks at stake, commanding protection for the guarantors in case of highly risky contracts as opposed to less ('normal') risky contracts. It has been argued that in this way the German Constitutional Court did not intend to foreclose access to credit by means of third-party guarantees for small businesses and start-ups, a foreclosure that would have resulted from the application of the right of cancellation of all guarantees regardless of the degree of the underlying risks involved—an argument this that falls in line with a full application of the ad hoc balancing approach. From this vantage point, allowing guarantors to cancel their guarantees in support of consumer loans in all circumstances, as the *Dietzinger* decision did, is as problematic as is the denial of protection for guarantors of commercial loans in all circumstances. In both cases, the Court under-optimised rights by embracing forms of balancing that either value guarantors' rights as important (the case of consumer guarantees) or otherwise (the case of commercial guarantees) in the abstract ('definitional balancing', that is, one interest is held to outweigh another) rather than considering the worthiness of the rights involved in the dispute ('ad hoc balancing').

ii. Under-Optimisation in *Schulte*

The case law on the right of cancellation applied to 'linked contracts' and specifically *Schulte* is another illustration of under-optimisation.[45] Here it is counterintuitive not to allow the investor-consumer to be released from the whole set of obligations entailed in the investment package, including property-related ones,[46] whenever this means making his position worse off than it would been if no right of cancellation had been applied at all (considering that the debtor is left with the obligation to repay the loan in full and at once rather than in instalments). Here having allowed cancellation in relation to the loan only, on the basis of the higher

balancing (ad hoc balancing as a practice of rights' optimisation insofar as it is about weighing the degree of relative importance of rights vis-à-vis each other) whilst *definitional balancing* stands for those particular decisions in which the Court holds some interests to outweigh others once and for all, without engaging in weighing their degree of importance relative to other interests as a practice needed for concretising the objective of rights' optimisation.

[44] This is why I must consider *Dietzinger* to have been decided on the basis of a 'definitional balancing' reasoning pattern that under-optimises rights.

[45] Case C-350/03 *Schulte* [2005] ECR I-9215.

[46] Critical in this sense it Reich, 'Balancing', above n 1.

importance of the position of the consumer than that of the counterparty, but having denied it in relation to property rights via textualism (denial of protection on the basis of the text of the Directive that 'expressly and unequivocally excludes contracts for the sale of immovable property from its scope' whilst not containing any possible textual basis for including in its scope of application 'connected contracts') causes grave disregard for the worth of rights. There is need for judicial opinions that void the whole package instead of making consumers worse off. Avoiding the deployment of 'ad hoc balancing' and clinging instead to textualism—combined with a form of 'definitional balancing'[47]—leads to a situation in which rights-protection is worsened, rather than optimised.

iii. Under-Optimisation in *Freiburger*

Balancing as deployed in *Freiburger* is equally a case that under-optimises rights. In the sense that the Court here chose one set of values (business orientated) which it interpreted as being higher in importance relative to those of the buyers (in the mode of 'definitional balancing'), rather than entertaining a balancing exercise that considers the worth of the rights involved in the dispute relative to each other (ad hoc balancing). The consumers claimed a right to 'quality' (not to be obliged to pay before performance) based on German default private law codified rules (albeit not mandatory rules), a position that the Court simply disregarded rather than weighing it against the interest of the business according to a judgement of the relative importance and sacrifice of the rights at stake. This is particularly striking considering that the case comes from a context in which regulators have traditionally developed a trust-based, consumer paternalistic policy, sceptical of exchanging guarantees (or lower prices) for rights-in-kind such as the right to pay after the counterparty's performance.[48] From this vantage point, the sacrifice of the rights-in-kind of the consumers in

[47] Here my critical remarks apply to the denial of the right of cancellation in relation to property rights. Insofar as the decision follows the precedent of *Heininger* in relation to obligatory (loan) rights, that portion of the decision could be justified on the ground of ad hoc balancing (as I argue in the remainder that it is in the case of *Heininger*) but the fact that the Court ultimately excluded full protection for Mr and Mrs Schulte as requested by the German lower courts' reference by embracing textualism turns that act of balancing in 'definitional' (ultimately, the CJEU decision holds that the interests of the consumers weigh lower than those of the counterparty). This is one more reason (that is, the Court having 'balanced' but then having ultimately 'limited' the potential for optimisation by embracing textualism), alongside the reason explained earlier at nn 43 and 44 above, why I consider also *Dietzinger* to have been based on a 'definitional' type of balancing.

[48] See eg G Teubner, 'Legal Irritants: Good Faith in British Law or How Unifying Law End Up in New Divergencies' (1998) 61 *Modern Law Review* 1. For a critical analysis of para 21 of Freiburger ('the consequences of the term *under the law applicable to the contract* must also be taken into account', which requires that 'consideration be given to the *national law*'.) see Niglia, 'The Rules Dilemma', n 37 above, at 141 et seq.

Freiburger is counterintuitive. Also, generally speaking, regulatory contexts vary, for there may be markets for goods or services in which consumers appear to be more interested in quality of contracts and less in lower prices,[49] or in which consumers may be interested in (extended) guarantees rather than no guarantees at all. Courts need to consider these factors in deciding which right is worthier than another, so as to avoid making a rigid kind of definitional balancing such as the one operationalised in *Freiburger*, which, in foreclosing consideration of the conflicting interests at stake, ends up with under-optimising rights. In order to pursue rights' optimisation, a more complex consideration of the circumstantial degrees of importance and sacrifice of the relevant rights would have been required, that is, ad hoc balancing.

Reading key private consumer law cases of the CJEU through the looking-glass of balancing, rather than just textualism,[50] has made them really intelligible in two key senses. First, and descriptively, one realises that the case law consists less of just textualist decisions and more of balancing decisions, with balancing being sometimes mixed up with textualism. Secondly, and critically, one realises that deciding the relevant cases via textualism or, alternatively or concurrently, via definitional balancing, rather than employing ad hoc balancing, has meant denying rights effective protection—in the sense that avoiding ad hoc balancing under-determines (no consideration of the circumstantial importance of rights relative to each other) and, as a result, under-optimises rights. In the cases considered above, the CJEU could have gone as far as incorporating ad hoc balancing so as to take private law rights seriously. The rights of Mr and Mrs Hofstetter to pay after performance (in *Freiburger*) or of Mr Dietzinger to cancel the guarantee or of Mr and Mrs Schulte to cancel the whole package of the investment contract or—to recall once more the case regarding the Company Directive—that of the creditors-depositors to obtain the restructuring of the bank-debtor, should not have been outrightly disregarded through textualism, or definitional balancing, but considered explicitly in relation to their 'weighing' relative to the position of the rights of the counterparts, with decisions made according to judgements regarding

[49] Cf eg, in a vast literature, and for a recent re-edition of this now classical law-and-economic argument, see O Bar-Gill and O Ben Shadar, 'Regulatory Techniques in Consumer Protection. A Critique of European Consumer Contract Law' (2012) 50 *Common Market Law Review* at 113–14 ('[C]onsumers are a heterogeneous group, with different preferences and different budgets'; [w]hilst some consumers may prefer to pay high prices for strong protections, others may prefer the low-price-low-protection combination' and '[a]mong the latter group are some consumers who would be priced out of the high-protection market').

[50] The same criticism applies to the textualist variant of purposivism as discussed above at n 36.

the higher or lower degree of importance of the relative rights so as to give all rights involved their due weight.

IV. OF BALANCING AND THE COURT OF JUSTICE OF THE EUROPEAN UNION II: OPTIMISING RIGHTS

The point of criticism coming from the *2004 Manifesto*, that is, their scepticism vis-à-vis the 'haphazard practice of national courts making references' to the CJEU to 'secure legitimacy for a system of European contract law' towards implementing 'a complex balance between the values of private autonomy and social justice',[51] was not really elaborated in any detail,[52] but, if considered in relation to *Dietzinger*, *Freiburger* and *Schulte*, it turns out to be appropriate overall in the sense that the CJEU cannot claim to have offered satisfactory (optimising) solutions in terms of balancing.[53] However, such explanation would no longer be truthful were one to apply it to the wider private consumer protection case law of the CEJU. For there is a remarkable mismatch between, on the one hand, the three cases considered up to now and, on the other hand, two lines of CJEU cases characterised by the common trait of optimising rights.

A. Balancing as Rights' Optimisation I: Protecting the Consumer in *Heininger*

A first line of CJEU cases is one in which the Court has reached a consumer protectionist output in circumstances in which the 'consumer' is self-evidently placed in a starkly weaker position relative to that of the other party, making the consumer protectionist decisions of the Court intelligible in the light of ad hoc balancing arguments and thus justified in terms of

[51] For the note that the writers of the *2004 Manifesto* had directed this criticism to the CJEU for not being the best branch for implementing the balancing of market and social elements in contract law see P Mengozzi, 'Il rapporto tra stati e individui nella giurisprudenza comunitaria' in *La Formazione del Diritto Europeo. Giornata di Studio per Alberto Trabucchi nel centenario della nascita Quaderni della Rivista di Diritto Civile* (Padua, Cedam, 2008) 111 as discussed below.

[52] It was addressed to the role of national courts and the CJEU in European private law in general, with no reference to specific cases towards substantiating the writers' opinion.

[53] For critical views see Collins, *The European Civil Code*, as discussed above at n 36 (regarding *Dietzinger*); Hesselink, 'Toolbox', as discussed above at n 24 (regarding *Hamilton*); Reich, 'Balancing', above at n 1 (regarding *Dietzinger*); Van Gerven, 'The ECJ Case-law' as discussed above at n 21 et seq (regarding *Panagis Pafitis*); Weatherill, 'Consumer Protection', above n 3 (as discussed in the remainder in relation to *Gonzáles*).

rights' optimisation. An illustration is *Heininger*.[54] Here, it is in relation to the 'weak position' of the consumer that the Court held that the consumer-contractor should be allowed to cancel a secured-credit agreement on the basis of the argument that:

> [T]he doorstep-selling directive is, as pointed out earlier, designed to protect consumers against the risks arising from the conclusion of contracts away from the trader's premises and, second, that that protection is assured by the introduction of a right of cancellation. [para 38]

Such right should be acknowledged until Mr and Mrs Heininger are made aware of it, whatever the timing, a position that the Court defends with the following argument that balances (in 'ad hoc' mode) legal certainty and protectionist objectives, that is:

> [A]s regards the argument that it is essential, for reasons of legal certainty, to restrict the period within which the right of cancellation may be exercised, such reasons cannot prevail since they imply a limitation of the rights expressly conferred on consumers by the doorstep-selling directive in order to protect them against the risks arising from the fact that the credit institutions have chosen to enter into agreements away from their business premises. If those institutions choose such methods in order to market their services, they can easily safeguard both the interests of consumers and their own requirements as to legal certainty by complying with their duty to supply consumers with information. [para 47]

Restriction of the period within which the right of cancellation may be exercised, understood as a way to further the goal of legal certainty, is a reason balanced not just against the textual provision of the right of cancellation but against all of the risks entailed in choosing a particular method of negotiation. The importance of the freedom of institutions to provide their services in the circumstances is graded lower than the risks being placed on the consumer, that is, compared with the importance of the right to cancel the secured-credit agreement, considering that the provider of services can 'easily' avoid those risks, that is, 'safeguard both the interests of consumers and their own requirements as to legal certainty' by offering the required information. To say it from the perspective of the consumer, the importance of satisfying the right of cancellation of the consumer is judged to be comparatively greater than the value of avoiding the detriment to the position of the credit institution entailed in the enforcement of the right of cancellation.

[54] See notably representative cases such as C-481/99, *Heininger v Bayerische Hypo- und Vereinsbank AG*, [2001] ECR I-9945 as discussed above, at n 33; Cases C-240/98 to 244/98 *Oceano Grupo Editorial SA v Rocio Murciano Quintero* [2000] ECR I-4941.

B. Balancing as Rights' Optimisation II: Not Protecting the Consumer in *Hamilton*

A second line of CJEU cases that contrasts with those considered in Section III is one in which the Court has reached a non-protectionist output (similarly to those of Section III) but in which it has nevertheless 'carefully explained' the reasons why it has chosen to value the interest of the consumer less highly than that of legal certainty, exercising an explicit form of ad hoc balancing.[55] For example, *Hamilton* has been decided 'against the consumer' on the basis of the argument that it is for the sake of the value of legal certainty that it makes sense for the national legislature to limit the right of cancellation at a certain point in time after full performance, legal certainty being adjudged ('ad hoc') as more important relative to the right of the consumer to cancel the contract, ultimately making of the performance of the contract a reasonable term *a quo* for national legislatures to then discretionally limit the invocation of the right of cancellation. In the words of Weatherill:

> [w]hereas one might have taken the 'Heininger logic' and argued that even after full performance the consumer is entitled to withdraw from the contract given that the trader has deprived the consumer of the necessary knowledge about his or her option to withdraw, the Court chose not to sharpen the deterrent effect attached to failure to provide information in this way. It treated consumer protection as not 'absolute' and 'subject to certain limits'.[56]

Whilst the Court has in this way increasingly shown a tendency to carefully consider and weigh the importance of the reasons behind its balancing acts, as demonstrated in particular by its post-2005 case law,[57] its case law does not remain immune from returning to its 'original sin'—as it fell upon the Court in the three cases regarding the Unfair Terms Directive and the Doorstep Selling Directive as considered above, decided in the decade 1995–2005—of playing down and under-optimising the interests of the consumers. Indeed, such eventuality has recently materialised with

[55] See eg Case 412/06 *Annelore Hamilton v Volksbank Filder* [2008] ECR I-2383; Case C-215/08, *E Friz GmbH v Carsten von der Heyden* [2010] ECR I-2947; Case C-40/08 *Asturcom Telecomunicaciones SL v Nogueira*[2009] ECR I-9579. For discussion see Weatherill, 'Consumer Protection', above n 3, at 231 ('In Hamilton, Friz and Asturcom Telecomunicaciones the Court uses the observation that consumer protection is not absolute as an introduction to a *careful examination of whether the pro-consumer interpretative presumption is apt to prevail over competing concerns such as legal certainty* and a fair division of risk. *This is already an intriguing exercise in balancing principles and priorities, but here is not the place to explore that dimension*' (emphasis added)), whose reading and note on 'careful examination' I am reconstructing in the vocabulary of ad hoc balancing.

[56] Weatherill, 'Consumer Protection', above n 3, at 227.

[57] See cases mentioned at n 55 above—considering the timing of the sequence of cases that under-optimise rights, that is, *Dietzinger* (1998), *Freiburger* (2004) and *Schulte* (2005).

González,[58] where the Court held it not to be manifestly incorrect to regard insurance contracts linked to investment funds as 'insurance contracts' for the purpose of their legislative exclusion from the scope of the Directive.[59] The consumer buying an insurance-linked investment appears to be in no less vulnerable position than the position of the guarantor of consumer loans that the Court chose to protect in *Dietzinger*. In adopting a definitional balancing mode of reasoning (in the sense that the interests of the insurers are held to outweigh those of the consumer) that categorically considers insurance contracts linked to investment funds to be excluded from the scope of the Directive in all circumstances,[60] *González* is less 'accident'[61] and more eternal return of an interpretative position that keeps conflicting with the rights' optimising orientation that comes from the rest of the CJEU decisions whenever they act out of ad hoc balancing. Seen in this perspective, the challenge is both about (negatively) *not* going too far and unnecessarily into the argument that consumer protection is 'not absolute', avoiding making of it a dogmatic tenet (considering the Court's holding for the right of cancellation never to apply to 'linked insurance contracts'),[62] and about (positively) convincing the Court to adjudicate on the consumer private law directives via implementing ad hoc balancing (optimisation) consistently throughout its case law. For, arguing for the 'non-absolute' character of consumer protection is deep down about articulating a balancing mode of reasoning as opposed to attributing value to consumer protection in absolute terms, and about engaging with testing the position of the consumer in terms of the objective of optimising rights. Consumer protection comes from a comparative assessment of the relative

[58] Case *Ángel Lorenzo González Alonso v Nationale Nederlanden Vida Cia De Seguros y Reaseguros SAE* 166/11, judgment of 1 March 2012. For critique of this decision see Weatherill, 'Consumer Protection', above n 3 (warning that 'the Court's declaration for the third time in recent years that the protection of consumers pursued by the EU's rules is not absolute and is subject to certain limits' ... 'should not be elevated to an interpretative principle apt to challenge the long-standing and constitutionally proper assumption that the EU's legislative *acquis* shall benefit from a pro-consumer interpretation').

[59] See *González*, ibid, at para 28 (on the basis of the argument that exclusions should be interpreted narrowly, at para 27).

[60] See Weatherill, 'Consumer Protection', above n 3, rightly denouncing *González* as a problematic decision in its clinging on a textualist interpretation of the legislative exclusions based on the background argument of 'no absolute protection' for the consumer. I understand *González* to be a decision based on 'definitional balancing' (the interest of the insurer as protected by the Directive's textual exclusion of 'insurance contracts' considered to outweigh that of the consumer to cancel the linked insurance contract in all circumstances) in that it holds that the argument for 'no absolute protection' runs counter to any attempt at arguing for the reversal of the legislative decision to exclude insurance contracts from the scope of the Doorstep Selling Directive.

[61] I agree with Weatherill, ibid at 233 ('probably an accident' and warning that 'the ruling González Alonso should therefore be festooned with red warning lights and not relied upon in future').

[62] An argument convincingly made by Weatherill, ibid, in relation to the ambiguous use of the argument from 'no absolute protection' for consumers made by the Court in *González*.

degree of importance of the involved rights. Overall, there is an unresolved, problematic tension within the case law of the CJEU between criptic (textualist)[63] and explicitly value-orientated (balancing) reasoning patterns, and, within balancing, between balancing decisions that optimise rights (ad hoc) and those that do not (definitional). It is a tension that is related less to who actually decides,[64] or to a supposedly implicit narrative of progression whereby the case law would 'improve' as it moves along decades (*González* disproves this hypothesis), and more to the power of epistemic dynamics *qua* reasoning structures in the work of judges.[65] Awareness of this tension should be a decisive starting point for creating a new interpretative environment in which private law rights can be subject to the assessment of optimisation and thus taken really seriously.

V. CONCLUSION: OF 'OPTIMISATION' IN EUROPE'S PLURAL CONTEXT

The argument put forward in 'response' to scholarly positions sceptical of judicial balancing in European private law[66]—whereby what makes the Court's decisions really credible is their orientation towards the value of 'protecting the individual', and, specifically, the individual in a 'weak' position[67]—turns out to be appropriate, considering that, in the language adopted in this chapter, the CJEU manages to optimise rights in most cases. To put it strongly, that argument entails that any stepping back from the rights' optimisation vocation of the CJEU turns out to be detrimental to the *exigencia existencial* of the Court to protect the individual in a weak position,[68] let alone that any such 'stepping back' exacerbates the problem of how to respond to those who hold that judicially driven rights'

[63] Cf A Von Bogdandy, 'Founding Principles of EU Law: A Theoretical and Doctrinal Sketch' (2010) 16 *European Law Journal* 95, at 103, as quoted at n 73 below.

[64] For the weakness of this argument see Weatherill, 'Consumer Protection', above n 3.

[65] For a recent interdisciplinary synthesis of sociological and political writings regarding legal epistemic conditions, see eg Britta Rehder, *Rechtsprechung als Politik: der Beitrag des Bundesarbeitsgerichts zur Entwicklung der Arbeitsbeziehungen in Deutschland* (Schriften des Max-Planck-Instituts für Gesellschaftsforschung, Köln, Bd 74) (Frankfurt, Campus Verlag, 2011) at 65 et seq._

[66] P Mengozzi, 'Il rapporto tra stati e individui nella giurisprudenza comunitaria' in *La Formazione del Diritto Europeo. Giornata di Studio per Alberto Trabucchi nel centenario della nascita Quaderni della Rivista di Diritto Civile* (Padua, Cedam, 2008) 111, at 113–14 (criticising the position of the *2004 Manifesto* insofar as sceptical of leaving it to courts to balance social justice and market orientated objectives; arguing that the case law of the CJEU is about producing solutions 'che non si limitano a stabilire la disciplina del mercato ma vanno largamente nella direzione della protezione dei singoli'; referring to *Courage* (n 32 above) as a model decision in that respect.

[67] Ibid.

[68] To paraphrase an argument of the *Tribunal Constitutional*, Spain, Decision 1/2004 (acknowledgement of primacy as *exigencia existential* of European law).

optimisation cannot be all that matters for the law to be fully credible and legitimate.[69] From this vantage point, not to employ ad hoc balancing on the part of the CJEU in key cases, from *Dietzinger* to *Freiburger*, *Schulte* and *González*, is a worrying practice. Private law is in need of a Court that does not betray its rights' protectionist vocation (as per *González*); it needs a Court that firmly engages with the challenge of providing protection for the individual, as this is institutionally the task of any court, and of constitutional courts in particular[70] and above all and no less so of the CJEU.[71]

A shift in scholarship towards looking at the private consumer case law as a cluster of balancing decisions to be evaluated on the basis of their optimising or otherwise of rights is bound to create a new interpretative climate: a climate in which to convince the Court to align all of its decisions in the subject area around balancing techniques that optimise rights, and to resist the tendency to under-optimise rights as re-enacted in *González*, where the Court has counter-intuitively refused to engage in an open exercise of ad hoc balancing by excluding 'linked insurance contracts' once and for all from the right of cancellation. The threefold reference to the notion that consumer protection 'is not absolute' contained in the CJEU case law will remain particularly worrying for the time being,[72] until the Court articulates all of its decisions in the vocabulary of rights' optimisation via ad hoc balancing. Scholarship can help counter the Court's pattern of sliding into under-optimising rights by reading the case law for what it is (a balancing case law) and by articulating critique in relation to the plasticity of the balancing exercise, that is, its lending itself to being more or less about optimising rights and, as such, requiring strict public scrutiny.[73] For there is no reason for scholarship to be sceptical of judge-made balancing,[74] not only in consideration of the structural need for judicial opinions to enforce norms for norms to become operational but, above all, for the consideration that, in a world characterised by increasing privatisation of power, balancing interventions of the courts on issues like

[69] Notably, in general, the critique of Jürgen Habermas *Between Facts and Norms* (trans W Rehg) (Cambridge, Polity Press, 1996 [1st edn 1992]) 256 et seq.

[70] See C Moellers, *The Three Branches* (Oxford, OUP, 2013) at 135 (critically commenting on the notion that '[t]he protection of basic rights is the most significant and most debated function of constitutional courts').

[71] See Mengozzi, 'Il rapporto tra stati e individui' as commented above at n 66 above.

[72] For the critical note see Weatherill, 'Consumer Protection', n 3 above.

[73] On the need for public scrutiny in relation to the value choice being made at the judicial level in the context of the EU see A Von Bogdandy, 'Founding Principles of EU Law: A Theoretical and Doctrinal Sketch' (2010) 16 *European Law Journal* 95, at 103: 'a judicial decision which employs the balancing of principles is more intelligible for most citizens than a 'legal-technical' reasoning phrased in hermetic language which obscures the valuations of the court. To devise legal controversies as conflicts of principles allows for a politicisation which should be welcomed in light of the principle of democracy, since it promotes the public discourse on judicial decisions'.

[74] For references see n 4 above.

loan, guarantee and investment contracts such as those involved in the private law CJEU case law can only be positive ways for (European) law to improve its democratic responsiveness.[75] Adopting the perspective of rights' optimisation on the part of scholarship is an interpretative strategy that serves this worthy purpose. With one qualification, however, that is: that the work of the CJEU, whenever it optimises rights, should be seen as an important yet only 'first-step' exercise in judicial deliberation insofar as there remains the challenge of assessing the measure of rights' optimisation as established by the CJEU from the vantage point of the ways in which national constitutional courts themselves optimise rights. For the CJEU operates in a plural context in which optimisation of private law rights must be measured against the voices of the national constitutional courts understood as guardians of Europe's wider constitutional heritage.[76] Indeed, as the CJEU handles material (the language of rights' optimisation) which originates from the national realm, 'drawing inspiration' from the national heritage, the latter must remain the ultimate reference axiological point for the practice of rights' optimisation. In a plural context of overlapping constitutional realms—one in which balancing translates into a practice of hybridisation of the European and the national level,[77] and in which proportionality increasingly translates in a balancing exercise[78]—there must be no end to the search for balancing interpretative combinations that engage with the challenge of optimising rights—even those CJEU decisions which optimise rights are about quasi-optimisation. As the CJEU embraces the judicial practice of rights' optimisation and thus totalises private law,[79] it remains part and parcel of a broader constitutional landscape whose

[75] Von Bogdandy, 'Founding Principles', n 73 above (on balancing as enhancing democracy through promotion of the public discourse on judicial decisions); S Rodota, 'Il Codice civile e il processo costituente europeo' in V Roppo (ed), *A European Civil Code? Perspectives and Problems* (Milan, Giuffrè, 2005) 183, at 193 (in the context of arguments in favour of the role of private law adjudication, arguing that a critique of 'judicial activism' would be about abstracting from real-life problems, and it would even be ideological , for it would not consider the real modalities of production of private law norms which are heavily privatised; defending judicial intervention in that respect as being undoubtedly good for democracy).

[76] I am thinking of the established CJEU practice of deriving fundamental rights from, and respecting, the domestic constitutional realms, which entails a constitutional requirement on the part of the CJEU to follow standards of 'optimisation' based on nationally established constitutional values *qua* fundamental rights: see the decision *Solange II* of the *BVerfG* and the related debate on constitutional pluralism: for discussion on constitutional *and* private law pluralism see L Niglia (ed), *Pluralism and European Private Law* (Oxford, Hart Publishing, 2013).

[77] On balancing as a practice of hybridization see also the perspective of P Mengozzi, 'The Judicial Protection of Individual Rights and the Principle of Proportionality after the Lisbon Treaty' in this *Symposium*, above at p 339.

[78] T Tridimas 'Fundamental Rights' (in this *Symposium*).

[79] In the sense discussed for example in M Kumm, 'Who is Afraid of the Total Constitution? Constitutional Rights as Principles and the Constitutionalization of Private Law' (2006) 7 *German Law Journal* 341.

boundaries need to be critically considered not only in relation to the issue of competences but also in relation to the substantive determinations being made by the CJEU.[80] This chapter sets the stage for this new way of 'seeing the world' freed from textual, formal constraints and thus paving the way for reaching optimal balanced interpretations of the relevant Directives and their provisions before the European courtrooms.

[80] I address this problematic of 'quasi-optimisation' in the third instalment of this series of essays on the state of European constitutional law. See also L Niglia, *The Struggle for European Private Law: A Critique of Codification* (Oxford, Hart Publishing, 2015).

Index